Fifth Edition

REALITY THROUGH THE ARTS

DENNIS J. SPORRE

PRENTICE HALL, UPPER SADDLE RIVER, NJ 07458

Published 2004 by Prentice Hall Inc.
A Division of Pearson Education
Upper Saddle River, New Jersey 07458

10 9 8 7 6 5 4 3 2

ISBN 0-13-183114-3

This book was designed and produced by
Laurence King Publishing Ltd, London
www.laurenceking.co.uk

Editor: Christine Davis
Senior Managing Editor: Richard Mason
Designers: Melinda Welch/Design Deluxe and Andrew Shoolbred
Picture Researcher: Emma Brown
Typesetter: Fakenham Photosetting Ltd, Fakenham, Norfolk
Printed in Hong Kong

Front cover: Ando Hiroshige, *Maple Leaves at the Tekona Shrine, Mamma*, 1857. British Museum, London.
Page 8: Diego Rivera, *Slavery in the Sugar Plantation, Tealtenago, Morelos* (detail), 1930–1. Palace of Cortez, Cuernavaca, Mexico.

CONTENTS

PART II: THE STYLES OF THE ARTS
How Artists Portray "Reality" 193

PREFACE

This book teaches basic principles and practices of the arts—drawing, painting, printmaking, sculpture, music, theatre, dance, cinema, literature, and architecture—in Western and other cultures. Designed for individuals whose experience of and in the arts is limited, it treats definitions and concepts in Part I in a cursory fashion, using general terms that can apply readily to the diverse cultural materials examined in Part II. The overall approach seeks to provide a convenient, one-volume outline with sufficient flexibility to serve a variety of classroom purposes.

Part I examines the media of the arts, defining and explaining important terminology, discussing how artworks are composed, and suggesting ways in which art can effect responses. The primary purpose of this compendium approach is to assist readers in polishing skills of observation and gaining confidence in sharing responses. Selection of materials is arbitrary. This text is neither a comprehensive history nor an introduction to aesthetic theory.

Part II is arranged chronologically in order to present a snapshot of arts from around the world that occurred at roughly the same time in history. The focus of Part II, however, is style, not history, and not every culture has been included. Decisions as to what to omit or include were made for two reasons: feedback from instructors and the practicalities of size set by the publisher.

This work is a product of many sources. In many instances it reflects the general knowledge of its author, who has spent nearly fifty years in formal and experiential relationship with the arts in the classroom and around the world. It reflects notes taken here and there as well as formal research. In the interest of readability, however, and in recognition of its generalized purpose, the text avoids footnoting wherever possible. I hope that the method selected for presentation and documentation of others' works meets the needs of both responsibility and practicality. The bibliography gives a comprehensive list of works consulted.

This edition, the fifth, contains several new features. First is a new Introduction which overviews the text and presents a more thorough and transparent approach than previous editions. Each chapter ends with a new "Thinking Critically" feature to assist in developing analysis and insight. That is followed by a "Cyber Study" section for finding additional materials on the Internet.

Within the chapters, an in-text pronunciation guide has been added so that readers can pronounce names and terms without having to look elsewhere for assistance. Also, each of the thirteen chapters contains a "Personal Journey" essay designed to give a personalized view of a specific work of art (designed, however, so as not to break the flow of the text). The intent is to show how experiencing artworks outside the classroom can become a meaningful part of one's life. In addition, a Humanities CD-ROM is available to bring to life several concepts, styles, and processes in the arts. The CD-ROM includes narration and fourteen video clips, with a listing of key terms and definitions that students can download to their hard drive for creating study notes and easy reference material. A web site, developed specifically for the CD-ROM, contains web links specific to each discipline. The CD-ROM also contains a starter kit for each discipline which provides general information for the arts genres, explaining why they are studied and how to study them effectively. Finally, a new section on Latino Art has been added to Chapter 13 in order to bring a better balance of materials to the realities of the contemporary classroom. The music CD available with previous editions continues to this edition. References to its selections are noted as "music CD."

In 1977, when I wrote *Perceiving the Arts* (Prentice Hall, 7th edition, 2002), I asked Ellis Grove, my colleague at The Pennsylvania State University, to prepare a chapter on film. Ten years later, that formed the basis for Chapter 5 of this book. In twenty-five years of revisions of these two texts, much of Ellis's original work has been altered. Nonetheless, the basics belong to him. Any deterioration of his work is the result of my tinkering, and I am indebted to him and to more than a score of colleagues whose insights, encouragement, and criticism have, I hope, made each edition of *Reality Through the Arts* better than its predecessor. I also owe much to Bud Therien at Prentice Hall, my friend, editor, and publisher for nearly twenty-five years, to the editors and copy-editors at Laurence King, Ltd., in London, England, and to my wife, Hilda, whose patience, love, understanding, proofreading, note-taking, and research assistance have provided me with a solid foundation from which to generate my own part of the project.

Dennis J. Sporre
Spring 2002

INTRODUCTION

USING THIS BOOK AND LEARNING ABOUT ART

Driving a car for the first time usually requires a preoccupation with mechanics and an intense concentration on keeping the car moving in a straight line. As technical details become habitual, drivers can attend to more important details of driving.

Experiencing art is somewhat like driving a car. When the experience is new and when studious attempts are made at doing it "right," or amassing materials for a classroom assignment, the details often can interfere with the larger experience. Obsession with finding specific details—what a book or a teacher has indicated should be the objects of looking—frequently robs the occasion of its pleasure and meaning. Nonetheless, with practice the details do fall into place and heightened enjoyment, and the sense of personal achievement—sophistication, some might say—expands exponentially.

Getting to that point, however, requires a beginning. Perceiving anything requires an understanding of what can be perceived. This book provides a usable outline of the basics: things that can be seen, heard, and responded to in works of visual and performing art and architecture (Part I: The Media of the Arts). In addition, the book serves as a reference for understanding the fundamental qualities of artistic style (Part II: The Styles of the Arts). The chapters treating history of the arts comprise a basic outline of styles with Internet hyperlinks to additional study examples.

CONNECTING TO THE WORLD WIDE WEB

When using this book in the "cyber" world, you will find URLs (web addresses) to connect with the world wide web. These serve as springboards for further investigation. Most of the URLs lead to artists and, from there, hyperlinks lead to numerous works of art. The artworks further illustrate the principles and styles discussed and illustrated in the text. Some of the web sites yield more detailed information about artists, styles, periods, general history, and so on. With regard to URLs, however, a warning is necessary. First, things change. A web site that was active when this book went to press may no longer exist. Second, an initial attempt to link to a site may prove unsuccessful: "Unable to connect to remote host." A rule of thumb is to try to connect to the site three successive times before trying another URL. Be careful to type the URL exactly. Any incorrect character will cause the connection to fail (capital letters matter).

In addition to the specific web addresses listed in the text, some general sites can provide a wealth of additional information. An easy and vast reference for visual art and architecture is the Artcyclopedia at http://www.artcyclopedia.com/index.html. Here, individual artists can be referenced along with their artworks, and searches can be done by style, medium, subject, and nationality. For music, a comprehensive MIDI library is located at http://www.classicalarchives.com/. Although these examples are all instrumental and digitally synthesized, the available selections are impressive. Several large text sites for literature exist, and these are noted at the ends of appropriate chapters.

PRONOUNCING NAMES AND TERMS

Study of the arts brings us face to face with many challenging terms (many of them in a foreign language) and names. To assist acquaintanceship, each term or name not pronounced exactly as it appears is followed, in parentheses, by a pronunciation guide. This guide has two features. First, it uses familiar English consonant and vowel representations, rather than International Phonetics. Second, emphasis is indicated by capital letters. A long "I" sound ("eye") will occasionally be represented by the letter "y." A word of warning: Pronunciation is not always universally agreed upon. Pronunciations in this text have been drawn from respected encyclopedic and dictionary sources. Even so, some may appear to flout common usage, especially of names that enjoy widespread Anglicization.

USING THE ACCOMPANYING CD-ROM

Available with this book is a CD-ROM that puts into sound and motion illustrations of material in the text. The CD-ROM contains fourteen tracks dealing with subjects such as musical forms and instruments, rhythm, perspective, subtractive and ceramic sculpture, theatre terminology, modern dance, ballet, Classical, medieval, and modern architecture, and poetry. Each track also includes a list of important terms, hyperlinks for additional study on the web, and space for note-making. The CD-ROM can be viewed as a whole or particular tracks may be called up as they are referenced in the text.

The realm of art holds potential for great personal enrichment and excitement. Hopefully, this book will stimulate curiosity and lead to finding so much in works of art that the world will no longer appear as it once did. Hopefully, too, the contents of this book and the aesthetic experiences they treat will become like old friends and comfortable, lifelong companions. Using this book will prove an exercise in empowerment. When its contents have been mastered, meeting works of art and sharing experiences with works of art can be undertaken with assurance. Artworks, terms, and names will no longer seem arcane or intimidating. Likewise, using technical vocabulary correctly and pronouncing foreign names and terms will make for liberating and confident conversation.

PUTTING THIS STUDY IN CONTEXT

For centuries, scholars, philosophers, and aestheticians have debated without general resolution a definition of "art." The challenging range of arguments encompasses, among other considerations, opposing points of view which insist on one hand that "art" must meet a criterion of functionality—that is, be of some societal use—and, on the other hand, that "art" exists for its own sake. This text seeks to survey rather than dispute. Thus, the dilemma of art's definition remains unsolved here, despite the energizing effect that such a discussion might engender. We can, however, examine some characteristics of the arts that enhance understanding.

Art has and has had a profound effect on the quality of human life, and its study requires seriousness of purpose. Having said that, however, we must not confuse seriousness of purpose in the study of art with a sweeping sanctification of works of art. Some art is serious, some art is profound, and some art is highly sacred. Yet some art is light, some is humorous, and some is downright silly, superficial, and self-serving for its artists.

The remainder of this section—"Putting this Study in Context"—treats five general subjects: (1) *The Arts and Ways of Knowing* (2) *What Are Art's Main Concerns?* (3) *What Are Art's Purposes and Functions?* (4) *How Should We Perceive and Respond?* and (5) *How Do We Live with Art?*

THE ARTS AND WAYS OF KNOWING

Humans are a creative species. Whether in science, politics, business, technology, or the arts, we depend on our creativity almost as much as anything else to meet the demands of daily life. Any book about the arts is a story about us: Our perceptions of the world as we have come to see and respond to it, and the ways we have communicated our understandings to each other for thousands of years (Fig. **0.1**).

Our study in this text will focus on vocabulary and perception, as well as on history. First, however, we need to have an overview of where the arts fall within the general scope of human endeavor.

We live in buildings and listen to music constantly. We hang pictures on our walls and react like personal friends to characters in television, film, and live dramas. We escape to parks, engross ourselves in novels, wonder about a statue in front of a public building, and dance

0.1 Cave chamber at Lascaux, France, early Stone Age (c. 15,000 B.C.E.).

through the night. All these situations involve forms called "art," in which we engage and are engaged in daily. Curiously, as close to us as these "art" activities are, in many ways they remain mysteries. How do they, in fact, fit into the larger picture of the human reality that we experience?

Since the human species began, we have learned a great deal about our world and how it functions, and we have changed our patterns of existence. However, the fundamental characteristics that make us human—our ability to intuit and to symbolize—have not changed. Art, the major remaining evidence we have of our earliest times, reflects these unchanged human characteristics in inescapable terms and helps us to understand the beliefs of cultures, including our own, and to express the universal qualities of humans.

As we begin this text, learning more about our humanness through art, let us start where we are. That has two implications. First, it means relying on the perceptive capabilities we already have. Applying our current abilities to perceive will develop confidence in approaching works of art. Second, starting where we are means learning how art fits into the general scheme of the way people

examine, communicate, and respond to the world around them. A course in the arts, designed to fulfill a requirement for a specified curriculum, demonstrates that the arts fit into an academic context that divides up the ways people acquire knowledge. Consequently, the first step in this exploration of the arts requires placing them in some kind of relationship with other categories of knowledge. Visual art, architecture, music, theatre, dance, and film belong in a broad category of pursuit called the "humanities," and that is where we begin.

The humanities, as opposed, for example, to the sciences, can very broadly be defined as those aspects of culture that look into what it means to be human. The sciences seek essentially to describe reality whereas the humanities seek to express humankind's subjective experiences of reality, to interpret reality, to transform our interior experience into tangible forms, and to comment upon reality, to judge and evaluate. But despite our desire to categorize, few clear boundaries exist between the humanities and the sciences. The basic difference lies in the approach that separates investigation of the natural universe, technology, and social science from the search for truth about the universe undertaken by artists.

Within the educational system, the humanities have traditionally included the fine arts (painting, sculpture, architecture, music, theatre, dance, and cinema), literature, philosophy, and, sometimes, history. Basically, these subjects explore what it means to be human, what human beings think and feel, what motivates their actions and shapes their thoughts. Many answers lie in the millions of artworks all around the globe, from the earliest sculpted fertility figures to the video and cyber art of today. These artifacts and images are themselves expressions of the humanities, not merely illustrations of past or present ways of life.

Change in the arts differs from change in the sciences in one significant way: New scientific discovery and technology usually displaces the old, but new art does not invalidate earlier human expression. The art of Picasso cannot make the art of Rembrandt a curiosity of history in the way that the theories of Einstein did the views of William Paley. Nonetheless, much about art has changed over the centuries. Part II of this text, "The Styles of the Arts," illustrates how the role of the artist can shift with the nature of the age. Using a spectrum developed by Susan Lacy in *Mapping the Terrain: New Genre Public Art* (1994), we learn that at one time an artist may be an *experiencer*; at another, a *reporter*; at another, an *analyst*; and at still another time, an *activist*. Further, the nature of how art historians see art has changed over the centuries—for example, today historians do not credit an artist's biography with all of the motivations for his or her work, and they now include in their studies works of art from previously marginalized groups such as women and minorities. These shifts in the discipline of arts history itself are important considerations in understanding the nature of art.

Works of art can be approached with the same subtleties we normally apply to human relationships. We know that people cannot simply be categorized as "good" or "bad," as "friends," "acquaintances," or "enemies." We relate to others in complex ways. Some friendships are pleasant but superficial, some people are easy to work with, and others (but few) are lifelong companions. Similarly, when we have gone beyond textbook categories and learned how to approach art with this sort of sensitivity, we find that art, like friendship, has a major place in enriching quality of life.

WHAT ARE ART'S MAIN CONCERNS?

Among other areas, art has typically concerned creativity, aesthetic communication, symbols, and the fine arts and crafts. Let's look briefly at each of these.

Creativity

Art has always evidenced creativity—the act of bringing forth new forces and forms. How creativity functions is a subject for debate. Nonetheless, something happens in which humankind takes chaos, formlessness, vagueness, and the unknown and crystallizes them into form, design, inventions, and ideas. Creativity underlies our existence. It allows scientists to intuit a possible path to a cure for cancer, for example, or to invent a computer. The same process allows artists to find new ways to express ideas through processes in which creative action, thought, material, and technique combine in a medium to create something new. That "new thing," often without words, triggers human experience—that is, our response to the artwork.

In the midst of this creative process is the art medium. Although most people can readily acknowledge the traditional media—for example, painting, sculpture, and printmaking—occasionally, when a medium of expression does not conform to expectations or experiences, many question whether the work qualifies as art. For example, Figure **0.2A** and **B** shows one gigantic installation in two parts, of blue and yellow umbrellas in Japan and the United States, respectively, created (and entirely financed) by the artists Christo and Jeanne-Claude. The umbrellas constituted the physical manifestation of a larger idea that the artists considered the whole work. People disagreed as to whether these constructions constituted an artistic medium or a work of art.

Aesthetic Communication

Art usually involves communication. Arguably, artists need people with whom they can share their perceptions. When artworks and humans interact, many possibilities arise. Interaction may be casual and fleeting, as in the first meeting of two people, when one or both are not at all interested in each other. Similarly, an artist may not have much to say, or may not say it very well. For example, a poorly written or produced play will probably not excite an audience. Similarly, an audience member's preoccupations with other things may make perception of the play's message impossible, thus short-circuiting that part of the artistic experience. On the other hand, optimum conditions may result in a profoundly exciting and meaningful experience. The play may treat a significant subject in a unique manner, the production artists may exhibit excellent skills in manipulating the medium, and the audience may be receptive. Or the interaction may fall somewhere between these two extremes.

Throughout history, artistic communication has involved *aesthetics*. Aesthetics is the study of the nature of

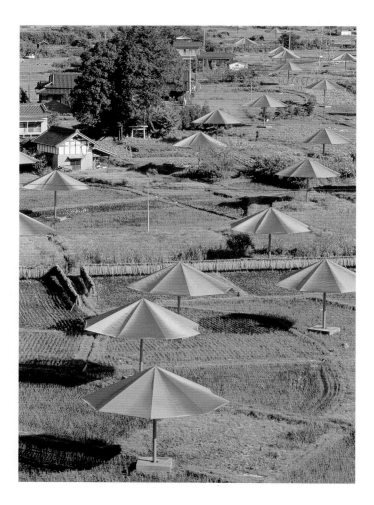

0.2A and **B** Christo and Jeanne-Claude, *The Umbrellas, Japan–USA*, 1984–91. (A) Valley north of Los Angeles, California, detail of 1,760 yellow umbrellas; (B) Valley in prefecture of Ibaraki, Japan, detail of 1,340 blue umbrellas. Nylon and aluminum, height of each umbrella including base, 19 ft 8¼ ins (6 m); combined length 30 miles (48 km).

beauty and of art and comprises one of the five Classical fields of philosophical inquiry—along with epistemology (the nature and origin of knowledge), ethics (the general nature of morals and of the specific moral choices to be made by the individual in relationship with others), logic (the principles of reasoning), and metaphysics (the nature of first principles and problems of ultimate reality). The term *aesthetics* (from the Greek for "sense perception") was coined by the German philosopher Alexander Baumgarten (1714–62) in the mid-eighteenth century, but interest in what constitutes the beautiful and in the relationship between art and nature goes back at least to the ancient Greeks. Both Plato and Aristotle saw art as *imitation* and beauty as the expression of a universal quality. For the Greeks, the concept of "art" embraced all handcrafts and the rules of symmetry, proportion, and unity applied equally to weaving, pottery, poetry, and sculpture. In the late eighteenth century, the philosopher Immanuel Kant (kahnt; 1724–1804) revolutionized aesthetics in his *Critique of Judgment* (1790) by viewing aesthetic appreciation not simply as the perception of intrinsic beauty, but as involving a judgment—subjective, but informed. Since Kant, the primary focus of aesthetics has shifted from the consideration of beauty *per se* to the nature of the artist, the role of art, and the relationship between the viewer and the work of art.

Symbols

Art is also concerned with symbols. Symbols are usually a tangible emblem of something abstract: a mundane object evoking a higher realm. They differ from signs, which suggest a fact or condition. Symbols carry deeper, wider, and richer meanings. Look at Figure **0.3**. Some people might identify this as a plus sign in arithmetic. But it might also be a Greek Cross, in which case it becomes a symbol because it suggests many images, meanings, and implications. Artworks use a variety of symbols to convey meaning. Symbols make artworks into doorways leading to enriched understanding.

Symbols occur in literature, art, and ritual. They can be based on conventional relationships such as a rose standing for courtly love in a medieval romance. A symbol can suggest physical or other similarities between itself and its reference (the red rose representing blood) or personal associations—for example, the Irish poet William Butler Yeats's use of the rose to symbolize death, ideal perfection, Ireland, and so on. Symbols also occur in linguistics wherein words are considered arbitrary symbols and in psychoanalysis where symbols, particularly images in dreams, are regarded as repressed, subconscious desires and fears. In Judaism, the contents of the feast table and

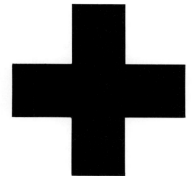

0.3 Greek Cross (?).

the ceremony performed at the Jewish Passover seder (the feast celebrating the exodus from slavery in Egypt) are symbolic of the events surrounding the Israelites' deliverance from Egypt. In Christian art, the lamb symbolizes the sacrifice of Christ.

Fine and Applied Art

One last consideration in understanding art's concerns involves the difference between *fine art* and *applied art*. The "fine arts"—generally meaning painting, sculpture, architecture, music, theatre, dance, and, in the twentieth century, cinema—are prized for their purely aesthetic qualities. During the Renaissance (see Chapter 11), these arts rose to superior status because Renaissance values lauded individual expression and unique aesthetic interpretations of ideas. The term "applied art" sometimes includes architecture and the "decorative arts" and refers to art forms that have a primarily decorative rather than expressive or emotional purpose. The decorative arts (a name first used in 1791) include handcrafts by skilled artisans, such as ornamental work in metal, stone, wood, and glass, as well as textiles, pottery, and bookbinding. They may also encompass aspects of interior design and personal objects such as jewelry, weaponry, tools, and costumes. Even mechanical appliances and other products of industrial design can be considered part of the category. Many decorative arts, such as weaving, basketry, and pottery, are also commonly considered "crafts," but the definitions of the terms are somewhat arbitrary and without sharp distinction.

WHAT ARE ART'S PURPOSES AND FUNCTIONS?

We can also expand our understanding of art by examining some of its purposes and functions. In terms of the former—its purposes—we are asking, What does art do? In terms of the latter—art's functions—we are asking, How does it do it?

Purposes

Essentially, art does four things: (1) It provides a record; (2) it gives visible or other form to feelings; (3) it reveals metaphysical or spiritual truths; and (4) it helps people to see the world in new ways. Art can do any or all of these. They are not mutually exclusive.

Until the invention of the camera, one of art's principal purposes was to enact a record of the world. Although we cannot know for sure, it is very likely that cave art of the earliest times did this. Egyptian art, ancient Greek art, Roman art, and so on until the invention of the camera all undertook, at times, to create pictorial records.

Art can give form to feelings. Perhaps the most explicit example comes in the Expressionist style of the early twentieth century (see Chapter 13). Here the emotions of the artist toward the work's content form a primary role in the work. "Feelings" can be referenced in works of art through technique—for instance, brush stroke—and through color (to isolate two visual examples), both of which have long associations with emotional content.

A third purpose of art can be the revelation of metaphysical or spiritual truths. Here we can turn to plainchant and the Gothic cathedrals of medieval Europe (see Chapter 10), whose light and space perfectly embodied medieval spirituality. A tribal totem, such as a Bakota ancestor (see Fig. 2.6), deals almost exclusively in spiritual and metaphysical revelation.

Finally, as a fourth purpose, most art, if well done, can assist us in seeing the world around us in new and surprising ways. Art that has abstract content may reveal a new way of understanding the interaction of life forces, as does the work of Piet Mondrian (peet MAWN-dree-ahn); see Figure 1.43 and the associated discussion.

Functions

In addition to its purposes (what it does), art also has many functions (how it does what it does), including (1) enjoyment, (2) political and social commentary, and (3) artifact. No one function is more important than the others. Nor are they mutually exclusive; one artwork may fill many functions. Neither are the three functions just mentioned the only ones. Rather, they serve as indicators of how art has functioned in the past and can function in the present. Like the types and styles of art that have occurred through history, these three functions and others are options for artists and depend on what artists wish to do with their artworks—as well as how we perceive and respond to them.

Plays, paintings, and concerts can provide escape from everyday cares, treat us to a pleasant time, and engage us in social occasions. Works of art that provide enjoyment

0.4 Grant Wood, *American Gothic*, 1930. Oil on beaver board, 30 × 25 ins (76 × 63 cm). Art Institute of Chicago (Friends of American Art Collection).

may perform other functions as well. The same artworks we enjoy may also create insights into human experience. We can glimpse the conditions of other cultures, and we can find healing therapy in enjoyment.

An artwork in which one individual finds only enjoyment may function as a profound social and personal comment to another. A Mozart symphony, for example, may relax us and allow us to escape our cares. It may also comment on the life of the composer and/or the conditions of eighteenth-century Austria. Grant Wood's *American Gothic* (Fig. **0.4**) may amuse us, and/or provide a tongue-in-cheek commentary about rural America, and/or move us deeply. The result depends on the artist, the artwork, and us. We can note here, as well, that implicit in our discussion of enjoyment as a function of art is the concept that art can exist for its own sake, alone. That is to say that many people believe that art need not have any "function" at all. "Art for art's sake" is the phrase used to describe their viewpoint, and the issue of whether art should be functional or exist purely for its own sake is worthy of discussion.

Art used to bring about political change or to modify the behavior of large groups of people has political or

social functions. In ancient Rome, for example, the authorities used music and theatre to keep masses of unemployed people occupied in order to quell urban unrest. At the same time, Roman playwrights used their public platform to attack incompetent or corrupt officials. The Greek playwright Aristophanes, in such plays as *The Birds*, saw that comedy could be employed as a means of challenging the political ideas of the leaders of ancient Athenian society. In *Lysistrata*, he puts his message over by creating a story in which all the women of Athens go on a sex strike until Athens is rid of war and warmongers.

In nineteenth-century Norway, the playwright Henrik Ibsen used *An Enemy of the People* as a platform for airing the conflict of priorities between pollution control and economic wellbeing. In the United States today, many artworks act as vehicles to advance social and political causes, or to sensitize viewers, listeners, or readers to particular cultural situations like racial prejudice and AIDS.

Art also functions as an artifact: A product of a particular time and place, an artwork represents the ideas and technology of that specific environment. Artworks often provide not only striking examples but occasionally the only tangible records of some peoples. Artifacts like paintings, sculptures, poems, plays, and buildings, enhance our insights into many cultures, including our own. Consider, for example, the many revelations we find in a sophisticated work like the roped pot on a stand from Igbo-Ukwu (Fig. **0.5**). This ritual water pot from a village in eastern Nigeria was cast using the *cire-perdue* or "lost-wax" process (see p. 68) and is amazing in its virtuosity. It reveals the sophisticated vision and technical accomplishment of this ninth- and tenth-century African society.

The Igbo-Ukwu pot suggests that when we examine art in the context of cultural artifact, one of the issues we face concerns the use of artworks in religious *ritual*. We could consider ritual as a separate function of art. In fact, we may not think of religious ritual as art at all; but ritual often expresses human communication through an artistic medium. Music, for example, when part of a religious ceremony, does this, and theatre—if seen as an occasion planned and intended for presentation—would include religious rituals as well as events that take place in theatres. Often, as a survey of art history would confirm, we cannot discern when ritual stops and secular production starts. For example, ancient Greek tragedy seems clearly to have evolved from, and maintained, ritualistic practices as it changed from choric dance to formal theatre. When ritual, planned and intended for presentation, uses traditionally artistic media like music, dance, and theatre, we can legitimately study it as art, and see it also as an artifact of its particular culture.

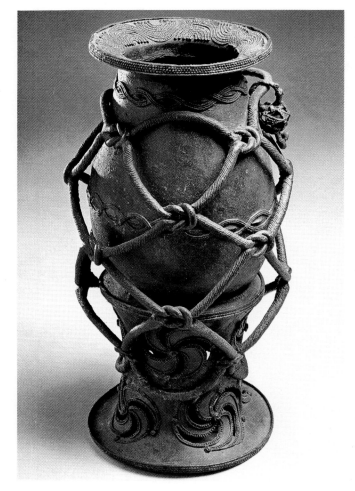

0.5 Roped pot on a stand, from Igbo-Ukwu, eastern Nigeria, 9th–10th century. Leaded bronze, height 12½ ins (32 cm). National Museum, Lagos.

HOW SHOULD WE PERCEIVE AND RESPOND?

Thus far, in putting the arts in context, we have examined The Arts and Ways of Knowing, What Are Art's Main Concerns? and What Are Art's Purposes and Functions? Now we deal with the challenge of how we approach studying them—How Should We Perceive and Respond? We have chosen a method of study that can act as a springboard into confident and rewarding engagement with the arts. In the first half of the book, we will examine the various media artists use to transform their visions of human reality into works of art. In the second half of the book we will travel through history and around the world to examine the choices artists make while using their media to give artworks their particular appearance. The first half of the book is more technical than the second, and it deals, basically, with the question, What can we see and hear in works of art? To put that question

in different terms, How can we sharpen our aesthetic perception? The answer is threefold.

- First of all, we must identify those items that can be seen and heard in works of art and literature.
- Second, we must learn some of the terminology relating to those items—just as we learn any subject.
- Third, we must understand why and how what we perceive relates to our response.

It is, after all, our response to an artwork that interests us. We can *perceive* an object. We *choose* to *respond* to it in aesthetic terms.

In Chapters 1–8 we need to employ a consistent method as we pass from one art discipline to another. We will ask three questions: (1) What is it? (2) How is it put together? (3) How does it stimulate the senses? We will study these questions in each of the art disciplines. As we will see, these are also the basic questions we can ask about individual artworks.

When we respond to the question, What is it? we make a formal response. We recognize that we are perceiving the two-dimensional space of a picture (Fig. 0.6), the three-dimensional space of a sculpture or a piece of architecture, or perhaps time and sound, or time and space in dance. We also recognize the form of the item—for example, a still life, a human figure, a tragedy, a ballet, a concerto, a narrative film, or a residence. The term *form* is a broad one: There are art forms, forms of arts, and forms in art.

When we respond to the question, How is it put together? we respond to the technical elements of the artwork. We recognize and respond to, for instance, the fact that the picture has been painted in oil, made by a print-making technique, or created as a watercolor. We also recognize and respond to other technical elements that constitute the work and which we define in subsequent chapters, for example, items of composition—line, form or shape, mass, color, repetition, harmony—and the unity that results from all of these. What devices have been employed, and how does each part relate to the others to make a whole? A concerto is composed of melody, harmony, timbre, tone, and more; a tragedy utilizes language, *mise-en-scène*, exposition, complication, dénouement; a ballet has formalized movement, *mise-en-scène*, line, and idea content.

Moving to the third question, we examine how the work stimulates our senses—and why. In other words, how do the particular formal and technical arrangements (whether conscious or unconscious on the part of the artist) elicit a sense response from us? Here we deal with physical and mental properties. For example, our

0.6 *Hercules and Telephos*, from Herculaneum, Italy, 2nd century B.C.E. Roman copy of a Greek work. Wall painting, height 5 ft 7 ins (1.17 m). Museo Archeologico Nazionale, Naples.

0.7 *Dionysus (Heracles?)*, from the east pediment of the Parthenon, Athens, c. 438–432 B.C.E. Marble, over life-size. British Museum, London.

response to sculpture can be physical. We can touch a piece of sculpture and sense its smoothness or its hardness (Fig. 0.7). In contrast we experience sense responses that are essentially mental. For example, upright triangles give us a sense of solidity. When we perceive the colors green and blue, we call them "cool"; reds and yellows are "warm" colors. Pictures that are predominantly horizontal or composed of broad curves are said to be "soft" or placid. Angular, diagonal, or short, broken lines stimulate a sense of movement. Music that utilizes undulating melodic contours can be "smooth"; music that is highly consonant can be "warm" or "rich." These and other sense responses tend to be universal.

We can also ask a fourth question about a work of art: What does the work mean? We might answer that question in strictly personal terms, for example, a painting may remind us of some personal experience. However, we cannot dismiss the question, What does it mean? as a reference to purely personal experience, as we will discover in Chapters 9–13. Response to an artwork, meaning, and experience go beyond opinion to encompass attempts to understand what the artist may have had in mind and what circumstances may have shaped the work. Meaning in an artwork often can be enhanced by understanding cultural or historical contexts, including biography.

When we have finished our examination of the two units of this text—*The Media of the Arts: What Artists Use to Express "Reality"* and *The Styles of the Arts: How Artists Portray "Reality"*—our own human reality will have broader horizons and deeper insights. We will also approach and communicate these issues with greater confidence.

HOW DO WE LIVE WITH ART?

Our final examination on the topic of putting the arts in context concerns the relationship of the arts to everyday life. Because of unfamiliarity, many individuals are uncomfortable approaching the arts and literature. That unfamiliarity, perhaps, has been fostered by individuals, both within the disciplines and without, who try to make involvement in the arts and literature elitist, and art galleries, museums, concert halls, theatres, and opera houses open only to the knowledgeable and the sophisticated. Nothing could be further from actuality. The arts are elements of life with which we can and must deal and to which we must respond every day. We live with the arts because the principles of *aesthetics* permeate our existence. Specifically, the aesthetic experience is a way of knowing and communicating in and of itself, separate from other ways of knowing and communicating. It forms a significant part of our experience. Cutting ourselves off from the part of our existence that deals with aesthetic communication and knowledge forces us to cope with life with only half of our available survival tools.

The arts also play important roles in making the world around us more interesting and habitable. Artistic ideas join with *conventions* to make everyday objects attractive and pleasurable. We use the term "convention" repeatedly in this text. A convention is a set of rules or mutually accepted conditions. For example, the plug on electrical appliances is a practical convention to which those who have traveled abroad can testify. A more relevant example of a convention might be the keyboard and tuning of a piano. In any case, conventions play important roles in everyday life.

Figure 0.8, a scale drawing of an eighteenth-century highboy, illustrates how art and convention combine in everyday items. The maker of the high chest conceived it to fill a practical purpose—to provide for storage of household objects in an easily accessible, yet hidden, place. However, while designing an object to accommodate that practical need, the cabinetmakers felt the additional need to provide an interesting and attractive object. If we perceive with discrimination and imagination, we enter an enlightening and challenging experience with this piece of furniture.

First of all, a convention that dictates a consistent height for tables and desks controls the design. So the lower portion of the chest, from point A to point B, designs space within a height that will harmonize with other furniture in the room. If we look carefully, we can also see that the parts of the chest are designed with a sophisticated and interesting series of proportional and progressive relationships. The distance from A to B is

0.8 Scale drawing of an 18th-century highboy.

strong repetition of the oval. We need only look at the various parts of the Bug to see variation on this theme. Later models differ from this version and reflect the intrusion of conventions, again, into the world of design. As safety standards called for larger bumpers, the oval design of the motor-compartment hood was flattened so a larger bumper could clear it. The rear window was enlarged and squared to accommodate the need for increased rear vision. The intrusion of these conventions changed the design of the Beetle by breaking down the strong unity of the original composition.

Finally, as Edwin J. Delattre states when he compares the purpose for studying technical subjects to the purpose for studying the humanities or the arts, "When a person studies the mechanics of internal combustion engines the intended result is that he should be better able to understand, design, build, or repair such engines, and sometimes he should be better able to find employment because of his skills, and thus better his life. ... When a person studies the humanities [the arts] the intended result is that he should be better able to understand, design, build, or repair a life—for living is a vocation we have in common despite our differences.

"The humanities provide us with opportunity to become more capable in thought, judgment, communication, appreciation, and action." Delattre goes on to say that these provisions enable us to think more rigorously and to imagine more abundantly. "These activities free us to possibilities that are new, at least to us, and they unbind us from portions of our ignorance about living well. ... Without exposure to the cultural ... traditions that are our heritage, we are excluded from a common world that crosses generations."[1] The poet Archibald MacLeish is more succinct: "Without the Arts, how can the university teach the Truth?"

APPLYING CRITICAL SKILLS

We all seem to want to opine on the quality of works of art. Whatever the form or medium, judgments about the quality of an artwork vary from one extreme to another, ranging from "I like it" and "interesting" to specific reasons for its effectiveness or ineffectiveness.

Because the word *criticism* implies many things to many people, we must first agree what it means—or what it does not. Criticism is not necessarily saying negative things about a work of art. All too often we think of critics as people who pass judgments, giving their opinions

twice the distance from A to D and is equal to the distance from B to C. The distances from A to F and C to E bear no recognizable relationship to the previous dimensions but are, however, equal to each other and to the distances from G to H, H to I, and I to J. In addition, the size of the drawers in the upper chest decreases at an even and proportional rate from bottom to top.

The Volkswagen shown in Figure 0.9 forms another example. Here repetition of form reflects a concern for unity, one of the fundamental characteristics of art. The design of the early Volkswagen Beetle (or "Bug") used

0.9 Volkswagen Beetle, 1938.

on the value of a painting, sculpture, work of architecture, and so on. Personal judgment may result from criticism, but criticism implies more than passing judgment.

Criticism *should* be a *detailed process of analysis to gain understanding and appreciation*. Identifying the formal elements of an artwork—learning what to look for—is the first step of art criticism. We *describe* an artwork by examining its many facets and then we try to understand how they work together to create meaning or experience. We then try to state what that meaning or experience is. Only when that process is complete should criticism move to judgment.

Professional critics usually bring to the process a set of standards developed from personal experience. Whenever personal standards are applied, the process of criticism becomes complicated. First of all, knowledge of the art form may be shallow. Second, perceptual skills may be faulty; and, finally, the range of personal experience may be limited. In addition, the application of personal standards can be problematic if judgment is based on pre-established criteria: If someone believes that, say, "beauty" and/or usefulness are essential elements of a work of art, then any work that does not meet those criteria will be judged as faulty, despite other qualities that may make the work unique and profound. Pre-established criteria often deny critical acclaim to new or experimental approaches in art.

History resounds with examples of new artistic attempts that met with terrible receptions from so-called experts, whose idea of what an artwork ought to be could not allow for experimentation or departures from accepted practice. In 1912, when Vaslav Nijinsky (nih-JIN-skee) choreographed the ballet *Rite of Spring* to music by Igor Stravinsky (strah-VIN-skee), the unconventional music and choreography actually caused a riot: Audiences and critics could not tolerate that it did not conform to accepted musical and balletic standards. Today, both the music and choreography are considered masterpieces.

Similarly, Samuel Beckett's play, *Waiting for Godot* (1953) (Fig. **0.10**) does not have a plot, characters, or ideas that are expressed in a conventional manner. In this play, two tramps wait beside the road by a withered tree for the arrival of someone named Godot. The tramps tell stories to each other, argue, eat some food, and are interrupted by a character named Pozzo leading a slave, Lucky, by a rope. After a brief conversation, Lucky and Pozzo leave. At the end of the first act, a boy enters to announce that Godot will not come today. In Act 2, much the same sequence of events occurs. Then Lucky leads in a blind Pozzo. The tree has sprouted a few leaves. The play ends as the young boy returns to indicate Godot will not arrive that day either. If your standards require a successful play to have a carefully fashioned plot wrapped around fully developed characters and a clear message, then *Waiting*

0.10 Samuel Beckett, *Waiting for Godot*, Utah Shakespearean Festival, 1990. Director: Tom Marlens.

for Godot cannot possibly be a good play. Some people agree with such an assertion; others disagree vehemently. What, then, are we to conclude? What if my criteria do not match yours? What if two experts disagree on the quality of a movie? Does that make any difference to our experience of it?

Value judgments are intensely personal, but some opinions are more informed than others and represent more authoritative judgment. Sometimes, even knowledgeable people disagree. Disagreements about quality, however, can enhance our experience of a work of art when they lead us to think about why the differences exist. In this way, we gain a deeper understanding of the artwork. Nonetheless, *criticism* can be exercised without involving any judgment. We can thoroughly dissect any work of art—for example, we can describe and analyze line, color, melody, harmony, texture, plot, character, and/or message. We can observe how all of these factors affect people and their responses. We can spend a significant amount of time doing this and never pass a value judgment at all.

Does this discussion mean all artworks are equal in value? Not at all. It means that in order to understand what criticism involves, we must separate descriptive analysis, which can be satisfying in and of itself, from the act of passing value judgments. We may not like the work we have analyzed, but we may have understood something we did not understand before. Passing judgment may play no role whatsoever in our understanding of an artwork. But we are still involved in criticism. As an exercise in understanding, criticism is necessary. We must investigate and describe. We must experience the need to know enough about the process, product, and experience of art if we are to have perceptions to share.

Now that we have examined briefly what criticism is and why we might try it, what approaches can we use?

TYPES OF CRITICISM

There are several types of criticism. Here we will examine four: formal criticism, contextual criticism, structuralism, and deconstruction.

Formal Criticism

Formal criticism is analysis that applies no external conditions or information. It attempts to explain a work's total formal aesthetic organization. When we use formal criticism, we analyze the artwork just as we find it: If it is a painting, we look only within the frame; if it is a play, we analyze only what we see and hear. Formal criticism approaches the artwork as a self-contained entity, and the work must stand on its own merits. Formal criticism is exemplified in the work of the "New Critics" such as Allen Tate (1899–1979), who insisted on the intrinsic value of a work of art and focused attention on the work alone as an independent unit of meaning. As an example of how we might go about formal criticism, consider this brief analysis of Molière's comedy *Tartuffe* (Fig. **0.11**).

Orgon, a rich bourgeois, has allowed a religious con man, Tartuffe, to gain complete control over him. Tartuffe has moved into Orgon's house and tries to seduce Orgon's wife while at the same time planning to marry Orgon's daughter. Tartuffe is unmasked, and Orgon orders him out. Tartuffe seeks his revenge by claiming title to Orgon's house and blackmailing him with some secret papers. At the very last instant, Tartuffe's plans are foiled by the intervention of the king, and the play ends happily.

We have just described a story. Were we to go one step further and analyze the plot, we would look, among other things, for points at which *crises* occur and cause important decisions to be made by the characters; we would also want to know how those decisions moved the play from one point to the next. In addition, we would try to locate the extreme crisis, the *climax*. Meanwhile, we would discover auxiliary parts of the plot such as *reversals*—for example, when Tartuffe is discovered and the characters become aware of the true situation. Depending on how detailed our criticism were to become, we could work our way through each and every aspect of the plot. We might then devote some time to describing and analyzing the driving force—the *character*—of each person in the play and how the characters relate to each other. Has Molière created fully developed characters? Are they types or do they seem to behave more or less like real individuals? In examining the *thematic* elements of the play, we would no doubt conclude that the play deals with religious hypocrisy, and that Molière had a particular point of view on that subject.

In this formal approach, information about the playwright, previous performances, historic relationships, and

0.11 Jean-Baptiste Molière, *Tartuffe*, University of Arizona Theatre, 1990. Director: Charles O'Connor.

so on, are irrelevant. Thus the formal approach helps us to analyze how an artwork operates and to decide why the artwork produces the responses it does. We can apply this form of criticism to any work of art and come away with a variety of conclusions. Of course, knowledge about how artworks are put together, what they are, and how they stimulate the senses (topics of the first half of this text) enhances the critical process. Knowing the basic elements that comprise these formal and technical elements of the artwork gives us a ready outline on which to begin a formal analysis.

Contextual Criticism

Another general approach, contextual criticism, seeks meaning by adding to formal criticism an examination of related information outside the artwork, such as facts about the artist's life, his or her culture, social and political conditions and philosophies, and public and critical responses to the work. These can be researched and applied to the work in order to enhance perception and understanding. Contextual criticism views the artwork as an artifact generated from particular contextual needs, conditions, and/or attitudes. If we carry our criticism of *Tartuffe* in this direction, we would note that certain historical events help clarify the play. For example, the object of Molière's attention was probably the Company of the Holy Sacrament, a secret, conspiratorial, and influential religious society in France at the time. Like many fanatical religious sects—including those of our own time—the society sought to enforce its own view of morality by spying on the lives of others and seeking out heresies—in this case, in the Roman Catholic Church. Its followers were religious fanatics, and they had considerable impact on the lives of the citizenry at large. If we were to follow this path of criticism, we would pursue any and all contextual matters that might illuminate or clarify what happens in the play. Contextual criticism may also employ the same kind of internal examination followed in the formal approach.

Structuralism

Structuralism is a European critical movement of the mid-twentieth century, based on the linguistic theories of Ferdinand de Saussure (soh-SUHR). It applies to the artwork a broader significance, insisting that individual phenomena—in this case works of art—can be understood only within the context of the overall structures of which they are a part. These structures represent universal sets of relationships which derive meaning from their contrasts and interactions within a specific context.

Structuralist criticism, associated with Roland Barthes (bahrt; 1915–80), derives by analogy from structural linguistics, which sees a "text" as a system of self-contained signs whose meaning is derived from the pattern of their interactions rather than from any external reference. This approach opposes critical positions that seek to determine an artist's intent, for example. Thus, the meaning of Molière's *Tartuffe* lies not in what Molière may have had in mind, but in the patterns of contextual relationships that work within the play. Structuralism opposes approaches, such as deconstruction, that deny the existence of uniform patterns and definite meanings.

Deconstruction

Deconstruction, associated with the French philosopher Jacques Derrida (dare-ee-DAH; b. 1930), was also originally associated with literary criticism, but has been applied to other disciplines. Derrida used the term *text*, for example, to include any subject to which critical analysis can be applied. Deconstructing something means "taking it apart." The process of deconstruction implies on the one hand drawing out all the threads of a work to identify its multitude of meanings and, on the other hand, undoing the "constructs" of ideology or convention that have imposed meaning on the work. All of this leads to the conclusion that there is no such thing as a single meaning in a work of art, nor can it claim any absolute truth. Inasmuch as a work can outlast its author, its meanings transcend any original intentions. In other words, the viewer or listener brings as much to the work as the artist; thus, there are no facts, only interpretations. The story of *Tartuffe*, for example, becomes only a sidebar to the interpretation that we bring to it based on our own experiences and circumstances.

Both structuralism and deconstruction are much more complex and philosophically and sociologically involved than the limited space available in this text allows us to discuss in detail. However, they illustrate the diversity of theories and approaches that are possible when encountering works of art. These theories—as well as the simple processes of formal and contextual criticism—merit further exploration and classroom discussion as ways in which we can engage, analyze, come to know as best we can, and, ultimately, judge works of art.

MAKING JUDGMENTS

Now that we have made a rough definition of criticism and noted some approaches criticism can take in pursuit of understanding and enjoyment of works of art, we can make a few brief comments about making judgments.

While artworks may be judged on many levels and by many criteria, two particular characteristics stand out: Artisanship and communication. Judgment of a work of art's quality probably ought to include consideration of both of these.

Artisanship

Judging a work's artisanship means judging how it is crafted or made. Generally, such judgments require knowledge about the medium of the artwork. It is, for example, difficult to judge how a musical symphony is crafted without having some knowledge of musical composition. The same may be said of judging how well a painting, sculpture, building, or play is made. Nonetheless, some criteria exist that allow general judgment of artisanship. These criteria include *clarity* and *interest*.

Applying the standard of clarity means deciding whether the work has coherence. Even the most complex works of art need handles that allow us to approach them and begin to understand how they work. This standard of judgment has stood the test of time. Artworks have sometimes been compared to onions in that the well-made ones allow respondents to peel away translucent layers, with removal of each layer moving us closer to the core. Some people are able to peel away all the layers, and some people are able to peel away only one or two, but a masterfully crafted work of art will have a coherence that allows virtually anyone to grasp on to some layer, if only the outer one.

Applying the standard of interest is similar to, and perhaps overlaps, applying the standard of clarity in that artists use layers of devices or qualities to capture and hold our interest. Masterfully crafted works of art employ such devices and qualities as: (1) universality (the artist's ability to touch a common experience or feeling within us), (2) carefully developed structures or focal points that lead us where the artist intends us to go, and (3) freshness of approach that makes us curious to investigate further. When we watch a tired and trite mystery, we know what is going to happen: The characters are stale clichés, and we lose interest almost immediately. A masterfully crafted work will hold us—even if we know the story. Such is the case with plays like Sophocles' *Oedipus the King* or Shakespeare's *Hamlet*.

If a work of art does not appear clear or interesting, we may wish to examine whether the fault lies in the work or in ourselves before rendering judgment.

Communication

Evaluating what an artwork is trying to say offers more immediate opportunity for judgment and less need for expertise. Johann Wolfgang von Goethe, the nineteenth-century poet, novelist, and playwright, set out a basic, commonsense approach to evaluating communication. Because Goethe's approach provides an organized means for discovering an artwork's communication by progressing from analytical to judgmental functions, it is a helpful way to end our discussion on criticism. Goethe suggests that we approach the critical process by asking three questions: What is the artist trying to say? Does he or she succeed? Was the artwork worth the effort? These questions focus on the artist's communication. The third question, of whether or not the project was worth the effort, raises issues such as uniqueness or profundity. A well-crafted work of art that merely restates obvious insights about the human condition lacks quality in its communicative component. One that offers profound and unique insights exhibits quality.

We should think of the arts somewhat as we think of people. An adequate adjustment to the world cannot be made from social responses that simply divide the "good people" from the "bad people." We should be skeptical even of such categories as "the people I like" and "the people I don't like." If we do maintain such divisions, we find individuals constantly moving from one group to the other. Eventually we find human differences too subtle for easy classification, and the web of our relationships becomes too complex for analysis. We try to move toward more and more sensitive discrimination, so that there are those we can learn from, those we can work with, those good for an evening of light talk, those we can depend on for a little affection, and so on—with perhaps those very few with whom we can sustain a relationship for a lifetime. When we have learned this same sensitivity and adjustment to works of art—when we have gone beyond the easy categories of the textbooks and have learned to regard our art relationships as part of our own growth—then we shall have achieved a dimension in living that is as deep and as irreplaceable as friendship.

THINKING CRITICALLY

- The artist Andy Warhol (WAHR-hall; 1928–87) reportedly said that "Art is anything you can get away with." Some people believe that art is whatever an artist says it is. Others contend that art is a vision of human reality expressed in a particular medium and shared with others. What do you agree or disagree with in these definitions? Formulate your own definition.

- The ancient Greek philosopher Aristotle (AIR-his-taht-uhl; 384–322 B.C.E.), divided the arts into "high art" and "low art." In terms of the arts of the twenty-first century, how would such a division apply? What reasons might there be, today, to separate "popular culture" from "art"?

- Some cities require new office buildings to set aside a certain percentage of their cost for artworks, such as sculptures, to be incorporated into the building. Make an argument for and against such policies.

- Public monies are often utilized to buy art, subsidize symphonies, and support individual artists. The intent is to keep art at the center of our public lives. Why would you agree or disagree with such practices? What stipulations should or should not be attached to public money used to support artistic activities?

- Do you believe that art should serve some kind of societal function, or should it exist solely for its own sake? Make a case for both sides of the argument.

- Locate an object in your home that has primarily a utilitarian purpose but also exhibits some kind of artistic design. Describe how the design of the object prompts a pleasurable, aesthetic experience for you.

PART I

THE MEDIA OF THE ARTS

What Artists Use to Express "Reality"

THE MEDIA OF THE ARTS

What Artists Use to Express "Reality"

MEDIA

The arts can be powerful means of expression, and, as we suggested earlier, we live with them on a daily basis, in and out of museums, concert halls, and theatres. We need to understand from the outset that we cannot recognize, understand, or communicate how art affects us without using language. It is important, therefore, that we become *literate* in the languages of the arts. Getting Started, then, means preparing to travel in the land of basic terminology. In other words, we are about to sample some of the things that will help us to identify and communicate important characteristics appropriate to works of art.

In the chapters of Part I of this text, we will meet the traditional art disciplines of drawing, painting, printmaking, photography, sculpture, music, theatre, cinema, dance, architecture, and literature. Each of these disciplines has its own language, and these chapters introduce us to those languages. Thus, Chapters 1–8 comprise mostly a catalogue of terms and definitions. Some are short and sweet, others are more complicated and conceptual. Many of the terms and concepts are recognizable, and you will find yourself thinking, "I know that." At other times you will wonder about the need for the technicality of what is presented. It is at these points that discussion in and out of class will be necessary. Reference to the music CD and careful study of the visual examples will be required. In the end, tremendous satisfaction and confidence will result when, on the street and elsewhere, works of art can be engaged and discussed with accurate terminology and enhanced perception. The ability to do this will result in amazing rewards.

APPROACHING PART I OF THE TEXT

FEATURE BOXES

Inserted at various points in the text are feature boxes. These inserts are intended to supplement the material in the text. They allow for more detailed discussion and analysis, and their purpose is to engage you and make the experience of the arts more personal and rewarding. Because of the way textbooks need to be designed, these boxes do not always appear in the most convenient places. That is to say, you will occasionally encounter a feature box in a place that breaks the flow of the text. Try not to break the flow of your reading when that happens. Continue with the text until you come to a natural break. Summarize what you have been reading, and then return to the feature box to absorb its message.

PART I OUTLINE

CHAPTER ONE: Pictures: Drawing, Painting, Printmaking, and Photography
CHAPTER TWO: Sculpture
CHAPTER THREE: Music
CHAPTER FOUR: Theatre
CHAPTER FIVE: Cinema
CHAPTER SIX: Dance
CHAPTER SEVEN: Architecture
CHAPTER EIGHT: Literature

CHAPTER ONE

PICTURES

Drawing, Painting, Printmaking, and Photography

WHAT ARE THEY?

HOW ARE THEY PUT TOGETHER?

MEDIA
  Drawing
  Painting
  Printmaking
  Photography
COMPOSITION
  Elements
  Principles
Profile: Pablo Picasso
OTHER FACTORS
  Perspective
  Chiaroscuro
  Content
*Painting and Human Reality:
  Géricault,* **The Raft of the
  "Medusa"**

HOW DO THEY STIMULATE THE SENSES?

CONTRASTS
A Personal Journey: Picasso,
  Guernica
DYNAMICS
TROMPE L'OEIL
JUXTAPOSITION
FOCUS
OBJECTIVITY
Thinking Critically
Cyber Study

IMPORTANT TERMS

Intaglio The printmaking process
  in which ink is transferred
  from the grooves of a metal
  plate to paper by extreme
  pressure.
Lithography A printmaking
  technique, based on the
  principle that oil and water do
  not mix, in which ink is
  applied to a piece of paper
  from a specially prepared
  stone.

Composition The arrangement of
  line, form, mass, color, and
  so forth in a work of art.
Line The basic building block of
  visual design; for example, a
  thin mark, a color edge, or
  implied.
Form The shape of an object
  within a composition.
Hue The spectrum notation of
  color.
Value The relationship of lights to
  darks in a visual composition.
Intensity The degree of purity of
  a color.
Variation The relationship of
  repeated items in a
  composition to each other.
Symmetry The balancing of like
  forms and colors on opposite
  sides of the vertical axis of a
  composition.
Perspective The creation of the
  illusion of distance in a
  picture through the use of
  line, atmosphere, and so on.
Chiaroscuro Light and shade; the
  balance of light and shade
  across the whole picture.

Pictures of family, friends, rock and sports stars, copies of artistic masterpieces, and original paintings and prints adorn our personal spaces. Dorm rooms, bedrooms, and living rooms seem coldly empty and depersonalized without pictures of some kind. Pictures have always been important to us. People who lived in caves 20,000 years ago drew pictures on their walls. In this chapter we shall learn about the many ways pictures can be made and how artists use two-dimensional qualities to speak to us.

WHAT ARE THEY?

Drawings, paintings, photographs, and prints are pictures, differing primarily in the technique of their execution. They are all two-dimensional. We respond initially to their content. A picture might be a landscape, seascape, portrait, still life, religious icon, non-objective (nonrepresentational), abstract—or something else. So, our initial encounter and response involves observation.

HOW ARE THEY PUT TOGETHER?

MEDIA

Our technical level of response is more complex. Our first response to how a work is put together is to the medium used by the artist to execute it.

Drawing

Drawing, considered the foundation of two-dimensional art, involves a wide variety of materials traditionally divided into two groups: *dry media* and *wet media*. In the discussion that follows we will note the dry media of chalk, charcoal, graphite, and pastel, and the wet media of pen and ink and wash and brush.

DRY MEDIA *Chalk* developed as a drawing medium by the middle of the sixteenth century. Artists first used it in its natural state, derived from ocher hematite, white soapstone, or black carbonaceous shale, placing it in a holder and sharpening it to a point. Chalk is a fairly flexible medium. A wide variety of tonal areas can be created, with extremely subtle transitions between them. Chalk can be applied with heavy or light pressure. It can be worked with the fingers once it is on the paper to create

the exact image the artist desires, as exemplified by *Prudence* (Fig. **1.1**) by Cherubino Alberti (chair-oo-BEE-no al-BAIR-tee).

Charcoal, a burnt wood product (preferably hardwood), is like chalk in that it requires a paper with a relatively rough surface—tooth—for the medium to adhere. Charcoal has a tendency to smudge easily, which dampened its early use as a drawing medium. It found wide use, however, as a means of drawing details, for example, on walls, and for murals that were eventually painted or frescoed. Today, resin fixatives sprayed over charcoal drawings can eliminate smudging, and charcoal has become a popular medium because artists find it extremely expressive. Like chalk, charcoal can achieve a variety of tonalities. The medium appears in a range of shapes and densities—for example, in sharpened sticks that work like pencils either hard or soft, as seen in George Bellows's *Study for "Nude with Hexagonal Quilt"* (Fig. **1.2**).

Graphite is a form of carbon, like coal, and is most commonly used in pencil leads. As a drawing medium it can be manufactured in various degrees of hardness. The harder the lead, the lighter and more delicate its mark, as seen in Oscar F. Bluemner's *Study for a Painting* (Fig. **1.3**).

Pastel, essentially a chalk medium, combines colored pigment and a non-greasy binder. Typically, pastels come in sticks about the diameter of a finger and in degrees of hardness: soft, medium, hard. Hardness is increased by adding more binder, with the result that the harder the stick, the less intense its color. In fact, the name "pastel" implies pale colors. Intense colors require soft pastels, but soft pastels are quite difficult to work with. A special ribbed paper helps to grab the powdery pastel, and a sprayed fixative holds the powder in place permanently

1.1 (*opposite top left*) Cherubino Alberti, *Prudence*, c. 1601. Red chalk on paper, 11¼ × 7 ins (28.7 × 17.7 cm). National Gallery of Art, Washington, D.C. (Gift of William B. O'Neal, in Honor of the 50th Anniversary of the National Gallery of Art).

1.2 (*opposite below left*) George Bellows, *Study for "Nude with Hexagonal Quilt,"* 1924. Charcoal and black crayon on paper, 21⅞ × 26⅞ ins (55.5 × 68.2 cm). National Gallery of Art, Washington, D.C. (Gift of Mr. and Mrs. Raymond J. Horowitz).

1.3 (*opposite top right*) Oscar F. Bluemner, *Study for a Painting*, probably 1928. Graphite on tracing paper, 19¹³⁄₁₆ × 13½ ins (50.3 × 34.2 cm). National Gallery of Art, Washington, D.C. (John Davis Hatch Collection).

1.4 (*opposite bottom right*) Beverly Buchanan, *Monroe County House with Yellow Datura*, 1994. Oil pastel on paper, 5 ft × 6 ft 7 ins (1.52 × 2 m). Bernice Steinbaum Gallery, Miami (Collection Dr. and Mrs. Harold Steinbaum).

1.5 Rembrandt van Rijn, *Lot and His Family Leaving Sodom*, c. 1655. Pen and light brown ink, 8⅛ × 11⅝ ins (20.5 × 29.5 cm). National Gallery of Art, Washington, D.C. (Widener Collection).

1.6 Chu Ta (Zhu Da) (Pata-shan-jen), *Lotus*, 1705. Brush and ink, 6½ × 28 ins (17 × 71 cm). Palmer Museum of Art, Pennsylvania State University.

on the paper. Beverly Buchanan's *Monroe County House with Yellow Datura* (Fig. **1.4**) illustrates not only the breadth of color intensity possible with pastels, but also the intricacy resulting from application by a skilled hand.

LIQUID MEDIA *Pen and ink* is a fairly flexible medium compared to graphite, for example. Although linear, pen and ink gives the artist the possibility of variation in line and texture. Shading can be achieved by diluting the ink, and the overall qualities of the medium are fluidity and expressiveness, as we can see in Rembrandt's *Lot and His Family Leaving Sodom* (Fig. **1.5**).

Wash and brush is created by diluting ink with water and applying it with a brush. Its characteristics are similar to watercolor, which we discuss in the next section on painting media. Although difficult to control, wash and brush creates effects nearly impossible to achieve in any other medium. Because it must be worked quickly and freely, it has a spontaneous and appealing quality, as suggested in *Lotus* (Fig. **1.6**) by Chu Ta (choo-tah).

In addition to the media just described (which may be combined in infinite variety) there exist a wide range of possibilities of an experimental and innovative nature. These include the computer, when it is used as an electronic sketchpad.

Painting

Like drawing media, painting media each have their own characteristics and, to a great extent, this dictates what the artist can or cannot achieve as an end result. In the following section we will examine six painting media: oils, watercolor, tempera, acrylics, fresco, and gouache.

Oils are perhaps the most popular of the painting media, and have been so since their development around the beginning of the fifteenth century. The popularity of oils stems principally from the fact that they offer a tremendous range of color possibilities; they can be reworked; they present many options for textural manipulation; and they are durable. If we compare two oil paintings, *The Starry Night* (Fig. **1.7**) by van Gogh (Vahn GOH) and *Holy Family with St. John* (Fig. **1.8**) by Giovanni Vanni (VAH-nee), the importance of the medium in each case can be seen. Vanni creates light and shade in the Baroque tradition, and his *chiaroscuro* (key-AR-ohs-SKOO-roh) depends upon the capacity of the medium to blend smoothly among color areas. Van Gogh, on the other hand, requires a medium that will form obvious brushstrokes. Vanni demands the paint to be flesh and cloth. Van Gogh demands the paint to be paint, and to call attention to itself.

Watercolor is a broad category that includes any color medium that uses water as a thinner. The term has traditionally referred to a transparent paint usually applied to paper. Because watercolors are transparent, an artist must be very careful to control them. If one area of color overlaps another, the overlap will show as a third area combining the previous hues. Their transparency gives watercolors a delicacy that cannot be produced in any other medium, with the possible exception of wash and brush.

Tempera is an opaque watercolor medium. It was employed by the ancient Egyptians, and is still used today. Tempera refers to ground pigments and their color binders—for example, gum or glue—but is best known in egg tempera form. It is a fast-drying medium that virtually eliminates brushstroke, and gives extremely sharp detail. Colors in tempera paintings appear almost gemlike in their clarity and brilliance.

1.7 Vincent van Gogh, *The Starry Night*, 1889. Oil on canvas, 29 × 36¼ ins (73.7 × 92.1 cm). The Museum of Modern Art, New York.

1.8 Giovanni Battista Vanni, *Holy Family with St. John*. Oil on canvas, 5 ft 10 ins × 4 ft 10 ins (1.78 × 1.47 m). Palmer Museum of Art, Pennsylvania State University.

Acrylics, in contrast with tempera, are modern, synthetic products. Most acrylics can be dissolved in water (but are water-impermeable when dry) and the binding agent for the pigment is an acrylic polymer. Flexible-media, acrylics offer artists a wide range of possibilities in both color and technique. An acrylic paint can be either opaque or transparent, depending upon dilution. It dries fast, thin, and resistant to cracking under extremes of temperature and humidity. It is perhaps less permanent than some other media but adheres to a wider variety of surfaces. It does not darken or yellow with age, as does oil.

Fresco is a wall-painting technique in which pigments suspended in water are applied to fresh wet plaster. Michelangelo's Sistine Chapel frescoes (see Fig. **11.10**) are the best-known examples of this technique. Because the end result becomes part of the plaster wall rather than being painted on it, fresco is long-lasting. However, it is an extremely difficult process, and once the pigments are applied, no changes can be made without replastering the entire section of the wall.

Gouache (gwash) is a watercolor medium in which gum is added to ground opaque colors mixed with water. Transparent watercolors can be made into gouache by adding Chinese white, which is a special opaque, water-soluble paint. The final product, in contrast to watercolor, is opaque.

Printmaking

Printmaking falls generally into three main categories, based essentially on the nature of the printing surface. First is *relief printing*, such as woodcut, wood engraving, and linoleum cut. Second is *intaglio* (in-TAH-lyoh) including etching, aquatint, and drypoint. Third is the *planographic process*, which includes lithography, silkscreen (serigraphy), and other forms of stenciling. Printmakers also use other combinations.

To begin, we need to ask, What is a print? A print is a hand-produced picture transferred from a printing surface to a piece of paper. An artist prepares the printing surface and directs the printing process. The unique value of a print lies in the fact that the artist usually destroys the block or surface after making the desired number of prints. In contrast, a reproduction is not an original, but a copy of an original painting or other artwork, reproduced usually by a photographic process. As a copy, the reproduction does not bear the handiwork of an artist.

Every print has a number. On some the number may appear as a fraction—for example, $^{36}/_{100}$. The denominator indicates how many prints were produced from the plate or block. This number is called the issue number, or

edition number. The numerator indicates where in the series the individual print was produced. If only a single number, such as 500, appears, it simply indicates the total number of prints in the series; this is also called an edition number. The numerator is an item of curiosity only; it has nothing to do with a print's value, monetarily or qualitatively. The issue number does have some value in comparing, for example, an issue of 25 with one of 500, and is usually reflected in the price of a print. However, the issue number is not the sole factor in determining the value of a print. Its quality and the reputation of the artist are more important considerations.

RELIEF PRINTING In relief printing (Fig. **1.10**), an artist transfers the image to paper by cutting away nonimage areas and inking the surface that remains. The image protrudes in relief from the block or plate, and produces a picture reversed from the image carved by the artist. This reversal characterizes all printmaking media. Figure **1.9** illustrates the linearity of the woodcut, and shows the precision and delicacy possible in the hands of an expert.

1.9 Albrecht Dürer, *Lamentation*, c. 1497–1500. Woodcut, 15½ × 11¼ ins (39 × 29 cm). Palmer Museum of Art, Pennsylvania State University (Gift of the Friends of the Museum of Art).

1.10 Relief printing.

1.11 Intaglio process.

INTAGLIO In the intaglio process (Fig. 1.11) (the opposite of relief printing), the artist transfers ink to the paper not from raised areas, but from grooves cut into a metal plate. Line engraving, etching, drypoint, and aquatint are some of the methods of intaglio.

Line engraving involves cutting grooves into the metal plate with special sharp tools. It requires great muscular control because the pressure must be continuous and constant if the grooves are to produce the desired image. The line-engraving process produces very precise images and represents the most difficult and demanding of the intaglio processes.

In the *etching* process, the artist removes the surface of the plate by exposing it to an acid bath. First the artist covers the plate with a thin, waxlike, acid-resistant substance called a *ground*. The artist scratches away parts of the ground to produce the desired lines then immerses the plate in acid, which burns away the exposed areas. The longer a plate is left in the acid, the deeper the resulting etches; the deeper the etch, the darker the final image. Artists wishing to produce lines or areas of differing darkness must cover the lines they do not want to be more deeply cut before further immersions in the acid. Repetition of the process yields a plate producing a print with the desired differences in light and dark lines.

Figure **1.12** consists only of individual lines, either single or in combination. The lighter lines required less time in the acid than the darker ones. Because of the precision and clarity of the lines, it is difficult to determine whether this print is an etching or an engraving. Drypoint, on the other hand, can be distinguished because it produces lines with less sharp edges.

In *drypoint* the printmaker scratches the surface of a metal plate with a needle. Unlike line engraving, which gives a clean, sharp line, the drypoint technique leaves a ridge, called a burr, on either side of the groove, resulting in a somewhat fuzzy line.

Aquatint can create a range of values from lightest gray to black and thus is useful for shading. The intaglio methods already noted consist of various means of cutting lines into a metal plate. Sometimes, though, an artist may wish to create large areas of subdued tonality. Such shadowy areas cannot be produced effectively with lines. Therefore, the artist dusts the plate with a resin substance and heats it, which affixes the resin. She then puts it into an acid bath. A rough surface, like sandpaper, results and the print has tonal areas that reflect this texture, making aquatint very recognizable.

Once prepared, whether by line engraving, etching, drypoint, aquatint, or a combination of methods, the plate goes into a press along with a special dampened paper. Padding is placed on the paper, and then a roller forces the plate and the paper together with great pressure. The carefully applied ink, remaining only in the grooves, transfers as the paper is forced into the grooves by the roller of the press. Even if no ink had been applied to the plate, the paper would still receive an image. This *embossing* effect or *platemark* marks an intaglio process.

1.12 Daniel Hopfer, *Ceiling Ornament*. Etching, 10 × 8¾ ins (25 × 22 cm). Palmer Museum of Art, Pennsylvania State University.

1.13 Planographic process.

1.14 Thomas Hart Benton, *Cradling Wheat*, 1938. Lithograph, 9½ × 12 ins (24 × 30 cm). Palmer Museum of Art, Pennsylvania State University (Gift of Carolyn Wose Hull).

PLANOGRAPHIC PROCESSES In a planographic process (Fig. **1.13**), the artist prints from a plane surface—neither relief nor intaglio. *Lithography* (the term's literal meaning is "stone writing") rests on the principle that water and grease do not mix. To create a lithograph, artists begin with a porous stone—usually limestone—and grind one side until absolutely smooth. They then draw an image on the stone with a greasy substance. They can control the darkness of the final image by varying the amount of grease used: The more grease, the darker the image. After drawing the image, the artist treats the stone with gum arabic and nitric acid, and then rinses it with a petrol product that removes the image. However, the water, gum, and acid have impressed the grease on the stone, and when it is wetted it absorbs water only in the ungreased areas. Finally, a grease-based ink is applied to the stone. It, in turn, will not adhere to the water-soaked areas, but only where the artist has drawn. As a result, the stone can be placed in a press and the image will be transferred to the waiting paper.

In Figures **1.14** and **1.15** we see the characteristic most attributable to lithography—a crayon-drawing appearance. Because the lithographer usually draws with crayonlike material on the stone, the final print has exactly that quality. Compare these prints with Figure **1.16**, a pastel drawing, and the point is clear.

Silkscreening is the most common of the stenciling processes. Silkscreens are made from a finely meshed silk fabric mounted on a wooden frame. The nonimage areas are blocked out by a variety of methods, including glue or cut paper. The stencil goes into the frame and ink is applied. A rubber instrument, called a squeegee, forces ink through the openings of the stencil, through the screen, and onto the paper below. This technique allows the printmaker to achieve large, flat, uniform areas, as can be seen in Figure **1.17**. Here the artist has, through

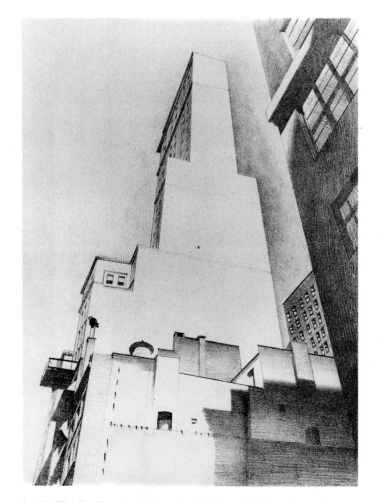

1.15 Charles Sheeler, *Delmonico Building*, 1925. Lithograph, 10 × 7⅛ ins (25 × 18 cm). Palmer Museum of Art, Pennsylvania State University.

1.16 Hobson Pittman, *Violets No. 1*, 1971. Pastel, 9½ × 10¼ ins (24 × 26 cm). Palmer Museum of Art, Pennsylvania State University.

1.17 Nancy McIntyre, *Barbershop Mirror*, 1976. Silkscreen, 26½ × 19 ins (67 × 48 cm). Palmer Museum of Art, Pennsylvania State University.

successive applications of ink, built up a complex composition, with highly lifelike detail.

Prints reflect recognizable differences in technique. It is not always possible to discern the technique that has been used in executing a print, and some prints reflect a combination of techniques. However, in determining the method of execution, we add another layer of potential response to a work.

Photography

Photographic images (and images of still photography's subsequent developments—motion pictures and video) are primarily informational. Cameras record the world around us, but, in addition, through editing, a photographer can take the camera's image and change the reality of life as we see it to a reality of the imagination. In one sense, photography is a simplification of reality that substitutes two-dimensional images for the three-dimensional images around us. It also can be an amplification of reality when a photographer takes a snapshot of one moment in time and transforms it, by altering the photographic image and/or artificially emphasizing one of its parts, into something quite different. In some cases, photography is merely a matter of personal record, executed with equipment of varying degrees of expense and sophistication (Fig. **1.18**). Certainly, photography as a matter of pictorial record, or even as *photojournalism*, may lack the qualities we believe are requisite to art. A photograph of a baseball player sliding into second base, or of Aunt Mabel cooking hamburgers at the family reunion, may trigger expressive responses for us, but the photographers

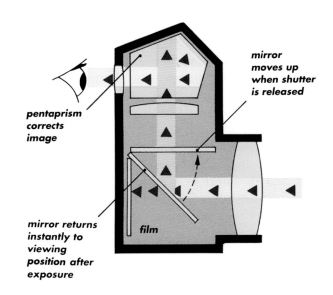

mirror
moves up
when shutter
is released

pentaprism
corrects
image

mirror returns
instantly to
viewing
position after
exposure

film

1.18 The single-lens reflex (SLR) camera.

PROFILE

Pablo Picasso

Pablo Picasso (1881–1973), born in Málaga, on the Mediterranean coast of Spain, studied at the Academy of Fine Arts in Barcelona but had already mastered realistic technique, however, and had little use for school. At sixteen he had his own studio in Barcelona. In 1900 he first visited Paris, and in 1904 he settled there. His personal style began to form in the years from 1901 to 1904, a period often referred to as his Blue Period because of the pervasive blue tones he used in his paintings at that time. In 1905, as he became more successful, Picasso altered his palette, and the blue tones gave way to a terra-cotta color, a shade of deep pinkish red. At the same time his subject matter grew less melancholy and included dancers, acrobats, and harlequins. The paintings he did during the years between 1905 and 1907 are said to belong to his Rose Period.

Picasso played an important part in the sequence of different artistic movements in the twentieth century. Because he and his work played significant roles in those movements, many people consider him the most important artist of the twentieth century. He said that to repeat oneself is to go against "the constant flight forward of the spirit." Primarily a painter, he also became a fine sculptor, engraver, and ceramist. In 1917 Picasso went to Rome to design costumes and scenery for Sergei Diaghilev's Ballets Russes. This work stimulated another departure in Picasso's work, and he began to paint the works now referred to as belonging to his Classic Period, which lasted from about 1918 until 1925.

At the same time as he was working on designs for the ballet, Picasso also continued to develop the Cubist technique (see Chapter 13), making it less rigorous and austere.

His painting *Girl Before a Mirror* (Fig. 1.19) gives us an opportunity to study his use of color in contrast to form. For example, Picasso chose red and green perhaps because they are complementary colors and perhaps, as art historian H. W. Janson suggests, because Picasso intended the green spot in the middle of the forehead of the mirror's image as a symbol of the girl's psyche, or inner self, which she confronts with apparent anguish.

Guernica (gair-NEE-kah; Fig. 1.36), his moving vision of the Spanish Civil War, also depends on curved forms. In this painting, however, the forms are intended to be fundamental because Picasso uses no color, only whites, grays, and black. *Guernica*, a huge painting, was Picasso's response to the 1937 bombing by the Fascist forces of the small Basque town of Guernica. The distortions of form that can be seen in this painting approach those of Surrealism (see Dali's *The Persistence of Memory*, Fig. 1.34), but Picasso never called himself a Surrealist. He continued to work with incredible speed and versatility—as painter, ceramist, sculptor, designer, and graphic artist—into his nineties.

---

probably did not have aesthetic communication or design in mind when they snapped the shutter. On the other hand, a carefully composed and sensitively designed photograph can contain every attribute of human expression possible in any art form.

Ansel Adams saw the photographer as an interpretative artist: He likened a photographic negative to a musical score, and the print to a performance. Despite all the choices the artist may make in committing an image to film, they are only the beginning of the artistic process. The photographer still has the choice of *size, texture,* and *value contrast (tonality).* A photograph of the grain of a piece of wood, for example, has an enormous range of aesthetic possibilities depending upon how the artist employs and combines these three elements.

COMPOSITION

A discussion of how any artwork is put together eventually results in a discussion of how it is composed. The elements and principles of *composition* are basic to all the arts, and we shall return to them time and time again as we proceed.

Elements

LINE The basic building block of a visual design is line. To most of us, a line is a thin mark: ————. In two-dimensional art, "line" is defined by its three physical characteristics. Line is (1) a linear form in which length dominates over width, (2) a color edge, and (3) an

1.19 Pablo Picasso, *Girl Before a Mirror*, Boisgeloup, March 1932. Oil on canvas, 5 ft 4 ins × 4 ft 3¼ ins (1.62 × 1.3 m).
The Museum of Modern Art, New York (Gift of Mrs. Simon Guggenheim).

1.20 Joan Miró, *Composition*, 1933. Oil on canvas, 4 ft 3⅜ ins × 5 ft 4 ins (1.31 × 1.65 m). Wadsworth Atheneum, Hartford, Connecticut.

implication of continued direction. Line as a linear form in which length dominates over width can be seen in several places in *Girl Before a Mirror* (Fig. **1.19**) by Pablo Picasso (pee-KAH-soh)—for example, in defining the diamond shapes in the background, along the back of the girl's head, and down her back. In *Composition* (Fig. **1.20**) by Joan Miró (hoh-ahn mee-ROH), the figures defined by the thin outlines also represent this characteristic. Second, line is an edge: The place where one object or plane stops and another begins. Again in Figure **1.20**, the edges where the white, black, and red color areas stop and the gray and gold backgrounds begin are lines.

The third characteristic, implication, is illustrated by the three rectangles in Figure **1.21**. They create a horizontal "line" that extends across the design. There is no physical line between the tops of the forms, but their spatial arrangement creates one by implication. A similar use of line occurs in Figure **1.7**, where we can see a definite linear movement from the upper left border through a series of swirls to the right border. That line is quite clear although it is composed not of a form edge or outline but of a carefully developed relationship of numerous color areas. This treatment of line appears in Figure **1.22**, although in a much more subtle and sophisticated way. By dripping paint onto canvas—a task not as easily

executed as it might appear—the artist subordinated form, in the sense of recognizable and distinct areas, and thereby *focal areas*, to form a dynamic network of complex lines. The effect of this technique has a strong relationship to the actual force and speed with which the pigment was applied.

An artist uses line to control our vision, to create unity and emotional value, and ultimately to develop meaning. In pursuing those ends, and by employing the three

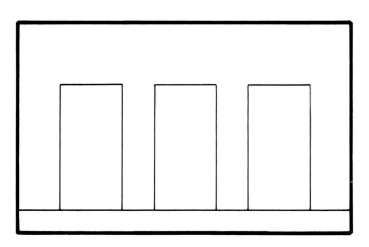

1.21 Outline and implied line.

1.22 Jackson Pollock, *Number 1, 1948*, 1948. Oil and enamel on unprimed canvas, 5 ft 8 ins × 8 ft 8 ins (1.73 × 2.64 m). The Museum of Modern Art, New York (Purchase).

aspects noted above, the artist finds that line has one of two simple characteristics: It is *curved* or *straight*. Whether expressed as an outline, as a boundary, or by implication, and whether simple or in combination, a line is some derivative of straightness or curvedness.

FORM *Form* and line relate closely both in definition and in effect. Form is the *shape* of an object within the composition, and the word shape is often used as a synonym for form. Form constitutes the space described by line. In a drawing, a building is a form. So is a tree. We perceive them as buildings or trees, and we also perceive their individual details because of the line by which they are composed. Form cannot be separated from line in two-dimensional design.

COLOR Many ways exist by which to approach the compositional concept of color. We could begin with color as electromagnetic energy, discuss the psychology of color perception, and/or approach color in terms of how artists use it. The first two possibilities are extremely interesting,

and the physics and psychology of color provide many potential crossovers between art and science and life. Nonetheless, we will limit our investigation to the last of these. The discussion that follows focuses on three color components: hue, value, and intensity.

Hue denotes the measurable wavelength of a specific color. The visible range of the color spectrum or range of colors we can actually distinguish extends from violet on one end to red on the other (Fig. **1.23**). The traditional color spectrum consists of seven basic hues (red, orange, yellow, green, blue, indigo, and violet). These are *primary hues* (red, blue, and yellow) and *secondary hues* that are direct derivatives of the primaries. In all, there are (depending on which color theory one follows) from ten to twenty-four perceivably different hues, including these seven.

Assuming, for the sake of clarity and illustration, that there are twelve basic hues, we can arrange them in a series (Fig. **1.24**) or turn them into a *color wheel* (Fig. **1.25**). With this visualization, artists' choices with regard to color become clearer. First, an artist can mix the

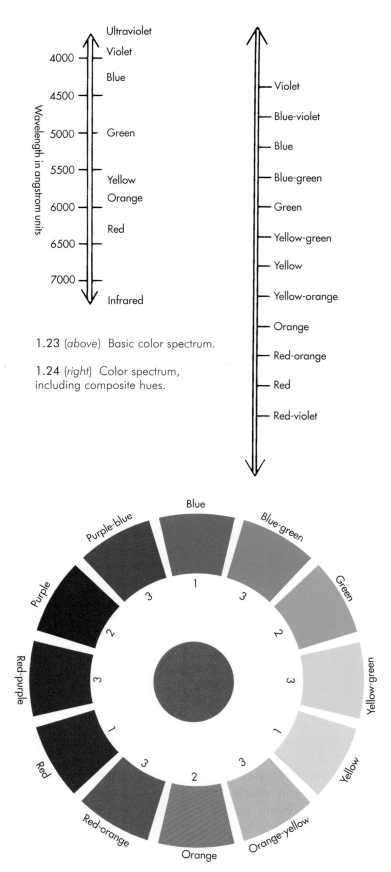

1.23 (*above*) Basic color spectrum.

1.24 (*right*) Color spectrum, including composite hues.

1.25 Color wheel: 1: primary hues; 2: secondary hues; 3: tertiary hues.

primary hues of the spectrum, two at a time in varying proportions, creating the other hues of the spectrum. For example, red and yellow in equal proportions make orange, a secondary hue. Varying the proportions—adding more red or more yellow—makes yellow-orange or red-orange, which are tertiary (TUHR-shee-air-ee) hues. Yellow and blue make green, and also blue-green and yellow-green. Red and blue make violet, blue-violet, and red-violet. Hues directly opposite each other on the color wheel are complementary. When they are mixed together in equal proportions, they produce gray.

Value, sometimes called key, is the relationship of blacks to whites and grays. The range of possibilities from black to white forms the value scale (Fig. **1.26**), which has black at one end, white at the other, and medium gray in the middle. The perceivable tones between black and white are designated light or dark. The lighter, or whiter, a color is, the higher its value. Likewise, the darker a color, the lower its value. For example, light pink is high in value, while dark red is low in value, even though they both have the same primary red as their base. Adding white to a hue (like primary red) creates a tint of that *hue*. Adding black creates a *shade*.

Some hues are intrinsically brighter than others, a factor we will discuss momentarily, but it is possible to have a brightness difference in the same color. The brightness may involve a change in value, as just discussed—that is, a pink versus a grayed or dull red. Brightness may also involve surface reflectance, a factor of considerable importance to all visual artists. A highly reflective surface creates a brighter color (and therefore a different response from the viewer) than does a surface of lesser reflectance, all other factors being equal. This is the difference between high gloss, semi-gloss, and flat paints, for example. Probably surface reflectance concerns texture more than color. Nonetheless, the term *brilliance* is often used to describe not only surface gloss but also characteristics synonymous with value. As just mentioned, some hues are intrinsically darker than others. That applies to the concept we discuss next: intensity.

Intensity, sometimes called chroma or saturation, is the degree of purity of a hue. Every hue has its own value—in its pure state each hue falls somewhere on the value scale, as in Figure **1.27**. The color wheel (see Fig. **1.25**) illustrates how movement around the wheel can create change in hue. Movements across the wheel alter intensity. For example, adding green to red grays the red. Therefore, because graying a hue is a value change, the terms intensity and value are occasionally used interchangeably. Some sources use the terms independently but state that changing a hue's value automatically changes its intensity. Graying a hue by using its comple-

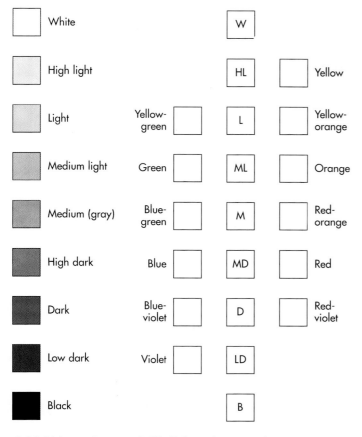

1.26 Value scale.   1.27 Color-value equivalents..

an artist applies pigment thickly with a palette knife. The texture of a picture falls anywhere within these two extremes. Texture may be illusory, in that the surface of a picture may be absolutely flat but the image gives the impression of three-dimensionality, so the term can be applied to the pictorial arts either literally or figuratively.

Principles

REPETITION Probably the essence of any design is repetition: how the basic elements in the picture are repeated or alternated. The three terms used are rhythm, harmony, and variation.

Rhythm, in technical language, is the recurrence of elements in a composition. In other words, rhythm is the repetition of lines, shapes, and objects in a picture. If the repeated elements, like the diamonds in Picasso's *Girl Before a Mirror* (see Fig. **1.19**), are of the same size or importance, then their rhythm is called regular. If the repeated elements, like the circular shapes in *St. Mark* (Fig. **1.28**) are of differing size and/or importance, then their rhythm is called irregular.

Harmony is the logic of the repetition. Harmonious relationships are those whose components appear to join naturally and comfortably. If the artist employs forms, colors, or other elements that appear incongruous or illogical, then we would use a musical term and say the picture is *dissonant*. However, we need to understand that ideas and ideals often reflect cultural conditioning or arbitrary understandings.

Variation is the relationship of repeated items to each other, like theme and variation in music. How does an artist take a basic element in the composition and use it again with slight or major changes? Picasso, the artist of Figure **1.19**, has used two geometric forms, the diamond and the oval, and created a complex painting via repetition. The diamond with a circle at its center repeats over and over to form the background. Variation occurs in the color given to these shapes. Similarly, the oval of the mirror repeats with variations in the composition of the girl. The circular motif is also repeated throughout the painting, with variations in color and size.

BALANCE is the achievement of equilibrium in a work of art. Determining whether a work is balanced or not is like dividing it into halves and evaluating whether one half or the other dominates. If the two halves seem equal, the work is balanced. As we shall see, many factors combine to affect a picture's balance, and line, form, and color all play a role. There are two general types of balance: symmetrical (formal) and asymmetrical (informal or psychological).

ment differs from graying a hue by adding black (or gray derived from black and white). Gray derived from complementaries, because it has hue, is far livelier than gray derived from black and white, which does not have hue.

The overall use of color by the artist is termed *palette*. An artist's palette can be broad, restricted, or somewhere in between, depending upon whether the artist has utilized the full range of the color spectrum and/or whether he or she explores the full range of *tonalities*—brights and dulls, lights and darks.

MASS is the physical volume and density of an object. In two-dimensional art such as drawing, painting, printmaking, and photography, mass must be implied. The use of light and shade, texture, and perspective (see p. 49) give the figures and objects in Giovanni Vanni's *Holy Family with St. John* (see Fig. **1.8**) the appearance of fully rounded, solid mass. Vanni does all in his power to create depth of space, thus drawing attention away from the fact that the picture exists in only two dimensions.

TEXTURE, a picture's apparent roughness or smoothness, ranges from the shine of a glossy photo to the three-dimensionality of *impasto*, a painting technique wherein

1.28 *St. Mark*, from the Gospel Book of St. Médard of Soissons, France, early 9th century. Paint on vellum, 14⅜ × 10¼ ins (37 × 26 cm). Bibliothèque Nationale, Paris.

1.29 Closed composition (composition kept within the frame).

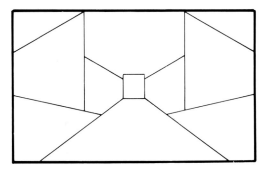

1.30 Open composition (composition allowed to escape the frame).

The most mechanical method of achieving balance is *symmetry*, specifically bilateral symmetry—the balancing of like forms, mass, and colors on opposite sides of the vertical axis (see Fig. **1.12**). Pictures employing absolute symmetry tend toward stability and stolidity. Many works approach symmetry, but nearly all retreat from placing mirror images on opposite sides of the centerline.

Asymmetrical balance, sometimes referred to as psychological balance, carefully arranges unlike items (Fig. **1.20**). Every painting illustrated in this chapter is asymmetrical. Comparative discussion as to how balance has been achieved is a useful exercise, especially if colors are considered. Often color is employed to balance line and form. Because some hues, such as yellow, have great eye attraction, they can counterbalance tremendous mass and activity.

UNITY An important characteristic in a work of art is the means by which it achieves unity. All of the elements of composition work together toward meaning. Often, compositional elements juxtapose in unusual fashions to achieve particular effects. Nonetheless, those effects usually entail a conscious attempt at making a unified statement. Critical analysis of the elements of a painting should lead us to a judgment about whether the total statement comprises a unified one.

With regard to unity, some may speak of *closed composition*, in which use of line and form always directs the eye into the painting (Fig. **1.29**), as unified, and *open composition*, in which the eye is allowed to wander off the canvas, or escape the frame (Fig. **1.30**), as disunified. Such is not the case. Keeping the artwork within the frame is a stylistic device that has an important bearing on the artwork's meaning. For example, painting following *Classical* standards stays predominantly within the frame, illustrating a concern for the self-containment of the artwork and for precise structuring. *Anticlassical* design forces the eye to escape the frame, suggesting perhaps the

world or universe outside, or the individual's place within an overwhelming cosmos. Unity does not depend on either condition.

FOCAL AREAS When we look at a picture for the first time, our eye moves around it, pausing briefly at those areas that seem to be of greatest visual appeal. These are *focal areas*. A painting may have a single focal area from which the eye will stray only with conscious effort. Or it may have an infinite number of focal points whereby the eye bounces from one point to another on the picture—in this way, the elements vie for our attention.

Artists achieve focal areas in a number of ways—through confluence of line, by encirclement (Fig. **1.28**), or by color, to name just a few. To draw attention to a particular point in the picture by confluence of line, the artist may make all lines lead to that point, as in Leonardo da Vinci's *Last Supper* (Fig. **11.8**). To create encirclement, the focal object or area may be placed in the center of a ring of objects. Focus by color means using a color that demands our attention more than the other colors in the picture. For example, bright yellows attract our eye more readily than dark blues.

OTHER FACTORS

Perspective

Perspective is a tool for indicating spatial relationships. It is based on the phenomenon of distant objects appearing smaller and less distinct than objects that are situated in the foreground.

There are a number of types of perspective. We will discuss three: linear, atmospheric, and shifting. *Linear perspective* (Fig. **1.31**) is characterized by the phenomenon of standing on railroad tracks and watching the two rails apparently come together at the horizon (known as the *vanishing point*). Very simply, linear perspective creates the illusion of distance in a two-dimensional

1.31 Linear perspective.

artwork through the convention of line and foreshortening—that is, the illusion that parallel lines come together in the distance. Linear perspective, also called scientific, mathematical one-point, or Renaissance perspective, developed in fifteenth-century Italy (see Chapter 11). Linear perspective is the system most people in Euro-American cultures think of as perspective, because it is the visual code they are accustomed to seeing. (See the Humanities CD: Perspective.)

Atmospheric perspective indicates distance through the use of light and atmosphere. For example, mountains in the background of a picture appear distant through less detail. In the upper left of Figure **1.8**, a castle appears at a great distance. We know it is distant because it is smaller and, more important, because it is indistinct.

Shifting perspective is found especially in Chinese landscapes and is affected by additional factors of culture and convention. The painting *Buddhist Monastery by Stream and Mountains* by Chü-jan (Fig. **1.32**) divides the picture into two basic units—foreground and background. The foreground of the painting consists of details reaching back toward the middle ground. At that point a division occurs, so that the background and the foreground are separated by an openness in what might have been a deep middle ground. The foreground represents the nearby,

1.32 Chü-jan, *Buddhist Monastery by Stream and Mountains*, c. 960–85 C.E. Ink on silk, 33⅜ × 22⅝ ins (85.5 × 57.5 cm). Cleveland Museum of Art (Gift of Katharine Holden Thayer).

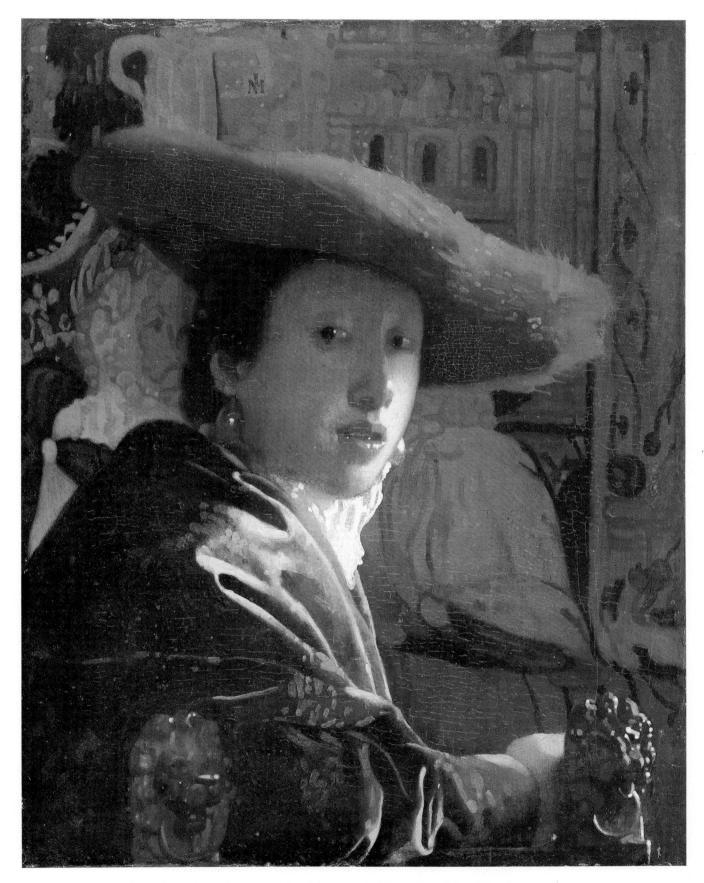

1.33 Jan Vermeer, *The Girl with the Red Hat*, c. 1665. Oil on wood, 9⅛ × 7⅛ ins (23 × 18 cm).
National Gallery of Art, Washington, D.C. (Andrew W. Mellon Collection).

and its rich detail causes us to pause and ponder on numerous elements, including the artist's use of brushstroke in creating foliage, rocks, and water. Then there is a break, and the background appears to loom up or be suspended—almost as if it were a separate entity. Although the foreground gives us a sense of dimension—of space receding from the front plane of the painting—the background appears flat, a factor that serves to enhance further the sense of height of the mountains. The apparent shift in perspective, however, results from the concept that truth to natural appearance should not occur at the expense of a pictorial examination of how nature works. The viewer is invited to enter the painting and examine its various parts, but not to take a panoramic view from a single position. Rather, the artist reveals each part as though the viewer were walking through the landscape. Shifting perspective allows for a personal journey and can lead to a strong personal, spiritual impact on the viewer.

Chiaroscuro

Chiaroscuro, whose meaning in Italian is "light and shade," is the suggestion of three-dimensional forms via light and shadow without the use of outline. It is a device used by artists to make their forms appear *plastic*—that is, three-dimensional. Making two-dimensional objects appear three-dimensional depends on the artist's ability to render highlight and shadow effectively. Without them, all forms are two-dimensional in appearance.

Chiaroscuro gives a picture much of its character. For example, the dynamic and dramatic treatment of light and shade in Figure 1.33 gives this painting a quality quite different from what would have resulted had the artist chosen to give full, flat, front light to the face. The highlights, falling as they do, create not only a dramatic effect but also a compositional triangle extending from shoulder to cheek, down to the hand, and then across the sleeve and back to the shoulder. Consider the substantial change in character had highlight and shadow been executed in a different manner. The treatment of chiaroscuro in a highly lifelike fashion in Figure 1.34 helps give the painting its strangely real yet dreamlike appearance.

In contrast, works that do not employ chiaroscuro have a two-dimensional quality. This can be seen to a large extent in Figure 1.7 and also in Figures 1.19 and 1.36.

Content

Arguably, all works of art pursue verisimilitude (vair-ih-sih-MIHL-ih-tood), and they do so with a variety of treatments of content. We can regard treatment of content as ranging from naturalism to stylization. Included are such concepts as abstract, representational, and nonobjective (see Glossary). The word versimilitude comes from the Latin, *verisimilitudo*, and it means plausibility. Aristotle,

1.34 Salvador Dalí, *The Persistence of Memory*, 1931. Oil on canvas, 9½ × 13 ins (24.1 × 33 cm). The Museum of Modern Art, New York (Given anonymously).

1.35 (opposite) Théodore Géricault, *The Raft of the "Medusa,"* 1819. Oil on canvas, 16 ft × 23 ft 6 ins (4.91 × 7.16 m). Louvre, Paris.

Géricault, *The Raft of the "Medusa"*

The Raft of the "Medusa" (meh-DOO-suh; Fig. **1.35**) by Théodore Géricault (zhay-ree-KOH) illustrates a criticism of social institutions in general. The painting tells a story of governmental incompetence that resulted in tragedy. In 1816, the French government allowed an unseaworthy ship, the *Medusa*, to leave port, and it was wrecked. Aboard a makeshift raft, the survivors endured tremendous suffering, and were eventually driven to cannibalism. In preparing for the work, Géricault interviewed the survivors, read newspaper accounts, and went so far as to paint corpses and the heads of guillotined criminals.

Géricault's painting captures the ordeal in Romantic style, tempered by Classical and even High Renaissance influences (see Chapters 11 and 12). He creates firmly modeled flesh, lifelike figures, and a precise play of light and shade (chiaroscuro). In contrast to other paintings of the time, which expressed Classical tendencies and, hence, two-dimensionality

and order, Géricault used a complex and fragmented compositional structure. He chose to base the design on two triangles rather than on one strong central triangle. In *The Raft of the "Medusa,"* the left triangle's apex is the makeshift mast, which points back toward despair and death. The other triangle moves up to the right to the figure waving the fabric, pointing toward hope and life as a rescue ship appears in the distance.

Géricault captures the moment that a potential rescue ship is sighted and sails on by. The play of light and shade heightens the dramatic effect and the composition builds upward from the bodies of the dead and dying in the foreground to the dynamic group whose final energies are summoned to support the figure waving to the ship. Thus, the painting surges with unbridled emotional response to the horror of the experience and the heroism of the survivors. It is hope followed by despair.

in his *Poetics*, insisted that art should reflect nature—for example, even highly idealized representations should possess recognizable qualities—and that the probable should take precedence over the merely possible. This has come to mean that the search for a portrayal of truth can sometimes mean a distortion of what we observe around us in favor of an image that, while perhaps not being life-like, better speaks to the underlying truth of human existence than mere lifelikeness does. So, the verisimilar, whether lifelike or not, becomes acceptable or convincing according to the respondent's own experience or knowledge. In some cases, this means enticing the respondent into suspending disbelief and accepting improbability within the framework of the work of art.

HOW DO THEY STIMULATE THE SENSES?

We do not touch pictures, and so we cannot feel their roughness or their smoothness, their coolness or their warmth. We cannot hear pictures and we cannot smell them. Concluding that a picture affects our senses in a particular way means responding in terms of visual stimuli that change into mental images of touch, taste, and sound.

CONTRASTS

The colors of an artist's palette are referred to as warm or cool depending upon which end of the color spectrum they fall. Reds, oranges, and yellows are said to be warm colors. They are the colors of the sun and therefore call to mind our primary source of heat, so they carry strong implications of warmth. Colors falling at the opposite end of the spectrum—blues and greens—are cool colors because they imply shade, or lack of light and warmth. As we will notice frequently, this mental stimulation has a physical basis.

Tonality and color contrast also affect our senses. The stark value contrasts of Figure **1.36** contribute significantly to the harsh and dynamic qualities of the work. The colorlessness of this monochromatic black, white, and gray is a horrifying comment on the tragic bombing of Guernica. In the opposite vein, the soft yet dramatic tonal contrasts of Figure **1.33** and the strong warmth and soft texture of the red hat create a completely different set of stimuli.

Many of the sense-affecting stimuli work in inseparable concert. We have already noted some of the effects of chiaroscuro, but one of the most interesting is its application to the treatment of flesh. Some flesh appears like stone, other flesh appears soft and true to life. Our response to whatever treatment has been given is tactile—we want to touch, or we believe we know what we would feel if we did touch. Chiaroscuro is essential to achieve

1.36 Pablo Picasso, *Guernica*, 1937. Oil on canvas, 11 ft 5 ins × 25 ft 5¾ ins (3.48 × 7.77 m). Museo Nacional Centro de Arte Reina Sofia, Madrid.

A Personal Journey

PICASSO, *GUERNICA*

Sunlight filtered through the trees around the Prado Museum in Madrid, Spain. I was headed to the museum's annex building to see Picasso's painting, *Guernica* (Fig. 1.36). Outside the annex, an old man stood in the shade. Dressed in a worker's cap and dark, cloth coat, he was grizzled and unshaven; stains blotted his coat and trousers. In his hand he held a large notebook and, as I approached, he opened the notebook to display newspaper articles and pictures about the village of Guernica as well as Picasso's painting. He seemed agitated, and I hesitated to become involved in whatever he wished to tell or show me. So, as politely as I could, I waved him off and continued up the hill toward the museum. His English was no better than my Spanish, and communication was difficult except for the fact that he wanted to engage me, and I wanted not to be engaged. What was clear was his passion about Guernica and the rendition Picasso had made of the bombing. As I moved by him, he began to shout at me, deeply upset that I had not heard him out. Most of the words were unintelligible, but I could discern "Fascist!" among them. The encounter unsettled and confused me, but I wondered how this person was connected to the bombing of Guernica and exactly what my transgression had been in relation to him and it.

Inside the museum, behind a glass shield and occupying an entire wall, Picasso's painting had an overpowering presence. Nearly 26 feet (8 m) wide and more than 11 feet (3 m) tall, it had a scale possessing a power I could not have imagined from seeing it previously only in pictures. My experience of the passion of the old man on the street gave the painting a curious combination of art and life that made the artwork come strangely alive with a human connection. Was the old man somewhere among the distorted figures in the painting? The starkness of the black-and-white color scheme infused the work with cold authority that gripped my emotions.

I knew the story—the saturation bombing of the northern Spanish Basque village of Guernica—but my experience of the old man's passion on the street outside gave the story a new relevance. Had he been there? Which side of the Spanish Civil War had he fought on? His calling me a fascist implied he was a loyalist, like Picasso, and I saw the story in personal terms. The old man's hardened face and raspy voice echoed through the room like explosions from the bombs portrayed in the painting.

Previously, I had thought of the universality of *Guernica*, the painting, applied to the prospects of nuclear holocaust, although Picasso had painted it years before the invention of the atomic bomb. (Since September 11, *Guernica* has taken on a new relevance.) But these were applications in the abstract, symbolism unintended by the artist. The work, because of this chance meeting on a sidewalk, spoke directly, in human ways. The figures, so distorted by Picasso's style, evoked torturous pain suffered by flesh-and-blood humans like the old man whose passion I had encountered

When I left the museum, I wanted to go back to the old man, to listen to his story, and perhaps find even greater meaning from the first-hand experiences that might have surrounded the creation of this work of art. Unfortunately, when I returned, the old man had gone.

1.37 Sir Peter Paul Rubens, *Rape of the Daughters of Leucippus*, c. 1616–17. Oil on canvas, 7 ft 3½ ins × 6 ft 10¼ ins (2.22 × 2.09 m). Alte Pinakothek, Munich.

1.38 Upright-triangular composition.

1.39 Inverted-triangular composition.

1.40 Curved line.

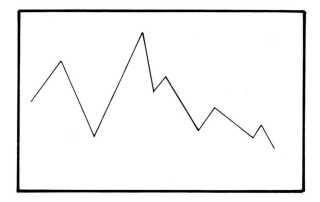

1.41 Broken line.

those effects. Harsh shadow and strong contrasts create one set of responses; diffused shadows and subdued contrasts create another. *Rape of the Daughters of Leucippus* (loo-SIH-puhs; Fig. **1.37**) by Rubens (ROO-behns) presents softly modeled flesh whose warmth and softness come from color and chiaroscuro. Highlight and shadow create softness, and predominantly red hues warm the composition; our sensual response is heightened dramatically.

DYNAMICS

Although static, pictures can stimulate a sense of movement and activity and create a sense of stable solidity. The artist stimulates these sensations by using certain conventional devices. Principally vertical composition can express, for example, a sense of dignity and grandeur (Fig. **1.45**; see also Fig. **0.4**). Horizontality can elicit a sense of stability and placidity. The triangle, for example, has interesting engineering possibilities because of its structural qualities. In art it has significant psychological qualities. If we place a triangle so that its base forms the bottom of a picture, we create a definite sense of solidity and immovability (Fig. **1.38**). If that triangle were a

1.42 Giotto, *The Lamentation*, 1305–6. Fresco, 7 ft 7 ins × 6 ft 7½ ins (2.31 × 2.02 m). Arena Chapel, Padua.

pyramid sitting on a level plane, a great deal of effort would be required to tip it over. If we invert the triangle so that it balances on its apex, a sensation of instability and action results (Figs. 1.39 and 1.42). Although we can feel clearly the sensations stimulated by these simple geometric forms, we should not conclude that such devices are either explicit or limited in their communication. Nonverbal communication in the arts is not that simple. Nonetheless, basic compositional devices do influence our response and impact our perceptions.

The use of line also affects sense response. Figure 1.40 illustrates curved line and a sense of relaxation. The broken line in Figure 1.41 creates a much more dynamic and violent sensation. We can also feel that the upright triangle in Figure 1.38, although solid and stable, is more dynamic than a horizontal composition because it uses

strong diagonal line, which tends to stimulate a sense of movement. Precision of linear execution can also create sharply defined forms or soft, fuzzy images. Figure 1.43 shows how straight lines and right angles can create the basic principles of life itself. Vertical lines signify vitality and life; horizontal lines signify tranquillity and death. The intersection of vertical and horizontal lines represents life's tensions.

TROMPE L'OEIL

Trompe l'oeil (tromp-LUH-yuh), or "trick the eye," gives the artist a varied set of stimuli by which to affect our sensory response. It is a form of illusionistic painting that attempts to represent an object as existing in three dimensions at the surface of the painting.

1.43 Piet Mondrian, *Composition in White, Black, and Red,* 1936. Oil on canvas, 3 ft 4¼ ins × 3 ft 5 ins (1.02 × 1.04 m). The Museum of Modern Art, New York (Gift of the Advisory Committee).

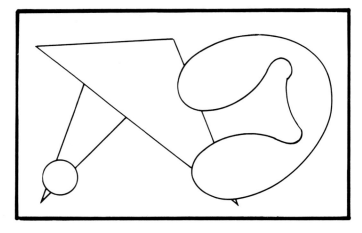

1.44 Juxtaposition of inharmonious forms.

JUXTAPOSITION

We can also receive stimuli from the results of juxtaposing curved and straight lines, which results in linear dissonance or consonance. Figure **1.44** illustrates the juxtaposing of inharmonious forms, which creates instability. Careful use of this device can stimulate some very interesting and specific sense responses.

The metaphysical fantasies of Giorgio de Chirico (KEE-ree-koh; 1888–1978) have Surrealist associations (see Chapter 13). Works such as *The Nostalgia of the Infinite*

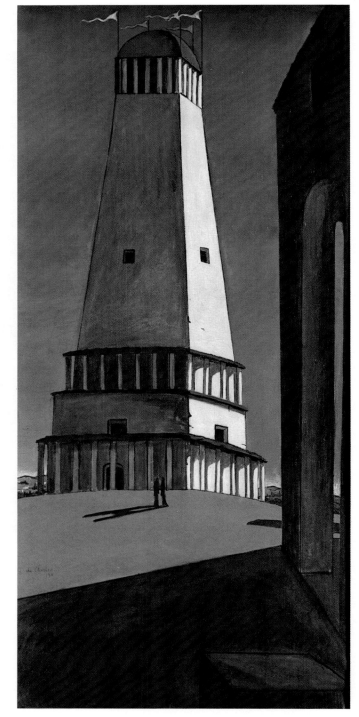

1.45 Giorgio de Chirico, *The Nostalgia of the Infinite,* 1913–14?, dated 1911 on the painting. Oil on canvas, 53¼ × 25½ ins (135.2 × 64.8 cm). The Museum of Modern Art, New York (Purchase).

(Fig. **1.45**) contain no rational explanation for their juxtaposition of strange objects. They have a dreamlike quality, associating objects that are not normally grouped together. Such works are not rational, and show a world humankind does not control. In them, "there is only what I see with my eyes open, and, even better, closed."

1.46 Francisco Goya, *Execution of the Citizens of Madrid, May 3, 1808*, 1814. Oil on canvas, 8 ft 6 ins × 11 ft 4 ins (2.59 × 3.45 m). Prado, Madrid.

FOCUS

The work of François Boucher (boo-SHAY; 1703–70) in the Rococo tradition (see Chapter 11) gives a taste of the decorative, mundane, and slightly erotic painting popular in the early and mid-eighteenth century. As a protégé of Madame de Pompadour, mistress of King Louis XV, Boucher enjoyed great popularity. His work has a highly decorative surface, and portrays pastoral and mythological settings such as shown in Figure 1.47. Boucher's figures appear amid exquisitely detailed drapery. His rendering technique is nearly flawless, and his displays of painterly virtuosity provide a fussily pretty work whose main subject competes with its decorative background for our attention. Each detail takes on a separate focus of its own and leads the eye first in one direction and then another.

OBJECTIVITY

Content, which involves any or all of the characteristics we have discussed, is a powerful device for effecting both sensory responses and more intense, subjective responses. The use of lifelikeness and nonobjectivity are noticeable stimulants of individual response. It would seem logical for individuals to respond intellectually to nonobjective pictures, because the subject matter should be neutral, with no inherent expressive stimuli. However, the opposite tends to occur. When asked whether they feel more comfortable with the content of Figure 1.8 or that of Figure 1.22, most individuals choose the former.

The works of the Spanish painter and printmaker Francisco de Goya (1746–1828) often reveal humanity and nature at their most malevolent. Figure 1.46 also tells a story of an actual event, when on May 3, 1808 the citizens of Madrid rebelled against Napoleon's army. Many individuals were arbitrarily arrested and executed. The focal attraction, the man in white, is one such individual. Goya's strong value contrasts force the eye to the victim; only the lantern behind the soldiers keeps the composition in balance.

So, does an explicit appeal cause a more profound response? Or does the stimulation provided by the unfamiliar cause us to think more deeply and respond more fully, because our imagination is left free to wander? The answers to these questions are worth considering as we perceive artworks, many of whose keys to response are not immediately obvious.

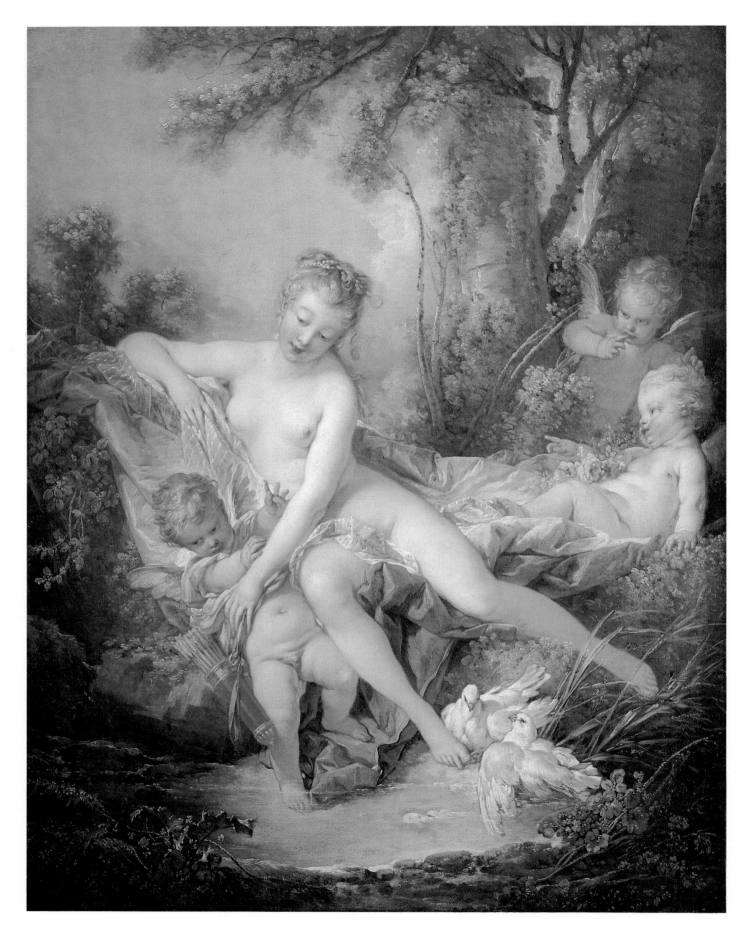

THINKING CRITICALLY

Do a *basic analysis* of a drawing, painting, or print: Pick a work of two-dimensional art and ask yourself how it reflects the qualities appropriate to the specific topics discussed in Chapter 1. Begin with the following:

- Reaction. Does the artist present clues in the work as to any response he or she might seek to achieve? In what ways does the artist stimulate emotional and intellectual response? What was your response and what means does the artist employ to evoke it?

Now build a *comparative analysis* by choosing two or more works and detailing how they reflect specific qualities described in the chapter. For example:

- Medium. What medium does van Gogh use in *The Starry Night* (Fig 1.7)? What medium does McIntyre use in *Barbershop Mirror* (Fig. 1.17)? Compare how the particular qualities of the media influence the final composition and appearance of the works.

- Line. Compare how Dürer (*Lamentation*, Fig. 1.9) and Vermeer (*The Girl with the Red Hat*, Fig. 1.33) employ the various qualities of line. How does their use of implied line, edge, and rectilinear line affect the dynamic workings of the pieces?

- Color. Compare the use of color in Vanni's *Holy Family with St. John* (Fig. 1.8) and Géricault's *The Raft of the "Medusa"* (Fig. 1.35). How do hue, value, intensity, and contrast contribute to the overall palette of each work, and how do the palettes compare?

CYBER STUDY

DRAWING (Charcoal):
—Georgia O'Keefe, *The Shell*
http://www.nga.gov/cgi-bin/pinfo?Object=56395+0+none

LINE ENGRAVING:
—Albrecht Dürer, *Angel with the Key to the Bottomless Pit*
http://sunsite.auc.dk/cgfa/durer/p-durer5.htm

LITHOGRAPHY:
—Robert Indiana, *South Bend*
http://www.nga.gov/cgi-bin/pinfo?Object=56441+0+none

PRINTMAKING (general):
http://www.artcyclopedia.com/media/Printmaker.html

ENGRAVING (general):
http://www.artcyclopedia.com/media/Engraver.html

PHOTOGRAPHY (general):
http://www.artcyclopedia.com/media/Photographer.html

1.47 François Boucher, *Venus Consoling Love*, 1751. Oil on canvas, 42⅛ × 33⅜ ins (107 × 85 cm). National Gallery of Art, Washington, D.C. (Chester Dale Collection).

CHAPTER TWO

SCULPTURE

WHAT IS IT?

HOW IS IT PUT TOGETHER?

DIMENSIONALITY
  Full-Round
  Relief
  Linear
METHODS OF EXECUTION
  Subtraction
  Addition
  Substitution
  Manipulation
  Found
  Ephemeral
A Personal Journey: The Elgin Marbles
COMPOSITION
  Elements
  Principles
Sculpture and Human Reality: Michelangelo, David
Profile: Michelangelo
OTHER FACTORS
  Articulation
  Focal Area (Emphasis)

HOW DOES IT STIMULATE THE SENSES?

TOUCH
TEMPERATURE AND AGE
DYNAMICS
SIZE
LIGHTING AND
  ENVIRONMENT
Thinking Critically
Cyber Study

IMPORTANT TERMS

Full-round Sculptural works that explore full three-dimensionality.

Relief Sculptural works attached to a background and seen from one side only.

Subtraction A method of execution in sculpture in which works are carved.

Addition A method of execution in sculpture in which works are constructed, or built, by one element being added to another.

Substitution A method of execution in sculpture in which works are transformed from a molten to a solid state.

Manipulation A method of execution in sculpture in which works are shaped by skilled use of the hands.

Articulation The manner of movement from one element in an artwork to another.

Proportion The relationship of shapes in a work of visual art.

Sculpture, in contrast to pictures, seems less personal and more public. In fact, we are likely to finds works of sculpture mostly in public spaces. Outside city halls and in parks and corporate office buildings we find statues of local dignitaries and constructions of wood, stone, and metal that appear to represent nothing at all. We might even wonder why our tax dollars were spent to buy them. Today, as throughout history, sculpture (and other forms of art) are often the subject of public pride and controversy. Because of its permanence, sculpture often represents the only artifact of entire civilizations. In this chapter we see not only how sculpture is made and how it works, but our examples will reveal ideas of artists from ancient history, contemporary times, and many cultures.

WHAT IS IT?

Sculpture is a three-dimensional art. It may take the form of whatever it seeks to represent, from pure, or nonobjective, form to lifelike depiction of people or any other entity. Sometimes sculpture, because of its three-dimensionality, comes very close to reality in its depiction. Duane Hanson and John DeAndrea, for example (see Cyber Study), use plastics to render the human form so naturalistically that the viewer must approach the artwork and examine it closely to determine that it is not a real person.

HOW IS IT PUT TOGETHER?

DIMENSIONALITY

Sculpture may be *full-round*, *relief*, or *linear*. Full-round works are freestanding and fully three-dimensional (Figs. 2.1 and 2.2). Relief works can be viewed from only one side—that is, projecting from a background (Fig. 2.3). A work utilizing materials two-dimensionally is called linear (Fig. 2.4). A sculptor's choice of full round, relief, or linearity as a mode of expression dictates to a large extent what he or she can and cannot do, both aesthetically and practically.

2.1 (*left*) Auguste Rodin, *The Burghers of Calais*, 1866. Bronze, height 6 ft 10½ ins (2.09 m). Hirshhorn Museum and Sculpture Garden, Smithsonian Institution, Washington, D.C. (Gift of Joseph J. Hirshhorn).

2.2 (*right*) Giovanni Bologna, *Samson Slaying a Philistine*, c. 1562. Victoria & Albert Museum, London.

2.3 East frieze, from Halicarnassus (modern Bodrum), Turkey. British Museum, London.

2.4 Alexander Calder, *Spring Blossoms*, 1965. Painted metal and heavy wire, extends 4 ft 4 ins × 8 ft 6 ins (1.35 × 2.59 m). Palmer Museum of Art, Pennsylvania State University (Gift of the class of 1965).

Full-Round

Full-round sculptural works explore full three-dimensionality and intend viewing from any angle (Fig. 2.1). Some subjects and styles pose certain constraints in this regard, however. Painters, printmakers, and photographers have virtually unlimited choice of subject matter and compositional arrangements. Full-round sculptures dealing with such subjects as clouds, oceans, and panoramic landscapes are problematic for the sculptor, though. Freestanding and three-dimensional sculpture forces sculptors to concern themselves with the practical-

ities of engineering and gravity. They cannot, for example, create a work with great mass at the top unless they can find a way (within the bounds of acceptable composition) to keep the statue from falling over. After we have viewed numerous full-round works, we begin to note the small animals, branches, tree stumps, rocks, and other devices that have been employed to give practical stability to a work.

Relief

The sculptor who creates a work in relief (Fig. 2.3) does not have quite so many restrictions. Since the work is attached to a background, he or she has freer choice of subjects and need not worry about their positions or supports. Clouds, seas, and perspective landscapes remain within the relief sculptor's reach, since the work requires viewing from only one side. Relief sculpture, then, is three-dimensional. However, because it protrudes from a background, it maintains a two-dimensional quality, as compared to full-round sculpture. There are cases in which relief sculpture can almost reach the point of full-roundness, as the jamb statues of saints from the west portal of Chartres (shartr) Cathedral in France illustrate (Fig. 2.5). Later jamb statues from another portal of the same cathedral (see Fig. 10.59) exhibit an even greater sense of emergence from their background. Relief sculptures that project only a small distance from their base, such as the Halicarnassus frieze (Fig. 2.3) are called *low*

2.5 Jamb statues, west portal, Chartres Cathedral, begun 1145.

relief. Sculptures such as those from Chartres Cathedral that project by at least half their depth are termed *high relief.* The French terms *bas-relief* (bah-ruh-leef), for the former, and *haut-relief* (oh-ruh-leef), for the latter, are also used.

Linear

The third category of sculpture, linear sculpture, emphasizes construction with linear items such as wire or neon tubing, as we might see in a mobile like Figure **2.4.** Artworks using linear materials and occupying three-dimensional space will occasionally puzzle us as we try to decide whether they are really linear or full-round. Here again, absolute definition is less important than the process of analysis and aesthetic experience and response.

METHODS OF EXECUTION

In general, we may say that sculpture is executed using subtractive, additive, substitute, or manipulative techniques, or any combination of these. A fifth category, that of found sculpture, may or may not be considered a "method" of execution, as we shall see later. For convenience, in this section we also will examine the topic "Ephemeral Sculpture," which may include any or all of the methods of execution.

Subtraction

Subtractive, or carved, works (see the Humanities CD: Sculpture) usually begin with a large block, typically of wood or stone, from which the sculptor cuts away (subtracts) the unwanted material. In previous eras, and to some extent today, sculptors had to work with whatever materials were at hand. Wood carvings emanated from forested regions, soapstone carvings from the Arctic, and great works of marble from the regions surrounding the quarries of the Mediterranean. Anything that can yield to the carver's tools can be formed into a work of sculpture. However, stone, with its promise of immortality, has proven to be the most popular material.

Three types of rock hold potential for the carver. *Igneous* rock—for example, granite—has hard mass and potential immortality. However, sculptors find it difficult to carve and therefore not desirable. *Sedimentary* rock such as limestone lasts a relatively long time, carves easily, and polishes ideally. Beautifully smooth and lustrous surfaces result from sedimentary rock. *Metamorphic* rock, including marble, appears the sculptor's ideal. It lasts, carves pleasurably, and exists in a broad range of colors. Whatever the artist's choice, one requirement must be met: The material to be carved, whether wood, stone, or a bar of soap, must be free of flaws.

A sculptor who sets about carving a work does not begin simply by imagining a *Samson Slaying a Philistine* (Fig. **2.2**) and then attacking the stone. The first step involves creating a model, usually smaller than the intended sculpture. The model, made of clay, plaster, wax, or some other material, reflects the precise details—in miniature—of the final product.

Once the likeness of the model has been enlarged and transferred, the artist begins to rough out the actual image ("knocking away the waste material," as Michelangelo put it). In this stage of the sculpting process, the artist carves to within two or three inches of what is to be the finished area, using specific tools designed for the purpose. Then, using a different set of carving tools, she or he carefully takes the material down to the precise detail. Finishing work and polishing follow.

Addition

In contrast with carving from a large block of material, the sculptor using an additive process starts with a small amount of raw material and adds element to element until the work is finished. The term *built sculpture* often

2.6 Bakota ancestor figure, from Gabon, late 19th century. Wood and copper sheeting, height 26¾ ins (68 cm). British Museum, London.

2.7 Giovanni Bologna, *Mercury*, c. 1567. Bronze, height 5 ft 9 ins (1.75 m). Museo Nazionale del Bargello, Florence.

A Personal Journey

THE ELGIN MARBLES

Calling the pediment statues from the Parthenon (Figs. **2.8** and **2.11**) the Elgin (EHL-ghihn) Marbles will not endear me to my Greek friends, because their dislocation from the Parthenon (see Fig. **7.2**) and transport to England by Lord Elgin in the nineteenth century remains a subject of dispute. The Greek government has tried repeatedly and unsuccessfully to have them returned. But there they were, set on a high platform across the end of their own room in the British Museum. Over the years I have visited them frequently. (The editors of this book have their offices across the street from the museum.) Nonetheless, my first visit had the greatest impact. On my very first trip abroad, I felt an excitement that only maiden voyages can induce.

London, England, sweeps through more than 2,000 years of history, whose evidence stood around me in stone. Inside the museum the artifacts of even more ancient times kept my camera clicking constantly.

The statues recreate the space of the Parthenon's pediment (the triangular gable above the columns on the front of the temple). The three goddesses at the right of Figure **2.11** form the left edge of the right side of the space. To their right, and continuing the diminution of space toward the outer corner, is one additional figure and one horse's head. To the left of that group, and comprising the left side of the pediment, are another set of four figures and a horse's head. As a group, they seem disconnected. It would take me ten years from this first encounter to visit the Parthenon in Athens (see p. 150), but I had seen pictures and understood their original placement. The statues, now separate from the building, seemed to long for reunification with their home, where they could cling to the marble and take refuge under the lip of the cornice. Although in the British Museum the statues are displayed on a plain dais in front of a plain wall, in a room lit by incandescent bulbs, it is easy to imagine them high on their original lofty perch in the bright Athenian sunlight.

That return will, doubtless, never happen, and even if it did, these works—which have been spared the ravages of modern pollution that have disfigured other statuary on the Athenian Acropolis—would simply find a home in another museum, albeit in Athens. The conditions of smog and the deterioration of time have been too savage ever to allow reunification of building and sculptures as their makers originally had them. Some things, sadly, can never be as they once were.

Nevertheless, whenever I visit the British Museum, I pay them a courtesy call. After nearly thirty years, they seem like old friends—a happy result often produced by the repeated experiencing of art.

2.8 Detail from the east pediment sculptures of the Parthenon, showing the goddesses Persephone and Demeter.

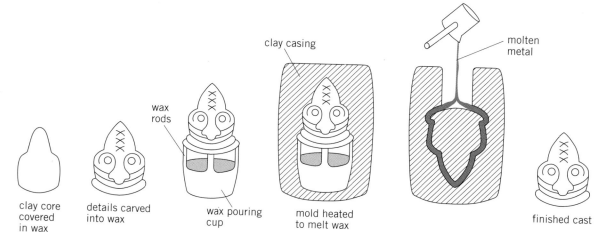

clay casing

molten metal

wax rods

clay core covered in wax

details carved into wax

wax pouring cup

mold heated to melt wax

finished cast

2.9 Lost-wax process.

describes works executed in an additive technique. The materials employed in this process can be plastics, metals such as aluminum or steel, terracottas (clay), epoxy resins, or wood. Many times materials are combined (Fig. 2.6). Sculptors commonly combine methods as well. For example, built sections of metal or plastic may be combined with carved sections of stone.

Substitution

Any material that can be transformed from a plastic, molten, or fluid state into a solid state can be molded or *cast* into a work of sculpture. The creation of a piece of cast sculpture always involves the use of a mold. First, the artist creates an identically sized model of the intended sculpture. This *positive* she then covers with a material, such as plaster of Paris, which when hardened and removed will retain the surface configurations of the positive. Called a *negative*, this form becomes the mold for the actual sculpture. The artist pours molten or fluid material into the negative and allows it to solidify. When the mold is removed, the work of sculpture emerges. Surface polishing, if desired, brings the work to its final form (Fig. 2.7).

One example of substitution is the ancient technique called "lost-wax" or *cire-perdue* (seer pair-DOO; Fig. 2.9). In this method of casting the artist creates the basic mold by using a wax model, which he then melts to leave the desired space in the mold. The artist then covers the heat-resistant "core" of clay—approximately the shape of the sculpture—with a layer of wax approximately the thickness of the final work. The sculptor carves the details in the wax. Rods and a pouring cup made of wax attach to the model, followed by thick layers of clay. When the clay dries, the artist heats the mold to melt the wax. Molten metal can then be poured into the mold. When the molten metal has dried, the clay mold is broken and removed, which means that the sculpture cannot be duplicated.

Very often sculpture is cast so it is hollow. This saves money, since it requires less material. It also results in a work less prone to crack, since it is less susceptible to expansion and contraction resulting from changes in temperature. Hollow sculpture is, naturally, lighter and thus more easily shipped and handled.

Manipulation

In this technique, materials such as clay are shaped by skilled use of the hands. A term of similar meaning is *modeling* (see the Humanities CD: Sculpture). The difference between this technique and addition is clear when an artist takes a single lump of clay and skillfully transforms it, as it turns on a potter's wheel, into a final shape like the lekythos (LEHK-ih-thohs) in Figure 10.1.

Found

This category of sculpture is exactly what its name implies. Very often natural objects, whether shaped by human hands or not, for some reason take on characteristics that stimulate aesthetic response. They become *objets d'art* (ahb-zheh dart) not because an artist puts them together (although an artist may combine found objects to create a work), but because an artist chooses to take them from their original surroundings and hold them up to the rest of us as vehicles for aesthetic communication. In other words, an "artist" decides that such an object says something aesthetically. As a result, it is presented in that vein.

Some may have concern about such a category, however, because it removes skill from the artistic process. As a result, objects such as driftwood and interesting rocks can assume perhaps an unwarranted place as art products or objects. Nonetheless, if a "found" object is altered in some way to produce an artwork, then the process probably falls under one of our previously noted methods, and the product can be termed an artwork in the fullest sense of the word.

Ephemeral

Ephemeral art has many different expressions and includes the works of the conceptualists, who insist that "art is an activity of change, of disorientation and shift, of violent discontinuity and mutability." Designed to be transitory, ephemeral art makes its statement and then, eventually, ceases to exist. Undoubtedly the largest work of sculpture ever designed was based on that concept. Christo and Jeanne-Claude's *Running Fence* (Fig. **2.10**) was an event and a process, as well as a sculptural work. In a sense such works are conceptual in that they call attention to the experience of art in opposition to its actual form. At the end of a two-week viewing period, *Running Fence* was dismantled completely.

COMPOSITION

Composition in sculpture comprises the same elements and principles as composition in the pictorial arts—line, form, color, mass, texture, repetition, balance, unity, and focal areas. Sculptors' uses of these elements and principles differ significantly from those of pictorial artists, however, since they work in three dimensions.

Elements

Unlike a picture, a sculpture has literal *mass*. It takes up three-dimensional *space*, and its materials have *density*. Mass in pictures is relative mass: The mass of forms in a picture has application principally in relation to other forms within the same picture. In sculpture, however, mass is literal and consists of actual volume and density. So, the mass of a sculpture 20 ft (6 m) high, 8 ft (2.5 m) wide, and 10 ft (3 m) deep, but made of balsa wood, appears less than a sculpture 10 ft (3 m) high, 4 ft (1.25 m) wide, and 3 ft (1 m) deep, made of lead. Space and density must both be considered. What if the material of a statue is disguised to look and feel like a different material? We will discuss this later in the chapter, when we look at how a sculpture affects our senses.

As stated in the previous chapter, *line* and *form* are closely related. We can separate them (with some difficulty) when we discuss pictures, because in two dimensions an artist uses line to define form. In painting, line is a construction tool. In sculpture form draws our interest,

2.10 Christo and Jeanne-Claude, *Running Fence, Sonoma and Marin Counties, California*, 1972–6. Woven nylon fabric and steel cables, height 18 ft (5.49 m), length 24½ miles (39.2 km).

2.11 (*right and opposite*) Part of the east pediment of the Parthenon, Athens, c. 438–432 B.C.E. Left to right: Persephone, Demeter, Isis, Hestia(?), Dione, and Aphrodite ("Three Seated Goddesses"). Marble, over life-size. British Museum, London.

and when we discuss line in sculpture, we do so in terms of how it is revealed in form.

When we view a sculpture its elements direct our eye from one point to another, just as focal points do, via line and color, in a picture (Fig. **2.11**). In some works the eye is directed through the piece and then off into space. Such sculptures have an *open* form. The sculptor of Figure **2.12** directs the eye outward from the work in the same fashion as composition that escapes the frame in painting. If, on the other hand, the work directs the eye continually back into the form, we say the form is *closed*. If we allow our eye to follow the linear detail of Figure **2.13**, we find that we are continually led back into the work. This is similar to composition kept within the frame in painting and to closed forms in music, which we will discuss in Chapter 3. Often it is difficult to fit a work precisely into one or the other of these categories.

Obviously, not all sculptures are completely solid; they may have openings. We call any such holes in a sculpture *negative space*, and we can discuss this characteristic in terms of its role in the overall composition. In some works negative space is inconsequential; in others it is quite significant. We must decide which, and determine how negative space contributes to the overall piece.

Perhaps *color* does not seem particularly important to us as we think of sculpture. We tend to see ancient sculpture as white and modern sculpture as natural wood or rusty iron. But color is as important to the sculptor as it is to the painter. In some cases the material itself may be chosen because of its color; in others, such as terracottas, the sculpture may be painted. The lifelike sculptures of Duane Hanson depend on color for their effect. They are so lifelike that one could easily confuse them with real persons. Finally, still other materials may be chosen or treated so that nature will provide the final color through oxidation or weathering.

2.12 Alberto Giacometti, *Man Pointing*, 1947. Bronze, 70½ × 40¾ × 16⅜ ins (179 × 103.4 × 41.5 cm), at base 12 × 13¼ ins (30.5 × 33.7 cm). The Museum of Modern Art, New York (Gift of Mrs. John D. Rockefeller 3rd).

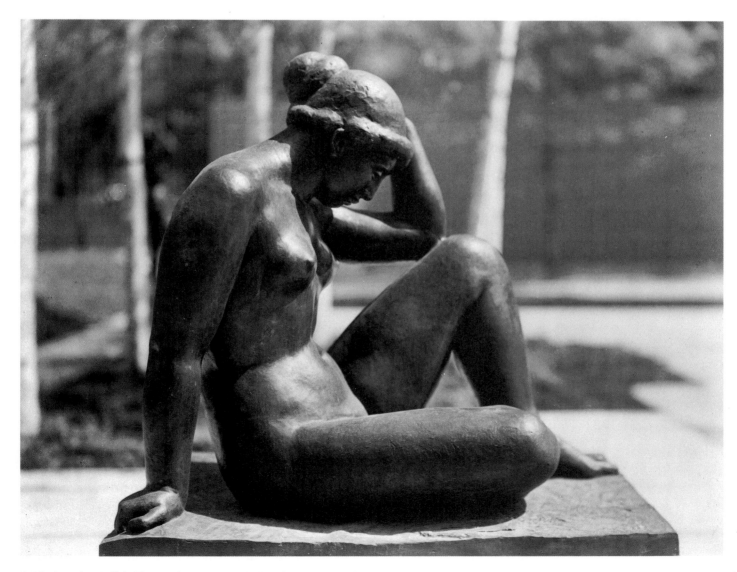

2.13 Aristide Maillol, *The Mediterranean*, 1902–5 (cast 1951–53). Bronze, 41 × 45 × 29¾ ins (104.1 × 114.3 × 75.6 cm), including base. The Museum of Modern Art, New York (Gift of Stephen C. Clark).

2.14 Kouros, c. 615 B.C.E. Marble, height 6 ft 4 ins (1.93 m). Metropolitan Museum of Art, New York (Fletcher Fund, 1932).

Texture, the roughness or smoothness of a surface, is a tangible characteristic of sculpture. Sculpture is unique in that we can perceive its texture through our sense of touch. Even when we cannot touch a work of sculpture, we can perceive and respond to texture, which can be both physical and suggested. Sculptors go to great lengths to achieve the texture they desire. In fact, much of a sculptor's technical mastery manifests itself in that final ability to impart a surface to the work. We will examine texture more fully in our discussion of sense responses.

Principles

Proportion is the relationship of shapes. Just as we have a seemingly innate sense of balance, so we have a feeling of proportion. That feeling tells us that each form in the sculpture exists in proper relationship to the others. As any student of art history will tell us, proportion—or the ideal of relationships—has varied from one civilization or culture to another. For example, such a seemingly obviously proportioned entity as the human body has varied greatly in its proportions as sculptors over the centuries have depicted it. Study the differences in proportion in the human body among Michelangelo's *David* (Fig. **2.15**), the Chartres saints (Fig. **2.5**), an ancient Greek kouros figure (Fig. **2.14**), and Giacometti's *Man Pointing* (Fig. **2.12**). Each depicts the human form, but each utilizes differing proportions. This difference in proportion helps transmit the message the artist wishes to communicate about his or her subject matter.

Rhythm, harmony, and variation constitute *repetition* in sculpture, as they did in the pictorial arts. In sculpture, though, we must look more carefully and closely to determine how the artist has employed these elements because they ocur more subtly. If we reduce a sculpture to its components of line and form, we begin to see how (as in music) rhythmic patterns—regular and irregular—occur. In Figure **2.3**, for example, a regular rhythmic pattern is established in space as the eye moves from figure to figure and from leg to leg of the figures. We can also see whether the components are consonant or dissonant. For instance, again in Figure **2.3**, a sense of dynamics—that is, action of movement—is created by the dissonance that results from juxtaposing the strong triangles of the stances and groupings with the *biomorphic* lines of the human body. On the other hand, unity of the curves in Figure **2.16** provides us with a consonant series of relationships. Finally, we can see how line and form are used in theme and variation. We noted the repetition of triangles in Figure **2.3**. In contrast, the sculptor of Figure **2.16** varies his motif, the oval, as the eye moves from the child's face to the upper arm, the hand, and finally the cat's face.

Michelangelo, *David*

Towering some 18 feet (5.5 m) above the floor on its base, Michelangelo's *David* (Fig. **2.15**) awesomely exemplifies *terribilità* (tay-ree-bee-lee-TAH), Michelangelo's particular tendency to create awe-inspiring characters. This nude champion exudes a pent-up energy as the body seems to exist merely as an earthly prison for the soul. The upper body moves in opposition to the lower. As the viewer's eye travels downward along the right arm and leg and then up along the left arm, a subtle thrust and counterthrust of movement emerges.

Much of the effect of *David*—the bulging muscles, exaggerated rib cage, heavy hair, undercut eyes, and frowning brow—may be due to the fact that these features were intended to be read from a distance. The work was originally meant to be placed high above the ground on a buttress for Florence Cathedral. Instead, the city leaders put it in front of the Palazzo Vecchio, believing it too magnificent to be placed so high.

The political symbolism of the work was recognized from the outset. *David* stood for the valiant Florentine Republic. It also stood for all of humanity, elevated to a new and superhuman power, beauty, and grandeur. However, its "total and triumphant nudity," which reflected Michelangelo's belief in the divinity of the human body, kept it hidden from the public for two months. When it did appear, a brass girdle with twenty-eight copper leaves hung around the waist.

Inspired by the Hellenistic sculptures he had seen in Rome (see pp. 234–7), Michelangelo set out in pursuit of an emotion-charged, heroic ideal. The scale, musculature, emotion, and stunning beauty and power of those earlier works became a part of Michelangelo's style. However, in contrast to the Hellenistic approach, in which the "body 'acts' out the spirit's agony" (compare the *Laocoön* (lay-AH-koh-ahn), by Hagesandrus, Polydorus, and Athenodorus, see Fig. **10.13**), *David* remains controlled, exhibiting action-in-repose for which Michelangelo is famous.

2.15 Michelangelo, *David*, 1501–4. Marble, height 13 ft 5 ins (4.08 m). Accademia, Florence.

Michelangelo

Michelangelo (1475–1564) was a sculptor, painter, and architect and perhaps the greatest artist in a time of greatness. He lived during the Italian Renaissance, a period known for its creative activity, and his contemporaries included Leonardo da Vinci and Raphael (rah-fah-AYL). In art, the age's great achievement, Michelangelo led all others. He had a remarkable ability to concentrate his thoughts and energy. Often while working he would eat only a little bread, sleep on the floor or on a cot beside his unfinished painting or statue, and continue to wear the same clothes until his work was finished.

Michelangelo's birthplace, Caprese, Italy, was a tiny village that belonged to the nearby city-state of Florence. He attended school in Florence, but his mind was on art, not on his studies. Even as a young child he was fascinated by painters and sculptors at work.

After gaining the patronage of Lorenzo de' Medici (MEH-dee-chee; Lorenzo the Magnificent), the young Michelangelo lived at the Medici Palace. One day Lorenzo saw him carving a marble faun's head and liked it so much that he took Michelangelo to live with him in his palace, treating the boy like a son. Lorenzo died in 1492, and Florence changed almost overnight. Savonarola (sah-voh-nah-ROHL-uh), a Dominican monk, rose to power and held the people under the spell of his sermons. Michelangelo feared Savonarola's influence and his art commissions dried up. Thus, he decided to leave Florence.

In 1496 Michelangelo was in Rome for the first time. There he was commissioned to carve a marble group showing the Virgin Mary supporting the dead Christ on her knees. This superb sculpture, known as the *Pietà* (pee-ay-TAH), won him wide fame. One of the few works signed by Michelangelo, it now stands in St. Peter's Basilica in Rome.

When he was twenty-six, Michelangelo returned to Florence. He was given an 18-foot (5.5-m) marble block that another sculptor had already started to carve. The block was nearly ruined. Michelangelo worked on it for more than two years. Out of its huge mass, and in spite of the difficulties caused by the first sculptor's work, he carved his youthful, courageous *David* (Fig. **2.15**).

Between 1508 and 1512 Michelangelo painted the vaulted ceiling of the Sistine Chapel in Rome (see Figs. **11.9** and **11.10**) with hundreds of giant figures that made up his vision of the world's creation.

Painting and sculpture, however, did not absorb all Michelangelo's genius. When Florence was in danger of attack, he superintended its fortification. He also wrote many sonnets. In his last years he designed the dome of St. Peter's Basilica in Rome, which has been called the finest architectural achievement of the Italian Renaissance. Michelangelo worked with many of the leaders of his time. He knew and competed with Leonardo da Vinci and Raphael. He died in 1564, at the age of eighty-nine, and was buried in the church of Santa Croce (kroh-chay) in Florence.

OTHER FACTORS

Articulation

Important, also, in viewing sculpture is noting the manner by which we move from one element to the next. That manner of movement is called *articulation*, and it applies to sculpture, painting, photography, and all the other arts. As an example, let us step outside the arts to consider human speech. Sentences, phrases, and individual words are nothing more than sound syllables (vowels) articulated (that is, joined together) by consonants. We understand what someone says because that individual articulates as he or she speaks. Let us put the five vowel sounds side by side: EH–EE–AH–O–OO. As yet we do not have a sentence. Articulate those vowels with consonants,

and we have meaning: "Say, she must go too." The nature of an artwork depends on how the artist has repeated, varied, harmonized, and related its parts and how he or she has articulated the movement from one part to another—that is, how he or she indicates where one stops and the other begins.

Focal Area (Emphasis)

Sculptors, like painters or any other visual artists, must concern themselves with drawing the viewer's eye to those areas of their work that are central to what they wish to communicate. They must also provide the means by which the eye can move around the work. However, their task is much more complicated, because they deal in three dimensions and they have little control over the

HOW DOES IT STIMULATE THE SENSES?

TOUCH

We can touch sculpture and feel its roughness or its smoothness, its coolness or perhaps its warmth. Even if museum regulations prohibit us from touching a sculpture, we can see the surface texture and translate the image of that texture into an imaginary tactile sensation. Any work of sculpture cries out to be touched, and tactility plays a greater role in our response to sculpture than to other arts.

TEMPERATURE AND AGE

Color in sculpture stimulates our response by utilizing the same universal symbols as it does in paintings, photographs, and prints. Reds, oranges, and yellows stimulate sensations of warmth; blues and greens, sensations of coolness. In sculpture, color can result from the conscious choice of the artist, either in the selection of material or in the selection of the pigment with which the material is painted. Or, as we indicated earlier, color may result from the artist's choice to let nature color the work through wind, water, sun, and so forth.

This weathering effect, of course, creates very interesting patterns, but in addition it gives the sculpture the attribute not only of space but also of time, because the work will change as nature performs its wonders. A copper sculpture early in its existence will be a different work, a different set of stimuli, from what it will be five, ten, or twenty years hence. This is not entirely accidental; artists choose copper knowing what weathering will do to it. They obviously cannot predict the exact nature of the weathering or the exact hues of the sculpture at any given time in the future, but such predictability is irrelevant.

The effects of age on a sculpture may shape our response. Ancient objects possess a great deal of charm and character. A wooden icon such as that in Figure 2.17 might have extra emotional impact because of the effects of age on its surfaces.

DYNAMICS

Line, form, and juxtaposition create dynamics in works of sculpture. The activity of a sculpture tends to be heightened because of its three-dimensionality. In addition, we

2.16 William Zorach, *Child with Cat*, 1926. Bronze, 17½ × 10 × 7½ ins (44 × 25 × 19 cm). Palmer Museum of Art, Pennsylvania State University.

direction from which one will first perceive the piece; the entire 360-degree view contributes to the total message communicated by the work.

The devices of convergence of line, encirclement, and color work for sculptors just as they do for painters. The encircling line in Figure 2.16 causes us, however we proceed to scan the work, to focus ultimately on the child's face.

One further device is available—movement, or kinesthesis. Sculptors have the option of placing moving objects in their work. Such an object immediately becomes a focal point of the sculpture. A mobile (see Fig. 2.4) presents many ephemeral patterns of focus as it turns at the whim of the breezes.

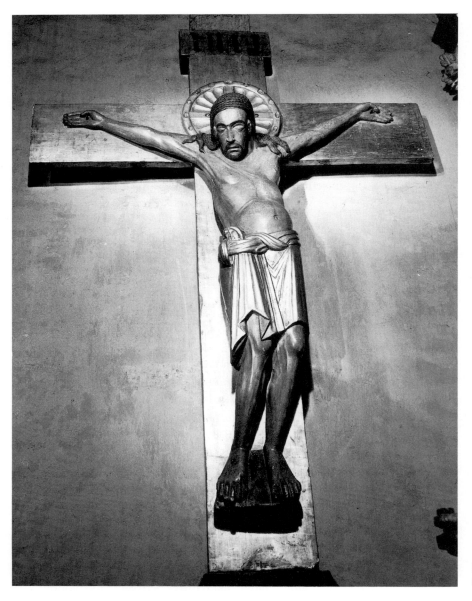

2.17 *Gero Crucifix*, Cologne Cathedral, c. 975–1000. Wood, height 6 ft 2 ins (1.87 m).

experience a certain sense of dynamics as we move around them. Although we are moving, rather than the sculpture, we perceive and respond to what seems to be movement in the work itself.

SIZE

Because sculpture has mass—that is, takes up space and has density—our senses respond to the weight and/or the scale of a work. Egyptian sculpture, which is solid, stable, and oversized (Fig. 2.18), has mass and proportion as well as line and form that make it appear heavier than a non-Egyptian work of basically the same size, such as Figure 2.7. Moreover, the very same treatment of texture, lifelikeness, and subject elicits a completely different sense response if one work is 3 feet (1 m) and another 130 feet (39.6 m) tall.

Exaggerated size and anatomical form, for symbolic effect, may also be seen in a colossal bust of Emperor Constantine (see Fig. 10.17), a gigantic representation—the head is over 8 feet (2.4 m) tall—exhibiting a stark and expressive realism that is countered by caricatured, ill-proportioned intensity. This likeness is not a portrait of Constantine—it is the artist's view both of Constantine's presentation of himself as emperor and of the office of emperor itself.

Early in the chapter we mentioned the possibility of an artist's disguising the material from which the work is made. Marble polished to appear like skin, or wood polished to look like fabric, can change the appearance of mass of a sculpture and significantly affect our response to it.

We must also consider the purpose of disguising material. For example, does the detailing of the sculpture reflect a formal concern for design, or does it reflect a concern for the greatest lifelikeness? Examine the cloth represented in *The Burghers of Calais* (see Fig. **2.1**) and the Chartres saints (see Fig. **2.5**). In both cases the sculptor has disguised the material by making stone appear to be cloth. In Figure **2.1** the cloth is detailed to reflect reality. It drapes as real cloth would drape, and as a result its effect in the composition depends upon the subtlety of line characteristic of draped cloth. However, in Figure **2.5** the sculptor has depicted cloth in such a way that its effect in the design is not dependent upon how cloth drapes, but rather upon the decorative function of line as the sculptor wishes to use it. Real cloth cannot drape as the sculptor has depicted it. Nor, probably, did the sculptor care. The main concern here was for decoration, for using line (that looks like cloth) to emphasize the rhythm of the work. When sculpture de-emphasizes lifelikeness in order to draw attention to the substance from which it is made, we call it *glyptic* (glihp-tihk). Glyptic sculpture emphasizes the material from which the work is created and usually retains the fundamental geometric qualities of that material.

LIGHTING AND ENVIRONMENT

One final factor that significantly influences our sense response to a sculpture, a factor that we very often do not consider and that is outside the control of the artist unless he or she personally supervises every exhibition in which the work is displayed, is lighting and environment. As we will see in Chapter 4, light plays a basic role in our perception of and thereby our response to three-dimensional objects. The direction and number of sources of light striking a three-dimensional work can change the entire composition of that work. Whether the work is displayed outdoors or indoors, the method of lighting affects the overall presentation. Diffuse room lighting allows us to see all aspects of a sculpture without external influence. However, if the work is placed in a darkened room and illuminated from particular directions by spotlights, it becomes much more dramatic and our response is affected accordingly.

The question of where and how a work is exhibited also contributes to our response. The response to a sculpture placed in a carefully designed environment that screens our vision from distracting or competing visual stimuli will change if the sculpture is exhibited among other works amid the bustle of a public park, for instance.

2.18 Egyptian statuary. Metropolitan Museum of Art, New York (Gift of Edward S. Harkness).

THINKING CRITICALLY

- Examine Giacometti's *Man Pointing* (Fig. **2.12**) and compare it with the archaic Greek kouros in Figure **2.14**. What visions of humankind do you find in each work and how are they similar or different?

Do a basic analysis of a work of sculpture by using the topics in this chapter as an outline. Begin with the following:

- Reaction. Does the artist present clues in the work as to any response he or she might seek to achieve? In what ways does the artist stimulate emotional and intellectual response? What was your response and what means does the artist employ to evoke it?

Now build a comparative analysis by choosing two or more works and detailing how they reflect specific qualities described in the chapter. For example:

- Dimensionality. How does the dimensionality of Maillol's *The Mediterranean* (Fig. **2.13**) change your perception as compared with the "Three Goddesses" from the Parthenon (Fig. **2.11**)? What is the dimensionality of each work? How does that dimensionality contribute to each work's overall design and effect? Try to imagine the original location of the *Three Goddesses* as you frame your analysis.

- Method of execution. What method of execution is employed by Michelangelo (*David*; Fig. **2.15**) and Giovanni (*Mercury*; Fig. **2.7**)? How do the methods of execution and materials create a final effect, and how do those considerations differ in each work?

- Focal areas. Compare the west portal jamb statues from Chartres Cathedral (Fig. **2.5**) with the *Gero Crucifix* (Fig. **2.17**) in terms of how the areas of interest work to move the eye around the sculptures. Which areas are primary and which are secondary?

CYBER STUDY

Duane Hanson, *Side By Side*
http://norton.org/exhibit/archive/sideby/hanson.htm
John DeAndrea
http://www.johndeandrea.com

SCULPTURE IN THE ROUND:
—Deborah Brown, *Cock Bob*
http://www.decordova.org/decordova/sculp_park/brown.html

BUILT SCULPTURE:
—Mary Mead, *Advancing Slowly*
http://www.decordova.org/decordova/sculp_park/mead.html

CAST SCULPTURE:
—Magdalena Abakanowicz, *Puellae* (Girls)
http://www.nga.gov/cgi-bin/pinfo?Object=108121+0+none

CHAPTER THREE

MUSIC

WHAT IS IT?

MASS
CANTATA
MOTET
OPERA
ORATORIO
ART SONG
FUGUE
SONATA
SYMPHONY
CONCERTO
CONCERT OVERTURE
SUITE

HOW IS IT PUT TOGETHER?

SOUND
Pitch
Dynamics
Tone Color
Duration
RHYTHM
Beat
Meter
Tempo
MELODY
Profile: Wolfgang Amadeus Mozart
HARMONY
TONALITY
TEXTURE

Monophony
Polyphony
Homophony
FORM
Closed Forms
Open Forms

HOW DOES IT STIMULATE THE SENSES?

OUR PRIMAL RESPONSES
THE MUSICAL PERFORMANCE

OPERA

TYPES OF OPERA
THE OPERA PRODUCTION
A Personal Journey: Verdi's Don Carlos
Music and Human Reality: Bizet, Carmen
Thinking Critically
Cyber Study

IMPORTANT TERMS

Oratorio A large choral work for soloists, chorus, and orchestra, developed in the Baroque period.

Fugue A musical composition in a fixed form in which a theme is developed by counterpoint.

Symphony A lengthy orchestral composition, usually in four movements.

Concerto A composition for one or more solo instruments, accompanied by an orchestra, typically in three movements.

Suite A set of dance-inspired movements written in the same key but differing in tempo, meter, and character.

Melody A succession of sounds with rhythmic and tonal organization.

Monophony A type of musical texture using a single musical line without accompaniment

Polyphony A type of musical texture utilizing two or more melodic lines of relatively equal interest performed at the same time.

Homophony A type of musical texture in which chords accompany one main melody.

Sonata form A type of musical structure employing exposition, development, and recapitulation sections.

Opera A staged, musical/theatrical work in which music predominates.

We all have favorite forms of music. They might be tejano, reggae, rock, rhythm and blues, rap, gospel, or Classical. Occasionally we are surprised to find that our favorite tune or musical form was once something else: a rock tune that first was an operatic aria, or an ethnic style that combines styles from other ethnic traditions. Whatever the case, all music comprises rhythms and melodies—they differ only in the ways they are put together. In this chapter we shall concentrate first on some traditional forms, but after that we discuss qualities that apply to all music.

Music has often been described as the purest of the art forms because it is free from the physical restrictions of space that apply to the other arts. However, the freedom enjoyed by the composer becomes a constraint for us listeners because music places significant responsibility on us. That responsibility is especially critical when we try to learn and apply musical terminology, because we have only a fleeting moment to capture many of the characteristics of music. A painting or a sculpture stands still for us; it does not change or disappear, despite the length of time it takes us to examine and appreciate.

We live in a very aural society, but aural perceptions usually do not require any kind of active listening. We hear music constantly on the radio, on the television, and in the movies, but nearly always place it in a peripheral role. Therefore we hardly ever undertake the kind of practice that we need in order to be deeply attentive to music and to perceive it in detail. However, like any skill, the ability to hear perceptively is enhanced through repetition and training. If we have had limited experience in responding to music, we will find challenge in the concert hall hearing what there is to hear in a piece of music that passes in just a few seconds.

WHAT IS IT?

At a formal level, our experience of a musical work begins with its type, or form. The term *form* is a very broad one. In addition to the forms we identify momentarily, all of which are associated with what we call "classical" (serious, or "high" art) music, we can also identify broader "forms" of music of which "classical" is only one—for example, the musical forms of jazz, pop/rock, and so on (play the Humanities CD: Music, Musical Forms). As we will see in Chapter 11, the term Classical also refers to a specific style of music within this broad "classical" form.

The basic form of a music composition shapes our initial encounter by providing us with some specific parameters for understanding. Unlike our experience in the theatre, we are likely to find an identification of the musical composition, by type, in the concert program. Here are a few of the more common forms we are likely to encounter. The first six are vocal forms; the second six are instrumental. Because many musical forms are period- or style-specific—that is, they grew out of a specific stylistic tradition, some of our descriptions may include brief historical references.

MASS

The mass is a sacred choral composition consisting of five sections: Kyrie, Gloria, Credo, Sanctus, and Agnus Dei (KEE-ree-ay; KRAY-doh; SAHNK-toos; AHN-yoos-day-ee). These also form the parts of the mass ordinary—that is, the Roman Catholic church texts that remain the same from day to day throughout most of the year. The Kyrie text implores, "Lord, have mercy upon us. Christ, have mercy upon us. Lord, have mercy upon us." The Gloria text begins, "Glory be to God on High, and on earth peace, good will towards men." The Credo states the creed: "We believe in one God, the Father, the Almighty, maker of heaven and earth," and so on. The Sanctus confirms, "Holy, holy, holy, Lord God of Hosts: Heaven and earth are full of thy glory. Glory be to thee, O Lord Most High." The Agnus Dei (Lamb of God), implores, "O Lamb of God, that takest away the sins of the world, have mercy upon us. O Lamb of God, that takest away the sins of the world, have mercy upon us. O Lamb of God, that takest away the sins of the world, grant us thy peace." (Listen to "Kyrie" from the *Pope Marcellus Mass* by Palestrina [Pa-leh-STREE-nah], music CD track 7.) The requiem mass, which often comprises a musical program, is a special mass for the dead.

CANTATA

A cantata is usually a choral work with one or more soloists and an instrumental ensemble. Written in several movements, it is typified by the church cantata of the Lutheran church of the Baroque period and often includes chorales and organ accompaniment. The word cantata originally meant a piece that was sung—in contrast to a sonata (see below), which was played. The Lutheran church cantata (exemplified by those of Johann Sebastian Bach) uses a religious text, which can be either original or drawn from the Bible or based on familiar hymns—chorales. In essence, it served as a sermon in music, drawn from the lectionary (prescribed Bible readings for the day and on which the sermon is based). A typical cantata might last twenty-five minutes and include several different movements—choruses, recitatives, arias, and duets. (Listen to Bach's *Cantata No. 80*, final chorale, music CD track 9.)

MOTET

A motet (moh-TEHT) is a polyphonic (two or more melodic lines of relatively equal importance performed at the same time) choral work employing a sacred Latin text other than that of the mass. With, but shorter than, the mass, the motet was one of the two main forms of sacred music during the Renaissance (late fourteenth to sixteenth centuries; see Chapter 11).

OPERA

Opera is a blending of music and theatre in which music plays the dominant role. We give special treatment to this form of music later in the chapter.

ORATORIO

An oratorio is a large-scale composition using chorus, vocal soloists, and orchestra. Normally an oratorio sets a narrative text (usually biblical), but does not employ acting, scenery, or costumes. The oratorio was a major achievement of the Baroque period. This type of musical composition unfolds through a series of choruses, arias, duets, recitatives, and orchestral interludes. The chorus of an oratorio is especially important and can comment on or participate in the dramatic exposition. Another feature of the oratorio is the use of a narrator, whose recitatives (vocal lines imitating the rhythms and inflections of normal speech) tell the story and connect the various parts. Like operas, oratorios can last more than two hours. (Listen to Handel's "Hallelujah Chorus" from the oratorio *Messiah*, music CD track 10.)

ART SONG

An art song is a setting of a poem for solo voice and piano. Typically, it adapts the poem's mood and imagery into music. Art song is a distinctive form of music growing out of the Romantic style of the nineteenth century. That is to say, it has an emotional tendency, and its themes often encompass lost love, nature, legend, and the far-away and long ago. In this type of composition, the accompaniment is an important part of the composer's interpretation and acts as an equal partner with the voice. In this form, important words are emphasized by stressed tones or melodic climaxes. (Listen to Schubert's "The Erlking," music CD track 14.)

FUGUE

The fugue is a polyphonic composition based on one main theme, or subject. It can be written for a group of instruments or voices or for a single instrument like an organ or harpsichord. Throughout the composition, different melodic lines, called "voices," imitate the subject. The top melodic line is the soprano and the bottom line, the bass. A fugue usually includes three, four, or five voices. The composer's exploration of the subject typically passes through different keys and combines with different melodic and rhythmic ideas. Fugal form is extremely flexible: the only constant feature is the beginning, in which a single, unaccompanied voice states the theme. The listener's task, then, is to remember that subject and follow it through the various manipulations that follow.

SONATA

An outgrowth of the Baroque period, a sonata is an instrumental composition in several movements written for from one to eight players. After the Baroque period, the sonata changed to a form typically for one or two players. The trio sonata of the Baroque period had three melodic lines (hence its name). It actually uses four players. (Listen to Mozart's *Piano Sonata No. 11 in A*, K. 331—Rondo: alla turca, music CD track 12.)

This general type of musical composition should not be confused with *sonata form*, which is a specific form for a single movement of a musical composition. Sonata form consists of three main sections: the *exposition* (the A part), in which themes are presented; the *development* (the B part), in which themes are treated in new ways; and the *recapitulation* (the A part revisited), in which the themes return. A concluding section, called a *coda*, often follows the recapitulation. (Listen to Beethoven's *Symphony No. 5 in C minor*—first movement, music CD track 13.)

SYMPHONY

An orchestral composition, usually in four movements, a symphony typically lasts between twenty and forty-five minutes. In this large work, the composer explores the full dynamic and tonal range of the orchestral ensemble. The symphony is a product of the Classical period of the late eighteenth century and evokes a wide range of carefully structured emotions through contrasts of tempo and mood. The sequence of movements usually begins with an active fast movement, changes to a lyrical slow movement, moves to a dancelike movement, and closes with a bold fast movement. The opening movement is almost always in sonata form (see Sonata). In most Classical symphonies, each movement is self-contained with its own set of themes. Unity in a symphony occurs partly from the use of the same key in three of the movements and also from careful emotional and musical complement among the movements. (Listen to Berlioz's *Symphonie Fantastique*—fourth movement ["The March to the Scaffold"], music CD track 16; also Beethoven's *Symphony No. 5 in C minor*—first movement, music CD track 13. In the Berlioz listen for the theme's mood. In the Beethoven, listen for repetition of the theme.)

CONCERTO

A solo concerto (kahn-CHAIR-toh) is an extended composition for an instrumental soloist and orchestra. Reaching its zenith during the Classical period of the eighteenth century, it typically contains three movements, in which the first is fast, the second, slow, and the third, fast. Concertos join a soloist's virtuosity and interpretive skills with the wide-ranging dynamics and tonal colors of an orchestra. The concerto thus provides a dramatic contrast of musical ideas and sound in which the soloist is the star. Typically, concertos present great challenge to the soloist and great reward to the listener, who can delight in the soloist's meeting of the technical and interpretive challenges of the work. Nonetheless, the concerto is a balanced work in which the orchestra and soloist act as partners. The interplay between orchestra and soloist provides the listener with fertile ground for involvement and discernment. Concertos can last from twenty to forty-five minutes. Typically, during the first movement, and sometimes the third, of a Classical concerto, the soloist has an unaccompanied showpiece called a cadenza.

Common in the late Baroque period of the seventeenth century (see Chapter 11), the concerto grosso is a composition for several instrumental soloists and small orchestra (in contrast to the solo concerto—see above). In the Baroque style contrast between loud and soft sounds and large and small groups of performers was typical. In a concerto grosso, a small group of soloists (two to four) contrasts a larger group called the *tutti* consisting of from eight to twenty players. Most often a concerto grosso contains three movements contrasting in tempo and character. The first movement is fast; the second, slow; and the third, fast. The opening movement, usually bold, explores the contrasts between *tutti* and soloists. The slow movement is more lyrical, quiet, and intimate. The final movement is lively, lighthearted, and sometimes dancelike. (Listen to Vivaldi's "Spring" from *The Four Seasons*—first movement, music CD track 11.)

CONCERT OVERTURE

A concert overture is an independent composition for orchestra. It contains one movement, composed in sonata form (see Sonata). The concert overture is modeled after the opera overture, similarly a one-movement work, that establishes the mood of an opera. Unlike the opera overture, however, the concert overture is not intended as the introduction to anything. It stands on its own as an independent composition.

SUITE

A suite comprises a set of dance-inspired movements written in the same key but differing in tempo, meter, and character. An outgrowth of the Baroque period, a suite can employ solo instruments, small ensembles, or an entire orchestra. The movements of a suite typically are in two parts, with each section repeated (AABB). The A section opens in the tonic key and modulates to the dominant (the fifth tone of the scale). The B section begins in the dominant and returns to the tonic. Both sections employ the same thematic material and exhibit little by way of contrast.

HOW IS IT PUT TOGETHER?

Understanding vocabulary and being able to identify its application in a musical work help us to comprehend communication using the musical language, and thereby to understand the creative communicative intent of the composer and the musicians who bring the composition to life. The ways in which musical artists shape the characteristics that follow bring us experiences which can challenge our intellects and excite our emotions. As in all communication, meaning depends upon each of the parties involved; communicators and listeners must assume responsibility for facility in the language utilized.

Among the basic elements by which music is put together, we will identify and discuss seven: (1) Sound; (2) Rhythm; (3) Melody; (4) Harmony; (5) Tonality; (6) Texture; and (7) Form.

SOUND

Musical composers design sounds and silences. In the broadest sense, sound is anything that excites the auditory nerve: sirens, speech, crying babies, jet engines, falling trees, and so on. We might even call such sources noise. Musical composition, although it can employ even "noise," usually depends on controlled and shaped sound, consistent in quality. We distinguish music from other sounds by recognizing four basic properties: (1) pitch; (2) dynamics; (3) tone color; and (4) duration.

Pitch

Pitch is a physical phenomenon measurable in vibrations per second. So, when we describe differences in pitch we describe recognizable and measurable differences in sound waves. A pitch has a steady, constant frequency. A faster frequency produces a higher pitch, a slower frequency, a lower pitch. Making a sounding body—a vibrating string, for example—smaller makes it vibrate more rapidly. Musical instruments designed to produce high pitches, such as the piccolo, therefore tend to be small. Instruments designed to produce low pitches tend to be large—for instance, bass viols and tubas. In music, a sound that has a definite pitch is called a *tone*.

In Chapter 1 we discussed color. It comprises a range of light waves within a visible spectrum. Sound also comprises a spectrum, whose audible pitches range from 16 to 38,000 vibrations per second. We can perceive 11,000 different pitches! Obviously that exceeds practicality for musical composition. Therefore, by convention musicians divide the sound spectrum into at least ninety equally spaced frequencies comprising seven and a half *octaves*.

The piano keyboard, consisting of eighty-eight keys (seven octaves plus two additional notes) representing the same number of equally spaced pitches, serves as an illustration (Fig. 3.1).

A *scale*—an arrangement of pitches played in ascending or descending order—is a conventional organization of the frequencies of the sound spectrum. The thirteen equally spaced pitches in an octave comprise a *chromatic scale*. However, the scales that sound most familiar to us are the major and minor scales, each of which consists of an octave of eight pitches. The distance between any two pitches is an *interval*. Intervals between two adjacent pitches are half steps. Intervals of two half steps are whole

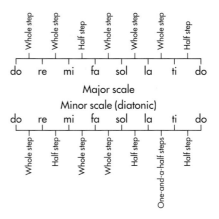

3.2 The major and minor scales.

steps. The major scale—*do re mi fa sol la ti do* (recall the song, "Doe, a deer ..." from *The Sound of Music*)—has a specific arrangement of whole and half steps (Fig. 3.2). Lowering the third and sixth notes of the major scale gives us the harmonic (the most common) minor scale.

Not all music conforms to the conventions of Western scales. European music prior to approximately 1600 C.E. does not, nor does Eastern music, which makes great use of quarter tones. In addition, some contemporary Western music departs completely from the conventions of *tonality*. Listen to tracks 1–3 on the music CD. These examples are from cultures whose music does not conform to the Western conventions of pitch, scale, and tonality. There are, however, other characteristics that make this music sound different from the music of Bach, for example (track 9). At the end of our discussion of musical elements, identify the additional ways in which these three tracks differ from traditional Western music.

Dynamics

Degrees of loudness or softness in music are called *dynamics*. Any tone can be loud, soft, or anywhere in between. Dynamics describe the decibel level of the tones, and depend upon the physical phenomenon of amplitude of vibration. Employing greater force in the production of a tone creates wider sound waves and causes greater stimulation of the auditory nerves. The size of the sound wave, not its number of vibrations per second, is changed.

Composers indicate dynamic level with a series of specific notations:

pp	pianissimo (pee-yah-NEE-see-moh)	very soft
p	piano	soft
mp	mezzo (MEHT-zoh) piano	moderately soft
mf	mezzo forte (FOR-tay)	moderately loud
f	forte	loud
ff	fortissimo	very loud

3.1 Part of the piano keyboard, with pitches.

The notations of dynamics that apply to an individual tone, such as *p*, *mp*, and *f*, may also apply to a section of music. Changes in dynamics may be abrupt, gradual, wide, or small. A series of symbols also governs this aspect of music:

⬉	crescendo	becoming louder
⬊	decrescendo	becoming softer
> ∧ *sfz*	sforzando (sfort-ZAHN-doh)	"with force"; a strong accent often followed by *p*

As we listen to and compare musical compositions we can consider the use and breadth of dynamics in the same sense that we consider the use and breadth of palette in painting.

Tone Color

Tone color, or timbre (TAM-ber), is the characteristic of tone that allows us to distinguish a pitch played on a violin, for example, from the same pitch played on a piano. In addition to identifying characteristic differences among sound-producing sources, tone color can also refer to differences in quality of tones produced by the same source. Here the analogy of "tone color" is particularly appropriate. A tone produced with an excess of air—for example, by a breathy human voice—is described as "white." Figure 3.6 illustrates some of the various sources that produce musical tone and account for its variety of tone colors (see the Humanities CD: Music, Instruments).

In the keyboard family, the piano could be considered either a stringed or a percussion instrument since it produces its sound by vibrating strings struck by hammers. The harpsichord's strings are set in motion by plucking, and the organ's sound is made by air.

Electronically produced music, available since the development of the RCA synthesizer at the Columbia-Princeton Electronics Music Center, has become a standard source in assisting contemporary composers. Originally electronic music fell into two categories: (1) the electronic altering of acoustically produced sounds, which came to be labeled as *musique concrète,* and (2) electronically generated sounds. However, advances in technology have blurred those differences over the years.

Note Values

♩ ♩ ♩ ♪ ♪ ♪ ♪
Whole Half Quarter Eighth Sixteenth Thirty-second Sixty-fourth

Rests

Whole Half Quarter Eighth Sixteenth Thirty-second Sixty-fourth

3.3 Musical notation.

Duration

Another characteristic of sound is duration: the length of time vibration continues without interruption. Duration in musical composition is designed with a set of conventions called notation (Fig. 3.3). This system consists of a series of symbols (notes) by which the composer indicates the relative duration of each tone. The system is progressive—that is, each note's duration is either double or half the duration of the adjacent note. Musical notation also includes a series of symbols that denote the duration of silences in a composition. These symbols are called *rests*, and have the same values as the symbols for duration of tone.

RHYTHM

Rhythm comprises recurring pulses and accents that create identifiable patterns. Without rhythm we have only an aimless rising and falling of tones. Composing music means placing each tone into a time or rhythmical relationship with every other tone. As with the dots and dashes of the Morse code we can "play" the rhythm of a musical composition without reference to its tones. Each symbol of the musical notation system denotes a duration relative to each other symbol in the system. Rhythm consists of: (1) beat; (2) meter; and (3) tempo (see the Humanities CD: Music, Rhythm).

Beat

The individual pulses we hear are called *beats*. Beats may be grouped into rhythmic patterns by placing accents every few beats. Beats are basic units of time and form the background against which the composer places notes of various lengths.

Meter

Normal musical practice groups clusters of beats into units called *measures*. When these groupings are regular and reasonably equal they comprise *simple* meters. When the number of beats in a measure equals three or two it constitutes *triple* or *duple* meter. We, as listeners, can distinguish between duple and triple meters because of their different *accent* patterns. In triple meter we hear an accent every third beat—ONE two three, ONE two three—and in duple meter the accent is every other beat—ONE two, ONE two. If there are four beats in a measure (sometimes called quadruple meter), the second accent is weaker than the first—ONE two THREE four, ONE two THREE four.

Listen to music CD track 15, *Nocturne in E-Flat Major,* Op. 9, No. 2 by Chopin (SHOH-pan), and note the triple meter. Compare that with Louis Armstrong's "Mack the Knife" (CD track 22), which illustrates the martial character of quadruple meter.

When accent occurs on normally unaccented beats, we have *syncopation*, as occurs in Duke Ellington's "It Don't Mean a Thing" (music CD track 23). Here the basic meter is duple, but the orchestra provides counterpoint for the vocalist with strong off-beat accents.

Sometimes repetitive patterning or strict metrical development does not occur. Listen to music CD tracks 4, 5, 8, and 19 in sequence. In track 4, an example of Gregorian chant, the rhythm is free-flowing with undistinguishable meter. The same is true of track 5, also a composition from the Middle Ages, by Hildegard of Bingen. In contrast, Thomas Morley's "Now is the Month of Maying" (track 8) is written in a strict, lively quadruple meter. Its repetitive pattern of 1, 2, 3, 4 is very obvious. On the other hand, Debussy's *Prelude to the Afternoon of a Faun* (music CD track 19) changes meter so frequently that the patterns virtually disappear (a faun—pronounced fawn—is a mythological creature with the body of a man and the horns, ears, tail, and sometimes legs of a goat).

Tempo

Tempo is the rate of speed of the composition. A composer may notate tempo in two ways. The first is by a *metronome marking*, such as ♩ = 60. This means that the piece is to be played at the rate of sixty quarter notes (♩) per minute. Such notation is precise. The other method is less precise and involves more descriptive terminology in Italian:

Largo (broad)	⎫	
Grave (grahv) (grave, solemn)	⎬	Very slow
Lento (slow)	⎫	
Adagio (ah-DAH-zhee-oh) (leisurely)	⎬	Slow
Andante (at a walking pace)	⎫	
Andantino (somewhat faster	⎬	Moderate
than andante)		
Moderato (moderate)		
Allegretto (briskly)	⎫	
Allegro (cheerful, faster than allegretto)	⎬	Fast

Vivace (vee-VAH-chay) (vivacious)	⎫	
Presto (very quick)	⎬	Very fast
Prestissimo (as fast as possible)	⎭	

The tempo may be quickened or slowed, and the composer indicates this by the words *accelerando* (accelerate) and *ritardando* (retard, slow down). A performer who takes liberties with the tempo uses *rubato* (roo-BAH-toh).

MELODY

Melody is a succession of sounds with rhythmic and tonal organization. We can visualize melody as linear and essentially horizontal. Two other terms, *tune* and *theme*, relate to melody as parts to a whole. For example, the tune in Figure 3.4 is a melody.

However, a melody is not always a tune. In general, the term tune implies singability, and there are many melodies that cannot be considered singable. A theme is also a melody. However, in musical composition it specifically means a central musical idea, which may be restated and varied throughout a piece. Thus a melody is not necessarily a theme.

Related to theme and melody is the *motif* (moh-TEEF), or *motive*, a short melodic or rhythmic idea around which a composer may design a composition. For example, in Beethoven's *Symphony No. 5 in C minor* (music CD track 13) the first movement develops around a motif of four notes.

In listening for how a composer develops melody, theme, and motif we can use two terms to describe what we hear: *conjunct* and *disjunct*. Conjunct melodies comprise notes close together, stepwise, on the musical scale. For example, the interval between the opening notes of the soprano line of J. S. Bach's chorale "Jesu Joy of Man's Desiring" from *Cantata 147* (Fig. 3.5) is never more than a whole step. Disjunct melodies contain intervals of two steps or more. However, no formula exists for determining disjunct or conjunct characteristics; there is no line at which a melody ceases to be disjunct and becomes conjunct. These are relative, discriptive terms. For example, the opening melody of "The Star-Spangled Banner" (Fig. 3.4) is more disjunct than the opening melody of "Jesu Joy of Man's Desiring"—or the latter is more conjunct than the former. Listen at http://www.classicalarchives.com/cgi-bin/n.cgi//prep./jesu_j1.mid.

3.4 "The Star-Spangled Banner" (excerpt).

3.5 "Jesu Joy of Man's Desiring" (excerpt).

3.6 The key sources of musical tone in an orchestra (instruments not to scale).

Wolfgang Amadeus Mozart

Wolfgang Amadeus Mozart (MOHT-zahrt; 1756–91) is often considered the greatest musical genius of all time. His output—especially in view of his short life—was enormous and included sixteen operas, forty-one symphonies, twenty-seven piano and five violin concertos, twenty-five string quartets, nineteen masses, and other works in every form popular in his time. Perhaps his greatest single achievement is in the characterization of his operatic figures.

Mozart was born on January 27, 1756, in Salzburg, Austria. His father, Leopold Mozart, held the position of composer to the archbishop and was a well-known violinist and author of a celebrated theoretical treatise on playing the instrument. When Wolfgang was only six years old, his father took him and his older sister, Maria Anna (called Nannerl) on tours throughout Europe during which they performed as harpsichordists and pianists—separately and together. They gave public concerts and played at the various courts. In Paris in 1764, Wolfgang wrote his first published works, four violin sonatas. In London he came under the influence of Johann Christian Bach. In 1768 young Mozart became honorary concertmaster for the archbishop of Salzburg.

In 1772, however, a new archbishop came to power, and the cordial relationship Mozart enjoyed with the previous archbishop came to an end. By 1777 the situation became so strained that the young composer asked to be relieved of his duties, and the archbishop grudgingly agreed.

In 1777 Mozart traveled with his mother to Munich and Mannheim, Germany, and to Paris, where she died. On this trip alone, Mozart composed seven violin sonatas, seven piano sonatas, a ballet, and three symphonic works, including the *Paris Symphony*.

The final break between Mozart and the archbishop occurred in 1781, but before that time Mozart had unsuccessfully sought another position. Six years later, in 1787, Emperor Joseph II finally engaged him as chamber composer—at a salary considerably smaller than that of his predecessor. Mozart's financial situation worsened steadily, and he incurred significant debts that hounded him until his death.

Meanwhile, his opera *The Abduction from the Seraglio* (suh-RAH-lee-oh) enjoyed great success in 1782; in the same year he married Constanze Weber, the daughter of friends. He composed his great *Mass in C Minor* for her, and she was soprano soloist in its premiere.

During the last ten years of his life, Mozart produced most of his great piano concertos; the four horn concertos; the *Haffner*, *Prague*, *Linz*, and *Jupiter* symphonies; the six string quartets dedicated to Haydn; five string quintets; and the major operas, *The Marriage of Figaro*, *Don Giovanni*, *Cosi Fan Tutte*, *La Clemenza di Tito*, and *The Magic Flute*. Mozart was unable to complete his final work, the Requiem, because of illness. He died in Vienna on December 5, 1791, and was buried in a multiple grave. Although the exact nature of his illness is unknown, there is no evidence that Mozart's death was deliberately caused (as the popular movie, *Amadeus*, implies).

HARMONY

When two or more tones sound at the same time, we have harmony. This is essentially a vertical arrangement, in contrast with the horizontal arrangement of melody. However, harmony also has a horizontal property: movement forward in time. In listening for harmony we are interested in how simultaneous tones sound together.

Two tones played simultaneously are an interval; three or more form a *chord*. When we hear an interval or a chord our first response is to its *consonance* or *dissonance*. Consonant harmonies sound pleasant and stable in their arrangement, while dissonant harmonies are tense and unstable. Consonance and dissonance, however, are not absolute properties. Essentially they are conventional and, to a large extent, cultural. What is dissonant to our ears may not be so to someone else's, and vice versa. What is important in musical response is determining *how* the composer utilizes these two properties. Most Western music is primarily consonant. Dissonance, on the other

Full   Half   Deceptive

3.7 Full, half, and deceptive cadences.

hand, can be used for contrast, to draw attention to itself, or as a normal part of *harmonic progression*.

As its name implies, harmonic progression involves the movement forward in time of harmonies. In discussing pitch we noted the convention of the major and minor scales—that is, the arrangement of the chromatic scale into a system of *tonality*. When we play or sing a major or minor scale we note a particular phenomenon: Our movement from *do* to *re* to *mi* to *fa* to *sol* to *la* is smooth and seems natural. But when we reach the seventh tone of the scale, *ti*, something happens. It seems as though we *must* continue back to *do*, the *tonic* of the scale. Try it! Sing a major scale and stop at *ti*. You feel uncomfortable. Your mind tells you that you must resolve that discomfort by returning to *do*. That same sense of tonality—that sense of the tonic—applies also to harmony. Within any scale a series of chords may be developed on the basis of the individual tones of the scale. Each of the chords has a subtle relationship to each of the other chords and to the tonic. That relationship creates a sense of progression that leads back to the chord based on the tonic.

The harmonic movement toward, and either resolving or not resolving to, the tonic is called *cadence*. Three different cadences are shown in Figure 3.7.

The use of cadence is one way of articulating sections of a composition or of surprising us by upsetting our expectations. A composer using a full cadence uses a harmonic progression that resolves just as our ear tells us it should. We have a sense of ending, of completeness. However, when a deceptive cadence is used, the expected progression is upset and the musical development moves in an unexpected direction.

In some compositions tonal centers are blurred because composers frequently *modulate*—that is, change from one *key* to another. In the twentieth century many composers—some using purely mathematical formulas to utilize all tones of the chromatic scale equally—removed tonality as an arranging factor and developed *atonal* music, or music without tonality (see Chapter 13).

TONALITY

Utilization of tonality or key has taken composers in various directions over the centuries. Conventional tonality, employing the major and minor scales and keys discussed previously relative to pitch, forms the basis for most sixteenth- to twentieth-century Western music, as well as traditionally oriented music of the twentieth century.

In the early twentieth century, traditional tonality was abandoned by some composers. Atonal compositions sought the freedom of any combination of tones without the necessity of having to resolve chordal progressions. Typically such compositions begin in a home key, modulate away, and return at the end.

TEXTURE

The aspect of musical relationships known as texture is treated differently by different sources. The term itself has various spatial connotations, and using a spatial term to describe a nonspatial phenomenon creates part of the divergence of treatment. Texture in painting and sculpture denotes surface quality—that is, roughness or smoothness. Texture in weaving denotes the interrelationship of the warp and the woof—that is, the horizontal and vertical threads in fabric. The organization in Figure 3.8 would be described as open or loose texture; that in Figure 3.9, closed or tight. There really is no single musical arrangement that corresponds to either of these spatial concepts. The characteristic called *sonority* comes the closest. Sonority describes the relationship of tones played at the same time. A chord with large intervals between its members would have a more open, or thinner, sonority (or texture) than a chord with small intervals between its tones; that chord would have a tight, thick, or close sonority or texture. Sonority is a term that does not have universal application; some sources do not mention it at all. Composers can vary textures within their pieces, as Handel does in the "Hallelujah Chorus" (music CD track 10). This creates an even richer fabric of sound for us to respond to. Let's examine three basic musical textures: monophony, polyphony, and homophony.

3.8 Open (loose) texture.   3.9 Closed (tight) texture.

Monophony

When a single musical line exists without accompaniment, the piece has a monophonic texture. Many voices or instruments may play at the same time, as in the Gregorian chant illustrated on music CD track 4, but as long as they sing the same notes at the same time—that is, in unison—the texture remains monophonic. In Handel's "Hallelujah Chorus" (music CD track 10), there occur instances in which men and women sing the same notes in different octaves. This still represents monophony.

Polyphony

Polyphony means "many-sounding," and it occurs when two or more melodic lines of relatively equal interest are performed at the same time. This combining technique also is called counterpoint. We can hear it in a very simple statement in "Ave Maria . . . Virgo Serena" by Josquin Desprez (day-PRAY) (music CD track 6). Palestrina's "Kyrie" from the *Pope Marcellus Mass* (music CD track 7) is more complex. When the counterpoint uses an immediate restatement of the musical idea, as in the Desprez, then the composer is utilizing *imitation*.

Homophony

When chords accompany one main melody, we have homophonic texture. Here the composer focuses attention on the melody by supporting it with subordinate sounds. The Bach chorale on music CD track 9 illustrates this type of texture very well. In this example all four voices sing together in simultaneous rhythm. The main melody is in the soprano, or top, part. The lower parts sing melodies of their own, which are different from the main melody, but, rather than being independent as would be the case in polyphony, they support the soprano melody and move with it in a progression of chords related to the syllables of the text.

FORM

Tones and rhythms that proceed without purpose or stop arbitrarily make little sense to the listener. Therefore, just as the painter, sculptor, or any other artist must try to develop a design that has focus and meaning, the musician must attempt to create a coherent composition of sounds and silences. The principal means by which artists create coherence is repetition. As we noted in the Introduction, the Volkswagen (see Fig. **0.9**) achieved unity through the use of strong geometric repetition which varied only in size. Music achieves coherence or unity through repetition in a similar fashion. However, since music deals with time as opposed to space, repetition in music usually involves recognizable themes.

Form can thus be seen as organization through repetition to create unity. Form may be divided into two categories: *closed form* and *open form*. These terms are somewhat similar to those used in sculpture and painting. Closed form directs the "musical eye" back into the composition by restating music from the beginning of the piece at the end. Open form allows the ear to escape the composition by utilizing repetition of thematic material only as a departure point for further development, and by ending without repetition of the opening. A few of the more common examples of closed and open forms follow.

Closed Forms

Binary form, as the name implies, consists of two parts: the opening section of the composition and a second part which often acts as an answer to the first: AB.

Ternary form is three-part structure in which the opening section is repeated after a different second section: ABA.

Ritornello (rih-tor-NELL-loh), which developed in the Baroque period, and *rondo* (RAHN-doh), which developed in the Classical period, are continuous structures which return repeatedly to the opening theme after statements of additional themes. Ritornello alternates orchestral and solo passages. Rondo alternates a main theme in the tonic key with subordinate themes in contrasting keys: ABACADA.

Sonata form, or *sonata-allegro form*, which we introduced earlier, takes its name from the conventional treatment of the first movement of the sonata. It is also the form of the first movement of many symphonies. The basic pattern is ABA or AABA. The first A section is a statement of two main themes, known as the *exposition*. It starts in the tonic and moves to a related key. To cement the perception of section A, the composer may repeat it: AA. The B section, the *development*, takes the original themes and develops them, usually with fragmentations and key changes. The A section then returns; this final section is called the *recapitulation*. The recapitulation is not an exact repetition of the opening section, because it needs to finish in the tonic key.

Open Forms

The *fugue*, again which we introduced earlier, is a polyphonic development of one, two, or sometimes three short themes. Fugal form, which takes its name from the Latin *fuga* ("flight"), has a traditional, though not a necessary, scheme of development. Two characteristics are common to all fugues: (1) counterpoint, and (2) a clear dominant–tonic relationship—that is, imitation of the theme at the fifth above or below the tonic. Each voice in a fugue (as many as five or more) develops the basic subject independent from the other voices, and passes through as many of the basic elements as the composer deems necessary. The composer achieves unification not by return to an opening section, as in closed form, but by the varying recurrences of the subject throughout.

The *canon* is a contrapuntal form based on note-for-note imitation of one voice by another. The voices are separated by a brief time interval—for example (the use of letters here does *not* indicate structure as above):

Voice 1: a b c d e f g
Voice 2:　a b c d e f g
Voice 3:　　a b c d e f g

The interval of separation is not always the same among the voices. The canon differs from a *round* such as "Row, row, row your boat." A round also repeats melody exactly; however, the canon develops new material indefinitely, while the round repeats the same phrases over and over. The interval of separation in the round stays constant—one phrase apart.

Theme and variations is a compositional structure in which an initial musical idea, the theme, repeats over and over and changes each time through melodic, rhythmic, and harmonic treatments, usually each more elaborate than the last.

How does it Stimulate the Senses?

OUR PRIMAL RESPONSES

We can find no better means of illustrating the sensual effect of music than to contrast two totally different musical pieces. The Chopin Nocturne we noted earlier (music CD track 15) provides us with an example of how musical elements can combine to give us a relaxing and soothing experience. Here, the tone color of the piano, added to the elements of a constant beat in triple meter, consonant harmonies, subtle dynamic contrasts, and extended duration of the tones combine in a richly subdued experience that engages us but lulls us at the same time. In contrast, listen to Stravinsky's "Auguries of Spring: Dances of the Youths and Maidens" from *The Rite of Spring* (music CD track 20). Here the driving rhythms, strong syncopation,

dissonant harmonies, wildly contrasting dynamics, and the broad tonal palette of the orchestra rivet us and ratchet up our excitement level. It is virtually impossible to listen to this piece without experiencing a rise in pulse rate. In both cases, our senses have responded at an extremely basic level over which we have, it would seem, little control.

Music contains a sensual attraction difficult to deny. At every turn it causes us to tap our toes, drum our fingers, or bounce in our seats in a purely physical response. This involuntary motor response is perhaps the most primitive aspect of our sensual involvement—as primitive as the images in Stravinsky's *The Rite of Spring*. If the rhythm is irregular and the beat divided or syncopated, as in this piece of music, we may find one part of our body doing one thing and another part doing something else. Having compared the Chopin and Stravinsky pieces, do we have any doubt that a composer's choices have the power to manipulate us sensually?

From time to time throughout this chapter, we have referred to certain historical conventions that permeate the world of music. Some of these have a potential effect on our sense response. Some notational patterns can be a kind of musical shorthand, or perhaps mime, that conveys certain kinds of emotion to the listener. This, of course, has little meaning for us unless we take the time and effort to study music history. Some of Mozart's string quartets indulge in exactly this kind of communication—another illustration of how expanded knowledge can increase the depth, value, and enjoyment of the aesthetic experience.

THE MUSICAL PERFORMANCE

A certain part of our sense response to music occurs as a result of the nature of the performance itself. As we suggested earlier in the chapter, the scale of a symphony orchestra gives a composer a tremendously variable canvas on which to paint. Let's pause, momentarily, to familiarize ourselves with this fundamental aspect of the musical equation. As we face the stage in an orchestral concert, we note perhaps as many as one hundred instrumentalists facing back at us. Their arrangement from one concert to another is fairly standard, as illustrated in Figure 3.10.

A large symphony orchestra can overwhelm us with diverse timbres and volumes; a string quartet cannot. Our expectations and our focus may change as we perceive the performance of one or the other. Because, for example, we know our perceptual experience with a string quartet will not involve the broad possibilities of an orchestra, we tune ourselves to seek the subtler, more personal mess-

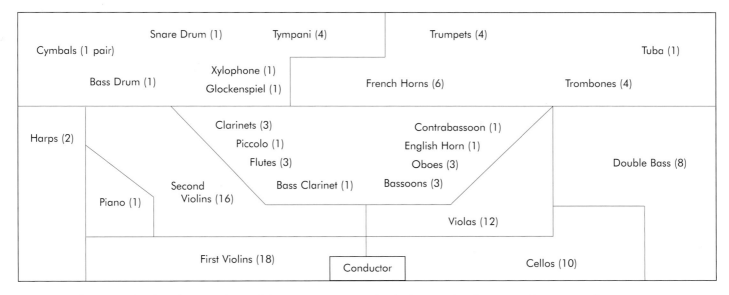

3.10 Typical seating plan for a large orchestra (about 100 instrumentalists), showing the placement of instrumental sections.

ages within that particular medium. The difference between listening to an orchestra and listening to a quartet is similar to the difference between viewing a museum painting of monumental scale and the exquisite technique of a miniature.

Textural suggestion can have much to do with sensual response to a musical work. Debussy's *Prelude to the Afternoon of a Faun* (music CD track 19) elicits images of Pan frolicking through the woodlands and cavorting with the nymphs on a sunny afternoon. Of course, much of what we imagine has been stimulated by the title of the composition. Our perception is heightened further if we are familiar with the poem by Mallarmé (mah-lahr-MAY) on which the symphonic poem is based. This piece represents program music, which comprises instrumental music associated with a story, poem, idea, or scene. Absolute music comprises instrumental music without a program. Titles, and especially text, in musical compositions may be the strongest devices a composer has for communicating directly with us. Images are triggered by words, and they can stimulate our imaginations and senses to wander freely "in tune" with the musical development. Johannes Brahms called a movement in his *German Requiem* "All Mortal Flesh is as the Grass"; we certainly receive a philosophical and religious communication from that title. Moreover, when the chorus ceases to sing and the orchestra plays alone, the instrumental melodies stimulate images of fields of grass blowing in the wind.

Harmony and tonality are both of considerable importance in stimulating our senses. Just as paintings and sculpture stimulate sensations of rest and comfort or action and discomfort, so harmonies create a feeling of repose and stability if they are consonant and a sensation

of restlessness and instability if they are dissonant. Harmonic progression that leads to a full cadential resolution leaves us feeling fulfilled; unresolved cadences are puzzling and perhaps irritating. Major or minor tonalities have significantly differing effects: Major sounds positive; minor, sad or mysterious. The former seems close to home, and the latter exotic. Atonal music sets us adrift to find the unifying thread of the composition.

Melody, rhythm, and tempo have close parallels to the use of line in painting, and the term *melodic contour* could be seen as a musical analogue to this element of painting. When the tones of a melody are conjunct and undulate slowly and smoothly, they trace a pattern having the same sensual effect as their linear visual counterpart—that is, soft, comfortable, and placid.

When melodic contours are disjunct and tempos rapid, the pattern and response change:

In conclusion, it remains for us as we respond to music to analyze how each of the elements available to the composer has in fact become a part of the channel of communication, and how the composer, consciously or unconsciously, has put together a work that elicits sensory responses from us. The "Thinking Critically" section at the end of this chapter offers suggestions on effective listening.

OPERA

The composer Pietro Mascagni (mahs-KAH-nyee) reportedly said, "In my operas do not look for melody or beauty . . . look only for blood." Mascagni represented a style of late-nineteenth-century opera called *verismo* (vay-REEZ-moh), a word with the same root as verisimilitude, meaning true to life. *Verismo* opera treated themes, characters, and events from life in a down-to-earth fashion. In Mascagni's operas and the operas of other composers of the *verismo* style, we find plenty of blood, but we also find fine drama and music, and the combination of drama and music into a single artistic form constitutes opera. In basic terms, opera is drama sung to orchestral accompaniment. In opera, music comprises the predominant element, but the addition of a story line, scenery, costumes, and staging makes opera significantly different from other forms of music.

In one sense, we could describe opera as the purest integration of all the arts. It contains music, drama, poetry, and visual arts. It even includes architecture, because an opera house constitutes a particular architectural entity with very specific requirements for orchestra, audience, and stage space, as well as stage machinery. In its wide variety of applications, opera ranges from tragedies of spectacular proportions, involving several hundred people, to intimate music dramas and comedies with two or three characters (Figs. **3.11–3.13**).

In an opera, unlike theatre, the production reveals character and plot through song rather than speech. This convention removes opera from the lifelikeness we might expect in the theatre and asks us to suspend our disbelief so we can enjoy magnificent music and the heightening of dramatic experience that music's contribution to mood, character, and dramatic action affords us.

Central to an opera are performers who can sing and act simultaneously. These include major characters played by star performers as well as secondary solo singers and chorus members plus supernumeraries—"supers" or "extras"—who do not sing but merely flesh out crowd scenes (Figs. **3.11–3.13**).

TYPES OF OPERA

In Italian, the word opera means *work*. In Florence, Italy, in the late sixteenth century, artists, writers, and archi-

3.11 Giacomo Puccini, *Manon Lescaut*. Opera Company of Philadelphia. Photo by Trudy Cohen.

3.12 Giuseppe Galli da Bibiena, *Scene design for an opera*, 1719. Contemporary engraving. Metropolitan Museum of Art, New York (Elisha Whittelsey Fund).

tects eagerly revived the culture of ancient Greece and Rome. Opera was an attempt by a group known as the *camerata* (Italian for fellowship or society) to re-create the effect of ancient Greek drama, in which, scholars believed, the words were chanted or sung as well as spoken. Through succeeding centuries, various applications of the fundamental concept of opera have arisen, and among these applications are four basic types of opera: (1) grand opera; (2) opéra comique; (3) opera buffa; and (4) operetta.

Grand opera, used synonymously with "opera," refers to serious or tragic opera, usually in five acts. Another name for this type of opera is *opera seria* (oh-pay-RAH SAY-ree-ah) (serious opera), which treats heroic subjects usually in a highly stylized manner—for example, the gods and heroes of ancient times.

Opéra comique (oh-pay-RAH coh-MEEK) is opera, regardless of subject matter, that has spoken dialogue. This type of opera must not be confused with comic opera.

Opera buffa (oh-pay-RAH BOO-fah) is comic opera (again, not to be confused with opéra comique), which usually does not have spoken dialogue. It usually uses satire to treat a serious topic with humor—for example, Mozart's *The Marriage of Figaro*.

Operetta also has spoken dialogue, but it has come to refer to a light style of opera characterized by popular themes, a romantic mood, and often a humorous tone. It is frequently considered more theatrical than musical, and its story line is usually frivolous and sentimental.

THE OPERA PRODUCTION

Like theatre, opera is a collaborative art, joining the efforts of a composer, a dramatist, a stage director, and a musical director. At its beginnings, an opera emerges when a composer sets to music a text, called a *libretto* (and written by a *librettist*). As suggested earlier, the range of subjects and characters in opera may be extremely broad, from mythological to everyday. All characters come to life through performers who combine singing and acting. Opera includes the basic voice ranges of soprano, alto, tenor, and bass, but divides them more precisely. Below are some of the categories.

Coloratura soprano	Very high range; capable of executing rapid scales and trills.
Lyric soprano	Fairly light voice; cast in roles requiring grace and charm.
Dramatic soprano	Full, powerful voice, capable of passionate intensity.
Lyric tenor	Relatively light, bright voice.
Dramatic tenor	Powerful voice, capable of heroic expression.
Basso buffo	Cast in comic roles; can sing very rapidly.
Basso profundo	Extremely low range capable of power; cast in roles requiring great dignity.

Since the large majority of operas in the contemporary repertoire are not of American origin, the American respondent usually has to overcome the language barrier to understand the dialogue and thereby the plot. A desire for snobbery or exclusivity does not cause the lack of English-translation performances; much of it is pure practicality. For example, performing operas in their original language makes it possible for the best singers to be heard around the world. Imagine the complications if a great singer had to learn a single opera in the language of every country in which he or she performed it. In addition, opera loses much of its musical character in translation. We spoke of tone color, or timbre, earlier in this chapter. Timbre characteristics implicit in the Russian, German, and Italian languages vanish when translated into English. In addition, inasmuch as opera is in a sense the Olympic Games of the vocal-music world—that is, the demands made on the human voice by the composers of opera call for the highest degree of skill and training of any vocal medium—tone, placement, and the vowels and consonants requisite to that placement, become very important to the singer. It is one thing for a tenor to sing the vowel "eh" on high B-flat in the original Italian. If the translated word to be sung on the same note employs an "oo" vowel, the technical demand is changed considerably. So, the translation of opera from its original tongue into English causes more difficult and complex problems than simply providing an accurate translation for a portion of the audience that does not know the text—as important as that may seem. Translation must concern itself with tone quality, color, and the execution of tones in the *tessitura*, or normal range, of the human voice.

Experienced operagoers may study the score before attending a performance. However, every concert program contains a plot synopsis (even when the production is in English), so that everyone can follow what is happening. Opera plots, unlike mysteries, have few surprise endings, and knowing the plot ahead of time does not diminish the experience of responding to the opera. To assist the audience, often opera companies project the translated lyrics on a screen above the stage, much like subtitles in a foreign film.

The opening element in opera is the *overture*. This orchestral introduction may have two characteristics. First, it may set the mood or tone of the opera. Here the composer works directly with our sense responses, putting us in the proper frame of mind for what follows. In his overture to *I Pagliacci* (ee pahl-YAH-chee), for example, Ruggiero Leoncavallo creates a tonal story foretelling comedy, tragedy, action, and romance, using only the orchestra. Listening to this overture, we can identify these elements, and in so doing understand the relative unimportance of English to comprehension of the work. Add to the "musical language" the language of body and mime, and we can understand even complex ideas and character relationships—*without* words. In addition to this type of introduction, an overture may provide melodic introductions—passages introducing the *arias* and *recitatives* (reh-sih-tah-TEEV) that will follow.

The plot of an opera unfolds through recitative, or sung dialogue. Recitative moves the plot along from one section to another; it usually has little emotional content to speak of, and the words are more important than the music. There are two kinds of recitative. In the first, *recitativo secco* (ray-chee-tah-TEE-voh say-koh), the singer has very little musical accompaniment, or none at all. Any accompaniment is usually in the form of light chording under the voice. The second type, *recitativo stromento* (ray-chee-tah-TEE-voh stroh-MEHN-toh), has full musical accompaniment.

The real emotion and poetry of an opera lie in its arias. Musically and poetically, an aria reflects high dramatic feeling. The great opera songs with which we are likely to be familiar are arias such as "La Donna è Mobile" from *Rigoletto* by Giuseppe Verdi (music CD track 17).

Every opera contains ensemble pieces such as duets, trios, and quartets, as well as chorus sections in which everyone gets into the act. In addition, ballet or dance interludes are not uncommon. These may have nothing to do with the development of the plot, but are put in to add more life and interest to the dramatic production, and in some cases to provide a link from one scene into another.

Bel canto, as its name implies, is a style of singing emphasizing the beauty of sound. Its most successful

A Personal Journey

VERDI, *DON CARLOS*

Tbilisi, Georgia, in the old Soviet Union was a beautiful city. A long civil war, however, has pockmarked its buildings and devastated its inhabitants. Before the fall of communism, I was strolling along a tree-lined street when a glass-encased sign, similar to those in front of churches in the United States, caught my attention. Among its words (in the Cyrillic alphabet of the Russian language), I could read "Verdi: Don Carlos." I gazed at the building: a large, green stucco Neoclassical façade betraying nothing of what might be inside. The sign implied that it was an opera house, but nothing else about the building suggested its use. The dates indicated that *Don Carlos* was playing that night. I hurried to my hotel to inquire how I might secure tickets and hoped the price would not destroy my budget. As was typical of Soviet bureaucracy, the command "come back in one hour" answered my query. One hour later I returned to the desk, receiving two tickets at ten dollars each (U.S. currency—cash—only) and instructions to arrive at the opera house by 7.30 p.m.

At precisely 7.30 p.m., my wife and I climbed the steps of the green building and entered a fantasyland of shining marble, gold, and glittering crystal chandeliers. A grand staircase rose from the lobby, and anterooms of colorful inlaid marble surrounded sumptuous hallways leading to the auditorium: a typical European opera house of tiered balconies. An immense crystal chandelier that would have done credit to *The Phantom of the Opera* dominated the building's interior.

As curtain time approached, I devoted my attention to the stage. The proscenium arch stood open, without a grand drape; the stage yawned, barren and black. My heart sank. I concluded that we were about to witness a stripped-down, communist version of Verdi's work. No wonder the tickets were only ten dollars (as opposed to more than one hundred in most other European operas—Prague, Czech Republic being a notable exception). We were, to my amazement, occupying the best seats in the sold-out house. As the lights dimmed, a man (actor? singer? stagehand?) moved to center stage, reached down, grabbed a handful of the black fabric that covered the stage, and pulled. As he did, mountains of cloth fell from everywhere and a lavish setting, dominated by three 30-foot (9-m) gold statues of Hercules, came to life. The audience gasped (me included), and applause echoed through the auditorium.

The opera's story takes place in sixteenth-century Madrid and involves Don Carlos, grandson of Holy Roman Emperor Charles V, and his love for Elizabeth of Valois, who loved Carlos, but who was forced, for political reasons, to marry Carlos' father, Philip II of Spain. Meeting a veiled lady whom Carlos believes to be Elizabeth, but who in fact is Princess Eboli (who also loves Carlos), Carlos proclaims his love and is rewarded by the fury of a woman scorned.

The plot twists further as things evolve, with revenge, counter-revenge, intrigue, imprisonment, and death following in swift order. The opera closes with Don Carlos dragged into his grandfather's tomb by a mysterious priest whom everyone assumes to be the ghost of Charles V.

It was a momentous evening, with singing as sumptuous as the setting, which reminded me how easily a great adventure can slip by for want of a little curiosity and effort—in this case, a question asked, an hour waited, and twenty dollars spent.

MUSIC AND HUMAN REALITY

Bizet, *Carmen*

George Bizet's (bee-ZEH) opera *Carmen* takes its libretto from a literary classic, a story by Prosper Mérimée. Its heroine, Carmen, is a seductive employee in a cigarette factory in nineteenth-century Seville. She flirts with Don Jose, a soldier, and completely enraptures him to the point where he deserts his service to follow her first to her haunt, a disreputable tavern, and then to a mountain pass where gypsy smugglers have made their hideout. But Carmen soon tires of Don Jose and becomes interested in the great toreador Escamillo (ehs-kah-MEEL-yoh). On the day of a bullfight in Seville, Carmen arrives with Escamillo, the latter welcomed as a hero. After Escamillo enters the bullring, Don Jose appears, dishevelled and distraught. In vain he pleads with Carmen to return to him. When she refuses, he stabs her fatally with a dagger. Emerging from the bullfight, Escamillo finds Don Jose weeping over Carmen's dead body.

Carmen began as *opéra comique*. When Bizet first wrote his score, he used spoken dialogue, and this is the way *Carmen* was heard at the Opéra Comique in Paris on March 3, 1875. Incidentally, it is still played that way at that house. But elsewhere, dialogue was replaced by recitatives, sung dialogues prepared not by the composer himself but by Ernest Guiraud.

Today a number of ballet sequences are interpolated (using background music from other Bizet compositions). *Carmen* had no ballets.

As a character and as a woman, Carmen fascinates. Bizet uses her as a symbol of "woman." Every passage Carmen sings is a new mask, mirroring the man she is addressing. Her receptive nature is portrayed with uncanny realism in her change of tone as she addresses the passers-by, Jose, Zuniga, the smugglers, and Escamillo. For each of the men, she alters the sound of her voice, the character of her melody, her mood, her tempo.

There was much in *Carmen* to disturb audiences in 1875. The vivid portrayal of such an immoral character caused shock. Never before had an opera presented women onstage smoking cigarettes. Some listeners objected to the music, thinking it was too much like Wagner, because Bizet assigned such importance to the orchestra and on random occasions used a leading-motif (*leitmotif*) technique. Nevertheless, *Carmen* was by no means the total failure that some of Bizet's early biographers suggested. As a matter of fact, some critics hailed it, a publisher paid a handsome price for the publication rights, and the opera company kept it in its repertory the following season.

3.13 Georges Bizet, *Carmen*. Opera Company of Philadelphia. Composite photo by Trudy Cohen.

composer, Gioacchino Rossini, had a great sense of melody and sought to develop the *art song* to its highest level. In *bel canto* singing the melody is the focus.

In the nineteenth century Richard Wagner (REE-kahrd VAHG-nuhr) (music CD track 18) gave opera and theatre a prototype that still continues to influence theatrical production—*organic unity*. Every element of his productions was integral and shaped to create a *Gesamtkunstwerk* (geh-ZAHMT-koonst-vairk), a work of total unity. Wagner also used *Leitmotif* (lite-moh-TEEF), a common element in contemporary film. A leitmotif is a musical theme associated with a particular person or idea. Each time that person appears or is thought of, or each time the idea surfaces, the leitmotif is played.

THINKING CRITICALLY

When listening to music, guide your listening, sharpen your perceptions, associate what you hear with musical terms, and critically analyze the selection by asking yourself the following questions. (As an example, listen to Bach's *Prelude and Fugue No. 1 in C*, BWV 846) at http://www.classicalarchives.com/cgi-bin/n.cgi/prep/b/bwv846.mid)

- Subject. Does the composition try to convey a subject or does it represent only that which is pure (absolute music)? Does the title of the piece suggest something (program music)?

- Function. Was the piece composed with any particular purpose in mind (march, lullaby, serenade, waltz)? Was it composed for some particular occasion? Does the piece introduce something or set the mood for some activity (prelude, overture)?

- Form. Does the title of the piece identify its form? How does it follow the characteristics of the form?

- Sound. How does the piece explore dynamics? Using the specific musical terms—for example, pianissimo, forte—describe the progression of the piece from beginning to end. In what ways does the music explore tone color?

- Rhythm. What is the meter? Do any changes occur? If so, where and how?

- Tempo. In what ways does the tempo of the piece affect your response? Using the specific musical terms—for example, largo, andante—describe the progression of speeds from beginning to end.

- Texture. What textures does the music explore? Where do changes, if any, in texture occur?

CYBER STUDY

SONATA:
—Franz Joseph Haydn, *Piano Sonata No. 20 in C minor*, 1. Allegro Moderato
http://www.classicalarchives.com/cgi-bin/n/cgi/prep/6/hay-p20a.mid

SYMPHONY:
—Ludwig van Beethoven, *Symphony No. 3 in E flat major*, "Eroica," Op. 55, 1. Allegro con brio
http://www.classicalarchives.com/cgi-bin/n.cig/prep/6/eroica-1.mid

CONCERTO:
—George Frederick Handel, *Concerto Grosso Op. 6, No. 12 in B minor*
http://www.classicalarchives.com/cgi-bin/n.cgi/prep/7/op6n12b-.mid

SUITE:
—Johann Sebastian Bach, *Orchestral Suite No. 2 in B minor*, BWV 1067
http://www.kt.rim.or.jp/~moclin/data/ba_air.mid

CHAPTER FOUR

THEATRE

IMPORTANT TERMS

Tragedy A serious drama or other literary work in which conflict between a protagonist and a superior force (often fate) concludes in disaster for the protagonist.

Comedy A genre of complex qualities involving humor. Comedy may or may not involve laughter and may or may not end "happily."

Melodrama A genre characterized by stereotyped characters, implausible plots, and an emphasis on spectacle.

Performance art A theatrical-type performance that combines elements from fields in the humanities and the arts.

Script A written document containing the words of the play.

Exposition A part of plot containing necessary background information

Complication A part of plot containing a series of conflicts and decisions by the characters.

Dénouement A part of plot containing the final resolution.

Protagonist The main character of a play.

Aesthetic distance The mental and physical separation of the audience from the performance.

Of all the arts, theatre comes the closest to personalizing the love, rejection, disappointment, betrayal, joy, elation, and suffering that we experience in our daily lives. It does so because theatre uses live people acting out situations that very often look and sound like real life. Theatre once functioned in society like television and movies do today. Many of the qualities of all three forms are identical. We shall find in this chapter the ways that theatre, which frequently relies on *drama* (a written script), takes lifelike circumstances and compresses them into organized episodes. The result, although looking like reality, goes far beyond it in order to help us find in its characters pieces of ourselves.

The word *theatre* comes from the Greek *theatron*—the part of the Greek theatre where the audience sat. Its literal meaning is "a place for seeing," but for the Greeks this implied more than the sense experience of vision (which, indeed, is an important part of the theatrical production). To the ancient Greeks, "to see" also might include comprehension and understanding. Thus, witnessing—seeing and hearing—a theatrical production was felt with the emotions and mediated by the intelligence of the mind, leading to an understanding of the importance of the play. Further, for the ancient Greeks, *theatron*, while a physical part of the theatre building, implied a non-physical place—a special state of being of those who together watched the lives of the persons of the drama.

Like the other performing arts, theatre is an interpretive discipline. Between the playwright and the audience stand the director, the designers, and the actors. Although each functions as an individual artist, each also serves to communicate the playwright's vision to the audience. Sometimes the play becomes subordinate to the expressive work of its interpreters; sometimes the concept of director as master artist places the playwright in a subordinate position. Nonetheless, a theatrical production always requires the interpretation of a concept through spectacle and sound by theatre artists.

WHAT IS IT?

Theatre represents an attempt to reveal a vision of human life through time, sound, and space. It gives us flesh-and-blood human beings involved in human action—we must occasionally remind ourselves that the dramatic experience is not reality: It is an imitation of reality, acting as a symbol to communicate something about the human condition. Theatre is make-believe: Through gesture and movement, language, character, thought, and spectacle, it imitates action. However, if this were all theatre consisted

of, we would not find it as captivating as we do, and as we have for more than 2,500 years.

At the formal level, theatre comprises *genre*—or type of play—from which the production evolves. Some of the genres of theatre are *tragedy, comedy, tragicomedy, melodrama*, and *performance art*. Some are products of specific periods of history, and illustrate trends that no longer exist; others are still developing and as yet lack definite form. Our response to genre differs from our formal response or identification in music, for example, because we seldom find generic identification in the theatre program. Some plays are well-known examples of a specific genre, for example, the tragedy *Oedipus the King* by Sophocles. In these cases, as with a symphony, we can see how the production develops the conventions of genre. Other plays, however, are not well known or may be open to interpretation. As a result, we can draw our conclusions only after the performance has finished.

TRAGEDY

We commonly describe tragedy as a play with an unhappy ending. Aristotle treats this subject in detail in *The Poetics*. The playwright Arthur Miller describes tragedy as "the consequences of a man's total compulsion to evaluate himself justly; his destruction in the attempt posits a wrong or an evil in his environment." In the centuries since its inception, tragedy has undergone many variations as a means by which the playwright makes a statement about human frailty and failing.

Typically, tragic heroes make free choices that bring about suffering, defeat, and, sometimes, triumph as a result of defeat. The protagonist often undergoes a struggle that ends disastrously. In Greek Classical tragedy of the fifth century B.C.E. (see Chapter 10), the hero or heroine was generally a larger-than-life figure who gained a moral victory amid physical defeat. Classical heroes usually suffer from a tragic flaw—some defect that causes them to contribute to their own downfall. In a typical Classical tragedy, the climax occurs as the hero or heroine recognizes his or her role and accepts destiny. In the years from ancient Greece to the present, however, writers have employed many different approaches. Arthur Miller argues the case for tragic heroes of "common stuff," suggesting that "the tragic right is a condition of life, a condition in which the human personality is able to flower and realize itself." See Cyber Study for examples.

COMEDY

The word comedy comes from the Greek *komoidia* (koh-mee-DEE-ah), which is a derivative of the Greek word for a singer in a revel, from *kômos* (KOH-mohs), meaning "a band of revelers." Comedy deals with light or amusing subjects or with serious and profound subjects in a light, familiar, or satirical manner. As a consequence, it is more complex than tragedy and more complicated to define precisely. The genre dates to the fifth century B.C.E., when it was associated with the revelry linked to worship of the god Dionysus (dy-uh-NY-suhs). The first period of Greek comedy, known as Old Comedy, is represented by the comedies of Aristophanes (air-ih-STAH-fuh-neez; see Chapter 10, p. 232). These were mostly satires of public officials. By Roman times, comedy shifted its focus to ordinary citizens portrayed as stock characters. The plots were usually formularized. For the most part disappearing until the Middle Ages, comedy reappeared as simply a story with a happy ending. In more recent times, the genre has taken divergent paths, depending on the attitude of its authors toward their subject matter. As a result, we find, for example, satirical comedy, in which the author intends to ridicule. When the ridicule focuses on individuals, the result is *comedy of character*. When the satire is on social conventions, *comedy of manners* results. This genre was especially popular and well developed in the eighteenth century in England. Satire of conventional thinking produces *comedy of ideas*. A few more types include: *romantic comedy* (the progress from troubles to triumphs in love) and *comedy of intrigue* (amusement and excitement through an intricate plot of reversals with artificial, contrived situations—for example, the Spanish comedies of Lope de Vega (vay gah) and Tirso de Molina (moh-LEE-nah)). *Sentimental comedy* entails exploitation of potentially serious issues without approaching the truly tragic aspects of the subject or examining its underlying significance. See Cyber Study for examples.

TRAGICOMEDY

As the name suggests, tragicomedy is a mixed form of theatre, which, like the other types, has been defined in different terms in different periods. Until the nineteenth century, the ending was the criterion for this form. Traditionally, characters reflect diverse social standings—kings (as in tragedy) and common folk (as in comedy)—and reversals go from bad to good and good to bad. The genre also includes language appropriate to both tragedy and comedy. Early tragicomedies were serious plays that ended, if not happily, then at least by avoiding catastrophe. In the past century-and-a-half, the term has been adapted to describe plays in which the mood may shift from light to heavy, or in which endings are neither exclusively tragic nor comic. See Cyber Study for an example.

MELODRAMA

Melodrama is another mixed form. It takes its name from the terms *melo* (Greek for "music") and "drama." Melodrama first appeared in the late eighteenth century, when dialogue took place against a musical background. In the nineteenth century, the term was applied to serious plays without music. Melodrama uses stereotypical characters involved in serious situations in which suspense, pathos, terror, and occasionally hatred are aroused. It portrays the forces of good and evil battling in exaggerated circumstances. As a rule, the issues involved are simplified and uncomplicated: Good is good and evil is evil; there are no ambiguities.

Geared largely for a popular audience, the form concerns itself primarily with situation and plot. Conventional in its morality, melodrama tends toward optimism—good always triumphs in the end. Typically, the hero or heroine is placed in life-threatening situations by the acts of a villain and then rescued at the last instant. The forces against which the characters struggle are external ones—caused by an unfriendly world rather than by inner conflicts. Probably because melodrama took root in the nineteenth century, at a time when spectacular scenic effects were in vogue, many melodramas depend on sensation scenes for much of their effect. The popular nineteenth-century adaptation of Harriet Beecher Stowe's novel *Uncle Tom's Cabin* reflects this fondness for spectacle, as Eliza and the baby, Little Eva, escape from the plantation and are pursued across a raging, ice-filled river. These effects taxed the capacities of theatres to their maximum, but gave the audience spectacle. Not all melodramas use such extreme scenic devices, but their use was so frequent that they have become identified with the type.

PERFORMANCE ART

The late twentieth century produced a form of theatrical presentation called Performance Art. Performance Art pushes the traditional theatre envelope in a variety of directions, some of which deny traditional concepts of theatrical production itself. It is a type of performance that combines elements from fields in the humanities and arts, from urban anthropology to folklore, and dance to feminism. Performance Art pieces called *Happenings* grew out of the pop-art movement of the 1960s and were designed as critiques of consumer culture. European performance artists were influenced by the early twentieth-century movement of Dadaism and tended to be more political than their American counterparts. The central focus of many Happenings was the idea that art and life should be connected.

Because of its hybrid and diverse nature, there is no "typical" performance artist or work we can study as an illustration. We can, however, note three brief examples, which, if they do not typify, at least illumine this movement. The Hittite Empire, an all-male performance art group, performs *The Undersiege Stories*, which focuses on nonverbal communication and dance and includes confrontational scenarios. Performance artist Kathy Rose blends dance and film animation in unique ways. In one performance in New York, she creatively combined exotic dances with a wide variety of styles that included German Expressionism (see p. 382) and science fiction. The *New York Times* called her performance "visual astonishments." Playwright Rezo Abdoh's *Quotations from a Ruined City*, an intense and kinetic piece, features ten actors who act out outrage in fascinating, energetic fashion. The complicated, overlapping scenes, tableaux, and dances are punctuated by loud but unintelligible prerecorded voices. The piece combines elements depicting brutality, sadism, and sexuality. In the 1990s, Performance Art saw some difficult times because many people viewed it as rebellious and controversial for its own sake.

HOW IS IT PUT TOGETHER?

Theatre consists of a complex combination of elements that form a single entity called a performance or a production. Understanding theatre production as a work of art can be enhanced if we have some tools for approaching it. The following come to us from the distant past.

Writing 2,400 years ago in the *Poetics*, Aristotle argued that tragedy consisted of plot, character, diction, music, thought, and spectacle. We can use and expand upon Aristotle's terminology to describe the basic parts of a production. These six parts—and their descriptive terminology—still cover the entire theatrical product. We shall reshape Aristotle's terms into language more familiar to us, explain what they mean, and learn how we can use them to understand how a theatrical production works— things to look and listen for in a production. First, we will examine the script, and include in that discussion Aristotle's concept of diction, or language. Next, we will examine plot, thought—themes and ideas—character, and spectacle, which we shall call the visual elements. That will be followed by a brief discussion of what Aristotle called music but which, to avoid confusion, we will call aural elements.

SCRIPT

A playwright creates a written document called a script, which contains the dialogue used by the actors. Aristotle called the words written by the playwright *diction*; we will refer to this part of a production as its *language*. The playwright's language tells us at least part of what we can expect from the play. For example, if everyday speech has been used, we generally expect the action to resemble everyday truth, or reality. In the play *Fences* (1986), playwright August Wilson uses everyday language to bring the characters to life in the context of the period:

(Act I, scene iii. Troy is talking to his son.)

Like you? I go out of here every morning . . . bust my butt . . . putting up with them crackers everyday . . . cause I like you? You about the biggest fool I ever saw.
 (Pause)
 It's my job. It's my responsibility! You understand that? A man got to take care of his family. You live in my house . . . sleep you behind on my bedclothes . . . fill you belly up with my food . . . cause you my son.[1]

Poetic language, on the other hand, usually indicates less realism and perhaps stronger symbolism. Compare the language of *Fences* with the poetry used by Pierre Corneille (kohr-NAY), a seventeenth-century dramatist, in *Le Cid* (luh seed) to create a mythical hero who is larger than life:

(Act III, scene iv)

Rodrigue: I'll do your bidding, yet still do I desire
To end my wretched life, at your dear hand.
But this you must not ask, that I renounce
My worthy act in cowardly repentance.
The fatal outcome of too swift an anger
Disgraced my father, covered me with shame.[2]

In both plays, we use language and its tone to aid us in determining the implication of the words. Language helps to create the overall tone and style of the play. It can also reveal character, theme, and historical context.

PLOT

Plot is the structure of the play, the skeleton that gives the play shape, and on which the other elements hang. The nature of the plot determines how a play works: how it moves from one moment to another, how conflicts are structured, and how the experience ultimately comes to an end. We can examine the workings of plot by seeing

A Personal Journey

FRANCIS GOODRICH AND ALBERT HASKETT, *THE DIARY OF ANNE FRANK*

A November wind races up the canal, buffeting dry leaves along the street in Amsterdam, The Netherlands. I lean against the railing and watch the water ripple to the cadence of the breeze. The bell-and-step gables of the narrow houses create a visual counterpoint against the blue sky. The sun tries to reach the street but does not quite do so. A group of tourists stands on the steps of one of the buildings, the Anne Frank House. I'm trying to decide whether to join them.

Anne Frank was sixteen when she died in the German concentration camp at Bergen-Belsen. As I look at the house, I have difficulty reconciling the events that took place there with the "live and let live" attitude of the Dutch of Amsterdam and the constant gaggle of tourists. Anne Frank and her family were Jewish. In 1933 they left Nazi Germany and settled in Amsterdam. In July 1942, after the Nazis invaded Holland, the Franks' oldest daughter, Margot, received a notice to report for deportation to a labor camp. The family went into hiding the next day in the sealed-off back room of this building, which was an office at the time. Soon, three members of the van Vels family and Fritz Pfeffer joined them. For more than two years, Dutch sympathizers, business associates, and former employees of Mr. Frank protected the eight fugitives and brought them food and other necessities. In August 1944 their hiding place was discovered, and they were taken into custody and shipped to concentration camps. Anne died of typhus less than one year later, in March of 1945. Her father, Otto, was the only member of the family to survive.

For her thirteenth birthday, Anne received a diary, which she faithfully kept until she was arrested.

After the war, the diary was found in its hiding place in the building. Given to Mr. Frank, who had it published as *The House Behind*, it was translated and published in the United States under the title, *Anne Frank: The Diary of a Young Girl*. It was then dramatized into a play titled *The Diary of Anne Frank* by Francis Goodrich and Albert Haskett. The play, seen through the eyes of Anne's father, captures the humor and love underpinning those two years of seclusion. But it is a tragic tale, nonetheless, because, despite Anne's optimism, we know the ending—even though Anne doesn't. Her entry of July 15, 1944 reads: "I can feel the sufferings of millions and yet, if I look up to the heavens, I think that it will all come right, that this cruelty too will end, and that peace and tranquility will return again."

A few more tourists have joined the line outside the Anne Frank House. The settings for the productions of the play that I have seen have all been carefully researched and, in great detail, faithfully reproduced the spaces of that annex in which the two families and Mr. Pfeffer played out their own drama—sometimes in peace and sometimes in conflict. (Recently released pages of the diary, withheld by Mr. Frank until after his death, detail more conflict in the Frank family than the original play presents.) Nonetheless, I know the physical spaces intimately. Can the actual rooms and their ghosts touch me more than the scenic rooms of the theatre? Or will the presence of curious tourists lessen the effect to one of idle voyeurism in contrast to the dramatic involvement of the theatre? In the end, which experience would be more real? A cold blast of wind off the canal strikes a shiver in my spine. I turn and walk away.

the play somewhat as a timeline, beginning as the script or production begins, and ending at the final curtain, or the end of the script. In many plays plot tends to operate like a climactic pyramid (Fig. **4.1**). In order to keep our attention, the dynamics of the play rise in intensity until they reach the ultimate crisis—the *climax*—after which they relax, through a resolution called the *dénouement* (day-noo-MAWN; French for "untangling"), to the end of the play.

Depending on the playwright's purpose, plot may be shaped with or without some of the features described below. Sometimes plot may be so de-emphasized that it virtually disappears. However, as we try to evaluate a play critically, the elements of plot give us things to look for—if only to note that they do not exist in the play at hand.

Exposition

Exposition provides necessary background information. Through it the playwright introduces the characters—their personalities, relationships, backgrounds, and present situation. Exposition is frequently a recognizable section at the beginning of a play. It can be presented through dialogue, narration, setting, lighting, costume—or any device the playwright or director chooses. The amount of exposition in a play depends very much on where the playwright takes up the story, called the *point of attack*. A play told chronologically may need fairly little expositional material, while others require a good bit of prior summary.

Complication

Drama is about conflict. Although not every play fits that definition, conflict of some sort is a fundamental dramatic device in order to interest an audience. At some point in the play, someone or something frustrates the expected course of events, giving the audience reason to be interested in what transpires. At a specific moment, an action someone takes or a decision someone makes upsets the current state of affairs. This is sometimes called the *inciting incident* and it opens the middle part of the plot—the *complication*. The complication is the meat of the play, and it comprises a series of conflicts and decisions, called crises (from the Greek *krisis*, meaning "to decide"), that rise in intensity until they reach a turning point—the climax—that constitutes the end of the complication section (see Fig. **4.1**).

Dénouement

The dénouement is the final resolution of the plot. It is the period of time during which the audience is allowed to sense that the action is ending—a period of adjustment, downward in intensity, from the climax. Ideally, the dénouement brings about a clear and ordered resolution.

Exposition, complication, and dénouement comprise a time-frame in which the remaining parts of the play operate. This structural picture is not always so neat, though. Some plays do not conform to this kind of plot structure, yet that does not make them poorly constructed or of inferior quality. Nor does it mean that these concepts cannot generally be used as a means for describing and analyzing how a play is put together.

Foreshadowing

Preparation for subsequent action—foreshadowing—provides credibility for future action, keeps the plot logical, and avoids confusion. It builds tension and suspense: The audience is allowed to sense that something is about to happen, but because they do not know exactly what or when, anticipation builds suspense and tension. In the movie *Jaws* a rhythmic musical theme foreshadows the presence of the shark. Just as the audience becomes comfortable with that device, the shark suddenly appears—without the music. As a result, uncertainty as to the next shark attack is heightened immensely. Foreshadowing also moves the play forward by pointing toward events that will occur later.

Discovery

Discovery is the revelation of information about characters, their personalities, relationships, and feelings. Hamlet discovers from his father's ghost that his father was murdered by Claudius, and is urged to avenge the killing—a discovery without which the play cannot proceed. The skill of the playwright in structuring the revelation of such information in large part determines the overall impact of the play on the audience.

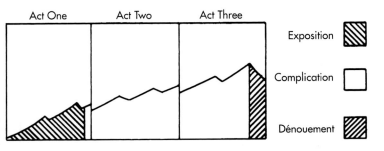

4.1 Hypothetical dynamic and structural development of a three-act play.

Reversal

Reversal is any turn of fortune; for example, Oedipus falls from power and prosperity to blindness and exile; Shakespeare's King Lear goes from ruler to victim of disaster. In comedy, reversal often changes the roles of social classes, as peasants jump to the upper class, and vice versa.

CHARACTER

Character is the psychological motivation of the people in the play. In most plays, the audience focuses on why individuals do what they do, how they change, and how they interact with other individuals, as the plot unfolds.

Plays reveal a wide variety of characters—both persons and motivating psychological forces. In every play there are characters who fulfill major functions and on whom the playwright wishes to focus. There are also minor characters. They may interact with the major characters, and their actions constitute subordinate plot lines. Much of the interest created by the drama lies in the exploration of how people with specific character motivations react to circumstances. For example, when Rodrigue in *Le Cid* discovers that his father has been humiliated, what is it in his character that makes him decide to avenge the insult, even though it means killing the father of the woman he loves, thereby jeopardizing that love? Such responses, driven by character, drive plays forward.

PROTAGONIST

Inside the structural pattern of a play some kind of action must take place. We must ask ourselves how the play works. How do we get from the beginning to the end? Most of the time, we take that journey via the actions and decisions of the *protagonist*, or central personage. Deciding on the protagonist of a play often poses challenging choices. However, understanding the play requires ascertaining the central character. In Terence Rattigan's *Cause Célèbre* three different responses are possible, depending upon whom the director decided was the protagonist. There are two central female roles. A good case could be made for either as the central personage of the play. Or they could be equal.

Often in drama a character appears in order to accentuate or contrast qualities in another character, particularly the protagonist. Such a contrasting character is called a *foil*. One of the best and best-known examples is Dr. Watson in Sir Arthur Conan Doyle's Sherlock Holmes stories. Here, Dr. Watson's obtuseness makes Holmes's deductions appear all the more brilliant.

THEMES

Themes and ideas comprise the intellectual content of a play (Aristotle used the term "thought"). In Lanford Wilson's *Burn This* (1987), for example, a young dancer, Anna, lives in a Manhattan loft with two gay roommates, Larry and Robby. As the play opens, we learn that Robby has been killed in a boating accident. Anna has just returned from the funeral and a set of bizarre encounters with Robby's family. Larry, a sardonic advertising executive, and Burton, Anna's boyfriend, maintain a constant animosity. Into the scene bursts Pale, Robby's brother and a threatening, violent figure. Anna is both afraid of and irresistibly attracted to Pale; the conflict of their relationship drives the play forward to its climax.

The above brief description summarizes the *plot* of a play. However, what the play is about—its *themes*—remains for us to discover and develop. Some might say it is about loneliness, anger, and the way not belonging is manifested in human behavior. Others might focus on abusive relationships, and others on how it deals with hetero- and homosexual conflicts and issues. The process of coming to conclusions about meaning involves several layers of interpretation. One involves the playwright's interpretation of the ideas through the characters, language, and plot. A second lies in the director's decisions about what the playwright has in mind, which is balanced by what the director wishes to communicate because, or in spite, of the playwright. Finally, we interpret what we actually see and hear in the production.

VISUAL ELEMENTS

The director takes the playwright's language, plot, and characters and translates them into action by using, among other things, what Aristotle called "spectacle," or what the French call *mise-en-scène* (meez-ahn-sehn), but which we can simply call the visual elements. The visual elements of a production include, first of all, the physical relationship established between actors and audience. The actor–audience relationship can take any number of shapes. For example, the audience might sit surrounding, or perhaps on only one side of, the stage. The visual elements also include stage settings, lighting, costumes, and properties, as well as the actors and their movements. Whatever the audience can see contributes to this aspect of the theatrical production.

Theatre Types

Part of our response to a production is shaped by the design of the space in which the play is produced. The

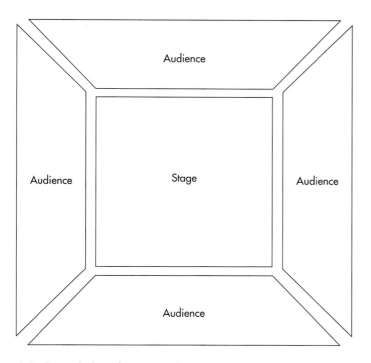

4.2 Ground plan of an arena theatre.

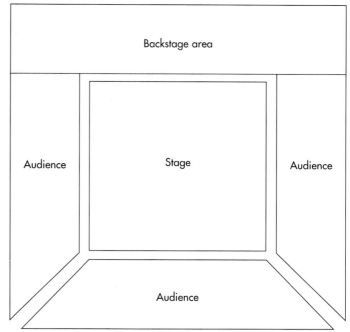

4.3 Ground plan of a thrust theatre.

earliest and most natural arrangement is the theatre-in-the-round, or *arena* theatre (Fig. **4.2**), in which the audience surrounds the playing area on all sides. Whether the stage is circular, square, or rectangular is irrelevant. Some argue that the closeness of the audience to the actors in an arena theatre provides the most intimate kind of theatrical experience. A second possibility is the *thrust*, or three-quarter, theatre (Fig. **4.3**), in which the audience surrounds the playing area on three sides. The most familiar example of this type of theatre is what we understand to have been the theatre of the Shakespearean period. The third format, and the one most widely used in the twentieth century, is the *proscenium* theatre, in which the audience sits on only one side and views the action through a frame (Fig. **4.4**).

There are also various experimental arrangements of audience and stage space. Sometimes acting areas are placed in the middle of the audience, creating little island stages. In certain circumstances, these small stages create quite an interesting set of responses and relationships between actors and audience.

Common experience indicates that the physical relationship of the acting area to the audience has an effect on the depth of audience involvement. It has also been found that some separation is necessary for certain kinds of emotional responses. This mental and physical separation is called *aesthetic distance*. The proper aesthetic distance allows us to become involved in what we know is fictitious and even unbelievable.

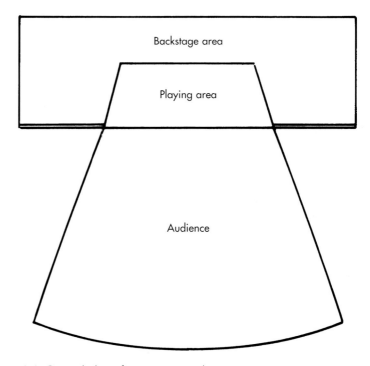

4.4 Ground plan of a proscenium theatre.

The visual elements may or may not have independent communication with the audience; this is one of the options of the director and designers. Before the nineteenth century, there was no coordination of the various elements of a theatre production. This, of course, had all kinds of curious, and in some cases catastrophic,

William Shakespeare

William Shakespeare (1564–1616) was one of the world's greatest literary geniuses. Most of his work was for the theatre, but he left a remarkable sequence of sonnets in which he pushed the resources of the English language to breathtaking extremes. In his works for the theatre, Shakespeare represents the Elizabethan love of drama, and the theatres of London were patronized by lords and commoners alike. They sought and found, usually in the same play, action, spectacle, comedy, character, and intellectual stimulation deeply reflective of the human condition. Thus it was with Shakespeare, the preeminent Elizabethan playwright. His appreciation of the Italian Renaissance—which he shared with his audience—can be seen in the settings of many of his plays. With true Renaissance breadth, Shakespeare went back into history, both British and Classical, and far beyond, to the fantasy world of *The Tempest*. Like most playwrights of his age, Shakespeare wrote for a specific professional company of which he became a partial owner. The need for new plays to keep the company alive from season to season provided much of the impetus for his prolific output.

Although we know only a little of his life, the principal facts are well established. He was baptized in the parish church of Stratford-upon-Avon on April 26, 1564, and probably attended the local grammar school. We next learn of him in his marriage to Ann Hathaway in 1582, when a special action was necessary to allow the marriage without delay. The reason is clear—five months later, Ann gave birth to their first daughter, Susanna. The next public mention comes in 1592, when his reputation as a playwright was sufficient to warrant a malicious comment from another playwright, Robert Greene. From then on, there are many records of his activities as dramatist, actor, and businessman. In addition to his steady output of plays, he also published a narrative poem entitled *Venus and Adonis*, which was popular enough to have nine printings in the next few years. His standing as a lyric poet was established with the publication of 154 Sonnets in 1609.

In 1594 he was a founder of a theatrical company called the Lord Chamberlain's Company, in which he functioned as shareholder, actor, and playwright. In 1599, the company built its own theatre, the Globe, which came directly under the patronage of James I when he assumed the throne in 1603. (A faithful reproduction of Shakespeare's Globe Theatre was completed in London in 1998.) Shakespeare died in 1616, shortly after executing a detailed will. His will, still in existence, bequeathed most of his property to Susanna and her daughter. He left small mementoes to friends. He mentioned his wife only once, leaving her his "second best bed" with its furnishings.

Playwrights were not highly esteemed in England in the sixteenth century, and there was virtually no reason to write about them. We do, however, know more about Shakespeare than we do most of his contemporaries.

consequences. However, for the past century, most theatre productions have adhered to the *organic theory* of play production: Everything, visual and aural, is designed with a single purpose. Each production has a specific goal in terms of audience response, and all of the elements in the production attempt to achieve this. Watch the Humanities CD: Theatre.

Scene Design

Simply stated, the purpose of scene design in the theatre is to create an environment suitable for achieving the aims of the production. Scene designers use the same tools of composition—line, form, mass, color, repetition, and unity—as painters. In addition, since a stage design occupies three-dimensional space and must allow for the movement of the actors in, on, through, and around the elements of scenery, the scene designer becomes a sculptor as well. Figures 4.5 and 4.6 illustrate how emphasis on certain elements of design highlights different characteristics in the production. Thomas Grieve's *Richard II* (Fig. 4.5) is formal, but light and spacious. His regular rhythms and repetition of arches create a completely different feeling from that elicited by Robert Burroughs's design for *Peer Gynt* (peer ghihnt; Fig. 4.6), where the zigzagging diagonals juxtaposed among verticals create a sense of action. Scene designers are limited by the stage space, the concepts of the director, the amount of time

4.5 Shakespeare, *Richard II*, Act II, scene ii (entrance into St. Stephen's Chapel). Producer: Charles Kean, London, 1857. Scene designer: Thomas Grieve. Victoria & Albert Museum, London.

and budget available for the execution of the design, and elements of practicality—for example, can the design withstand the wear and tear the actors will cause? Scene designers are also limited by the talent and abilities of the staff available to execute the design. A complex setting requiring sophisticated painting and delicate carpentry may be impossible if the only staff available are unskilled. These are the constraints, and also the challenges, of scene design.

A *scenic environment* occurs wherever theatre takes place: Any physical surrounding for a production is a scenic design because someone makes an artistic choice in its selection. In the contemporary theatre, scene designers function as creative partners in determining the direction and appearance of a theatre production. Ultimately, scene design must have something of its own

to say to the audience. Stage design is first and foremost a visual art, and the fundamental artistic tools of the scene designer are those of the visual artist we studied in Chapter 1: the elements and principles of composition, such as line and color.

Lighting Design

Lighting designers are perhaps the most crucial of all the theatre artists in modern productions. Without their art nothing done by the actors, the costume designer, the property master or mistress, the director, or the scene designer would be seen by the audience. Yet lighting designers work in an ephemeral medium. They must sculpt with light and create shadows that fall where they desire them to fall; they must "paint" over the colors

4.6 Scenic design for Ibsen, *Peer Gynt*, University of Arizona Theatre. Director: Peter R. Marroney. Scene designer: Robert C. Burroughs.

provided by the other designers. In doing so, they use lighting instruments with imperfect optical qualities. They do their work in their minds, unlike scene designers, who can paint a design mock-up and then calculate the end product in feet and inches. Lighting designers must imagine what their light will do to an actor, to a costume, to a set. They must enhance the color of a costume, accent the physique of an actor, and reinforce the plasticity of a setting. They also try to reinforce the dramatic structure and dynamics of the play. They work within the framework of light and shade. Without shadows and highlights, the human face and body become imperceptible: A human face without shadows cannot be seen clearly more than a few feet away. In a theatre, such small movements as the raising of an eyebrow must be seen clearly as much as 100 feet (30.5 m) away. The lighting designer makes this possible. In the contemporary theatre, with computerized movement of lighting instruments a reality, stage lighting has assumed an even more important role in theatre productions.

In summary, lighting design serves four functions or purposes: (1) *selective visibility*; lighting helps us see what the production requires of us, with proper focus on actors and settings, and enhancement of our perception of forms and depth; (2) *rhythm and structure*; changes in lighting help move the play and indicate the rises and falls in action from which we perceive the play's meaning; (3) *mood*; lighting is, arguably, our most important clue to the atmosphere of the play; (4) *illusion and motivation*; by creating sunlight, lamplight, moonlight, and other sources of light, lighting helps us experience the time and place of the action.

Costume Design

It is tempting to think of theatrical costumes merely as clothing that has to be researched to reflect a particular historical period and constructed to fit particular actors. But costuming goes beyond that. Costume designers work with the entire body of the actor. They design hair styles and clothing and sometimes makeup to suit a specific person or occasion, a character, a locale.

Stage costuming has three functions. First, it *accents*—that is, it shows the audience which personages are the most important in a scene, and it shows the relationship between people.

4.7 Costume designs for Shakespeare, *Twelfth Night*, Old Globe Theatre, San Diego, California. Director: Craig Noel. Costume designer: Peggy J. Kellner.

Second, it *reflects*—a particular era, time of day, climate, season, location, or occasion. The designs in Figure 4.7 reflect a historical period. We recognize different eras primarily through silhouette, or outline. Costume designers may merely suggest full detail or may actually provide it, as is the case in Figure 4.7. Evident here is the designer's concern not only for the period but also for character in her choice of details, color, texture, jewelry, and hair style. Notice the length to which the designer goes to indicate detail, providing both front and back views of the costume, as well as a head study showing the hair without a covering.

Third, stage costuming *reveals* the characters of the personages as well as their social position, profession, cleanliness, age, physique, and health. In Figure 4.8 the concern of the designer is clearly less with historical period than with production style and character. This costume design reveals the high emotional content of the particular scene, and we see at first glance the deteriorated health and condition of King Lear as he goes mad on the heath. The contrast provided by the king in such a state heightens the effect of the scene, and details such as the bare feet, the winter furs, and the storm-ravaged cape are precise indicators of the pathos we are expected to find and respond to. Costume designers work, as do scene and lighting designers, with the same general elements as painters and sculptors: the elements of composition. A stage costume is an actor's skin: It allows her to move as she must, and occasionally it restricts her from moving as she should not.

4.8 Costume design for Shakespeare, *King Lear*, Old Globe Theatre, San Diego, California.
Director: Edward Payson Call. Costume designer: Peggy J. Kellner.

Properties

Properties fall into two general groups: *set props* and *hand props*. Set properties are part of the scene design: furniture, pictures, rugs, fireplace accessories, and so on. Along with the larger elements of the set, they identify the mood of the play and the tastes of those who inhabit this world. Hand properties used by the actors in stage business—cigarettes, papers, glasses, and so forth—also help to portray characters. The use of properties reveals significant information toward our understanding of a play. For example, if at the opening curtain all properties appear to be neat and in order, but as the play develops the actors disrupt them, so that at the end the entire scene is in disarray, that simple transition illustrates and enhances what has happened in the play. As in all artworks, details make important statements.

AURAL ELEMENTS

What we hear contributes to our understanding and enjoyment of a production. The aural elements, whether the actors' voices, the background music, or the clashing of swords, function importantly in a theatrical production. How a production sounds represents a series of conscious choices on the part of all the artists involved: playwright, director, actors, and designers. Just as a composer of a musical piece creates harmonies, dynamics, rhythms, and melodies, the director, working with the actors and sound designer, makes the production develop in an aural sense so the audience has the proper mood, is drawn in the appropriate emotional direction, and is captured by meaningful attention points.

DYNAMICS

Every production has its own dynamic patterns, which we can chart (as in Fig. 4.1). They make the structural pattern of a play clear, and help to hold the interest of the audience. Scientific studies indicate that attention or interest functions intermittently; human beings can concentrate on specific items only for very brief periods. Therefore, holding audience attention over the two-hour span of a production requires employing devices whereby from time to time interest or attention can peak and then relax. The peaks must be carefully controlled. A production should build to a high point of dramatic interest—the climax. However, each scene or act has its own peak of development—again, to maintain interest. Thus the path from the beginning of the play to the high point of dramatic interest is not a steady rise, but a series of peaks and valleys. Each successive peak is closer to the ultimate one. The director controls where and how high these peaks are by controlling the dynamics of the actors—volume and intensity, both bodily and vocal.

ACTORS

Although we cannot always determine easily which functions in a production are the playwright's, which the director's, and which the actor's, the main channel of communication between the playwright and the audience remains the actors. Through their movements and speech an audience perceives the play.

Looking for two elements among many in an actor's portrayal of a role enhances our understanding and response. The first is *speech*. Language should be understood as the playwright's words, and speech is the manner in which the actor delivers those words. Speech, like language, can range from high lifelikeness to high theatricality. If an actor's speech adheres to normal conversational rhythms, durations, and inflections, we respond in one way. If it utilizes extended vowel emphasis, long, sliding inflections, and dramatic pauses, we respond quite

4.9 Proscenium setting for Jean Kerr, *Mary, Mary*, University of Arizona Theatre.
Director: H. Wynn Pearce. Scene and lighting designer: Dennis J. Sporre.

4.10 Arena setting for Tennessee Williams, *The Glass Menagerie*, State University of New York at Plattsburgh.
Director: H. Charles Kline. Scene and lighting designer: Dennis J. Sporre.

differently—even though the playwright's words are identical in both cases.

The second element of an actor's portrayal that aids our understanding is the physical reinforcement he or she gives to the character's basic motivation. Most actors try to identify a single basic motivation for their character. That motivation is called a *spine*, or *superobjective*. Everything that pertains to the decisions the person makes is kept consistent because it all stems from this basic drive. Actors will translate the drive into something physical that they can do throughout the play. For example Blanche, in Tennessee Williams's *A Streetcar Named Desire*, is driven by an immense desire to clean everything she encounters, because of the way she regards herself and the world around her. Ideally, the actress playing Blanche will discover that element of Blanche's personality as she reads the play and develops the role. But to make that spine clear to us in the audience, she will need to translate it into physical action. Therefore, we will see Blanche constantly smoothing her hair, rearranging and straightening her dress, cleaning the furniture, brushing imaginary dust from others' shoulders, and so forth. Nearly every physical move she makes will relate somehow to the act of cleaning. Of course, these movements will be subtle; if we are attentive, we will notice them, but even if we do not pick them up we are likely to perceive them subconsciously and so understand the nature of the character portrayed. Watch the Humanities CD: Theatre, The Director.

LIFELIKENESS

In describing the relationship of the visual elements to the play, we have noted the designers' use of compositional elements. The use of these elements relative to life can be placed on a continuum, one end of which is theatricality and the other lifelikeness. Items high in lifelikeness are those with which we deal in everyday life: language, movements, furniture, trees. As we progress toward theatricality, the elements of the production express less and less relationship to everyday life. They become distorted, exaggerated, and perhaps even nonobjective. Poetry, as we noted, is high in theatricality; everyday speech is high in lifelikeness. The position of the various elements of a production on this continuum suggests the style of the play, in the same sense that brushstroke, line, and palette indicate style in painting.

Figures 4.9–4.14 illustrate the range between lifelikeness and theatricality. Figure 4.9 is a proscenium setting high in lifelikeness—including a full ceiling over the setting. Figure 4.10 is an arena setting high in lifelikeness; it reflects the style of the presentation. However, the requirement of the arena configuration that there be no walls moves the production away from lifelikeness. Note

4.11 Proscenium setting for Oscar Wilde, *The Importance of Being Earnest*, University of Arizona Theatre.
Director: William Lang. Costume designer: Helen Workman Currie. Scene and lighting designer: Dennis J. Sporre.

4.12 Proscenium setting for Stephen Sondheim musical, *Company*, University of Arizona Theatre. Director: Peter R. Marroney. Scene and lighting designer: Dennis J. Sporre.

4.13 Scene design for Euripides, *The Bacchae*, University of Illinois at Chicago Circle. Director: William Raffeld. Scene and lighting designer: Dennis J. Sporre.

that some theatricality—specifically, the empty picture frame—occurs in the decoration of this set. In Figure 4.11, although the set props are high in lifelikeness and the setting is representational, the designer has attempted to heighten the theatrical nature of the production by using open space where one might expect solid walls in this proscenium production.

The setting in Figure 4.14 moves further toward theatricality, and indicates clearly through exaggerated detail and two-dimensionality the whimsical nature of the pro-

duction. The design in Figure 4.12 creates a purely formal environment. Various areas of the set serve as locations and have realistic furniture, and this use of representational detail keeps the setting tied to the overall approach of the actors. Finally, in Figure 4.13, neither time nor place is indicated nor remotely suggested. Here the emphasis is on reinforcement of the high action of the production. The steep ramps throughout the set make it impossible for the actors to walk from one level to the next; the setting forces them to run.

4.14 Scene design for Jerry Devine and Bruce Montgomery, *The Amorous Flea*, University of Iowa Theatre. Director: David Knauf. Scene and lighting designer: Dennis J. Sporre.

In most arts the artist's style is unique—a recognizable mark on his or her artwork. Some artists change their style, but they do so by their own choice. Interpretive artists such as costume, scene, and lighting designers, and to a degree conductors as well, must submerge their personal style in favor of that of the work with which they are involved. Playwrights or directors set the style, and scene designers adapt to it and make their design reflect it.

HOW DOES IT STIMULATE THE SENSES?

In each of the elements just discussed, our senses are stimulated in a particular manner. We respond to the play's structure and how it works; we respond to dynamics. We are stimulated by the theatricality or lifelikeness of the language of the playwright and the movements and speech of the actors. We find our response shaped by the relationship of the stage space to the audience, and by the sets, lights, properties, and costumes. All of these elements bombard us simultaneously with complex visual and aural stimuli. How we respond, and how much we are able to respond, determines our ultimate understanding of and reaction to a production.

The theatre is unique in its ability to stimulate our senses, because only the theatre makes a direct appeal to our emotions through the live portrayal of other individuals involved directly in the human condition. Being in the presence of live actors gives us more of life in two hours than we could experience outside the theatre in that same time span. The term we use to describe our reaction to and involvement with what we experience in a theatrical production is *empathy*. Empathy causes us to cry when individuals whom we know are only actors become involved in tragic or emotional situations. Empathy makes us wince when an actor slaps the face of another one, or when two football players collide at full speed. Empathy is our mental and physical involvement in situations in which we are not direct participants.

Now let us examine a few of the more obvious ways a production can appeal to our senses. In plays that deal in conventions, *language* may act as virtually the entire stimulant of our senses. Through language the playwright sets the time, place, atmosphere, and even small details of decoration. We become our own scene, lighting, and even costume designer, imagining what the playwright tells us ought to be there. In the opening scene of *Hamlet* we find Bernardo and Francisco, two guards. The hour is midnight; it is bitter cold; a ghost appears, in "warlike form." How do we know all of this? In a modern production we might see it all through the work of the costume and set designers. But such need not be the case, because the playwright gives us all of this information in the dialogue. Shakespeare wrote for a theatre that had no lighting save for the sun. His theatre (such as we know of it) probably used no scenery. The actors' costumes were the street clothes of the day. The theatrical environment was the same whether the company was playing *Hamlet, Richard III,* or *The Tempest.* So what needed to be seen needed to be imagined. The play's language provided the stimuli for the audience.

We also respond to what we *see.* A sword fight performed with flashing action, swift movements, and great intensity sets us on the edge of our chair. Although we know the action is staged and the incident fictitious, we are caught in the excitement of the moment.

We can also be gripped and manipulated by events of a quite different dynamic quality. In many plays we witness character assassination, as one life after another is laid bare before us. The intense but subtle *movements* of the actors—both bodily and vocal—can pull us here and push us there emotionally, and perhaps cause us to leave the theatre feeling emotionally drained. Part of our response is caused by subject matter, part by language—but much of it is the result of careful manipulation of *dynamics.*

Mood is an important factor in theatrical communication. Before the curtain is up, our senses are tickled by

THEATRE AND HUMAN REALITY

David Rabe, *Hurly-Burly*

David Rabe (b. 1940; Fig. **4.15**) is one of America's foremost contemporary playwrights. A Vietnam veteran, Rabe has treated themes of physical and emotional violence—sometimes controversially—in plays that use war as a backdrop. *Hurly-Burly* (1984) is about drug- and people-abuse in Hollywood. As in many of his plays, the male hero, Eddie, has a hoodlum, demented quality. Such treatment suggests that Rabe likes to create a world in which people are defined by a particular "lingo." He has a very "masculine" vision of his heroes. The way they speak makes them who they are. That is Rabe's dramatic strategy, as he puts it: a choice.

In *Hurly-Burly* the characters speak the language of high tech and Hollywood. Rabe uses the language as a kind of stage poetry, metaphorically and stylistically, rather than trying to reflect reality. Eddie rants against television, and Rabe wants the audience to see Eddie's distress—the brilliance of his mind, and the waste of it. Rabe wants the audience to be drawn to Eddie, to recognize Eddie's ideas, and to develop a sympathetic chord in Eddie's sensibility. Eddie has a kind of innocence and gullibility. He is very open.

From Eddie's character and from the play, David Rabe tries to point out to the audience that, although somewhat off-centered, the people of *Hurly-Burly* can be found anywhere—not just in Hollywood. They could be from Wall Street, Washington, D.C., or professional athletics. From Rabe's point of view, everybody is addicted: "Cocaine and TV are both drugs."

For Rabe, human reality lies not in where a play is set or whether the language appears contemporary. Rather, it is defined by the cause-and-effect at work in human events. "Realism is sane—everybody is sane in realism, no matter how crazy they are."[3]

4.15 David Rabe in 1972.

stimuli designed to put us in the mood for what follows. The houselights in the theatre may be very low, or we may see a cool or warm light on the front curtain. Music fills the theatre. We may recognize the raucous tones of a 1930s jazz piece, or a melancholy ballad. Whatever the stimuli, they are all carefully designed to prepare us for the way the director wishes us to react. Once the curtain is up, the assault on our senses continues. The palette utilized by the scene, lighting, and costume designers helps communicate the mood of the play and other messages about it. The rhythm and variation in the visual elements capture our interest and reinforce the rhythmic structure of the play. For example, in Figure 4.6, the use of line and form as well as color provides a formal atmosphere reflecting the epic grandeur of Ibsen's *Peer Gynt*.

The degree of plasticity or three-dimensionality created by the lighting designer's illumination of the actors and the set causes us to respond in many ways. If the primary lighting instruments are directly in front of the stage,

plasticity will be diminished and the actors will appear washed out or two-dimensional. We respond quite differently to the maximum plasticity and shadow that results from lighting coming nearly from the side.

We also react to the mass of a setting. Scenery that towers over the actors and appears heavy is different in effect from scenery that seems minuscule relative to the human form. The settings in Figures **4.11** and **4.16** are different from one another in scale, and each places the actors in a different relationship with their surroundings.

Finally, focus and line act on our senses. Careful composition can create movement, outlines, and shadows that are sharp. Or it can create images that are soft, or blurred. Each of these devices is a stimulant; each has the potential to elicit a relatively predictable response. Perhaps in no other art are such devices so available and full of potential for the artist. We, as audience, benefit through nearly total involvement in the life situation that comes to us over the footlights.

4.16 Scene design (probably an alternative design) for Charles Fechter's revival of Shakespeare, *Hamlet*, Lyceum Theatre, London, 1864. Designer: William Telbin. Victoria & Albert Museum, London.

THINKING CRITICALLY

Create a basic analysis of a theatre production by using the following outline of concepts from the text as a guide.

- Genre. In what genre was the play? How did it exhibit the characteristics of tragedy, comedy, melodrama, etc.?

- Plot. How did the plot work? Where in the play would you say the exposition ended? Where was the climax? Where were the crises? What instances of foreshadowing, discovery, and reversal were present? Was the plot a significant part of the play or not? Why?

- Protagonist. Who was the protagonist? How did his or her actions and decisions move the plot? Was the protagonist active or passive?

- Character. How did the playwright draw the characters? Were they three-dimensional? Did you find any of them identifiable with your own life and feelings?

- Themes. What ideas did the play pursue? In what ways did the playwright or the production make you aware of the point of view being presented?

- Theatre form. In what theatre form was the play produced? What effect on your response to the play did the form create? Would you have had a different response if the production had utilized a different physical arrangement—for example, thrust, arena, or proscenium?

- Visual elements. In what ways did the settings, costumes, and lighting reinforce the message and style of the play? How did the visual elements provide historical or structural information to the audience?

- Language. How did the playwright's language and the actors' speech create meaning for you?

- Reaction. How did the previous elements combine to create a reaction in you? In other words, what drew your attention? What was your emotional response to the production, and what caused that reaction?

CYBER STUDY

TRAGEDY:
—Sophocles, *Oedipus the King.*
http://etext.lib.virginia.edu/cgibin/browse-mixed?id=SopOedi&tag=public&images=images/modeng&data=/lv1/Archive/eng-parsed
—William Shakespeare, *King Lear.*
http://www.infomotions.com/etexts/literature/english/1600-1699/shakespeare-king-45.txt

TRAGICOMEDY:
—Henrik Ibsen, *The Wild Duck.*
http://etext.lib.virginia.edu/cgibin/browse-mixed?id=IbsWild&tag=public&images=images/modeng&data=/lv1/Archive/eng-parsed

COMEDY:
—Aristophanes, *Lysistrata.*
http://www.litrix.com/lysis/lysis001.htm
—William Shakespeare, *Comedy of Errors.*
http://etext.lib.virginia.edu/cgibin/browse-mixed?id=HulCome&tag=public&images=images/modeng&data=/lv1/Archive/eng-parsed
—Richard Brinsley Sheridan, *The School for Scandal.*
http://www.bartleby.com/18/2/
—Molière, *The School for Wives.*
http://www.ipl.org/cgi-bin/common/redirect?http://www.bibliomania.com/Drama/Moliere/Plays/ch1act01.html

CHAPTER FIVE

CINEMA

WHAT IS IT?

NARRATIVE FILM
DOCUMENTARY FILM
ABSOLUTE FILM

HOW IS IT PUT TOGETHER?

EDITING
CAMERA VIEWPOINT
　Objectivity
A Personal Journey: Tian Zhuangzhuang, Lan Fengzheng (The Blue Kite)
　The Shot
Cinema and Human Reality: Sergei Eisenstein, Battleship Potemkin
CUTTING WITHIN THE FRAME
DISSOLVES
FOCUS
MOVEMENT
LIGHTING
Profile: D. W. Griffith

HOW DOES IT STIMULATE THE SENSES?

CROSSCUTTING
TENSION BUILD-UP AND RELEASE
DIRECT ADDRESS
MAGNITUDE AND CONVENTION
STRUCTURAL RHYTHM
　Audio Techniques
Thinking Critically
Cyber Study

IMPORTANT TERMS

Narrative film Film that tells a story.

Documentary film Film that records actual events.

Absolute film Film that exists for its own aesthetic sake.

Editing The process of assembling the various pieces or shots of a film.

Master shot A single shot of an entire piece of action, taken to facilitate the assembly of the film in the editing process.

Cutting within the frame A method of shooting the film that avoids the necessity of editing.

Dissolve A means of ending a scene.

Crosscutting An alternation between two separate actions that are related by theme, mood, or plot but occur at the same time.

Direct address A technique whereby the actors appear to address the audience directly.

Structural rhythm The manner in which various shots in a film are joined together and juxtaposed with other cinematic images, visual and aural.

Like theatre, but without the spontaneity of "live" performers, cinema can confront us with life very nearly as we find it on our streets. On the other hand, through the magic of sophisticated special effects, films can take us to new worlds open to no other form of art. Film, also, because of its status in popular culture, possesses a unique ability to fulfill the function of art, discussed in the Introduction, as a social and political weapon. In this regard, film reminds us of how we can be influenced by works of art, sometimes subtly, and sometimes blatantly. For example, director James Cameron has admitted that he made his movie *Titanic* (1997) as a Marxist-Socialist critique of America. Consequently, we need to reflect on the meanings and implications of the works we encounter and enjoy. Part of our task in developing critical perception of works of art includes identifying how they can not only entertain us but can create changes in our culture as well.

Cinema, the most familiar and most easily accessible art form, is usually accepted almost without conscious thought, at least in terms of the story line or the star image presented or the basic entertainment value of the product. Yet all these elements are carefully crafted out of editing techniques, camera usage, juxtaposition of image, and structural rhythms. These details of cinematic construction can enhance our viewing and raise film from mere entertainment into the realm of serious art. Bernard Shaw once observed, "Details are important; they make comments." It is not as easy as it might seem to perceive the details of a film because, while we search them out, the entertainment elements of the film are drawing our attention away from the search.

WHAT IS IT?

Cinema is aesthetic communication through the design of time and three-dimensional space compressed into a two-dimensional image. Once the principles of photography had evolved and the mechanics of recording and projecting cinematic images were understood, society was ready for the production of pictures that could move, be presented in color, and eventually talk.

If we examine a strip of film, we notice that it is only a series of still pictures running the length of the strip. Each of these pictures, or *frames*, is about ⅚ inch (22 mm) wide and ⅗ inch (16 mm) high. If we study the frames in relation to one another, we see that even though each may seem to show exactly the same scene, the position of the objects is slightly different. This film contains sixteen frames per foot (30 cm). When it is running on a project-

ing device and passed before a light source at the rate of twenty-four frames per second (sixteen to eighteen frames per second for silent films), a magnifying lens is used to enlarge the frames printed on it. Projected onto a screen, the images appear to move. However, the motion picture, as film is popularly called, does not really move but only seems to. This is due to an optical phenomenon called *persistence of vision*, which according to legend was discovered by the astronomer Ptolemy in the second century C.E. The theory is that the eyes take a fraction of a second to record an impression of an image and send it to the brain. Once the impression is received, the eye retains it on the retina for about one-tenth of a second after the actual image has disappeared.

The film projector pulls the film between the light source and a lens in a stop-and-go fashion, the film pausing long enough at each frame to let the eye take in the picture. Then a shutter on the projector closes, the retina retains the image, and the projection mechanism pulls the film ahead to the next frame. Perforations along the right-hand side of the filmstrip enable the teeth on the gear of the driving mechanism to grasp the film and not only move it along frame by frame but also hold it steady in the gate (the slot between the light source and the magnifying lens). This stop-and-go motion gives the impression of continuous movement. If the film did not pause at each frame, the eye would receive a blurred image.

The motion picture was originally invented as a device for recording and depicting motion. But once this goal was realized, it was quickly discovered that the projector could also record and present stories—in particular, stories that made use of the unique qualities of the medium of film.

Our formal response to film recognizes three basic techniques of presentation. These are narrative film, documentary film, and absolute film.

NARRATIVE FILM

Narrative film tells a story; in many ways it uses the technique of theatre. It follows the rules of literary construction in that it begins with expository material, adds levels of complications, builds to a climax, and ends with a resolution of all the plot elements. As in theatre, the personages in the story are portrayed by professional actors under the guidance of a director. The action of the plot takes place within a setting designed and constructed primarily for the action of the story but allowing the camera to move freely in photographing the action. Many narrative films are genre films, constructed out of familiar literary styles—the western, the detective story, and the horror story, among others. In these films the story elements are so familiar to the audience that they usually know the outcome of the plot before it begins. The final showdown between the "good guy" and the "bad guy," the destruction of a city by an unstoppable monster, and the identification of the murderer by the detective are all familiar plot elements that have become clichés or stereotypes within the genre; their use fulfills audience expectations. Film versions of popular novels and stories written especially for the screen are also part of the narrative-film form, but since film is a major part of the mass entertainment industry the narrative presented is usually material that will attract a large audience and thus assure a profit. In a film of this genre the narrative can also be interpreted symbolically. Regardless of the story, principles of universality apply. *E.T.: The Extra-Terrestrial* (1982), for example, tells a story of fantasy that also symbolizes the innocence and beauty of childhood. E.T. says goodbye to his friend Eliot, and Eliot will likewise outgrow his childhood. The memories, however, remain. Narrative films may also include elements from documentary and absolute film (see below).

DOCUMENTARY FILM

Documentary film is an attempt to record actuality using primarily either a sociological or a journalistic approach. It is normally not reenacted by professional actors and is often shot as the event is occurring—at the time and place of its occurrence. The film may use a narrative structure, and some of the events may be ordered or compressed for dramatic reasons, but its presentation gives the illusion of reality. The footage shown on the evening television news, programming concerned with current events or problems, and full coverage either by television or film companies of a worldwide event, such as the Olympics, are all kinds of documentary film. All convey a sense of reality as well as a recording of time and place. A classic example of documentary film is Leni Riefenstahl's (REE-fehn-shtahl; b. 1902) *Olympia* (1936). For more information, visit http://www.german-way.com/cinema/rief.html.

ABSOLUTE FILM

Absolute film is simply film that exists for its own sake, for its record of movement or form. It does not use narrative techniques, although documentary techniques can be used in some instances. Created neither in the camera nor on location, absolute film is built carefully, piece by piece, on the editing table or through special effects and multiple-printing techniques. It tells no story but exists solely as movement or form. Absolute film is rarely longer

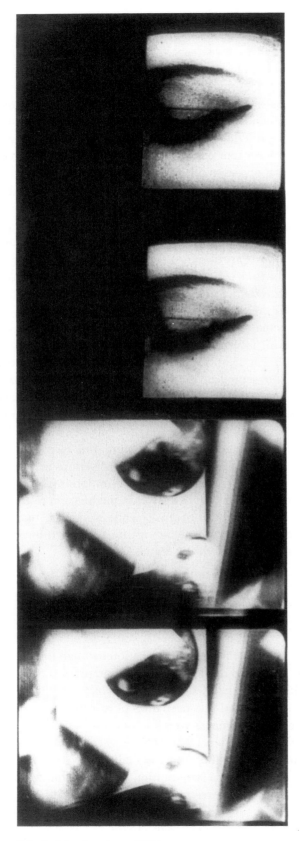

5.1 *Ballet mécanique*, 1924.
Director: Fernand Léger.

than twelve minutes (one reel) in length, and it is not usually created for commercial intent but is meant only as an artistic experience. Narrative or documentary films may contain sections that can be labeled absolute, and these can be studied either in or out of the context of the whole film. An excellent example of absolute film is Fernand Léger's (lay-zhay; 1881–1955) *Ballet mécanique* (may-kah-NEEK; 1924; Fig. **5.1**). For more images and study questions, visit http://www.english.uiuc.edu/mardorossian/DOCS/films/filmpages/ballet.html.

HOW IS IT PUT TOGETHER?

EDITING

Film is rarely recorded in the order of its final presentation. It is filmed in bits and pieces and put together, after all the photography is finished, as one puts together a jigsaw puzzle or builds a house. The force or strength of the final product depends upon the editing process, the manner in which the camera and the lighting are handled, and the movement of the actors before the camera. Naturally, the success of a film depends equally on the strength of the story presented and the ability of the writers, actors, directors, and technicians who have worked on the film. However, this level of success is based on the personal taste of the audience and the depth of perception of the individual, and therefore does not lie within the boundaries of this discussion.

Perhaps the greatest difference between film and the other arts discussed within this volume is *plasticity*—the quality of film that enables it to be cut, spliced, and ordered according to the needs of the film and the desires of the filmmaker. If twenty people were presented with all the footage shot of a presidential inauguration and asked to make a film commemorating the event, you would probably end up with twenty completely different films. Each filmmaker would order the event according to his or her own views and artistic ideas. This concept of plasticity is, then, one of the major advantages of the use of the machine in consort with an art form.

The filmmaker must be able to synthesize a product out of many diverse elements. The editing process creates or builds the film, and within that process are many ways of joining shots and scenes to make a whole. Let's examine some of these basic techniques. *Cutting* is simply joining together shots during the editing process. A *jump cut* is a cut that breaks the continuity of time by moving forward from one part of the action to another that is obviously separated from the first by an interval of time, location, or camera position. It is often used for shock effect or to call attention to a detail, as in commercial advertising on television. The *form cut* cuts from one image to another—a different object that has a similar shape or contour; it is used primarily to make a smoother transition from one shot to another. For example, in D.W. Griffith's silent film *Intolerance*, attackers are using a battering ram to smash in the gates of Babylon. The camera shows the circular frontal area of the ram as it is advanced toward the gate. The scene cuts to a view of a circular shield, which in the framing of the shot is placed in exactly the same position as the front view of the ram.

Montage (mahn-TAHZH) can be considered the most aesthetic use of the cut in film. It is handled in two basic ways: first, as an indication of compression or elongation of time and, second, as a rapid succession of images to illustrate an association of ideas. A series of stills from Léger's *Ballet mécanique* (Fig. **5.1**) illustrates how images are juxtaposed to create comparisons. For example, a couple goes out to spend an evening on the town, dining and dancing. The film then presents a series of cuts of the pair—in a restaurant, then dancing, then driving to another spot, then drinking, and then more dancing. In this way the audience sees the couple's activities in an abridged manner. Elongation of time can be achieved in the same way.

Montage also allows the filmmaker to depict complex ideas or draw a metaphor visually. Sergei Eisenstein, the Russian film director (see p. 123), presents a shot in one of his early films of a Russian army officer walking out of the room, his back to the camera and his hands crossed behind him. Eisenstein cuts immediately to a peacock strutting away from the camera and spreading its tail. These two images are juxtaposed, and the audience is allowed to make the association that the officer is as proud as a peacock.

CAMERA VIEWPOINT

Camera position and viewpoint are as important to the structure of the film as is the editing process. In the earliest days of the silent film the camera was merely set up in one basic position; the actors moved before it as if they were performing before an audience on a stage in a theatre. However, watching all the action from one position became dull, and the early filmmakers were forced to move the camera in order to add variety. Out of this emerged the many angle shots that open up a range of possible comments on the subject being filmed.

A Personal Journey

TIAN ZHUANGZHUANG, *LAN FENGZHENG (THE BLUE KITE)*

Children and mud puddles evoke something magical. On the week between Christmas and New Year, a Saturday night, I'm in Hong Kong—on the Kowloon side. Holiday lights bedeck and brilliantly illumine buildings on both sides of the harbor, outlining them into huge red, green, blue, and yellow boxes. Countless families stroll up and down the streets and plazas, taking photographs of their fancily dressed children. The children, notwithstanding their bandbox clothing, seem to find fascination only in the mud puddles remaining from a recent rain. The temperature is comfortable, and the puddles, irresistible. One pair after another of brand new leather shoes receives baptism with a forceful leap into the middle of a shallow pool: a white pair—splash! a brown pair—kerwhop! Shrill giggles fill the air as the act of spreading water as far and wide as possible repeats itself, over and over again. As the return of Hong Kong to communist China nears, I wonder if there is a Tietou among these children.

Tietou is the child who narrates Tian Zhuangzhuang's film *Lan Fengzheng (The Blue Kite*, 1992). The film introduces him as an infant in the unsettled 1950s and 60s in China and follows him through adolescence as he comments on the emotional turmoil occurring within his family. *The Blue Kite* examines the impact of politics and revolution on people and families.

The film opens with the wedding of the couple who are later to become Tietou's parents. His father is a teacher; his mother, a librarian. Soon after Tietou's birth, a Chinese nationalistic movement begins, and the intrusive hand of the Communist Party reaches into everyone's lives.

The blue kite symbolizes the freedom to develop with the natural ebb and flow of life, an occurrence the filmmaker finds absent in life under the communists. The kite sails through the sky, its directions determined by the wind alone. On earth, Tietou, his family, and everyone else evolve only in response to the constantly changing political correctness of Maoism. The revolution that was supposed to improve their lives serves only to plunge them into chaos. Titetou's father is sent to a labor camp where he eventually dies. A friend cares for Tietou and his mother, and she later marries him. When he dies, she marries again, this time an elderly party member. As a consequence, Tietou grows into a disaffected teen, thrown into even greater turmoil by the Cultural Revolution in 1967.

The Blue Kite challenges the hypocrisy of communist theory by contrasting it with communist reality. The film questions the entire purpose of revolution when basic human needs (not to mention common civility and compassion) take a back seat to revolution. The only difference, according to the film, is those who are in power. The chasm between the haves and the have-nots remains the same.

The children's squeals of delight are infectious on this holiday evening, and, yet, something sobering boils beneath it. Before long, communism will control Hong Kong, and life, always a bit unsettled in this city, will become even more so. I wonder how well "reel" life actually captures "real" life. I look at the children. Tietou, are you there?

The Shot

The shot is what the camera records over a particular period of time and is the basic unit of filmmaking. Several varieties are used. The *master shot* is a single shot of an entire piece of action, taken to facilitate the assembly of the component shots of which the scene will finally be composed. The *establishing shot* is a long shot (see below) introduced at the beginning of a scene to establish the interrelationship of details, a time, or a place.

The *long shot* is taken with the camera a considerable distance from the subject, the *medium shot* is taken nearer to the subject, and the *close-up* even nearer. A close-up of two people within the frame is known as a *two-shot*, and a *bridging shot* is one inserted in the editing of a scene to cover a brief break in continuity.

CINEMA AND HUMAN REALITY

Sergei Eisenstein, *Battleship Potemkin*

Sergei M. Eisenstein's (eye-zehn-stine) *Battleship Potemkin* (1925) remains one of the most influential films ever made. It is a great classic of film art. When it was released, it brought instant fame both to Eisenstein and to a newly emerging film industry in the former Soviet Union. Among other things, it added a new dimension to film language: montage editing.

After the Bolshevik Revolution in 1917, the Soviet government took control of the country's film industry and decreed that film would serve the purpose of education and propaganda to indoctrinate the Russian masses and promote class consciousness throughout the world. Originally designed to celebrate the twentieth anniversary of the unsuccessful 1905 Revolution against the Czar, *Battleship Potemkin* was limited by Eisenstein to narrating a single episode in the struggle—the mutiny of the *Potemkin* and the subsequent massacre of civilians on the steps leading down to the harbor in Odessa (Fig. **5.2**).

The film has a number of qualities that give it the appearance of a documentary. Eisenstein engaged non-professionals who looked like the type of character he wished to portray. The film was shot on location. Its collective hero is the Russian people—represented by the people of Odessa, the mutineers, and the sailors on other ships who rebelled against Czarist oppression.

Eisenstein's use of montage, featuring juxtaposing shots and lighting, camera angle, and subject movement, creates meaning by incorporating shots within shots. His cuts between shots were intentionally jarring and designed to create shock and agitation in the audience. He identified five types of montage and used each in the film: (1) *metric montage*—conflict caused by the length of shots; (2) *rhythmic montage*—conflict generated by the rhythm of movement within the shots; (3) *tonal montage*—arrangement of shots by their "tone" or "emotional sound"; (4) *overtonal montage*—a synthesis of the previous three types; and (5) *intellectual montage*—the juxtaposition of images to create visual metaphor.

In the Soviet Union, the film did not immediately gain favor. Eisenstein was accused of being overly formal—that is, being concerned with aesthetic form rather than ideological content. Once they noted that it received universal acclaim outside the Soviet Union, the Soviet authorities changed their tune and supported the film enthusiastically.

5.2 *Battleship Potemkin,* still from the "Odessa steps" sequence, 1925. Director: Sergei M. Eisenstein.

Objectivity

An equally important variable of camera viewpoint is whether the scene is shot from an objective or subjective viewpoint. The *objective viewpoint* is that of an omnipotent viewer, roughly analogous to the technique of third-person narrative in literature. In this way filmmakers allow their audience to watch the action through the eyes of a universal spectator. However, those who wish to involve their audience more deeply in a scene may use the *subjective viewpoint:* The scene is presented as if the audience were actually participating in it, and the action is viewed from the filmmaker's perspective. This is analogous to the first-person narrative technique, and is usually found in the films of more talented directors.

CUTTING WITHIN THE FRAME

Cutting within the frame is a method used to avoid the editing process. It can be created by actor movement, camera movement, or a combination of the two. It allows the scene to progress smoothly and is used most often on television. In a scene in John Ford's classic *Stagecoach*, the coach and its passengers have just passed through hostile territory without being attacked; the driver and his passengers all express relief. Ford cuts to a long shot of the coach moving across the desert and *pans*, or follows, it as it moves from right to left on the screen. This movement of the camera suddenly reveals in the foreground, and in close-up, the face of a hostile warrior watching the passage of the coach. In other words, the filmmaker has moved smoothly from a long shot to a close-up without needing the editing process. He has also established a spatial relationship.

In a scene from *Jaws* (Fig. **5.3**) the camera also moves from distant objects to the face in the foreground, finally including them both in the frame; the pan across the scene is thus accomplished without editing of the film. Directors choose to cut or to cut within the frame because the results of each option create psychological overtones that cause responses in the viewer. In the arena scene from *Gladiator* (DreamWorks Pictures, 2000), Russell Crowe's gladiator character confronts another gladiator and a tiger. Director Ridley Scott cuts back and forth from Russell Crowe to the tiger and the other gladiator to create suspense. When he combines them all in one shot, however, he produces the maximum sense of danger.

DISSOLVES

During the printing of the film negative, transitional devices can be worked into a scene. They are generally used to indicated the end of one scene and the beginning of another. The camera can cut or jump to the next scene, but the transition is smoother if the scene fades out into black and the next scene fades in. This is called a *dissolve*. A *lap dissolve* occurs when the fade-out and the fade-in are done simultaneously and the scene momentarily overlaps. A *wipe* is a form of optical transition in which an invisible line moves across the screen, eliminating one shot and revealing the next, much in the way a windshield wiper moves across the windshield of a car. In silent film the transition could also be created by closing or opening the aperture of the lens; this process is called an *iris-out* or an *iris-in*.

5.3 *Jaws*, 1975. Universal Pictures.
Director: Steven Spielberg.

FOCUS

Even the manner in which the lens is focused can add to the meaning of the scene. If both near and distant objects are shown clearly at the same time, the camera is using *depth of focus*. In Figure 5.3 foreground and background are equally in focus. In this situation actors can move without necessitating a change of camera position. Many television shows photographed before an audience use this kind of focus.

If the main object of interest is photographed clearly while the remainder of the scene is blurred or out of focus, the camera is using *rack* or *differential focus*. With this technique the filmmaker can draw the audience's attention to one element within a shot.

MOVEMENT

The movement of the camera as well as its position can add variety or impact to a shot or scene. There are many kinds of physical (as opposed to apparent) camera movement. The *track* is a shot taken as the camera is moving in the same direction, at the same speed, and in the same place as the object being photographed. A *pan* is taken by rotating the camera horizontally while keeping it fixed vertically. It is usually employed in enclosed areas, particularly television studios. The *tilt* is taken by moving the camera vertically or diagonally, and is used to add variety to a sequence. Moving the camera toward or away from the subject is known as a *dolly shot*. Modern sophisticated lenses can achieve the same effect by changing the focal length—this negates the need for camera movement and is known as a *zoom shot*.

LIGHTING

The camera cannot photograph a scene without light, whether it be natural or artificial. Most television productions shot before a live audience require a flat, general illumination pattern. For close-ups, stronger and more

5.4 *The Birth of a Nation*, 1915.
Director: D. W. Griffith.

D. W. Griffith

David Lewelyn Wark Griffith (1875–1948) was the first giant of the motion-picture industry and a genius of film credited with making film an art form. As a director, D. W. Griffith never needed a script. He improvised new ways to use the camera and to cut the celluloid, which redefined the craft for the next generation of directors.

D. W. Griffith was born on January 22, 1875, in Floydsfork, Kentucky, near Louisville. His aristocratic Southern family had been impoverished by the American Civil War, and much of his early education came in a one-room schoolhouse or at home. His father, a former Confederate colonel, told him battle stories that may have affected the tone of Griffith's early films.

When Griffith was seven, his father died and the family moved to Louisville. He quit school at sixteen to go to work as a bookstore clerk. In the bookstore he met some actors from a Louisville theatre. This acquaintanceship led to work with amateur theatre groups and to tours with stock companies. He tried playwrighting, but his first play failed on opening night in Washington, D.C. He also attempted writing screenplays, but his first scenario for a motion picture also met with rejection. While acting for New York studios, however, he did sell some scripts for one-reel films, and when the Biograph Company had an opening for a director in 1908, Griffith was hired.

During the five years with Biograph, Griffith introduced or refined all the basic techniques of filmmaking. His innovations in cinematography included the close-up, the fade-in and fade-out, soft focus, high- and low-angle shots, and panning (moving the camera in panoramic long shots). In film editing, he invented the techniques of flashback and crosscutting—interweaving bits of scenes to give an impression of simultaneous action.

Griffith also expanded the horizon of film with social commentary. Of the nearly 500 films he directed or produced, his first full-length work was his most sensational. *The Birth of a Nation* (first shown as *The Clansman* in 1915; see Fig. **5.4**) was hailed for its radical technique but condemned for its racism. As a response to censorship of *The Birth of a Nation*, he produced *Intolerance* (1916), an epic integrating four separate themes.

After *Intolerance* Griffith may have turned away from the epic film because of the financial obstacles, but his gifted performers more than made up for this loss, for they were giants in their own right. Among the talented stars he introduced to the industry were Dorothy and Lillian Gish, Mack Sennett, and Lionel Barrymore.

In 1919 Griffith formed a motion picture distribution company called United Artists with Mary Pickford, Charlie Chaplin, and Douglas Fairbanks.

Griffith's stature within the Hollywood hierarchy was one of respect and integrity. He became one of the three linchpins of the ambitious Triangle Studios, along with Thomas Ince and Mack Sennett.

---

definitely focused lights are required to highlight features, eliminate shadows, and add a feeling of depth. Cast shadows or atmospheric lighting (in art, chiaroscuro) are often used to create a mood, particularly in black-and-white films (Fig. **5.4**). Lighting at a particular angle can heighten the feeling of texture, just as an extremely close shot can. These techniques add visual variety to a sequence.

If natural or outdoor lighting is used and the camera is hand-held, the film appears unsteady; this technique and effect is called *cinéma vérité*. Such camera work and natural lighting are found most often in documentary films or sequences photographed for newsreels or television news programming. It is one of the conventions of current-events reporting and adds to the sense of reality and immediacy suitable for this kind of film recording. Contemporary portrayals of war such as *Saving Private Ryan* (1998) and *We Were Soldiers* (2002) utilize the techniques of *cinéma vérité* masterfully, in addition, ironically, to applying computer-generated scenography.

These techniques and many others are used to ease technical problems, to make films smoother or more static, depending upon the needs of the story line, or to add an element of commentary. One school of cinematic thought believes that camera technique is best when it is not noticeable; another, more recent way of thinking asserts that the obviousness of all the technical aspects of film adds meaning to the concept of cinema. In any case, camera technique is present in every kind of film and is used to add variety and commentary, meaning and method, to the shot, the scene, and the film.

HOW DOES IT STIMULATE THE SENSES?

The basic aim of film, as with any art, is to involve the audience in its product, either emotionally or intellectually. There is nothing like a good plot with well-written dialogue delivered by trained actors to create audience interest. But there are other ways in which filmmakers can enhance their final product—techniques that manipulate the audience toward a deeper involvement or a heightened intellectual response.

Perception is most important in the area of technical detail. We should begin to cultivate the habit of noticing even the tiniest details in a scene, for often these add a commentary that the average member of an audience misses. For example, in Hitchcock's *Psycho*, when the caretaker of the motel (Tony Perkins) wishes to spy upon the guests in cabin 1, he pushes aside a picture that hides a peephole. The picture is a reproduction of Giovanni Bologna's statue *Rape of the Sabine Woman*—Hitchcock's irony is obvious. Thus, perception becomes the method through which viewers of film find its deeper meanings as well as its basic styles.

CROSSCUTTING

The most familiar and most easily identified filmmaking technique used to heighten feeling is *crosscutting*. This is an alternation between two separate actions that are related by theme, mood, or plot but are usually occurring at the same time. Its most common function is to create suspense. Consider this familiar cliché. Pioneers going west in a wagon train are besieged by hostile Native Americans. The settlers are holding them off, but ammunition is running low. The hero has been able to find a cavalry troop, and they are riding to the rescue. The film alternates between pioneers fighting for their lives and soldiers galloping across the countryside toward them. The film continues to cut back and forth, the pace of cutting increasing until the sequence builds to a climax—then the cavalry arrives in time to save the wagon train. The famous chase scene in *The French Connection*, the final sequences in *Wait Until Dark*, and the sequences of the girl entering the fruit cellar in *Psycho* are each built for suspense through techniques of crosscutting.

A more subtle case of crosscutting—*parallel development*—occurs in *The Godfather, Part I*. At the close of that film Michael Corleone is acting as godfather for his sister's son; at the same time his men are destroying all his enemies. The film alternates between views of Michael at the religious service and sequences showing violent death. This parallel construction is used to draw an ironic comparison; the juxtaposition allows the audience to draw their own inferences and added meaning.

TENSION BUILD-UP AND RELEASE

If the plot of a film is believable, the actors competent, and the director and film editor talented and knowledgeable, a feeling of tension will be built up. If this tension becomes too great, the audience will seek some sort of release, and an odd-sounding laugh, a sudden noise, or a loud comment from a member of the audience may cause the rest of the viewers to laugh, thus breaking the tension and in a sense destroying the atmosphere so carefully created. Wise filmmakers therefore build into their film a *tension release* that deliberately draws laughter from the audience, but at a place in the film where they wish them to laugh. This can be engineered by a comical way of moving, a gurgle as a car sinks into a swamp, or merely a comic line. It does not have to be too obvious, but it should be present in some manner. After a suspenseful sequence the audience needs to be relaxed; once the tension release does its job, they can be drawn into another exciting situation.

Sometimes, to shock the audience or maintain their attention, a filmmaker may break a deliberately created pattern or convention of film. In *Jaws*, for example, each time the shark is about to appear, a four-note musical motif is played. The audience thereby grows to believe that they will hear this warning before each appearance, and so they relax. However, toward the end of the film the shark suddenly appears without benefit of the motif, shocking the audience. From that point until the end of the film they can no longer relax, and their full attention is directed to it.

DIRECT ADDRESS

Another method used to draw attention is that of *direct address*. In most films, the actors rarely look at or talk directly to the audience. However, in *Tom Jones*, while Tom and his landlady are arguing over money, Tom suddenly turns to the audience and says, "You saw her take the money." The audience's attention is focused on the screen more strongly than ever after that. This technique

5.5 *Your Darn Tootin'*, 1928. A Hal Roach Production for Pathé Films.
Director: Edgar Kennedy.

has been effectively adapted by television for use in commercial messages. For example, a congenial man looks at the camera (and you) with evident interest and asks if you are feeling tired, rundown, and sluggish. He assumes you are and proceeds to suggest a remedy. In a sense, the aside of nineteenth-century melodrama and the soliloquy of Shakespeare were also ways of directly addressing an audience and drawing them into the performance.

In silent films, where this type of direct address to the audience could not be used, the device of titles was substituted. However, some of the silent comedians felt that they should have direct contact with their audience, and so they developed a *camera look* as a form of direct address. After an especially destructive moment in his films, Buster Keaton would look directly at the camera, his face immobile, and stare at the audience. When Charlie Chaplin achieved an adroit escape from catastrophe he might turn toward the camera and wink. Stan Laurel would look at the camera and gesture helplessly (Fig. 5.5), as if to say, "How did all this happen?" Oliver Hardy, after falling into an open manhole, would register disgust directly to the camera and the audience. These were all ways of letting the audience know that the comedians knew they were there. Some sound comedies

adapted this technique too. In the "road" pictures of Bob Hope and Bing Crosby both stars, as well as camels, bears, fish, and anyone else who happened to be around, would comment on the film or the action directly to the audience. However, this style may have been equally based on familiarity with radio programs in which the performer usually spoke directly to the home audience.

MAGNITUDE AND CONVENTION

In considering the magnitude of a film we must be aware of the means by which the film is to be communicated. In other words, was the film made for a television showing or for projection in a large theatre? Due to the size of the television screen, large panoramas or full-scale action sequences are not entirely effective on television—they become too condensed. To be truly effective, television films should be built around the close-up and around concentrated action and movement, because the television audience is closer to the screen than are the viewers in a large theatre. Scenes of multiple images with complex patterns of movement, or scenes of great violence, will become confusing because of the intimacy of television, and will seem more explicit than they really are. On the other hand, when close shots of intimate details are enlarged through projection in a theatre they may appear ridiculous. The nuance of a slightly raised eyebrow that is so effective in the living room will appear either silly or overly dramatic when magnified on a 60-foot (18-m) screen.

Film, as theatre, has certain conventions or customs that the viewer accepts without hesitation. When an exciting chase scene takes place, no one asks where the orchestra is that is playing the music that enhances the sequence. They merely accept the background music as part of the totality of the film. A film photographed in black-and-white is accepted as a recording of reality, even though the viewers know that the real world has color. When a performer sings and dances in the rain in the middle of a city street, none of the audience wonders whether the performer will be arrested for creating a public spectacle. The conventions of the musical film are equally acceptable to an audience that has been conditioned to accept them.

This consideration of convention is especially important to the acceptance of the silent film as a form of art. The silent film should not be thought of as a sound film without sound, but as a separate entity with its own special conventions. These revolve around the methods used to indicate sound and dialogue without actually using them. The exaggerated pantomime and acting styles, the use of titles, character stereotyping, and visual metaphors are all conventions that were accepted during the silent era but can appear ludicrous today, because of changes in style and taste and improvements in the devices used for recording and projecting film. The action in the silent film was recorded and presented at a speed of sixteen to eighteen frames per second; when it is presented today on a projector that operates at twenty-four frames per second, the movement becomes too fast and appears jerky and disconnected. However, once we learn to accept these antiquated conventions, we may find that the silent film is an equally effective form of cinematic art.

Visual metaphor, just mentioned, works the same as verbal metaphor (see p. 190)—that is, it uses a visual image to transfer an idea to another circumstance by inference. Metaphorical comparisons also create a kind of shock. For example, in *The Mission*, the priest's (Robert De Niro) entire ascent up the mountain while carrying the soldier's armor works as a visual metaphor for the internal awareness of guilt that the De Niro character feels; when he is forgiven and freed of his guilt, the weaponry is cut from him and tumbled down the mountain, offering him relief—from the weight of the armor and from his own guilt.

STRUCTURAL RHYTHM

Much of the effectiveness of a film relies on its success as a form as well as a style. Filmmakers create rhythms and patterns that are based on the way they choose to tell their stories or that indicate deeper meanings and relationships. The manner in which the various shots are joined together and juxtaposed with other cinematic images, both visual and aural, is known as *structural rhythm*.

Symbolic images in film range from the very obvious to the extremely subtle, but they are all useful in directing the attention of the audience to the ideas inherent in the philosophical approach underlying the film. This use of symbolic elements can be found in such clichés as the hero dressed in white and the villain dressed in black, in the more subtle use of water images in Fellini's *La Dolce Vita*, or even in the presence of an X whenever someone is about to be killed in *Scarface*. Symbols certainly imply additional meanings apparent to sensitive viewers.

Sometimes, symbolic references can be enhanced by form cutting—for example, cutting directly from the hero's gun to the villain's gun. Or the filmmaker may choose to repeat a familiar image in varying forms, using it as a composer would a motif in music. In *Fort Apache*, John Ford uses clouds of dust as a curtain to cover major events; the dust is also used to indicate the ultimate fate of the cavalry troop. Grass, cloud shapes, windblown trees, and patches of color have all been used symbolically and as motifs. Once such elements are perceived, serious students of film will find the deeper meanings of a film more evident and their appreciation heightened. George Lucas uses form cutting with obviousness in *Star Wars, Episode I: The Phantom Menace*.

Another part of structural rhythm is the repetition of certain visual patterns throughout a film. A circular image positioned against a rectangular one, a movement from right to left, an action repeated regularly throughout a sequence—all can become observable patterns or even thematic statements. The silent film made extreme use of thematic repetition. In *Intolerance*, D.W. Griffith develops four similar stories simultaneously and continually crosscuts among them. This particular use of form enabled him to develop the ideas of the similarity of intolerance throughout the ages. In their silent films Laurel and Hardy often built up a pattern of "You do this to me and I'll do that to you"; they called it "tit for tat." Their audience would be lulled into expecting this pattern, but at a certain point the film would present a variation on the familiar theme (a process quite similar to the use of theme and variation in musical composition). The unexpected breaking of the pattern would surprise the audience into laughter.

Parallel development, discussed earlier, can also be used to create form and pattern throughout a film. For example, Edwin S. Porter's *The Kleptomaniac* alternates between two stories: a wealthy woman caught shoplifting a piece of jewelry, and a poor woman who steals a loaf of bread. Each sequence alternately shows crime, arrest, and punishment; the wealthy woman's husband bribes the judge to let her off, while the poor woman is sent to jail. Porter's final shot shows the statue of justice holding her scales, one weighted down with a bag of gold. Her blindfold is raised over one eye, which is looking at the money. In this case, as in others, the form is the film.

Audio Techniques

When sound films became practicable, filmmakers found many ways of using the audio track creatively in addition to just recording dialogue. It could be used for symbolism, for motifs that reinforced the emotional quality of a scene, or for stronger emphasis or structural rhythm.

Some filmmakers believe that a more realistic feeling can be created if film is cut rather than dissolved. Abrupt cuts from scene to scene give the film a staccato rhythm that approaches the reality they hope to achieve. Dissolves, on the other hand, create a slower pace and tend to make the film's transitions smooth and thus more romantic. If the abrupt cutting is done to the beat of the sound track, a pulsating rhythm is created for the film sequence; this in turn adds a sense of urgency.

In Fred Zinnemann's *High Noon*, the sheriff waits for the midday train to arrive. The sequence, in montage, shows the townspeople, as well as the sheriff, waiting. Every eight beats of the musical track the shot changes. Then as noon approaches, the shot is changed every four beats. Tension mounts. The feeling of rhythm is enhanced by images of a clock's pendulum swinging to the beat of the sound track. Tension continues to build. The train's whistle sounds. A series of rapid cuts of faces turning and looking follows, but there is only silence on the sound track, which serves as a tension release. This last moment of the sequence is also used as transition between the music and silence. In other films the track may shift from music to natural sounds and back to the music again. Or a pattern may be created of natural sound, silence, and a musical track. All depends on the mood the filmmaker is trying to create. In Hitchcock's films, music is often used as a tension release or an afterthought, as he usually relies on the force of his visual elements to create structural rhythm.

Earlier in this chapter we mentioned the use of motif in *Jaws*. Many films opt for an audio *motif* to introduce visual elements or to convey meaning symbolically. Walt Disney, particularly in his pre-1940 cartoons, often uses his sound track in this manner. For example, Donald Duck is trying to catch a pesky fly, but the fly always manages to elude him. In desperation Donald sprays the fly with insecticide. The fly coughs and falls to the ground. But on the sound track we hear an airplane motor coughing and sputtering, and finally diving to the ground and crashing. In juxtaposing these different visual and audio elements, Disney is using his track symbolically.

John Ford often underlines sentimental moments in his films by accompanying the dialogue of a sequence with traditional melodies. As the sequence comes to a close the music swells and then fades away to match the fading out of the scene. In *The Grapes of Wrath*, when Tom Joad says goodbye to his mother, "Red River Valley" is played on a concertina; as Tom walks over the hill the music becomes louder, and when he disappears from view it fades out. Throughout the film, this familiar folk song serves as a thematic reference to the Joads' home in Oklahoma and also boosts the audience's feelings of nostalgia.

In *She Wore a Yellow Ribbon*, the title of the film is underlined by the song of the same name, but through the use of different tempos and timbres its mood is changed each time it is heard. In the graveyard sequences the tune is played by strings and woodwinds in $\frac{2}{4}$ time in slow tempo, which makes the song melancholy and sentimental. As the cavalry troop rides out of the fort the song is played in a strong $\frac{4}{4}$ meter with a heavy emphasis on the brass; the sequence is cut to the beat of the track. Again, in the climactic fight sequence in *The Quiet Man*, John Ford cuts to the beat of a sprightly Irish jig, which enriches the comic elements of the scene and plays down the violence.

A pivotal step in the use of music in film occurred with George Lucas's first film of the *Star Wars* trilogy (1977). Lucas revived the use of bold symphonic accompaniment to heighten the dramatic effect of the scenes. As Robert Giannetti notes in *Understanding Movies* (p. 224), "John Williams's score is brassy, powerful, and richly orchestrated, very much in the manner of the lushly romantic and full-bodied scores of Hollywood's golden age. Critic Frank Spotnitz noted that 'the score is like a second screenplay, commenting on and enriching the first.'" Indeed, the recollection of older cinematic traditions recurs repeatedly in *Star Wars*' visual and dialogue allusions.

Our discussion in these last few paragraphs touches only the surface of the techniques and uses of sound in film; there are many other ways of using sound and the other elements discussed thus far. But part of the challenge of the film as an art form is the discovery by the viewer of the varying uses to which film technique can be put, and this in turn enhances further perceptions.

THINKING CRITICALLY

Create a basic analysis of a work of film by using the following outline of concepts from the text as a guide.

- Genres. What was the genre of the film? If it was a narrative film, how did the elements of plot work? Where did the crises, climax, and dénouement occur? If it was an absolute film, what artistic elements such as composition were evident, and how did the filmmaker use them to create specific effects? If the film was a documentary, what characteristics of that genre did the filmmaker explore?

- Editing. What elements of editing were utilized, and how did those elements control viewer response or affect the rhythm and pace of the film?

- Shots. What shots did the filmmaker seem to emphasize? How did that emphasis create a basic sense of spectacle in the film?

- Cutting. How did the editor make use of cutting to create rhythmic flow in the film? What specific effects did the cutting techniques have on the mood, structure, and meaning of the film?

- Dissolves. Did the filmmaker use any particular types of dissolve for specific effects? If so, what were they?

- Focus. How did the use of focus seek to control your attention? Was it successful?

- Camera movement. In what ways did camera movement contribute to the overall effect of the film?

- Reaction. How did the previous elements combine to create a reaction in you? In other words, what drew your attention? What was your emotional response to the film, and what caused that reaction?

CYBER STUDY

GREAT FILMS BY DECADE:
http://www.filmsite.org/pre20sintro.html
http://www.filmsite.org/20sintro.html
http://www.filmsite.org/30sintro.html
http://www.filmsite.org/40sintro.html
http://www.filmsite.org/50sintro.html
http://www.filmsite.org/60sintro.html
http://www.filmsite.org/70sintro.html
http://www.filmsite.org/80sintro.html
http://www.filmsite.org/90sintro.html

THE AMERICAN FILM INSTITUTE WEBSITE:
http://www.afi.com/membership/scripts/JoinAFI.asp

CHAPTER SIX

DANCE

WHAT IS IT?

BALLET
MODERN DANCE
WORLD CONCERT/
RITUAL DANCE
FOLK DANCE
JAZZ DANCE

HOW IS IT PUT TOGETHER?

FORMALIZED MOVEMENT
LINE, FORM, AND
REPETITION
Profile: Martha Graham
RHYTHM
MIME AND PANTOMIME
THEME, IMAGE, AND STORY
LINE

*A Personal Journey: The
Stuttgart Ballet, Romeo and
Juliet*
MUSIC
MISE-EN-SCÈNE
LIGHTING

HOW DOES IT STIMULATE THE SENSES?

MOVING IMAGES
*Dance and Human Reality:
Martha Graham,
Appalachian Spring*
FORCE
SIGN LANGUAGE
COLOR
Thinking Critically
Cyber Study

IMPORTANT TERMS

Ballet "Classical" or formal dance.
Modern dance Highly individualized twentieth-century dance works essentially antiballetic in philosophy.
World concert/ritual dance Concert and ceremonial dances specific to a country or culture.
Jazz dance A variety of styles of movement originating in the African American experience.
Folk dance A body of group dances performed to traditional music.
First position The basic position for all movements in ballet. The heels are together and the toes "open" and out to the side.
Plié A bending of the knees with the feet in first position.
Choreographer The artist who creates a dance work.
Mime Bodily movement that suggests the actions of people or animals.
Pantomime The acting out of dramatic action without words.
Mise-en-scène The visual elements supporting a dance work, including settings, lighting, and costumes.

Every December, Tchaikovsky's *Nutcracker* ballet rivals Handel's *Messiah* and television reruns of the Jimmy Stewart movie *It's a Wonderful Life* as a holiday tradition. Dance is one of the most natural and universal of human activities. In virtually every culture, regardless of location or level of sophistication, we find some form of dance. Dance appears to have sprung from humans' religious needs. For example, scholars are relatively certain that the theatre of ancient Greece developed out of that society's religious tribal dance rituals. It is without doubt that dance is part of human communication at its most fundamental level. We can see this expression even in little children who, before they begin to paint, sing, or imitate, begin to dance.

Carved and painted scenes dating from antiquity to the beginning of the era of film give us only the scantiest means by which to study the history of dance, an ephemeral art of movement—something we will notice as we move through Chapters 9–13 of this book. Dance is also a social activity and, although this text takes a fairly relativistic view of what comprises art, discussion of dance in this text is limited to what may be called "theatre dance"—dance that involves a performer, a performance, and an audience.

WHAT IS IT?

Dance focuses on the human form in time and space. It can follow numerous directions and traditions, including ballet, modern, world concert/ritual, folk, jazz, tap, and musical comedy. The discussion that follows treats five of these: ballet, modern, world concert/ritual, folk, and jazz dance.

BALLET

Ballet comprises what can be called "classical" or formal dance. Its rich tradition rests heavily upon a set of prescribed movements and actions. In general, ballet is a highly theatrical dance presentation consisting of solo dancers, duets, and choruses, or the *corps de ballet* (cohr-duh-bah-LAY). According to Anatole Chujoy in the *Dance Encyclopedia*, the basic principle in ballet is "the reduction of human gesture to bare essentials, heightened and developed into meaningful patterns." George Balanchine saw the single steps of a ballet as analogous to single frames in a motion picture. Ballet, then, became a fluid succession of images, existing within specialized codes of movement. As with all dance and indeed all the arts, ballet expresses basic human experiences and desires. Play the Humanities CD: Dance, Ballet.

MODERN DANCE

Modern dance is a label given to a broad variety of highly individualized dance works beginning in the twentieth century, American in derivation, and antiballetic in philosophy. It began as a revolt against the stylized and tradition-bound elements of ballet. The basic principle of modern dance could be stated as an exploration of natural and spontaneous or uninhibited movement, in strong contrast with the conventionalized and specified movement of ballet. The earliest modern dancers found stylized ballet incompatible with their need to communicate in twentieth-century terms. As Martha Graham characterized it, "There are no general rules. Each work of art creates its own code." Nonetheless, in its attempts to be nonballetic, it has accrued certain conventions and characteristics. While there are narrative elements in many modern dances, there may be less emphasis on them than in traditional ballet. There also are differences in the use of the body (particularly in the angularity of line expressed in modern dance), use of the dance floor (which in modern dance becomes more interactive with the dancer rather than being just a surface from which to spring and then return), and interaction with the visual elements. Play the Humanities CD: Dance.

WORLD CONCERT/RITUAL DANCE

Out of a plethora of scholarly arguments about how to label and define certain types of dance emerged the term "world dance." This name describes dances specific to a particular country. Within or alongside the category of world dance exists another label: *ritual dance*. In other words, among the dances classified as "world" there exist dances based in ritual—dances having ceremonial functions, formal characteristics, and particular prescribed procedures—which pass from generation to generation. Perhaps complicating the definition further, some of the dances falling in such a category have public presentation as their objective, and some have both ritualistic and public performance aims. Further, some ritual dances would never be performed for an audience because of their sacredness.

World concert/ritual dances typically center around topics important to single cultures—for example, "religion, moral values, work ethics or historical information relating to a culture" (Nora Ambrosio, *Learning About Dance*, p. 94). Some of the dances involve cultural communication, and others—such as those in the Japanese *Noh* and *Kabuki* traditions—are theatrical. World concert/ritual dance is an important element of many African and Asian cultures. At least in general terms, world concert/ritual dance can be differentiated from the next category, *folk dance*, although the boundaries are often blurred.

FOLK DANCE

Folk dance, somewhat like folk music, is a body of group dances performed to traditional music. It is similar to folk music in that we do not know the artists who developed it; no choreographer is recorded for folk dances. They began as a necessary or informative part of certain societies, and their characteristics are always stylistically identifiable with a given culture. They developed over a period of years, passing from one generation to another. They have prescribed movements, prescribed rhythms, and prescribed music and costume. At one time or another they may have become formalized—that is, committed to some form of record. But they are part of a heritage, and usually not the creative result of an artist or a group of interpretative artists, as is the case with the other forms of dance. Likewise, they exist more to involve participants than to entertain an audience (Fig. **6.1**).

Folk dancing establishes an individual sense of participation in society, the tribe, or a mass movement. "The group becomes one in conscious strength and purpose, and each individual experiences a heightened power as part of it ... [a] feeling of oneness with one's fellows which is established by collective dancing."[1]

JAZZ DANCE

Jazz dance traces its origins to Africa prior to the arrival of African slaves on the American continent. Today it exists in a variety of forums including popular theatre, concert stage, movies, and television. The rhythms of African music found their way into dances performed for enjoyment and entertainment. The foundations they provided led to the Minstrel shows in which dances were performed by white entertainers in blackface. By the late twentieth century, jazz dance had evolved into a variety of styles of movement, lacking a precise definition other than that of a vital, theatrical dance rooted in jazz and the African heritage. Jazz dance relies heavily on improvisation and syncopation.

HOW IS IT PUT TOGETHER?

Dance is an art of time and space which utilizes many of the elements of the other arts. In the setting and in the line and form of the human body it involves many of the compositional elements of pictures, sculpture, and theatre. Dance also relies heavily on the elements of music—whether or not music accompanies the dance presentation. However, the essential ingredient of dance is the human body and its varieties of expression.

6.1 The Csárdás, a traditional Hungarian folk dance.

6.2A First position.   6.2B Second position.   6.2C Third position.   6.2D Fourth position.   6.2E Fifth position.

6.2 The five ballet positions.

FORMALIZED MOVEMENT

The most obvious repository of formalized movement in dance is ballet. All movement in ballet is based upon five basic leg, foot, and arm positions. In the *first position* (Fig. **6.2A**) the dancer stands with weight equally distributed between the feet, heels together, and toes open and out to the side. In ballet all movements evolved from this basic "open" position; the feet are never parallel to each other with both pointing straight forward. The *second position* (Fig. **6.2B**) is achieved by opening the first position the length of one's foot, again with the weight placed evenly on both feet. In the *third position* (Fig. **6.2C**) the heel of the front foot touches the instep of the back foot; the legs and feet must be well turned out. The heel of the front foot is opposite the toe of the back foot in the *fourth position* (Fig. **6.2D**). The feet are parallel and separated by the length of the dancer's foot; again, the weight is placed evenly on both feet. The *fifth position* (Fig. **6.2E**) is the most frequently used of the basic ballet positions. The feet

are close together with the front heel touching the toe of the back foot. The legs and the feet must be well turned out to achieve this position correctly, and the weight is placed evenly on both feet. As is clear from Figure **6.2**, each position changes the attitude of the arms as well as that of the legs and feet. From these five basic positions a series of fundamental movements and poses is developed, and they are the core of every movement of the human body in formal ballet.

Many variations can be made upon the five basic positions. For example, the *grande seconde* (Fig. **6.3**) is a variation upon second position in which one leg is elevated to full height. One leg also is elevated in the *demi-hauteur* (deh-mee-oh-TUHR), or "half-height" (Fig. **6.4**). Full height requires extension of the leg at a 90-degree angle to the ground; half height requires a 45-degree extension.

Movements carry the same potential for variety. For example, in the *ronds de jambe à terre* (ruhn duh zhamb ah tair; Fig. **6.5**) the leg from the knee to and including the foot is rotated in a semicircle. As we develop expertise

6.3 *Grande seconde.*   6.4 *Demi-hauteur.*   6.5 *Ronds de jambe à terre.*

6.6 On point.

6.7 On point, detail.

in perceiving dance, it will become obvious in watching formal ballet (and, to a lesser degree, modern dance) that we see a limited number of movements and poses, turns and leaps, done over and over again. Thus these bodily compositions form a kind of theme with variations, and in that respect they are interesting in themselves.

In addition, it is possible to find a great deal of excitement in the bodily movements of formal ballet if for no other reason than the physical skills required for their execution. Just as in gymnastics or figure skating, the strength and grace of individuals in large part determine their qualitative achievement. Yet ballet is far more than just a series of gymnastic exercises.

Perhaps the most familiar element of ballet is the female dancer's toe work or dancing *on point* (Fig. **6.6**). A special kind of footgear is required (Fig. **6.7**). Dancing on point is a fundamental part of the female dancer's development, but it usually takes a minimum of two years of thorough training and development before a dancer can begin. Certain kinds of turns are not possible without toeshoes—for example, spinning on point or being spun by a partner.

We have focused on ballet in this discussion of formalized movement because it is the most familiar of the traditional, formalized dance forms. Ballet, however, is not alone in adhering to formalized patterns of movement. It is, in part, formalized movement that allows us to distinguish folk and other dances, such as the *pavane*, the *galliard*, the *waltz*, and the *mambo*. All have formal or conventional patterns of movement. Perhaps only modern dance resists formal movement, and even then not completely.

LINE, FORM, AND REPETITION

The compositional elements of line, form, and repetition apply to the use of the human body in exactly the same sense that they apply to painting and sculpture—the latter especially. The body of the dancer can be analyzed as a sculptural, three-dimensional form which reflects the use of line, even though the dancer is continually in motion. The body as a sculptural form moves from one pose to another, and if we were to take a stop-action movie of a dance, we could analyze, frame by frame or second by second, the compositional qualities of the human body. The human form in every illustration in this chapter, including those that show groupings of dancers, can be analyzed as a composition of line and shape. Dance, therefore, can be seen at two levels: first, as a type of pictorial communication employing symbols that occur only for a moment and, second, as the design of transition with movement between those moments.

Martha Graham

Martha Graham (1893–1991), arguably, contributed more to the art of modern dance as an innovative choreographer and teacher than any other individual. Her techniques were rooted in the muscular and nerve-muscle responses of the body to inner and outer stimuli. She created the most demanding body-training method in the field of modern dancing.

Born in Pittsburgh on May 11, 1893, Graham spent her early years there and in Santa Barbara, California. As a teenager she began studying dance at Denishawn, a dance company founded by Ruth St. Denis and Ted Shawn. Her dance debut came in *Xochitl* (ZOH-chee-tuhl), a ballet choreographed by St. Denis and based on an Aztec theme. It proved a great success both in vaudeville and concert performances.

Graham left Denishawn in 1923 to become a featured dancer in the Greenwich Village Follies. She also taught for a time at the Eastman School of Music in Rochester, N.Y. She debuted in New York City as an independent artist in 1926. One year later, her program included the dance piece *Revolt*, probably the first dance of protest and social comment in the United States.

Graham became interested in social comment as a legitimate theme in the arena of the arts, and combined it with her attraction to the early history of America. The result was her most famous ballet, *Appalachian Spring*, in which Graham herself danced the principal role of The Bride. Other roles included The Revivalist, The Husbandman, The Pioneering Woman, and The Followers. Perhaps the best loved of Graham's works, and the one with the finest score, *Appalachian Spring* takes as its pretext a wedding on the American frontier. The dance is like no actual ceremony or party, however. The movement not only expresses individual character and emotion, but it has a clarity, spaciousness, and definition that relate to the open frontier, which must be fenced and tamed. During the dance, the characters emerge to make solo statements; the action of the dance is suspended while they reveal what is in their hearts. The Bride's two solos suggest not only joy but trepidation for the future. (See box p. 143.)

In a career spanning seventy years, Martha Graham created 180 dance works. Some of these were based on Greek legends: *Night Journey*, first performed in 1947, about Jocasta, the mother of Oedipus; *Clytemnestra* (kly-tehm-NEH-struh; 1958); and *Cave of the Heart* (1946), about the tragedy of Medea. *Letter to the World* (1940) was based on the life of poet Emily Dickinson. *Seraphic Dialogue* (1955) dealt with Joan of Arc, and *Embattled Garden* (1962) took up the Garden of Eden legend. Among her other works were *Alcestis* (1960); *Acrobats of God* (1960); and *Maple Leaf Rag* (1990). Graham announced her retirement in 1970, but she continued to create new dances until her death from cardiac arrest in New York City on April 1, 1991.

Because dancers move through time, the concept of repetition becomes an important consideration in analyzing how a dance work is put together. The relationship of the movements to each other as the dance progresses shows us a repetitional pattern that is very similar to theme and variation in music. *Choreographers* plan these patterns using individual dancers' bodies as well as combinations of dancers in duets, trios, or the entire *corps de ballet* (Figs. 6.8 and 6.9). Watching a dance should focus on how movements, ensembles, scenery, and individual bodies explore diagonal, curved, or asymmetric lines, just in the same way that responding to a painting or work of sculpture involves perceiving and evaluating how those same elements of composition have been explored by the artist.

RHYTHM

As we watch a dance we can see that the steps are related and coherent. Dance phrases are held together by their rhythm, in the same sense as in musical rhythm. Sequences of long and short motions occur which are highlighted by accents. In a visual sense dance rhythms occur in spatial arrangements, up and down, back and forth, curved and linear, large and small. We can also perceive rhythmic relationships in the ebb and flow of dancers' energy levels. Energy, of course, calls to mind dynamics in the sense the term is used in music and theatre, and the rhythm of dynamics often creates a pyramidal form rising to a peak and tapering to a resolution. Play the Humanities CD: Music and Dance, Rhythm.

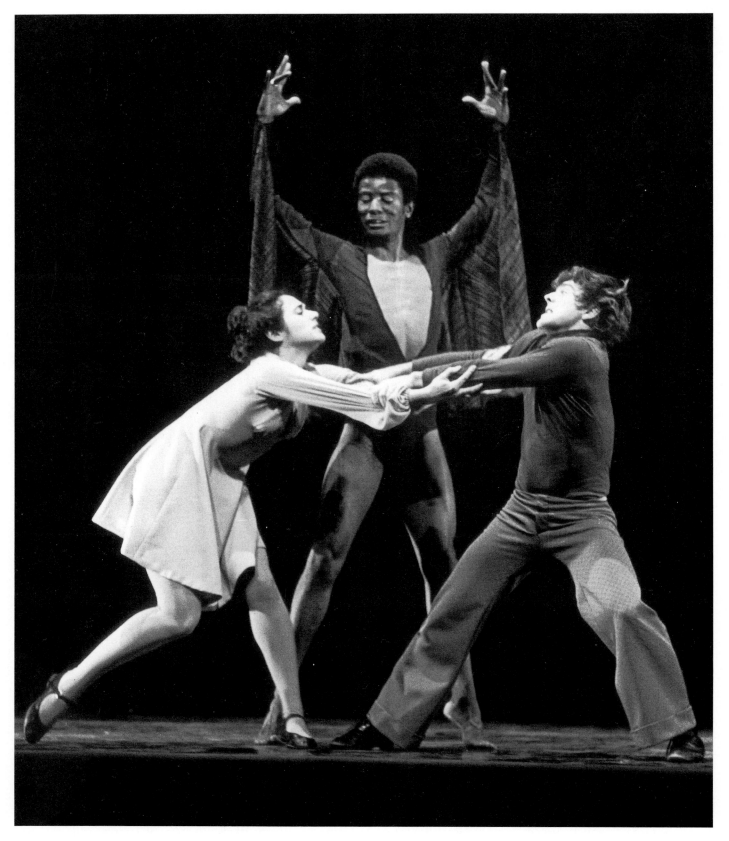

6.8 *Family Tree*, Jazz Dance Theatre at Penn State, Pennsylvania State University. Choreographer: Jean Sabatine.

6.9 *Nameless Hour*, Jazz Dance Theatre at Penn State, Pennsylvania State University. Choreographer: Jean Sabatine.

MIME AND PANTOMIME

Within any dance form there may be elements of bodily movement that we call *mime* and *pantomime*. Bodily movement is mimetic whenever it suggests the kinds of movements we associate with people or animals. It is also mimetic if it employs any of the forms of conventional sign language, such as the Delsarte system. And if there are narrative elements in the dance and the dancer actually portrays a character in the theatrical sense, there also may be pantomimetic action. Pantomime is the "acting out" of dramatic action without words. In the romantic style of ballet, for example, pantomime helps to carry forward the story line. We sense the emotions and character relationship in the dancers' steps, gestures, movements, and facial expressions. Only when the movement of the dance is purely an emotional expression of the dancer can we say that it is free of mime or pantomime.

THEME, IMAGE, AND STORY LINE

Our consideration of the presence or absence of mime leads us to a consideration of how dance communicates its idea content. There are three general possibilities. First, the dance may contain *narrative* elements—that is, it may tell a story. Romantic ballet usually has strong narrative elements. Second, the dance may communicate through *abstract* ideas. There is a specific theme to be communicated but no story line—the ideas relate to some aspect of human emotion or the human condition. Modern ballet—that is, twentieth-century ballet—has dealt increasingly with abstract ideas. Modern dance,

A Personal Journey

THE STUTTGART BALLET, *ROMEO* AND *JULIET*

Many cities have arts complexes, and their designers always pay close attention to the public spaces. Attending a play, a concert, a ballet, or an opera is a public experience—just like attending a rock concert. Perhaps more subdued than a rock concert, these more formal kinds of performing arts events bring people together, and the grandness of the situation usually begins outside on the street in a plaza like New York City's Lincoln Center. The large, open square, bounded by Broadway on one side and the New York State Theatre, Avery Fisher Hall, and the Metropolitan Opera House on the other three, ushers us into a grand setting. I was heading to the Metropolitan Opera House for a performance by the Stuttgart Ballet of Germany of the ballet based on Shakespeare's play *Romeo and Juliet*.

I like Shakespeare's play. I've seen it many times, and it never ceases to move me. It speaks to the soul, but much of what makes it speak is undoubtedly Shakespeare's language. Tonight I would discover whether the story, told in the pantomime of dance, could involve me and affect me as deeply as its prototype. Frankly, I was doubtful.

Inside the Metropolitan Opera House, the cavernous auditorium, with its plush red carpets and seats and tiers of balconies stacked one atop the other, creates a feeling of grandeur. The huge proscenium arch suggests that the production will be something big. Usually, in that space, it is opera, with its larger-than-life settings and characters, with music swelling throughout the house. Theatre, in contrast, is more intimate, and it is easy to lose important aspects of a play in a space as large as an opera house. I wondered how the dancers would fare without songs to give them prominence.

I needn't have worried. When the curtain opened, an Italian Renaissance setting peopled with characters in rich period clothing sparkled. A fan of gymnastics, I marveled at the power of the dancers' bodies, the height of their leaps, and the grace of their movement. As the story unfolded, each detail communicated clearly in dance pantomime. Even had I not known the story beforehand, I would have understood the visual narrative. Romeo's love for Juliet; her love for him; the hostility of the two families—the Montagues and the Capulets; Tibault's brashness; Friar Lawrence's interventions. All were communicated clearly from the stage. The sword fights flashed and clanged—thrilling in action and painful in death. The intimacy of the tomb, where the two lovers meet their tragic deaths, gripped as forcefully in dance as it did when clothed in Shakespeare's dialogue.

The ballet proved as effective as a production of the play. The moves of the dancers were graceful, precise, and communicative. They were also, on occasion, big, strong, and athletic, like Michael Jordan, leaving the floor and suspended in mid-air until the laws of gravity seemed destroyed.

---

especially, tends to explore human psychology and behavior. Social themes occur frequently, as do impressions or expressions from plays, poems, and novels. Religious and folk themes can be found too. A variation of abstract idea content in dance is *ethnic influence*. It is interesting to note how elements of dance reflect sociocultural background. Jazz dance, for example, may stimulate us to consider the African American heritage in the United States. The third possibility is the absence of any narrative or abstract communication. The work may be a *divertissement* (dee-vair-TEES-mawn; French for "diversion")—some ballets are *divertissements*.

Participating as an audience member for dance requires active involvement, and determining the meaning involved in the themes, images, and story line of a dance requires evaluation of the feeling the choreographer is trying to establish. In addition, we should attempt to discover what the choreographer is trying to say through the elements of the dance. Are the dancers portraying a character, transmitting an emotion, or some combination?

6.10 Traditional tights and tutu.

MUSIC

Dance is associated with music as a matter of course. Music usually serves as a basis for the bodily movement of the work we are perceiving, although it is not absolutely necessary for dance to be accompanied by music. However, it is impossible to have dance without one element of music—rhythm. Every action of a dancer's body has some relationship in time to every other movement, and those relationships establish rhythmic patterns that are musical regardless of the presence or absence of sound.

When we hear music accompanying a dance we can respond to the relationship of the dance to the musical score. The most obvious link we see and hear is that between the gestures and footfalls of the dancer and the beat of the music. In some cases the two are in strict accord—the beat-for-beat relationship is one to one—in other cases not.

Another relationship is that of the *dynamics* of the dance to those of the music. Of prime importance in this relationship is the intensity, or force, of the dance. Moments of great intensity can manifest themselves in rapid movement and forceful leaps. Or they may be reflected in other qualities. The same kind of analysis can be used in dance as that used in theatre to plot dynamic levels and overall structure. For maximum interest there must be variety of intensity. If we chart the relationship of the peaks and valleys of dynamics, we are likely to conclude that the dynamic structure of a dance is similar to the dynamic structure of a play: it tends to be pyramidal, building to a high point and then relaxing to a conclusion. This applies whether or not narrative elements are present.

MISE-EN-SCÈNE

Because dance is essentially a visual and theatrical experience, part of our response must be to those theatrical elements of dance that are manifested in the environment of the presentation. In other words, we can respond to the *mise-en-scène* of the dance (Fig. 6.8). We can note elements of verisimilitude and how they reflect or otherwise relate to the aural and visual elements of the dance. A principal consideration here is the interrelationship of the dance with properties, settings, and the floor of the theatrical environment. Some dances employ massive stage designs. Others have no setting at all; they are performed in a neutral environment. A principal difference between formal ballet and modern dance lies in the use of the *dance floor*. In formal ballet the floor acts principally as an agent from which dancers spring and to which they return. But in modern dance the floor assumes an integral role in the performance, and we are likely to see the dancers sitting on the floor, rolling on it—in short, *interacting* with the floor. Consideration of the floor in dance also concerns how its use relates to the themes and images of the dance.

Crucial to understanding a dance is perception of how the choreographer utilizes space. Changing levels, directions, shapes, and floor patterns form a fundamental part of how dance works, and understanding a dance and responding to it involves active perception and evaluation of how the entirety of the physical space and the dancers' space interact and communicate.

In discussing the relationship of *costume* to dance, we would do well to return to the section on costume design in Chapter 4 to note the purposes of costume, because they apply equally to dance as to theatrical productions. In some dances costume will be traditional, conventional, and neutral. There would be little representation of story line or character in the tights and *tutu* of the female dancer shown in Figure 6.10. However, in many dances we are likely to see costumes high in verisimilitude. They may help portray character, locality, and other aspects of the dance (Figs. 6.8 and 6.9).

It is especially important that costumes should allow dancers to do whatever it is that the choreographer expects of them. In fact, costume may become an integral part of the dance itself. An example of this is Martha Graham's *Lamentation*, in which a single dancer is costumed in what could best be described as a tube of fabric—no arms, no legs, just a large envelope of cloth. Every movement of the dancer stretches the cloth so that the line and form is not that of a human body but rather of a human body enveloped in a moving fabric.

The final element of the dance costume to be considered, and one of great significance, is footgear. Dancers' footgear ranges from the simple, soft, and supple ballet slipper to the specialized toeshoe of formal ballet, with street shoes, character Oxfords, and a variety of representational or symbolic footwear in between. Modern dance is often done barefoot. The fundamental requirements of footgear are comfort and enough flexibility to allow the dancer to dance. Footgear must be appropriate to the surface of the stage floor, whether toeshoe, ballet slipper, or character Oxford. Great care must be taken to ensure that the dance floor is not too hard, too soft, too rough, too slippery, or too sticky. The floor is so important that many touring companies take their own floor with them to ensure that they will be able to execute their movements properly. There have been cases in which professional dance companies have refused to perform in local auditoriums because the floor was dangerous for the dancers.

LIGHTING

Inasmuch as the entire perception of a dance relies on viewing the human body as a three-dimensional form, the work of the lighting designer is of critical importance. How we perceive the human form in space depends on how that body is lit. Certainly our emotional and sense response is highly shaped by the nature of the lighting that plays on the dancer and the dance floor.

HOW DOES IT STIMULATE THE SENSES?

The complex properties of dance make possible diverse and intense communicative stimuli. It is possible to respond at different levels to an artwork. To some extent we can respond even at a level of total ignorance. There will be levels of understanding, levels of meaning, levels of potential response for the uninitiated as well as the thoroughly sophisticated viewer. The more sophisticated a *balletomane* one becomes, the fuller one's understanding and response will be.

MOVING IMAGES

Like every other artwork that exists in space, dance appeals to our senses through the compositional qualities of line and form. These exist not only in the human body but in the visual elements of the *mise-en-scène*. Essentially, horizontal lines stimulate a sense of calm and repose. Vertical lines suggest grandeur and elegance. Diagonal lines stimulate a feeling of action and movement (see Fig. 6.8), and curved lines, grace. As we react to a dance work we respond to how the human body expresses line and form—when it is standing still and when it moves through space. If we are alert and perceptive

DANCE AND HUMAN REALITY

Martha Graham, *Appalachian Spring*

Social criticism as an artistic message came into vogue in the United States during the Great Depression of the 1930s. During the same period, modern dance pioneer Martha Graham began to pursue topical themes in her dances. Her interest in the shaping of America led to a now renowned dance piece set to the music of Aaron Copland, *Appalachian Spring* (1944; Fig. **6.11**). It deals, among other things, with the triumph of love and common sense over the fire-and-brimstone of American puritanism at that time.

Appalachian Spring came about as a result of a commission funded by Elizabeth Sprague Coolidge and had its première on October 30 at the Library of Congress as part of its concert series. Its story deals with a pioneer frontier marriage. The characters are a young bride, a young groom, an older woman who is their advisor and protector, and a preacher—a fire-and-brimstone frontier evangelist who prophesies hellfire and damnation for all who do not agree with him. Around the preacher flock a group of young spinsters who worship him and whom Martha Graham used as a source of comedy in the dance. She treated the young couple and their taking over of a new house and a new farm with moving and sensitive simplicity. Overall, the work read like a "love letter, a dance of hope, budding, fresh, and beautiful."[2] *Appalachian Spring* has become perhaps the most admired work in the Graham company repertoire. Its music has become an American classic, and the stunning set by sculptor Isamu Noguchi (see p. 388) a benchmark in theatrical design.

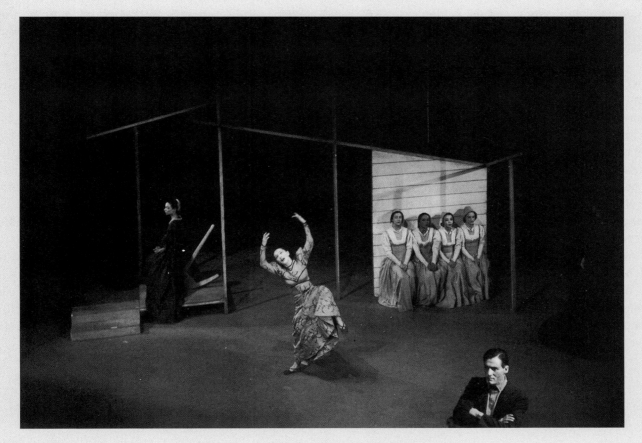

6.11 *Martha Graham in* Appalachian Spring, *1954. Choreographer: Martha Graham.*

we will recognize not only how lines and forms are created but also how they are repeated from dancer to dancer and from dancer to *mise-en-scène*.

Often, the kind of line created by the body of a dancer is the key to understanding the work of the choreographer. George Balanchine, for example, insisted that his dancers be almost skin and bone; you would not see a corpulent or overly developed physique in his company. Thus bodies, too, affect our perception, and choreographers capitalize on that in their dance conceptions.

FORCE

We noted in Chapter 3 that the beat of music makes a fundamental appeal to our senses. Beat is the aspect of music that sets our toes tapping and our fingers drumming. Probably our most basic responses to a dance are to the dynamics expressed by the dancers and in the music. A dancer's use of vigorous and forceful action, high leaps, graceful turns, or extended pirouettes appeals directly to us, as does the tempo of the dance. Variety in dynamics—the louds and softs and the highs and lows of bodily intensity as well as musical sound—is the dancer's and choreographer's means of providing interest, just as it is the actor's, the director's, and the painter's.

SIGN LANGUAGE

Dancers, like actors, can stimulate us directly because they are human beings and can employ many symbols of communication. Most human communication requires us to learn a set of symbols—we can respond to dance at this level only when we have mastered its language. There are systems of sign language, such as the Delsarte, in which the positions of the arms, hands, and head have meanings. Likewise, each of the hand movements of the hula dance communicates an idea, and it is these on which we should concentrate, not the vigorous hip movements.

However, there is a set of universal body symbols to which all of us respond (so psychologists tell us), regardless of our level of familiarity or understanding. For example, the gesture of acceptance in which the arms are held outward with the palms up has the same meaning universally. Rejection is shown by holding the hands in front of the body with the palms out as if to push away. When dancers employ universal symbols we respond to their appeal to our senses just as we would to the nonverbals or body language in everyday conversation.

COLOR

Although dancers use facial and bodily expressions to communicate some aspects of the human condition, we do not receive as direct a message from them as we do from the words of actors. So, to enhance the dancer's communication the costume, lighting, and set designers must strongly reinforce the mood of the dance through the *mise-en-scène* they create. The principal means of expression of mood is color. Because lifelikeness is not as important in dance as in the theatre, lighting designers are free to work in much more obvious ways with color. They may not have to worry if the face of a dancer is red or blue or green—which would be disastrous in a play. So we often see much stronger, more colorful, and more suggestive lighting in dance than in theatre. Colors are more saturated, intensity much higher, and the qualities of the human body, as form, are explored much more strongly by light from various directions. The same is true of costumes and settings. Because dancers do not portray roles with high verisimilitude, their costumes can communicate in an abstract way.

On the other hand, scene designers must be careful to utilize color so as to focus on the dancer in the stage environment—that is, unless a synthesis of the dancer with the environment is intended, as in the case, for example, of some works by choreographer Merce Cunningham. In any but the smallest of stage spaces it is very easy for the human body to be overpowered by the elements of the setting, since the latter occupies so much more space. Nevertheless, scene designers use color as forcefully as they can to help reinforce the overall mood of the dance.

These examples of how dance affects our senses are rudimentary ones. Perhaps more than any other art, dance causes us to ascend beyond our three cognitive questions—What is it? How is it put together? How does it affect the senses?—and dwell on a fourth level of response—What does it mean?

THINKING CRITICALLY

Create a basic analysis of a dance work by using the following outline of concepts from the text as a guide.

- Genre. In what ways did the dance piece pursue the characteristics of a particular genre—for example, ballet, modern, world concert/ritual, folk, or jazz dance?

- Formalized movement. In what ways did elements of formalized movement shape the piece? What recognizable explorations of first, second, third, fourth, and fifth positions occurred?

- Line, form, and repetition. How did the dancers, individually and as a group, create visual forms and repetitions? What were these forms—for example, were they rounded, angular, vertical, horizontal—and how did they create an emotional or intellectual impact?

- Rhythm. What was the rhythmic structure of the piece?

- Mime and pantomime. What, if any, elements of mime and pantomime were in the dance? What, if any, was the story line or symbolism of the dancers' movements?

- Theme, image, and story line. What kind of message or experience was the dance trying to communicate? Did it succeed; why or why not?

- Music. How did the dance relate to the music that accompanied it? If there was no musical accompaniment, what effect did that have on your experience of the work?

- Mise-en-scène. What role did the elements of the mise-en-scène play in the dance? How did the settings, lighting, and costumes work in conjunction with the movements of the dancers to create a total experience? In what ways did changes in lighting enhance or detract from your experience of the piece?

- Reaction. How did the previous elements combine to create a reaction in you? What drew your attention, and why? What were your emotional and intellectual responses to the dance piece, and what caused them?

CYBER STUDY

ANCIENT GREECE:
http://www.firstnethou.com/annam/dancehis.html/history/index.html

BALLET:
http://balletdance.about.com/gi/dynamic/offsite.htm?site=http%3A%2F%2Fwww.ccs.neu.edu%2Fhome%2Fyiannis%2Fdance%2Fhistory.html

MODERN:
http://click.hotbot.com/director.asp?id=6&target=http://www.encyclopedia.com/articles/08601.html&query=modern+dance&rsource=LCOSW2
—Martha Graham:
http://www.pathfinder.com/photo/gallery/arts/morgan/cap02.htm)

CHAPTER SEVEN

ARCHITECTURE

WHAT IS IT?

HOW IS IT PUT TOGETHER?

STRUCTURE
Post-and-lintel
Arch
Cantilever
Bearing-Wall
Skeleton Frame
A Personal Journey: The Parthenon
BUILDING MATERIALS
Stone
Concrete
Wood
Steel
LINE, REPETITION, AND BALANCE
SCALE AND PROPORTION
CONTEXT
Profile: Frank Lloyd Wright
SPACE
CLIMATE

HOW DOES IT STIMULATE THE SENSES?

CONTROLLED VISION AND SYMBOLISM
Architecture and Human Reality: Le Corbusier, Villa Savoye
STYLE
APPARENT FUNCTION
DYNAMICS
SCALE
Thinking Critically
Cyber Study

IMPORTANT TERMS

Post-and-lintel An architectural structure consisting of horizontal beams laid across open spaces between vertical supports.

Tunnel vault Arches placed back to back to enclose space.

Arcade Several arches placed side by side.

Groin vault Tunnel vaults meeting at right angles.

Cantilever An overhanging beam or floor supported at only one end.

Bearing-wall A system of architectural structure in which the walls support themselves.

Skeleton frame A system of architectural structure in which a framework supports the building and the walls are attached to the frame.

Scale The relationship of the size of a building to the human form.

Context The environment surrounding a work of architecture.

Function The basic purpose of a building.

Prestressed concrete Concrete using metal rods and wires under stress or tension to cause structural forces to flow in predetermined directions.

Ferroconcrete Concrete cast in place with metal reinforcement embedded in the concrete.

Every street in our towns represents a museum of ideas and engineering. The houses, churches, and commercial buildings we pass every day reflect appearances and techniques almost as old as the human race itself. We go in and out of these buildings, often without noticing them, and yet they frequently dictate actions we can or cannot take.

In approaching architecture as an art, we really cannot separate aesthetic properties from practical or functional properties. In other words, architects first have a particular function to achieve in their building. That function is their principal concern. The aesthetics of the building are important, but they must be tailored to overall practical considerations. For example, when architects set about designing a 110-story skyscraper, they are locked into an aesthetic form that will be vertical rather than horizontal in emphasis. They may attempt to counter verticality with strong horizontal elements, but the physical fact that the building will be taller than it is wide is the basis from which the architects must work. Their structural design must take into account all the practical needs implicit in the building's use. Nonetheless, considerable room for aesthetics remains. Treatment of space, texture, line, and proportion can give us buildings of unique style and character—or of unimaginative sameness.

Architecture is often described as the art of sheltering. To consider it as such we must use the term "sheltering" very broadly. Obviously there are types of architecture within which people do not dwell and under which they cannot escape the rain. Architecture encompasses more than buildings. So, we can consider architecture as the art of sheltering people both physically and spiritually from the raw elements of the unaltered world.

In this chapter, as in previous ones, attention focuses predominantly on technical, definitional matters. Understanding these basics gives us tools to get more out of experiencing architectural structures and pleasure in communicating our reactions to others. Later in the text (Chapters 10–14) the history of architecture unfolds and some of its meaning for humankind emerges.

WHAT IS IT?

As well as the art of sheltering, architecture comprises design of three-dimensional space to create practical enclosure. Its basic forms include residences, places of worship, and commercial buildings. Each can take innumerable shapes, from single-family residences to the ornate palaces of kings to high-rise condominiums and apartments. The categorization of architectural forms can also be expanded to include bridges, walls, monuments, and so forth.

HOW IS IT PUT TOGETHER?

In examining how a work of architecture is put together we will limit ourselves to ten fundamental elements: structure, building materials, line, repetition, balance, scale, proportion, context, space, and climate.

STRUCTURE

Although many systems of construction or structural support exist, the text that follows treats only a few: *post-and-lintel, arch, cantilever, bearing-wall,* and *skeleton frame.*

7.1 Stonehenge, Salisbury Plain, England, c. 1800–1400 B.C.E.

7.2 Parthenon, Acropolis, Athens, 448–432 B.C.E.

Post-and-Lintel

Post-and-lintel structures consist of horizontal beams (lintels) laid across the open spaces between vertical supports (posts) traditionally of stone. They are similar to *post-and-beam* structures, in which series of vertical posts are joined by horizontal members, traditionally of wood. The wooden members of post-and-beam structures are held together by nails, pegs, or lap joints.

The lack of *tensile strength* in their fundamental material, stone, limits post-and-lintel structures in their ability to define space. Tensile strength is the ability of a material to withstand bending. If a slab of stone supported at each end bridges an opening, it can span only a narrow space before it cracks in the middle and falls to the ground. On the other hand, stone has great *compressive strength*—the ability to withstand compression or crushing.

A very early example of a post-and-lintel structure is Stonehenge, that ancient and mysterious religious configuration of giant stones in Great Britain (Fig. **7.1**). The ancient Greeks refined this system to high elegance; the most familiar of their post-and-lintel creations is the Parthenon in Athens (Fig. **7.2**).

The Greek post-and-lintel structure has served as a *prototype* for buildings throughout the world and down the centuries. One of its most interesting aspects rests in the treatment of *columns* and *capitals*. Figure **7.3**

Greek Doric		Ionic		Corinthian	
A Entablature	D Frieze	G Shaft	1 Guttae	4 Abacus	7 Fluting
B Column	E Architrave	H Base	2 Metope	5 Echinus	8 Dentils
C Cornice	F Capital	I Plinth	3 Triglyph	6 Volute	9 Fascia

7.3 Greek columns and capitals: (*left*) Doric, (*center*) Ionic, (*right*) Corinthian.

shows the three basic Greek orders—*Doric*, *Ionic*, and *Corinthian*. These are not the only styles possible— column capitals can be as varied as the imagination of the architect who has designed them. Their primary purpose is to act as a transition for the eye as it moves from post to lintel. The columns themselves also vary in shape and detail. A final element, present in some columns, is *fluting*—vertical ridges cut into the column.

Arch

A second type of architectural structure is the arch. Post-and-lintel structure limits the amount of unencumbered space it can cross, but the arch can define large spaces because its stresses transfer outward from the center (the *keystone*) to its legs (piers, columns, or door and window jambs). It does not depend solely on the tensile strength of its material.

Many different styles of arch exist, some of which appear in Figure 7.4. The characteristics of different arches may have structural as well as decorative functions. As an example, examine St. Alban's Cathedral (Fig. 7.5), built in the English Norman style. This style of building, with its accent on rounded arches, was loosely based on the Classical architecture of Roman times.

The transfer of stress from the center of an arch outward and downward dictates the need for a strong support to keep the legs from caving outward. Such a reinforcement is called a *buttress* (Fig. 7.6). The designers of Gothic cathedrals sought to achieve a sense of lightness. Since stone was their basic building material, they recognized that some system had to be developed that would overcome the bulk of a stone buttress. Therefore they developed a system of buttresses that accomplished structural ends but were light in appearance. These are called *flying buttresses* (Fig. 7.7).

Several arches placed side by side form an *arcade* (Fig. 7.8). Arches placed back to back to enclose space form a *tunnel vault* (Fig. 7.11). When two tunnel vaults intersect at right angles, they form a *groin vault* (Fig. 7.9). The protruding masonry indicating diagonal juncture of arches in a groin vault is *rib vaulting* (Figs. 7.10 and 7.12).

When arches join at the top, with their legs forming a circle, a *dome* results (Figs. 7.13 and 7.14). Through intersecting arches, this allows for more expansive, freer space within the structure. If the structures that support the dome form a circle, the result is a circular building such as the Pantheon in Rome. To permit squared space beneath a dome, the architect needs to transfer weight and stress through the use of *pendentives* (Fig. 7.15).

The problems architects face in utilizing one form or another for structural support are illustrated by the story

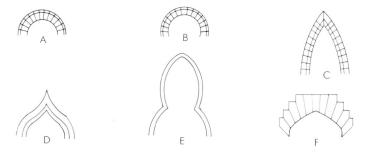

7.4 The arch: (A) round (Roman), (B) horseshoe (Moorish), (C) lancet (pointed, Gothic), (D) ogee, (E) trefoil, (F) Tudor.

7.5 St. Alban's Cathedral, England, nave, facing east.

7.6 The buttress: any projecting structure, generally of stone, built against a wall to support it.

A Personal Journey

THE PARTHENON

Athens sprawls almost to the horizons. Nonetheless, the Acropolis rises majestically in the center of it all. Opening the drapes at my hotel window provided one of those rare and hoped-for but entirely serendipitous happenings. I was staying at the foot of the Acropolis and I could see the ruins of the Parthenon. Two days would pass, however, before I climbed to it.

There was some method to such madness. I wanted the Acropolis and the Parthenon to comprise the apex of my discoveries in Athens, just as they sat as the apex of Athenian civilization nearly 2,400 years earlier. Working my way around the city, which crowds the base of the plateau forming the Acropolis, gave me the opportunity to see the Parthenon, and the Erechtheum, Propylaea, and Temple of Athena Nike, from every angle possible. Besides, there is more to Athens than the Parthenon.

Nearest my hotel rose the remains of the Theatre of Dionysus where Aeschylus, Sophocles, Euripides, and Aristophanes' plays witnessed their productions (see Chapter 10). I could almost hear 20,000 Athenians applauding those playwrights and the many others whose works have been lost, but who also competed, and won, against those four great playwrights whose works are the only ones to survive.

On the opposite side of the Acropolis, I wandered through the ruins of the ancient *agora*—the marketplace—and imagined Socrates teaching his students by asking them questions and drawing from them answers to life's mysteries. Higher up was the rocky outcrop where St. Paul preached Christianity to the Athenians a scant 500 years later. The agora lies below current street level, and in it I felt strangely apart from today and in communion with the ancients.

Leaving the agora, I began my climb to the top. It's a modest slope, but when I reached the steps of the Propylaea (see the Humanities CD: Architecture, Classical)—the structure that serves as an entrance portal for the top of the Acropolis and the Parthenon—I realized I wasn't "in Kansas anymore." The steps were broken and irregular. No handrails existed to steady the step. The Occupational, Safety, and Health Act had not reached the ancient temples of Athens. As I passed through the Propylaea and its sprawling, unfinished buildings spilling out on the awkward, sloping site, the Parthenon (Fig. 7.2) slowly came into view.

The temple sits at a slight angle to the Propylaea, and so the view revealed is of two sides sloping away. It looked the same as in photographs, and I was fortunate to see it before, like so many ancient monuments, it disappeared behind a mountain of scaffolding. Looking up at the front pediment, I studied the blank space that once contained the Elgin Marbles now residing in the British Museum (p. 67). I tried to place them as they had been: Helios and the horses of his chariot team, Dionysus, Persephone, Demeter, and Iris on one side, and Hestia(?), Dione, Aphrodite, Selene, and one of the horses from her chariot on the other (see Fig. 2.11). I wondered if Lord Elgin had, indeed, despoiled this great temple when he removed the statues or if he had, truly, saved them from obliteration by neglect and the awful etching away of stone perpetrated by Athens's modern smog.

7.7 Notre Dame, Paris, flying buttresses.

7.9 Groin vault.

7.10 Rib vault.

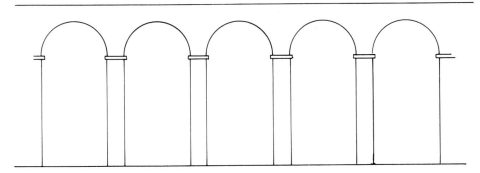

7.8 Arcade.

7.11 Tunnel vault.

7.12 Canterbury Cathedral, England, choir showing rib vaulting.

of St. Paul's Cathedral, London. Its dome measures 112 feet (34 m) in diameter and stands 365 feet (110 m) tall at the top of the cross. The lantern and cross alone weigh 700 tons (711 tonnes), while the dome and its super-structure weigh in at 64,000 tons (65,000 tonnes). In designing this cathedral Wren was faced with seemingly insurmountable problems of supporting such a tremen-dous load. His ingenious solution turns the dome into a timber shell covered in lead, with the actual weight of the dome only a fraction of what it would have been in stone. This allowed Wren to create a wonderful silhouette on the outside and to have a high ceiling in the interior (Fig. 7.16).

Cantilever

A cantilever is an overhanging beam or floor supported at only one end (Fig. 7.18). Although it is not a twentieth-century innovation—many nineteenth-century barns in the central and eastern parts of the US employed it—the most dramatic uses of cantilevers have emerged with the introduction of modern materials such as steel beams and *prestressed concrete*. The possibilities of cantilever as a structure reveal themselves in Edouardo Torroja's (tohr-ROH-hah) soaring Zarzuela Grandstand (Fig. 7.17). The most fascinating example of this structural system emerges in Frank Lloyd Wright's Fallingwater (Fig. 7.26).

7.13 Giovanni Paolo Panini, *The Interior of the Pantheon, Rome*, c. 1734/5. Oil on canvas, 50½ × 39 ins (128 × 99 cm). National Gallery of Art, Washington, D.C. (Samuel H. Kress Collection).

7.14 Christopher Wren, St. Paul's Cathedral, London, west façade, 1675–1710.

7.15 Dome with pendentives (P).

7.16 Christopher Wren, St. Paul's Cathedral, London, cross-section.

7.17 Eduardo Torroja, Zarzuela Race Track Grandstand, Madrid, 1935.

7.18 Cantilever.

Bearing-Wall

In this system, the wall supports itself, the floors, and the roof. Log cabins are examples of bearing-wall construction; so are solid masonry buildings, in which the walls are the structure. In variations of bearing-wall construction, such as Figure 7.35, the wall material is continuous—that is, not jointed or pieced together—in a system called *monolithic construction.*

Skeleton Frame

Here a framework supports the building. The walls attach to the frame, forming an exterior skin. When skeleton framing utilizes wood, as in house construction, the technique is called *balloon construction.* When metal forms the frame, as in skyscrapers, it is known as *steel-cage construction.*

BUILDING MATERIALS

Historic and contemporary architectural practices and traditions often center on specific materials, and to understand architecture further, we need to note a few.

Stone

The use of stone as a material turns us back to post-and-lintel systems and Figures 7.1 and 7.2. When stone is used in conjunction with mortar—for example, in arch

7.19 Pont du Gard, near Nîmes, France, 1st century B.C.E.

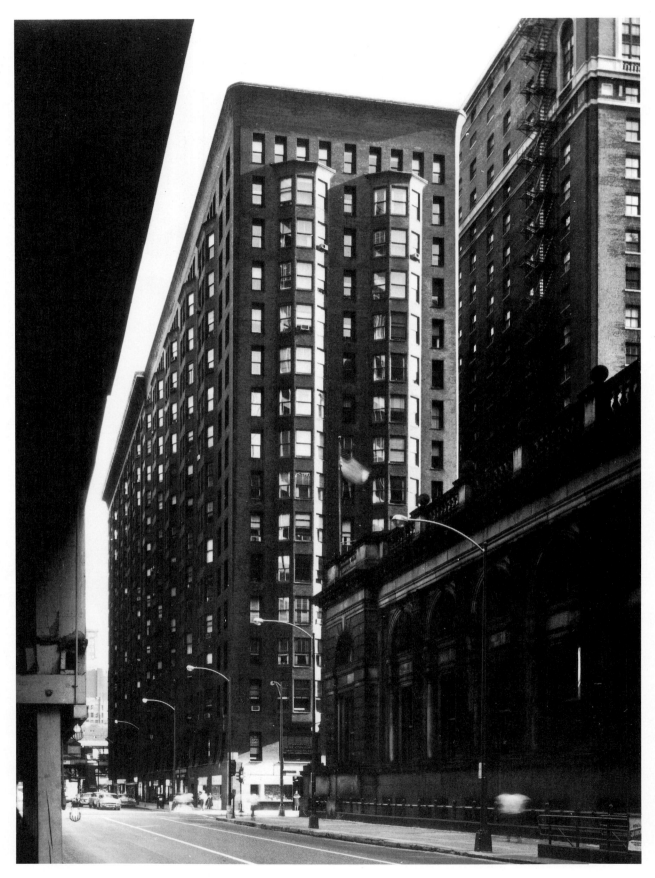

7.20 Burnham & Root, Monadnock Building, Chicago, 1889–91.

7.21 Richard Buckminster Fuller, geodesic dome, Climatron, St. Louis, Missouri, 1959.

construction—that combination is called *masonry construction*. The most obvious example of masonry, however, is the brick wall. Masonry construction utilizes stones, bricks, or blocks joined together with mortar, one on top of the other, to provide standard, structural, weight-bearing walls (Fig. 7.19). The pressures that play on the joints between blocks and mortar and the foundation on which they rest limit what can be accomplished with masonry. However, when one considers that office buildings such as Chicago's Monadnock Building (Fig. 7.20) are skyscrapers and that their walls are built solely of masonry—that is, no hidden steel reinforces the walls—it becomes obvious that this elemental combination of stone and mortar has numerous potentials.

Concrete

The use of concrete is central to much contemporary architectural practice, but it was also significant as far back in the past as ancient Rome. The Pantheon (see Fig. 7.13) comprises a masterful structure of concrete with a massive concrete dome, 142 feet (43 m) in diameter, resting on concrete walls 20 feet (6 m) thick. In contemporary architecture, we find *precast concrete*, which is cast in

place using wooden forms around a steel framework. *Ferroconcrete (reinforced concrete)* has metal reinforcement embedded in the concrete. Such a technique combines the tensile strength of the metal with the compressive strength of the concrete. *Prestressed* and *post-tensioned concrete* use metal rods and wires under stress or tension to cause structural forces to flow in predetermined directions. Both are extremely versatile building materials.

Wood

Whether in balloon framing or in laminated beaming, wood has played a pivotal role in architecture, especially in the United States. As new technologies emerge to make engineered beams from what was once scrapwood, it seems that it will remain a viable building product—and being a renewable resource, it also has a less negative impact on the environment than do many other materials. In domestic architecture dimensional lumber remains predominant as framing, even though it costs more than steel. This is largely due to the conservatism of the building trade, which is reluctant to adopt new techniques or invest in tools to employ other materials.

7.22 Frank Lloyd Wright, Marin County Courthouse, California, 1957–63.

Steel

Steel gives almost limitless possibilities for construction. Its introduction into the nineteenth-century industrial age forever changed style and scale in architecture. We noted steel-cage and cantilever construction earlier. *Suspension construction* in structures such as bridges, superdomes, and aerial walkways has carried architects to the safe limits of space spansion—and sometimes beyond. The *geodesic dome* (Fig. **7.21**), invented by an American architect, R. Buckminster Fuller, uses materials in a unique way. Consisting of a network of metal rods and hexagonal plates, the geodesic dome provides a light, inexpensive, yet strong and easily assembled building. Although it has no apparent size limit (Fuller claimed that he could roof New York City, given the funds), its potential for variation and aesthetic expressiveness seems somewhat limited.

7.23 Hampton Court Palace, England, Wren façade, 1689.

LINE, REPETITION, AND BALANCE

Line and repetition perform the same compositional functions in architecture as in painting and sculpture. In his Marin County Courthouse in California (Fig. 7.22), Frank Lloyd Wright takes a single motif—the arc—and varies only its size, repeating it almost endlessly with dynamic and fascinating results.

Christopher Wren, the architect of St. Paul's Cathedral (see Figs. 7.14 and 7.16), also designed one of the façades of Hampton Court Palace outside of London, England (Fig. 7.23), in the classically oriented style of the English Baroque (see Chapter 11). Wren's use of line, repetition, and balance results in a sophisticated visual design and engaging perceptual experience. Note first the symmetrical façade. The outward wing at the far left of the photograph duplicates at the right. In the center of the building four attached columns surround three windows. The middle window forms the exact center of the design, with mirror-image repetition on each side. Above the main windows appear a series of relief sculptures, *pediments* (triangular casings), and circular windows. Return to the main row of windows at the left border of the picture and

count toward the center. The outer wing contains four windows; then seven windows, then the central three; then seven; and finally four. Patterns of threes and sevens are very popular in architecture and carry religious and mythological symbolism. Wren has established a pattern of four in the outer wing, three in the center, and then repeated it within each of the seven-window groups to create yet three additional patterns of three! How is it possible to create patterns of three with only seven windows? First, locate the center window of the seven. It has a pediment and a relief sculpture above it. On each side of this window are three windows (a total of six) without pediments. So, we have two groupings of three windows each. A circular window rests above each of the outside four windows. The window on each side of the center window does not have a circular one above it. Rather, it has a relief sculpture, the presence of which joins these two windows with the center window to give us our third grouping of three. Line, repetition, and balance in this façade form a marvelous perceptual exercise and experience.

Buckingham Palace, London (Fig. 7.24), and the Palace of Versailles (Fig. 7.25) illustrate different treatments of line and repetition. Buckingham Palace uses

7.24 Buckingham Palace, London, c. 1825.

straight line almost exclusively, with repetition of recti-linear and triangular form. Like Hampton Court Palace, it exhibits *fenestration* groupings of threes and sevens, and the building itself is symmetrical and divided by three pedimented, porticolike protrusions. Notice how three major pediments break the predominantly horizontal line of the building while the window pediments and the verticality of the attached columns give interest and contrast across its full length.

Compare Buckingham Palace with the Palace of Versailles, in which repetition occurs in groupings of threes and fives. Contrast is provided by juxtaposition and repetition of curved lines in the arched windows and Baroque statuary. Notice how the horizontal shape of the

building, despite three porticoes, remains virtually undis-turbed, in contrast with that of Buckingham Palace.

SCALE AND PROPORTION

Scale in architecture refers to a building's size and the relationship of the building and its decorative elements to the human form. Scale may range from the intimacy of a domestic bungalow to the towering power of a skyscraper such as the Sears Tower (see Fig. 7.39). Proportion, or the relationship of individual elements to each other, also plays an important role in a building's visual effect. In this case, the elements of concern are the parts of the building in juxtaposition and their intended effects—such as the

7.25 Louis Le Vau and Jules Hardouin-Mansart, Palace of Versailles, France, 1669–85.

relationships just discussed relative to Hampton Court Palace. Proportion and scale are tools with which the architect can create straightforward or deceptive relationships. We must decide how these elements are used and to what effect. In addition, proportion in many buildings is mathematical: The relationships of one part to another often are based on ratios of three to two, one to two, one to three, and so on. Discovering such relationships in a building is one of the fascinating challenges facing us whenever we encounter a work of architecture.

CONTEXT

An architectural design should take into account its context, or environment. In many cases context is essential to the statement made by the design. For example, Chartres Cathedral (Fig. **7.27**) sits at the center of and on the highest point in the town of Chartres. Its placement at that particular location had a purpose for the medieval artisans

and clerics responsible for its design. The centrality of the cathedral to the community was an essential statement of the centrality of the church in the life of the medieval community. Context also has a psychological bearing on scale. A skyscraper in the midst of skyscrapers has great mass but does not appear as massive as it would in isolation. A cathedral, alongside a skyscraper, looks relatively small in scale. However, one standing at the center of a community of small houses appears quite the opposite.

Context is also important in terms of the design of line, form, and texture relative to the physical environment. Sometimes the environment can be shaped according to the compositional qualities of the building, during or after its construction. Perhaps the best illustration of that principle is Louis XIV's palace at Versailles, whose formal symmetry is reflected in the design of thousands of acres around it.

On the other hand, a building may be designed so as to reflect the natural characteristics of its environment.

PROFILE

Frank Lloyd Wright

Frank Lloyd Wright (1867–1959) pioneered ideas in architecture far ahead of his time and became probably the most influential architect of the twentieth century. Born in Richland Center, Wisconsin, Wright grew up under strong influences of his clergyman father's love of Bach and Beethoven. He entered the University of Wisconsin at fifteen, forced to study engineering because the school had no architecture program.

In 1887 Wright took a job as a draughtsman in Chicago and, the next year, joined the firm of Adler and Sullivan. In short order Wright became Louis Sullivan's chief assistant. As Sullivan's assistant Wright handled most of the firm's designing of houses. Deep in debt, Wright moonlighted by designing for private clients on his own. When Sullivan objected, Wright left the firm to set up his own private practice.

As an independent architect, Wright led the way in a style of architecture called the Prairie school. Houses designed in this style have low-pitched roofs and strong horizontal lines reflecting the flat landscape of the American prairie. These houses also reflect Wright's philosophy that interior and exterior spaces blend together.

In 1904 Wright designed the strong, functional, Larkin Building in Buffalo, New York, and in 1906 the Unity Temple in Oak Park, Illinois. After traveling to Japan and Europe, he returned to America in 1911 to build a house on his grandfather's farm, Taliesin (Ta-lee-AY-zuhn), which is Welsh for "shining brow."

In 1916 Wright designed the Imperial Hotel in Tokyo, floating the structure on an underlying sea of mud. As a consequence, when the catastrophic earthquake of 1923 occurred, the hotel suffered very little damage.

The Great Depression of the 1930s greatly curtailed new building projects, and Wright spent his time writing and lecturing. In 1932 he established the Taliesin Fellowship, a school in which students learned by working with building materials and problems of design and construction. In winter the school moved from Wisconsin to Taliesin West, a desert camp near Phoenix, Arizona.

The mid-1930s represented a period of intense creative output for Wright, and some of his most famous designs occurred during those years. Perhaps his most dramatic project, the Kaufmann House—Fallingwater—in Bear Run, Pennsylvania (Fig. 7.26) emerged in 1936–7. Another famous project during this period was the S. C. Johnson and Son Administration Building in Racine, Wisconsin.

Two other significant buildings, among many, came later. The Solomon R. Guggenheim Museum (Fig. 7.38) began in 1942 with completion in 1957, and the Marin County Courthouse, California (Fig. 7.22), followed over the period 1957–63.

Wright's work was always controversial, and he lived a flamboyant life full of personal tragedy and financial difficulty. Married three times, he had seven children and died in Phoenix, Arizona on April 9, 1959.

Frank Lloyd Wright's Fallingwater, in Pennsylvania (Fig. 7.26), illustrates this principle. Many architects have advanced such an idea, especially in residences where large expanses of glass allow us to feel a part of the outside while we are inside. The interior decoration of such houses often takes as its theme the colors, textures, lines, and forms of the environment surrounding the home. Natural fibers, earth tones, delicate wooden furniture, pictures that reflect the surroundings, large open spaces—together they form the core of the design, selection, and placement of nearly every item in the home, from walls to furniture to silverware.

SPACE

It seems almost absurdly logical to state that architecture must concern space—for what else, by definition, is architecture? However, the world is overwhelmed with examples of architectural design that have not met that need. Design of space essentially means the design and flow of contiguous spaces relative to function. Take, for example, a sports arena. Of primary concern is the space

necessary for the sports intended to occupy the building. Will it play host to basketball, hockey, track, football, or baseball? Each of these sports places a design restriction on the architect, and curious results occur when functions not intended by the design are forced into its parameters. When the Brooklyn Dodgers moved to Los Angeles, they played for a time in the Los Angeles Coliseum, a facility designed for the Olympic Games and track and field, and reasonably suited to the addition of football. However, the imposition of baseball created ridiculous effects; the left-field fence was only slightly over 200 feet (61 m) from home plate!

In addition to the requirements of the game, a sports arena must accommodate the requirements of the spectators. Pillars that obstruct the spectator's view do not create goodwill and discourage the purchase of tickets. Likewise, attempting to put too many seats in a confined space can create severe discomfort. It is not easy to determine where to drawn the line between more seats and fan comfort. The old Montreal Forum, in which anyone over the height of 5 feet 2 inches (1.58 m) was forced to sit with their knees under their chin, was not deleterious to

7.26 Frank Lloyd Wright, Fallingwater, Bear Run, Pennsylvania, 1936–7.

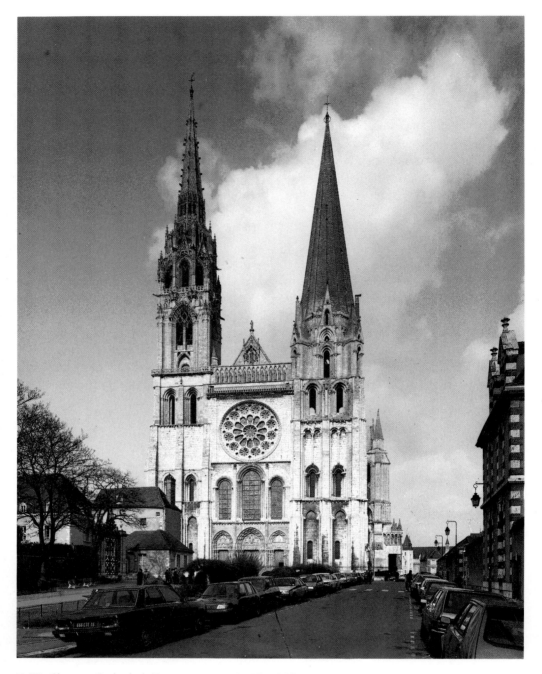

7.27 Chartres Cathedral, France, exterior, 1145–1220.

ticket sales for the Montreal Canadiens hockey team. However, such space design might be disastrous for a franchise in a less hockey-oriented city.

Finally, the design of space should take into account various needs peripheral to the primary functions of the building, such as rest rooms and concession stands.

Once functional concerns have been met, the architect can start to consider aesthetic aspects of space design. Eero Saarinen's Trans-World Airline Terminal in New York City takes the dramatic shape of flight in curved lines and carefully designed spaces, which accommodate large masses of people and channel them to and from waiting aircraft. (Such shapes can be executed only using modern construction techniques and materials such as reinforced concrete.) Flight has also been suggested by Le Corbusier's dynamic church Notre-Dame-du-Haut (nah-truh-dahm-doo-OH; Fig. **7.28**). However, this pilgrimage church appears more like a work of sculpture than a building. Here the building's function cannot be surmised from its form. Rather, the juxtaposed *rectilinear* windows

7.28 Le Corbusier, Notre-Dame-du-Haut, France, from the southeast, 1950–4.

and *curvilinear* walls and the overwhelming roof nestled lightly on thin pillars above the walls all appear as a "pure creation of the spirit."

CLIMATE

Climate has always been a factor in architectural design in zones of severe temperature, either hot or cold. As the world's energy supplies diminish, this factor will grow in importance. In the temperate climate of much of the United States, solar systems and designs that make use of the moderating influence of the earth are common. These are *passive* systems—that is, their design accommodates natural phenomena rather than adding technological devices such as solar collectors.

For example, in the colder areas of the United States an energy-efficient building can be made by creating a design with no glass, or minimal glass, on its north-facing side. Windows looking south can be covered in the summer and then uncovered to catch sunlight in midwinter, when it still provides considerable warmth.

Since temperatures at the shallow depth of 5 feet (1.6 m) below the earth's surface rarely go above or below 50°F (10°C), regardless of season, the earth presents a gold mine of potential for design. Houses built into the sides of hills or recessed below the earth's surface require much less heating or cooling than those standing fully exposed—whatever the extremes of climate. Even in zones of uniform and moderate temperature, design must consider climate. The "California lifestyle" requires design that accommodates easy access to the out-of-doors and large, open spaces with free-flowing traffic patterns.

HOW DOES IT STIMULATE THE SENSES?

As should be clear by this point, sensual response to aesthetic design is a composite experience. The individual characteristics we have discussed previously provide the stimuli for our response. Lately, color has become an especially important tool for the Postmodern architect in stimulating sense responses. The effects of color in the Piazza d'Italia (Fig. **7.29**) turn architecture into an exotic sensual experience.

CONTROLLED VISION AND SYMBOLISM

The Gothic cathedral has been described as the perfect synthesis of intellect, spirituality, and engineering. The upward, striving line of the Gothic arch makes a simple yet powerful statement of medieval people's striving to understand their earthly relation to the spiritual unknown. Even today the simplicity and grace of that design have an effect on most who view a Gothic cathedral such as Notre Dame, Paris (Fig. **7.32**).

The cathedral at Amiens (Fig. **7.33**) is similar in basic composition to Notre Dame, but rather than creating a sense of foursquare power, it gives an impression of delicacy. Amiens Cathedral illustrates a late development of Gothic style. The differences between Amiens and Notre Dame provide an important lesson in the ways design can be used to elicit a response. At Amiens, greater detail, as opposed to flat stone, focuses our attention. Both cathedrals are divided into three obvious horizontal and vertical sections of roughly the same proportion. Notre Dame

appears to rest heavily on its lowest section, whose proportions are diminished by the horizontal band of sculptures above the portals. Amiens, on the other hand, carries its portals upward to the full height of the lower section. In fact, the central portal, much larger than the central portal of Notre Dame, reinforces the line of the side portals to form a pyramid whose apex penetrates into the section above. The roughly equal size of the three portals of Notre Dame reinforces its horizontal sense, thereby giving it stability. Similarly, each use of line, form, and proportion in Amiens reinforces lightness and action, as compared with stability and strength in Notre Dame. This is not to imply that one design is better than the other. Each is valid on its own terms and simply displays a different approach.

Together with the grandeur of simple vertical line in Gothic cathedrals is an ethereal lightness which defies the material from which they were constructed. The medieval architect created in stone not the heavy yet elegant composition of the early Greeks, which focused upon treatment of stone, but rather a construction that focuses on space—the ultimate mystery. Inside the cathedrals, the stained glass high above the worshipers' heads so controls the light entering as to produce an overwhelming effect of mystery. Line, form, scale, color, structure, balance, proportion, context, and space all combine to form unified compositions that have stood for hundreds of years as symbols of the Christian experience.

7.29 Charles Moore, Piazza d'Italia, New Orleans, 1978–9.

ARCHITECTURE AND HUMAN REALITY

Le Corbusier, Villa Savoye

Art and architecture of the early twentieth century began to exhibit a simple, straightforward, and practical approach. That quality found an exponent in the Swiss painter–architect Charles-Edouard Jeanneret (1887–1965), known by his pseudonym Le Corbusier (luh kohr-boo-SYAY). Le Corbusier defined a house as "a machine for living." By that he did not mean that a house ought to be an artless, empty mechanical environment fit only for robots to inhabit. Rather, as was fairly typical of his time, he saw machines as beneficial to human needs. Le Corbusier believed that a house should be conceived, designed, and produced in the same rational manner as are tools, cars, and airplanes. He thought that traditional houses were irrational in design and frustrated the promise of the new age and the good life that machines would bring.

As a result, Le Corbusier attempted to design simple buildings whose structure and inner logic were clear and void of any surface decoration. The function of a building was to be clearly recognizable in the relation of its forms. Le Corbusier's realization of his philosophy came in the Villa Savoye, just outside Paris (Fig. **7.31**). Villa Savoye uses ferroconcrete, which exploits the possibilities offered by skeleton framing to create free and open spaces in the interior. The cube on pillars of reinforced concrete called pilotis (Fig. **7.30**) was a favorite device of Le Corbusier because it allowed space to flow under and through the building and enhanced its sense of volume. Hollowed out on three sides, Villa Savoye allows sunlight to flood the center of the building. Without load-bearing walls in the interior, free space abounds. The building has no "front" or "back" because it is open on every side. Thus it achieves Le Corbusier's objective of total interpenetration of outer and interior space.

7.30 Section of the Villa Savoye.

7.31 Le Corbusier, Villa Savoye, Poissy, France, 1928–30.

7.32 Notre Dame, Paris, west front, 1163–1250.

7.33 Amiens Cathedral, France, west front, c. 1220–59.

A totally different appeal to the emotions emerges from the ornate German Baroque Kaisersaal Residenz in Würzburg (Fig. 7.34), wherein opulence is the message conveyed by line and form, materials and color.

STYLE

The Christian experience also determines the design of Conrad & Fleishman's the Holy Family Church in Parma, Ohio (Fig. 7.35). However, despite the upward-striving power of its composition linking it with its medieval predecessors, this church has a modern clarity of line and sophistication, which perhaps speaks more of our own conception of space as less unknowable and more conquerable. The juxtaposing of straight and curved lines creates an active and dynamic response in a modern style that prompts abruptness rather than mystery. The composition is cool, and its material calls attention to itself by starkness and lack of decoration.

Each part of the church remains distinct and not quite subordinate to the totality of the design. This building perhaps represents a philosophy and style intermediate between that underlying Chartres Cathedral, whose entire design can be reduced to a single motif—the Gothic arch—and that of the Baroque, as seen in the Hall of Mirrors of the Palace of Versailles (Fig. 7.36). No single part of the design of this hall epitomizes the whole, yet each part subordinates to the whole. Ornate complexity calls for involvement and investigation and intends to overwhelm with opulence. Here, as in most art, the expression and stimuli reflect the patron. Chartres Cathedral reflects the medieval church; the Church of the

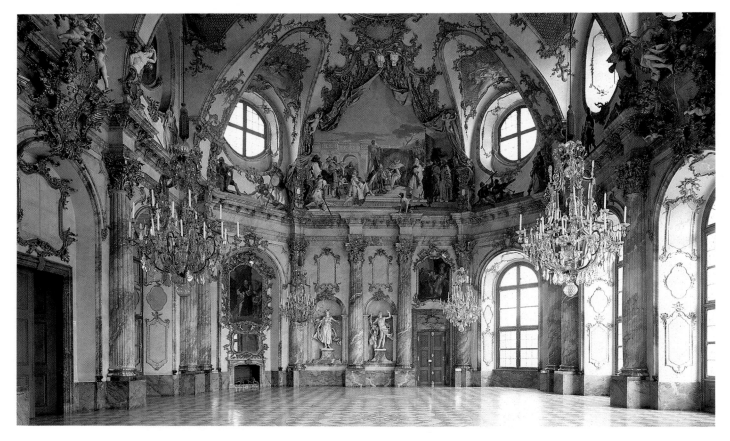

7.34 Balthasar Neumann, Kaisersaal Residenz, Würzburg, Germany, 1719–44.

7.35 Conrad & Fleishman, Holy Family Church, Parma, Ohio, 1965.

7.36 Jules Hardouin-Mansart and Charles Le Brun, Palace of Versailles, France, Hall of Mirrors, 1680.

7.37 United States Capitol Building, Washington, D.C., 1792–1856.

7.38 Frank Lloyd Wright, Guggenheim Museum, New York, 1942–59.

Holy Family, the contemporary church; and Versailles, King Louis XIV. Versailles is complex, highly active, and yet warm. The richness of its textures, the warmth of its colors, and its curvilinear softness create a certain kind of comfort despite its scale and formality.

In the United States Capitol, a Neoclassical house of government (Fig. 7.37), formality creates a foursquare, solid response. The symmetry of its design and the weight of its material give us a sense of impersonal power, heightened by the crushing weight of the dome. No longer do we see the upward-striving spiritual release of the Gothic arch, or even the powerful elegance of the Greek post-and-lintel. The Capitol Building, based on a Roman prototype, elicits a sense of struggle. This effect results from upward columnar thrust (heightened by the context provided by Capitol Hill) and downward thrust (of the dome), focused toward the interior.

APPARENT FUNCTION

The architect Louis Sullivan (of whom Frank Lloyd Wright was a pupil) is credited with the concept that form follows function. This means that the form or shape or design of any building must grow from the function the building serves. When someone looks at a building, they should recognize at the outset the purpose of that building. Sullivan here inadvertently edges against one of art's great debates: should art serve a purpose, or exist out of

its own needs exclusively? By his maxim "form follows function," Sullivan meant that purpose should be the first (but not the only) consideration in design. This principle, which also implied that beauty resides in the purity of unornamented form, was applied in a great deal of modernist design in the period following World War I (see Chapter 13).

This philosophy stood in contrast to aestheticism, an artistic movement characterized by the slogan "art for art's sake." Those who championed this cause reacted against Victorian notions that a work of art must be uplifting, educational, or otherwise socially or morally beneficial. They argued that artworks are independent and self-justifying and need no reason for being, other than the fact of being beautiful. This is the championing of form over function or purpose.

To a degree we have seen that concept in the previous examples, even though, with the exception of the Church of the Holy Family, they all precede Sullivan in time. A worthy question concerning the Guggenheim Museum in New York City (Fig. 7.38) might be how well Wright followed his teacher's philosophy. A story exists that Wright hated New York City because of unpleasant experiences he had had with the city fathers during previous projects. As a result, the Guggenheim, designed late in his life, became his final gesture of derision to the city. This center of contemporary culture and art, with its single, circular ramp from street level to roof, was built (so the story goes) from the plans for a parking garage. Be that as it may, its line and form create a simple, smoothly flowing, leisurely, upward movement juxtaposed against another stark and dynamic rectilinear form. The building's line and color and the feeling they produce make contemporary statements appropriate to the contemporary art the museum houses. Its modernity stands in contrast with the Classical proportions of the Metropolitan Museum of Art, just down the street, which houses great works of ancient and modern art. The Guggenheim expresses its interior design outwardly in the ramp, and one can argue whether its slowly curving, unbroken line reinforces the manner and pace that one should pursue when going through a museum.

DYNAMICS

Leisurely progress is not what one would imagine when confronted by the cantilevered roof of the grandstand at Zarzuela Race Track in Spain (see Fig. 7.17). Speed, power, and flight are its preeminent concerns. The sense of dynamic instability inherent in the structural form—cantilever—and this particular application of it mirror the dynamic instability and forward power of the race horse at full speed. However, despite the form and strong diagonals, this design remains controlled. The architect has created unity by repeating the track-level arcade in the arched line of the cantilevered roof. The design is dynamic and yet humanized in the softness of its curves and the control of its scale.

SCALE

Nothing symbolizes the technological achievement of modern humans more than the skyscraper. Also, nothing symbolizes the subordination of humans to their technology more than the scale of this monumental type of building (Fig. 7.39). Designed with rectangular components placed side by side, Chicago's Sears Tower is a glass and steel monolith overwhelming in its scale and proportions and cold in its materials. As a point of departure, its appeal to our senses raises the question of what comes next—the conquest of space, or a return to respect for its natural mysteries?

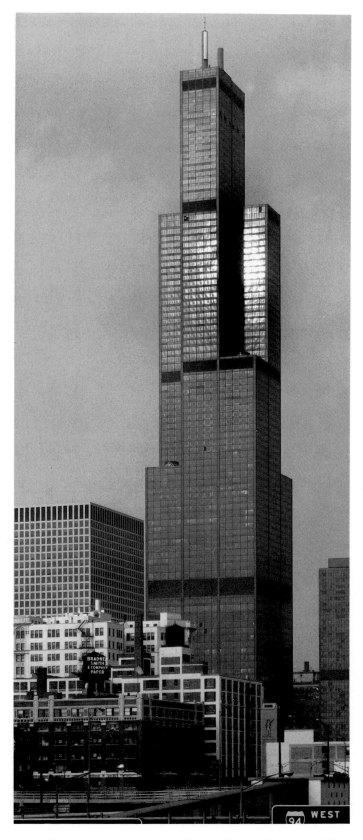

7.39 Skidmore, Owings, & Merrill, Sears Tower, Chicago, 1971.

THINKING CRITICALLY

As mentioned in the opening of this chapter, understanding terms and concepts brings experience to more confident and pleasurable levels. You can enhance your response and build a basic critical analysis of a work of architecture by using the topics in this chapter as an outline. Pick an example such as St. Paul's Cathedral (Fig. 7.14) and ask yourself how it reflects the qualities appropriate to the specific topics. Begin with the following:

- Reaction. This building was designed to create a reaction. What elements discussed in the chapter combine to create your reaction? What are your intellectual and emotional responses to the architectural work, and what causes them?

Now build a comparative analysis by choosing two or more works and detailing how they reflect specific qualities described in the chapter. For example:

- Structure. Describe the structures basic to the Monadnock Building (Fig. 7.20) and Fallingwater (Fig. 7.26). How do the elements you can see suggest how the building is supported and how do the two examples differ in the way they use their structures to form their visual appeal?

- Scale and proportion. Using the same two examples, how do the sizes of the examples relate to the human form? Describe and compare how proportion works in each example.

- Context. How does the Palace of Versailles (Fig. 7.25) explore its context? What is the environment in which the example stands?

CYBER STUDY

ARCHITECTURAL EXAMPLES INDEXED BY ARCHITECT:
—With dates and nation
http://www.artcyclopedia.com/media/Architect.html
—With cross-index of date and period
http://www.bluffton.edu/~sullivanm/index/index2.html#B

CHAPTER EIGHT

LITERATURE

WHAT IS IT?

FICTION
  Novels
  Short Stories
    Saki (H. H. Munro), "The
    Blood-feud of Toad-Water: A
    West-country Epic"
*Literature and Human Reality:
Alice Walker, "Roselilly"*
POETRY
  Narrative
    Geoffrey Chaucer, *The
    Canterbury Tales*, "The Cook's
    Prologue" and "The Cook's
    Tale"
  Dramatic
  Lyric
    William Shakespeare,
    Sonnet XIX
Profile: Toni Morrison
BIOGRAPHY
  John Wesley, *God Brought Me Safe*
ESSAY
  Informal
  Formal
    Oliver Goldsmith, "The
    Benefits of Luxury in Making a
    People More Wise and Happy"
DRAMA

HOW IS IT PUT TOGETHER?

FICTION
  Point of View

Appearance and Reality
Tone
Character
Plot
Theme
Symbols
*A Personal Journey: Franz
Kafka, "Description of a
Struggle"*
POETRY
  Language
    William Shakespeare,
    "The Seven Ages of
    Man"
    Robert Frost, "Stopping
    by Woods on a Snowy
    Evening"
  Structure
  Sound Structures
  Meter
BIOGRAPHY
  Facts
  Anecdotes

HOW DOES IT STIMULATE THE SENSES?

PICTURES
SOUNDS
EMOTIONS
Thinking Critically
Cyber Study

IMPORTANT TERMS

Fiction A work of literature created
from the author's imagination
rather than from fact.
Narrative poetry Poetry that tells a
story.
Lyric poetry A brief, subjective
work employing strong
imagination, melody, and feeling.
Point of view The perspective of a
work of fiction: first person,
epistolary, third person, stream of
consciousness.
Plot The structure of a work of
literature.
Imagery A verbal representation of a
sensory experience.
Figures The use of language to take
words beyond their literal
meaning.
Metaphors Figures of speech that
give new implications to words;
they are implied comparisons.
Meter The type and number of
rhythmic units in a line of
poetry.
Anecdotes Stories or observations
about moments in a biography.

Read any good books lately? Ever tried to write poetry? From the earliest of times, cultures have been defined by their literature, whose medium is language. Today, before there can be a movie or a soap opera, there must be a story and, usually, a script. Such things comprise literature, whose greatest characteristic is the arousal of the imagination and the emotions by means of speech and writing.

WHAT IS IT?

Traditionally literature falls into two categories: utilitarian and creative. Creative literature has a different approach than utilitarian literature. The approach determines the category—that is, creative or utilitarian—in the same sense that one picture (composed of line, form, and color) can be termed "art," whereas another picture composed of those same elements, but whose purpose is merely to provide a visual copy, can be termed "illustration." This text focuses on creative literature—literature pursuing excellence of form or expression and presenting ideas of permanent or universal interest.

People read creative literature because they expect it to hold their interest and provide pleasure—for the same reasons they watch athletic contests or go to movies. Common experience maintains that reading creative literature is good for us, but, in all honesty, we read for the immediate reward of the pleasure it provides. Some rewards of reading may lie in the future, but immediate rewards come from the experience of participating. Creative literature takes us out of ourselves while we engage in it.

This chapter, like the preceding ones, focuses on fundamentals. History comes later. It helps to know the categories of literature and how literature is put together in order to get the most out of reading and to share experiences with others using the proper descriptive terminology. As do artists in all the arts, writers utilize the formal and technical details discussed here to shape their material in order to effect responses in their readers. They choose their words very carefully to provide maximum impact. Our initial response (What is it?) to works of literature, made up of those carefully chosen words and devices, begins, as it does in the other arts, with formal divisions or genres. The formal divisions of literature are fiction, poetry, biography, essay, and drama.

FICTION

Fiction emanates from the author's imagination rather than from fact. Normally it takes one of two approaches to its subject matter: *realistic*—that is, the appearance of observable, true-to-life details; or *nonrealistic*—that is, fantasy. Fictional elements can appear in narrative poetry, drama, and even biography and epic poetry. Traditionally, however, fiction is divided into two categories, *novels* and *short stories*.

Novels

The novel is a fictional prose narrative of considerable length which has a plot that unfolds from the actions, speech, and thoughts of the characters. Normally novels treat events within the range of ordinary experience and draw upon original subject matter rather than traditional or mythic subjects. Novels typically have numerous characters and employ normal, daily speech. Their subject matter can be divided into two general categories: *sociological-panoramic*, covering a wide-ranging story of many years and various settings; and *dramatic-intimate*, which is restricted in time and setting.

Often, novels are formally classified by their subject, a few of which include:

epistolary Told through the medium of letters written by one or more of the characters, for example, Samuel Richarson, *Pamela* (1740).

Gothic Pseudo-medieval fiction with a prevailing atmosphere of mystery and terror, for example, Ann Radcliffe, *The Mysteries of Udolpho* (1794).

historical Set in a period of history and attempting to portray the spirit, manners, and social conditions of the time with realistic detail and faithfulness to historical fact, for example, Robert Graves, *I, Claudius* (1934).

manners Finely detailed observations of the customs, values, and mores of a highly developed and complex society, for example, Jane Austen, *Pride and Prejudice* (1813).

picaresque The adventures of a rogue or lowborn adventurer, for example, Thomas Nash, *The Unfortunate Traveller* (1594).

psychological Depicting the thoughts, feelings, and motivations of the characters as equal to or greater than the external action of the narrative. The internal states of the characters are influenced by and in turn trigger external events, for example, Leo Tolstoy, *War and Peace* (1864–9).

sentimental Exploiting the reader's capacity for tenderness, compassion, or sympathy to a disproportionate degree by presenting an unrealistic view of its subject, for example, once again, Samuel Richardson, *Pamela* (1740).

Short Stories

As the name implies, short stories are short prose fictional works focusing on unity of characterization, theme, and effect. In the short story "The Blood-feud of Toad-Water: A West-country Epic," the Scottish writer H. H. Munro, who wrote under the pseudonym of Saki, describes a scene of Edwardian England. He uses flippancy, wit, and invention to satirize social pretension, unkindness, and stupidity.

The Blood-feud of Toad-Water: a West-country Epic
Saki (H. H. Munro)
1870–1916

The Cricks lived at Toad-Water; and in the same lonely upland spot Fate had pitched the home of the Saunderses, and for miles around these two dwellings there was never a neighbour or a chimney or even a burying-ground to bring a sense of cheerful communion or social intercourse. Nothing but fields and spinneys and barns, lanes and waste-lands. Such was Toad-Water; and, even so, Toad-Water had its history. Thrust away in the benighted hinterland of a scattered market district, it might have been supposed that these two detached items of the Great Human Family would have leaned towards one another in a fellowship begotten of kindred circumstances and a common isolation from the outer world. And perhaps it had been so once, but the way of things had brought it otherwise. Indeed, otherwise. Fate, which had linked the two families in such unavoidable association of habitat, had ordained that the Crick household should nourish and maintain among its earthly possessions sundry head of domestic fowls, while to the Saunderses was given a disposition towards the cultivation of garden crops. Herein lay the material, ready to hand, for the coming of feud and ill-blood. For the grudge between the man of herbs and the man of live stock is no new thing; you will find traces of it in the fourth chapter of Genesis. And one sunny afternoon in late spring-time the feud came—came, as such things mostly do come, with seeming aimlessness and triviality. One of the Crick hens, in obedience to the nomadic instincts of her kind, wearied of her legitimate scratching-ground, and flew over the low wall that divided the holdings of the neighbours. And there, on the yonder side, with a hurried consciousness that her time and opportunities might be limited, the misguided bird scratched and scraped and beaked and delved in the soft yielding bed that had been prepared for the solace and well-being of a colony of seedling onions. Little showers of earth-mould and root-fibres went spraying before the hen and behind her, and every minute the area of her operations widened. The onions suffered considerably. Mrs. Saunders, sauntering at this luckless moment down the garden path, in order to fill her soul with reproaches at the iniquity of the weeds, which grew faster than she or her good man cared to remove them, stopped in mute discomfiture before the presence of a more magnificent grievance. And then, in the hour of her calamity, she turned instinctively to the Great Mother, and gathered in her capacious hands large clods of the hard brown soil that lay at her feet. With a terrible sincerity of purpose, though with a contemptible inadequacy of aim, she rained her earth bolts at the marauder, and the bursting pellets called forth a flood of cackling protest and panic from the hastily departing fowl. Calmness under misfortune is not an attribute of either hen-folk or womenkind, and while Mrs. Saunders declaimed over her onion bed such portions of the slang dictionary as are permitted by the Nonconformist conscience to be said or sung, the Vasco da Gama fowl was waking the echoes of Toad-Water with crescendo bursts of throat music which compelled attention to her griefs. Mrs. Crick had a long family, and was therefore licensed, in the eyes of her world, to have a short temper, and when some of her ubiquitous offspring had informed her, with the authority of eye-witnesses, that her neighbour had so far forgotten herself as to heave stones at her hen—her best hen, the best layer in the countryside—her thoughts clothed themselves in language "unbecoming to a Christian woman"—so at least said Mrs. Saunders, to whom most of the language was applied. Nor was she, on her part, surprised at Mrs. Crick's conduct in letting her hens stray into other body's gardens, and then abusing of them, seeing as how she remembered things against Mrs. Crick—and the latter simultaneously had recollections of lurking episodes in the past of Susan Saunders that were nothing to her credit. "Fond memory, when all things fade we fly to thee," and in the paling light of an April afternoon the two women confronted each other from their respective sides of the party wall, recalling with shuddering breath the blots and blemishes of their neighbour's family record. There was that aunt of Mrs. Crick's who had died a pauper in Exeter workhouse—every one knew that Mrs. Saunders' uncle on her mother's side drank himself to death—then there was that Bristol cousin of Mrs. Crick's! From the shrill triumph with which his name was dragged in, his crime must have been pilfering from a cathedral at least, but as both remembrancers were speaking at once it was difficult to distinguish his infamy from the scandal which beclouded the memory of Mrs. Saunders' brother's wife's mother—who may have been a regicide, and was certainly not a nice person as Mrs. Crick painted her. And then, with an air of accumulating and irresistible conviction, each belligerent informed the other that she was no lady—after which they withdrew in a great silence, feeling that nothing further remained to be said. The chaffinches clinked in the apple trees and the bees droned round the berberis bushes, and the waning sunlight slanted pleasantly across the garden plots, but between the neighbour households had sprung up a barrier of hate, permeating and permanent. The male heads of the families were necessarily ♦ drawn into the

LITERATURE AND HUMAN REALITY

Alice Walker, "Roselilly"

Wit and irony are tools used by the black American author Alice Walker (Fig. 8.1) in her novels, poetry, and critical writings. The battles she fights are for rights for blacks and women. However, she is prone to satirize political activists just as much as their opponents. Her life and writing reflect the tensions and ideals of a "womanist"—a word she has coined for a black feminist. The "twin afflictions" of the civil rights and black power movements and the women's movement are the focus of her work.

Walker came from a family of Georgia sharecroppers and was one of eight children. Because a childhood accident left her blind in one eye, she was able to attend Spelman College, a prestigious black women's college in Atlanta, on a state rehabilitation scholarship. She continued her education at Sarah Lawrence in New York and graduated in 1965. Her identity as a black and a woman was challenged by an unwanted pregnancy, an abortion, and a trip to South Africa. She returned to the South and married a Jewish civil rights leader, from whom she was divorced in 1976.

Her short stories indicate a preoccupation with "the oppressions, the insanities, the loyalties, and the triumphs of black women." Her technique is subtle and experimental, and we can see some of that in the way that she weaves together the ritual of the marriage ceremony and the thoughts of her female character in "Roselilly" as a counterpoint to her theme of the distance between promise and fulfillment.

Roselilly
Alice Walker
(b. 1944)

Dearly Beloved.
She dreams; dragging herself across the world. A small girl in her mother's white robe and veil, knee raised waist high through a bowl of quicksand soup. The man who stands beside her is against this standing on the front porch of her house, being married to the sound of cars whizzing by on highway 61.

We are gathered here
Like cotton to be weighed. Her fingers at the last minute busily removing dry leaves and twigs. Aware it is a superficial sweep. She knows he blames Mississippi for the respectful way the men turn their heads up in the yard, the women stand waiting and knowledgeable, their children held from mischief by teachings from the wrong God. He glares beyond them to the occupants of the cars, white faces glued to promises beyond a country wedding, noses thrust forward like dogs on a track. For him they usurp the wedding.

in the sight of God
Yes, open house. That is what country black folks like. She dreams she does not already have three children. A squeeze around the flowers in her hands chokes off three and four and five years of breath. Instantly she is ashamed and frightened in her superstition. She looks for the first time at the preacher, forces humility into her eyes, as if she believes he is, in fact, a man of God. She can imagine God, a small black boy, timidly pulling the preacher's coattail.

to join this man and this woman
She thinks of ropes, chains, handcuffs, his religion. His place of worship. Where she will be required to sit apart with covered head. In Chicago, a word she hears when thinking of smoke, from his description of what a cinder was, which they never had in Panther Burn. She sees hovering over the heads of the clean neighbors in her front yard black specks falling, clinging from the sky. But in Chicago. Respect, a chance to build. Her children at last from underneath the detrimental wheel. A chance to be on top. What a relief, she thinks. What a vision, a view, from up so high.

in holy matrimony
Her fourth child she gave away to the child's father who had some money. Certainly a good job. Had gone to Harvard. Was a good man but weak because good language meant so much to him he could not live with Roselilly. Could not abide TV in the living room, five beds in three rooms, no Bach except from four to six on Sunday afternoons. No chess at all. She does not forget to worry about her son among

8.1 Alice Walker reading excerpts from her Pulitzer Prizewinning novel *The Color Purple* in 1985.

his father's people. She wonders if the New England climate will agree with him. If he will ever come down to Mississippi, as his father did, to try to right the country's wrongs. She wonders if he will be stronger than his father. His father cried off and on throughout her pregnancy. Went to skin and bones. Suffered nightmares, retching and falling out of bed. Tried to kill himself. Later told his wife he found the right baby through friends. Vouched for, the sterling qualities that would make up his character.

It is not her nature to blame. Still, she is not entirely thankful. She supposes New England, the North, to be quite different from what she knows. It seems right somehow to her that people who move there to live return home completely changed. She thinks of the air, the smoke, the cinders. Imagines cinders big as hailstones; heavy, weighing on the people. Wonders how this pressure finds its way into the veins, roping the springs of laughter.

If there's anybody here that knows a reason why

But of course they know no reason why beyond what they daily have to know. She thinks of the man who will be her husband, feels shut away from him because of the stiff severity of his plain black suit. His religion. A lifetime of black and white. Of veils. Covered head. It is as if her children are already gone from her. Not dead, but exalted on a pedestal, a stalk that has no roots. She wonders how to make new roots. It is beyond her. She wonders what one does with memories in a brand-new life. This had seemed easy, until she thought of it. "The reasons why ... the people who" ... she thinks, and does not wonder where the thought is from.

these two should not be joined

She thinks of her mother, who is dead. Dead, but still her mother. Joined. This is confusing. Of her father. A gray old man who sold wild mink, rabbit, fox skins to Sears, Roebuck. He stands in the yard, like a man waiting for a train. Her young sisters stand behind her in smooth green dresses, with flowers in their hands and hair. They giggle, she feels, at the absurdity of the wedding. They are ready for something new. She thinks the man beside her should marry one of them. She feels old. Yoked. An arm seems to reach out from behind her and snatch her backward. She thinks of cemeteries and the long sleep of grandparents mingling in the dirt. She believes that she believes in ghosts. In the soil giving back what it takes.

together

In the city. He sees her in a new way. This she knows, and is grateful. But is it enough? She cannot always be a bride and virgin, wearing robes and veil. Even now her body itches to be free of satin and voile, organdy and lily of the valley. Memories crash against her. Memories of being bare to the sun. She wonders what it will be like. Not to have to go to a job. Not to work in a sewing plant. Not to worry about learning to sew straight seams in working-men's overalls, jeans, and dress pants. Her place will be in the home, he has said, repeatedly, promising her rest she had prayed for. But now she wonders. When she is rested, what will she do? They will make babies—she thinks practically about her fine brown body, his strong black one. They will be inevitable. Her hands will be full. Full of what? Babies. She is not comforted.

let him speak

She wishes she had asked him to explain more of what he meant. But she was impatient. Impatient to be done with sewing. With doing everything for three children, alone. Impatient to leave the girls she had known since childhood, their children growing up, their husbands hanging around her, already old, seedy. Nothing about them that she wanted, or needed. The fathers of her children driving by, waiving, not waving; reminders of times she would just as soon forget. Impatient to see the South Side, where they would live and build and be respectable and respected and free. Her husband would free her. A romantic hush. Proposal. Promises. A new life! Respectable, reclaimed, renewed. Free! In robe and veil.

or forever hold

She does not even know if she loves him. She loves his sobriety. His refusal to sing just because he knows the tune. She loves his pride. His blackness and his gray car. She loves his understanding of her *condition*. She thinks she loves the effort he will make to redo her into what he truly wants. His love of her makes her completely conscious of how unloved she was before. This is something; though it makes her unbearably sad. Melancholy. She blinks her eyes. Remembers she is finally being married, like other girls. Like other girls, women? Something strains upward behind her eyes. She thinks of the something as a rat trapped, cornered, scurrying to and fro in her head, peering through the windows of her eyes. She wants to live for once. But doesn't know quite what that means. Wonders if she has ever done it. If she ever will. The preacher is odious to her. She wants to strike him out of the way, out of her light, with the back of her hand. It seems to her he has always been standing in front of her, barring her way.

his peace

The rest she does not hear. She feels a kiss, passionate, rousing, within the general pandemonium. Cars drive up blowing their horns. Firecrackers go off. Dogs come from under the house and begin to yelp and bark. Her husband's hand is like the clasp of an iron gate. People congratulate. Her children press against her. They look with awe and distaste mixed with hope at their new father. He stands curiously apart, in spite of the people crowding about to grasp his free hand. He smiles at them all but his eyes are as if turned inward. He knows they cannot understand that he is not a Christian. He will not explain himself. He feels different, he looks it. The old women thought he was like one of their sons except that he had somehow got away from them. Still a son, not a son. Changed.

She thinks how it will be later in the night in the silvery gray car. How they will spin through the darkness of Mississippi and in the morning be in Chicago, Illinois. She thinks of Lincoln, the president. That is all she knows about the place. She feels ignorant, *wrong*, backward. She presses her worried fingers into his palm. He is standing in front of her. In the crush of well-wishing people, he does not look back.[1]

quarrel, and the children on either side were forbidden to have anything to do with the unhallowed offspring of the other party. As they had to travel a good three miles along the same road to school every day, this was awkward, but such things have to be. Thus all communication between the households was sundered. Except the cats. Much as Mrs. Saunders might deplore it, rumour persistently pointed to the Crick he-cat as the presumable father of sundry kittens of which the Saunders she-cat was indisputably the mother. Mrs. Saunders drowned the kittens, but the disgrace remained. Summer succeeded spring, and winter summer, but the feud outlasted the waning seasons. Once, indeed, it seemed as though the healing influences of religion might restore to Toad-Water its erstwhile peace; the hostile families found themselves side by side in the soul-kindling atmosphere of a Revival Tea, where hymns were blended with a beverage that came of tea-leaves and hot water and took after the latter parent, and where ghostly counsel was tempered by garnishings of solidly fashioned buns—and here, wrought up by the environment of festive piety, Mrs. Saunders so far unbent as to remark guardedly to Mrs. Crick that the evening had been a fine one. Mrs. Crick, under the influence of her ninth cup of tea and her fourth hymn, ventured on the hope that it might continue fine, but a maladroit allusion on the part of the Saunders good man to the backwardness of garden crops brought the Feud stalking forth from its

corner with all its old bitterness. Mrs. Saunders joined heartily in the singing of the final hymn, which told of peace and joy and archangels and golden glories; but her thoughts were dwelling on the pauper aunt of Exeter. Years have rolled away, and some of the actors in this wayside drama have passed into the Unknown; other onions have arisen, have flourished, have gone their way, and the offending hen has long since expiated her misdeeds and lain with trussed feet and a look of ineffable peace under the arched roof of Barnstaple market. But the Blood-feud of Toad-Water survives to this day.[2]

POETRY

Poetry is designed to convey a vivid and imaginative sense of experience. It uses condensed language selected for its sound, suggestive power, and meaning, and employs specific technical devices such as meter, rhyme, and metaphor. Poetry can be divided into three major types: *narrative, dramatic*, and *lyric*.

Narrative

Narrative poetry tells a story. *Epic* poetry is narrative poetry of substantial length and elevated style. It uses strong symbolism, and has a central figure of heroic proportions. A *ballad* is a sung or recited narrative, and a *metrical romance* is a long narrative, romantic tale in verse. Chaucer's *The Canterbury Tales* illustrate narrative poetry.

The Canterbury Tales
Geoffrey Chaucer
c. 1340–1400

THE COOK'S PROLOGUE

The cook from London, while the reeve yet spoke,
Patted his back with pleasure at the joke.
"Ha, ha!" laughed he, "by Christ's great suffering,
This miller had a mighty sharp ending
Upon his argument of harbourage!
For well says Solomon, in his language,
'Bring thou not every man into thine house';
For harbouring by night is dangerous.
Well ought a man to know the man that he
Has brought into his own security.
I pray God give me sorrow and much care
If ever, since I have been Hodge of Ware,
Heard I of miller better brought to mark.
A wicked jest was played him in the dark.
But God forbid that we should leave off here;
And therefore, if you'll lend me now an ear,
From what I know, who am but a poor man,
I will relate, as well as ever I can,
A little trick was played in our city."
    Our host replied: "I grant it readily.
Now tell on, Roger; see that it be good;
For many a pasty have you robbed of blood,
And many a Jack of Dover have you sold
That has been heated twice and twice grown cold.
From many a pilgrim have you had Christ's curse,
For of your parsley they yet fare the worse,
Which they have eaten with your stubble goose;
For in your shop full many a fly is loose.
Now tell on, gentle Roger, by your name.
But yet, I pray, don't mind if I make game,
A man may tell the truth when it's in play."
    "You say the truth," quoth Roger, "by my fay!
But 'true jest, bad jest' as the Fleming saith.
    And therefore, Harry Bailey, on your faith,
Be you not angry ere we finish here,
If my tale should concern an inn-keeper.
Nevertheless, I'll tell not that one yet.
But ere we part your jokes will I upset."
    And thereon did he laugh, in great good cheer,
And told his tale, as you shall straightway hear.

Thus ends the prologue of the cook's tale

THE COOK'S TALE

There lived a 'prentice, once, in our city,
And of the craft of victuallers was he;
Happy he was as goldfinch in the glade,
Brown as a berry, short, and thickly made,
With black hair that he combed right prettily.
He could dance well, and that so jollily,
That he was nicknamed Perkin Reveller.
He was as full of love, I may aver,
As is a beehive full of honey sweet;
Well for the wench that with him chanced to meet.
At every bridal would he sing and hop,
Loving the tavern better than the shop.
    When there was any festival in Cheap,
Out of the shop and thither would he leap,
And, till the whole procession he had seen,
And danced his fill, he'd not return again.
He gathered many fellows of his sort
To dance and sing and make all kinds of sport.
And they would have appointments for to meet
And play at dice in such, or such, a street.
For in the whole town was no apprentice
Who better knew the way to throw the dice
Than Perkin; and therefore he was right free
With money, when in chosen company.
His master found this out in business there;
For often-times he found the till was bare.
For certainly a revelling bond-boy
Who loves dice, wine, dancing, and girls of joy—
His master, in his shop, shall feel the effect,
Though no part have he in this said respect;
For theft and riot always comrades are,
And each alike he played on gay guitar.
Revels and truth, in one of low degree,
Do battle always, as all men may see.
    This 'prentice shared his master's fair abode
Till he was nigh out of his 'prenticehood,
Though he was checked and scolded early and late
And sometimes led, for drinking, to Newgate;
But at the last his master did take thought,
Upon a day, when he his ledger sought,
On an old proverb wherein is found this word:
"Better take rotten apple from the hoard
Than let it lie to spoil the good ones there."
So with a drunken servant should it fare;
It is less ill to let him go, apace,
Than ruin all the others in the place.
Therefore he freed and cast him loose to go
His own road unto future care and woe;
And thus this jolly 'prentice had his leave.
Now let him riot all night long, or thieve.
    But since there's never thief without a buck
To help him waste his money and to suck
All he can steal or borrow by the way,
Anon he sent his bed and his array

To one he knew, a fellow of his sort,
Who loved the dice and revels and all sport,
And had a wife that kept, for countenance,
A shop, and whored to gain her sustenance.

Of this cook's tale Chaucer made no more.[3]

Dramatic

Dramatic poetry utilizes dramatic form or technique. It is, typically, a portrayal of life or character or the telling of a story usually involving conflicts and emotions through action and dialogue (drama can also utilize prose). The major form of dramatic poetry is the dramatic monologue, which is a poem written in the form of a speech of an individual character to an imaginary audience. It develops a narrative sense of the speaker's history and psychological insights into his or her character in a single vivid scene. Perhaps its greatest practitioner is Robert Browning in such poems as "My Last Duchess" (http://eserver.org/poetry/dramatic-romances.txt; scroll through the examples until you reach "My Last Duchess").

Lyric

Lyric poetry was originally intended to be sung and accompanied by a lyre. It is a brief, subjective work employing strong imagination, melody, and feeling to create a single, unified, and intense impression of the personal emotion of the poet. The most finished form of lyric poetry is the sonnet, which has two principal types: Petrarchan (Italian) and Shakespearean (English).

Sonnet XIX
William Shakespeare
1564–1616

Devouring Time, blunt thou the lion's paws,
And make the earth devour her own sweet brood;
Pluck the keen teeth from the fierce tiger's jaws,
And burn the long-lived phoenix in her blood;
Make glad and sorry seasons as thou fleets,
And do whate'er thou wilt, swift-footed Time,
To the wide world and all her fading sweets;
But I forbid thee one most heinous crime:
O, carve not with thy hours my love's fair brow,
Nor draw no lines there with thine antique pen;
Him in thy course untainted do allow
For beauty's pattern to succeeding men.
Yet, do thy worst, old Time: despite thy wrong,
My love shall in my verse ever live young.[4]

BIOGRAPHY

Biography is a written account of a person's life. Over the centuries it has taken many forms and witnessed many techniques and intentions, including literary narratives, catalogues of achievement, and psychological portraits. Accounts of the lives of saints and other religious figures are called *hagiographies*. John Wesley (1703–91), the Anglican clergyman who founded the Methodist Church, provides a sample of the elements of biography in *God Brought Me Safe*.

God Brought Me Safe
John Wesley
1703–91

[Oct. 1743]

Thur. 20.—After preaching to a small, attentive congregation, I rode to Wednesbury. At twelve I preached in a ground near the middle of the town to a far larger congregation than was expected, on "Jesus Christ, the same yesterday, and to-day, and for ever." I believe every one present felt the power of God; and no creature offered to molest us, either going or coming; but the Lord fought for us, and we held our peace.

I was writing at Francis Ward's in the afternoon when the cry arose that the mob had beset the house. We prayed that God would disperse them, and it was so. One went this way, and another that; so that, in half an hour, not a man was left. I told our brethren, "Now is the time for us to go"; but they pressed me exceedingly to stay; so, that I might not offend them, I sat down, though I foresaw what would follow. Before five the mob surrounded the house again in greater numbers than ever. The cry of one and all was, "Bring out the minister; we will have the minister." I desired one to take their captain by the hand and bring him into the house. After a few sentences interchanged between us the lion became a lamb. I desired him to go and bring one or two more of the most angry of his companions. He brought in two, who were ready to swallow the ground with rage; but in two minutes they were as calm as he. I then bade them make way, that I might go out among the people. As soon as I was in the midst of them I called for a chair, and, standing up, asked, "What do any of you want with me?" Some said, "We want you to go with us to the Justice." I replied, "That I will with all my heart." I then spoke a few words, which God applied; so that they cried out with might and main, "The gentleman is an honest gentleman, and we will spill our blood in his defence." I asked, "Shall we go to the Justice to-night, or in the morning?" Most of them cried, "To-night, to-night"; on which I went before, and two or three hundred followed, the rest returning whence them came.

Toni Morrison

Toni Morrison (b. 1931) was born in Lorain, Ohio, as Chloe Anthony Wofford. She was the second of four children of George Wofford, a shipyard welder, and Ramah Willis Wofford. Her parents moved to Ohio from the South to escape racism and to find better opportunities in the North. At home, Chloe heard many songs and tales of Southern black folklore. The Woffords were proud of their heritage. Lorain was a small industrial town populated with immigrant Europeans, Mexicans, and Southern blacks who lived next to each other. Chloe attended an integrated school. In her first grade, she was the only black student in her class and the only child who could read. She was friends with many of her white schoolmates and did not encounter discrimination until she started dating. In college at Howard University in Washington, D.C., she majored in English, and because many people couldn't pronounce her first name correctly, she changed it to Toni, a shortened version of her middle name.

Later she taught at Howard, where she joined a small writers' group as refuge from an unhappy marriage to a Jamaican architect, Harold Morrison. Today Ms Morrison is one of America's most celebrated authors. Her six major novels, *The Bluest Eye* (1969), *Sula* (1973), *Song of Solomon* (1977), *Tar Baby* (1981), *Beloved* (1987), and *Jazz* (1992), have received extensive national acclaim. She received the National Book Critics Circle Award in 1977 for *Song of Solomon* and the 1988 Pulitzer Prize for *Beloved*. In 1993 Morrison was awarded the Nobel Prize for literature. She is an editor at Random House and a visiting lecturer at Yale University.

She is noted for her spare but poetic language, emotional intensity, and sensitive observation of African American life. Her novel *Jazz* is meant to follow *Beloved* as the second volume of a projected trilogy, although *Jazz* doesn't extend the story told in *Beloved* in a conventional way. The characters are new, and so is the location. Even the narrative approach is different. In terms of chronology, however, *Jazz* begins roughly where *Beloved* ended and continues the greater story. Morrison wishes to tell of her people passing through their American experience, from the days of slavery in the 1900s to the present. The individuals struggle to establish and sustain a personal identity without abandoning their own history, while individual and community interests clash. *Jazz* reads like a blues ballad from the musical age it suggests.

The night came on before we had walked a mile, together with heavy rain. However, on we went to Bentley Hall, two miles from Wednesbury. One or two ran before to tell Mr. Lane they had brought Mr. Wesley before his Worship. Mr Lane replied, "What have I to do with Mr. Wesley? Go and carry him back again." By this time the main body came up, and began knocking at the door. A servant told them Mr. Lane was in bed. His son followed, and asked what was the matter. One replied, "Why an't please you, they sing psalms all day; nay, and make folks rise at five in the morning. And what would your Worship advise us to do?" "To go home," said Mr Lane, "and be quiet."

Here they were at a full stop, till one advised to go to Justice Persehouse at Walsall. All agreed to do this; so we hastened on, and about seven came to his house. But Mr. P. likewise sent word that he was in bed. Now they were at a stand again; but at last they all thought it the wisest course to make the best of their way home. About fifty of them undertook to convoy me. But we had not gone a hundred yards when the mob of Walsall came, pouring in like a

flood, and bore down all before them. The Darlaston mob made what defense they could; but they were weary, as well as outnumbered; so that in a short time, many being knocked down, the rest ran away, and left me in their hands.

To attempt speaking was vain, for the noise on every side was like the roaring of the sea. So they dragged me along till we came to the town, where, seeing the door of a large house open, I attempted to go in; but a man, catching me by the hair, pulled me back into the middle of the mob. They made no more stop till they had carried me through the main street, from one end of the town to the other. I continued speaking all the time to those within hearing, feeling no pain or weariness. At the west end of the town, seeing a door half open, I made toward it, and would have gone in, but a gentleman in the shop would not suffer me, saying they would pull the house down to the ground. However, I stood at the door and asked, "Are you willing to hear me speak?" Many cried out, "No, no, knock his brains out; down with him; kill him at once." Others said, "Nay, but we will hear him first." I began asking, "What evil have I done? Which of you all have I wronged in word or deed?"

and continued speaking for above a quarter of an hour, till my voice suddenly failed. Then the floods began to lift up their voice again, many crying out, "Bring him away! Bring him away!"

In the meantime my strength and my voice returned, and I broke out aloud into prayer. And now the man who had just before headed the mob turned and said, "Sir, I will spend my life for you: follow me, and not one soul here shall touch a hair of your head." Two or three of his fellows confirmed his words, and got close to me immediately. At the same time, the gentleman in the shop cried out, "For shame, for shame! Let him go." An honest butcher, who was a little farther off, said it was a shame they should do thus; and pulled back four or five, one after another, who were running on the most fiercely. The people then, as if it had been by common consent, fell to the right and left; while those three or four men took me between them, and carried me through them all. But on the bridge the mob rallied again: we therefore went on one side over the mill-dam, and thence through the meadows, till, a little before ten, God brought me safe to Wednesbury, having lost only one flap of my waistcoat and a little skin from one of my hands.[5]

ESSAY

The essay is a non-fictional literary composition on a single subject, usually presenting the personal views of the author. The word comes from the French, meaning "to try" and the vulgar Latin, meaning "to weigh." Essays include many subforms and a variety of styles, but they are characteristically marked by clarity, grace, good humor, wit, urbanity, and tolerance. For the most part, essays are brief, but occasionally they are much longer works, such as *The Federalist Papers* by Alexander Hamilton, John Jay, and James Madison (1787). Traditionally, essays fall into two categories: *informal* or *formal*.

Informal

Informal essays tend to be brief, conversational in tone, and loose in structure. They can be categorized as *familiar* (or *personal*) and *character*. The personal essay presents an aspect of the author's personality as he or she reacts to an event. Character essays describe individuals, isolating their dominant traits, for example.

Formal

Formal essays are longer and more tightly structured than informal ones. They tend to focus on impersonal subjects and place less emphasis on the personality of the author. Oliver Goldsmith provides an example.

The Benefits of Luxury, in Making a People More Wise and Happy
Oliver Goldsmith
1730?–74

From such a picture of nature in primeval simplicity, tell me, my much respected friend, are you in love with fatigue and solitude? Do you sigh for the severe frugality of the wandering Tartar, or regret being born amidst the luxury and dissimulation of the polite? Rather tell me, has not every kind of life vices peculiarly its own? Is it not a truth, that refined countries have more vices, but those not so terrible; barbarous nations few, and they of the most hideous complexion? Perfidy and fraud are the vices of civilized nations, credulity and violence those of the inhabitants of the desert. Does the luxury of the one produce half the evils of the inhumanity of the other? Certainly those philosophers who declaim against luxury have but little understood its benefits; they seem insensible, that to luxury we owe not only the greatest part of our knowledge, but even of our virtues.

It may sound fine in the mouth of a declaimer, when he talks of subduing our appetites, of teaching every sense to be content with a bare sufficiency, and of supplying only the wants of nature; but is there not more satisfaction in indulging those appetites, if with innocence and safety, than in restraining them? Am not I better pleased in enjoyment than in the sullen satisfaction of thinking that I can live without enjoyment? The more various our artificial necessities, the wider is our circle of pleasure; for all pleasure consists in obviating necessities as they rise; luxury, therefore, as it increases our wants, increases our capacity for happiness.

Examine the history of any country remarkable for opulence and wisdom, you will find they would never have been wise had they not been first luxurious; you will find poets, philosophers, and even patriots, marching in luxury's train. The reason is obvious: We then only are curious after knowledge, when we find it connected with sensual happiness. The senses ever point out the way, and reflection comments upon the discovery. Inform a native of the desert of Kobi, of the exact measure of the parallax of the moon, he finds no satisfaction at all in the information; he wonders how any could take such pains, and lay out such treasures, in order to solve so useless a difficulty: but connect it with his happiness, by showing that it improves navigation, that by such an investigation he may have a warmer coat, a better gun, or a finer knife, and he is instantly in raptures at so great an improvement. In short, we only desire to know what we desire to possess; and whatever we may talk against it, luxury adds the spur to curiosity, and gives us a desire to becoming more wise.

But not our knowledge only, but our virtues are improved by luxury. Observe the brown savage of Thibet, to whom the fruits of the spreading pomegranate supply food, and its branches are habitation. Such a character has few vices, I grant, but those he has are of the most hideous nature; rapine and cruelty are scarcely crimes in his eye; neither pity nor tenderness, which ennoble every virtue, have any place in his heart; he hates his enemies, and kills those he subdues. On the other hand, the polite Chinese and civilized European seem even to love their enemies. I have just now seen an instance where the English have succoured those enemies, whom their own countrymen actually refused to relieve.

The greater the luxuries of every country, the more closely, politically speaking, is that country united. Luxury is the child of society alone; the luxurious man stands in need of a thousand different artists to furnish out his happiness; it is more likely, therefore, that he should be a good citizen who is connected by motives of self-interest with so many, than the abstemious man who is united to none.

In whatsoever light, therefore, we consider luxury, whether as employing a number of hands naturally too feeble for more laborious employment; as finding a variety of occupation for others who might be totally idle; or as furnishing out new inlets to happiness, without encroaching on mutual property; in whatever light we regard it, we shall have reason to stand up in its defence, and the sentiment of Confucius still remains unshaken: *that we should enjoy as many of the luxuries of life as are consistent with our own safety, and the prosperity of others; and that he who finds out a new pleasure is one of the most useful members of society.*[6]

DRAMA

Drama is the written script, or play, upon which a theatre performance may be based (see Chapter 4).

HOW IS IT PUT TOGETHER?

FICTION

Point of View

Fiction is a story told by someone at a particular time and place to a particular audience. So it has a definite perspective, and, therefore, certain limitations of objectivity. It raises questions about the right way of seeing things. The "point of view" is a device to objectify the circumstances. Four types of narrative point of view are (1) *first person*; (2) *epistolary*—that is, told through the use of

letters written by the characters; (3) *omniscient narration* or "third person"; and (4) *stream of consciousness* or "interior monologue"—a flow of thoughts, feelings, and memories coming from a specific character's psyche. These arbitrary definitions may vary, or may be combined by authors to suit their own purposes. Point of view, as we have discussed it here, means merely that one of the means by which fiction is put together is usable by an author in several ways, at several levels, to communicate meaning.

Appearance and Reality

Fiction claims to be true to actuality, but it is built on invented sequences of events. It refers back on itself, layering the fictional and the factual.

Tone

Tone may also be known as the atmosphere of the story. In essence, it is the author's attitude toward the story's literal facts. Reading is much like listening to conversation. That is, the words carry meaning, but the way in which they are said—their tone—shapes meaning much more than we realize. In addition, the atmosphere of the story sometimes includes the setting or the physical environment. In many stories, atmosphere is psychological as well as physical, and when all of these characteristics of tone are taken together, they provide subtle and powerful suggestions leading to fuller understanding of the work.

Character

Literature appeals through its people, but not just people alone. It draws our interest because we see a human character struggling with some important problem. Authors write to that potential interest and usually strive to focus our attention, and to achieve unity, by drawing a central character with whose actions, decisions, growth, and development we can identify, and in whom we can find an indication of some broader aspect of the human condition. As we noted in Chapter 4, the term character goes beyond the mere identification of a "person." Character means the psychological spine of individuals, the driving force that makes them respond the way they do when faced with a given set of circumstances. Character is what we are interested in: Given a set of troubling or challenging circumstances, what does the character of the individual lead him or her to do?

In developing character, an author has numerous choices, depending, again, on purpose. Character may be fully three-dimensional and highly individual—that is, as

A Personal Journey

FRANZ KAFKA, "DESCRIPTION OF A STRUGGLE"

Two very late middle-aged, otherwise cautious adults have squeezed through a hole in a wooden fence atop a precipice over the Vltava river in Prague, Czech Republic. Sliding downward on the loose rocks, they nervously inch their way for a good view of a ruin called Libusa's Bath, jutting out of the cliff. This bizarre, heart-pounding behavior came in the name of research. My wife was preparing a story about Libuše, a legendary, medieval Czech queen. The adventure seemed to me—a willing participant, if not instigator of the climbing—as I grabbed an outcrop on my way back to the top and to safety, absolutely and appropriately *kafkaesque*.

"Kafkaesque" means of, relating to, or suggestive of Franz Kafka or his writings—having, especially, a nightmarishly complex, bizarre, or illogical quality. Thus, our outlandish behavior over Libusa's Bath reminded me that Franz Kafka (1883–1924) lived and wrote on the top of another of Prague's hills, in a little house tucked into the wall of Prague Castle. Kafka had his roots in the soil of Prague. The mystical magic of Old Prague and the mixture of its people charmed Kafka's poetic soul. His short story "Description of a Struggle," written when he was twenty, utilizes real places in Prague. It is the twisted tale of a young man who is beset by a stranger at a party, and who ends up walking the late-night streets of Prague with this stranger. As he does so, he imagines all kinds of bizarre relationships developing between himself and the stranger, including his own murder by the stranger. At first, he can't understand why he left the party in his new acquaintance's company—even though it was his own suggestion. He puzzles over the man's mood and behavior: "I realized that my acquaintance had begun to hum a melody from the *Dollar Princess*. It was low, but I could hear it distinctly. What did this mean? Was he trying to insult me?" The imaginings emerge in a characteristically "kafkaesque" exploration of the anxieties and alienation of twentieth-century humankind which was so typical of Kafka's writings. "Obviously, this is the time for the murder. I'll stay with him and slowly he'll draw the dagger—the handle of which he is already holding in his pocket—along his coat, and then plunge it into me. It's unlikely that he'll be surprised at the simplicity of it all—yet maybe he will, who knows? I won't scream, I'll just stare at him as long as my eyes can stand it."

The cold of the late night of the story takes the two companions to Charles Bridge, Prague's famous landmark. And that was where I found myself on a pleasant spring afternoon, having safely ascended the cliff above Libusa's Bath, escaped Vyšehrad Park without arrest, and taken a quick subway ride to Staré Mesto (Old Town). To reach Kafka's house, one must either climb up from below Prague Castle or take the tram to Hradcany and walk down. Preferring the ease of the latter, I entered the castle by the front series of gates and found my way around St. Vitus Cathedral to the street of small houses called the Golden Lane, where, in number 22, Kafka lived and wrote. The cramped little house reminds me of Kafka's story and the strange acts we humans often commit upon ourselves.

complex as the restrictions of the medium allow. Novels, because of their length and the fact that the reader can go back to double-check a fact or description, allow much more complex character development or individuality than do plays, whose important points must be found by the audience the moment they are presented. Also, a change of narrative viewpoint, appropriate to a novel but not to a play (unless a narrator is used, as in *Our Town*), can give the reader aspects of character in a more efficient manner than can revelation through action or dialogue.

On the other hand, the author's purpose may be served by presenting character not as a fully developed individual but as a type. Occasionally, however, two-dimensionality of character development reveals a qualitative lack in the writer. Whatever the author's choice, the nature of character development tells much about the meaning of the work.

Plot

Plot is the structure of the work. It is more than the story line or the facts of the piece. In literature, as in the theatre, we find our interest dependent upon action. The action of a literary work is designed to dramatize a fully realized theme, situation, or character. Plot is the structure of that action. It creates unity in the work and thereby helps us to find meaning. Plot is the skeleton that determines the ultimate shape of the piece, once the elements of flesh have been added to it.

Plot may be the major or a subordinate focus in a work, and it can be open or closed. Closed plots rely on the Aristotelian model of pyramidal action with an exposition, a complication, and a resolution or dénouement. An open plot has little or no resolution. We merely leave the characters at a convenient point and imagine them continuing as their personalities will dictate.

Theme

Most good stories have an overriding idea or theme by which the other elements are shaped. Quality in works of art rests at least partly on artists' ability to utilize the tools of their medium, as well as on whether they have something worthwhile to say. Some critics argue that the quality of a theme is less important than what the author does with it. Yet the conclusion is inescapable: The best artworks are those in which the author has taken a meaningful theme and developed it exceptionally. The theme or idea of a work is thus what the author has to say. Theme may mean a definite intellectual concept, or it may indicate a highly complex situation. Clues to understanding the idea can come as early as our exposure to the title. Beyond that, the theme is usually revealed in small pieces as we move from beginning to conclusion.

Symbols

As we discussed in the Introduction, symbols stand for or suggest something else by reason of relationship, association, convention, or accidental resemblance. They are often a visible sign of something invisible (for example, the lion is a symbol of courage and the cross is a symbol of Christianity). In this sense, all words can be called symbols. The symbols used in literature are often private or personal in that their significance is only evident in the context of the work in which they appear. For example, the optician's trade sign of a huge pair of spectacles in F. Scott Fitzgerald's *The Great Gatsby* (1925) is a piece of scenic detail, but it can also be understood as a symbol of divine nearsightedness. A symbol can have more than one meaning. It can be hidden, profound, or simple. Symbols function in literature, as in all art, as devices that expand the content of a work beyond specifics to universals. In literature, symbols give a work its richness and much of its appeal. When we realize that a character in a story, for example, is a symbol, regardless of how much of an individual the writer may have portrayed, the story takes on new meaning because the character symbolizes us as humans—that is, some aspect of our complex and often contradictory natures.

POETRY

Language

Rhythm in poetry consists of the flow of sound through accents and syllables. For example, in Robert Frost's "Stopping by Woods on a Snowy Evening" (see below) each line contains eight syllables with an accent on every other syllable. Rhythms, like Frost's, that depend on a fixed number of syllables per line, are called *accentual-syllabic*. Contrast that with the freely flowing rhythm of Shakespeare's "The Seven Ages of Man," from Act II of *As You Like It*, in which rhythmic flow uses naturally occurring stresses in the words. This use of stress to create rhythm is called *accentual*.

The Seven Ages of Man
William Shakespeare
1564–1616

All the world's a stage,
And all the men and women merely players.
They have their exits and their entrances,
And one man in his time plays many parts,
His acts being seven ages. At first the infant
Mewling[i] and puking in the nurse's arms.
Then the whining schoolboy, with his satchel
And shining morning face, creeping like snail
Unwillingly to school. And then the lover,
Sighing like furnace, with a woeful ballad[ii]
Made to his mistress' eyebrow. Then a soldier,
Full of strange oaths and bearded like the pard,[iii]
Jealous in honor,[iv] sudden and quick in quarrel,
Seeking the bubble reputation[v]
Even in the cannon's mouth. And then the justice,
In fair round belly with good capon lined,[vi]
With eyes severe and beard of formal cut,
Full of wise saws[vii] and modern instances,[viii]
And so he plays his part. The sixth age shifts
Into the lean and slippered Pantaloon,[ix]
With spectacles on nose and pouch on side;
His youthful hose, well saved, a world too wide
For his shrunk shank, and his big manly voice,
Turning again toward childish treble, pipes

And whistles in his sound. Last scene of all,
That ends this strange eventful history,
Is second childishness and mere oblivion,
Sans[x] teeth, sans eyes, sans taste, sans everything.[7]

[i] Whimpering.
[ii] Poem.
[iii] Leopard.
[iv] Sensitive about honor.
[v] As quickly burst as a bubble.
[vi] Magistrate bribed with a chicken.
[vii] Sayings.
[viii] Commonplace illustrations.
[ix] The foolish old man of Italian comedy.
[x] Without.

Imagery is a verbal representation of objects, feelings, or ideas. It can be *literal* or *figurative*. In the former there is no change or extension in meaning; for example, "green eyes" are simply eyes that are a green color. In the latter, there is a change in literal meaning; for example, green eyes might become "green orbs."

Figures, like images, take words beyond their literal meaning. Much of poetic meaning comes in comparing objects in ways that go beyond the literal. For example, in Robert Frost's "Stopping by Woods on a Snowy Evening," snowflakes are described as "downy," which endows them with the figurative quality of soft, fluffy feathers on a young bird. In the same sense, Frost uses "sweep" and "easy" to describe the wind.

Stopping by Woods on a Snowy Evening
Robert Frost
1874–1963

Whose woods these are I think I know.
His house is in the village though;
He will not see me stopping here
To watch his woods fill up with snow.

My little horse must think it queer
To stop without a farmhouse near
Between the woods and frozen lake
The darkest evening of the year.

He gives his harness bells a shake
To ask if there is some mistake.
The only other sound's the sweep
Of easy wind and downy flake.

The woods are lovely, dark and deep.
But I have promises to keep.
And miles to go before I sleep.
And miles to go before I sleep.[8]

Metaphors are figures of speech by which new implications are given to words. Thus the expression "the twilight of life" applies the word "twilight" to the concept of life to create an entirely new image and meaning. Metaphors are implied but not explicit comparisons.

Symbols are also often associated with figures of speech, but not all figures are symbols, and not all symbols are figures. Symbolism is critical to poetry, which uses compressed language to express, and carry us into, its meanings. In poetry "the whole poem helps to determine the meaning of its parts, and in turn, each part helps to determine the meaning of the whole poem."[9] Watch the Humanities CD: Literature.

Structure

Form or structure in poetry derives from fitting together lines of similar structure and length tied to other lines by end rhyme. For example, the sonnet has fourteen lines of iambic pentameters rhymed 1–3, 2–4, 5–7, 6–8, 9–11, 10–12, 13–14 (see "Meter" below).

Stanzas, which are any recurring groupings of two or more lines in terms of length, meter, and rhyme, are part of structure. A stanza usually presents a unit of poetic experience, and if the poem has more than one stanza, the pattern is usually repeated.

Sound Structures

Rhyme—the coupling of words that sound alike—is the most common sound structure in poetry. Its function is to tie the sense together with the sound. Rhyme can be *masculine, feminine,* or *triple.* Masculine rhyme is based on single-syllable vowels such as "hate" and "mate." Feminine rhyme is based on sounds between accented and unaccented syllables, for example, "hating" and "mating." Triple rhyme has a correspondence over three syllables, such as "despondent" and "respondent."

Alliteration is a second type of sound structure in which an initial sound is repeated for effect: for example, *fancy free.*

Assonance is a similarity among vowels but not consonants, for example, "quite like."

Consonance is the repetition or recurrence of identical or similar consonants, as in Shakespeare's song "The ousel cock so black of hue." It is often combined with assonance and alliteration.

Meter

Meter refers to the type and number of rhythmic units in a line. Rhythmic units are called *feet.* Four common kinds of feet are *iambic, trochaic, anapestic,* and *dactylic.* Iambic meter alternates one unstressed and one stressed syllable; trochaic alternates one stressed and one unstressed syllable; anapestic alternates two unstressed and one stressed syllable; and dactylic alternates one stressed and two unstressed syllables.

Line, also called *verse,* determines the basic rhythmic pattern of the poem. Lines are named by the number of feet they contain. One foot is monometer; two, dimeter; three, trimeter; four, tetrameter; five, pentameter; six, hexameter; seven, heptameter; and eight, octameter.

BIOGRAPHY

Facts

Facts are the verifiable details around which a biography is shaped. However, facts, other than matters such as birth, death, marriage, and other date-related occurrences, often have a way of becoming elusive. They can turn out to be observations filtered through the personality of the observer. Incontrovertible facts may comprise a chronological or skeletal framework for a biography, but they may well not create much interest. Frequently they do not provide much of a skeleton either. Few facts are recorded about many of the individuals who arouse our curiosity.

On the other hand, the lives of other important individuals have been chronicled in such great detail that almost too many facts exist. Artistry entails selection and composition, and many facts may have to be omitted from the narrative to maintain the reader's interest. Another issue is the question of what the author should actually do with the facts. If they are injurious, should they be used? In what context? Whatever the situation, facts alone are not sufficient for an artistic or interesting biography.

Anecdotes

Anecdotes are stories or observations about moments in a biography. They take the basic facts and expand them for illustrative purposes, thereby creating interest. Anecdotes may be true or untrue. Their purpose is often to create a memorable generalization. They may also generate debate or controversy.

Quotations form part of anecdotal experience. They are used to create interest by changing the presentational format to that of dialogue. In the sense that dialogue creates the impression that we are part of the scene, as opposed to being third parties listening to someone else describe a situation, it brings us closer to the subjects of the biography.

HOW DOES IT STIMULATE THE SENSES?

Literature, like all the arts, appeals to our senses by the way in which the writer uses the tools of the medium. Specifically, literature utilizes words. What we see and hear in literature results from the skill of the writer in turning words into sensual stimuli.

PICTURES

Skillful wordplay opens many sensual vistas. The very words of the title of Saki's short story—Toad-Water—conjure pictures. Perhaps the image of this place depends on our having had some experience of toads, so for those who have not, toad-water brings to mind a soggy primeval place hovering somewhere around the level of squalor. Toads, with their warts and other unlovely features, are denizens of dank, unlovely places. Alice Walker paints a devastating picture when she describes Roselilly's reaction to her husband's religion as "ropes, chains, handcuffs." Her effective use of simile turns the touch of his hand into "the clasp of an iron gate."

SOUNDS

We hear real sounds stimulated by words. Again, Alice Walker evokes an auditory scene as she writes in "Roselilly": "the general pandemonium. Cars drive up blowing their horns. Firecrackers go off. Dogs come from under the house and begin to yelp and bark." William Shakespeare creates sounds of a different kind as he draws a portrait of old age in "The Seven Ages of Man": "For his shrunk shank, and his big manly voice,/Turning again toward childish treble, pipes/And whistles in his sound."

EMOTIONS

The mood evoked by a piece of literature can turn us in on ourselves, stimulating sensations that can range from pleasure to pain. We may or may not understand why we react as we do, but we do understand vividly the power of words to invade our personal world and to move us. Visceral reactions, arguably, form the top layer of the "onion" comprising our response to literary stimuli. When we peel the top layer away and delve into those layers beneath, real pleasure and sense of accomplishment result. Examining the "whats" of artistic stimulation provides a significant challenge. Determining the "whys" multiplies the reward exponentially.

THINKING CRITICALLY

Build a basic critical analysis of a work of literature by using the topics in this chapter as an outline: Pick an example and ask yourself hard questions about the work's performance and significance.

- Reaction. What purpose does the author have in mind in this work? How do you react? Does the work probe a significant subject?
- Genre. Is the work fictional, poetic, narrative, dramatic, lyric, or biographical? What characteristics lead you to that conclusion?
- Fiction. If the work is one of fiction, is it a novel or short story? Explain how point of view, appearance and reality, tone, character, plot, theme, and symbols are developed.
- Poetry. If the work is poetic, describe the use of rhythm, imagery, figures, metaphors, structure, sound structures, and meter.
- Biography. If the work is biographical, how has the author utilized facts and anecdotes?
- Essay. If the work is an essay, explain how either formality or informality is expressed.

CYBER STUDY

LITERATURE INDEXED BY GENRE:
—Fiction
Louisa May Alcott's *Little Women*, Jane Austen's *Pride and Prejudice*, Mariano Azuela's *The Underdogs*, Emily Bronte's *Wuthering Heights*, James Joyce's *Dubliners*, and Virginia Woolf's *Night and Day*
—Poetry
Samuel Taylor Coleridge's, *The Rime of the Ancient Mariner*, Dante Alighieri's *The Divine Comedy*, T. S. Eliot's *The Wasteland*, Homer's *The Iliad*, Amy Lowell's *Sword Blades and Poppy Seed*, Naidu Sarojini's *The Golden Threshold*, William Shakespeare's *Sonnets*, Sara Teasdale's *Rivers to the Sea*, and William Butler Yeats's *A Poet to His Beloved*.
http://www.inform.umd.edu/EdRes/ReadingRoom/

LITERATURE INDEXED BY AUTHOR AND/OR TITLE:
http://www.infomotions.com/alex/

LITERATURE INDEXED BY AUTHOR, TITLE, OR SUBJECT:
http://digital.library.upenn.edu/books/titles.html

LITERATURE INDEXED BY AUTHOR, TITLE, OR DEWEY DECIMAL CLASSIFICATION:
http://www.ipl.org/reading/books/

PART II

THE STYLES OF THE ARTS

How Artists Portray "Reality"

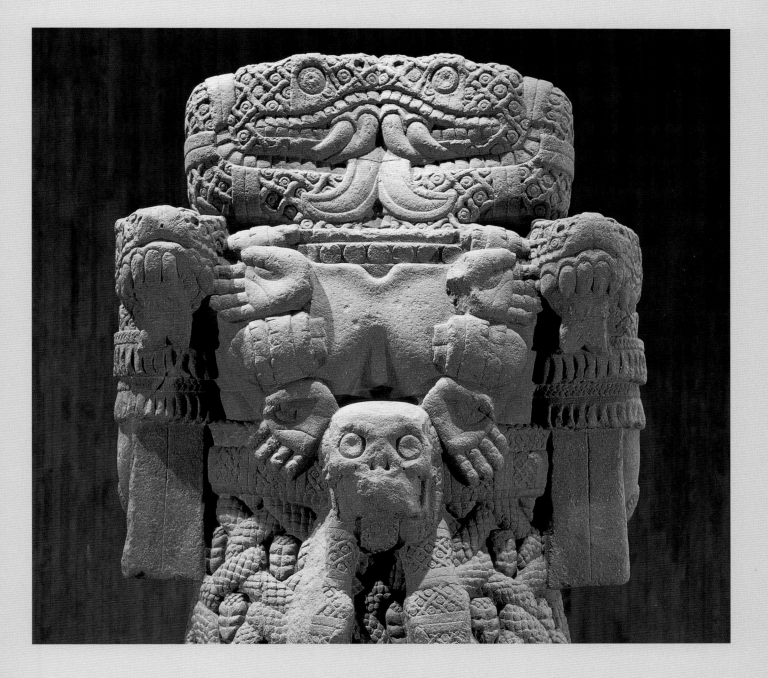

THE STYLES OF THE ARTS

How Artists Portray "Reality"

STYLE

The manner in which artists express themselves constitutes their style. Style is tantamount to the personality of an artwork. It is the body of characteristics that identifies an artwork with an individual, a historical period, a "school" of artists, or a nation. Often, styles are derived from philosophical ideas, and there may be theories of expression that underlie styles such as Classicism, Romanticism, and Postmodernism, to name a few. We will discuss these as they appear in the text. In the meantime, we can benefit from some general observations. To begin, arriving at an artwork's style involves a process. It means assimilating materials, making comparisons, and drawing conclusions.

The style of any artwork can be determined by analyzing how the artist has arranged the characteristics of the medium. If the usage is similar to that of others, we might conclude that they exemplify the same style. For example, Bach and Handel typify the Baroque style in music; Haydn and Mozart, the Classical. Listening to works by these composers quickly leads to the conclusion that the ornate melodic shapes and rhythmic patterns of Bach are like those of Handel, and quite different from the flowing themes and precise concern for structure of Mozart and Haydn. The precision and symmetry of the Parthenon compared with the ornate opulence of the Palace of Versailles suggest that, in line and form, the architects of these buildings treated their medium differently. Yet the design of the Parthenon is very much a visual companion, stylistically, of Mozart and Haydn; Versailles reflects an approach to design similar to that of Bach and Handel.

HOW CAN WE ANALYZE STYLE?

Let us take our examination one step further and stylistically analyze four paintings. The first three were done by three different artists; the fourth, by one of those three. By stylistic analysis, we will determine the painter of the fourth.

The first painting (Fig. **II.1**), *A View Near Volterra,* is by Corot (kuh-ROH). Corot has primarily used curved *line* to create the edges of the forms or shapes in the painting. Many of the forms—the rocks, trees, clouds—do not have crisp, clear edges. Color areas tend to blend with each other, giving the painting a somewhat fuzzy or out-of-focus appearance. This comfortable effect is heightened by Corot's use of palette. Palette, as we noted, encompasses the total use of color and contrast; since these illustrations are black-and-white, we can deal with only one aspect of palette: *value contrast*. As with his use of line, Corot maintains subtlety in his value contrast—that is, in the relationship of blacks to white. Movement from light to dark is gradual, and he avoids stark contrasts. He employs a full range of black, grays, and whites, but does so without calling attention to their positioning. Corot's *brushstroke* is somewhat apparent: If we look carefully, we can see brush marks—individual strokes where paint has been applied—throughout the painting. We can tell that the foliage was executed by *stippling* (by dabbing the brush to the canvas as one would dot an "i" with a pencil). Thus, even though the objects portrayed are lifelike, the artist has not made any attempt to hide the fact that the picture has been painted. The overall effect is lifelike but we can see in every area the spontaneity with which it was executed.

The second painting (Fig. II.2) is Picasso's *Guernica*. We hardly need be an expert to tell that this painting is by a different painter—or at least in a different style from the previous one. Picasso has joined curved and straight lines, placing them in such relationships that they create movement and dissonance. The edges of color areas and forms are sharp and distinct; nothing here is soft or fuzzy. Likewise, the value contrasts are stark and extreme. Areas of the highest value—that is, white—are forced against areas of the lowest value—black. In fact, the range of tonalities is far narrower than in the previous work. Mid or medium (gray) tones are here, but they play a minor role in the effect of the palette. Tonal areas are flat, and the starkness of the work is reinforced by brushstroke, which is noteworthy for its near *absence* of effect.

The third painting (Fig. II.3) is van Gogh's *Starry Night*. Use of line is highly active although uniformly curved. Forms and color areas have both hard and soft edges, and van Gogh, like Picasso, uses outlining to strengthen his images and reduce their reality. The overall effect of line is a sweeping and undulating movement, highly dynamic and yet far removed from the starkness of the Picasso. In contrast, van Gogh's curvilinearity and

softened edges are quite different in effect from the relaxed quality of the Corot. Van Gogh's value contrasts are broad, but moderate. He ranges from darks through medium grays to white, all virtually equal in importance. Even when movement from one area to another is across a hard edge to a highly contrasting value, the result is moderate: not soft, not stark. It is, however, brushstroke that gives the painting its unique personality. We can see thousands of individual brush marks where the artist applied paint to canvas. The nervous, almost frenetic use of brushstrokes makes the painting come alive.

Now that we have examined three paintings in different styles and by different artists, can you determine which of the three painted Figure II.4? First, examine the use of line. Form and color edges are hard. Outlining is used. Curved and straight lines are juxtaposed. The effect is active and stark: unlike Corot, a bit like van Gogh, and very much like Picasso. Next, examine palette. Darks, grays, and whites are used broadly. However, the principal impression is of strong contrast—the darkest darks against the whitest whites. This is not like Corot, a bit like van Gogh, and most like Picasso. Finally, brushstroke is generally unobtrusive. Tonal areas are mostly flat. This is

II.1 Jean-Baptiste-Camille Corot, *A View Near Volterra*, 1838. Oil on canvas, 27⅜ x 37½ ins (70 x 95 cm). National Gallery of Art, Washington, D.C. (Chester Dale Collection).

II.2 Pablo Picasso, *Guernica*, 1937. Oil on canvas, 11 ft 5 ins x 25 ft 5¾ ins (3.48 x 7.77 m).
Museo Nacional Centro de Arte Reina Sofía, Madrid.

II.3 Vincent van Gogh, *The Starry Night*, 1889. Oil on canvas, 29 x 36¼ ins (73.7 x 92.1 cm).
The Museum of Modern Art, New York.

II.4 Exercise painting (see p. 43 for identification).

definitely not a van Gogh and probably not a Corot. Three votes out of three go to Picasso—and the style is so distinctive that you probably had no difficulty deciding, even without the written analysis. However, would you have been so certain if asked whether Picasso painted Figure 1.20? A work by another Cubist painter might pose even greater difficulty. Some differences in style are obvious; others are subtler. It is quite a challenge to distinguish the work of one artist from another who designs in a similar fashion. However, the analytical process we just completed indicates how we can approach artworks to determine in what ways they exemplify a given style.

STYLE AND CULTURE

We sometimes recognize differences in style without thinking much about it. Our experience or formal training need not be extensive for us to recognize that the buildings in Figures II.6 and II.7 reflect different cultural circumstances. The Russian Orthodox church in Figure II.6 is distinguishable by its characteristic domes and the icons that decorate its walls (Fig. II.5). The tomb in Figure II.7 is, similarly, typically Muslim, identifiable by

its arch. The decorative embellishment, in contrast to the icons of the Orthodox Church, reflects the Islamic prohibition against depicting human form in an architectural decoration.

HOW DOES A STYLE GET ITS NAME?

Why is some art called Classical, some Pop, some Baroque, and some Impressionist? Some styles were named hundreds of years after they occurred—the definition resulted from extended, common usage or a historical viewpoint. For example, the Athenian Greeks, whose works we know as Classical, were centuries removed from the naming of their style. Some labels, such as Surrealist, were coined by artists themselves. Many are attributed to individual critics who, having experienced the emerging works of several artists and noting a common or different approach, invented a term (sometimes a derogatory one) to describe it. Because of the influence of the critic or the catchiness of the term, the name was adopted by others. Thus, a style was born.

We must be careful, however, when we use labels for artworks. Occasionally they imply stylistic characteristics; sometimes they identify attitudes or tendencies that are not really stylistic. Often debate exists as to which is which. For example, Romanticism has stylistic characteristics in some art disciplines, but the term also describes a broad philosophy of life. A style label can be a composite of several elements with dissimilar characteristics but identical objectives—for example, Post-Impressionism (see p. 360). Terminology is convenient but is not universally agreed upon in fine detail. Occasionally experts

II.5 Church of Nikolai Khamovnik, Moscow, detail of front portal.

II.6 Church of Nikolai Khamovnik, Moscow, Russia,1679–82.

II.7 Tomb of the Shirvanshah, Baku, Azerbaijan, 15th century.

disagree as to whether certain artworks fall within the descriptive parameters of one style or another, even while agreeing on the definition of the style itself.

In addition, we can ask how the same label might identify stylistic characteristics of two or more unrelated art disciplines, such as painting and music. Is there an aural equivalent to visual characteristics, or vice versa? These are challenging questions, and the answers are debatable. More often than not, similarity of objectives results in the same stylistic label being used for works in quite different disciplines.

Styles do not start and stop on specific dates, nor do they recognize national boundaries. Some reflect deeply held convictions or creative insights; some are imitations of previous styles. Many styles are profound; others are superficial. Some are intensely individual.

Merely dissecting artistic or stylistic characteristics is not an end in itself. What makes analysis come alive is the actual experience of artworks, as we describe our reactions and attempt to find the deepest level of meaning possible. Every artwork reflects the attempt of another human being to express some view of the human condition we all share. We can try to place that viewpoint in the context of the time or the specific biography that produced it and speculate upon why its style is as it is. We can attempt to compare those contexts with our own. We may never know the precise stimuli that caused a particular artistic reflection, but our attempts at understanding make our responses more informed and exciting, and our understanding of our own existence more profound.

APPROACHING PART II OF THE TEXT

"REALITY"

In the chapters that remain we examine the manner in which artists have portrayed and continue to portray "reality." We must remember that "reality" in terms of this textbook includes subject matter that we will never find in the world around us. Indeed, the products of our wildest fantasies can be forms of "reality" in its very broadest sense. But our purpose here is not to debate definitions but to experience works of art in a reasonably convenient way. The fact of the matter is that artists use certain tools that, in Part I, we have called "media" to create artistic visions of something—call it "reality" or call it something else. Whatever we believe it reflects or reveals, that creation is an artwork, and it has a specific

signature that we call "style." In the remainder of the text, we will look at a variety of styles from around the world from the earliest times to the present.

ORGANIZATION

There probably is no perfect way to organize a study of the diverse styles we are about to discover. For the simple reason that chronology is familiar and convenient, we have chosen to proceed with an organization that focuses on style but does so in a roughly chronological fashion. However, rather than a true "history" of the arts, the material in these chapters constitutes a series of snapshots only—a sampling of the art humankind has produced over 35,000 years and the labels by which we have come to identify it. This gives us many styles to examine but precious few examples to describe them. Indeed, many artistic styles from around the world do not appear at all.

Thus, as we make our way through the remainder of the book, we will take some pretty dizzying jumps—geographically and time-wise. Think of it as an elaborate artistic buffet. The chronological arrangement is a way of keeping the meats together and the salads likewise. It is not the only way we could have organized the smorgasbord, but it is a helpful way of sorting out several hundred examples of humankind's artistic output. At a formal meal in a conventional restaurant, in contrast to a buffet, we would not find tables with fried potatoes sitting next to carrot salads or with seven different meats and ten different desserts. Think of a typical history book as a conventional restaurant where we can find specialization and concentrated details. At a buffet, on the other hand, we can sample many items and come away enlightened and satisfied even though we may have eaten only a tablespoonful of any dish. If we are fortunate, we may discover, in the wide array, a dish or two that we might go to a traditional restaurant and order as a regular course in a more formal meal.

This book is a buffet, and a potpourri of presentation and discovery is what Part II intends, and what you should expect. If you concentrate on the names and characteristics of the styles, or approaches, presented, and compare one style's characteristics with those of another, regardless of when or where they occurred, you will succeed nicely. Such concentration and comparison not only will yield interesting results but also will polish your confidence and ability to respond to works of art that you will experience when this book has long been forgotten. Do not, however, try to find a continuum of artistic development as the material in Part II spins out. You won't find one; none is intended, even though the material has a chronological framework, and although it is extremely helpful to know, for example, that Greek Classicism occurred during the fifth century B.C.E., or that modern dance is a twentieth-century movement.

ART FROM MANY CULTURES

As if a sweep through 35,000 years of art in 200 pages weren't enough, we have the added factor of diverse cultures with which to contend. That need not be troublesome. As the text unfolds, very little in the way of background is presented. Nevertheless, as we noted in the Introduction, we can analyze art in both formal and contextual ways. Arguably, perhaps, we can never see a work of art outside our own culture in the way that someone nurtured in that culture can. We cannot hope to know the historic works of our own culture in the way they were known in their own times.

On the other hand, questions of style, organization, aesthetic flavor, and comparison can be addressed by purely formal means, and that is what this text emphasizes. At the bottom line, the unique and unforgettable quality of a work of art is the way it looks and sounds. And we can analyze, compare, and relate those qualities even if we do not know much about the context or culture that produced them. Fundamentally, formal skills of analysis and observation are what we are called upon to use most of the time when we experience art outside the world of the textbook and the classroom. When we meet a work of art for the first time, we can engage it formally and at great depth—luckily so, because most of the time we do not have contextual materials, as valuable as they might be, to call upon.

Finally, there is one general factor to note as we progress through Part II of this text. That is the changing emphasis on space and volume. We can see this within single cultures and among the diverse cultures examined here. The exercise in comparing the use of line, form, and color we just finished is an exercise to be performed repeatedly in comparing works of art within the European tradition and with works from Asia, Africa, and Native America. That exercise alone will yield critical insights of significant consequence.

PART II OUTLINE

CHAPTER NINE

ANCIENT APPROACHES

c. 30,000 to c. 480 B.C.E.

IMPORTANT TERMS

Venus figure A feminine figurine
from the Paleolithic period.

Stylized A type of depiction in
which lifelikeness has been
altered for artistic effect.

Bible From the Greek word for
books, and referring to the
town of Byblos.

Torah The Hebrew Bible's book of
the Law, comprising the books
of Genesis, Exodus, Leviticus,
Numbers, and Deuteronomy.

Psalm From the Psalter, the
hymnal of ancient Israel.

Pao-chia system The ancient
Chinese system of mutual
responsibility.

Pre-Columbian Native American
art that predates the arrival of
Columbus in 1492.

Archaic style A style of Greek vase
painting and sculpture dating to
the sixth century B.C.E.

Doric style A style of Greek
architecture marked by heavy,
slanted columns with a flat slab
for a capital.

Kouros Referring to Archaic
sculpture of Greek youth.

PALEOLITHIC EUROPEAN ART

SCULPTURE

Humankind's first known sculpture dates from the period from approximately 30,000 to 15,000 B.C.E.[1] The head and body of a man carved from mammoth ivory were found in a burial site at Brno in the Czech Republic (Fig. **9.1**). Although many body parts are missing, the head of the sculpture reveals an apparent attention to anatomical details. The hair is closely cropped, the brow is low, and the eyes are deeply set.

Western European art probably began approximately 25,000 to 30,000 years before the Common Era and, at its earliest, consisted of simple lines scratched in damp clay. The people making these scratchings lived in caves and seem, eventually, to have elaborated them into the outlines of animals. This development—from what appears to be idle doodling into sophisticated art—seems to have come in three phases. Black outline drawings of animals with a single colored filler mark the first. Next came the addition of a second color within the outline, to create a sense of light and shade, or modeling. As we shall see, these depictions often incorporated projecting portions of

9.1 Man from Brno, c. 27,000–20,000 B.C.E. Ivory, height 9 ins (20 cm). Moravian Museum, Brno, Czech Republic.

the cave walls to add a sense of three-dimensionality. In many cases it appears as though the artist picked a specific rock protrusion or configuration for the animal drawing. The third phase in the development of early art consists of exciting multicolored paintings in impressive realistic style. In this category are the well-known paintings at Altamira in Spain (Fig. **9.2**). Here the artists

9.2 Bison, from Altamira, Spain, c. 14,000–10,000 B.C.E. Paint, length 8 ft 3 ins (2.51 m).

9.3 Woman from Willendorf, Lower Austria, c. 30,000–25,000 B.C.E. Limestone, height 4⅓ ins (11 cm). Naturhistorisches Museum, Vienna.

features and are remarkably similar in overall design. They may be symbolic fertility figures—hence modern scholars have named them after the Roman goddess of love and beauty—or they may be no more than objects for exchange or recognition. Whatever the case, each figure has the same tapering legs, wide hips, and tapering shoulders and head, forming a diamond-shaped silhouette.

The Woman from Willendorf (Fig. **9.3**) is the best-known example of a Venus figure. Emphasis on swollen thighs and breasts and prominent genitals implies that the image is a fertility symbol. Some have gone so far as to suggest that these works reveal their makers' obsessions with sexual ideas. Carved from limestone, the Woman from Willendorf was originally colored red—the color of blood—perhaps symbolizing life itself. Many early peoples painted corpses red.

Although faceless, Venus figures usually have hair, often wear bracelets, beads, aprons, or a waist band, and sometimes show markings that may represent tattoos. Although a male hunting ethos dominated the culture that made them, only women are represented in the statuary that survives. Emphasis on their sexuality, the mystery and apparent miracle of birth, and the uniquely female role therein clearly influenced the carvers' perception of reality.

captured detail, essence, mass, and a remarkable sense of movement, using only earth colors and charcoal.

The earliest artists seem to have shied away from the difficulties of drawing three-dimensionality, keeping their subjects in profile (as, much later, the Egyptians were to do). Only an occasional turning of head or antlers tests the artist's skill at portraying depth.

So-called Venus figures have been found on burial sites in a band stretching approximately 1,100 miles (1,833 km) from western France to the central Russian plain. Many scholars believe that these figures are the first works in a representational style. They share certain stylistic

CAVE PAINTING

The cave of Lascaux (lah-SKOH) lies slightly over a mile from the little French town of Montignac, in the valley of the Vézère river. A group of children, investigating a tree

9.4 Main hall, or Hall of Bulls, Lascaux, France. Paint on limestone, 30 × 100 ft (9 × 30 m).

uprooted by a storm, scrambled down a fissure into a world undisturbed for thousands of years and discovered the cave. Hundreds of paintings were found there, as elsewhere in France, Spain, and other parts of Europe. The significance of the Lascaux works lies in the quantity and the quality of an intact group.

An overwhelming sense of power and emerges from the main hall or "Hall of Bulls" (Fig. 9.4). The thundering herd moves below a sky of rolling contours formed in the stone ceiling. At the entrance of the hall an 8-foot (2.5-m) unicorn begins a monumental montage of bulls, horses, and deer, whose shapes intermingle and whose colors radiate warmth and power, with heights of up to 12 feet (3.5 m). Although the paintings in the main hall were created over a long period and by a succession of artists, the cumulative effect of this 30- by 100-foot (9- × 30-m) domed gallery is of a single work, carefully composed for maximum impact.

A Personal Journey

THE CAVE OF LASCAUX

The short drive from the district capital of Brive-la-Gaillarde (breev lah guy-YARD) to the medieval village of Montignac (muhn-tihn-YAHK) winds along the banks of the Vézère (vay-zair) river. In that part of France, the Vézère is called the *Vallée de l'homme* (the Valley of Man) because it has been inhabited continuously since Neanderthal and Cro-Magnon times. It is a pretty place with a temperate climate and plenty of water, and I couldn't help thinking that it must have seemed a good place to live, even 20,000 years ago. So, with an early November sun highlighting trees still replete with colorful foliage, I made my way to a hill above Montignac to a place called Lascaux and a cave discovered by local children to reveal a world undisturbed for thousands of years.

Literally and figuratively, a trip to Lascaux (Fig. 9.4) is a journey of a lifetime. In a literal sense, Lascaux was a journey I decided to take after learning about the cave in a high-school humanities class in the 1950s. My humanities instructor was correct when he opined that such courses do not merely concern the material they cover, but also concern the rest of one's life. Unfortunately, the cave was closed to the public in 1963, before I could make the trip. In the late 1970s, the opening of Lascaux II, an exact replica only 660 feet (200 m) from the original, allowed me to fulfill my dream—at least to the degree an imitation would allow. Artistic copies rarely carry the impact of the original, but Lascaux II may be a notable exception.

In the figurative sense of a "journey of a lifetime," Lascaux represents an excursion to one of the earliest human records—a journey across the recorded lifetime of humanity. Although not unique—there are nearly 300 sites of Ice Age cave painting spreading from Spain to Russia—Lascaux is, arguably, the most spectacular.

The cave itself suits the display it presents very well. The walls curve gently outward and upward from the floor to a height of approximately 6 feet (1.8 m). They are rough and undecorated. At that height the line of the stone abruptly changes direction and rises to form a shallow dome perhaps 12 feet (3.5 m) across and 10 feet (3 m) high at its apex. On this dome Paleolithic humans painted, with ocher for reds and manganese oxide for blacks, vibrant portrayals of animals, some of whose types exist today. On these surfaces, smoother in texture than the lower walls, four large bulls encircle the chamber, and smaller animal figures provide a counterpoint. Human representations are virtually non-existent, and when they do appear, they are as stick figures, in contrast to the lifelikeness of the animals. The artists of Lascaux were creative and inventive. They executed some of the details using the curvatures of the hand as a stencil, with the pigment blown onto the surface.

I felt a personal communion, even in the replica cave, with the humanness of the people who created the figures in the original, and felt what it might have been like to be there with them all that time ago. Although I will never know what the paintings meant to those who created them, I found in the figures a meeting with the human spirit of the makers.

SUMER

Some time around 6000 B.C.E. the first recognizable civilization appeared in that part of the Near East we call Mesopotamia—the region between the Tigris and Euphrates rivers (in present-day Iraq)—and the earliest recognizable culture to emerge in this area was that of Sumer (soo-muhr). Sumerians lived in villages and organized themselves around several important religious centers, which grew rapidly into cities. Sumerian mathematics employed a system of counting based on sixty and that system was used to measure time (we still have sixty minutes in one hour) and circles, divided into 360 degrees. The wheel appeared in Sumer as early as 3000 B.C.E.

The majority of surviving artworks from Mesopotamia prior to 3000 B.C.E. are painted pots and stamp seals. Decoration of pottery served to satisfy the creative urge while providing functional objects. Decoration was abstract. Stamp seals, although clearly functional, went beyond tool status and were also regarded as surfaces ideally suited to exercise artists' creative ingenuity. Early seals were round or rectangular; later, for reasons unknown to us, cylindrical ones came into being. A carved wooden roller was applied to wet clay to produce a ribbonlike design of indefinite length. The creative possibilities inherent in cylinder seal design were far greater than in the other shapes. The way that intricate design can be repeated infinitely seems to have fascinated the Sumerians. Scenes of sacrifice, hunting, and battle all appear in the examples of cylinder seal art that have survived. Figure 9.6 combines two Sumerian fertility symbols: the lioness and the intertwined snake. This design appears repeatedly in Sumerian art.

In *low-relief* art of the early Sumerians such as Figure 9.5 we find a preoccupation with ritual and the gods. This

9.5 Vase with ritual scene, from E-anna, Uruk (modern Warka), Iraq, c. 3500–3100 B.C.E. Alabaster relief, height 36 ins (91 cm). Iraq Museum, Baghdad.

large alabaster vase celebrates the cult of E-anna, goddess of fertility and love. Divided into four bands, it commemorates the marriage of the goddess, which was re-enacted to ensure fertility. The bottom band has alternate stalks of

9.6 Cylinder seal and impression, showing snake-necked lions, from Mesopotamia, c. 3300 B.C.E. Green jasper, height 1¾ ins (4 cm). Louvre, Paris.

9.7 (*above*) Soundbox panel of the royal lyre, from the tomb of Queen Puabi, Ur, Iraq, 2650–2550 B.C.E. Shell inlay set in bitumen, height 13 ins (33 cm). University of Pennsylvania Museum, Philadelphia.

9.8 (*right*) Royal lyre, from the tomb of Queen Puabi, Ur. Wood with gold, lapis lazuli, and shell inlay. University of Pennsylvania Museum, Philadelphia.

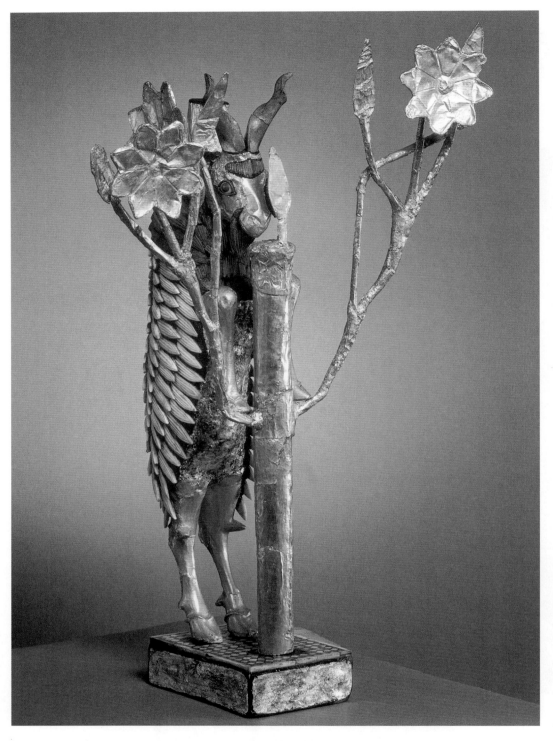

9.9 He-goat, from Ur, c. 2600 B.C.E. Wood with gold and lapis lazuli overlay, height 20 ins (51 cm). University of Pennsylvania Museum, Philadelphia.

barley and date palms; above it are rams and ewes. In the second band, naked worshipers carry baskets of fruit and other offerings. At the top the goddess herself stands before her shrine—two coiled bundles of reeds—to receive a worshiper or priest, also nude, whose tribute basket brims with fruit. The composition exhibits an alternating flow of movement: from left to right in the rams and ewes, and right to left in the worshipers. Conventions of figure portrayal are similar to but not as rigid as those in Egyptian art (see pp. 214–15).

Other works from this period such as Figures **9.7** and **9.8** illustrate the splendor of the Sumerian court. Inlaid in gold and laden with the symbolism of masculine fertility, the dazzling golden goat from the royal graves at Ur (Fig. 9.9) manifests the basic Sumerian belief in a pantheon of gods personifying nature. The elegantly depicted goat represents Tammuz, one of the gods of vegetation.

Religion and government shared a close relationship in Sumer. Religion permeated the social, political, and economic, as well as the spiritual and ethical life of society. A long epic poem, the *Gilgamesh* (GHIL-ghuh-mesh) *Epic* reveals Sumerian religion, around which Sumerian society was organized. The epic tells of a southern Mesopotamian ruler probably from the first half of the third millennium B.C.E., although there is no historical evidence for the exploits narrated in the epic. Parallels exist, however, between the *Gilgamesh Epic* and stories found in the Hebrew Bible (Old Testament of the Christian Bible)—for example, the story of the flood.

ASSYRIA

By the year 1000 B.C.E., a new power had arisen in Mesopotamia—the Assyrians. Northern peoples from Ashur on the River Tigris, they had both military power and skill that enabled them to maintain supremacy over the region, including Syria, the Sinai peninsula, and as far as lower Egypt. For nearly 400 years they appear to have engaged in almost continuous warfare, ruthlessly destroying their enemies and leveling conquered cities. Finally, they, too, felt the conqueror's sword, and all their cities were utterly destroyed.

Under Sargon II, who came to power in 722 B.C.E., the high priests regained many of the privileges they had lost under previous kings, and the Assyrian Empire reached the peak of its power. Early in his reign he founded the city of Dur Sharrukin (door shah-ROO-kihn; on the site of modern Khorsabad), about 9 miles (15 km) northeast of Nineveh. His vast royal citadel, occupying an area of some quarter of a million square feet, was built as an image not only of his empire but of the cosmos itself. The reconstruction of the citadel in Figure **9.10** shows the style of architecture at the time and illustrates the priorities of Assyrian civilization. Clearly, in Sargon's new city, secular architecture took precedence over temple architecture. The rulers seem to have been far more preoccupied with building fortifications and pretentious palaces than with erecting religious shrines. Dur Sharrukin was built, occupied, and abandoned within a single generation.

9.10 Sargon II's citadel, Dur Sharrukin (modern Khorsabad), Iraq, reconstruction.

MASTERWORK

The Tell Asmar Statues

Undoubtedly the most striking features of these Sumerian votive figures (made as an act of worship to the gods) are their enormous, staring eyes, with their dramatic exaggeration (Fig. 9.11). Arguably representing Abu, the quasi-divine king (the large figure), a goddess assumed to be his spouse, and a crowd of worshipers, the statues occupied places around the inner walls of an early temple, in prayer, awaiting the divine presence. The figures have great dignity, despite the stylization and somewhat crude execution. In addition to the staring eyes, our attention is drawn to the distinctive carving of the arms, which are separate from the body. The composition is closed and self-contained, reflecting the characteristics of prayer.

Certain geometric and expressive qualities characterize these statues. In typical Sumerian style, each form is based on a cone or cylinder, and the arms and legs are stylized and pipe-like, rather than lifelike depictions of the subtle curves of human limbs. They are made of gypsum, a very fragile material.

The god Abu and the mother goddess may be distinguished from the rest by their size and by the large diameter of their eyes. The meaning in these statues clearly bears out what we know of Mesopotamian religious thought. The gods were believed to be present in their images. The statues of the worshipers were substitutes for the real worshipers, even though there appears to have been no attempt to make the statues look like any particular individual: Every detail is simplified, focusing attention on the remarkable eyes constructed from shell, lapis lazuli, and black limestone.

Large and expressive eyes appear to be a basic convention of Sumerian art—although it is a convention found in other ancient art as well. Its basis is unknown, but the idea of the eye as a source of power permeates ancient folk-wisdom. The eye could act as a hypnotizing, controlling force, for good or for evil, hence the term "evil eye," which is still used today. Symbolic references to the eye range from "windows of the soul" to the "all-seeing" vigilance of the gods.

The Sumerians used art, like language, to communicate through conventions. Sumerian art took lifelikeness, as it was perceived by the artist, and reduced it to a few conventional forms. These statues also established social hierarchy and, to those who understood the conventions, communicated larger truths about the world.

9.11 Statues of worshipers and deities from the Square Temple at Tell Asmar, Iraq, c. 2750 B.C.E. Gypsum, tallest figure 30 ins (76 cm). Iraq Museum, Baghdad, and Oriental Institute, University of Chicago.

9.12 Sargon II's citadel, Khorsabad (during excavation), gate with pair of winged and human-headed bulls, 8th century B.C.E. Limestone.

The citadel, representing the ordered world, rises like the hierarchy of Assyrian gods, from the lowest levels of the city, through a transitional level, to the king's palace, which stands on its own elevated terrace. Two gates connect the walled citadel to the outside world. The first was undecorated; the second was adorned with and guarded by winged bulls and genii (Fig. **9.12**).

Remarkably, excavations at the site have revealed fairly inadequate construction methods. In addition, buildings are arranged haphazardly, and within the inner walls five minor palaces were crowded with obvious difficulty into the available space.

The main palace comprises an arrangement of ceremonial apartments around a central courtyard. Winged bulls and other figures guarded entrances to the throne room. The walls of the room itself, decorated with floor-to-ceiling murals, stood approximately 40 feet (12 m) high. Three small temples adjoined the palace and beside these rose a *ziggurat* (zih-goo-RAT) with successive stages painted in different colors, connected by a spiral staircase. Construction was of mud brick, laid without mortar while still damp and pliable, and of dressed and undressed stone. Some roof structures used brick barrel vaulting, although the majority appear to have had flat ceilings with painted beams.

Corresponding to the vast scale of the buildings are the great guardian figures represented by Figure **9.12**.

Undoubtedly symbolizing the supernatural powers of the king, these colossal hybrids are majestically powerful in stature and scale. Carved partly in relief and partly in the round, they are rationalized to be seen from front or side. The sculptor has provided each figure with a fifth leg, with the result that the viewer can always see four. Each of these monoliths was carved from a single block of stone upward of 15 feet (4.5 m) square.

HEBREWS, ISRAELITES, AND JEWS

The people who wrote and collected the books of the Old Testament, the offspring of the Patriarchs, are known variously as Hebrews, Israelites, and Jews. They began as an identifiable group around 1200 B.C.E., and they described themselves as both a religious and a national entity. The word *Hebrew* refers to Abraham's ethnic group. Eventually Abraham's descendants came to be called *Israel* (after Abraham's grandson). Around 922 B.C.E., the kingdom of Israel divided and the Northern Kingdom was destroyed. When in 587 B.C.E. Babylon destroyed the surviving Southern Kingdom, Judah (named for its major tribe), the people of the nation of Judah were taken into

9.13 Reconstruction drawing of Solomon's Temple, Jerusalem. The significance of the two bronze pillars is uncertain, but some scholars suggest that they may have represented the twin pillars of fire and smoke that guided the Israelites during their wanderings in the desert after the Exodus from Egypt.

captivity in Babylon. Later, the expression of Israelite religion became known as Judaism, from which came the words *Jew* and *Jewish*, meaning followers of Judaism and/or members of the ethnic group from which Judaism originated.

THE TEMPLE OF SOLOMON

The Temple in Jerusalem was the symbol of Hebrew faith as early as its third King, Solomon (c. 1000 B.C.E.). Described in the Bible in I Kings 5–9, the Temple of Solomon was primarily the house of the Lord God, rather than a place for the common people to come to worship.

The temple itself, as reconstructed in Figure 9.13, stood on a platform with a dominating entrance of huge wooden doors flanked by two bronze pillars about 18 feet (5.5 m) tall. The doors were decorated with carved palms, flowers, and cherubim (guardian winged beasts sometimes shown with human or animal faces). The entrance hall, or vestibule, measured approximately 15 by 30 feet (4.5 m × 9 m). Inside the temple proper was a Holy Place, or *Hekal*, about 45 feet (13.5 m) high, 60 feet (18 m) long, and 30 feet (9 m) wide. The paneled walls, made from cedars of Lebanon and carved in rich floral designs, were pierced at the top by small rectangular windows that allowed light to enter the temple. The room itself had various sacred furnishings: ten large lampstands, an inlaid table for priestly offerings, and a cedarwood altar covered with gold.

From a staircase behind the altar the High Priest entered the Holy of Holies, the most sacred part of the Temple, a windowless cubicle 30 feet (9 m) square. It contained the Ark of the Covenant, the symbol of God's presence, which the Jews had carried with them from the wilderness. Two large cherubim flanked the Ark.

THE HEBREW BIBLE

The word "bible" comes from the Greek word for book, and it refers to the town of Byblos, which exported the papyrus reed used in the ancient world for making books. The Jews compiled the history of their culture and religion into a collection of sacred writings called scriptures. The compilation grew from the oral traditions of the Hebrew people and took shape over a period of years as it was assembled, transcribed, and verified by state officials and scholars. The Bible has been handed down in a variety of forms. The Hebrew Bible, often called the Masoretic Text (MT), is a collection of twenty-four books written in Hebrew, with a few passages in Aramaic.

The earliest written Bible probably dates to the United Monarchy of King David in the tenth century B.C.E. It is composed of an assemblage of history, songs, stories, and prophecy. The current Hebrew Bible, canonized by the Council of Jamnia in 90 C.E., contains three parts: the Law (Torah), the Prophets, and the Writings. Briefly, the Torah comprises the books of Genesis, Exodus, Leviticus, Numbers, and Deuteronomy. The Prophets include Joshua, Judges, Samuel, Kings, Isaiah, Jeremiah, Ezekiel, and the twelve minor prophets. The Writings, which contain a variety of literary forms, including poetry and apocalyptic visions, comprise the biblical books of Psalms, Proverbs, Job, Song of Songs, Ruth, Lamentations, Ecclesiastes, Esther, Daniel, Ezra, Nehemiah, and Chronicles.

The Psalter is the hymnal of ancient Israel. Most of the Psalms were probably composed to accompany worship in the temple. They can be divided into various categories such as hymns, enthronement hymns, songs of Zion, laments, songs of trust, thanksgiving, sacred history, royal psalms, wisdom psalms, and liturgies. Here we include Psalm 22 (a psalm of David), and Psalms 130 and 133 (Songs of Ascent).[2]

Psalm 22

My God, my God, why hast thou forsaken me?
    Why art thou so far from helping me, from the words of
    my groaning?
2 O my God, I cry by day, but thou dost not answer;
    and by night, but find no rest.
3 Yet thou art holy,
    enthroned on the praises of Israel.
4 In thee our fathers trusted;
    they trusted, and thou didst deliver them.
5 To thee they cried, and were saved;
    in thee they trusted, and were not disappointed.

⁶ But I am a worm, and no man;
   scorned by men, and despised by the people.
⁷ All those who see me mock at me,
   they make mouths at me, they wag their heads;
⁸ "He committed his cause to the Lord; let him deliver
   him,
   let him rescue him, for he delights in him!"

⁹ Yet thou art he who took me from the womb;
   thou didst keep me safe upon my mother's breasts.
¹⁰ Upon thee was I cast from my birth,
   and since my mother bore me thou hast been my God.
¹¹ Be not far from me,
   for trouble is near
   and there is none to help.

¹² Many bulls encompass me,
   strong bulls of Bashan surround me;
¹³ they open wide their mouths at me,
   like a ravening and roaring lion.
¹⁴ I am poured out like water,
   and all my bones are out of joint;
   my heart is like wax,
   it is melted within my breast;
¹⁵ my strength is dried up like a potsherd,
   and my tongue cleaves to my jaws;
   thou dost lay me in the dust of death.

¹⁶ Yea, dogs are round about me;
   a company of evildoers encircle me;
   they have pierced my hands and feet—
¹⁷ I can count all my bones—
   they stare and gloat over me;
¹⁸ They divide my garments among them,
   and for my raiment they cast lots.

¹⁹ But thou, O Lord, be not far off!
   O thou my help, hasten to my aid!
²⁰ Deliver my soul from the sword,
   my life from the power of the dog!
²¹ Save me from the mouth of the lion,
   my afflicted soul from the horns of the wild oxen!
²² I will tell of thy name to my brethren;
   in the midst of the congregation I will praise thee:
²³ You who fear the Lord, praise him!
   all you sons of Jacob, glorify him,
   and stand in awe of him, all you sons of Israel!
²⁴ For he has not despised or abhorred
   the affliction of the afflicted;
   and he has not hid his face from him,
   but has heard, when he cried to him.

²⁵ From thee comes my praise in the great congregation;
   my vows I will pay before those who fear him.
²⁶ The afflicted shall eat and be satisfied;
   those who seek him shall praise the Lord!
   May your hearts live for ever!

²⁷ All the ends of the earth shall remember
   and turn to the Lord;
   and all the families of the nations
   shall worship before him.
²⁸ For dominion belongs to the Lord,
   and he rules over the nations.

²⁹ Yea, to him shall all the proud of the earth bow down;
   before him shall bow all who go down to the dust,
   and he who cannot keep himself alive.
³⁰ Posterity shall serve him;
   men shall tell of the Lord to the coming generation,
³¹ And proclaim his deliverance to a people yet unborn,
   that he has wrought it.

Psalm 130

Out of the depths I cry to thee, O Lord!
   Lord, hear my voice!
² Let thy ears be attentive
   to the voice of my supplications!

³ If thou, O Lord, shouldst mark iniquities,
   Lord, who could stand?
⁴ But there is forgiveness with thee,
   that thou mayest be feared.

⁵ I wait for the Lord, my soul waits,
   and in his word I hope;
⁶ My soul waits for the Lord
   more than watchmen for the morning,
   more than watchmen for the morning.

⁷ O Israel, hope in the Lord!
   For with the Lord there is steadfast love,
   and with him is plenteous redemption.
⁸ And he will redeem Israel from all his iniquities.

Psalm 133

Behold, how good and pleasant it is
   when brothers dwell in unity!
² It is like the precious oil upon the head,
   running down upon the beard,
   upon the beard of Aaron,
   running down on the collar of his robes!
³ It is like the dew of Hermon,
   which falls on the mountains of Zion!
   For there the Lord has commanded the blessing,
   life for evermore.

These poetic examples represent the section of the Bible where humans express their feelings to God. Psalm 22, which many believe Jesus quoted as he hung on the cross, develops from despair to trust and praise, as the psalmist pours out his troubles and then recognizes his own frailty and the greatness and unfailing love of God. The imagery is powerful: "I am poured out like water, and all my bones are out of joint; my heart is like wax, it is melted within my breast." Psalm 130, likewise, develops from trouble to hope. Typical of Hebrew tradition, things are stated twice, in different words: (1) "Out of the depths I cry to thee, O Lord! Lord, hear my voice." (2) "Let thy ears be attentive to the voice of my supplications!" Finally, Psalm 133 speaks of the benefits of peace, again with vivid imagery. When brothers dwell in unity, it is better than an excess of the most expensive commodities: "It is like precious oil upon the head, running down the beard."

ANCIENT EGYPT

The other ancient culture in this part of the world was that of Egypt. Protected by deserts and confined to the narrow Nile valley, ancient Egypt remained relatively isolated for thousands of years. It had a unified civilization, under the control of an absolute monarch (pharaoh). As a rural society, it depended uniquely upon the regular annual flooding of its single river, the Nile. Ancient Egyptian history divides into three periods, or kingdoms: Old, Middle, and New, beginning in about 2800 B.C.E. The other basic organizational unit, the dynasty, conforms to the period of a particular family of rulers.

Death—or, rather, everlasting life in the hereafter— was the focus of much of the art of the Egyptians. Appearing mostly in the service of the cult of a god or to glorify the power and wealth of a pharaoh, art and architecture centered on the provision of an eternal dwelling-place for the dead.

OLD KINGDOM

Sculpture was the major art form of the Egyptians. It not only furnished the "other self" for the tomb of the deceased, to provide immortality, but also stood in temples. By the time of the Old Kingdom (c. 2800–c. 2400 B.C.E.), sculptors had overcome many of the technical difficulties that plagued their predecessors. Possibly, religious tenets had also confounded sculptors during earlier times. (Many so-called primitive peoples throughout history have regarded lifelike portrayal of the human figure as inviting danger—making a likeness of an individual was thought to capture the soul.)

Old Kingdom sculpture shows technical mastery and strong artisanship. Life-size pieces capture the human form in exquisite detail. At the same time, certain conventions are used to idealize royalty. Egyptian belief in the divinity of the pharaoh dictated a dignified and majestic portrayal. Although rigidity of treatment lessened as time went on, softening and human-centered qualities never completely divested the pharaonic statue of its divine repose.

Rahotep and Nofret

The dual sculpture of Prince Rahotep and his wife Nofret (Fig. **9.14**) comes from the tomb of the prince. The stylized posture represents a trademark of Egyptian art, with its intellectual or conceptual, as opposed to lifelike or visual, nature. The statues' striking colors exemplify the Egyptian tendency to use paint to provide a decorative surface for sculpture. The eyelids of both figures are painted black, and their eyes are dull and light-colored quartz. In line with convention, the skin tones of the woman are several shades lighter than those of the man. A woman's skin was traditionally creamy yellow, whereas a man's ranged from light to dark brown.

In Dynasty IV the kings rose from peasant stock, an ancestry which is apparent in the sturdy, broad-shouldered, well-muscled physique of the prince. At the same time his facial characteristics—particularly the eyes and expression—exhibit alertness, wisdom, strength, and capacity. The portrayal of Nofret expresses similar individuality. Probably for the first time in Egyptian art, we find full development of the three-dimensional female body. Nofret wears the typical gown of the period, cut to reveal voluptuous breasts. The artist has meticulously observed and depicted detail here, as in all the details of the upper portion of both statues.

Egyptian admiration for the human body reveals itself clearly in both statues. Precise modeling and attention to detail occur in the smallest items. In the statue of Nofret the gown at once covers and reveals the graceful contours of the body beneath. She has a sensual and pampered face. Her hair is a wig shaped in the style of the day, and beneath the constricting headband we can see Nofret's own hair, of much finer texture, parted in the middle and swept back beneath the wig. A precise and delicate treatment of the hand held open against the body reveals the

9.14 Prince Rahotep (*left*) and his wife Nofret (*opposite*), from Medum, Egypt, c. 2580 B.C.E. Painted limestone, height 3 ft 11½ ins (1.2 m). Egyptian Museum, Cairo.

9.15 Great Pyramid of Cheops (Khufu), Giza, Egypt, 2680–2565 B.C.E.

artist's perception. Small dimples decorate the fingers and the unpainted nails are correctly portrayed as lighter than normal skin tone.

The Pyramids

The years around 2700 B.C.E. brought forth the most remarkable edifices of Egyptian civilization—the pyramid area of Giza. In addition to the three most obvious pyramids, the area comprises burial places for almost all of the important individuals of Dynasties IV and V. Each pyramid complex has four buildings. The largest pyramid, that of Cheops (Fig. 9.15), measures approximately 750 feet (228 m) square (440 cubits) and rises at an angle of approximately 51 degrees to a height of 481 feet (146 m). The burial chamber of the pharaoh lay hidden in the middle (Fig. 9.16). Construction consisted of irregularly placed, rough-hewn stone blocks covered by a carefully dressed limestone facing approximately 17 feet (5 m)

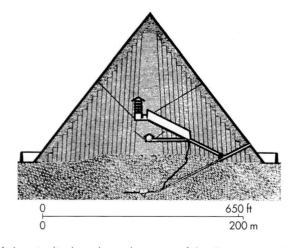

9.16 Longitudinal south–north section of the Great Pyramid of Cheops.

thick. The famous Sphinx (Fig. 9.17) is a colossal figure carved from natural rock, lying at the head of the causeway leading from the funerary temple adjoining the pyramid of Cheops' son Chephren, whose pyramid originally measured 707 feet (215 m) square, and rose at an angle of 52 degrees to a height of 471 feet (143 m).

Egypt's pyramids are the oldest existing buildings in the world. These ancient tombs are also among the world's largest structures. The largest stands taller than a forty-story building and covers an area greater than that of ten football fields. More than eighty pyramids still exist, and their once smooth limestone surfaces hide secret passageways and rooms. The pyramids of ancient Egypt served a vital purpose: to protect the pharaohs' bodies after death. Each pyramid held not only a pharaoh's preserved body but also all the goods he would need in his life after death.

NEW KINGDOM

The Temple at Luxor

Leaving the pyramids behind, we move to the New Kingdom (c. 1575–c. 1100 B.C.E.) and a building of great luxury and splendor: the temple at Luxor (Fig. 9.18). It approaches more nearly the modern conception of architecture—as a useful place for humankind to spend the present, rather than eternity. Built by Amenhotep III, the temple is dedicated to the Theban Triad of Amun, Mut, and Chons. It served two purposes. First, it was the place of worship for Amun, Mut, and Chons. Second, during the great feast of the middle of the flood, the barques of these gods were anchored there for several days.

Amenhotep III was a great builder and his taste for splendid buildings drew sustenance from a number of

9.17 (*above*) The Sphinx,
Giza, c. 2650 B.C.E.

9.18 Temple at Luxor, Egypt,
1417–1397 B.C.E.

N

9.19 Temple at Luxor, plan.

PROFILE

Nefertiti

Nefertiti (neh-fuhr-TEE-tee; c. 1372–1350 B.C.E.; Fig. **9.20**) was Akhenaton's (ah-keh-NAH-tuhn) Great Royal Wife. Scholars debate whether she was a princess from another land or an Egyptian. Those believing her to be of Egyptian origin are also divided. One group claims she was the daughter of Aye and Tiy, and the other claims her as the oldest daughter of Amenhotep III and another wife, possibly Sitamun. Whatever her parentage, Nefertiti was married to Akhenaton and while living in Memphis gave birth to six daughters. It is possible that she also had sons, although no record has been found of this. It was a practice in Egyptian art not to portray the male heirs as children. Possibly she was Tutankhamun's mother. Nefertiti achieved a prominence unknown to other Egyptian queens; there are, in fact, more statues and drawings of her than of Akhenaton. Some have even claimed that Nefertiti, not Akhenaton, instigated the monotheistic religion of Aton. Around year 15 of Akhenaton's reign, Nefertiti mysteriously disappeared from view. Perhaps she died, but no indication of this can be found. Some scholars think that she was banished for some reason, and lived the rest of her years in the northern palace, raising Tutankhamun. Whatever may have happened, she was replaced by her oldest daughter, Meritaten, and disappeared from history.

Akhenaton's own words describe Nefertiti: "The Hereditary Princess, Great of Favor, Mistress of Happiness, Gay with the two feathers, at hearing

9.20 *Nofretete (Nefertiti),* c. 1360 B.C.E. Painted limestone, height 19 ins (48 cm). Egyptian Museum, Berlin.

whose voice one rejoices, Soothing the heart of the king at home, pleased at all that is said, the Great and Beloved Wife of the King, Lady of the Two Lands, Neferu-aton Nefertiti, living forever."

---

excellent architects. Notable among these was Athribis, whose likeness at age eighty is preserved in a magnificent statue showing he retained his intellectual and physical abilities and that he expected to reach the age of 110, which the Egyptians considered to be the natural human life span.

People entered the temple through a vestibule full of giant pillars with palm-shaped capitals (Fig. **9.19**). From the vestibule they progressed to a huge courtyard surrounded by bunched columns, then to the *hypostyle* room, and, finally, the Holy of Holies. We cannot escape the loveliness of the columns. The balance between the open spaces and the mass of the columns creates a beautiful play of light and shade. The proportions were mass-

ive: The seven pairs of central pillars in the Hall of Pillars are nearly 52 feet (15.8 m) high. Surviving the centuries, the temple grew when Rameses II added a forecourt ringed with columns and covered walkways as well as containing two colossal statues of the king and a pair of obelisks. The walls of the courtyard present relief sculptures of Rameses and his family. Later, the inner enclosure served as a sanctuary for Alexander the Great, and in early Christian times it was used as a Christian church.

Theban Rock Tombs

Tomb paintings and low-relief carvings functioned to furnish the dead with an "eternal castle" and thus to

9.21 Tomb of Queen Nefertari-mi-en-Mat, Thebes, Egypt, ground plan, 1290–1224 B.C.E.

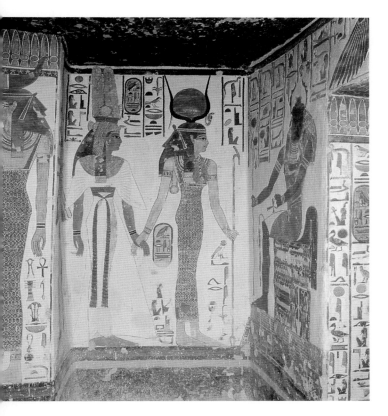

9.22 *Queen Nefertari Guided by Isis*, from the First Room of the tomb of Queen Nefertari, Thebes.

to the south lies the Main Room or offering chamber. Connected to these chambers is the major part of the tomb, in which the Hall of Pillars or Sarcophagus Chamber provides the central focus. Off and surrounding the Hall of Pillars lie three side rooms.

The northeast wall of the First Room houses a vibrant painting showing the goddess Selkis on the extreme left, with a scorpion on her head (Fig. **9.22**). On the extreme right appears the goddess Maat. Her hieroglyph, the feather, rests on her head. Over the door to the Main Room is the vulture goddess Nekhbet of El-Kab (partly visible in the top right corner of the illustration). Her claws hold the shen-sign, which symbolizes eternity and sovereignty. The rear wall of the recess depicts Queen Nefertari led by the goddess Isis toward the beetle-headed Khepri—a form assumed by the sun god implying his everlasting resurrection. On her crown Isis wears the horns of a cow, surrounded by the sun-disc from which hangs a cobra. In her left hand she carries the divine scepter. Queen Nefertari dresses according to the fashion

establish the status they had attained on earth, which they would continue to have in the hereafter. Most of what we now know about Egyptian painting of this period comes from the Theban rock tombs. Ceiling decorations are common and elaborate. The paintings portray the vivacity and humor of daily life.

The tomb of Queen Nefertari-mi-en-Mat, of Dynasty XIX (one of the four principal wives of King Rameses II and his favorite) lies in the Valley of Queens in western Thebes (now the west bank at Luxor), by precipitous cliffs at the end of the gloomy valley of Biban el Harin. The paintings adorning the walls of Nefertari's tomb exemplify a style of painting done in low relief, and show great elegance, charm, and vivacious color. The tomb (Fig. **9.21**) is entered through the First Room; off it and

9.23 Funerary mask of King Tutankhamun, c. 1340 B.C.E. Gold inlaid with enamel and semiprecious stones, height 21¼ ins (54 cm). Egyptian Museum, Cairo.

of the time, and over the vulture hood she wears the tall, feathered crown of the Divine Consort.

Rich, warm, and elegant, the paintings reveal high stylization. The limited palette uses four hues, which never change in value throughout the work. Yet the overall effect of this wall decoration is one of great variety. The human form is treated in flat profile—the conventionalized style established in Dynasty I. Eyes, hands, head, and feet show no attempt at lifelikeness. Quite the contrary: The fingers become extenuated designs, elongating the arms to balance the elegant and sweeping lines of legs and feet. The matching figures of Selkis and Maat (extreme left and right) even have arms of unequal length and proportion.

Akhenaton and Monotheism: The Tell el Amarna Period

The reign of Akhenaton marks a break in the continuity of artistic style in Egypt. Stiff poses disappear in favor of a more natural form of representation. Moreover, the pharaoh is depicted in intimate scenes of domestic life as well as in the formal ritual or military acts that were expected. He is no longer seen with the traditional human and animal gods of Egypt. Rather, he and his queen are depicted worshiping the disc of the sun, Aton, whose rays end in hands that either bless the royal pair or hold to their nostrils the *ankh*, the symbol of life. What accounts for this revolution is not certain.

In the fifth or sixth year of his reign, the king moved his court to a sandy desert ground on the east side of the Nile: the newly constructed city of Tell el Amarna. It was a new city for a new king intent on establishing a new order based on a new religion. Because the movement failed, leaving the city abandoned, we find an encapsulated artistic synthesis, including the city itself. Tell el Amarna lay away from cultivated land, and, once abandoned, was never built over.

The town itself is dominated by the large estates of the wealthy, who chose the best sites and laid them out in the style of Egyptian country houses, with large gardens and numerous outbuildings, enclosed within a wall. Between these large estates lay the smaller dwellings of the less wealthy. There was even a slum area outside the northern suburb. Nearby was the grand North Palace.

In many ways Amarna reflects the standard features of New Kingdom domestic architecture, but it seems much less sumptuous. Its lines and style are relatively simple. Structures are open, in contrast to the dark and secret character of the temple of Luxor, for example. At Amarna, numerous unroofed areas lead to Aton's altar, left open to provide access to the rays of his sun.

Sculpture at Amarna departed from tradition. It moved away from the strong emphasis on tombs and temples and became more a form of secular art. Amarna sculptors sought to represent the uniqueness and individuality of humankind through the human face. In one sense their sculptures are highly lifelike, and yet, in another, they depart into the realm of spirituality. The bust of Queen Nefertiti (Fig. **9.20**) illustrates these characteristics. Of course, we have no way of knowing how Queen Nefertiti actually looked, but the figure is so anatomically correct that it could be a lifelike representation. None the less, the line and proportions of the neck and head appear elongated, probably to increase her spiritual appearance.

Depictions of Akhenaton show that he apparently suffered from physical deformity. The artistic trends of the period and Akhenaton's desire for truth seem to have resulted in his graphic representation as a man with a misshapen body, an elongated head, and drooping jaw. Yet the eyes are deep and penetrative, producing the effect of a brooding genius.

Although his religious reforms failed, Akhenaton's experiment in monotheism left us with a clear portrait of an integrated scheme of life and culture.

Tutankhamun

One of the most popular artifacts from the succeeding period is an exquisite funerary mask from the tomb of Akhenaton's son Tutankhamun (Fig. 9.23), discovered in the Valley of Kings near Thebes. The mask is of solid beaten gold inlaid with semiprecious stones and colored glass. Designed to cover the face of the king's mummy, it contains the royal *nemes* headdress with two flaps hanging down at the sides. A ribbon holds his braid at the back. The hood formed by the headdress reveals two symbolic creatures: the uraeus serpent and the vulture goddess Nekhbet of El-Kab, divinities who protected Lower and Upper Egypt.

ANCIENT CHINA

From the earliest times, China witnessed the crowding of populations into tight-walled villages. That packing-in of people governed social and family relationships. The family—as opposed to the individual, state, or religious group—formed the most significant social unit. This was reinforced by the practice of ancestor worship. The family also formed the basic political unit. A scheme of mutual

9.24 Ritual wine vessel or *hu*, c. 1300–1100 B.C.E. Bronze, height 16 ins (40.6 cm), width 11 ins (27.9 cm). Nelson Atkins Museum of Art, Kansas City (Purchase: Nelson Trust).

9.25 Elephant feline head, from China, c. 1200 B.C.E. (Shang Dynasty). Jade, length 1⅝ ins (4 cm). Cleveland Museum of Art (Anonymous gift).

relief. Each line has perfectly perpendicular sides and a flat bottom, meeting at a precise 90-degree angle; this contrasts, for example, with incised decoration, which forms a groove. The bronze ritual vessel in a shape called *hu* (Fig. **9.24**) has subtle symmetrical patterns and delicate craftsmanship. Deftly placed ridges and gaps break the graceful curves and although the designs are delicate, the overall impression is one of solidity and stability.

Another innovation of the Shang culture was stone sculpture in high-relief or in the round. The most numerous objects to survive are small-scale images in jade. There is a broad range: from fish, owls, and tigers as single units to metamorphoses such as the elephant head of Figure **9.25**. This design combines simplicity with subtle detail. Its feline head has large, sharp teeth, an elephant's trunk, and bovine horns.

responsibility, called the *Pao-chia system*, made people in the same household answerable for each other's actions.

Within the family, a hierarchy existed. The position of each person was dictated by birth and marriage. (Marriages were arranged more as a union of families than of individuals.) Everyone was subordinate to the family and, in general, women were subordinate to men. Norms for social conduct, such as loyalty, sincerity, and benevolence, were inculcated in the family system. The greatest virtue was filial piety. Later (sixth century B.C.E.), the ethical system of Confucianism fulfilled the role played by law and religion in the West. The Chinese social model was authoritarian and class-conscious.

At a time slightly prior to the Israelites' enslavement in Egypt, verifiable Chinese history began: From approximately 1400 to 1100 B.C.E., the Shang Dynasty emerged. As in Egypt, the dynasty was the basic organizational unit of history.

The Shang Dynasty produced two types of bronzes: weapons and ceremonial vessels. Both are frequently covered with elaborate designs, either incised or in high-

NATIVE AMERICA

Native American art is labeled as either *pre-Columbian*—before Columbus, which we shall examine here,—or *post-Columbian* and encompasses weaving, metalsmithing, pottery, and architecture. Like all others, Native American artists developed their own set of conventions or ground rules. Some of these are quite different from the artistic conventions of Western culture. Those who do not come from the culture themselves may never—probably cannot ever—fully engage a work of art from this tradition, with all its subtleties, comprehending what it comprises in the understanding of its creators.

In many respects, however, Native American art is the same as Western, Chinese, or any other art: human, with visual, emotional, and psychological qualities.

Among many Native American groups there is no specific term equivalent to the word "art." In Native

9.26 Olmec-style head with trace of red paint inlay, from Xochipala, Guerrero, Mexico, 1250–750 B.C.E. Fragment of carved stone figurine, 3 × 1 ins (7.6 × 2.5 cm). National Museum of the American Indian, Smithsonian Institution, Washington, D.C.

American culture in general, however, art is anything technically well done or that has a well conceived end result. The effect could be magical or thought to bring power. In essence, an "artist" was merely one person who possessed greater skill at something than another. Only a few Indian tribes—for example the Northwest Coast, Mayan, and Inca—had a group of professionals who earned a living by producing art.

Within Native American culture exists a wide variety of expressions, approaches to materials, and general styles. The earliest identifiable art in Mexico comes from the Olmecs—the word means "dwellers in the land of rubber"—and can be dated to approximately 1000 B.C.E. The Olmecs constituted a major civilization, which traded extensively with parts of Mesoamerica at a considerable distance from the Olmec territory along the Gulf of Mexico. They carved a number of animal subjects, including jaguars and figures called were-jaguars that combined human and jaguar features. Their human carvings often have a characteristic turned-down mouth (Fig. 9.26). Even though much of the body of the tiny figure is missing, we can see the care with which details were carved on this green-gray stone effigy.

Olmec artists also carved on a colossal scale, producing stone heads some 8 feet (2.4 m) in diameter, again with turned-down mouths. These were crafted from basalt boulders moved to the gulf coast from the Tuxtla Mountains more than 60 miles (97 km) inland. Scholars believe they represent portraits of rulers.

Olmec architecture includes the Great Pyramid at La Venta, Mexico, an earth mound rising to a height of around 100 feet (30 m). Whether its rounded form has resulted from erosion or was intended to replicate a volcano remains unknown.

ARCHAIC GREECE

The time from approximately 800 to 480 B.C.E. is called the "Archaic period." Archaic Greece was preceded by two nearby civilizations, the Minoan (c. 3000 B.C.E. to c. 1500 B.C.E.) and the Mycenaean (c. 1400 B.C.E. to c. 1200 B.C.E.), whose styles we, unfortunately, do not have space to discuss.

Archaic Greek culture consisted of a collection of city-states or *poleis* (singular—*polis*) of self-governing people. Each had its own sense of self. Some, like Athens, had high esteem for the arts and philosophy; others, like Sparta, were militaristic and seemingly indifferent to high culture. There was, however, a unifying spirit among these independent poleis of Greek derivation—they saw themselves as "Hellenes" and shared a common language and calendar, which dated to the first Olympic games in 776 B.C.E.

9.27 Attic bowl showing Perseus and the gorgons, early 6th century B.C.E. Height 36½ ins (93 cm). Louvre, Paris.

ARCHAIC STYLE

By the middle of the sixth century B.C.E. Greek artists tried to portray the human body in a three-quarter position, between profile and full frontal. A new feeling for three-dimensional space emerged, and artists began to depict eyes more accurately. Fabric began to assume the drape and folds of real cloth. All these characteristics mark vase painting in a style called Archaic (Fig. **9.27**).

Most of the freestanding statues in the Archaic style are of nude youths, known as *kouroi* (koo-roy). The term means, simply, "male youth," and the singular form is *kouros* (koo-rohs; Fig. **9.28**). These statues focus on physicality and athleticism, and all exhibit a stiff, fully frontal pose. Most of the kouroi were sculpted as funerary and temple art. Many of them were signed by the artist: "So-and-so made me." In addition, the sculpture attempts to indicate movement. The left foot extends forward, giving a greater sense of motion than if both feet were side by side in the same plane.

ARCHITECTURE: THE DORIC STYLE

In the Archaic period, temples exhibited a new adaptation of post-and-lintel structure. The style of these temples was called Doric after one of the Hellenic peoples, the Dorians. We can sense the qualities and details of the Doric order by examining a reconstruction drawing of the west front of the Temple of Artemis at Corfu (Fig. **9.29**) and by referring to the drawing of the parts of the order in Figure **9.30**. We note especially the tapering columns that sit directly on the stylobate. The column shafts are fluted (vertically grooved), and the capital consists of a simple slab.

9.28 Kouros, c. 615 B.C.E. Marble, height 6 ft 4 ins (1.93 m). Metropolitan Museum of Art (Fletcher Fund, 1932).

9.29 Reconstruction drawing of the west front of the Temple of Artemis, Corfu [after Rodenwaldt].

9.30 The Doric order.

9.31 Attributed to the Eucharides Painter, amphora showing Apollo playing a lyre and Artemis holding an aulos before an altar, c. 490 B.C.E. Height 18½ ins (47 cm). Metropolitan Museum of Art, New York (Rogers Fund, 1907).

MUSIC

Surviving records tell us that Greek music consisted of a series of modes, the equivalent of our scales. Each mode—for example, the Dorian and Phrygian—had a name and a particular characteristic sound, not unlike the difference between our major and minor scales, and the Greeks attributed certain behavioral outcomes to each mode. Just as we say that minor scales sound sad or exotic, the Greeks held that the Dorian mode exhibited strong, even warlike, feelings, while the Phrygian elicited more sensual emotions.

We have a fairly good picture of what Greek musical instruments looked like from vase paintings such as Figure 9.31. The Greeks were particularly fond of vocal music, and used instruments mainly to accompany the voice. Some lyrics have survived, and these include songs to celebrate acts by the various gods, from whom some mortal had gained special favor.

LITERATURE

Homer is probably the best-known of the ancient Greek poets, but he was by no means the only one. By the end of the seventh century B.C.E. poets appeared who tell us their names, and sing of themselves, their travels, military adventures, homesickness, drinking parties, poverty, hates, and loves. The poet Sappho (born around 615 B.C.E.) lived all her life on the island of Lesbos. She gathered around her a coterie of young women interested in poetry. Many of Sappho's poems are written in honor of one or other of these young women. Sappho was called a lyrist or lyric poet because, as was the custom of the time, she wrote her poems to be performed with the accompaniment of a lyre. She was one of the first poets to write in the first person, describing love and loss as they affected her personally. Her style was sensual and melodic.

Homer's *Iliad* and *Odyssey* created the mythical history that later Greeks accepted as their historic heritage. They took the dark and unknown past and created in a literary, originally oral, form a cultural foundation for an entire people. They told of heroes and described the gods. They depicted places and events and did so in a form that represented a significant artistic achievement: *epic poetry* (see Chapter 8). Both poems deal with minor episodes in the story of the battle of Troy, which ended, with the destruction of the city, in about 1230 B.C.E. Divided into twenty-four books, the *Odyssey* tells the story of Odysseus, king of Ithaca, as he travels home from the Trojan War to recover his house and kingdom. Also set in twenty-four books, the *Iliad* explores the heroic ideal with all its contradictions. Homer develops events on the battlefield and behind the lines of both adversaries. From his descriptions, an elaborate evocation emerges of the splendor and tragedy of war and the inconsistencies of mortals and gods. The heroes are types, not real people, and legend established their characters long before Homer described them in this epic poem. Here is a brief extract:

The Iliad
Book XX
Homer
8th century B.C.E.

How Achilles made havoc among the men of Troy.

So by the beaked ships around thee, son of Peleus, hungry for war, the Achaians armed; and over against them the men of Troy, upon the high ground of the plain.

But Zeus bade Themis call the gods to council from many-folded Olympus' brow; and she ranged all about and bade them to the house of Zeus. …

Thus gathered they within the doors of Zeus; nor was the Earthshaker heedless of the goddess' call, but from the salt sea came up after the rest, and set him in the midst, and inquired concerning the purpose of Zeus: "Wherefore, O Lord of the bright lightning, hast thou called the gods again to council? Say, ponderest thou somewhat concerning the Trojans and Achaians? for lo, the war and the fighting of them are kindled very nigh."

And Zeus, who gathered the clouds, answered him, saying: "Thou knowest, O Earthshaker, the purpose within my breast, wherefor I gathered you hither; even in their perishing have I regard unto them. But for me I will abide here, sitting within a fold of Olympus, where I will gladden my heart with gazing; but go all ye forth that ye come among the Trojans and Achaians and succour these or those, howsoever each of you hath a mind. For if Achilles alone shall fight against the Trojans, not even a little while shall they hold back the son of Peleus, the fleet of foot. Nay, but even aforetime they trembled when they looked upon him; now therefore that his wrath for his friend is waxen terrible I fear me lest he overleap the bound of fate, and storm the wall."

Thus spake the son of Kronos, and roused unabating war.[3]

THINKING CRITICALLY

- Identify the fundamental characteristics of Egyptian, Assyrian, and Archaic Greek art. Choose one example from each period, and compare the examples by noting how they exemplify the characteristics of their time and how they are like or different from each other.

- From the evidence presented in the chapter, and from any other material you can find, evaluate the statement that the art of the Stone Age indicates that human beings were as fully developed in their humanity as current humans are.

- Drawing on notions of aesthetics as Western culture has developed them (see pp. 15–16), develop a comparison with Native American concepts of "art."

- Employing the concepts of line, form, mass, and articulation, do a comparative, formal analysis of the Tell Asmar statues (Fig. **9.11**) and the Archaic Greek kouros in Figure **9.28**.

CYBER STUDY

PREHISTORIC ART:
http://witcombe.sbc.edu/ARTHprehistoric.html#general

MESOPOTAMIA:
http://witcombe.sbc.edu/ARTHancient.html#AncNearEast

ANCIENT EGYPT:
http://witcombe.sbc.edu/ARTHancient.html#AncEgypt

NATIVE AMERICA:
http://doaks.org/PCWebSite/Gallery%20Tour/Gallery%20HTML%20pages/02gallery.html

ARCHAIC GREECE:
http://library.thinkquest.org/26264/art/periods/site004.htm

CHAPTER TEN

ARTISTIC REFLECTIONS IN THE PRE-MODERN WORLD

c. 600 B.C.E. to c. 1400 C.E.

CHINA

CHINESE SCULPTURAL STYLE
CHINESE ARCHITECTURAL
STYLE
CHINESE PAINTING STYLE

JAPAN

JAPANESE STYLE IN
ARCHITECTURE
JAPANESE STYLE IN
PAINTING AND
SCULPTURE
JAPANESE STYLE IN THEATRE
AND LITERATURE

MEDIEVAL EUROPE

MEDIEVAL MUSICAL STYLE
Chant
Profile: Hildegard of Bingen
Polyphony: Organum
ROMANESQUE STYLE IN
ARCHITECTURE
ROMANESQUE STYLE IN
SCULPTURE
*A Personal Journey: Autun
Cathedral Tympanum*

MEDIEVAL LITERATURE
The Song of Roland
Dante, *The Divine Comedy*,
from Canto V
GOTHIC STYLE IN
PAINTING
GOTHIC ARCHITECTURE:
THE CATHEDRAL
GOTHIC SCULPTURE
MEDIEVAL THEATRE

NATIVE AMERICA

Thinking Critically
Cyber Study

IMPORTANT TERMS

Classicism An artistic style dating
to fifth-century-B.C.E. Greece
and exhibiting simplicity,
clarity of structure, and appeal
to the intellect.

Contrapposto stance In sculpture,
the arrangement of body parts
so that the weight-bearing leg
is apart from the free leg,
thereby shifting the
hip/shoulder axis.

Diptych Two panels hinged
together.

Hieratic style A style in Byzantine
art presenting formalized,
almost rigid, depictions to
inspire reverence and
meditation.

Aryballus A shape in Inca pottery
containing a wide base and tall,
flanged neck.

Plainchant Also called chant and
plainsong (and sometimes,
Gregorian chant). A body of
sacred Christian monophonic
music.

Organum Polyphony developed
through the addition of
melodic lines to plainchant.

Romanesque style A broad style of
visual art and architecture
referring to vaulted medieval
architecture preceding the
Gothic style.

Gothic style A style of visual arts
and architecture most closely
associated with the pointed
arch and a sense of light and
space.

GREEK CLASSICISM

Under the ruler Pericles (PAIR-ih-kleez), Classical Greek culture reached its miraculous zenith in the fifth century B.C.E. In the brief span of time between approximately 600 and 200 B.C.E., Greek influence and civilization spread throughout the Mediterranean world. At its widest, under Alexander the Great (356–323 B.C.E.), it stretched—for the span of a single lifetime—from Spain to the River Indus. All this was achieved by a people whose culture, at its height, took as its measure the human intellect. In society, as in the arts, rationality, clarity, and beauty of form were the aim. However, as the style we call Hellenistic developed in the fourth century B.C.E., artists increasingly sought to imbue their works with the expression of feeling.

Classicism is an artistic style and cultural perspective based on principles associated with the art and thought of ancient Greece and Rome. Specifically, this means a striving for harmony, order, reason, intellect, objectivity, and

formal discipline. It contrasts with, for instance, Romanticism (see Chapter 12) and other "anti-classical" styles and directions such as the Baroque and Rococo (Chapter 11), which emphasize imagination, emotion, and free expression. Artworks in the Classical style—for example, Myron's *Discus Thrower* (see Fig. **10.3**)—represent idealized perfection rather than real life. As we will see, this embodies an ideal of beauty, sculpted according to the aesthetic principles of proportion, balance, and unity of form. Classicism is also an ideological viewpoint that reflects the idea of ancient Greece as the fount of civilization, later to be expanded to view western European culture as its ultimate fulfillment.

Style is generally related to treatment of form rather than content or subject matter, but often form and content cannot be separated. When Classicism was modified by a more individualized and lifelike treatment of form, its subject matter broadened to include the mundane.

Such expression, particularly in painting, reflects a technical advance as well as a change in attitude. Many of the problems of foreshortening—the perceivable diminution of size as the object recedes in space—had been solved and, as a result, figures have a new sense of depth. By the end of the fifth century B.C.E. the convention typified in Egyptian and Mesopotamian art—of putting all the figures along the baseline on the front plane of the design—gives way to suggestions of depth. Some figures are occasionally placed higher than others. By the end of the fourth century B.C.E. the problems of depth and foreshortening were fully overcome. Impressions of lifelikeness are also heightened in some cases by the use of light and shadow.

CLASSICAL PAINTING

Some records imply that mural painters of the Classical period were highly skillful in representation, but no examples have survived. What has come down to us is a wealth of vase painting. The restrictions inherent in the medium, however, preclude assessment of the true level of skill and development of the two-dimensional art of this period.

Fifth-century Athenian painting of the Classical style demonstrates the artists' concern for formal design—that is, logical, evident, and perfectly balanced organization of space. What separates Classical painting from earlier styles is a new sense of idealized reality in figure depiction.

The Achilles Painter (Fig. **10.1**) exemplifies use of idealization and dignity in the Classical style. The portrayal of feet in the frontal position reflects a new and significant skill in depicting space.

CLASSICAL SCULPTURE

The fifth century saw many of the most talented artists turn to sculpture and architecture. The age of Greek Classical style in sculpture probably begins with the sculptors Myron and Polyclitus (pah-lih-KLY-tuhs) in the middle of the fifth century B.C.E. Both contributed to the development of *cast* sculpture (see Chapter 2). Polyclitus reportedly achieved the ideal proportions of the male athlete (Fig. **10.2**). Note that the *Lance Bearer* by Polyclitus represents *the* male athlete, and not *a* male athlete. In this work the body's weight rests on one leg in the *contrapposto* stance (see Glossary). This simple but important new posture, characteristic of Greek Classical style, results in a sense of relaxation and controlled dynamics and a subtle play of curves.

Polyclitus developed a set of rules for constructing the ideal human figure that he laid out in his treatise *The*

10.1 Achilles Painter, White ground lekythos from Gela (?), showing woman and her maid, 440 B.C.E. Height 15 ins (38 cm). Museum of Fine Arts, Boston (Francis Bartlett Donation; © 2002 Museum of Fine Arts, Boston).

10.2 Polyclitus, *Doryphorus* (*Lance Bearer*), Roman copy after an original of c. 450–440 B.C.E. Marble, height 6 ft 6 ins (1.98 m). Museo Archeologico Nazionale, Naples.

Canon (*kanon* is the Greek word for "rule" or "law"). The *Lance Bearer* supposedly illustrates his theory, but because neither the treatise nor the original statue has survived, we do not know what set of proportions Polyclitus thought ideal. Probably, he used ratios between some basic unit and the length of some body part or parts. The best-known work by Myron is the *Discus Thrower* (Fig. 10.3).

Classical Greek statuary may be portraiture, but the features are always idealized. Man may be the measure of all things, as the Greek philosopher Protagoras argued, but Greek Classical artists raised him above human reality to the state of perfection found only in the gods.

CLASSICAL THEATRE

The theatre of Periclean Athens was a theatre of convention, and the term convention, as it applies here, takes on a new meaning. Every era and every style have their conventions—those underlying, accepted expectations and/or rules that influence artists subtly or otherwise. "Theatre of convention" implies a style of production lacking in illusion or stage realism. Theatre of convention is to a large extent freer to explore the ideal than theatre of illusion (in which scenic details are portrayed representationally) because dependence upon stage mechanics and historically accurate costume does not hamper the playwright. An audience simply accepts a poetic description in theatre of convention and does not demand to see it. Thus in imagination rests the key to theatre of convention. Greek dramatists found that with freedom from the restraints imposed by dependence on illusion or depiction, they were much better able to pursue the lofty moral themes fundamental to their perception of the universe.

Although some plays from the era have survived, and indicate what and how playwrights wrote, we do not

MASTERWORK

Myron, *Discus Thrower*

Myron's *Discus Thrower* (or *Discobolus*) (Fig. 10.3) exemplifies the Classical concern for restraint in its subdued vitality and subtle suggestion of movement coupled with balance. But it also expresses the sculptor's interest in the flesh of the idealized human form. This example of the *Discus Thrower* is, unfortunately, a much later marble copy. Myron's original was in bronze (cast sculpture, see Chapter 2), a medium that allowed more flexibility of pose than marble. A statue, as opposed to a relief sculpture, must stand on its own, and supporting the weight of the marble on a small area, such as one ankle, poses a significant structural problem. Metal has greater tensile strength (the ability to withstand bending and twisting), and thus this problem does not arise.

In *Discovery of the Mind: The Greek Origins of European Thought* Bruno Snell writes: "If we want to describe the statues of the fifth century in the words of their age, we should say that they represent beautiful or perfect men, or, to use a phrase employed in the early lyrics for the purposes of eulogy: 'god-like' men. Even for Plato the norm of judgment still rests with the gods, and not with men."

Myron's representation of this young athlete contributes a sense of dynamism to Greek sculpture. Here Myron tackles a vexing problem for the sculptor: how to condense a series of movements into a single pose without making the sculpture appear static or frozen. His solution dramatically intersects two opposing arcs: one created by the downward sweep of the arms and shoulders, the other by the forward thrust of the thighs, torso, and head.

As is typical of Greek freestanding statues, the *Discus Thrower* is designed to be seen from one direction only. It is thus a sort of freestanding, three-dimensional "super-relief." The beginnings of Classical style are represented by celebration of the powerful nude male figure. The suggestions of moral idealism, dignity, and self-control in the statue are all qualities inherent in Classicism. However, the *Discus Thrower* marks a step forward, in the increasing vitality of figure movement. Warm, full, and dynamic, Myron's human form achieves a new level of expressiveness and power. It is fully controlled and free of the unbridled emotion of later sculpture. For Myron, balanced composition remains the focus of the work, and form takes precedence over feeling.

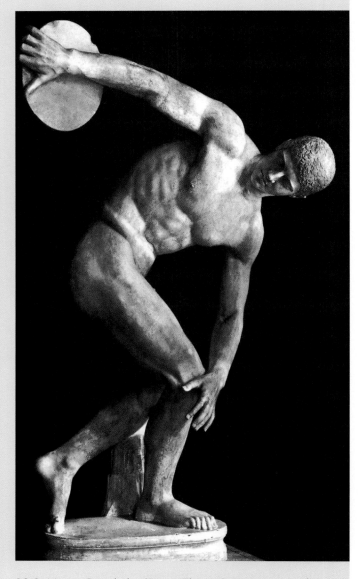

10.3 Myron, *Discobolus* (*Discus Thrower*), Roman copy after a bronze original of c. 450 B.C.E. Marble, life-size. Museo Nazionale Romano, Rome.

know specifically how those works became theatre—that is, a production. Nevertheless, we can build a picture of production from descriptions in the plays themselves, from other literary evidence, and from a few archeological examples.

Theatre productions in ancient Greece comprised part of religious festivals held three times a year: the City Dionysia, Rustic Dionysia, and Lenaea. The first of these was a festival of tragic plays and the last, of comic ones. The City Dionysia occurred in the theatre of Dionysus in Athens. Our knowledge of Greek theatre grows somewhat through the fact that, although we do not have most of the plays, we do know the titles and the names of the authors who won these contests from the earliest, in 534 B.C.E., to the final one. The records, inscribed in stone, show that three playwrights figured prominently and repeatedly as winners in the contests of the era:[1] Aeschylus, Sophocles, and Euripides (EH-skih-luhs; SAH-foh-kleez; yoo-RIH-pih-deez). All the complete tragedies to survive are by these three playwrights: seven by Aeschylus, seven by Sophocles, and eighteen by Euripides.

A playwright entering the contests for tragedy or comedy was required to submit the work to a panel of presiding officers, who selected just three authors for actual production. Early plays in the Classical style had only one actor plus a chorus, and at selection time the playwright was assigned the chief actor plus a *choregus*— a patron who paid all production expenses. The playwright was author, director, choreographer, and musical composer. He often also played the leading role.

Aeschylus (525–456 B.C.E.)

Aeschylus was the most famous poet of ancient Greece. Clearly fitting the Classical mold, he wrote magnificent tragedies of high poetic language and lofty moral themes. In *Agamemnon*, the first play in the *Oresteia* (ohr-eh-STY-uh) trilogy, Aeschylus's chorus warns us that success and wealth are insufficient without goodness.

Justice shines in sooty dwellings
Loving the righteous way of life,
But passes by with averted eyes
The house whose lord has hands unclean.
Be it built throughout of gold.
Caring naught for the weight of praise
Heaped upon wealth by the vain, but turning
All alike to its proper end.[2]

Aeschylus probed questions that we still ask: How responsible are we for our own actions? How much are we controlled by the will of the gods (or God)? His

characters are larger than life; they are types rather than individuals, in accordance with the idealism of the time. Yet they are also human. Aeschylus's early plays consist of the traditional single actor, plus a chorus of fifty. Later, he is credited with the addition of a second actor, and by the end of his career a third actor had been added and the chorus reduced to twelve.

Aeschylus's plays make a strong appeal to the intellect. He lived through the Persian invasions, witnessed the great Athenian victories, and fought at the battle of Marathon (490 B.C.E.). His plays reflect this experience and spirit.

Sophocles (496?–406 B.C.E.)

Sophocles' career overlapped that of Aeschylus, and he reached his peak at the zenith of the Greek Classical style with works like *Oedipus the King*. But he lived well beyond the death of Pericles in 429 B.C.E., experiencing the shame of Athenian defeat.

Sophocles' plots and characterizations illustrate a trend toward increasing realism. Yet the trend was not a progression toward theatre of illusion. Sophocles was a less formal poet than Aeschylus. His themes are more humane and his characters more subtle, although his exploration of the themes of human responsibility, dignity, and fate matches the intensity and seriousness of Aeschylus. His plots show increasing complexity, but within the formal restraints of the Classical spirit. Classical Greek theatre was mostly discussion and narration. Themes often dealt with bloodshed, but, though the play led up to violence, blood was never shed on stage.

Euripides (480?–406 B.C.E.)

Euripides was younger than Sophocles, although both men died in 406 B.C.E. They competed with each other but did not share the same style. Euripides' plays carry realism to the furthest extent we see in Greek tragedy. They deal with individual emotions rather than great events, and his language, though still basically poetic, comes closer to normal speech with much less formality than that of his predecessors.

Euripides experimented with, and ignored, many of the conventions of Greek theatre. He explored the mechanics of scene painting and depended less on the chorus than his rivals.[3] Sometimes he questioned the religion of his day. Strictly speaking, his plays are tragicomedies rather than pure tragedies. Some critics have described many of them as melodramas (see Chapter 4).

Plays such as *The Bacchae* reflect the changing Athenian spirit and dissatisfaction with contemporary events. Euripides was not particularly popular in his time, perhaps because his audience expected a more idealistic, formal, and conventional treatment of dramatic themes and characters. Was he perhaps too close to the reality of his age? His plays were received with enthusiasm, however, in later years.

Aristophanes (448?–380? B.C.E.)

Tragedies and satyr plays were not the only works produced in the theatre of the Classical era in Athens. The Athenians were extremely fond of comedy; unfortunately no examples survive from the Periclean period. Aristophanes was the most gifted of the comic poets, and his comedies of the post-Classical period, such as *Lysistrata*, are highly satirical, topical, sophisticated, and often sexually suggestive. Eleven of his plays have survived, and translated productions of them are still staged. As the personal and political targets of his invective are unknown to us, these modern productions are mere shadows of what took the stage at the turn of the fourth century B.C.E. As we noted in the Introduction, in *Lysistrata* Aristophanes creates a plot in which the women of Athens go on a sex strike to rid the city of war and war-mongers.

Theatre Design

The form of the Greek theatre owes much to the choral dances associated with the worship of Dionysus from which it originated. In 534 B.C.E. Thespis reportedly introduced a single actor to these dances, or dithyrambs. In 472 B.C.E., Aeschylus added a second actor, and in 458 B.C.E., Sophocles added a third.

Throughout its history the Greek theatre comprised a large circular *orchestra*—an acting and dancing area—with an altar at its center, and a semicircular *theatron*—an

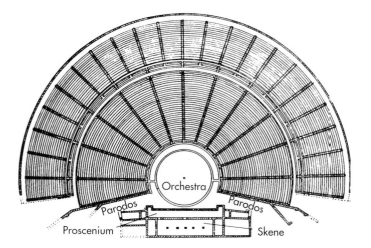

10.5 Polyclitus the Younger, Theatre at Epidaurus, Greece, c. 350 B.C.E., plan.

10.6 Theatre at Epidaurus. Diameter 373 ft (114 m), orchestra 80 ft (24 m) across.

auditorium or viewing place—usually cut into or occupying the slope of a hill. Since the actors played more than one role, they needed somewhere to change costume, and so a *skene* (skee-nay)—a scene building or retiring place—was added. The gradual development of the *skene* to include a raised stage is somewhat obscure, but clearly, by Hellenistic times it had emerged, and the building had become a rather elaborate affair with projecting wings at each end (Fig. 10.4).

The earliest surviving theatre, dating from the fifth century B.C.E., is the Theatre of Dionysus on the south slope of the Acropolis in Athens. It witnessed the plays of Aeschylus, Sophocles, Euripides, and Aristophanes. Its current form dates back to a period of reconstruction work around 338–326 B.C.E.

10.4 Reconstruction of the Hellenistic theatre at Ephesus, Turkey, c. 280 B.C.E., rebuilt c. 150 B.C.E.

The theatre at Epidaurus (Figs. **10.5** and **10.6**) is the best preserved ancient theatre. Built by Polyclitus the Younger about 350 B.C.E., 100 years after the end of the Classical period, it demonstrates by sheer size the monumental character the theatre had assumed by that time. The *orchestra* has a diameter of 80 feet (24 m) and an altar to Dionysus in the center. The auditorium—slightly more than a semicircle—is divided by an *ambulatory*, or covered walkway, about two-thirds of the way up, and by radiating stairways. All the seats were of stone. The first or lowest row was reserved for the dignitaries of Athens, and here the seats had backs and arms. Some were decorated with relief sculptures.

Undoubtedly variation existed in the design of theatres in different locations but, again, time has removed most examples from our grasp. The many theories of how Greek theatre productions worked, how scenery was or was not used, and when a raised stage appeared make fascinating reading.

CLASSICAL ARCHITECTURE

The arts of the Western world have returned over the past 2,400 years to the style of Classical Greek architecture, and nothing brings that style so clearly to mind as the Greek temple. Most people have an amazingly accurate concept of its structure and proportions. The art historian H. W. Janson suggests that the crystallization of the characteristics of a Greek temple is so complete that when we think of one Greek temple, we basically think of all Greek temples.

The Classical Greek temple, as seen in Figure **10.7**, has a structure of horizontal blocks of stone laid across vertical columns. This *post-and-lintel construction* is not unique to Greece, but certainly the Greeks refined it to its highest aesthetic level. As we saw in Chapter 7, this type of structure creates some very basic problems. Stone is not high in tensile strength—the ability to withstand bending and twisting—although high in compressive strength—the ability to withstand crushing. Downward thrust works against tensile qualities in horizontal slabs (lintels) and works for compressive qualities in vertical columns (posts). As a result, columns can be relatively delicate, whereas lintels must be massive.

Only limited open space can result from this structural system. Such restriction did not concern the Greeks because their temples were seen and used from the outside. Exterior structure and aesthetics were the primary concerns.

Greek temples consist of three *orders*: Doric, Ionic, and Corinthian (see Fig. **7.3**). These are not just decorative and elevational conventions, but systems of proportion.

The first two are Classical; the third, though of Classical derivation, belongs to the later, Hellenistic style. The contrasts between these types make an important, if subtle, stylistic point. Simplicity was an important characteristic of the Greek Classical style, and the Doric and Ionic orders maintain clean and simple lines. The Corinthian order has more ornateness and complexity. There are differences in column bases and the configuration of the lintels, as well as in the columns and capitals.

The earlier of the two Classical types—the Doric—has a massive appearance compared to the Ionic. The Ionic, with a round base, has a curved profile which raises the column above the baseline of the building. The fluting (ridging) of the Ionic order, usually twenty-two per column, is deeper and separated by wider edges than is that of the Doric, giving the former a more delicate appearance. The Ionic capital is surrounded by a crown of hanging leaves, or *kymation*. The *architrave*—the section resting directly on the capitals—is divided into three parts, and each diminishes downward. This creates a much lighter impression than the more massive architrave of the Doric.

The Parthenon

Perched atop the Acropolis at Athens, the Parthenon (Fig. **10.7**) stands as the greatest temple built by the Greeks and the prototype for all Classical buildings thereafter. When the Persians sacked Athens in 480 B.C.E., they destroyed the then existing temple and its sculpture. Pericles rebuilt the Acropolis in the late fifth century B.C.E. Athens was at its zenith, and the Parthenon was its crowning glory.

In plan the Parthenon is a peripteral temple—that is, columns surround the interior room, or *cella*, and the number of columns on the sides equals twice the number across the front, plus one. The inside, divided into two parts, housed the 40-foot (12-m)-high ivory and gold statue of the goddess Athena Parthenos.

The Parthenon typifies every aspect of Greek Classical style in architecture. Doric in character and geometric in configuration, it achieves balance through symmetry, and the clean, simple line and plan hold the composition together perfectly.

The internal harmony of the design lies in the regular repetition of virtually unvaried form. Each column is alike and equidistant from its neighbor, except at the corners, where the spacing lessens in subtle, aesthetic adjustment. A great deal has been written about the so-called "refinements" of the Parthenon—the elements that intentionally depart from strict geometric regularity. According to some scholars, the slight outward curvature of horizontal

10.7 Ictinus and Callicrates, Parthenon, Acropolis, Athens, from the northwest, 447–438 B.C.E.

elements compensates for the tendency of the eye to perceive downward sagging if all elements are actually parallel. Each column swells about 7 inches (17 cm)—this is called *entasis*—supposedly to compensate for the tendency of vertical parallel lines to appear to curve inward. The columns also tilt inward at the top so as to appear upright. The *stylobate* (the foundation immediately below the row of columns) rises toward the center so as not to appear to sag under the immense weight of the stone columns and roof.

The white marble, which in other circumstances might appear stark, may have been chosen to harmonize with and reflect the intense Athenian sunlight. However, some parts of the temple and its statuary would originally have been brightly painted.

Here we have the perfect embodiment of Classical characteristics: *convention, order, balance, idealization, simplicity, grace,* and *restrained vitality*—of this earth but mingled with the divine. Watch the Humanities CD: Architecture, Classicism.

LATE CLASSICAL STYLE IN SCULPTURE

Sculpture of the fourth century B.C.E. illustrates the change in emphasis reflected in late Classical styles. Famous for his *individualism* and delicacy in choice of themes, Praxiteles created in the *Cnidian Aphrodite* (Fig.

10.8) an inward-looking style different from the formal detachment of earlier sculpture. (Note that this is a copy; the original has never been found.) Aphrodite's body bends to the left in the famous Praxitelean S-curve. Originally, she rested her weight on one foot. Strain on the ankle was minimized by attaching the arm to drapery and a vase.

The late fourth century found in the sculpture of Lysippus (a favourite of Alexander the Great) a dignified naturalness and a new concept of space. In the *Scraper* (Fig. 10.9) he attempts to put the figure into motion, in contrast to the posed figures at rest of earlier periods. The sculpture has a mundane theme—an athlete scraping dirt and oil from his body. The proportions of the figure reflect greater lifelikeness than those of Polyclitus. Style had moved a long way from earliest Classicism, but Classical influence remained.

HELLENISTIC STYLE

As the age of Pericles gave way to the Hellenistic period, the dominant characteristics of Classicism gradually modified to a less formal, more realistic, and more emotional style reflecting a diversity of approaches.

Like other media and art forms, vase painting around the year 400 B.C.E. had a highly ornate style. Thick lines, dark patterns on garments, and a generous use of white and yellow characterized compositions of crowded figures represented mainly in three-quarter views. Illustrative of

10.10 Attributed to the Suessula Painter, amphora showing combat of Greeks and Amazons, 5th–6th century B.C.E. Height 14 ins (36 cm). Metropolitan Museum of Art, New York (Fletcher Fund).

10.8 (*above*) Praxiteles, *Cnidian Aphrodite*, probably Hellenistic copy of 4th-century B.C.E. bronze original. Marble, height 5 ft ½ in (1.54 m). Metropolitan Museum of Art, New York (Fletcher Fund).

10.9 (*above middle*) Lysippus, *Apoxyomenus* (*Scraper*), Roman copy, probably after a bronze original of c. 330 B.C.E. Marble, Height 6 ft 9 ins (2.05 m). Musei Vaticani, Rome.

this change in style is the combat scene from an *amphora* (AM-fohr-uh), or storage jar, painted by the Suessula Painter (Fig. **10.10**). Here the figures step away from the baseline, creating an illusion of spatial depth.

In the Hellenistic era, everyday scenes—sometimes comic and vulgar—occurred in wall painting. These scenes are remarkable for their use of atmospheric and linear perspective (see Chapter 1) to indicate three-dimensional space. Unfortunately, the few surviving examples of Classical and Hellenistic two-dimensional art furnish us with only a glimpse of the two important painting styles, so closely linked, yet reflecting such different attitudes.

Hellenistic style in sculpture dominated the Mediterranean world for several centuries until the first century B.C.E. As time progressed, style changed to reflect an increasing interest in individual human differences. Hellenistic sculptors often turned to pathos, banality, trivia, and flights of individual virtuosity. The *Dying Gaul* (Fig. **10.11**) provides powerful expression of emotion and pathos, depicting a noble warrior on the verge of death. Representing a Gallic casualty in the wars between Pergamon and barbarian invaders, the man slowly bleeds to death from a chest wound. The figure sits on a stage, as

10.11 (*above*) *Dying Gaul*, Roman copy of a bronze original from Pergamon, Turkey, of c. 230–220 B.C.E. Marble, life-size. Museo Capitolino, Rome.

10.12 (*left*) *Nike of Samothrace* (*Winged Victory*), c. 190 B.C.E. Marble, height 8 ft (2.43 m). Louvre, Paris.

10.13 (*above*) Hagesandrus, Polydorus, and Athenodorus, *Laocoön and his Two Sons*, 1st century C.E. Marble, height 5 ft (1.52 m). Musei Vaticani, Rome.

if to act out a drama. The *Nike of Samothrace* (Fig. **10.12**), or *Winged Victory*, displays a dramatic, dynamic technical virtuosity. Symbolizing a triumph of one of Alexander's successors, the victory figure seems to defy its heavy marble material and rise weightless, at the same time presenting a sense of great strength and power. The sculptor has treated stone almost as if the work were a painting. As a result, a full, awesome reality of wind and sea emerges.

The common Hellenistic theme of suffering dominates the Laocoön (lay-AH-koh-ahn) group (Fig. **10.13**). The sculpture depicts the Trojan priest Laocoön and his sons strangled by sea serpents. Based on Greek myth, the subject reflects Laocoön's punishment for defying Poseidon, god of the sea, and warning the Trojans of the Greek strategy of the Trojan horse. Emotion and movement burst all restraint; muscles strain and veins bulge in stark realism.

The temple of the Olympian Zeus (Fig. **10.14**) illustrates Hellenistic modification of Classical style in architecture—similar to that in painting, sculpture, and theatre. Temple architecture in this style sought to produce an overpowering emotional experience. It is the product of an empire rather than a reflection of the aspirations of a free people in a city-state. Scale and complexity have increased, but order, balance, moderation, and consonant harmony remain. In these huge ruins we see a change in proportions from the Parthenon, and slender and ornate Corinthian columns replace the Doric ones. The first major Corinthian temple, begun by the architect Cossutius for King Antiochus IV of Syria, it was not completed until the second century C.E., under the Roman emperor Hadrian. The cause was its elaborate detail. The remaining ruins only vaguely suggest the scale and richness of the original building, which was surrounded by an immense, walled precinct.

IMPERIAL ROMAN CLASSICISM

Roman civilization developed parallel to that of Greece and progressed from Etruscan origins through a Republican form of government to an Empire. When Hellenistic culture waned after the death of Alexander the Great, the Romans emerged as the masters of the Mediterranean region and, eventually, over most of Europe. By 70 C.E. the Romans had destroyed the Temple of Solomon in Jerusalem and colonized Britain, spreading their pragmatic and pluralistic version of Hellenistic Mediterranean civilization to peoples of the Iron Age in northern and western Europe. Under Augustus, the first Roman emperor (63 B.C.E.–14 C.E.), Roman culture turned again to Greek Classicism and in that spirit glorified Rome, the emperor, and the Empire. Inventive and utilitarian, Roman culture left us roads, fortifications, viaducts, planned administration, and a sophisticated yet robust legal system.

ROMAN SCULPTURAL STYLE

Some Roman art appears to imitate Greek prototypes, but much displays vigorous, uniquely Roman creativity. Scholars are divided not only on what various works of Roman sculpture reveal but also on what motivated them. The *Portrait of an Unknown Roman* (Fig. **10.15**) shows a "veristic" or highly lifelike representation. Etruscan–Roman religious practice undoubtedly had a strong influence. Portraits were an integral part of household and ancestor worship, and the image of a departed ancestor was maintained in a wax death mask. Wax is not a substance ideally suited for immortality, and there is a possibility that the naturalism of this bust stems from the fact that it was made from a death mask. However, there may

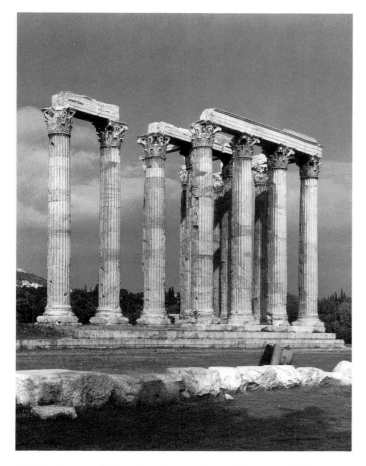

10.14 Temple of Olympian Zeus, Athens, 174 B.C.E.–130 C.E.

10.15 *Portrait of an Unknown Roman*, 1st century B.C.E. Marble, height 14⅜ ins (36 cm). Metropolitan Museum of Art, New York (Rogers Fund).

10.16 *Augustus of Primaporta*, early 1st century C.E. Marble, height 6 ft 8 ins (2.03 m). Musei Vaticani, Rome.

be more than mere portrait accuracy in this work, and some scholars point to an apparent selectivity of features and a reinforcement of an idea or ideal of ruggedness and character. A comparison with the Ife head of a queen (see Fig. 10.39) reveals a similarly realistic approach utilizing lifelikeness and selective details.

Hellenistic influence grew in the late first century B.C.E. Greek Classical influence dominated, but always with a Roman—that is, a more practical and individual—character. By the first century C.E., Classical influence had returned sculpture to the idealized style of Periclean Athens. Greek Classical form was duplicated, recast, and translated into vital forms of the present. It was also a common practice to copy the idealized body of a well-known Greek statue and add to it a portrait head of a contemporary Roman (Fig. 10.16). The aesthetics of sculptural depiction thus remained Greek, with Roman clothing added: The pose, rhythm, and movement of the body originated in the past. Much sculpture at this time portrayed the emperor, raising him to the status of a god, perhaps because a far-flung empire required assurances of stability and suprahuman characteristics in its leaders.

The reality that men are men and not gods was not long in returning to Roman consciousness, however, and third-century sculpture exhibits an expressive starkness. In the fourth century a new and powerful emperor took the

throne, and his likeness (Fig. 10.17)—part of a gigantic sculpture (the head is over 8 feet [2.5 m] tall)—shows an exaggerated, ill-proportioned intensity comparable with Expressionist works of the early twentieth century (see pp. 382–3). This work is not an actual likeness of Constantine. Instead, it is the artist's view of Constantine's perception of himself as emperor, and of the office of emperor itself. The exaggerated features of this work, however, do not reach the level of stylization witnessed, for example, in the bearded male figure from Djenne (see

Fig. **10.40**), but do show similarities to the approach taken in the head from Jemaa, Nigeria (see Fig. **10.38**).

LITERATURE

"Roman Literary Style"

At the time when literature became reasonably acceptable to the practical Romans, it was nurtured chiefly through the contributions of Greek slaves. At first, it imitated Greek literature and was written in Greek. Latin was initially seen as a peasant language with few words capable of expressing abstract notions. Credit for developing a Latin prose style and vocabulary for the expression of philosophical ideas is probably due to Cicero (106–43 B.C.E.). His contemporaries Lucretius and Catullus inaugurated the Golden Age of Latin literature with their poetry.

During the reign of Augustus, the poets Horace (65–8 B.C.E.) and Virgil (70–19 B.C.E.) wrote verses glorifying the emperor, on the origins of Rome, the simple honesty of rural life, patriotism, and the glory of dying for one's country. Livy (59 B.C.E.–17 C.E.) set about retelling Roman history in sweeping style. Virgil's *Aeneid* (ee-NEE-ihd) tells the story of the founding of Rome, in an epic account of the journey of Aeneas from the ruins of Troy to the shores of Italy. A section of Book 1 follows.

The Aeneid
Book 1
Virgil
70–19 B.C.E.

ARMS and the man I sing, who first made way
Predestined exile, from the Trojan shore
To Italy, the blest Lavinian strand.
Smitten of storms he was on land and sea
By violence of Heaven, to satisfy
Stern Juno's sleepless wrath; and much in war.
He suffered, seeking at the last to found
The city, and bring o'er his fathers' gods
To safe abode in Latium; whence arose
The Latin race, old Alba's reverend lords,
And from her hills wide-walled, imperial Rome.

O Muse, the causes tell! What sacrilege,
Or vengeful sorrow, moved the heavenly Queen
To thrust on dangers dark and endless toil
A man whose largest honor in men's eyes
Was serving Heaven? Can gods such anger feel?

In ages gone an ancient city stood—
Carthage, a Tyrian seat, which from afar

10.17 Head of Constantine the Great (part of an original colossal seated statue), 313 C.E. Marble, height 8 ft 6⅜ ins (2.61 m). Palazzo dei Conservatori, Rome.

Made front on Italy and on the mouths
Of Tiber's stream; its wealth and revenues
Were vast, and ruthless was its quest of war.
'T is said that Juno, of all lands she loved,
Most cherished this—not Samos' self so dear.
Here were her arms, her chariot; even then
A throne of power o'er nations near and far,
If Fate opposed not, 't was her darling hope
To 'stablish here; but anxiously she heard
That of the Trojan blood there was a breed
Then rising, which upon the destined day
Should utterly o'erwhelm her Tyrian towers;
A people of wide sway and conquest proud
Should compass Libya's doom;—such was the web
The Fatal Sisters spun.
                        Such was the fear
Of Saturn's daughter, who remembered well
What long and unavailing strife she waged
For her loved Greeks at Troy. Nor did she fail
To meditate th' occasions of her rage,
And cherish deep within her bosom proud
Its griefs and wrongs: the choice by Paris made;
Her scorned and slighted beauty; a whole race
Rebellious to her godhead; and Jove's smile
That beamed on eagle-ravished Ganymede.
With all these thoughts infuriate, her power
Pursued with tempests o'er the boundless main
The Trojans, though by Grecian victor spared
And fierce Achilles; so she thrust them far
From Latium; and they drifted, Heaven-impelled
Year after year, o'er many an unknown sea—
O labor vast, to found the Roman line!

Below th' horizon the Sicilian isle
Just sank from view, as for the open sea
With heart of hope they sailed, and every ship
Clove with its brazen beak the salt, white waves.
But Juno of her everlasting wound
Knew no surcease, but from her heart of pain
Thus darkly mused: "Must I, defeated, fail
Of what I will, not turn the Teucrian King
From Italy away? Can Fate oppose?
Had Pallas power to lay waste in flame
The Argive fleet and sink its mariners,
Revenging but the sacrilege obscene
By Ajax wrought, Oileus' desperate son?
She, from the clouds, herself Jove's lightning threw,
Scattered the ships, and ploughed the sea with storms.
Her foe, from his pierced breast out-breathing fire,
In whirlwind on a deadly rock she flung.
But I, who move among the gods a queen,
Jove's sister and his spouse, with one weak tribe
Make war so long! Who now on Juno calls?
What suppliant gifts henceforth her altars crown?"

So, in her fevered heart complaining still,
Unto the storm-cloud land the goddess came,
A region with wild whirlwinds in its womb,
Æolia named, where royal Æolus
In a high-vaulted cavern keeps control
O'er warring winds and loud concourse of storms.
There closely pent in chains and bastions strong,
They, scornful, make the vacant mountain roar,
Chafing against their bonds. But from a throne
Of lofty crag, their king with sceptred hand
Allays their fury and their rage confines.
Did he not so, our ocean, earth, and sky
Were whirled before them through the vast inane.
But over-ruling Jove, of this in fear,
Hid them in dungeon dark: then o'er them piled
Huge mountains, and ordained a lawful king
To hold them in firm sway, or know what time,
With Jove's consent, to loose them o'er the world.

To him proud Juno thus made lowly plea:
"Thou in whose hands the Father of all gods
And Sovereign of mankind confides the power
To calm the waters or with winds upturn,
Great Æolus! a race with me at war
Now sails the Tuscan main towards Italy,
Bringing their Ilium and its vanquished powers.
Uprouse thy gales! Strike that proud navy down!
Hurl far and wide, and strew the waves with dead!
Twice seven nymphs are mine, of rarest mould,
Of whom Deiopea, the most fair,
I give thee in true wedlock for thine own,
To mate thy noble worth; she at thy side
Shall pass long, happy years, and fruitful bring
Her beauteous offspring unto thee their sire."
Then Æolus: "'T is my sole task, O Queen,
To weigh thy wish and will. My fealty
Thy high behest obeys. This humble throne
Is of thy gift. Thy smiles for me obtain
Authority from Jove. Thy grace concedes
My station at your bright Olympian board,
And gives me lordship of the darkening storm."
Replying thus, he smote with spear reversed
The hollow mountain's wall; then rush the winds
Through that wide breach in long embattled line,
And sweep tumultuous from land to land:
With brooding pinions o'er the waters spread,
East wind and south, and boisterous Afric gale
Upturn the sea; vast billows shoreward roll;
The shout of mariners, the creak of cordage,
Follow the shock; low-hanging clouds conceal
From Trojan eyes all sight of heaven and day;
Night o'er the ocean broods; from sky to sky
The thunders roll, the ceaseless lightnings glare;
And all things mean swift death for mortal man.[4]

The influence of Horace, Virgil, and Livy on Western culture is difficult to overestimate; "they are so much a part of us that we take their values for granted and their epigrams for truisms."[5] As far as Augustus was concerned, they fully expressed the Roman tradition and Roman language. Horace, Virgil, and Livy created a literature that distracted the upper classes from Greek "free thought" and which the emperor could exploit to rally them to the ancient Roman order as represented in his person.

Throughout the literature of the Augustan period runs a moralizing Stoicism. This Greek philosophy held that God was the basis of the universe, that human souls were sparks of the divine fire, and that virtue was all-important. The most remarkable product of Stoicism in poetry was satire, which allowed writers to advocate morality with great popular appeal. Martial (c. 40–104 C.E.) and Juvenal (c. 60–130 C.E.) utilized poetry to attack vice—which gave them license to describe it in graphic detail. Petronius (fl. 1st century C.E.) produced satirical verse and prose novels describing the adventures of roguish heroes. Their details were as readable as Martial's and Juvenal's but void of their morality. Lucan (39–65 C.E.) and Apuleius (a-puh-LEE-uhs; fl. 2nd century C.E.) followed in the same literary tradition. Apuleius's *Golden Ass* creates a fictional biography describing how he was tried and condemned for the murder of three wineskins. He was brought back to life by a sorceress, and in the process of trying to follow her in the form of a bird, he was changed instead into an ass. The only cure for his affliction appeared to be the procurement of rose leaves, and in his search for these, he fell into some bizarre and fantastic adventures.

Latin was later to become the language of learning and of the Christian Church throughout Europe.

The Letters of St. Paul and Christianity

Although Constantine cleared the way for Christianity to proceed without overt persecution in the Roman Empire, St. Paul undoubtedly made it palatable to the more logical inclinations of a heritage that lay in Classicism.

Rooted in Judaism's post-exilic Messianic hopes, Christianity arose in what its central personage and its later believers professed was God's intervention in human history to establish a new covenant to supplant the covenant established with Moses. Jesus of Nazareth was the Christ—Messiah. The Apostle Paul was the most effective missionary of early Christianity and its first theologian. He is sometimes called the "second founder" of Christianity, having written more than one-fourth of the New Testament and having been responsible for translating Christianity into terms that could be accepted by Greek-thinking people of the Roman Empire. His theology

emerges from the many letters he wrote to the young churches throughout Asia Minor and Greece, but his Letter to the Romans probably stands as the greatest systemization of Christian theology ever produced. While acknowledging his theological debt to Judaism, Paul propounds a philosophy about the origin and shape of the universe (cosmology) that reflects that of the Hellenistic world.

Paul's favorite literary form is the Hellenistic discourse known as the *diatribe*. In this argumentative structure, the correspondent raises a series of questions and then answers them. Because Paul dictated his letters, their style is often awkward and, occasionally, difficult to comprehend. One of Paul's earliest letters, the Letter to the Corinthians, was written from Ephesus around 50 C.E. Among Paul's admonitions and theology come some truly great poetic passages, which have endured the test of time and endeared themselves to millions. Perhaps the best example is the "Hymn of Love" from I Corinthians 13:

First Letter to the Corinthians
St. Paul

I may speak with the tongues of men and of angels, but if I have not love, I am become no more than echoing brass or a clanging cymbal. I may have the gift of prophecy, I may understand all sacred secrets and all knowledge, I may have faith enough to remove mountains, but if I have not love I am nothing. I may dole out all that I have, I may surrender my body that I may be burned, but if I have not love it is no good to me.

Love is patient; love is kind; love knows no envy; love is no braggart; it is not inflated with its own importance; it does not behave gracelessly; it does not insist on its rights; it never flies into a temper; it does not store up the memory of any wrong it has received; it finds no pleasure in evil-doing; it rejoices with the truth; it can endure anything; it is completely trusting; it never ceases to hope; it bears everything with triumphant fortitude.

Love never fails. Whatever prophecies there are, they will vanish away. Whatever tongues there are, they will cease. Whatever knowledge we have, it will pass away. It is only part of the truth we know now and only part of the truth that we can foretell to others. But when that which is complete shall come, that which is incomplete will vanish away. When I was a child I used to speak like a child; I used to think like a child; I used to reason like a child. When I became a man I put an end to childish things. Now we see only reflections in a mirror which leaves us with nothing but riddles to solve, but then we shall see face to face. Now I know in part; but then I will know even as I am known. Now faith, hope, love remain—these three; but the greatest of these is love.[6]

10.18 Temple of Fortuna Virilis, Rome, late 2nd century B.C.E.

10.19 Colosseum, Rome, c. 70–82 C.E.

10.20 Colosseum, interior.

ROMAN ARCHITECTURAL STYLE

Given the practicality of the Roman viewpoint, it is not surprising that a distinctive Roman style in architecture emerged. The clear crystallization of form found in the post-and-lintel structure of the Classical Greek temple also appears in the Roman arch, and the Roman use of concrete—applied to create coffered domes, as we will see—made possible aesthetic and practical applications impossible for the Greeks.

Very little early Roman architecture remains, but what there is has Corinthian orders and fairly graceful lines, suggesting a strong Hellenistic influence. Notable differences arise, however. Hellenistic temples were built on an impressive scale, but Roman temples were even smaller than the Classical Greek ones, principally because Roman worship was mostly a private rather than a public matter. Roman temple architecture also employed engaged columns—columns partly embedded in the wall. As a result, on three sides Roman temples lacked the open colonnade of the Greek temple.

The Temple of Fortuna Virilis (Fig. **10.18**) is the oldest and best preserved example of its kind, dating from the second century B.C.E. The influence of Greek style can be seen in the delicate Ionic columns and entablature. The cella (main enclosed space), containing only one room, departs from an earlier convention of three rooms. Roman temples displayed trophies from military campaigns as well as housing the image of the deity.

As in the case of sculpture, the Augustan age refashioned Roman architecture in the light of Classical Greek style. This accounts for the dearth of surviving buildings from previous eras. Temples were built on Greek plans, but the proportions were significantly different. The first through fourth centuries witnessed typical Roman style. Its most significant characteristic is the use of the arch as a structural system in arcades and tunnel and groin vaults.

The Colosseum

The Colosseum (Figs. **10.19** and **10.20**), the best known of Roman buildings and one of the most stylistically typical, combines an arcaded exterior with vaulted corridors. It seated 50,000 spectators and was a marvel of engineering. Its aesthetics are reminiscent of Greek Classicism, but fully Roman in style. The circular sweep of the building is carefully countered by the vertical line of engaged columns flanking every arch. Doric, Ionic, and Corinthian

10.21 Arch of Titus, Roman Forum, Rome, 81 C.E. Marble.

columns each mark one level, progressing upward from heavy to lighter orders. The Colosseum was a new type of building called an "amphitheatre," in which two "theatres," facing each other, combined to form an arena surrounding an oval space.

Placed in the center of the city of Rome, the Colosseum housed gladiatorial games, including the martyrdom of Christians by turning lions loose on them as a gruesome "spectator sport." Emperors competed with their predecessors to produce the most lavish spectacles here. Originally a series of poles and ropes supported awnings to provide shade for the spectators. The space below the arena contained animal enclosures, barracks for gladiators, and machines for raising and lowering scenery.

The Arch of Titus

Roman triumphal arches comprised another type of impressive architectural monument. In the Arch of Titus (Fig. **10.21**), the Roman Classical style survives in a memorial to the emperor Titus (reigned 79–81 C.E.) raised by his younger brother, Domitian (reigned 81–96 C.E.). It records accomplishments that Titus shared with his father, Vespasian (reigned 69–79 C.E.), in the conquest of Jerusalem. The sculptural reliefs on the arch show Titus riding in his chariot in triumph. The reliefs are allegories of political reverence rather than illustrations of historical events. Accompanying Titus in them

are figures such as the *Genius Senatus* and the *Genius Populi Romani*—embodiments of the spirit of the Senate, or governing body, and the general populace. This work illustrates the contrast of external appearance—the richly and delicately ornamented façade—with the massive internal structure of the arch, a characteristic which reappeared in Renaissance architecture.

The Pantheon

The Pantheon (Figs. **10.22** and **10.23**; see also Fig. **7.13**) fuses Roman engineering, practicality, and style in a domed temple of unprecedented scale, dedicated, as its name indicates, to all the gods.

In both plan and section the Pantheon is round. From the exterior we glimpse a cella comprising a simple, unadorned cylinder capped by a gently curving dome. The entrance is a Hellenistic porch with huge Corinthian columns. Originally it was approached by a series of steps and attached to a rectangular forecourt, so we see only part of a more complex design.

Inside (see Fig. **7.13**), the scale and detail are overwhelming. The drum and dome consist of solid monolithic concrete reinforced with bands of vitrified tile. The vertical gravity loads are collected and distributed to the drum by arches incorporated in the concrete. The wall of the 20-foot-thick drum has alternating rectangular and curved niches cut into it, thus forming a series of massive radial buttresses. Originally, statues of the gods occupied these niches, which are carved out of the massive walls. Corinthian columns add grace and lightness to the lower level, and heavy horizontal moldings accentuate a feeling of open space made possible by the huge dome. It is 143 feet (43 m) in both diameter and height (from the floor to the *oculus* [AH-kyoo-luhs; Latin for "eye"], the round opening at the top of the dome). The circular walls supporting the dome are 20 feet (6 m) thick and 70 feet (21 m) high. Recessed square *coffers* on the underside of the dome give an added sense of lightness and reflect the framework into which concrete was poured. Originally the ceiling was gilded to suggest the golden dome of heaven.

How could the Romans have built such a colossal structure? Historians have argued that the key lies in a novel form of concrete containing a specific kind of cement developed near Naples. The secret, however, may rest with the mysterious rings around the dome, as suggested by a Princeton University study: "Probably they perform a function similar to the buttresses of a Gothic cathedral ... The extra weight of the rings ... helps stabilize the lower portion of the dome: Rather than functioning like a conventional dome, the Pantheon behaves like

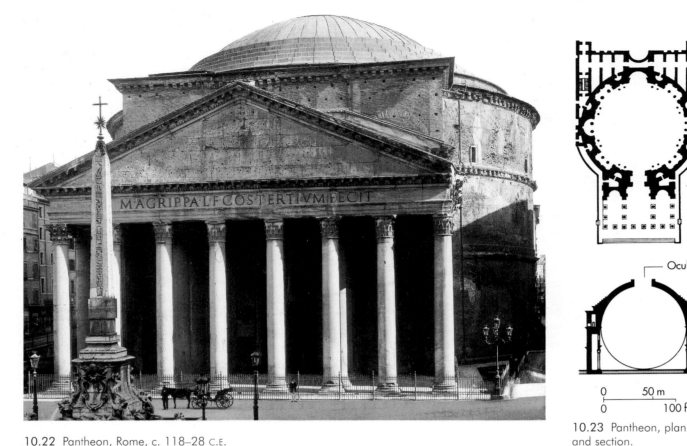

10.22 Pantheon, Rome, c. 118–28 C.E.

10.23 Pantheon, plan and section.

a circular array of arches, with the weight of the rings holding the end of each arch in place."[7]

BYZANTIUM

Astride the main land route from Europe to Asia and its riches, Byzantium possessed tremendous potential as a major metropolis. In addition, the city was a defensible deep-water port and controlled the passage between the Mediterranean and the Black Sea. Blessed with fertile agricultural surroundings, it formed the ideal "New Rome." For this was the objective of the emperor Constantine when he dedicated his new capital in 330 C.E. and changed its name to Constantinople (literally, "city of Constantine"). It prospered, and became the center of Orthodox Christianity and mother to a unique and intense style in the visual arts and architecture. When Rome fell to the Goths in 476 C.E. it had long since handed the torch of civilization to Constantinople. Here the arts and learning of the Classical world were preserved and nurtured, along with an Eastern orientation, while western Europe underwent the turmoil and destruction of barbarian invasion.

BYZANTINE STYLE

A fundamental characteristic of Byzantine visual art is the concept that art has the potential to interpret as well as to represent. Byzantine art and literature were both conservative and mainly anonymous and impersonal. Much Byzantine art remains undated, and questions concerning derivation of styles lie unresolved. Yet the development of narrative Christian art, with its relatively new approach, can be dated to the mid-fifth century, and early attempts at *iconography* (the pictorialization of sacred personages) can be traced to the third and fourth centuries.

The content and purpose of Byzantine art was always religious, although the style of representation underwent numerous changes. The period of Justinian (reigned 527–65 C.E.) marks an apparent deliberate break with the past. What is now described as the Byzantine style, with its anti-naturalistic character, began to take shape in the fifth and sixth centuries, although the Classical Hellenistic tradition seems to have survived as an undercurrent. Throughout the seventh century Classicism and decorative abstraction intermingled in Byzantine art.

By the eleventh century Byzantine style had adopted a *hierarchical* formula in wall painting and mosaics. The Church represented the kingdom of God: Moving up

10.24 San Vitale, Ravenna, Italy, 526–47 C.E.

1 Narthex
2 Ambulatory
3 Nave
4 Sanctuary
5 Apse

10.25 San Vitale, plan and transverse section.

10.26 San Vitale, interior.

the hierarchy, figures changed in form from human to divine. Thus placement in the composition depended upon religious, not spatial, relationships. A strictly two-dimensional, flat style appeared—elegant and decorative, without any perspective.

Stylization and dramatic intensity characterize twelfth-century Byzantine art; approaches further intensified in the thirteenth century with turbulent movement, architectural backdrops, and elongated figures. The fourteenth century produced small-scale, crowded works with narrative content. Their use of space is confused and perspective is irrational. Figures are distorted, with small heads and feet. A more intense spirituality comes across.

We can draw a few general conclusions with regard to Byzantine art (which, we must remember, encompasses nearly 1,000 years of history, and, thereby, several shifts in style). First, the *content* of Byzantine art focuses on human figures. Those figures reveal three main elements: (1) *holy figures*—Christ, the Virgin Mary, the saints, and the apostles with bishops and angels portrayed in their company; (2) *the emperor*—believed divinely sanctioned by God; (3) *the Classical heritage*—images of cherubs, mythological heroes, gods and goddesses, and personifications of virtues. In addition, the *form* of Byzantine two-dimensional art increasingly reflected a consciously-derived spirituality.

BYZANTINE ARCHITECTURE

Western Byzantium: San Vitale

The church of San Vitale in Ravenna, Italy (Figs. **10.24–10.26**), is the major Justinian monument in the West, and was probably built as a testament to Orthodox Christianity. The structure consists of two concentric octagons (Fig. **10.25**). The hemispherical dome rises 100

10.27 *Emperor Justinian and His Court*, San Vitale, Ravenna, c. 547 C.E. Wall mosaic.

feet (30.5 m) above the inner octagon, and floods the interior with light. Eight large piers alternate with columned niches to define the central space. An extraordinary feature is the placement of the *narthex* (porch) at an odd angle. Two possible explanations—one practical and one spiritual—are: (1) the narthex paralleled a street that existed when the building was under construction, and (2) it was designed in order to make worshipers reorient themselves on entering the complex arrangement of spaces, so that they would experience a transition from the outside world to the spiritual one.

On the second level of the *ambulatory* was a special gallery reserved for women—a standard feature of Byzantine churches. The aisles and galleries contrast strikingly with the calm area under the dome. Clerestory light reflects off the mosaic tiles with great richness. In fact, new construction techniques in the vaulting allow for windows on every level and open the sanctuary to much more light than was previously possible, or than was found in the West until the end of the Romanesque style and the advent of the Gothic.

The sanctuary itself comes alive with mosaics of the imperial court and sacred events. Figure **10.27** provides a vivid picture of the emperor. Particularly fascinating here is the stylistic contrast of two mosaics in the same church. *Abraham's Hospitality and the Sacrifice of Isaac*

10.28 *Abraham's Hospitality and the Sacrifice of Isaac*, San Vitale, Ravenna. Wall mosaic.

10.29 Anthemius of Tralles and Isidorus of Miletus, Hagia Sophia, 532–7 C.E.

10.30 Hagia Sophia, axonometric section (bird's eye view).

(Fig. **10.28**) demonstrates a relaxed realism whereas the mosaic depicting Justinian and his court demonstrates an orientialized style, more typically Byzantine, with the figures posed rigidly and frontally rather than realistically. The emperor has a golden halo with a red border, is robed in regal purple, and presents a golden bowl to Christ, pictured in the semidome above. The mosaics link the church to the Byzantine court, reflecting the connection of emperor to the faith, of Christianity to the state, and, indeed, the concept of the "Divine Emperor." Justinian and the empress, Theodora, are portrayed as analogous to Christ and the Virgin.

Eastern Byzantium: Hagia Sophia

If San Vitale praises the emperor and Orthodox Christianity in the West, the church of Hagia Sophia (Holy Wisdom) in Constantinople (modern Istanbul) represents a crowning memorial in the East (Figs. **10.29–10.32**). Characteristic of Justinian Byzantine style, Hagia Sophia uses Roman vaulting techniques with Hellenistic design and geometry, resulting in a richly colored building in an Eastern antique style. Basic to the

10.32 Hagia Sophia, plan.

10.31 Hagia Sophia, interior.

conception is the elevated central area with its domed image of heaven and large, open, and functional spaces.

Its architect, Anthemius (am-THEEM-ee-uhs), was a natural scientist and geometer from Tralles in Asia Minor, who built the church to replace an earlier basilica. For a long time this was the largest church in the world, yet it was completed in only five years and ten months. Byzantine masonry techniques were used, in which courses of brick alternate with courses of mortar equally thick as or thicker than the bricks. Given the speed of construction, this placed great weight on insufficiently dry mortar. As a result, arches buckled and buttresses had

to be erected almost at once. The eastern arch and part of the dome fell in 557 C.E., after two earthquakes. No one has since constructed such a large, flat dome. Also remarkable is the delicate proportioning of the vaults which support such great weight. The building suggests an intense spirituality and yet it can hold large numbers of worshipers; it creates a transcendental environment, where thoughts and emotions are wafted to a spiritual sphere. "It seemed as if the vault of heaven were suspended above one," wrote the sixth-century Byzantine historian Procopius.

Justinian's reign thus inaugurated the style called Byzantine, blending together previous styles—Eastern and Western—to create something new. Forms and relationships were given a spiritual essence built on Classical models but shaped uniquely. The wide range of works from the reign of Justinian synthesizes the relationships between God, the State, philosophy, and art. The emperor was the absolute monarch and also defender of the faith, seen to govern by and for the will of God. Reality was therefore spiritualized and was reflected in works of art that depicted earthly habitation in a *hieratic* ("holy" or "sacred") style.

BYZANTINE STYLE IN MOSAICS AND IVORIES

By about the year 500 C.E. the hieratic style appeared in Byzantine art and presented formalized, almost rigid depictions intended not so much to represent people as to inspire reverence and meditation (Fig. 10.27). (Do not confuse this style with the hierarchical formula discussed earlier. The hierarchical arrangement dealt with figure placement top to bottom. Hieratic style deals with figure proportion.) One formula of the hieratic style ordained that an individual should measure nine heads (seven heads would be our modern measurement). The hairline had to be a nose's length above the forehead. "If the man is naked, four noses' lengths are needed for half his width." By the thirteenth century, mosaics returned to more lifelike depictions, but still with a clear sense of spirituality.

Ivory, traditionally a luxury material, was always popular in Byzantium. A number of carved works of different styles provide evidence of the varying influences and degrees of technical ability in the Eastern Byzantine Empire. Many, but not all, Byzantine ivories are *diptychs* (DIHP-tick)—on two hinged panels. Ivories from the tenth century show delicate elegance and a highly finished style. The Harbaville Triptych (Fig. **10.33**) has been described as the most beautiful of all Byzantine ivories. Called a *triptych* because of its three sections (*tri*), it was probably intended as a portable altar or shrine. Each of the two wings folded shut across the center panel. In the top center Christ is enthroned and flanked by John

the Baptist and the Virgin Mary. They plead for mercy on behalf of all humanity. Five of the apostles appear below. An ornament, repeated with the addition of rosettes at the bottom border and three heads in the top border, divides the two *registers* of the central panel. On either side of Christ's head appear medallions depicting angels holding the symbols of the sun and the moon. The Harbaville Triptych exhibits the frontal pose, formality, solemnity, and slight elongation of form that typify the Byzantine hieratic style. Here it produces a sense of detachment from the world and evokes a deep spirituality. Byzantium remained the stronghold of Orthodox Christianity until the middle of the fifteenth century when it fell to the forces of Islam.

ISLAM

The Islamic tradition in art springs from the religion of Islam (meaning submission), of which Muhammad was the prophet. Adherents are called Muslims or Moslems. Muslims are those who submit to the will of God ("Allah"

10.33 *The Harbaville Triptych*, interior, late 10th century. Ivory, height 9½ ins (24 cm); width of central panel 5⅜ ins (14 cm). Louvre, Paris.

10.34 Al-Qasim ibn 'Ali al-Hariri, *Maqamat al-Hariri* (a book of stories), 1323. Mesopotamian manuscript. British Library, London (Oriental Collection).

10.35 Great Mosque, Damascus, details of mosaic decoration, c. 715 C.E.

in Arabic). The latest of the three great monotheistic religions, it drew upon the other two—Judaism and Christianity. Abraham and Jesus are in the list of prophets preceding Muhammad. Muslims generally believe that Jesus will return as the Mahdi—Messiah—at the end of the world. Islam is based on the sacred book the Koran, which Muslims believe was revealed by God to Muhammad. Five duties are prescribed for every Muslim; the last is a once-in-a-lifetime pilgrimage (Hajj) to Mecca. This has made the pilgrimage the greatest in the world and a great unifying force in Islam. In addition to the Koran, Islam accepts the Sunna—collections of moral sayings and anecdotes of Muhammad, collected as early as the ninth century. There appear to be contradictions in the Sunna, but they are resolved by the doctrine of Ijma: Every Muslim holds a belief that the greater part of Islam is infallibly true—a principle that has made the religion a flexible one.

Early in its history, a great split occurred in Islam between Sunnites and Shiites, and it has persisted. Originally it concerned the caliphate, the crowning institution of the structure of Islam—the placement of both religious and political leadership in the hands of a single ruler. The caliphs, successors—so-called deputies—of Muhammad, claimed authority resting on their descent from the families of the Prophet or his early associates. In Muslim countries the civil law entwines with religious law, though in some places secularism has modified the unity somewhat. Religion governs all aspects of life.

Islam spread rapidly in the seventh and eighth centuries and was soon dominant from Spain to India. Today, it spreads across Asia to the South Pacific, prevails in

North Africa, and is still gaining converts in the rest of Africa. Originally spread "by the sword," Islam appealed through its openness to everyone: It stresses the brotherhood of the faithful before God, regardless of race or culture. Interestingly, the Arab warriors who started out to conquer the world for Allah did not expect to make converts of conquered peoples—they merely expected the unbelievers to be obedient to them. Converts were expected to become Arabs: The Koran was not translated because it was believed to have been dictated by God to Muhammad in Arabic. Converts also had to submit to the social and legal systems of the Muslim community.

10.36 Dome of the Rock, Jerusalem, late 7th century C.E.

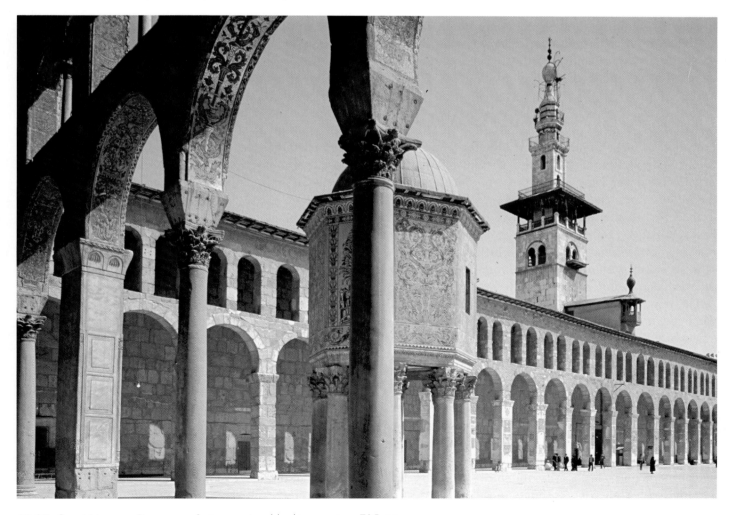

10.37 Great Mosque, Damascus, Syria, courtyard looking west, c. 715 C.E.

As a result, the conquering Arabs resisted the usual fate of conquerors—to be absorbed into the culture of the conquered.

ISLAMIC STYLE IN VISUAL ART

Theoretically, Islam prohibits all human and animal figures from art because of the Scriptural command against making images. In reality, images are widespread: The only prohibition seems to have been on objects intended for public display. In the courts of the caliphs, images of living things were commonplace. They were considered harmless if they did not cast a shadow, were small in scale, or appeared on everyday objects.

In the early years of Islam, there seems to have been some continuity in the visual arts. The Arabs obtained manuscripts from Byzantium and were tremendously interested in Greek science. A plethora of illustrated texts translated into Arabic resulted. Typical of this type of Arab illustration is a pen-and-ink sketch perhaps from a Mesopotamian manuscript of the fourteenth century (Fig. 10.34). The drawing has a clear presentation, with many of the strokes seeming to act as accents. The lines flow freely in subtle curving movements to establish a comfortable rhythm across the page. In very simple line, the artist is able to capture human character, thus showing strong observational ability. The witty flavor of the drawing goes far beyond mere illustration.

ISLAMIC STYLE IN LITERATURE

Probably the most familiar Islamic literature, besides the Koran, is a collection of tales called *The Arabian Nights* or *The Thousand and One Nights*. These accumulated during the Middle Ages, and as early as the tenth century they formed part of the oral traditions of Islam in the Near East. Over the years more tales were added, including a unifying device called a *frame-tale*, which places all of the separate stories within a large framework. By around 1450 the work had assumed its final form.

The frame-tale recounts the story of a jealous Sultan who, convinced that all women were unfaithful, married a new wife each evening and put her to death the following morning. A new bride, Shaharazad, gained a reprieve by beginning a story on her wedding night and artfully maintaining the Sultan's curiosity. She was able to gain a reprieve for 1,001 nights—during which time she produced three male heirs. After this the Sultan abandoned his original practice. The tales capture the spirit of Islamic life, its exotic setting, and its sensuality. Although no particular moral purpose underlies the stories, they do reflect a moral code. They cover a variety of subjects and range from fact to fiction, including stories of camel trains, desert riders, and insistent calls to prayer. They are supernatural, aristocratic, romantic, bawdy, and satiric.

ISLAMIC STYLE IN ARCHITECTURE

Work on the first major example of Islamic architecture—the Dome of the Rock in Jerusalem (Fig. 10.36)—was begun in 685 C.E. by Islamic emperors who were direct descendants of the Prophet's companions. Built near the site of the Temple of Solomon (see p. 212), it was designed as a special holy place—not an ordinary mosque. Its location is revered by Jews as the tomb of Adam and the place where Abraham prepared to sacrifice Isaac. According to Muslim tradition, it also is the place from which Muhammad ascended into heaven. Written accounts suggest its purpose was to overshadow a Christian church of similar construction on the other side of Jerusalem—the Holy Sepulchre. Caliph Abd al-Malik wanted a monument that would outshine the Christian churches of the area, and, perhaps, the Ka'ba in Mecca.

The Dome of the Rock is shaped as an octagon, and inside it contains two concentric ambulatories (walkways) surrounding a central space capped by the dome. The exterior was later decorated with the glazed blue tiles that give the façade its dazzling appearance; the interior glitters with gold, glass, and mother-of-pearl multi-colored mosaics.

Undoubtedly, the Dome of the Rock was intended to speak to Christians as well as Muslims, distracting the latter from the splendor of Christian churches. Inside the mosque is an inscription: "The Messiah Jesus Son of Mary is only an apostle of God, and His Word which he conveyed into Mary, and a Spirit proceeding from Him. Believe, therefore in God and his apostles and say not 'Three.' It will be better for you. God is only one God. Far be it from his glory that He should have a son."

Another excellent example of Islamic architecture is the Great Mosque in Damascus, Syria (Fig. 10.37). When the Muslims captured Damascus in 635 C.E., they adapted the precinct of a pagan temple, which had meanwhile been converted into a Christian church, into an open-air mosque. Seventy years later, Caliph al-Walid demolished the church and set about building Islam's largest mosque. The only feature of the original buildings left standing was the Roman wall, though the four original towers were metamorphosed into the first minarets, from which the faithful were called to prayer. Unfortunately, the centuries have not been kind to the Great Mosque. Sacked a number of times, it lost much of the splendor of its lavish decorations. However, some of its grandeur remains in

10.38 Head from Jemaa, Nigeria, c. 400 B.C.E. Terra-cotta, height 10 ins (25 cm). National Museum, Lagos.

the arcaded courtyard, with fine, gold-inlaid detailing visible in the returns of the arches (Fig. 10.37). Inside, colorful mosaics (Fig. 10.35) express great subtlety of detail and texture. These works rank among the most accomplished of mosaics and were probably produced by Byzantine craftsmen.

AFRICA

As Islamic culture spread across northern Africa and into Europe, the cultures of Sub-Saharan Africa continued traditions that had existed for thousands of years, over which time African artists and craftsmen created objects of sophisticated vision and masterful technique. The modern banalities of so-called primitive "airport art" sold to tourists belie the rich cultural history of the African continent. It traded with the Middle East and Asia as early as 600 C.E. Chinese Tang Dynasty coins found along the coast of East Africa document this fact. Climate, materials, and the nature of tribal culture doomed much of African art to extinction; only a small fraction remains. Nonetheless, what has survived traces a rich vision that

varies from culture to culture and, stylistically, runs from abstract to realistic. Its purposes range from magical to utilitarian, sometimes portraying human reality in ways that individuals from other cultural traditions may be ill-equipped to understand. Works from African traditions—as from any others—can nevertheless reward the viewer with great satisfaction.

NOK STYLE

During the first millennium B.C.E., on the Jos plateau of northern Nigeria, a nonliterate culture of farmers entered the Iron Age and developed an accomplished artistic style. Named the "Nok style" after the village of Nok where the first sculptures were discovered, it appeared in terra-cotta figures comparable to the Qin Dynasty warriors of China (see Fig. 10.43). The sculptures were boldly designed; some represent animals realistically and others portray life-sized human heads (Fig. 10.38). Although stylized, for example, with segmented lower eyelids, each work reveals individualized character. Facial expressions and hair styles differ and "it is this unusual combination of human individuality and artistic stylization which gives them their peculiar power."[8] These heads are probably portraits of ancestors of the ruling class. The technique and medium of execution seem to have been chosen to ensure permanence, for magical rather than artistic reasons. The Nok style appears to have influenced several West African styles.

10.39
Head of a queen, from Ife, Nigeria, 12th–13th century. Terra-cotta, height 10 ins (25 cm). Museum of Ife Antiquities, Ife.

10.40 Bearded male figure from Djenne, Mali, 14th century. Terra-cotta, height 15 ins (38 cm). Detroit Institute of Arts (Eleanor Clay Ford Fund for African Art).

IGBO-UKWU STYLE

The level of skill achieved by the ninth and tenth centuries C.E. can be seen in a ritual war pot from the village of Igbo-Ukwu in eastern Nigeria (see Fig. 0.5). Cast using the *cire-perdue* or lost-wax process, this leaded bronze artifact is amazing in its virtuosity. The graceful design of its curved lines and flaring base in itself is exquisite, but the addition of a delicate and detailed rope overlay reflects sophistication of both technique and vision.

IFE STYLE

A link between the Nok culture and that of Ife, also in Nigeria, may have existed to draw these two cultures together in their art across the centuries. Ife was an important cultural and religious center in the southwest. The accomplishments of its artists—their mastery of the terracotta medium, their rendering skills, and the depth

of their vision—suggest to some scholars a long developmental period, culminating in twelfth- to thirteenth-century works such as Figure 10.39. This terra-cotta head represents a mature artistic style. The anatomical detail is remarkable, and even today the textures are so exquisite that the figures seem ready to come to life. The full mouth and expressive eyes suggest extreme sensitivity. The high brow and minutely detailed headdress complete this portrait and bring to its surface the innermost qualities of the individual.

DJENNE STYLE

The styles of African art range from realistic to highly expressive and abstract. Some way up the Niger river at Djenne, in Mali, the latter is found in a small, fourteenth-century terracotta figure of a bearded male (Fig. 10.40). This example of manipulation technique (see Chapter 2) reveals a striking and stylized thrusting chin. The lower and upper jaws protrude grotesquely from a platelike appendage—probably a stylized beard—where the jaw would normally be. Lightly incised into the conical surface of the head are the man's eyes. The torso's proportions pinch inward, as if compressed by the undetached arms, and details of what could be armor show careful modeling. The sophisticated rendering of the entire form suggests that the artist intended to reflect internal psychological or spiritual qualities.

As noted, Africa had many early ties to China, and using that as a segue, we jump across the Indian Ocean to examine a few of the art styles existing in China during the period of history pertinent to this chapter. Beginning with a brief look at three of China's philosophical and religious directions, we move to the arts, beginning at a time roughly equivalent to the Hellenistic period of ancient Greece.

CHINA

Confucius (551–479 B.C.E.), probably the first professional teacher and philosopher in China, is also recognized as the greatest. His teaching is contained in five classical works (not all of which were actually written by him). One, the *Analects*, is probably an authentic collection of his sayings and conversations, in the format of questions and answers.

His thought rests more on a pragmatic level than an intellectual one. His primary interest lay in politics. He proposed a return to the ancient way, in which persons must play their proper, assigned roles subject to authority. But he saw government primarily as an ethical challenge. It was a ruler's virtue, rather than power, that yielded contentment in the people. He aimed to convince rulers to pursue ethical principles. Thus he became China's first moralist, and founder of a great ethical tradition.

In contrast to Confucianism, Daoism, or "The Way," teaches independence for the individual. It, too, emerged in the sixth century B.C.E. Confucianism is pragmatic; Daoism is mystical. The Daoist goal is profound, joyful, and practical harmony with the universe, and to this end meditation and simplicity are encouraged. Followers believe that *yin* (the feminine) balances *yang* (the masculine), and that all extreme positions revert to their opposites.

Buddhism, imported to China, is a system of philosophy and ethics founded by Gautama Siddhartha, the Buddha (563–483 B.C.E.), in northeast India. The Four Noble Truths of Buddha are: (1) existence is suffering; (2) the origin of suffering is desire; (3) suffering ceases when desire ceases; and (4) the way to reach the end of desire is to follow the Eightfold Path. This comprises right belief, right resolve (to renounce carnal pleasure, harm no living creature, and so on), right speech, right conduct, right occupation or living, right effort, right contemplation or right-mindedness, and right ecstasy. The final goal of the religious person is to gain enlightenment and so escape from existence into blissful nonexistence—*nirvana*. Buddhists believe that the substance of all objects is

10.41 Liurong Temple (Six Banyan Pagoda), Guangzhou, China, c. 989 C.E. (Song Dynasty).

10.42 Lintel and pediment of tomb, from China, 1st century B.C.E. (Han Dynasty). Gray earthenware; hollow tiles painted in ink and colors on a whitewashed ground, 29 × 80½ ins (73.8 × 204.7 cm). Museum of Fine Arts, Boston (Denman Waldo Ross Collection, and Gift of C. T. Loo).

10.43 Warriors, Tomb of Emperor Qin Shihuangdi, Lintong, near Xi'an (Shaanxi), China, c. 221–209 B.C.E. (Qin Dynasty). Terra-cotta, life-size figures.

10.44 Rider with saddled horse, from Tomb of Emperor Qin Shihuangdi, Lintong. Terra-cotta, life-size.

10.45 (right) Guanyin, The Bodhisattva of Compassion, from the Ku Shihto Ssu monastery, Sion, Shensi Province, China (Northern Chou-sui Dynasty). Limestone, height 6⅜ ins (16.2 cm).

10.46 Fo-kuang-ssu (Monastery of the Buddha's Halo), Mount Wu-t'ai, northern Shansi, China, front elevation and cross section of main hall, 9th century (Tang Dynasty).

illusion, and that it is greed, hatred, and delusion that separate people from reality and keep them tied to the cycle of earthly existence. It is from this cycle that they can escape by religious living.

CHINESE SCULPTURAL STYLE

By the third century B.C.E., the Chinese had reached a high level of technical accomplishment in sculpture. They had developed scientific manufacturing processes for pottery and knew how to control firing temperatures.

We know this because Emperor Qin Shihuangdi, who reigned for almost the whole of the Qin Dynasty (221–206 B.C.E.), spent most of his time preparing his palace and mausoleum. In March 1974, during the digging of a well at Lintong, some life-size and lifelike pottery figures were unearthed. Pits were found containing terra-cotta warriors, horses, and bronze chariots. In one vault alone (measuring 760 × 238 feet [231 × 72 m]), 6,000 terra-cotta warriors and horses were found. A total of three vaults contain over 8,000 figures (Fig. 10.43).

The warriors have various expressions. Some are dignified; others, vigorous; some are cheerful; others, debonair. Some appear lost in brooding, while still others look witty and handsome. Each figure displays an almost knowable character, as if some living form had been miraculously frozen in time through the consummate skill of the artists. Precise detailing reveals temperament, rank, and home province of these warriors. Common soldiers, for example, appear in short battle tunics or laceless armored suits. Their heads are covered by small round caps, and they wear square-toed sandals on their feet.

The horses appear well bred, and all look muscular and vigorous. Their proportions are perfect (Fig. 10.44) and even their expressions indicate the artists' strong insight, understanding, and skill. The eyes stare ahead intensely and the necks stretch in graceful curvature, reflecting energy and power. The hardness of the figures and their almost flaw-free condition testify to the superior clay-making technology (manipulation; see Chapter 2) of the Qin Dynasty.

The demand for Buddhist images in the sixth century C.E. made the period one of significant sculptural output. Probably the one great age of Chinese sculpture, it shows deep spirituality, reflecting stiff, austere abstraction (Fig. 10.45). In this stone carving of Guanyin, the Goddess of Mercy, we see a female Bodhisattva (bah-dih-SAHT-vah), or person who is going to attain enlightenment. The gentle curving flow of line from all points in the image directs the eye upward to the serene face. Repetition of deep curves unifies the composition, giving it grace, harmony, and softness. In this later feminine form, the Bodhisattva stays in this world to help others achieve salvation before passing onto *nirvana* herself; she becomes a gentle and compassionate protectress.

When in the following centuries Chinese interests turned in a more humanistic direction, sculpture reflected greater intimacy and humanity. Images became rounder and more lifelike, in line with contemporary Chinese concepts of human beauty.

CHINESE ARCHITECTURAL STYLE

Very little has survived of early Chinese architecture, partly because most of it was constructed of wood, and partly because there was a mass destruction of Buddhist monasteries, temples, and shrines in 845 C.E. We can capture a sense of its style, however, by examining a recon-struction drawing of the main hall of the ninth-century Fo-kuang-ssu (Monastery of the Buddha's Halo) on Mount Wu-t'ai (Fig. 10.46). Dating to the Tang Dynasty (618–906 C.E.), this is China's oldest wooden building. The curved roof lines, deep overhangs, and ornate decoration are all elements that have come to represent Asian style.

Also typical is the Liurong Temple or Six Banyan Pagoda of Guangzhou (Fig. 10.41). Built in its final form in approximately 989 C.E., in the early years of the Song Dynasty (960–1279), the pagoda rises 188 feet (57 m) in nine exterior stories. On the inside it contains seventeen stories. Richly painted in red, green, gold, and white, it was at one time called the Flowery Pagoda. The current name comes from the famous writer and calligrapher Su Dong-po, who visited it in 1100 and admired the six banyan trees surrounding it. The upward curving lines of the eaves and the colorful glazed roof tiles became characteristic of Chinese architecture from this time onward.

CHINESE PAINTING STYLE

Our quick survey gives us two examples of Chinese painting style separated by more than one thousand years. In the first, from the Han Dynasty (206 B.C.E.–220 C.E.), we find movement and lively depictions of, for example, mythical beings, dragons, and rabbits: The painted tile in Figure 10.42 exhibits skillfully rendered figures whose brushstroke suggests liveliness and movement. They appear in three-quarter poses, which gives the painting a sense of depth and action, and the diagonal sweep of the line adds to the sense of motion. The poses of the personages suggest character—that is, the psychology of the figure portrayed. Although the use of pose and direction reflects a sophisticated approach and technique, the figures stand on the same baseline, with no sense of placement in deeper space.

Since the Song Dynasty of the thirteenth century, the Chinese have regarded painting as their greatest art. The basic conventions were established then and painting reached a height that has probably never been surpassed. Buddhist influence remained strong, although secular art grew in prominence too. In secular painting emphasis was on landscapes, as opposed to human events and images. Figure 10.47, in a soft and atmospheric style, is part of a larger scroll entitled *Twelve Views from a Thatched Cottage* by Xia Gui (c. 1180–1230). It depicts a mountain range and a lake with boats. Each of the sections of the scroll carries an inscription—for example, "Distant Mountains and Wild Geese." Taken as a whole, the scroll reveals time as well as space as it moves from daylight to dusk.

Subtle technique merges soft washes with firm brush-strokes, and images move from sharp focus to indistinct

10.47 Xia Gui, *Twelve Views from a Thatched Cottage* (detail), c. 1200–30. Handscroll, ink on silk, height 11 ins (28 cm). Nelson Atkins Museum of Art, Kansas City (Purchase: Nelson Trust).

suggestion utilizing atmospheric perspective. The detailing gives the subject a degree of lifelikeness, but it goes beyond that to give a "sense" of nature. The images are impressions rather than depictions. The artist selects details carefully and concentrates on essences.

In the eleventh century, color mattered little. Most Chinese painting was monochromatic. For the Chinese, landscapes represent nature as a whole: Each small detail symbolizes the larger universe. In this painting an over-riding mysticism emerges, probably reflecting the Daoist belief system.

JAPAN

Across the Sea of Japan from China lies Japan, whose early history, religion, and artistry reflect strong Chinese influences. Chinese chronicles mention Japan for the first time in the first century C.E. By that time Japan had entered the Metals Age and had developed a major rice-growing economy. The first development of any major political center, however, appears to have occurred in the fourth century. The country was controlled by a strongly entrenched aristocracy, the Yamato, whose dominance continued throughout the fifth and sixth centuries. At this time Japan experienced strong Korean cultural influence.

Between the sixth and eighth centuries Japan passed from what historians call "protohistory" into civilization. The Yamato created a state centered on the Chinese model. Buddhism was introduced and adopted by the court sometime in the sixth century, although Shinto, Japan's ancient polytheistic nature cult, appears to have been maintained. Over the next 200 years the constitution was modeled on Confucian ethics, land reform transformed the aristocracy into a bureaucracy paid by the state, legal and penal codes were introduced, and historical chronicles developed. An official break with China in 894 C.E. testified to the divergence of Japanese culture.

Japanese aesthetics matured as well. By the fifteenth century, Japanese culture and society reached one of their highest points. Level local economies, technological advances, and a burgeoning sea trade each contributed their part. As in the Western world, a new middle class, or bourgeoisie, made a significant impact on Japanese culture. Zen gardens proliferated and the tea ceremony was invented. Architectural masterpieces were built and Noh theatre was founded. However, on the political front, Japan could not maintain a steady course. Centralized authority all but disappeared, and civil strife reigned. The shogunate—the hereditary officials who governed Japan at this period—became incapable of controlling the vassals, and became so weak that the opposite occurred. Despite prosperity and cultural accomplishment, Japan was a sorely divided state when the Portuguese arrived in 1543 bringing Christianity and firearms.

JAPANESE STYLE IN ARCHITECTURE

Buddhism made a significant impact on Japan during the Jogan or Early Heian (hy-ahn) period (794–897). Esoteric

10.48 Kondo of Muroji, Nara prefecture, Japan, 9th century (Early Heian period).

JAPANESE STYLE IN PAINTING AND SCULPTURE

In the thirteenth century, Japanese sculpture turned to a simple style which stressed strength and virility. A series of civil wars had led to the military dictatorship of the

10.49 Kumano Mandala, c. 1300 (Kamakura period). Color on silk. Cleveland Museum of Art (John L. Severance Fund).

Buddhism, or the Mikkyo, emphasized secrecy and mystery, and its precepts can be found in a monastery (Fig. 10.48) in a remote part of Nara prefecture. The secluded location of Muroji (-ji means "temple") removes the temple from "distractions and corruptions." The design of the *kondo* (kahn-doh), or main hall, is asymmetrical, with a close relationship to the natural site. Rising above a terrace and surrounded on the upper level by a porch, it has an almost modern contextual relationship. Its shingled roof sets it apart from the tiled-roof structures of Chinese influence (see Figs. **10.41** and **10.46**) and argues for a native Japanese style in temple architecture.

10.50 *Night Attack on the Sanjo Palace*, from the Heiji Monogatari scroll, detail, second half of 13th century (Kamakura period). Handscroll, ink and colors on paper, 16¼ ins × 23 ft (41.3 cm × 7 m). Museum of Fine Arts, Boston (Fenollosa-Weld Collection; © 2002 Museum of Fine Arts, Boston).

10.51 Unkei, *Nio*, Todaiji, Nara, 1203.
Wood, height 26 ft 6 ins (8 m).

delicately rendered landscape. The presentational style creates a shorthand of ideas and a beautiful design of delicate and active line, holding the entire work together and leading the eye from section to section. Notice that although the buildings seem to represent three dimensions, no convergence of lines toward vanishing points, as in true linear perspective, appears (see Chapter 1).

In contrast to the Kumano Mandala, with its mysticism, the Heiji Monogatari scroll (Fig. 10.50) depicts a dramatic fire scene replete with crowds and emotion. As the Sanjo Palace burns, figures and flames explode from the right border to the left. The artist creates a masterful stylized scene which is so tightly controlled compositionally that it could be a study for any painter of any age. The forceful diagonals and the powerful, horizontal, dark thrust of the palace roof meet to form an arrow shooting across the paper. In a design as intricate and powerful as any Baroque painting (see p. 305), this work builds detailed individual pieces, stimulating in their own right, into a large and complicated unity of contrasting colors, values, and textures. Straight and curved lines combine to create further conflict and dramatic tension.

JAPANESE STYLE IN THEATRE AND LITERATURE

Japan's two great dramatic forms, Noh and the later Kabuki (kah-BOO-kee; see p. 304), both originated from religious rituals dating to the late eighth and early ninth centuries, when drama was used as a teaching tool by Buddhist monks. The dramatizing of religious ritual in Buddhism slowly became more and more secularized, found its way out of the sanctuary, and gained in popularity, much as did miracle, mystery, and morality plays in medieval Europe (see p. 272). The results emerged as dramatic forms performed in markets as well as places of worship.

Noh drama matured during the fourteenth century into an original literary and performing art. Highly conventionalized, it emerged from two sources: simple dramas based on symbolic dances performed to music at the imperial court, and mimes popular with the common people. Its final form is credited to a Shinto priest named Kan'ami (1333–84) and his son Seami (1363–1443). They also founded one of the hereditary lines of Noh performers, the Kanze (kahn-zay), who still perform today.

Noh drama is performed on a simple, almost bare stage and, like early Classical Greek tragedy, uses only two actors. Also, as in Classical Greek drama, the actors wear elaborate masks and costumes, and a chorus functions

shoguns and their samurai (warriors) and to a broadly based feudal regime. This was reflected in the works of sculptors such as Unkei, whose demonic and colossal wooden Buddhist deities (Fig. 10.51) guard the entrance to the Todaiji at Nara, one-time capital of Japan. We are drawn both by the statue's power, expressed in the fierce facial expression and forbidding hand, and by its simplicity, through the clean lines of the swirling fabrics.

In the late thirteenth century, Japanese painting expanded its subject matter from individual portraiture to include landscape (Fig. 10.49). The Kumano Mandala draws into close proximity three Shinto shrines which are geographically many miles apart. Above them are *mandalas* (MAN-dah-lah) containing Buddhist deities. A *mandala* is a circular diagram of the cosmos used for meditation, ceremonial incantation, or magic. The presence of Buddhist deities in portrayals of Shinto shrines attests to the dominance of Buddhism at the time. Around and between the depiction of the shrines appears a as a narrator. Actors chant highly poetic dialogue to an orchestral accompaniment. All their actions suggest rather than depict, which gives the drama its stylization and conventionality; symbolism and restraint characterize both acting and staging.

Subjects range from stories of Shinto gods to Buddhist secular history, and usually center on the more popular Buddhist sects. The tone of Noh plays tends to be serious—appealing to the intellect—with a focus on the spirit of some historical person who wishes for salvation but is tied to this earth by worldly desires. The plays tend to be short, and an evening's performance encompasses several, interspersed with comic burlesques called Kyogen ("Crazy Words"). Although Noh drama is performed today and is extremely popular, it remains primarily a fourteenth-century form. Almost all of its canon of scripts (approximately 240) come from that period, with more than 100 written by Seami.

In general, Noh plays can be classified into five types, according to subject: (1) gods; (2) warriors; (3) women; (4) spirits or mad persons; and (5) demons. Traditionally, an evening's performance included all five types, performed in the order noted. Contemporary practice,however, has shortened the program to two or three.

At a time falling between two European literary works studied later in this chapter, the *Song of Roland* (see p. 265) and Dante's *Divine Comedy* (see p. 266) a significant writer arose in Japan: Lady Murasaki Shikibu (born c. 978 C.E.), part of a minor branch of a powerful family. Her name came partly from the title of the office her father held (Shikibu) and partly from a character in her book (Murasaki). Influenced by her father's strong scholarly abilities, although hampered by her expected role as a femininely ignorant woman, she developed tremendous knowledge but needed to hide it because it exceeded what a woman properly should know. After the death of her husband, Lady Murasaki became an attendant to the Empress Akiko, tutoring her in Chinese and reading Chinese poetry to her. Lady Murasaki kept a detailed diary of customs, court dress, and her own thoughts. Perhaps at the bequest of the Empress for something more entertaining than traditional stories, Lady Murasaki wrote the novel *The Tale of Genji*. The task took her perhaps as many as twenty years to complete.

The Tale of Genji, an intricate and detailed description of court life, tells the story of the son of the Emperor by his favorite consort. The Emperor tries to protect his son, who has no backing at court, by making him a Genji, a member of the nonroyal clan—that is, one who cannot be Emperor and, thus, poses no threat to anyone. Genji turns into the most handsome, talented, and charming person at court ("the shining Genji"). The book works its way

through Genji's life. The story continues into the next generation after Genji's death.

The book modeled its characters on actual persons at court and made it a particularly biting criticism. It reveals tremendous detail about the life of Heian Japan.

MEDIEVAL EUROPE

We call the period of time from the mid-fifth century C.E. until the mid- to late fourteenth century, the Middle Ages. It covers the period from the fall of Rome to the Italian Renaissance. In 732 C.E. Charles Martel repelled the threat of Islam and the Moorish conquest at the battle of Poitiers (pwah-TYAY) in France. His grandson, Charlemagne (SHAHR-luh-mayn), returned Europe to its first significant centralized political organization since the fall of Rome and created a brief flourishing of art and culture. Our study of the Middle Ages begins early on, with music known as chant.

MEDIEVAL MUSICAL STYLE

Chant

By around the year 500 C.E., a body of sacred—that is, religious—music called chant, *plainchant*, or *plainsong* had been developed for use in Christian worship services. (The terms, along with Gregorian chant, are commonly used as synonyms, although detailed study reveals differences.) Chant was vocal and took the form of a single melodic line (*monophony*) using notes relatively near each other on the musical scale. The haunting, undulating character of early chant possibly points to Near Eastern origins. Chants were sung in a flexible tempo with unmeasured rhythms following the natural accents of normal Latin speech. In one type of chant setting, called *syllabic*, each syllable of the chant was given one note. In another, called *melismatic* (mehl-iz-MAT-ik), each syllable was spread over several notes. The selection "Kyrie: Hodie Christus Resurrexit" (music CD track 4) lets us sense the flavor of the undulating and ethereal melody of the melismatic type. Kyrie is one of the five parts of the *mass ordinary* (see Chapter 3). These sections, sung by the choir, are alternated with the affirmation, "*Hodie Christus Resurrexit*" ("Today Christ is Risen"), sung by a soloist, which gives the piece an ABABA structure.

Plainchant is often called Gregorian chant because Pope Gregory I (540–604 C.E.) supposedly supervised the selection of melodies and texts he thought most appro-

PROFILE

Hildegard of Bingen

One of the significant musical and literary figures of the time, the German nun Hildegard of Bingen (1098–1179) was educated at the Benedictine cloister of Disibodenberg and became prioress there in 1136. Having experienced visions since she was a child, at age forty-three she consulted her confessor, who reported the matter to the archbishop of Mainz. A theological committee confirmed the authenticity of her visions, and a monk was appointed to help her record them in writing. The finished work, *Scivias* (1141–52), consisted of twenty-six visions, prophetic, symbolic, and apocalyptic in form. About 1147 Hildegard left Disibodenberg to found a convent at Rupertsberg, where she continued to prophesy and to record her visions in writing.

She is the first composer whose biography is known. She founded a convent, where her musical plays were performed. She wrote music and texts to her songs, mostly liturgical plainchant honoring saints and the Virgin Mary. She believed that music was the means of recapturing the original joy and beauty of paradise and that music was invented and musical instruments made in order to worship God appropriately. She wrote in the plainchant tradition of a single vocal melodic line that we have just discussed. She wrote seventy-seven chants and the first musical drama in history, which she entitled "The Ritual of the Virtues."

Hildegard of Bingen's music was written for performance by the nuns of the convent she headed. She combined all her music into a cycle called *The Symphony of the Harmony of the Heavenly Revelations*, from which the "Lauds of Saint Ursula" ("O Ecclesia" excerpt, music CD track 5) is one example. This music is sung by three sopranos accompanied by an instrumental drone, which serves as a sustained bass above which the voices soar in the chant-like melody. It celebrates St. Ursula, who, according to legend, was martyred with eleven thousand virgins in Cologne. Like Hildegard, Ursula devoted her life to God and headed a company of women.

Hildegard believed that many times a day, humans fall out of sorts and lose their way. Music was the sacred technology that could best redirect human hearts toward heaven. It could integrate mind, heart, and body and heal discord.

Hildegard's numerous other writings include a morality play, a book of saints' lives, two treatises on medicine and natural history, and extensive correspondence, in which are to be found further prophecies and allegorical treatises. Her lyrical poetry, gathered in *The Symphony of the Harmony of the Heavenly Revelations* (*Symphonia armonie celestium revelationum*), consists of seventy-seven poems (all with music), and together they form a liturgical cycle.

priate and compiled them for church services. Although Pope Gregory did not invent plainchant, his contributions of selection and codification were apparently such that the form acquired his name.

Polyphony: Organum

At some time between the eighth and tenth centuries, monks in monastery choirs began to add a second melodic line to the chant. At first the additional line paralleled the original at the interval of a fourth or a fifth. Medieval music that consists of Gregorian chant and an additional melodic line (or lines) is called *organum* (OHR-guh-nuhm). Between the tenth and thirteenth centuries organum became truly *polyphonic*. As time progressed,

the independent melodies became increasingly independent of each other and differed rhythmically as well as melodically.

ROMANESQUE STYLE IN ARCHITECTURE

At the beginning of the new millennium a new and radical style in architecture emerged. The Romanesque style took hold throughout Europe in a relatively short period. Originally meaning "debased Roman," it takes its name from the Roman-style round arches and columns of its doorways and windows. The term was invented in the early nineteenth century to describe medieval vaulted architecture that preceded the Gothic pointed arch. In

10.52 St.-Sernin, Toulouse, France, c. 1080–1120. (The top part of the tower was added in the 13th century.)

addition to arched doorways and windows, characteristic of this style was a massive, static quality—a further reflection of the barricaded mentality and lifestyle generally associated with the Middle Ages.

The Romanesque style nonetheless exemplified the power and wealth of the Church Militant and Triumphant. If the style mirrored the social and intellectual system that produced it, it also reflected a new religious fervor and a turning of the Church toward its growing flock. Romanesque churches were larger than their predecessors—Figures **10.52** and **10.53** give some impression of their scale. St.-Sernin is an example of southern French Romanesque, and it reflects a heavy elegance and complexity. The church plan is a *Roman cross*, and the side aisles extend beyond the crossing to create an ambulatory. Here pilgrims, who were mostly on their way to Spain, could walk around the altar without disturbing the service.

Significantly, the roof of this church is stone, whereas earlier buildings had wooden roofs. As we view the magnificent vaulted interior we wonder how the architect reconciled the conflicting forces of engineering, material, and aesthetics. Given the properties of stone and the increased force of added height, did he try to push his skills to the brink of practicality in order to create an interior of breathtaking scale? Did his efforts reflect the glory of God or the abilities of humankind?

Returning to the exterior view, we can see how some of the stress of the high tunnel vaulting was diffused. In a complex series of vaults, the tremendous weight and outward thrust of the central vault were transferred to the ground, leaving a high and unencumbered central space. If we compare this structural system with that of post-and-lintel and consider the compressive and tensile properties of stone, we can easily see the superiority of the arch as a structural device for creating open space. Watch the Humanities CD: Architecture, Romanesque and Gothic styles.

ROMANESQUE STYLE IN SCULPTURE

In the case of sculpture, Romanesque refers more to an era than to a style. Examples are so diverse that if most sculptural works were not decorations attached to Romanesque architecture, they probably could not be grouped under a stylistic label. However, we can draw some general conclusions. First, it is associated with Romanesque architecture. Second, it is heavy and solid.

10.53 St.-Sernin, interior.

10.54 Gislebertus, Last Judgment tympanum, Autun Cathedral, France, c. 1130–5.

Third, its medium is usually stone. Fourth, it is monumental. These last two characteristics represent a distinct departure from previous sculptural style. Monumental stone sculpture had all but disappeared in the fifth century. Its reemergence across Europe in such a short time was remarkable, indicating at least a beginning of an outward dissemination of knowledge from the cloistered world of the monastery to the general populace—for it was applied to the exterior of the building, where it could appeal to the lay worshiper. This artistic development almost certainly led to an increase in religious zeal among the laity.

The Last Judgment tympanum (TIHM-puh-nuhm) at Autun in France (Fig. 10.54), presents its message clearly. In the center of the composition, framed by a Roman-style arch, is an awe-inspiring figure of Christ. Beside him are a series of disproportional figures. The inscription of the artist, Gislebertus (zheez-lay-BAIR-tuhs), tells us that their purpose was "to let this horror appal those bound by earthly sin." Death was still central to medieval thought, and devils share the stage, gleefully pushing the damned into the flaming pit.

MEDIEVAL LITERATURE

St. Benedict (c. 480–c. 550 C.E.) was one of the few great scholars of the early medieval period. In the early Middle Ages, with the notable exception of the court of Charlemagne in the late eighth and early ninth centuries, the politically powerful cared little for culture, and for the most part could neither read nor write. Thanks to the efforts of the monastic community, and particularly Benedictine monks, important books and manuscripts were carefully preserved and copied.

Literature flourished in Spain, where Muslim contact with Greek scholarship led to the setting up of schools in Córdoba. Aristotle, Plato, and Euclid were on the curriculum alongside the Koran. Toledo and Seville were also centers of learning. Biblical literature, however, was the central focus of the Middle Ages in Christian Europe.

In addition, there were the poems of the traveling minstrels and court poets, who were popular throughout Europe. These professional storytellers produced fantastic legends and romances, such as the *Song of Roland* from France. In the *Song of Roland*, an unknown poet with fine but simple dramatic skills tells the story of a great battle between the emperor Charlemagne (742–814 C.E.) and the Saracens of Saragossa in Spain, which took place in the year 778 C.E. Charlemagne is deceived by the Saracens, draws his main army back into France, and leaves Roland with a rearguard to hold the mountain pass. The Saracens are aided by recreant Christian knights, and after a furious struggle, Roland and his entire army are killed. Our extract describes the battle between Roland's army and the Saracens.

The Song of Roland

King Marsilion comes along a valley
with all his men, the great host he assembled;
twenty divisions, formed and numbered by the King,
helmets ablaze with gems beset in gold,
and those bright shields, those hauberks sewn with brass.
Seven thousand clarions sound the pursuit,
and the great noise resounds across that country.
Said Roland then: "Oliver, Companion, Brother,
that traitor Ganelon has sworn our deaths:
it is treason, it cannot stay hidden,
the Emperor will take his terrible revenge.
We have this battle now, it will be bitter,
no man has ever seen the like of it.
I will fight here with Durendal, this sword,
and you, my companion, with Halteclere—
we've fought with them before, in many lands!
how many battles have we won with these two!
Let no one sing a bad song of our swords." AOI.[9]

When the French see the pagans so numerous,
the fields swarming with them on every side,
they call the names of Oliver, and Roland,
and the Twelve Peers: protect them, be their warranter.
The Archbishop told them how he saw things:
"Barons, my lords, do not think shameful thoughts,
do not, I beg you all in God's name, run.
Let no brave man sing shameful songs of us:
let us all die here fighting: that is far better.
We are promised: we shall soon find our deaths,
after today we won't be living here.
But here's one thing, and I am your witness:
Holy Paradise lies open to you,
you will take seats among the Innocents."
And with these words the Franks are filled with joy,
there is no man who does not shout Munjoie! AOI.

A Saracen was there of Saragossa,
half that city was in this pagan's keeping,
this Climborin, who fled before no man,
who took the word of Ganelon the Count,
kissed in friendship the mouth that spoke that word,
gave him a gift: his helmet and its carbuncle.
Now he will shame, says he, the Land of Fathers,
he will tear off the crown of the Emperor;
sits on the horse that he calls Barbamusche,
swifter than the sparrowhawk, than the swallow;
digs in his spurs, gives that war horse its head,
comes on to strike Engeler of Gascony,
whose shield and fine hauberk cannot save him;
gets the head of his spear into his body,
drives it in deep, gets all the iron through,
throws him back, dead, lance straight out, on the field.

• • •

The battle is fearful, there is no rest,
and the French strike with all their rage and strength,
cut through their fists and their sides and their spines,
cut through their gardments into the living flesh,
the bright blood flows in streams on the green grass.
The pagans cry: "We can't stand up to this!
Land of Fathers, Mahummet's curse on you!
Your men are hard, we never saw such men!"
There is not one who does not cry: "Marsilion!
Come to us, King! Ride! We are in need! Help!"

The battle is fearful and vast,
the men of France strike hard with burnished lances.
There you would have seen the great pain of warriors,
so many men dead and wounded and bleeding,
one lies face up, face down, on another.
The Saracens cannot endure it longer.
Willing and unwilling they quit the field.
The French pursue, with all their heart and strength. AOI.

• • •

Roland the Count calls out to Oliver:
"Lord, Companion, now you have to agree
the Archbishop is a good man on horse,
there's none better on earth or under heaven,
he knows his way with a lance and a spear."
The Count replies: "Right! Let us help him then."
And with these words the Franks began anew,
the blows strike hard, and the fighting is bitter;
there is a painful loss of Christian men.
To have seen them, Roland and Oliver,
these fighting men, striking down with their swords,
the Archbishop with them, striking with his lance!
One can recount the number these three killed:
it is written—in charters, in documents;
the Geste tells it: it was more than four thousand.
Through four assaults all went well with our men;
then comes the fifth, and that one crushes them.
They are all killed, all these warriors of France,
all but sixty, whom the Lord God has spared:
they will die too, but first sell themselves dear. AOI.

Count Roland sees the great loss of his men,
calls on his companion, on Oliver:
"Lord, companion, in God's name, what would you do?
All these good men you see stretched on the ground.
We can mourn for sweet France, fair land of France!
a desert now, stripped of such great vassals.
Oh King, and friend, if only you were here!
Oliver, Brother, how shall we manage it?
What shall we do to get word to the King?"
Said Oliver: "I don't see any way.
I would rather die now than hear us shamed." AOI.[10]

Another major literary accomplishment of the early Middle Ages, one with a completely different subject matter, was the German *Nibelungenlied* (nee-buh-LUHN-guhn-leed; "Song of the People of the Mists," meaning the dead). These early hero-stories of northern peoples, which took their final shape in southeast Germany c. 1200, are a rich mixture of history, magic, and myth.

The favorite Old English epic *Beowulf* (BAY-oh-wuhlf) is the earliest extant poem in a modern European language. Composed by an unknown author, it falls into separate episodes that incorporate old legends. Its three folk stories center on the hero Beowulf, and his exploits against the monster Grendel, Grendel's mother—a hideous water hag—and a fire-breathing dragon.

From the period of the Middle Ages corresponding to the Gothic style, came the Italian poet Dante (DAHN-tay), perhaps the greatest poet of the age. The major work of his life was *The Divine Comedy*. Its description of heaven, hell, and purgatory is a vision of the state of souls after death told in an allegory—that is, a dramatic device in which the superficial sense is accompanied by a deeper or more profound meaning. It works on several levels to demonstrate the human need for spiritual illumination and guidance. On a literal level, it describes the author's fears as a sinner and his hopes for eternal life. On deeper levels, it represents the quandaries and character of medieval society faced with, for example, balancing Classicism and Christianity. Here is a sample:

10.55 *David Harping*, from the Oscott Psalter, c. 1270. 7½ × 4¾ ins (20 × 11.1 cm). British Library, London.

The Divine Comedy
(Circle Two) Canto V
The Carnal
Dante
1265–1321

So we went down to the second ledge alone;
  a smaller circle of so much greater pain
  the voice of the damned rose in a bestial moan.

There Minos sits, grinning, grotesque, and hale.
  He examines each lost soul as it arrives
  and delivers his verdict with his coiling tail.

That is to say, when the ill-fated soul
  appears before him it confesses all,
  and that grim sorter of the dark and foul

decides which place in Hell shall be its end,
  then wraps his twitching tail about himself
  one coil for each degree it must descend.[11]

The late Middle Ages was the time of Geoffrey Chaucer, a sample of whose work we read in Chapter 8, and Christine de Pisan (c. 1365–c. 1463), who was a prolific and versatile French poet and author whose diverse writings include numerous poems of courtly love and several works championing women. Her works include *The Book of the City of Ladies* (1405), in which she described women known for their heroism and virtue.

Decameron, by Giovanni Boccaccio (boh-KAH-choh; 1313–75), uses a frame-tale (see Glossary) in which ten young people flee the plague in Florence in 1348 to sit out the danger in the countryside. To amuse themselves, they tell one hundred stories. The *Decameron* extols the virtue of humankind, proposing that to be noble, one must

A Personal Journey

AUTUN CATHEDRAL TYMPANUM

An intermittent rain splashed the windshield of the car as I drove the back road, descending steadily down the mountainside. I had just come from Vézelay (VAY-zeh-lay), France, a mountain retreat, abbey, and pilgrim church of Sainte Madeleine with a remarkable tympanum over the entry door. It was a medieval kind of day, dark and closed-in. I had spent the morning 30 miles (48 km) northwest in the village of Auxerre (oh-ZAIR), deep in the ninth-century crypts whose wall paintings reveal much of medieval monastic life. In another 40 miles (64 km) I would reach the subprefecture village of Autun (oh-TUHN), whose cathedral boasts another tympanum sculpture, this one by the artist Gislebertus (Fig. **10.54**). As was the case in Vézelay, finding the cathedral proved little problem. I merely kept going uphill until I ran into it. I thought it very convenient of our medieval ancestors to put their cathedrals in the center of town at the highest point. The symbolism inherent in such a placement is obvious. Nearly 900 years later, it also makes life a great deal simpler for tourists such as I to find these expressions of medieval philosophy, theology, and engineering. Sometimes it is difficult for Americans, whose country is barely 200 years old, to fathom fully buildings that date back 1,000 or more years and are still in use—as in Autun, Vézelay, Auxerre, and through-

out Europe and the Middle East. Autun was still a thriving, functioning center, and the cathedral, now a bit gray and soot-laden, perhaps, still occupied at least a semblance of its original centrality. The mid-April weather aided in finding a parking space at the rear of the church, and the rain conveniently subsided as I stepped into the street.

I walked toward the front of the cathedral. Above the doors, Gislebertus's statement about the Last Judgment looked down at me. I stood transfixed, my attention shifting slowly from section to section and figure to figure. The skill of the artist's handling of stone was obvious, and the details read clearly. I had no question about why Gislebertus chose to portray the figures in such a degree of exaggeration. He wanted to create an effect and to hammer home his message—or that of the medieval Church. Designed as an instruction book for the masses, the sculpture proclaimed the message of the Church loud and clear. At the center, framed by a Roman-style arch, stands an awe-inspiring Christ. Around him are a series of figures—some in Heaven and some in Hell, with an inscription, "to let this horror appal those bound by earthly sin."

As if to amplify the point, a thunderclap jolted me back to reality, and I moved quickly into the foyer lest a lightning bolt hasten me into the company of Gislebertus's subjects.

---

accept life as one finds it, without bitterness. Above all, one must accept the responsibility for, and consequences of, one's actions.

GOTHIC STYLE IN PAINTING

In the twelfth to the fifteenth centuries, traditional paintings in the form of frescoes and altar panels returned to prominence while manuscript illumination continued. The characteristics of Gothic style in painting include the beginning of three-dimensionality in figure representation and a striving to give figures mobility and life within three-dimensional space. Space is the essence of

Gothic style. Gothic painters and illuminators had not mastered perspective, and their compositions do not have the spatial rationality of later works, but if we compare them with their predecessors of the earlier medieval eras, we discover that they have more or less broken free from the static, frozen two-dimensionality of earlier styles. Gothic painting also shows spirituality, lyricism, and a new humanism (mercy, as opposed to the irrevocable judgment of the past). It is less crowded and frantic.

The Gothic style of two-dimensional art found magnificent expression in manuscript illumination. The courts of France and England produced some truly exquisite works. In *David Harping* (Fig. **10.55**) the curious pro-

10.56 Salisbury Cathedral, England, from the southwest, begun 1220.

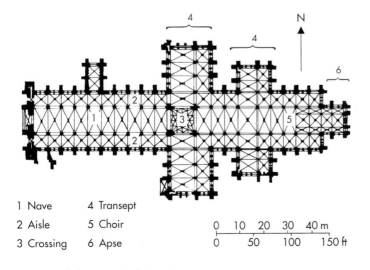

1 Nave   4 Transept
2 Aisle   5 Choir
3 Crossing 6 Apse

0 10 20 30 40 m
0   50   100   150 ft

10.57 Salisbury Cathedral, plan.

portions of the face and hands of David, and the awkward linear draping of fabric juxtaposed against the curves of the harp and chair, create a sense of unease and nervous tension. There is almost a carelessness about the layout of the background screen, and yet the repetition of the diamond forms (compare with Picasso's *Girl Before a Mirror*, Fig. **1**.19) provides a captivating counterpoint to the "X" shapes in the blue, orange, and beige border. The upward curving arcs at the top are intended to be symmetrical, but their hand-drawn quality is reinforced by the imprecision of the repetition of diamond shapes. A touch of realism appears in the curved harp string that David is plucking, and rudimentary use of highlight and shadow gives basic three-dimensionality to cloth and skin. While unbalanced in the interior space, the figure, nonetheless, does not appear to crowd the borders.

GOTHIC ARCHITECTURE: THE CATHEDRAL

Gothic style in architecture took many forms, but is best exemplified in the Gothic cathedral. The cathedral, in its synthesis of intellect, spirituality, and engineering, perfectly expresses the medieval mind. Gothic architectural style developed initially in a very localized way on the Île de France in the late twelfth century and spread outward to the rest of Europe. It had died as a style in some places before it was adopted in others. The "slipping, sliding, and overlapping" circumstances of artistic development were fully applicable to Gothic architecture.

Cathedrals were church buildings whose purpose was the service of God. However, civic pride as well as spirituality inspired their construction. Various local guilds contributed their services in financing or in the actual building work, and guilds were often memorialized in special chapels and stained-glass windows. Gothic cathedrals occupied the central, often elevated, area of the town or city. Their physical centrality and context symbolized the dominance of the universal Church over human affairs, both spiritual and secular. Probably no other style has exercised such an influence across the centuries or played such a central role, even in twentieth-century Christian architecture.

The beginnings of Gothic architecture can be pinpointed between 1137 and 1144 in the rebuilding of the royal Abbey Church of St.-Denis near Paris. Ample evidence exists that the Gothic style was a physical extension of philosophy, rather than a practical response to the structural limitations of the Romanesque style—that is, Gothic theory preceded its application. Abbot Suger, who was advisor to Louis VI and a driving force in the alteration of St.-Denis, held that harmony—the perfect relationship of parts—is the source of beauty, that Light Divine is a mystic revelation of God, and that space is symbolic of God's mystery. The composition of St.-Denis and subsequent Gothic churches expressed that philosophy and, as a result, Gothic architecture is more unified than Romanesque. Both in exterior spires and the pointed arch, Gothic cathedrals use refined, upward-striving line to symbolize humanity's striving to escape from earth into the mystery of space.

The pointed arch is the most easily identifiable characteristic of this style, and it represents not only a symbol of Gothic spirituality but also an engineering practicality. Compared with the round arch, it redistributes the thrust of downward force into more equal and controllable directions. The round arch places tremendous pressure on its *keystone*, which then transfers thrust outward to the sides and requires massive external buttressing, whereas the pointed arch controls thrust into a downward path through its legs. The pointed arch also makes design more flexible. Space encompassed by a round arch is limited to the radius of specific semicircles, whereas dimensions around a pointed arch can be adjusted to whatever practical and aesthetic parameters are desired.

Engineering advances implicit in the new form made possible larger *clerestory* (KLEER-stoh-ree; see Glossary) windows (hence more light) and more slender ribbing (hence a greater emphasis on space as opposed to mass). Outside, practical and aesthetic flying buttresses carry the outward thrust of the vaults through a delicate balance of ribs, vaults, and buttresses gracefully and comfortably to the ground. The importance of stained-glass windows in Gothic cathedrals cannot be overemphasized. Now that space and light replace bulky Romanesque walls, windows take the place of frescoes in telling the story of the gospels and the saints. They carefully control light entering the sanctuary, reinforcing a marvelous sense of mystery.

With the exception of St. Paul's Cathedral in London, Salisbury (Fig. **10.56**) is the only English cathedral whose entire interior structure was built to the design of a single architect and completed without a break, in 1265. However, the cathedral took another fifty-five years to complete, and the famous spire, built between 1285 and 1310, added an additional 404 feet (123 m) to a squat tower that rose only a few feet above the nave. The spire thus became the highest in England and the second highest in Europe. Unfortunately, the piers and foundations could not carry the additional 6,400 tons, and the masons were forced to add a strong stone vault at the crossing of the nave below the tower.

Compared to the soaring vertical cathedrals of France such as Notre Dame, Paris, and Amiens (see Figs. **7.32** and **7.33**), Salisbury seems long, low, and sprawling. The west front, wider than the nave, functions almost as a screen wall. Its horizontal bands of decoration emphasize the horizontal thrust of the building. The plan of the cathedral (Fig. **10.57**), with its double *transept*, retains features of the Romanesque style. The same emphasis on the horizontal appears in the interior, where the nave wall is made up of a succession of arches and supports. Watch the Humanities CD: Architecture, Romanesque and Gothic styles.

GOTHIC SCULPTURE

Gothic sculpture again reveals the changes in attitude of the period. It portrays serenity and idealization. Like Gothic painting, it has a human quality. Conceptions of Christ as a benevolent teacher and of God as beautiful

10.58 Chartres Cathedral, France, jamb statues on west portal, c. 1145–70.

10.59 Chartres Cathedral, jamb statues on south portal, c. 1215–20.

replace the vale of tears, death, and damnation typical of earlier in the Middle Ages. This style has a new order, symmetry, and clarity. Its visual images carry with distinctiveness over a distance. The figures of Gothic sculpture stand away from their backgrounds (Fig. 10.58).

Compositional unity changed from Early to Late Gothic. Early architectural sculpture was subordinate to the overall design of the building, but later work lost much of that integration as it gained in emotionalism (Fig. 10.59).

The sculptures of Chartres Cathedral, which bracket nearly a century, illustrate clearly the transition from Early to Late Gothic. The attenuated figures of Figure 10.58 display a relaxed tranquillity, idealization, and

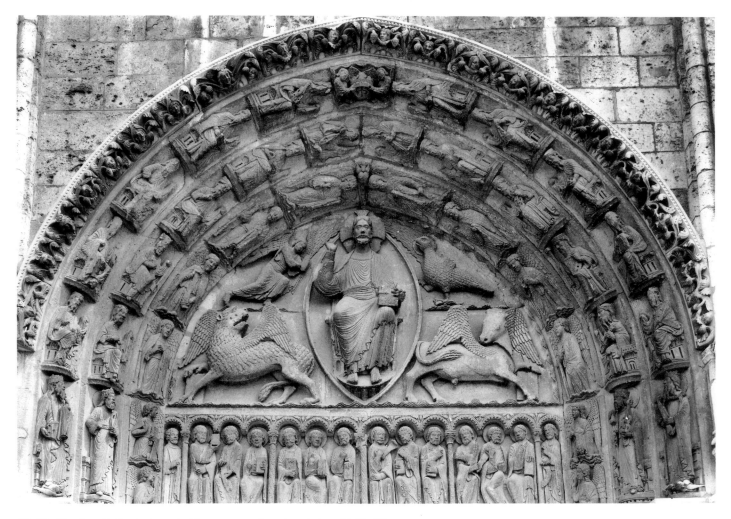

10.60 Chartres Cathedral, central tympanum of west portal, c. 1145–70.

simple realism. Although an integral part of the portal columns, they emerge from them, each statue in its own space. Detail is somewhat formalized and shallow, but we now see the human figure beneath the fabric—in contrast to previous uses of fabrics as mere compositional decoration.

Lifelikeness is even more pronounced in the figures of 100 years later (Fig. **10.59**). Here we can see the characteristics of the High Gothic style. Proportion is more lifelike, and the figures have only the most tenuous connection to the building. Figures are carved in subtle S-curves rather than as rigid perpendicular columns. Fabric drapes are much more naturally depicted, with deeper and softer folds. In contrast to the idealized older saints, these figures have the features of specific individuals expressing qualities of spirituality and determination.

The content of Gothic sculpture is also noteworthy. Like most church art, it was didactic, or designed to teach. Many of its lessons are fairly straightforward and can be appreciated by anyone with a basic knowledge of

the Bible. Christ appears as a ruler and judge of the universe above the main doorway of Chartres Cathedral (Fig. **10.60**), with a host of symbols of the apostles and others. Also decorating the portals are sculptures of the prophets and kings of the Old Testament, whose purpose is to proclaim the harmony of secular and spiritual rule by implying that the kings of France are the spiritual descendants of biblical rulers—in much the same sense as we noted in the art of Justinian at Ravenna (see pp. 245–7).

Other lessons of Gothic cathedral sculpture are more hidden. According to some scholars, specific conventions, codes, and sacred mathematics are involved. These factors relate to positioning, grouping, numbers, symmetry, and recognition of subjects. For example, the numbers three, four, and seven (often found in compositions of later periods) symbolize the Trinity, the Gospels, the sacraments, and the deadly sins. The positioning of the figures around Christ shows their relative importance—the place on his right is the most important. These codes and symbols are used on highly complex levels. All of this is consistent with the mysticism of the period, which held to strong beliefs in allegorical and hidden meanings in holy sources.

MEDIEVAL THEATRE

As the Middle Ages progressed, drama became associated with the Church. Its progression from sacred to secular began with the earliest church drama, which consisted of simple elaborations and illustrations of the mass (called tropes). Later drama included bible stories (mystery plays), lives of the saints (miracle plays), and didactic allegories (morality plays).

Mystery plays take their name from the Latin word meaning "service" or "occupation" rather than from the word for "mystery." The designation probably refers to the production of religious plays by the occupational guilds of the Middle Ages rather than the "mysteries" of revelation. Dating from the twelfth century, *The Representation of Adam* is the oldest known French mystery play. There were three parts, each with written dialogue: The Fall of Adam and Eve, the Murder of Abel, and the Prophecies of Christ. Latin instructions, which indicated scenery, costumes, and even actors' gestures, were written into the play: "Paradise shall be situated in a rather prominent place, and is to be hung all around with draperies and silk curtains."

Miracle plays presented a real or fictitious account of the life, miracles, or martyrdom of a saint. Almost all the surviving miracle plays concern either the Virgin Mary or St. Nicholas, the fourth-century bishop of Myra in Asia Minor, both of whom had active cults during the Middle Ages. The Mary plays consistently involve her coming to the aid of all who invoke her, be they worthy or wanton. The Nicholas plays are similar in content, usually chronicling the deliverance of a crusader or the conversion of a Saracen king.

Morality plays used allegorical characters such as Sloth, Gluttony, Lust, Pride, and Hatred to communicate their message. The most famous morality play (one which is still performed) is *Everyman*. In its story, Death summons Everyman to his final judgment. Everyman then seeks, as companions on his journey to judgment, the qualities (characters) of Fellowship, Kindred, Cousin, and Goods. Each refuses to join him. He finally asks Good Deeds, but Good Deeds is too weak from neglect to make the journey. Seeking advice from Knowledge, Everyman is told to do penance—an act that revives Good Deeds, who then takes up the journey with Everyman. Along the way, Five Wits also deserts him as he nears the grave. Good Deeds, however, stays with him until the end. So he is welcomed to Heaven.

NATIVE AMERICA

In very short order European attention would turn to the Americas, where native peoples had developed significant civilizations. In the last chapter we discussed the Olmecs of Mexico, one of many indigenous peoples, and noted their probable influences on the Mayan people. Further to the south another major culture emerged during the period we have studied in this chapter. They were the Incas, and we will discuss them in detail in the next chapter. Their art, however, conformed to some general characteristics we need to mention here. In general, Native American art tended to be portable and functional because the people were primarily nomadic, and practicality demanded that possessions be kept to a minimum and provide maximum utilization. If works of art—objects of beauty—were necessary, then they should fulfill their aesthetic functions as well as some domestic function. There were, nonetheless, some works of art designed for their own sake—for example, Figure **10.62**, an openwork vessel with a design representing a bird. This ceramic object, with cutout areas precluding it as a container, appears to be only aesthetic in function. In cultures such as those of the Plains Indians, Aztecs, and Incas, which were strongly militaristic, artistic expression found its way into ceremonial objects as well as costumes and weaponry.

In addition to following broad, general characteristics, Native American works of art also can reflect specific tribal characteristics. For example, characteristic of Inca art is a pottery shape called the *aryballus* (uh-RIH-buh-luhs), shown in Figure **10.61**. Delicate in design, this

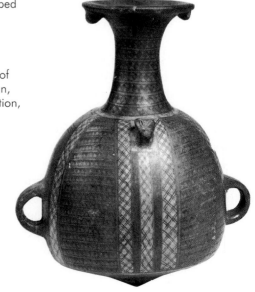

10.61 Arybal-shaped Inca vessel, from Bolivar, Ecuador, 10½ × 8¾ ins (26.7 × 22.2 cm). National Museum of the American Indian, Smithsonian Institution, Washington, D.C.

10.62 Openwork bird jar, from Ocklockonee Bay, Florida. Redware, with pre-fired "kill" hole in base, height 10½ ins (26.7 cm). National Museum of the American Indian, Smithsonian Institution, Washington, D.C.

multicolored ceramic urn features carefully painted small geometric patterns arranged symmetrically. The insect appended to the bowl creates an intriguing focal point and provides a visual counterpoint to the smooth and lustrous surface. The neck of the urn rises in a graceful curve and then splays outward into a disclike lip, divided symmetrically by underhung droplets. Aesthetic sensitivity and sophistication can be seen in the treatment of the lip. The asymmetrical handles placed below the centerline of the bowl give it a dynamic force and create additional interest for the viewer.

THINKING CRITICALLY

- Identify the basic characteristics of Greek Classicism and explain how the Parthenon (Fig 10.7) and two architectural examples from your own city or town exemplify those characteristics. In what ways are the local examples like or different from the Parthenon?

- Using line, form, mass, articulation, and your own personal, emotional reaction as points of comparison, analyze the *Scraper* (Fig. 10.9), the bearded figure from Djenne (Fig.10.40), and the *Bodhisattva of Compassion* (Fig. 10.45).

- Using your personal reaction and at least two characteristics of poetry (see Chapter 8), compare the excerpts from the *Aeneid* and the *Song of Roland*.

- Enumerate and compare the ways in which the Chinese painting *Twelve Views from a Thatched Cottage* (Fig. 10.47) and the Byzantine mosaic *Emperor Justinian and His Court* (Fig. 10.27) change what we would call photographic reality (lifelikeness) into something else. How do those changes from lifelikeness affect the ways in which you respond to the works?

- Explain the basic characteristics of Romanesque and Gothic art using illustrations from the text as examples. What kind of world do you think would have evoked the characteristics of each style?

CYBER STUDY

CLASSICAL GREECE:
http://library.thinkquest.org/26264/art/periods/site100.htm
http://witcombe.sbc.edu/ARTHgreecerome.html#Greek

ROME:
http://witcombe.sbc.edu/ARTHgreecerome.html#Roman

AFRICA:
http://artnetweb.com/guggenheim/africa/south.html

CHINA:
http://www.chinapage.com/paint1.html

JAPAN:
http://www.bergerfoundation.ch/wat1/frameset?pg=
japon&ref=First_japan82&babel=en

BYZANTINE STYLE:
http://witcombe.sbc.edu/ARTHmedieval.html#Byzantine

ISLAMIC STYLE:
http://witcombe.sbc.edu/ARTHmedieval.html#Islamic

ROMANESQUE STYLE:
http://witcombe.sbc.edu/ARTHmedieval.html#Romanesque

GOTHIC STYLE:
http://witcombe.sbc.edu/ARTHmedieval.html#Gothic
http://witcombe.sbc.edu/ARTHmedieval.html#LateGothic

CHAPTER ELEVEN

ARTISTIC STYLES IN THE EMERGING MODERN WORLD

c. 1400 to c. 1800

THE ENLIGHTENMENT IN EUROPE

ROCOCO STYLE IN PAINTING
LANDSCAPE AND PORTRAITURE
STILL LIFE AND *GENRE*
NEOCLASSICAL STYLE
    Painting
    Architecture
Masterwork: Jacques-Louis David,
    The Oath of the Horatii
MUSICAL CLASSICISM
    The Classical Sonata and Sonata
        Form
    The Classical Symphony
    Other Classical Forms
    Haydn
    Mozart
    Beethoven
LITERATURE
    Jonathan Swift, *A Modest*
        Proposal
    Alexander Pope, Epistle I, from
        An Essay on Man
    Phillis Wheatley, "On Virtue"
Thinking Critically
Cyber Study

IMPORTANT TERMS

Renaissance The period from approximately 1400 to 1527 that was seen as a rebirth of understanding after the Middle Ages.

High Renaissance The period between 1495 and 1527 encapsulated by the genius of Leonardo da Vinci, Michelangelo, and Raphael.

Word painting A musical technique in which the music attempts to enhance the meaning and emotion of a written text.

Mass The most important rite of the Roman Catholic liturgy. A musical form reflecting the parts of the mass.

Madrigal A musical setting of lyric poetry for four or five voices.

Baroque style A diverse seventeenth-century style in the visual and performing arts generally typified by largeness, ornateness, and emotional appeal.

Program music Music written to illustrate an external idea.

Absolute music Music that presents purely musical ideas.

Rococo style An eighteenth-century style typified by intricacy, grace, charm, and delicacy.

THE RENAISSANCE

The Renaissance was explictly seen by its leaders as a rebirth of our understanding of ourselves as social and creative beings. "Out of the sick Gothic night our eyes are opened to the glorious touch of the sun," was how the writer Rabelais (RAB-uh-lay) expressed what most of his educated contemporaries felt. Florence, the crucible of the Renaissance in Italy, was called the "New Athens," and it was here that the fine arts, or "liberal arts," were first redefined as art, in contrast to their status as crafts in the Middle Ages. Now accepted among the intellectual disciplines, the arts became an essential part of learning and literary culture. Artists, architects, composers, and writers gained confidence from their new status and from the technical mastery they were achieving. For the first time, it seemed possible not merely to imitate the works of the Classical world, but to surpass them.

Definitions of the Renaissance have been debated for centuries. The word certainly describes a new sense of self and self-awareness felt by Western European people, who had come to see themselves as no longer part of the "Middle Ages." But deciding where and how the Renaissance began, and what specifically it was, is as difficult as answering the question of where and how it ended—if it ended at all.

In the middle of the nineteenth century, a Swiss historian, Jacob Burckhardt, began what is formally known as Renaissance studies. He maintained—thus agreeing with fifteenth-century Italians—that an actual rebirth of ideas began in the 1400s after centuries of stagnation, and he asserted that in Italy during the fourteenth century there was a new spirit of inquiry and understanding in which the Classical world of Greece and Rome again

A Personal Journey

FLORENCE, *ET AL*

I'm standing in the Piazzale Michelangelo, across the Arno River from central Florence, looking down on the city. It's a spectacular view, dominated by Brunelleschi's dome on the cathedral (Fig. 11.6). Behind me, in the center of this *piazzale* (pee-aht-TZAH-lay), or square, is a monument with bronze copies of some of Michelangelo's marble statues, including *David*. This bronze copy begins my walking tour. In an attempt at symmetry, I'll end at the original statue of David. Although Florence spreads out widely below, a tremendous number of Renaissance treasures occupy a very small geographical area. I find it difficult to choose among them; today I'll just hit the highlights.

Down from the heights of the Piazzale Michelangelo the acrid air and the constant din of thousands of Vespa motor scooters reminds me that however grand the Florentine Quattrocento (the 1400s; the Renaissance in Florence) might have been, this is 500 years later. Still on the south side of the river, I stop first at the rather nondescript Church of Santa Maria del Carmine. That's the outside. Inside, in the Brancacci Chapel (brahn-KAHT-chee), is Masaccio's *Tribute Money* (Fig. 11.1). But it shares the chapel as part of a cycle of paintings titled *Scenes from the Life of St. Peter*. Another cycle, *Original Sin*, includes Masaccio's masterpiece *Expulsion from the Earthly Paradise*, which faces Masolino's *The Temptation of Adam and Eve*.

Out of the church and over the Ponte Vecchio (pahn-tuh VEH-kee-oh), to the north side of the Arno and just beside the bridge, I duck into the Uffizi (oo-FEET-zee) Gallery, the oldest art gallery in the world, to see Botticelli's *La Primavera* (Fig. 11.2). I'm tempted to spend the day, because the Uffizi offers so much to see; however, I find it easier to study one work at a time, and so I move on.

A short stroll east brings me to the Church of Santa Croce (kroh-chay; Holy Cross), with the Pazzi (paht-zee) Chapel tucked in its cloister (Fig. 11.7). The façade (the pronaos) has six Corinthian columns and a wide central arch between elegant inset panels of gray sandstone. Inside, a wide array of individual artworks awaits, but time doesn't permit lingering to study them, because I'm off to see Ghiberti's *Gates of Paradise* on the Baptistery across from the front entrance of the cathedral (Fig. 11.3).

Time slips away, and so, with a quick sprint, I cover the three blocks to the Bargello (bar-JAY-lo) Museum for a peek at Donatello's *David* (Fig. 11.4). This is another place to spend considerable time on another visit. The Bargello is dedicated to sculpture and the "minor" arts, and was once a palace famous for its grisly executions. I'm still a little out of breath from the run, but I'll have time to recover waiting in line outside the Gallery of the Academy to see Michelangelo's statue of David (Fig. 2.15), set in a large corner niche in the Tribuna of the Gallery.

I'm sorry I rushed so frantically, but there was a lot of ground to cover. Florence is rich in great art but, in reality, every street in every town has important human stories to tell in buildings and museums. A quick tasting often reveals a need to return to savor the details.

---

became the inspiration for a superior civilization, thus supplanting the "Middle" Ages.

However, many scholars in the mid-twentieth century felt that Burckhardt's viewpoint was over-simplistic, and that the period was nothing more than a natural extension of the previous times—that is, the clear break identified by Burckhardt had not occurred. The apparent change that took place in the fifteenth century was more of a shift in cultural and educational emphasis than it was a new discovery of the past. In addition, the Renaissance, rather than being a monolithic period, was really three or more periods, each with its own circumstances and—to a large degree—its own characteristics. We can identify an Early Renaissance, particularly that occurring in Florence; a High Renaissance, specifically in Rome and Venice; and a Renaissance that occurred outside Italy, particularly in the northern European states, which was highly influenced by—or at least related to—the Protestant Reformation.

In the past thirty years, a third viewpoint has emerged, which attests that the word "Renaissance" is strictly an educational and artistic label and is not particularly applicable to politics and society at large. According to this viewpoint, any label such as "Renaissance" does not do justice to the complex issues and circumstances that arose in such a diverse area as Europe over a period as long as 200 years.

RENAISSANCE PAINTING IN FLORENCE

In Italy, more precisely in Florence, the Renaissance found its early spark and heart in about 1400. Florence was a wealthy commercial center and, like Athens, leapt into a golden age on a soaring spirit of victory as the city successfully resisted the attempts of the Duke of Milan to subjugate it. The consequent outpouring of art made Florence the focal point of the Early Italian Renaissance.

During the first two decades of the fifteenth century, sculpture reigned as the premier visual art of the time. Painters, for the most part, were kept busy painting altarpieces for Florentine churches—generally in a variation of Gothic style. Unlike sculpture, painting showed little concern for the human spirit or for the stylistic problems that occupied sculptors. But ideas were developing, and came to fruition in the work of Masaccio (mah-ZAH-koh or mah-ZAHT-choh; Tommaso di Giovanni, 1401–29). The hallmark of Masaccio's invention and development of a "new" style is the way he employs deep space and rational foreshortening or perspective in his figures. Rational use of linear perspective, determined by Brunelleschi (broo-nuh-LES-kee; see p. 283) from his Classical models, was one of the great inventions of the Renaissance. In collaboration with the artist Masolino, Masaccio was summoned in 1425 to create a series of frescoes for the Brancacci Chapel of the Church of Santa Maria del Carmine in Florence. Watch the Humanities CD: Visual Art, Perspective.

Masaccio, The Tribute Money

The most famous of Masaccio's frescoes in the Brancacci family chapel is *The Tribute Money* (Fig. **11.1**). Its setting makes full use of the new discovery of linear perspective, as the rounded figures move freely in unencumbered deep space. It employs a technique called "continuous narration," unfolding a series of events across a single canvas—here the New Testament story from Matthew (17:24–7).

The figures in this fresco are remarkably accomplished. In the first place, they are dressed in fabric that falls like real cloth. Next, weight and volume are depicted entirely differently from how they were in Gothic painting: Each

11.1 Masaccio, *The Tribute Money*, Brancacci Chapel, Santa Maria del Carmine, Florence, c. 1427. Fresco (after restoration 1989), 8 ft 4 ins × 19 ft 8 ins (2.54 × 5.9 m).

11.2 *Sandro Botticelli, La Primavera (Spring),* c. 1478. Tempera on panel, 6 ft 8 ins × 10 ft 4 ins (2.03 × 3.15 m). Galleria degli Uffizi, Florence.

figure is in Classical *contrapposto* stance. The sense of motion is not particularly remarkable, but the accurate rendering of the feet makes these figures seem to stand on real ground. Masaccio uses light to reveal form and volume. The key is establishing a source for the light that strikes the figures and then rendering the objects in the painting so that all highlights and shadows occur as if caused by that single light source.

Masaccio's figures form a circular and three-dimensional grouping rather than a flat line across the surface of the work as in *La Primavera* by Botticelli (bah-tih-CHAY-lee) (Fig. 11.2). Even the haloes of the apostles appear in the new perspective and overlap at odd angles. Compositionally, the single vanishing point, by which the linear perspective is controlled, sits at the head of Christ—we will see this device for achieving focus again in Leonardo da Vinci's *Last Supper* (see Fig. 11.8). In addition, Masaccio utilizes atmospheric perspective, in which distance is indicated through diminution of light and blurring of outlines. This not only enhances dimensionality but provides a unifying device.

Botticelli, Spring

By the last third of the fifteenth century, most of the originators of Renaissance art were dead. The essences of the new art were well known and well established; it was a time for further exploration in other avenues. One of these turned inward toward the life of the spirit, and in its search created a lyrical expression, much more poetic than anything we have seen thus far. Outward reality was often ignored in favor of more abstract values. This tradition is best expressed in the paintings of Sandro Botticelli (Alessandro Filipepi, c. 1445–1510). The linear quality of *La Primavera*, or *Spring* (Fig. 11.2), suggests an artist apparently unconcerned with deep space or subtle plasticity in light and shade. Rather, forms emerge through outline. The composition moves gently across the picture through a lyrical combination of undulating curved lines, with focal areas in each grouping. Mercury, the Three Graces, Venus, Flora, Spring, and Zephyrus—each part of this human, mythical composition carries its own emotion: contemplation, sadness, or happiness. Note the apparently Classical and non-Christian subject matter. But, in fact, the painting uses *allegory* to equate Venus with the Virgin Mary. Beyond the immediate qualities, deeper symbolism relates also to the Medici family, the patron rulers of Florence.

Anatomically, Botticelli's figures are quite simple. He shows little concern for detailed musculature. Although he renders figures three-dimensionally and shades them subtly, they seem almost weightless, floating in space without anatomical definition.

RENAISSANCE SCULPTURE IN FLORENCE

An attempt to capture the essence of European sculpture in the Early Renaissance can, again, best be served by looking to fifteenth-century Florence, where sculpture also enjoyed the patronage of the Medici. The early Renaissance sculptors developed the skills to create images of high verisimilitude. The goal, however, was not the same as that of the Greeks, with their idealized reality of human form. Rather, Renaissance sculptors found their ideal in individualism. The ideal was the glorious—even if not quite perfect—individual. Sculpture of this style presented an uncompromising and stark view of humankind—complex, balanced, and full of action. Freestanding statuary, long out of favor, returned to dominance. The human form was built up layer by layer upon

its skeletal and muscular framework, reflecting scientific inquiry and interest in anatomy. Even when clothed, fifteenth-century sculpture revealed the body under the garments, quite unlike medieval works. And relief sculpture caught onto the new means of representing deep space through systematic, scientific perspective.

Notable and typical among fifteenth-century Italian sculptors were Lorenzo Ghiberti (ghee-BAIR-tee; 1378–1455) and Donatello (Donato de' Bardi, 1386–1466). Ghiberti's *Gates of Paradise*, from the doors of the Baptistery in Florence, show the same concern for rich detail, humanity, and feats of perspective evident in Florentine painting. Ghiberti, who trained as a goldsmith and painter, creates beautiful surfaces with delicate detail. He also conveys a tremendous sense of space in each of the ten panels. In *The Story of Jacob and Esau* (Fig. **11.3**),

11.4 Donatello, *David*, dated variously 1430–40. Bronze, height 5 ft 2¼ ins (1.58 m). Museo Nazionale del Bargello, Florence.

11.3 Lorenzo Ghiberti, *The Story of Jacob and Esau*, panel of the *Gates of Paradise*, Baptistery, Florence, c. 1435. Gilt bronze, 31¼ ins (79 cm) square.

11.5 Raphael, *Count Baldassare Castiglione*, 1514. Oil transferred from wood to canvas, 2 ft 9¾ ins × 2 ft 3½ ins (82 × 66 cm). Louvre, Paris.

RENAISSANCE LITERATURE

The sixteenth century witnessed the climax and close of what amounted to an Italian monopoly in Renaissance literature. The influence of the Italian Renaissance spread to the rest of Europe, reaching France in the middle third of the century and England in the last third of the century. The common factor everywhere was imitation of the classics. In Italy the writers of the High Renaissance were apparently indifferent to the tragic social and political events to which they bore witness. Most, like Castiglione, chose to ignore what was going on. However, it is reasonably clear that after the Spanish Sack of Rome in 1527, literature, with perhaps the exception of Torquato Tasso, slipped into mediocrity.

Baldassare Castiglione

In essence, the Renaissance state was monarchical. In fact, the whole movement of the Renaissance was toward monarchical government. In Italy, it may have seemed less so than in France and Spain, but it was nonetheless the case in the petty duchies and principalities, and the gentlemen and ladies of the Renaissance were courtiers. The Conte Baldassare Castiglione (kah-stee-lee-YOH-nee; 1478–1529) was himself the perfect courtier (Fig. 11.5), and his book *Il Cortegiano* or *The Courtier* became a universal guide to "goodly manners" and "civil conversation" of the court of the duchy of Urbino. In effect, he was the arbiter of courtly behavior for all of Europe. In this influential work, Castiglione suggests, through an imagined dialogue, a picture of an artistically ordered society, in which cultivated Italians regard social living as a fine art.

Castiglione was raised at the court of Duke Sforza of Milan. He studied Greek, Latin, and Italian poetry, music, painting, and horsemanship. As his portrait reveals, he was a handsome, intelligent man, who entered the service of the duke of Urbino in 1504, thereby entering an environment with a fabulous library that was the rendezvous of European scholars and artists. As a diplomat, he visited England, became an advisor of Pope Leo X, and papal nuncio of Pope Clement VII to the court of the Holy Roman Emperor Charles V. When the Emperor's troops sacked Rome, Castiglione became the subject of numerous rumors of treason.

The particular character of *The Courtier* lies in the realistic manner in which the conversations are handled and the way in which the various opinions of the participants are introduced. Above all, *The Courtier* propounds the humanist's ultimate ideals—of men and women of intellectual refinement, cultural grace, moral stability, spiritual insight, and social consciousness. It provided a model

for example, he uses receding arcades to create depth and perspective. The bold relief of these scenes took Ghiberti twenty-one years to complete.

The greatest masterpieces of fifteenth-century Italian Renaissance sculpture came from the unsurpassed master of the age, Donatello (doh-nah-TAY-loh or dahn-uh-TEHL-oh). He had a passion for antiquity, and began his career as an assistant on the Florentine Baptistery doors. His early statues were similar to medieval works in that they were architectural and designed to occupy niches. His magnificent *David* (Fig. 11.4) was the first freestanding nude since Classical times. Unlike Classical nudes, David is partially clothed. His armor and helmet, along with bony elbows and adolescent character, invest him with a highly individualized nature. Donatello has returned to Classical *contrapposto* stance, but the carefully executed form expresses a new humanity suggesting that the statue is almost capable of movement. The work symbolizes Christ's triumph over Satan. The laurel crown on the helmet and laurel wreath on which the work stands allude to the Medici family, in whose palace the statue was displayed in 1469.

of the ideal Renaissance society, but its values are timeless: true worth is determined "by character and intellect rather than by birth." The excerpt that follows, although brief, illustrates both the context of the time and the content of Castiglione's work.

The Courtier
On Women
Baldassare Castiglione
1478–1529

Leaving aside, therefore, those virtues of the mind which she must have in common with the courtier, such as prudence, magnanimity, continence and many others besides, and also the qualities that are common to all kinds of women, such as goodness and discretion, the ability to take good care, if she is married, of her husband's belongings and house and children, and the virtues belonging to a good mother, I say that the lady who is at Court should properly have, before all else, a certain pleasing affability whereby she will know how to entertain graciously every kind of man with charming and honest conversation, suited to the time and the place and the rank of the person with whom she is talking. And her sense and modest behavior, and the candor that ought to inform all her actions, should be accompanied by a quick and vivacious spirit by which she shows her freedom from boorishness; but with such a virtuous manner that she makes herself thought no less chaste, prudent and benign than she is pleasing, witty and discreet. Thus she must observe a certain difficult mean, composed as it were of contrasting qualities, and take care not to stray beyond certain fixed limits. Nor in her desire to be thought chaste and virtuous, should she appear withdrawn or run off if she dislikes the company she finds herself in or thinks the conversation improper. For it might easily be thought that she was pretending to be straitlaced simply to hide something she feared others could find out about her; and in any case, unsociable manners are always deplorable.[1]

Ludovico Ariosto

A second major literary figure of the time was Ludovico Ariosto (ah-ree-OH-stoh; 1474–1533). Ariosto was a courtier of the house of Este (EH-stay) at Ferrara, a civil servant and diplomat as well as court poet. Classically trained, he wrote most of his work in Latin until he was twenty-five years old. His father died when he was twenty-six, and he assumed responsibility for providing for his four brothers and five sisters. He spent fourteen years as confidential secretary to Cardinal d'Este, and during this time he traveled throughout Italy on political missions. In 1518, he entered the service of the cardinal's brother, the duke of Ferrara, eventually becoming the duke's director of entertainment. Under Ariosto's supervision, the court enjoyed pageants and dramatic productions, Ariosto himself designing the theatre and scenery and writing a number of the plays. As early as 1505 he began his masterpiece, *Orlando Furioso*, forty cantos (sections) of which were published in 1516. For nearly thirty years he continued to revise the work, which became one of the most influential poems of the Renaissance. *Orlando Furioso* ("Roland in a Mad Fury") is a romantic epic—its forty-six cantos total over 1,200 pages—of "Loves and Ladies, Knights and Arms ... Of Curtesies, and many a Daring Feat." Ariosto depended heavily on the Greco-Roman tradition of Homer and Virgil, and borrowed incidents, character types, and rhetorical devices, such as the catalogue of troops and extended simile. Designed for a sophisticated audience, it employs an ottava rima (a stanza of eight lines rhyming abababcc), and it has a polished, graceful style. It became a bestseller throughout Europe.

Orlando Furioso captivated its sixteenth-century readers with its elements of supernatural trips to the moon, allegorical incidents that taught modesty and chastity, and romantic adventure. However, the characters are shallow and two-dimensional, for Ariosto made no attempt to probe the depths of human behavior or to tackle important issues. Nonetheless, individual incidents are worked out with care and carried through to a climax, after which the next is taken up, and all the loose threads are tied together at the end. *Orlando Furioso* served the Renaissance as a model of the large-scale narrative poem that was written with technical skill, smoothness, and the gracefulness typical of the classics. Ariosto spent most of his adult life writing and revising this masterpiece.

RENAISSANCE ARCHITECTURE

Early Renaissance architecture centered in Florence and departed from medieval architecture in three significant ways. First was its concern with the revival of Classical models along technical lines. Ruins of Roman buildings were measured carefully and their proportions became those of Renaissance buildings. Rather than seeing Roman arches as limiting factors, Renaissance architects saw them as geometric devices by which a formally derived design could be composed. The second departure from the medieval was the application of decorative detail—nonstructural ornamentation—to the façade of the building. Third, and a manifestation of the second difference, was a radical change in the outer expression of structure. The outward form of a building was previously closely related to the structural support of the building—for

example, post-and-lintel, masonry, and the arch. In the Renaissance, these supporting elements were hidden from view and the external appearance was no longer sacrificed to structural concerns.

Early architecture of the period, such as the dome of Florence Cathedral (Fig. **11.6**), imitated Classical form appended to medieval structures. This curious design by Filippo Brunelleschi (1377–1446) was added to a fourteenth-century building in the fifteenth century. The soaring dome rises 180 feet (55 m) into the air, and its height is apparent from both outside and within.

Compared with the Pantheon (see Figs. **10.22** and **10.23**), Brunelleschi's departure from traditional practice becomes clear. The dome of the Pantheon is impressive only from the inside of the building, because its exterior supporting structure is so massive that it clutters the visual experience. On the exterior of Brunelleschi's dome, though, the supporting elements such as stone and timber girdles and lightweight ribbings are hidden, resulting in an aesthetic statement where visual appearance rivals structural considerations.

Classical ornamentation also marks Brunelleschi's Pazzi Chapel (Fig. **11.7**). It uses its walls as a plain background for surface decoration. Concern for proportion and geometric design is clear, but the overall composition is not a slave to pure arithmetical considerations. Rather, the Pazzi Chapel reflects Brunelleschi's sense of Classical aesthetics. Brunelleschi's influence was profound in the first half of the fifteenth century, and he served as a model and inspiration for later Renaissance architects.

THE HIGH RENAISSANCE IN ROME

As important and revolutionary as the fifteenth century was in Italy, the high point of the Renaissance came in the early sixteenth century. Its importance as the apex of Renaissance art has led scholars to call this period in the visual arts the High Renaissance. Painters of the High Renaissance included giants of Western visual art: Leonardo da Vinci, Michelangelo, Raphael, Giorgione, and Titian. A concept of particular importance to our overview of visual art in the High Renaissance style is the concept of genius. Genius was implicit in humanistic exploration of the individual's earthly potential and fulfillment. In Italy between 1495 and 1520 everything in visual art was subordinate to the overwhelming genius of two men, Leonardo da Vinci and Michelangelo

11.6 (*opposite*) Filippo Brunelleschi, Florence Cathedral, dome, 1420–36.

11.7 Filippo Brunelleschi, Pazzi Chapel, Santa Croce, Florence, c. 1440–61.

Buonarroti. Their impact has led many to debate whether the High Renaissance of visual art was a culmination of earlier Renaissance style or a new departure.

By 1500 the courts of the Italian princes had become important sources of patronage and cultural activity. In pursuit of their world of beauty, the Italian nobility needed artists, writers, and musicians. The arts of the Early Renaissance now seemed commonplace and naive. A more aristocratic, elegant, dignified, and exalted art was demanded. This new style was lofty.

The reestablishment of papal authority, the wealth of the popes, and their desire to rebuild and transform Rome on a grand scale also contributed significantly to the shift in style and the emergence of Rome as the center of High Renaissance patronage. Music came of age as a major art, finding a great patron in Pope Leo X. There was a revival of ancient Roman sculptural and architectural style. Important discoveries of ancient sculptures such as the *Apollo Belvedere* and the *Laocoön* (see Fig. **10.13**) were made. Because the artists of the High Renaissance had such a rich immediate inheritance of art and literature from the Early Renaissance and felt they had developed even further, they considered themselves on an equal footing with the artists of the antique period. Their approach to the antique in arts and letters was therefore different from that of their Early Renaissance predecessors.

High Renaissance painting sought a universal ideal achieved through impressive art, as opposed to over-emphasis on anatomy or tricks of perspective. Figures became types again, rather than individuals—godlike human beings in the Greek Classical tradition. Artists and writers of the High Renaissance sought to capture the essence of Classical art and literature without resorting to copying, which would have captured only the externals. They tried to emulate, and not to imitate. As a result, High Renaissance art idealizes all forms and delights in composition. It is stable without being static, varied without confusion, and clearly defined without dullness.

High Renaissance artists carefully observed how the ancients borrowed motifs from nature, and they then set out to develop a system of mathematically defined proportion and compositional beauty. Such faith in harmonious proportions reflected a belief among artists, writers, and composers that a harmonious universe and nature possessed perfect order. High Renaissance style departed from previous styles in its meticulously arranged composition, based almost exclusively on geometric devices, such as a central triangle or an oval. Composition was closed—line, color, and form kept the viewer's eye continually redirected into the work, as opposed to leading off the canvas.

Leonardo da Vinci

The work of Leonardo da Vinci (1452–1519) contains an ethereal quality which he achieved by blending light and shadow (called *sfumato* [sfoo-MAHT-oh]—literally, "smoked,"

from the Italian). His figures hover between reality and illusion as one form disappears into another, and only highlighted portions emerge. It is difficult to say which of Leonardo's paintings is the most popular or admired, but certainly *The Last Supper* (Fig. **11.8**) ranks among the greatest. It captures the drama of Christ's prophecy, "One of you shall betray me," at the moment when the apostles are responding with disbelief. Leonardo's choice of medium proved most unfortunate because his mixture of oil, varnish, and pigments (as opposed to fresco) was not suited to the damp wall. The painting began to flake and was reported to be perishing as early as 1517. Since then it has been clouded by retouching, defaced by a door cut through the wall at Christ's feet, and bombed during World War II. Miraculously, it survives.

In *The Last Supper*, human figures and not architecture are the focus. The figure of Christ dominates the center of the painting. All line, actual and implied, leads outward from his face, pauses at various subordinate focal areas, is directed back into the work, and returns to the central figure. Various postures, hand positions, and groupings of the disciples direct the eye from point to point. Figures emerge from the gloomy architectural background in strongly accented relief; nothing anchors them to the floor of the room where they sit. This typically geometric composition is amazing in that so much drama can be expressed within such a mathematical format. Yet, despite the drama, the mood in this work and others is calm, belying the conflict of Leonardo's own life and times.

11.8 Leonardo da Vinci, *The Last Supper*, Santa Maria delle Grazie, Milan, c. 1495–8.

Michelangelo

Perhaps the most dominant figure of the High Renaissance was Michelangelo Buonarroti (bwoh-nuh-ROH-tee; 1475–1564). While Leonardo was a skeptic, Michelangelo was a man of great faith. Leonardo was fascinated by science and natural objects; Michelangelo, by contrast, showed little interest in anything other than the human form.

Michelangelo's Sistine Chapel ceiling (Fig. 11.10) is a shining example of the ambition and genius of this era and its philosophies. Some scholars see in this monumental work a blending of Christian tradition and a *Neoplatonist* view of the soul's progressive ascent through contemplation and desire. In each of the triangles along the sides of the chapel the ancestors of Christ await the Redeemer. Between them, amidst painted pillars, are the sages of antiquity. In the corners Michelangelo depicts various biblical stories, and across the center of the ceiling he unfolds the episodes of the first book of the Bible, Genesis. The center of the ceiling captures the Creation of Adam (Fig. 11.9) at the moment of fulfillment, and does so in sculpturesque human form and beautifully modeled anatomical detail. God, in human form, stretches outward from his matrix of angels to a reclining but dynamic Adam, awaiting the divine infusion, the spark of the soul. The figures do not touch, and we are left with a supreme feeling of anticipation of what we imagine will be the power and electricity of God's physical contact with mortal man.

The Sistine Chapel ceiling creates a visual display of awesome proportions. It is not possible to get a comprehensive view of the entire ceiling standing at any point in the Chapel. If we look upward and read the scenes back toward the altar, the prophets and sibyls appear on their sides. If we view one side as upright, then the other appears upside down. These opposing directions are held together by the structure of simulated architecture, whose transverse arches and diagonal bands separate vault compartments. Twenty nudes appear at intersections and harmonize the composition because they can be read either with the prophets and sibyls below them or with the Genesis scenes, at whose corners they appear.

Michelangelo believed that the image from the artist's hand must spring from the idea in his or her mind. The idea is the reality, and it is revealed by the genius of the artist. The artist does not create the ideas, but finds them in the natural world, which reflects the absolute idea: beauty. So, to the Neoplatonist, imitation of nature in art reveals hidden truths within nature.

Michelangelo broke with earlier Renaissance artists in his insistence that measurement was subordinate to judgment. He believed that measurement and proportion should be kept "in the eyes," and so established a rationale for the release of genius to do what it would, free from any preestablished "rules." This enabled him to produce works such as *David* (see Fig. 2.15), a colossal figure and the earliest monumental sculpture of the High Renaissance.

11.9 Michelangelo, *The Creation of Adam*, Sistine Chapel ceiling (detail).

11.10 Michelangelo, Sistine Chapel ceiling, the Vatican, Rome, 1508–12.

Papal Splendor: The Vatican

Here for almost 2,000 years has been the center of a spiritual communion; in countries all over the world, Christians aspire to achieve a community of spirit with the successor to St. Peter. By comprehending this significance of the Vatican, one can also understand what it was that led Roman Catholicism to embellish the center of its spiritual power with the diversity of human knowledge, including the arts.[2]

Rome was the city of the arts in the fifteenth and sixteenth centuries. The Renaissance—and particularly the High Renaissance, when the papacy called all great artists to Rome—contributed most of the splendor of Vatican art and architecture. The papacy as a force and the Vatican as the symbol of that force represent a synthesis of Renaissance ideas and reflections. St. Peter's and the Vatican have earthly and heavenly qualities which reflect the reality of the Church on earth and the mystery of the spiritual church of Christ (Fig. **11.11**). The Church sponsored art on a grand scale to give glory to God and to draw the general populace closer to God.

Plans for replacement of the original basilica of Old St. Peter's were made by Nicholas V (reigned 1447–55) in the fifteenth century, but it was Pope Julius II (reigned 1503–13) who decided to put them into effect. Julius commissioned Donato Bramante (brah-MAHN-tay; 1444–1514) to construct the new basilica. Bramante's design called for a building in the form of a Greek cross (Fig. **11.12**). The work was planned as "an harmonious arrangement of architectural forms" in an "image of bright amplitude and picturesque liveliness." But Bramante died before his plans were carried out, and was succeeded by two of his assistants and Raphael (1483–1520). Changes were made, partly because the designs were then severely criticized by Michelangelo. Eventually Pope Paul III (reigned 1534–49) convinced Michelangelo to become chief architect. Michelangelo set aside liturgical considerations and returned to Bramante's original conception, which he described as "clear and pure, full of light ... whoever distances himself from Bramante, also distances himself from the truth" (Fig. **11.13**). Michelangelo's project was completed in May of 1590 as the last stone was added to the dome and a High Mass was celebrated. Work on thirty-six columns

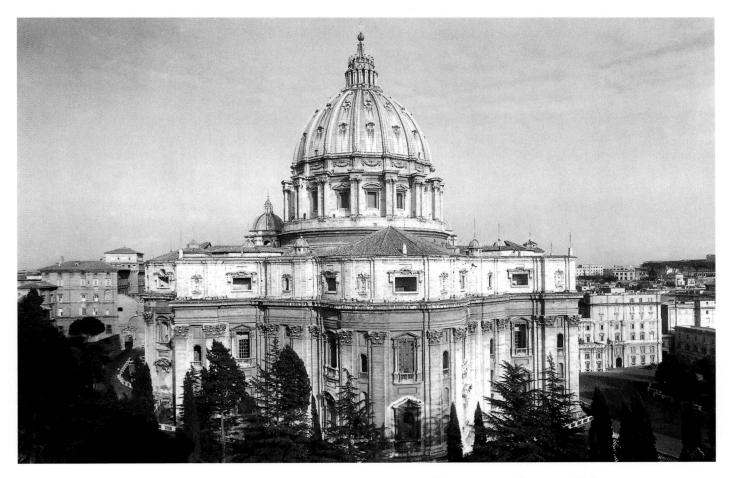

11.11 Michelangelo, St. Peter's, Rome, from the west, 1546–64 (dome completed by Giacomo della Porta, 1590).

→ N

0 100 ft
0 30 m

11.12 Bramante's design for St. Peter's, 1506.

11.13 Michelangelo's design for St. Peter's, 1547.

11.14 Plan of St. Peter's as built to Michelangelo's design, with alterations by Carlo Maderno, 1606–15.

continued, however, and was completed by Giacomo della Porta (c. 1522/3–1602) and Domenico Fontana (1543–1607) after Michelangelo's death. Full completion of the basilica as it stands today was under the direction of yet more architects, including Carlo Maderno (1556–1629). He was forced to yield to the wishes of the cardinals and change the original form of the Greek cross to a Latin cross (Fig. **11.14**). As a result, the Renaissance design of Michelangelo and Bramante, with its central altar, was rejected. It was replaced by Maderno's design, including a *travertine* façade of gigantic proportions and sober elegance. His extension of the basilica was influential in the development of Baroque architecture. The project was completed in 1614, over 150 years after the first plans were laid.

FLANDERS

In the north of Europe lies a small area known as the Low Countries where, in the fifteenth century, Flemish painters and musicians forged new approaches amid a dominant culture of Late Gothic architecture and sculpture. Here in Flanders they formed a link with their contemporaries in northern Italy—the heart of the Early Renaissance in art; they were to influence European painters and musicians for the next century. However, many scholars see early-fifteenth-century Flemish arts as remaining part of the Late Gothic style, despite the contact with Italy, and despite Italian admiration of Flemish painting.

Flemish painting of this period was revolutionary. Whereas painters of the Gothic style essentially retained a certain two-dimensional feeling, and little continuity in their perspective, Flemish painters achieved pictorial reality and rational perspective. The sense of completeness and continuity marks a new and clearly different style. Line, form, and color are painstakingly controlled to compose subtle, varied, three-dimensional, clear, and logically unified statements.

Part of the drastic change in Flemish painting stemmed from a new development in painting media—oil paint. Oil's versatile characteristics gave Flemish painters new opportunities to vary surface texture and brilliance, and to create far greater subtlety of form. Oil paint allowed blending of color areas, because it could be worked wet on the canvas, whereas egg tempera, the previous painting medium, dried almost immediately upon application. Gradual transitions between color areas made possible by oils allowed fifteenth-century Flemish painters to use *atmospheric perspective* and control this most effective indicator of deep space better than had previously been possible. Blending between color areas also enhanced chiaroscuro, by which all objects assume three-dimensionality, for without highlight and shadow the illusion of depth is lost. Early-fifteenth-century Flemish painters explored light and shade not only to heighten

11.15 (opposite) Jan van Eyck, *The Arnolfini Marriage* (*Giovanni Arnolfini and His Bride*), 1434. Oil on panel, 33 × 22½ ins (84 × 57 cm). National Gallery, London.

11.16 Albrecht Dürer, *The Four Horsemen (Apocalypse)*. c. 1497–8. Woodcut, proof before text, 15½ × 11 ins (39.4 × 28.1 cm). Museum of Fine Arts, Boston (Bequest of Francis Bullard; © 2002 Museum of Fine Arts, Boston).

three-dimensionality of form but also to achieve rational unity in their compositions, for example, by having consistent light sources and natural shadows on surrounding objects. This new unity and realistic three-dimensionality separated the fifteenth-century Flemish style from Gothic art and tied it to the Renaissance.

The Arnolfini Marriage, or *Giovanni Arnolfini and His Bride* (Fig. **11.15**), by Jan van Eyck (fahn YK; c. 1390–1441) illustrates the qualities of Flemish painting and also stimulates a marvelous range of aesthetic responses. Van Eyck used the full range of values from darkest darks to lightest lights and blended them with extreme subtlety to achieve a soft and lifelike appearance. His colors are rich, varied, and predominantly warm in feeling. All forms achieve three-dimensionality through subtle color blending and softened shadow edges. Natural highlights and shadows emanate from obvious sources, such as the windows, and tie the figures and objects together.

The painting depicts a young couple taking a marriage vow in the sanctity of the bridal chamber, and the painting is thus both a portrait and a marriage certificate. The

artist has signed the painting in legal script above the mirror "Johannes de Eyck fuit hic. 1434" (Jan van Eyck was here. 1434). In fact, we can see the artist and another witness reflected in the mirror.

GERMANY

As early as the late Middle Ages, southern Germany was positioned at the center of a thriving trade axis that connected the Netherlands with Italy. Throughout Europe, much of the wealth created in centers such as the Netherlands and Germany was used for the encouragement of arts and letters. By the late fifteenth century important artists such as Albrecht Dürer followed the trade routes back and forth to Italy, helping to bring the Renaissance to northern Europe.

Albrecht Dürer (DYOO-ruhr; 1471–1528), was, like Leonardo da Vinci, a transitional figure and, at the same time, innovator. Dürer shared Leonardo's deep curiosity about the natural world, a curiosity that is expressed especially in his drawings, which explore human figure and physiognomy, animals, plants, and landscapes. Unlike Leonardo, Dürer worked principally as an engraver and was tortured by religious problems during this time of the Protestant Reformation. We can see Dürer's skill as a printmaker and his remarkable artistic and religious insight in the woodcut *The Four Horsemen of the Apocalypse* (Fig. **11.16**; see also Fig. 1.9). Here are present the tensions evident in northern Europe at the end of the fifteenth century. The emotions of *The Four Horsemen of the Apocalypse* exhibit a medieval preoccupation with superstition, famine, fear, and death that typify German art of this period and place Dürer at a pivot point between medieval and Renaissance styles. This woodcut is the fourth work in a series, and this print presents a frightening vision of doomsday and the omens leading up to it, as described in the Revelation of St. John, the last book of the Bible. In the foreground, Death tramples a bishop, and working toward the background, Famine swings a scales, War brandishes a sword, and Pestilence draws a bow. Underneath, trampled by the horses' hoofs, lies the human race. The crowding and angularity of shapes are reminiscent of late Gothic style, and yet the perspective foreshortening and three-dimensionality of figures reflect the influence of the Italian Renaissance. We can read human character and emotion in the faces of the figures, which humanize them and give them a sense of reality and a proximity to life that adds depth to the meaning of the work. The technique of the woodcut gives the work its particular quality, and Dürer creates lines of tremendous delicacy, which combine into a poignantly complex picture.

LATE RENAISSANCE THEATRE IN ENGLAND

While Late Renaissance Italy prepared the way for our modern theatre building and certain acting techniques, sixteenth-century England produced a new theatre of convention, and history's foremost playwright.

We must always be careful when we try to draw conclusions about why the arts developed as they did within a particular historical context. While Italy and France saw the arts prosper under varying forms of extravagant patronage, England saw a theatre of great literary consequence prosper under a monarch who loved the theatre only as long as it did not impose upon her financially. Elizabeth I encouraged the arts not by patronage of the kind provided by the Medici or the Church but, rather, by benign neglect.

England's drama in the mid- to late sixteenth century was national in character, influenced by the severance of Church and state under Henry VIII. Nevertheless, there were also strong Italian literary influences in England at this time, and the theatre reflected them.

The Elizabethans loved drama, and the theatres of London saw prince and commoner together among their audiences. They sought and found—usually in the same play—action, spectacle, comedy, character, and intellectual stimulation so deeply reflective of the human condition that Elizabethan plays have found universal appeal through the centuries since their first production.

Shakespeare

William Shakespeare (1564–1616) was the preeminent Elizabethan playwright. His sensitivity to and appreciation of the Italian Renaissance can be seen in the settings of many of his plays. In a true spirit of Renaissance expansiveness, Shakespeare took his audiences back into history, both British and Classical, and far beyond, to the fantasy world of Caliban in *The Tempest*. We gain perspective on the Renaissance world's self-perception when we compare the placid, composed reflections of Italian painting with Shakespeare's tragic portraits of intrigue in Renaissance Italy.

Like most playwrights of his age, Shakespeare wrote for a specific professional company (of which he became partial owner). The need for new plays to keep the company alive from season to season provided much of the impetus for his prolific writing. There is a robust, peculiarly Elizabethan and Renaissance quality in Shakespeare's plays. His ideas have universal appeal because of his understanding of human motivation and character and his ability to probe deeply into emotion. He provided insights that are the equivalent of Rembrandt's visual probings. Shakespeare's plays reflect life and love, action and nationalism; and they present those qualities robustly, in magnificent poetry that explores the English language in unrivaled fashion. Shakespeare's use of tone, color, and complex or new word meanings gives his plays a musical as well as dramatic quality which appeals to every generation.

More is known about the theatres that Shakespeare played in than about his life, but that information is far from complete. They may have looked like the reconstruction in Figure **11.17**.

Shakespeare's plays fall into three distinct genres: comedies (including *Love's Labour's Lost*, *The Merchant of Venice*, and *Much Ado About Nothing*), tragedies, and histories. His history plays are large-scale dramatizations and glorifications of events that took place between 1200 and 1550. His greatest tragedy is *Hamlet* (first performed in 1601 and published in 1603). The Hamlet story was a widespread legend in northern Europe.

MASTERWORK

William Shakespeare, *Hamlet*

Hamlet, Shakespeare's most famous play, was first performed in 1601 and published in 1603. Shakespeare's source for the play may have been Belleforest's *Histoires Tragiques* (1559). Shakespeare's play may also have used as a source a lost play supposedly by Thomas Kyd, usually referred to as the *Ur-Hamlet*. *Hamlet*, however, has its own unique central element in Hamlet's tragic flaw, his hesitation to avenge his father's murder.

At the beginning of the play, Hamlet mourns the death of his father, who has been murdered, and also laments his mother's marriage to his uncle Claudius within a month of his father's death. Hamlet's father's ghost appears to Hamlet, telling him that he was poisoned by Claudius and asking him to avenge his death. Hamlet hesitates, requiring further evidence of foul play. His uncertainty and hesitancy make him increasingly moody, and everyone believes that Hamlet is going mad. The pompous old courtier Polonius believes Hamlet is lovesick over his daughter Ophelia.

Despite Claudius's apparent guilt, Hamlet still cannot act. Nevertheless, he terrorizes his mother and kills the eavesdropping Polonius. Fearing for his life, Claudius sends Hamlet to England with his friends Rosencrantz and Guildenstern, who have orders to have Hamlet killed. Discovering the orders, Hamlet arranges to have his friends killed instead. Returning to Denmark, Hamlet learns that Ophelia has killed herself, and her brother Laertes has vowed vengeance on Hamlet for Polonius's death. Claudius happily arranges the duel. Both Hamlet and Laertes are struck by the sword that Claudius has had dipped in poison. Gertrude mistakenly drinks from the cup of poison intended for Hamlet. Before Hamlet dies, he fatally stabs Claudius.

In the play, Shakespeare appears to suggest that traditional beliefs about revenge are over-simplified, arguing that revenge does not solve evil if evil lies in a complex situation: "The time is out of joint; O cursed spite/That ever I was born to set it right" (V.i.189–90). He also seems to maintain that revenge itself is morally wrong. In *Hamlet*, as well as the other tragedies (*Othello*, *King Lear*, and *Macbeth*), Shakespeare explores with great psychological sub-tlety how the personality flaws in the protagonist lead almost inevitably to his own destruction and the destruction of those around him.

Hamlet
Act III, scene i
William Shakespeare
1564–1616

Hamlet:
To be, or not to be: that is the question:
Whether 'tis nobler in the mind to suffer
The slings and arrows of outrageous fortune,
Or to take arms against a sea of troubles,
And by opposing end them? To die: to sleep:
No more; and by a sleep to say we end
The heartache and the thousand natural shocks
That flesh is heir to,—'tis a consummation
Devoutly to be wish'd. To die, to sleep;
To sleep: perchance to dream: ay, there's the rub:
For in that sleep of death what dreams may
    come,
When we have shuffled off this mortal coil,
Must give us pause: there's the respect
That makes calamity of so long life;
For who would bear the whips and scorns of
    time,
The oppressor's wrong, the proud man's
    contumely,
The pangs of despised love, the law's delay,
The insolence of office and the spurns
That patient merit of the unworthy takes,
When he himself might his quietus make
With a bare bodkin? Who would fardels bear,
To grunt and sweat under a weary life,
But that the dread of something after death,
The undiscover'd country from whose bourn
No traveller returns, puzzles the will
And makes us rather bear those ills we have
Than fly to others that we know not of?
Thus conscience does make cowards of us all;
And thus the native hue of resolution
Is sicklied o'er with the pale cast of thought,
And enterprises of great pith and moment
With this regard their currents turn awry,
And lose the name of action.[3]

11.17 The second Globe Theatre, London, as reconstructed, c. 1614.

Marlowe

Shakespeare was not the only significant playwright of the English Renaissance stage. The plays of Christopher Marlowe (1564–93) and Ben Jonson (1573–1637) still captivate theatre audiences. Marlowe's love of sound permeates his works, and if his character development is weak, his heroic grandeur has the Classical qualities of Aeschylus and Sophocles (see p. 231). His most famous play is *Doctor Faustus* (*The Tragical History of the Life and Death of Doctor Faustus*), first published in 1604. The story resembles the plot of a medieval morality play, using richly poetic language to narrate a man's temptation, fall, and damnation. His language was a breakthrough in drama of the time. His flexible use of blank verse and the brilliance of his imagery combine to stimulate emotion and rivet his audience's attention. The imagery of terror in the final scene is among the most powerful in all drama. In addition, Marlowe's language and imagery unify the play: The patterns in Faust's references to heaven subtly imply the force he cannot escape and yet which he must, at the beginning, deny. "He cannot escape from a world order and from responsibility, nor can he escape from a dream of unfettered domination. That is his tragedy."[4]

RENAISSANCE MUSIC

Renaissance music differed from medieval style particularly in features such as greater melodic and rhythmic integration, a more extended range, broader texture, and subjection to harmonic principles of order. In the sixteenth century this integrated style produced distinct vocal and instrumental idioms, and vocal music, under the influence of humanism, became increasingly intent on expressing a text. In fact, vocal music, because of the humanistic interest in language, was a more important musical idiom than instrumental music. Renaissance composers tried to enhance the meaning and emotion of the written text. In doing so, they often used what is called *word painting*—for example, if a text described a descent, then the music might utilize a descending melodic line. In sum, however, and despite the increased sense of emotion, Renaissance music remained restrained and balanced, avoiding extreme contrasts in dynamics, tone color, or rhythm.

The texture of Renaissance music was mostly polyphonic, with imitation among the voices being fairly common. There was also homophony, especially in light music such as dance. In addition, the musical texture of a piece might vary, with the contrast used to highlight the particular emotion of the composition.

Sacred Music

In Rome, the papal chapel was one of the central musical forces in Europe. There, the career of Giovanni Pierluigi da Palestrina (pah-lehs-TREE-nuh; 1526?–94) flourished. Palestrina enjoyed the grace and favor of popes and cardinals. Director of the Julian Chapel Choir from 1551 to 1555, he became a singer in the pontifical choir in the latter year and began to compose for the papal chapel. Because he was married, however, he was forced to leave his post when Pope Paul IV imposed a stricter discipline in choral appointments.

Palestrina's works are exclusively vocal and almost totally liturgical; the only exception is a single book of madrigals and a collection of spiritual madrigals. He wrote 105 masses. Palestrina became the most celebrated composer of his time. Palestrina's *Pope Marcellus Mass* is his most famous. It was dedicated to Pope Marcellus II, who reigned briefly in 1555, when Palestrina sang in the papal choir. The mass is written for six voice parts (*a cappella*—that is, without accompaniment): soprano, alto, two tenors, and two basses. Earlier we examined a Kyrie from Gregorian chant (music CD track 4). Let's now examine the Kyrie from Palestrina's *Pope Marcellus Mass* (music CD track 7).

The Kyrie has a rich, polyphonic texture in which the six voices imitate each other. The melodic contours are rounded, evoking images of the Gregorian chant. The melody is in the top voice, the cantus or soprano line. The Kyrie is in three sections:

1. *Kyrie eleison*   (Lord, have mercy upon us).

2. *Christe eleison*   (Christ, have mercy upon us).

3. *Kyrie eleison*   (Lord, have mercy upon us).

The words of this brief text are repeated with different melodic treatments and express calm supplication. Each section ends with all voices coming together on sustained chords.

Another important form of Renaissance sacred music is the *motet*, which is like the mass in style, but shorter than the mass. The Renaissance motet is a polyphonic choral work set to a Latin text other than the ordinary of the mass. Its most significant proponent was Flemish composer Josquin Desprez (day-pray; c. 1440–1521), whose four-voice motet, *Ave Maria . . . virgo serena* (music CD track 6), contains delicate and serene music.

Secular Music

The sixteenth century witnessed development of previous forms into the *madrigal*, a setting of lyric poetry for four or five voices. Madrigal is the name given to two important types of secular vocal music. One type was cultivated exclusively in fourteenth-century Italy; the other developed anew and flourished in Italy during the sixteenth century amid an explosion of Italian poetry. Poetically, the sixteenth-century madrigal normally comprises a text of from three to fourteen lines (of seven and eleven syllables in no particular order) arranged in a rhyme scheme of the poet's choosing. The musical setting emphasizes the mood and meaning of individual words and phrases of the text rather than formal structure.

Madrigals were composed for as few as three and as many as eight parts, although, in general, before 1650 a four-part texture was preferred. After that, a five-part composition predominated. Madrigals were often sung by solo voices, one per part, but also were performed with instruments substituting for some of the voices or doubling the various parts. By the second half of the sixteenth century, the madrigal had become established as the dominant form of secular music in Italy and the rest of Europe.

NATIVE AMERICA
THE AZTECS

Another aspect of the Renaissance in Europe was the rise of Spain as a power. In what has been called Spain's Golden Century (the sixteenth), the Spanish succeeded in driving out the Muslims, unifying the country, and exploring the New World. When the Spanish conquistadors came to the Americas, in the South Central region of present-day Mexico, they encountered the Aztecs, who lived in the highlands in an area of basins separated by eroded volcanic peaks and broken mountain ranges.

According to their own records, the Aztecs migrated from the north, probably around the early thirteenth century. At first they remained nomadic, struggling to survive. They traveled in search of a new home because their sun and war god ordered them to make a pilgrimage to a new land. He ordered them to settle in the first place they saw an eagle with a snake in its beak, sitting on a cactus. Around 1248 they saw the eagle on an island in the middle of Lake Chapultepec (chah-PUHL-tuh-pehk). For about a century the Aztecs lived peacefully. However, around 1325 they came into conflict with the neighboring tribes, who allied themselves against the Aztecs and defeated them. The conquering tribes enslaved most of them, but a small group managed to escape to an island on a nearby saltwater lake. According to some sources, this was the date and original location where the Aztecs saw the eagle sitting on the stem of a prickly pear cactus, holding a serpent in its talons with its wings open to the sun. In any case, the Aztecs saw this as an omen concerning where to build their future city and capital, Tenochtitlan (tay-NAWK-teet-lan). In order to build it, however, they needed to drain the swamps and the standing water around them and had to construct artificial islands for gardens.

In the beginning, Aztec life consisted of subsistence living by hunting, fishing, and gathering native plants. Eventually the Aztecs domesticated many crops, including cocoa, vanilla, bananas, squash, pumpkin, beans, chili, tobacco, onions, red tomatoes, green tomatoes, sweet potatoes, jicama, huautli, and maize.

Aztec leaders refused permanent friendship with other tribes because they believed they were the chosen people of their principal god and that he had forbidden alliances. This fostered a commitment to war that played a significant role in the rise of the Aztec Empire. It caused many tribes to declare war on the Aztecs and created the circumstances for the Aztecs to start their era of conquest. Raiding and warring often began simply to collect captives for use in sacrificial offerings. When the Aztecs conquered another tribe, they permitted them to retain their own religion and government. However, the Aztecs expected the vanquished tribes to pay tributes of food, textiles, pottery, and other items needed to support the nobles, priests, and administrators of the capital city.

The Aztec legend of the creation of humankind and origins of the Aztec tribe created the need for human sacrifice. Specifically, the gods sacrificed for humans, and, therefore, humans must sacrifice for the gods. In addition, the gods depended on human blood for their sustenance and required humans to provide it to them. The Aztec view of death included Heaven and Hell, each of which was ruled by a separate god. The world of the dead comprised nine levels below and thirteen levels above the earth. The dead spent a four-year period in Hell, and the Aztecs considered this time a journey during which the family of the deceased should present offerings and sacrifices to make the journey easier. Remnants of this belief persist today in the Mexican celebration of *Día De Los Muertos* (DEE-ah day lohs MWAIR-tohs; Day of the Dead), during which people set up altars for the deceased and make food offerings. In preparation for *Día De Los Muertos*, Mexicans buy candy skeletons and skeleton bread, relating to the fact that the Aztec god of the dead was a skeleton. The Aztecs believed that entrance to Heaven was earned by suffering during life. Thus, a baby

who died would go to Hell because he or she had not suffered enough during life. Individuals who had suffered— for example, warriors, sacrificial victims, mothers who died giving birth, and slaves—went to Heaven.

The Aztecs did not have a written language, yet they did make written records. They chiefly used direct representation and varieties of hieroglyphic painting. Although the Spanish destroyed most Aztec books, several facsimiles of their drawings appear in Spanish documents. A page from *Codex Mendoza* (Fig. **11.18**) illustrates an idealized representation of Tenochtitlan and its sacred ceremonial precinct. Central to the drawing, an eagle perched on a prickly pear plant symbolizes the city. Waterways divide the city into fourths, with seated figures representing the wards of each of the quarters. The warriors at the bottom of the page symbolize Aztec conquests, while the house at the top center of the drawing probably symbolizes the Great Pyramid, a double, stepped pyramid

11.18 *The Founding of Tenochtitlan*, page from *Codex Mendoza*, 16th century. Ink and color on paper, 12⁵⁄₁₆ × 8⁷⁄₁₆ ins (31.5 ×21.5 cm). Bodleian Library, University of Oxford.

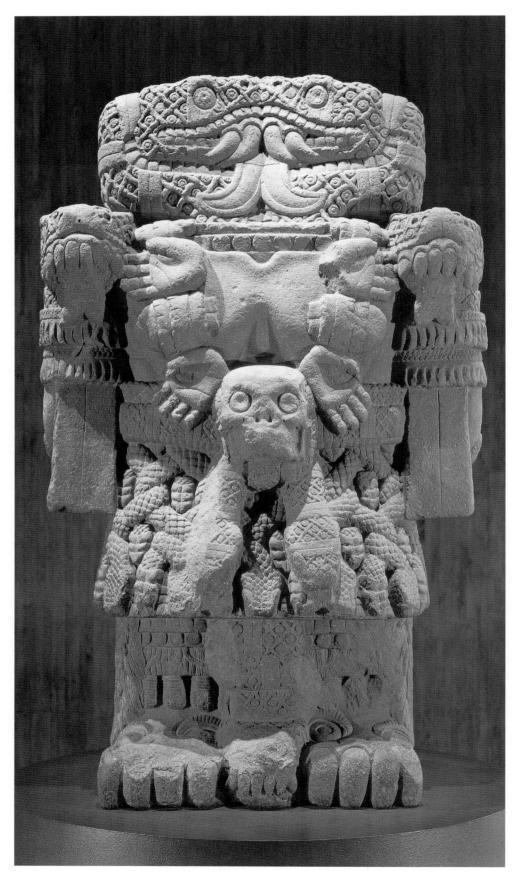

11.19 *The Mother Goddess, Coatlicue,* 15th century. Stone, height 8 ft 6 ins (2.65 m). Museo Nacional de Antropologia, Mexico City.

with two temples on top, one of which served as the site for human sacrifice.

The statue of the mother of the principal Aztec god pictured in Figure **11.19** probably played a part in the ritual of an Aztec temple. Records indicate conquistadors seeing similar statues covered with blood inside a temple. The goddess has clawed hands and feet and a skirt of twisted snakes. Around her cling a pair of serpents and symbols of gushing blood. Her necklace contains sacrificial offerings of hands, hearts, and a skull. Originally, the statue would have been vividly painted to heighten its effect.

THE INCAS

The Incas ruled the largest native empire of the Americas, eventually including an estimated 12 million people in much of what is now Peru and Ecuador as well as in large parts of Chile, Bolivia, and Argentina. Near the end of the fourteenth century the empire began to expand from its initial base in the Cuzco region of the southern Andes mountains of South America. It ended with the Spanish invasion led by Francisco Pizarro (pee-ZAH-roh) in 1532.

The term *Inca* refers to the ruler himself as well as to the people of the valley of Cuzco, the capital of the empire. The early years of the empire remain mysterious. The Spanish conquistadors received a version of early Incan history, but actual historical events remain inseparably entwined with myth and legend to the degree that fact cannot be separated from fiction. The Inca Empire probably began as a small kingdom, similar to many others in the Andes during the fourteenth century. A powerful state centered at Huari (WAH-ree; the current city of Ayacucho [eye-ah-KOO-choh], Peru, some distance north of Cuzco), probably controlled the area at one time, but by the tenth century the region consisted of small feuding kingdoms. How the Incas came to power remains unknown, nor can scholars determine for certain if Manco Capac (MAHN-koh KAH-pahk), supposedly the founding ruler, was a historical personage.

The Incas' remarkable territorial expansion really took off in the middle of the fifteenth century. They succeeded, at least in part, through a series of armed conquests consisting of bloody invasions of neighboring territories, crushing all resistance. Direct military action, however, did not account for all of the expansion. Some tribes joined in alliances with the Incas in response to peaceful overtures from the growing state. Others cooperated fearing that military intervention would result if an invitation to peaceful alliance were rejected.

In the early sixteenth century, the death of the Inca ruler plunged the empire into civil war. No system of succession had been determined. Atahualpa (ah-tah-WHAHL-pah) finally won the disastrous war and was on his way to Cuzco in 1532 to claim the whole kingdom when the Spanish conquistador Francisco Pizarro arrived. The Incas allowed Pizarro and a contingent of about 150 soldiers to enter the regional capital at Cajamarca (ky-ah-MAHR-kah), where Atahualpa and his army had camped. The Spaniards succeeded in taking Atahualpa captive and, thus, assured the collapse of the empire.

The Incas developed a functional style of architecture which exhibited strong engineering techniques and fine stone masonry (Fig. **11.20**). Their cities followed a plan based on broad avenues intersected by smaller streets converging on an open square lined by state buildings and temples. Structures were usually single-storied, displaying perfectly joined cut stones, although building materials differed from region to region. In mountainous

11.20 Inca building techniques.

11.21 Machu Picchu, Peru, 15th–16th century.

areas—for example, at Machu Picchu (mah-choo PEE-choo; Fig. **11.21**)—their architecture often contained ingenious adaptation to the context. Machu Picchu straddles a ridge between two high peaks. It consists of stone buildings situated around central plazas. Narrow terraces devoted to agriculture step down the mountainside.

The Incas developed excellent skills in metallurgy and, thus, in cast sculpture, as illustrated by the llama in Figure **11.22**. Unlike the Spanish, who sought gold and silver simply as materials of wealth, the Inca saw gold and silver as symbols of the sun and the moon respectively. This difference in philosophy accounts for the dearth of Inca statuary, which the conquistadors melted down for transport to Spain. For the Incas, gold was "the sweat of the sun" and silver the "tears of the moon." The llama, too, had significant religious meaning for the Incas, who connected it with the sun, rain, and fertility. Every morning and evening in the capital city of Cuzco, the Incas sacrificed a llama to the sun. A white llama kept in Cuzco symbolized the Incas themselves, and, bedecked with a red tunic and gold jewelry, it passed through the streets during religious celebrations.

11.22 Llama, from Bolivia or Peru, found near Lake Titicaca, Bolivia, 15th century. Cast silver with gold and cinnabar, 9 × 8½ × 1¾ ins (22.9 × 21.6 × 4.4 cm). American Museum of Natural History, New York.

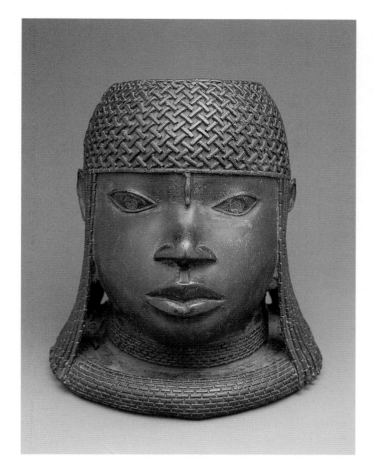

1⁻.23 Memorial head from Benin, c. 1400–1550. Bronze, height 9¼ ins (23.4 cm), width 8⅝ ins (22 cm). Metropolitan Museum of Art, New York (The Michael C. Rockefeller Memorial Collection, Bequest of Nelson A. Rockefeller, 1979).

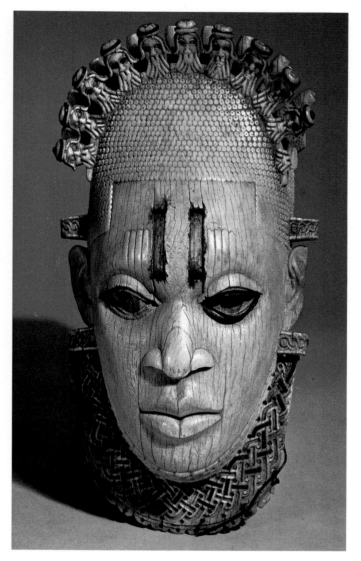

11.24 Pectoral or waist mask from Benin, early 16th century. Ivory, height 9¼ ins (25 cm). British Museum, London.

AFRICA

BENIN STYLE

The spirit of discovery that took the Spanish to the Americas also took the Portuguese to Africa in the late fifteenth century, and that made an impact on artistry as well as culture. In Chapter 10 we experienced the artistic style of Ife (see p. 254). That culture probably gave birth to the artistry of the great city-state of Benin (beh-NEEN), approximately 150 miles (240 km) to the southeast. Local tradition suggests that the Benin style originated from either a master from Ife or the Portuguese, with whom the Benin came into contact in the late fifteenth century. We see the style of Ife, as in Figure 10.39, represented some 200 years later in Benin in the memorial head pictured in Figure 11.23. Here the work reflects mastery of the sculptural technique of casting—in this case, brass. Only the

Oba, or King of Benin, could commission works in brass, and the tradition of casting memorial heads for the shrines of royalty continues today. Benin art developed into a widespread style of its own, marked by carefully executed lifelike features and a close attention to detail—as witnessed by the woven patterns of the headdress.

Another example of superb artistry in the Benin style occurs in the early sixteenth-century ivory mask pictured in Figure 11.24. The carver has obvious mastery of the medium. The elongated head and stylized features create expressiveness, while the details of the mask are precise and delicate. Into the headdress the artist has skillfully woven heads of Portuguese men with beards. Their appearance holds some symbolic, yet unclear, meaning.

11.25 Mark of Wan Li, covered jar, c. 1600. Porcelain, height 4 ins (10.2 cm). Cleveland Museum of Art (John L. Severance Fund).

ASIAN STYLES
CHINA

Ming Sculpture and Ceramics

Throughout the period of the Renaissance in Europe, the lengthy Ming Dynasty (1368–1644) brought about a centralization of power and money in the court of the emperor of China. As a result, the demand for decorative arts caused a tremendous increase in the number and quality of ceramic works. The celebrated Ming vases have become a symbol for the wide variety of ceramic ware produced during this period. Strong traditions in ceramic style and technique had been established much earlier. The Ming Dynasty capitalized on them and took ceramic art to even higher levels, especially in porcelains. By the fifteenth century an underglaze decoration of cobalt blue had been developed, and artisans achieved remarkable skill in color control. Familiar blue-and-white porcelains

had their classic period between 1426 and 1435. They were marked by clarity of detail and variety of shapes. Over the next 100 years the palette was enriched by adding multicolored enamels to the basic blue. The result can be seen in a five-color covered jar from the reign of Wan Li (wahn-lee; 1573–1620; Fig. **11.25**). The complex process of adding layers of color called for refined designs and repeated firings. First, blue designs were applied to the white ground and were glazed and fired. Over this glaze, the decoration was completed in red, green, yellow, and brown; the work was then refired. The process resulted in a rich and delicate ceramic with freely painted narrative scenes and floral compositions of charm, grace, and appeal. Their content gives them a human quality of warmth.

INDIA

Although Islam made incursions into India as early as the eighth century, with another push in the eleventh, during the period of the European Renaissance India witnessed a significant clash of cultures as Muslims (the Mughals) strove again to conquer this Hindu subcontinent. Meanwhile, both cultures contributed significantly to the arts of India, in some cases with remarkable symbiosis.

11.26 *Madhu Madhavi Ragini*, from Malwa, India, c. 1630–40. Color on paper, 7⁹⁄₁₆ × 5¹³⁄₁₆ ins (19.2 × 14.8 cm). Cleveland Museum of Art (Gift of J. H. Wade).

11.27 *Gajahamurti* (*Shiva and Devi on Gajasura Hide*), from Basohli, India, c. 1657–80. Color on paper, 9¼ × 6¼ ins (23.5 × 15.8 cm). Cleveland Museum of Art (Edward L. Whittemore Fund).

Rajput Style

One style of Indian painting is called the Rajput style, after a group of clans in northern and central India who fought vigorously against the Muslim invaders. Their art has a folk quality and takes much of its subject matter from Hindu literature. Its treatment ranges widely, from abstract to intellectual to concrete and emotional. Figure 11.26, *Madhu Madhavi Ragini*, is a typical example. Its primary characteristic is its distinctive dark blue background. The title of the painting refers both to a musical mode and to a representation of a heroine who goes into the night to meet her lover with peacocks flying around her and lightning flashing. However, there seems little here that is ominous. Space is limited to the surface plane. Crossing diagonals give the work a sense of movement, and strong colors and contrasts make the painting forceful and appealing. The conventions of figure portrayal are similar to those of Egypt (see p. 215).

Punjab Style

Another major school of Indian painting, the Punjab hills style, comes from the northwest of the Indian subcontinent. Its drawings are linear, in a gentle, lyrical mode. For example *Gajahamurti*, which means "after the death of the elephant-demon" (Fig. 11.27), presents deities posed formally in a perfectly balanced composition of gently curved forms and careful coloring. The gods Siva and Devi are presented in rigid formality, with Siva, the slayer of the demon, as the main focus. The two figures float in the sky on the elephant's hide. Swirling clouds seem to suggest a storm, especially in their strong contrast to the dark blue background. The sky takes predominance over a rather conventionally and sparsely illustrated earth. Nonetheless, the flowers show fine detailing and individuality. The ducks are also delicate and graceful, both in the water and in flight. Overall, the tone is subdued rather than violent.

Muslim and Hindu Architecture

The Mughal emperors of the seventeenth century were great patrons of architecture, and the most famous of all Indian architectural accomplishments—the Taj Mahal at Agra, near Delhi (Fig. 11.28)—is Islamic. It does, however, blend Persian and indigenous Indian styles. It was built by Shah Jahan (1592–1666) as a mausoleum for his favorite wife Mumtaz Mahal (1593–1631). Such a tomb for a wife was entirely without precedent in Islam, and it is possible that the building was also intended as an allegory of the day of resurrection: The building is a symbolic replica of the throne of God. Four intersecting waterways in the garden symbolize the four flowing rivers of Paradise, as described in the Koran. The scale of the building is immense, and yet the details—entirely geometric and nonfigurative—are exquisitely refined. Proportions are well-balanced and symmetrical. The effect of this huge, white, octagonal structure, with its impressive dome and flanking minarets, is nothing short of breathtaking.

By contrast, the Hindu architectural tradition is almost defiantly anti-Islamic, with an abundance of figurative sculpture celebrating a plurality of deities. Examples can be seen throughout India, but especially in the south, in the 10-square-mile city of Vijayanagar (vee-jay-YA-nah-ghar), formerly the center of a Hindu empire established in the fourteenth century. Here, huge and exquisite temples come alive with brilliantly colored sculpture depicting the Hindu pantheon (Fig. 11.29). Upward-striving terraces with ornate detail reach toward a vaulted pinnacle. In Vijayanagar the concept of the temple went beyond a single shrine and encompassed an entire complex of

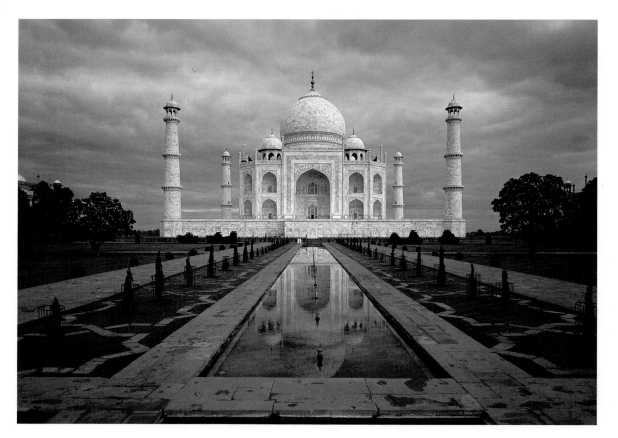

11.28 Ustad Ahmad Lahori (architect), Taj Mahal, Agra, India, 1632–48.

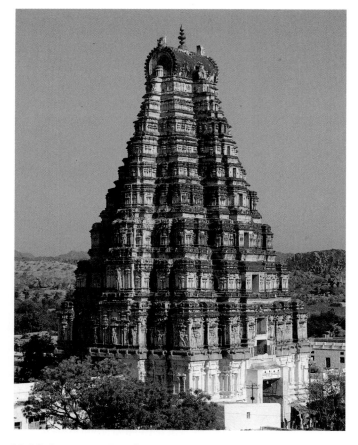

11.29 Pampapati Temple, Vijayanagar, India, *gopura* (gateway tower), 16th century (renovated in 17th century).

buildings within concentric enclosures. These were entered through tall gate towers called *gopuras*, which were packed with *friezes* of the Hindu gods, and which increased in size as one moved from inner to outer walls.

JAPAN

Seventeenth-century Japan witnessed impressive economic growth and a tripling of the population to more than 30 million. Samurai (warriors) were forced to live in towns near their masters. Sharply divided from other classes by their superior status, they became an administrative class responsible for managing the revenue of the shogun. They attended special schools where they were taught Neo-Confucianism, among other subjects. Japanese society became increasingly urban through the eighteenth century, and a strong middle class of merchants and artisans developed. The arts flourished; the puppet theatre and Kabuki theatre emerged. The reign of the Tokugawa shoguns (1603–1867) was at its peak.

Painting Style

Tawayara Sotatsu (soh-that-soo; d. 1643) was a highly creative painter of the late sixteenth and early seventeenth centuries. In contrast with other Japanese painters, who tended to use Chinese motifs and patterns, Sotatsu painted in a style that emphasized boldness, severity, and asymmetry, with simplified silhouettes. He deftly broadened the color palette and use of ink, developing a notable skill in fading the edges of color areas and in creating blurred and pooled effects in wet colors by allowing ink and color to run together. He looked to sources in Japanese traditions for his subject matter. His hanging paper scroll *The Zen Priest Choka* (Fig. **11.30**) shows the priest sitting in a tree. The remarkable aspect of this painting is its use of space—the subject occupies only a small portion of the work. Choka sits in a tree, but it is only faintly suggested at the left border: Its trunk and limbs ebb and flow up the boundary and give us a glimpse here and there of their presence, but mostly leave a full configuration to our imagination. The priest himself is curiously de-emphasized. Sotatsu portrays him with pale color and soft lines of medium tonality. Although most of the painting is void of images, it is fully in balance. Sotatsu has cleverly split the universe of this work into halves divided on the lower left/upper right diagonals. This is a fascinating example of how, both philosophically and visually, something can be balanced by nothing.

Imari Porcelain

The discovery of *porcelain* clay in Japan in the early seventeenth century, and the importation of Chinese techniques, led to some remarkable accomplishments in ceramic art. Typical of Japanese mastery of this medium is

11.30 Tawayara Sotatsu, *The Zen Priest Choka*, pre-1643. Ink on paper, 37¾ × 15¼ ins (95.9 × 38.7 cm). Cleveland Museum of Art (Norman O. Stone and Ella A. Stone Memorial Fund).

11.31 Imari ware Japanese vase, late 17th century. Porcelain, height 22 ins (55.9 cm). Cleveland Museum of Art (Gift of Ralph King).

an Imari porcelain vase from the late seventeenth century (Fig. **11.31**). The exquisite recurved silhouette of this piece has a relaxing flow. The proportions call attention to themselves as the design divides in half at the top of the lower bowl, is balanced by a gracefully slim neck that enlarges into an asymmetrical bulb, and ends in a delicate lip at the top. The ornate flowers have elegance and fine detail that give the vase delicacy and refinement. European figures often appear in this style of ceramics: Dutch and Portuguese men, and also Western ships.

In the Imari vase, a sophisticated plan of proportional adjustment brings together three registers—or bands—of unequal proportion to make a smoothly unified whole. This compositional arrangement is reminiscent of the high chest of drawers illustrated in the Introduction (Fig. 0.8), and also reflects the complexities of the Baroque style (see below).

Kabuki Theatre

Kabuki (kah-BOO-kee) drama began as "middle-class theatre" in the seventeenth century and, as such, was the object of contempt by the samurai and the court. The earliest Kabuki plays were simple sketches; two-act plays did not appear until the middle of the century. The most important Kabuki playwright was the legendary seventeenth-century writer Chikamatsu (1653–1724). By the mid-eighteenth century, the plays of the popular writer Takeda Izumo (1691–1756) had reached a length of eleven acts, and required a whole day to perform.

The focus of a Kabuki play tends to be a climactic moment, as opposed to the plot. Connections between scenes tend to be vague, in contrast with much of Western theatre, whose plot development runs according to cause and effect. A narrator and chorus play predominant roles in Kabuki productions, because although there is a musical accompaniment, the actors themselves do not sing. The narrator describes the scene, comments on the action, and even speaks portions of the dialogue. The overall style of Kabuki drama tends to fall somewhere between convention and depiction. Every location is portrayed scenically, and scenery is changed in full view of the audience.

Kabuki theatre has changed significantly since the mid-sixteenth century because of its ability to shift with the times and incorporate aspects of other theatre traditions. It has borrowed freely from Noh drama (see p. 260) and from the popular Japanese puppet theatre whose plays and stage machinery it incorporated. Productions continue to be lengthy, although the day-long practice of the eighteenth century has now been pared back to two five-hour performances per day.

BAROQUE STYLE IN EUROPE

Meanwhile in Europe, the seventeenth century brought an age of intellectual, spiritual, and physical action. Along with the new age came a tremendously diverse new style, the Baroque. (The word itself originally referred to a large, irregularly shaped pearl of the kind often used in the extremely fanciful jewelry of the post-Renaissance period.) In many cases, the Baroque meant opulence, intricacy, ornateness, and appeal to the emotions, and outdid previous styles in reflecting the grandiose expectations of its patrons. In other cases, it was intellectual and more subdued. The idea of proving one's position to one's peers using overwhelming art infected the aristocracy, the bourgeoisie (middle classes), and even the Roman Catholic Church. Its strategy for coping with the Reformation and the spread of Protestantism included attracting worshipers back into the Church with magnificent art, architecture, and music.

Systematic rationalism sprang forth as a means of explaining the universe in secular and scientific terms, and as an organizational concept for works of art. Thus in all Baroque art a sophisticated organizational scheme subordinates a multitude of single parts to the whole and carefully merges one part into the next to create an exceedingly complex but highly unified design. The world became more and more secularized as power shifted from the Church to more worldly institutions. Over all of them reigned the absolute or all-powerful monarch.

> The idea of absolutism dominated individual as well as collective psychology in the baroque age, each man governing his life like an absolute monarch. Balthasar Gracian advises the courtier: "Let all your actions be those of a king, or at least worthy of a king in due proportion to your estate." Every man was inwardly a king. The ego, or the superego, became an entity which recognized no limits beyond itself. ... The baroque artist exercises this sovereignty "in due proportion to his estate" as Balthasar Gracian would have any man do; that is, his art. The seventeenth century produced artists who, if not solitaries, were at least independent men ... who considered their art, even if it depended upon commissions, as a personal activity, allowing no limits to be placed on their creative power.[5]

In the Baroque, color and grandeur are emphasized, as is dramatic use of lights and darks that carry the viewer's eye off the canvas. Baroque art takes Renaissance clarity of form and recasts it into intricate patterns of geometry and fluid movement. Open composition symbolizes the notion of an expansive universe and a wider reality. The human figure, as an object or focus in painting, can be monumental in full Renaissance fashion, but can also now be a minuscule figure in a landscape—part of, but subordinate to, an overwhelming universe. Above all, Baroque style is characterized by intensely active compositions which emphasize feeling rather than form, emotion rather than intellect. Paintings exhibit clear individuality, and virtuosity emerged as artists sought to establish a style distinctly their own.

Baroque style in the visual arts had manifestations reaching into all segments of society: the Church, the aristocracy, and the middle classes. With reference to the Catholic Church, two terms are relevant: Counter-Reformation and Catholic Reformation. The desire for spiritual regeneration in the Roman Catholic Church in the late fifteenth and early sixteenth centuries eventually led to internal reform. This process is often called the Counter-Reformation, because its characteristics took shape in the 1540s and 1550s in loyalty to the Pope and opposition to Protestant doctrines and practices. There was, however, a Catholic Reformation that was more than a reaction against Protestantism. The impulse for renovation and purification and an internal rebirth of Catholic sensibility existed for more than a century before it transformed the papacy and made possible the codification of doctrine and discipline set out by the Council of Trent (1545–63).

Catholic Reformation Baroque art was art in the Baroque style that pursued the objectives and visions of regeneration in the Roman Catholic Church. There was also a strong use of art in the Baroque style to showcase the wealth and power of the aristocracy. Not to be outdone, the rising middle classes—with their own wealth at times outshining that of the aristocracy—also utilized Baroque style for their own purposes. Thus, in painting, sculpture, and architecture, Baroque style moved across the fabric of Europe.

PAINTING

Baroque painting is identifiable as a general style, although, as noted, its uses were diverse and pluralistic, not conforming to a simple mold. It spread throughout Europe with examples in every area between 1600 and 1725. Our examination encompasses three important painters in the Baroque style: Caravaggio (kah-rah-VAHD-joh), Rubens, and Rembrandt. There were many others, whose inclusion space does not permit, including Jan Vermeer (see Fig. 1.33) and the Spanish painter Diego Velázquez, whose well-known painting *Las Meninas* (*The Maids of Honor*) can be studied at http://museoprado.mcu.es/prado/html/imeni.html.

Caravaggio

In Rome—the center of early Baroque—papal patronage and the Catholic Reformation spirit brought artists together to make Rome the "most beautiful city of the entire Christian world." Caravaggio (Michelangelo Merisi, 1569–1609) was probably the most significant of the Roman Baroque painters. His extraordinary style carries lifelikeness to new heights. In *The Calling of St. Matthew* (Fig. **11.32**) highlight and shadow create a dynamic portrayal of the moment when the future apostle is touched by divine grace. Here a religious subject emerges in contemporary terms. Turning away from idealized Renaissance form, Caravaggio uses realistic imagery and an everyday setting. The call from Christ streams, in dramatic chiaroscuro, across the two groups of figures. This painting expresses central themes of Catholic Reformation belief: Faith and grace are open to all who have the courage and simplicity to transcend intellectual pride, and spiritual understanding is a personal, mysterious, and overpowering emotional experience.

Rubens

Peter Paul Rubens (1577–1640) is noted for his vast, overwhelming paintings and fleshy female nudes. In 1622–5, he painted a series of works as a commission from Maria de' Medici, a Florentine princess, the widow of the French king Henri IV, and regent during the minority of her son Louis XIII. *Henry IV Receiving the Portrait of Maria de' Medici* (Fig. **11.33**) is one of twenty-one canvases that give an allegorical version of the queen's life. In this painting, we see Rubens's ornate curvilinear composition, lively action, and complex color. Typical are the corpulent cupids (*putti*) and female flesh—it has a sense of softness and warmth found in the work of few other artists. Rubens's colors are warm, with deep rich blues throughout the picture. There is strong contrast, making for enhanced dynamics between lights and darks and between lively and more subdued tones. The composition sweeps from upper left to lower right and circles around the rectangular frame of Maria's portrait at the juncture of the vertical, horizontal, and diagonal axes. The painting seems to swirl before the viewer's eyes. It is rich in detail, but each finely rendered part is subordinate to the whole. Rubens leads the eye around the painting, upward, downward, inward, and outward, occasionally escaping the frame altogether. Nevertheless, the sophisticated

11.32 Caravaggio, *The Calling of St. Matthew*, c. 1596–8. Oil on canvas, 11 ft 1 in × 11 ft 5 ins (3.38 × 3.48 m). Contarelli Chapel, Santo Luigi dei Francesi, Rome.

composition beneath all this complexity holds the base of the painting solidly in place and leads the eye to the smiling face of Maria. The overall effect is one of richness, glamor, and optimism. It appeals directly to the emotions rather than the intellect.

The Classical allegory of the painting shows Minerva, the Roman goddess of wisdom, advising the aging King Henry IV (whose helmet and shield are being stolen by the cupids) to accept the Florentine princess as his second bride. Maria's portrait is presented by Mercury, god of commerce, while Juno and Jupiter, the principal Roman gods, look on approvingly. The painting depicts happy promises of divine intervention, radiant health, and grandeur.

Rubens produced works at a prolific rate, primarily because he ran what was virtually a painting factory where he employed numerous artists and apprentices to assist in his work. He priced his paintings on the basis of

their size and depending on how much actual work he, personally, had done on them. We should not be overly disturbed by this, especially when we consider the individual qualities and concepts expressed in his work. His unique Baroque style emerges from every painting, and many untrained observers can recognize a Rubens with relative ease. Clearly artistic value here lies in the conception, not merely in the handiwork.

Rembrandt

Rembrandt van Rijn (1606–69), in contrast to Rubens, could be called a middle-class artist. Born in Leiden in the Netherlands, he trained under local artists and then moved to Amsterdam. His early and rapid success gained him many commissions and students. Rembrandt became what can only be called a capitalist artist. He believed that art had value not only in itself but also in its market

11.33 Peter Paul Rubens, *Henry IV Receiving the Portrait of Maria de' Medici*, 1622–5. Oil on canvas, 13 ft × 9 ft 8 ins (3.96 × 2.95 m). Louvre, Paris.

11.34 (*below*) Rembrandt van Rijn, *The Night Watch* (*The Company of Captain Frans Banning Cocq*), 1642. Oil on canvas, 12 ft 2 ins × 14 ft 6 ins (3.7 × 4.44 m). Rijksmuseum, Amsterdam.

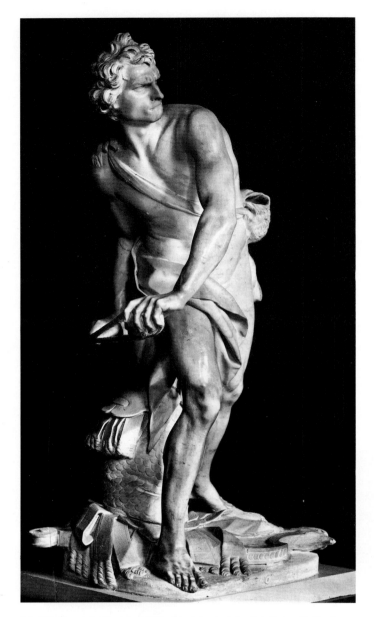

11.35 Bernini, *David*, 1623. Marble, height 5 ft 7 ins (1.7 m). Galleria Borghese, Rome.

worth. He reportedly spent huge sums of money buying his own works so as to increase their value.

Rembrandt's genius lay in depicting human emotions and characters. He suggests rather than depicts great detail, as seen in *The Night Watch*, one of his greatest works (Fig. **11.34**). He concentrates here on atmosphere and shadow, implication and emotion. As in most Baroque art, the viewer is invited to share in an emotion, to enter into an experience rather than to observe as an impartial witness.

The huge canvas now in the Rijksmuseum in Amsterdam is only a portion of the original, which was cut down in the eighteenth century to fit into a space in Amsterdam Town Hall. It no longer shows the bridge members of the watch were about to cross. Group portraits, especially of military units, were popular at the time. They usually showed the company in a social setting such as a gathering around a banquet table. Rembrandt chose to break with the norm and portrayed it as if on duty. It resulted in a scene of greater vigor and dramatic intensity, true to the Baroque spirit—but it displeased his patrons.

A recent cleaning has revealed the vivid color of the original, making it a good deal brighter than it was in its previous state. However, it has not explained its dramatic highlights and shadows—no analysis of light can solve the problem of how these figures are illuminated, for there is no natural light whatsoever in the scene. Another problem lies in the title of the work. It has been suggested that this is, in fact, a "Day Watch," so that the intense light at the center of the work can be explained as morning sunlight. But it seems that Rembrandt has made his choice of highlights for dramatic purposes only. While the figures are rendered with a fair degree of lifelikeness, no such claim can be made for the light sources.

SCULPTURE

Bernini

The Baroque style was particularly suited to sculpture. Form and space were charged with energy, carrying beyond the limits of actual physical confines. As with painting, sculpture appealed to the emotions by inviting participation rather than neutral observation. Feeling was the focus. Baroque sculpture also treated space pictorially, almost like a painting, to describe action scenes rather than single sculptural forms. The best examples we can draw upon belong to the sculptor Gianlorenzo Bernini (bair-NEE-nee; 1598–1680).

David (Fig. **11.35**) exudes dynamic power, action, and emotion as he curls to unleash his stone at an imagined Goliath standing some distance away. Our eyes sweep upward along a diagonally curved line and are propelled outward by the concentrated emotion of David's expression. Throughout the work the curving theme is repeated in deep, rich, and fully contoured form. A wealth of elegant and ornamental detail occupies the composition. Again the viewer participates emotionally, feels the drama, and responds to the sensuous contours of dramatically articulated muscles. Bernini's *David* flexes and contracts in action, rather than repressing pent-up energy as does Michelangelo's giant-slayer (see Fig. **2.15**).

ARCHITECTURE

Versailles

Probably no monarch better represents the *absolutism* of the Baroque era than the French King Louis XIV, known as the Sun King (reigned 1643–1715). No artwork better represents the magnificence and grandeur of the Baroque style than does the Palace of Versailles, near Paris, and its sculpture and grounds—a grand design of buildings and nature to reflect systematic rationalism. The great Versailles complex grew from the modest hunting lodge of Louis XIII into the grand palace of the Sun King over a number of years, involving several architects, and amid curious political and religious circumstances.

The Versailles *château* (French for "castle") was rebuilt in 1631 by Philibert Le Roy. The façade was decorated by Louis Le Vau with bricks and stone, sculpture, wrought iron, and gilt lead. In 1668 Louis XIV ordered Le Vau to enlarge the *château* by enclosing it in a stone envelope containing the king's and queen's apartments (Fig. 11.36). The city side of the building retains the spirit of Louis XIII, but the park side (see Fig. 7.25) reflects Classical French influence. François d'Orbay and, later, Jules Hardouin-Mansart expanded the *château* into a palace whose west façade extends over 2,000 feet (609 m). It became Louis XIV's permanent residence in 1682. French royalty was at the height of its power and Versailles was the symbol of the Divine Right of Kings—the absolute authority of the monarch.

As much care, elegance, and precision was employed on the interior as on the exterior. With the aim of developing French commerce, Louis XIV had his court live in unparalleled luxury. He also decided to furnish his palace permanently, something previously unheard of. The result was a fantastically rich and beautiful set of furnishings. Royal manufacturers produced mirrors, tapestries, and brocades. The highest quality was required, and these furnishings became highly sought after in Europe. Le Brun kept a meticulous eye on anything for the State Apartments, such as the creation of statues and the design of ceilings.

As a symbol and in practical fact, Versailles played a fundamental role in keeping France stable. Its symbolism as a magnificent testament to royal centrality and to France's sense of nationalism is fairly obvious. As a practical device, Versailles served the purpose of pulling the aristocracy out of Paris where they could foment discontent, and isolated them where Louis XIV could keep his eye on them and keep them busy. Versailles further served as a giant economic engine to develop and export French taste and the French luxury trades.

MUSIC

Baroque music did not differ from its visual cousins in that in many cases it was shaped by the needs of churches, which used its emotional and theatrical qualities to make worship more attractive and appealing. The term *Baroque* refers to music written during the period extending approximately from 1600 to 1750.

Baroque composers began to write for specific instruments, or for voices, in contrast to earlier music that might be equally sung or played. They also brought to their music new kinds of action and tension, for example, quick, strong contrasts in tone color or volume, and strict rhythms juxtaposed against free rhythms. The Baroque era was crucial to the development of modern musical language.

Instrumental Music

As Baroque composers began to write specifically for individual voices and instruments, instrumental music assumed a new importance, and musical instruments underwent technical development. A new system of "equal temperament," in which each half-step in the musical scale is equidistant from the preceding or following, was established and illustrated in a series of two sets of preludes and fugues in all possible keys (*The Well-Tempered Clavier* [klah-VEER]) by Johann Sebastian Bach, in 1722 and 1740. In this keyboard music, the fugue (see Chapter 3), with its formal structure and strict imitation, illustrates the complexity and virtuosity of Baroque composition.

SONATA The word *sonata* (suh-NAH-tuh) is one of the most elastic terms in music and has been used to refer to many different musical forms. The name itself comes from the Italian *sonare* (to sound) and came into use during the Baroque era to indicate any piece played on instruments, as distinct from the vocal *cantata*, which means "sung." Its most popular treatment during the seventeenth century became known as the trio sonata, with two high, intertwining parts for violins, flutes, or oboes played above a bass part for cello or bassoon. Usually an organist or harpsichordist played along to reinforce the bass and fill in harmonies indicated by numerals written in the bass part (a practice called "figured bass").

CONCERTO The concerto (see Chapter 3) was one of the forms contributed to Western music by the Baroque age. One of the masters of the concerto was Antonio Vivaldi (vee-VAHL-dee; 1675?–1741), who composed for specific occasions and usually for a specific company of

11.36 Palace of Versailles, Queen's Staircase.

performers. Probably his most familiar solo concerto is "Spring," one of four works in opus 8 (1725), *The Four Seasons*. *The Four Seasons* is an early example of *program music*, written to illustrate an external idea, in contrast with *absolute music*, which presents purely musical ideas. In "Spring" (music CD track 11), a series of individual pieces interlock to form an ornate whole. In the first movement (allegro) Vivaldi alternates an opening theme (A) with sections that depict bird song, a flowing brook, a storm, and the birds' return (ABACADAEA).

Vocal Music

CANTATA As we just noted, the Italian word *cantata* denotes "sung" (see Chapter 3). It comprises vocal compositions with instrumental accompaniment, with several movements based on related text segments. It developed from monody, or solo singing with a predominant vocal

11.37 J. S. Bach, "Ein feste Burg ist unser Gott" from Cantata No. 80.

line, centering on a text to which the music was subservient. These works, which consisted of many short, contrasting sections, were far less spectacular than opera, and they were designed to be written for solo soprano voice, although many used other voices and groups of voices. Two types of cantatas existed during the Baroque era: secular and religious.

In Germany, the cantata was a sacred work that grew out of the Lutheran chorale. The master of the sacred cantata was J. S. Bach who, under obligation as a choirmaster, composed a new cantata weekly; he wrote more than 200 between 1704 and 1740. His cantatas were primarily contrapuntal (polyphonic) in texture, usually scored for up to four soloists and a four-part chorus. An excellent example, whose theme is well known, is *Cantata No. 80*: "Ein feste Burg ist unser Gott" ("A Mighty Fortress is Our God," Fig. **11.37**). The chorale on which the cantata is based was written by Martin Luther (Luther probably wrote both words and music), and the chorale is a centerpiece of Protestant hymnology. Luther's words and melody are used in the first, second, fifth, and last movements. Salomo Franck, Bach's favorite librettist, wrote the remainder of the text. The first movement, a choral fugue, states the familiar theme and text:

> A mighty fortress is our God,
> A good defense and weapon;
> He helps free us from all the troubles
> That have now befallen us.
> Our ever evil foe,
> In earnest plots against us,
> With great strength and cunning
> He prepares his dreadful plans.
> Earth holds none like him.

PROFILE

Johann Sebastian Bach

Although currently considered one of the giants of music, Johann Sebastian Bach (1685–1750) was considered old-fashioned during his lifetime, and his works lay virtually dormant after his death. Not until the nineteenth century did he gain recognition as one of the greatest composers of the Western world. He was born in Thuringia, in what is now Germany, and when he was ten years old both his parents died. His oldest brother, Johann Christoph, took responsibility for raising and teaching him, and Johann Sebastian became a choirboy at the Michaelskirche in Luneburg when he was fifteen. He studied the organ and was appointed organist at Neukirche in Arnstadt, where he remained for four years. Then he took a similar post at Muhlhausen at about the same time as he married his cousin Maria Barbara Bach. One year later, he took the position of court organist at Weimar, remaining there until 1717, when Prince Leopold of Kothen hired him as his musical director. While he was serving as musical director to Prince Leopold, Bach completed the Brandenberg Concertos in 1721.

In 1720 Bach's wife died, and one year later he married Anna Magdalena Wilcken. In 1723 he moved to Leipzig as the city's musical director at the school attached to St Thomas's Church, and among his responsibilities to the city was the supply of performers for four churches. In 1747 he played at Potsdam for Frederick II the Great of Prussia but shortly thereafter his eyesight began to fail, and he went blind just before his death in 1750.

Bach's output as a composer was prodigious but also required as part of his responsibilities, especially at Leipzig. Over his career, he wrote more than 200 cantatas, the *Mass in B Minor*, and three settings of the Passion story, works that illustrate Bach's deep religious faith. His sacred music allowed him to explore and communicate the profound mysteries of the Christian faith and to glorify God. His cantatas typify the Baroque exploration of wide-ranging emotional development. They range from ecstatic expressions of joy to profound meditations on death. The Passions, of which the *St. Matthew Passion* is typical, tell the story of the trial and crucifixion of Jesus. Written in German rather than the traditional Latin, the Passions express Bach's devotion to Lutheranism.

In addition to his sacred works, Bach wrote a tremendous amount of important music for harpsichord and organ, including the forty-eight Preludes and Fugues, called *The Well-Tempered Clavier*, and the *Goldberg Variations*. In the fugues, he develops a single theme, which is then imitated and polyphonically developed among the voices of the composition. Among his many instrumental pieces are twenty concertos and twelve unaccompanied works—six for violin and six for cello.

The final movement (music CD track 9) rounds off the cantata. Luther's chorale is now sung in Bach's own four-part harmonization. Instruments double each voice, and the simple, powerful melody stands out against the lower parts:

Das Wort, sie sollen lassen stahn
 und kein Dank dazu haben.
Er ist bei uns wohl auf dem Plan
 mit seinem Geist und Gaben.
Nehmen sie uns den Leib,
Gut, Her, Kind und Weib,
 lass fahren dahin
 sie habens kein Gevinn
das Reich muss uns doch bleiben.

Now let the Word of God abide
 without further thought.
He is firmly on our side
 with His spirit and strength.
Though they deprive us of life,
Wealth, honor, child and wife,
 we will not complain,
 It will avail them nothing
For God's kingdom must prevail.

OPERA Baroque operas (see Chapter 3) grew out of late fifteenth-century madrigals. Many of these madrigals—some called "madrigal comedies" and some called *intermedi*—were written to be performed between the acts of theatre productions. They were fairly dramatic, and included pastoral scenes, narrative reflections, and amorous adventures. They gave rise to a new style of solo singing. The first surviving opera, *Euridice* (yoo-RID-ih-see), was written by Jacopo Peri (YAH-koh-poh PAY-ree; 1561–1633), based on a contemporary pastoral drama and using characters from Greek mythology. By the second half of the seventeenth century, opera had become an important art form, especially in Italy, but also in France, England, and Germany.

ORATORIO Another major development in the same vein was the oratorio. Broad in scale like an opera, it combined a sacred subject with a poetic text. Like a cantata, it was designed for concert performance, without scenery or costume. Many oratorios could be staged and have highly developed dramatic content with soloists portraying specific characters.

Oratorio began in Italy in the early seventeenth century, but its greatest master was George Frederick Handel (1685–1759). Although Handel was German by birth he lived in England and wrote oratorios in English. Most of his oratorios are highly dramatic in structure and contain exposition, conflict or complication, and dénouement or

resolution sections. Many could be staged in full operatic tradition (except for two outstanding examples, *Israel in Egypt* and *Messiah*). Handel's oratorios rely strongly on the chorus. The choral numbers are most frequently polyphonic, with soprano, alto, tenor, and bass parts each taking a turn with the same melody, although there are homophonic sections too. Most of the solo arias can stand on their own as performance pieces. They also fit magnificently together in a systematic development, usually following a portion of recitative, where the storyline is progressed.

Handel's works continue to enjoy wide popularity, and each year *Messiah* has thousands of performances around the world. Written in 1741 in twenty-four days, it is divided into three parts: the birth of Jesus; Jesus' death and resurrection; and the redemption of humanity. The music comprises an overture, choruses, recitatives, and arias, and is written for small orchestra, chorus, and soloists. The choruses provide some of the world's best-loved music, including the famous "Hallelujah Chorus."

The "Hallelujah Chorus" (music CD track 10) comprises the climax of the second part. The text proclaims a victorious Lord whose host is an army with banners. Handel creates infinite variety by sudden changes of texture among monophony, polyphony, and homophony. Words and phrases are repeated over and over again (Fig. **11.38**). In unison the voices and instruments proclaim, "for the Lord God omnipotent reigneth." Polyphony marks the repeated exclamations of "Hallelujah" and yields to homophony in the hymn-like "The kingdom of this world."

11.38 G. F. Handel, "Hallelujah Chorus" from the *Messiah*.

LITERATURE

Throughout the fifteenth century, medieval forms continued to dominate literature in Europe. The sixteenth century witnessed a true renaissance of national literatures. These were influenced in Protestant countries by the Reformation. For Roman Catholics, especially in Spain, the Counter-Reformation gave literature a deep religious emotion. Illustrative of the times was Miguel de Cervantes (sur-VAHN-tayz; 1547–1616), whose *Don Quixote* (dahn kee-HOH-tay) drew a composite picture of the Spanish people that captured their mixed philosophies of realism and idealism.

Born during the Spanish Golden Century previously noted in this chapter, Cervantes fought in the decisive sea battle against the Muslim Turks at Lepanto in 1571. During the battle he received a wound that permanently crippled his left hand, and en route back to Spain he was captured by the Turks and sold into slavery. Ransomed five years later, he returned to Spain to a tangled and difficult life during which he had some success writing poetry and short stories. *Don Quixote* saw immediate success and put Cervantes among literature's foremost men of letters. The book is now regarded as fundamental to the development of the modern novel.

Written in two parts (1605 and 1615), it has become one of the most read classics in Western literature. The novel has a realistic style that satirizes the chivalric romances popular at the time. Don Quixote, Cervantes' hero, has a head full of fantasies from reading romances as he sets off to seek adventure on his old horse Rosinante with his faithful and pragmatic squire Sancho Panza. Along the way, he finds love in the person of the peasant Dulcinea (duhl-sih-NAY-uh). Cervantes uses irony as a literary device throughout the work.

THE ENLIGHTENMENT IN EUROPE

In Europe, the eighteenth century was an age of change and revolution in some areas and prosperous stability in others. The idea of the absolute monarch was challenged—though with varying success. The middle classes rose to demand their place in society, and social philosophy attempted to make a place for all classes in the scheme of things. *Philosophes* (FIHL-oh-sawfs)—a group of writers and scholars—undertook the challenge of making the great ideas and texts of human intellect accessible to the general public. In short, they were popularizers. Knowledge, for them, was a transcendent and universal goal. The aristocracy found itself in decline, and the *Rococo* (roh-coh-COH) style reflected their increasingly superficial and delicate condition. The pendulum then swung back from exquisite refinement and artifice to intellectual seriousness, at least for a while. The structural clarity of Classicism returned in painting, sculpture, and architecture, and above all in music, in which a remarkable century culminated in works of emotional depth and formal inventiveness. The century closed in anticipation of the upheavals of *Sturm und Drang* (German for "storm and stress") and the Romantics.

ROCOCO STYLE IN PAINTING

The change from grand Baroque courtly life to that of the small salon and intimate townhouse was reflected in a new style of painting called Rococo. Among other characteristics, it satirized the customs of the age, but criticized with humor. Its intimate grace, charm, and delicate superficiality reflect the social ideals and manners of the period. Informality replaced formality in both life and painting. The logic and academic character of the Baroque style were found lacking in feeling and sensitivity. Its overwhelming scale and grandeur were too ponderous. In Rococo art, deeply dramatic action gives way to lively effervescence and melodrama. Love, sentiment, pleasure, and sincerity become predominant themes. None of these characteristics conflicts significantly with the overall tone of the Enlightenment, whose major goal was the refinement of humankind. The arts of the period dignified the human spirit through social consciousness and bourgeois social morality, as well as through the graceful gamesmanship of love. Delicacy, informality, lack of grandeur, and lack of action did not always imply superficiality or limp sentimentality.

The quandary of the declining aristocracy is reflected in the Rococo paintings of Antoine Watteau (wah-TOH; 1683–1721). Although largely sentimental, Watteau's work avoids frivolity. *Embarkation for Cythera* (SIH-theh-ruh; Fig. 11.39) gives an idealized picture of aristocratic social graces. Cythera is a mythological land of enchantment—the island of Venus, Roman goddess of love. Watteau portrays aristocrats waiting to depart, idling away their time in amorous pursuits. The fantasy quality of the landscape is created by fuzzy color areas and hazy atmosphere. A soft, undulating line underscores the human figures, all posed in slightly affected attitudes. Watteau's fussy details and decorative treatment of clothing stand in contrast to the diffused quality of the background. Each grouping of couples engages in graceful conversation and love games typical of the age. Delicacy pervades the scene, over which an armless bust of Venus presides. The doll-like figurines, which are only symbols, engage in sophisticated and elegant pleasure, but their usefulness is past, and the softness and affectation of the work counterbalance gaiety with languid sorrow.

LANDSCAPE AND PORTRAITURE

Portraiture and landscape painting became increasingly popular during the eighteenth century. One of the most

11.39 Antoine
Watteau,
*Embarkation for
Cythera*, 1717. Oil
on canvas, 4 ft 3 ins
× 6 ft 4½ ins
(1.3 × 1.94 m).
Louvre, Paris.

11.40 Jean-Baptiste
Siméon Chardin,
Menu de Gras, 1731.
Oil on canvas,
13 × 16⅛ ins
(33 × 41 cm).
Louvre, Paris.

11.41 Thomas Gainsborough, *The Market Cart*, 1786–7. Oil on canvas, 6 ft ½ in × 5 ft ¼ in (1.84 × 1.53 m). Tate Gallery, London.

influential English artists of the time was Thomas Gainsborough (1727–88), whose landscapes bridge the gap between Baroque and Romantic style and whose portraits range from Rococo lightheartedness to sensitive elegance.

The Market Cart (Fig. **11.41**) is reminiscent of Watteau and other Rococo painters from mainland Europe in its delicate use of color. Gainsborough's exploration of tonalities and shapes expresses a deep and almost mystical response to nature. Although pastoral, the composition derives energy from its diagonal character. The tree forms on the right border are twisted and gnarled. The foremost tree leads the viewer's eye up and to the left, to be caught by the downward circling line of the trees and clouds in the background and returned on the diagonal. Gainsborough does not wish us to become too interested in the humans in the picture—they are warmly rendered, but not as specific individuals. Their forms remain indistinct, suggesting that they are subordinate to the forces of nature which ebb and flow around and through them.

STILL LIFE AND *GENRE*

A new bourgeois flavor inhabits the mundane (*genre*) subjects of France's Jean-Baptiste Siméon Chardin (1699–1779). He was the finest still-life and genre painter of his time, on a par with Dutch masters of the previous century such as Jan Vermeer, whose technique we looked at in Chapter 1 (see Fig. **1.33**). His early works are almost exclusively still lifes. *Menu de Gras* (Fig. **11.40**) illustrates how the everyday can be imbued with interest. With gentle insight, the artist invests cooking pot, ladle, pitcher, bottles, cork, a slab of meat, and other small items with significance. Richness of texture and color combined with sensitive composition and the use of chiaroscuro make these humble items somehow noble. The eye moves slowly from point to point, carefully directed by shapes and angles, color and highlight. The work controls the speed of our viewing: Each new focus demands that we pause and savor its richness. There is pure poetry in Chardin's brush. We are subtly urged to go beyond the surface impression of the objects themselves into a deeper reality.

NEOCLASSICAL STYLE

Painting

The late eighteenth century went whirling back to antiquity, and in particular to nature, in the light of the discovery of the ruins of Pompeii, the art historian Winckelmann's interpretation of Greek Classicism, the philosopher Rousseau's concept of the Noble Savage, and the philosopher Baumgarten's invention of the term "aesthetics." Theoreticians of the eighteenth century saw history as a series of compartments—Antiquity, Middle Ages, Renaissance, and so on—rather than as a single, continuous cultural stream broken by a medieval collapse of Classical values.

One of the principal Neoclassical painters was Jacques-Louis David (dah-VEED; 1748–1825). His works illustrate the newly perceived grandeur of antiquity and its reflection in subject matter, composition, depiction, and historical accuracy. They show a Roman two-dimensionality and have a strong, classically simple compositional unity. But Classical detail and principles are treated selectively and adapted—the Neoclassicism of David and others is not confined to copying ancient works. David sought to inspire patriotism and democracy, and so some of his works are propagandist in tone (see Masterwork box, p. 318).

Architecture

In the mid-eighteenth century architecture changed entirely, embracing the complex philosophical concerns of the Enlightenment. Three important concepts emerged as a result. First was the archeological concept, which viewed the present as continually enriched by persistent inquiry into the past—the idea of *progress*. Second was *eclecticism*, which allowed artists to choose among styles or, more importantly, to combine elements of various styles. The third was *modernism*, which viewed the present as unique and, therefore, possible of expression in its own terms. These concepts fundamentally changed the basic premises of art from that time forward.

Basic to Neoclassicism in architecture are the identifiable forms of Greece and Rome. They found enthusiastic advocates in the Frenchman Abbé Laugier (loh-ZHAY; 1713–69) and the Italian Giovanni Battista Piranesi (pee-rah-NAY-zee; 1720–78). Laugier's *Essai sur l'architecture* (Paris, 1753) was strictly rationalistic and expressed Neoclassicism in a nutshell. He discarded the architectural language developed since the Renaissance. Rather, he urged architects to seek truth in principles demonstrated in the architecture of the ancient world. They should use those principles to design modern buildings along the same logical lines as the Classical temple. Laugier's Classicism descended directly from the ancient Greeks, with only passing reference to the Romans.

Piranesi, incensed that Laugier's arguments placed Greece above Rome, retaliated with an overwhelmingly detailed work, *Della Magnificenza ed Architettura dei Romani*, which professed to prove the superiority of Rome over Greece—perhaps by sheer weight of evidence. The

11.42 Thomas Jefferson, Monticello, Charlottesville, Virginia, 1770–84 (rebuilt 1796–1800).

revival of Classicism in architecture was seen in many quarters as a revolt against the frivolity of the Rococo with an art that was serious and moral.

The designs of colonial architects like Thomas Jefferson (1743–1826) reflect the complex interrelationships of this period. Jefferson's philosophy of architecture was founded on a belief that the architecture of antiquity embodied indisputable natural principles. He was highly influenced, too, by the Italian architect Andrea Palladio (1508–80), who enjoyed popularity in a significant revival in English villa architecture between 1710 and 1750. Jefferson felt that a theory of architecture could be built on a Palladian-style reconstruction of the Roman temple. Monticello (Fig. 11.42) has at its center superimposed Doric and Ionic *porticos* (porches). Short, low wings are attached by continuing Doric *entablatures*. The simplicity and refinement of Jefferson's building go beyond reconstruction of Classical prototypes and appeal directly to the intellect.

MUSICAL CLASSICISM

In 1785 Michel Paul de Chabanon (shah-bah-NAWN) wrote, "Today there is but one music in all of Europe." The basis of this statement was music composed to appeal not only to the aristocracy but to the broad middle classes

as well. The move toward equality and the popularizing of ideals typical of the *philosophes* had influenced artists, and they now aimed at a wider audience. Eighteenth-century rationalism regarded excessive ornamentation and excessive complexity (both Baroque characteristics) as unsuitable when trying to meet a broader social mix on its own terms. Against the background of Neoclassicism, this prompted a move to order, simplicity, and careful attention to form. In music the style is known as Classical (the term was not applied until the nineteenth century) rather than Neoclassical or Classical revival. This is because music had no known Classical antecedents to revive, whereas other arts returned (more or less) to Greek and Roman prototypes. Music thus turned to Classical ideals, though not to Classical models.

The Classical style in music had, among others, five basic characteristics. The first of these is variety and contrast in *mood*. In contrast to Baroque style, which typically dealt with a single emotion, Classical pieces typically explore contrasts between moods. There may be contrasting moods within movements and also within themes. Changes in mood may be gradual or sudden; they are, however, as one might expect of a style called "Classical," well controlled, unified, and logical.

A second characteristic of Classical style is flexibility of *rhythm*. Classical music explores a wide variety of

Jacques-Louis David, *The Oath of the Horatii*

David's famous painting *The Oath of the Horatii* (Fig. **11.43**) concerns the conflict between love and patriotism. In legend, the leaders of the Roman and Alban armies, on the verge of battle, decided to resolve their conflicts by means of an organized combat between three representatives from each side. The three Horatius brothers represented Rome; the Curatius sons represented the Albans. A sister of the Horatii was the fiancée of one of the Curatius brothers. David's painting depicts the Horatii as they swear on their swords to win or die for Rome, disregarding the anguish of their sister.

The work captures a directness and intensity of expression that were to play an important role in Romanticism. But the starkness of outline, the strong geometric composition (which juxtaposes straight line in the men and curved line in the women), and the smooth color areas and gradations hold it to the more formal, Classical tradition. The style represents academic Neoclassicism. The scene takes place in a shallow picture box, defined by a severely simple architectural framework. The costumes are historically correct. The musculature, even the arms and legs of the women, has a surface devoid of warmth or softness, like the drapery.

Ironically, David's work was admired and purchased by King Louis XVI, against whom David's revolutionary cries were later directed and whom David, as a member of the French Revolutionary Convention, would sentence to death. Neoclassicism increased in popularity and continued through the Napoleonic era and into the nineteenth century.

11.43 Jacques-Louis David, *The Oath of the Horatii*, 1784–5. Oil on canvas, approx. 14 × 11 ft (4.27 × 3.35 m). Louvre, Paris.

rhythms, utilizing unexpected pauses, syncopations, and frequent changes from long to shorter notes. As in mood, changes in rhythm may be sudden or gradual. A third characteristic of Classical style is a predominantly homophonic *texture*. Nonetheless, texture also is flexible, with sudden and gradual shifts from one texture to another. In general, the texture of Classical pieces is simpler than that of Baroque ones. However, a work may begin homophonically, with a melody and simple accompaniment, and then shift to complex polyphony featuring two or more simultaneous melodies or melodic fragments imitated among the instruments.

A fourth characteristic is memorable *melody*. The themes of Classical music often have a folk or popular flavor. Classical melodies tend toward balance and symmetry, again what one would expect of "Classical" works as we have seen them since the Athenian Greeks. Frequently Classical themes have two phrases of equal length. The second phrase often begins like the first but ends more decisively.

A fifth characteristic of Classical style is gradual changes in *dynamics*, in contrast to Baroque music, which employs sudden changes in dynamics (*step dynamics*). One of the consequences of this direction in composition was the replacement of the harpsichord with the piano, which was more capable of handling the subtlety of Classical dynamic patterns.

The Classical Sonata and Sonata Form

As we noted earlier, "sonata" has been used to refer to many different musical forms, from a short piece for a single instrument to complex works in many sections or movements, for a large ensemble. By the middle of the eighteenth century, however, the sonata for one or two keyboard instruments, or for another instrument accompanied by keyboard, was utilized as an instrumental genre comparable to the symphony, which we discuss momentarily. These genres share a flexible multi-movement design that music analysts call the *sonata cycle*. The term *sonata form* refers to the form of a *single movement* and should not be confused with the term *sonata*, which describes a composition made of several movements. The sonata form, the most important musical structure of the Classical period, was used in symphonies, sonatas, and other genres mostly in the first movement, although sometimes in other movements as well.

The Classical Symphony

Franz Josef Haydn (Hy-duhn; see below) began composing symphonies in the Classical sense about 1757. In his long life he solidified and enriched symphonic style, culminating in a set of twelve works composed for London in 1791–5 (called the "Salomon Symphonies," after the German impresario J. P. Salomon, who, in 1790, persuaded Haydn to go to England). Haydn wrote 104 symphonies (some scholars put the number higher), which were widely performed and imitated during his lifetime. Wolfgang Amadeus Mozart wrote forty-one symphonies, and his last six—No. 35 in D (*Haffner*), No. 36 in C (*Linz*), No. 38 in D (*Prague*), No. 39 in E-flat, No. 40 in G Minor, and No. 41 in C (*Jupiter*)—are complex in design and rich in orchestration, wedding formal perfection and expressive depth. Ludwig van Beethoven wrote only nine symphonies (1800–24), but in them he greatly increased the form's weight and size.

The Classical orchestra, which performed the Classical symphony, was typified by the supreme orchestra of the time, the court orchestra at Mannheim, Germany, which flourished in the third quarter of the century. It had approximately thirty string players and helped to standardize the remaining instrumental complement, specifically, two flutes, two oboes, two bassoons, two horns, two trumpets, two kettledrums, and a new instrument, the clarinet. Beethoven increased the technical demands on every Classical orchestra by writing parts for piccolo, trombones, and contrabassoon. The finale of his *Symphony No. 9* also requires triangle, cymbals, and bass drum (in addition to choral voices).

Other Classical Forms

Although the sonata and symphony were the most important musical forms of this period, there were others. One form called *theme and variations* was widely used as an independent piece or as one movement of a symphony, sonata, or string quartet. In a theme and variations the theme (a basic musical idea) is repeated over and over, each time with some change—for example, mood, rhythm, dynamics and so on.

A form known as *minuet and trio*, or *minuet*, often occurs as the third movement of a symphony, string quartet, or other works. The form originated as a stately dance, but in Classical music it is designed for listening, not dancing. It has triple meter and, usually, a moderate tempo. Its ABA form consists of a minuet (A), trio (B), and minuet (A). The trio (B) section utilizes fewer instruments than the minuet (A) sections. Another form popular in the Classical time was the *rondo*. It features a melodic main theme (A) that returns several times, alternating with other themes. Other forms such as the concerto witnessed their own transformation into Classical characteristics at this time.

Haydn

Austrian-born Franz Joseph Haydn (1732–1809) pioneered the development of the symphony from a short, simple work into a longer, more sophisticated one. Haydn's symphonies are diverse and numerous. Many of the early ones use the pre-Classical three-movement form. His middle symphonies, from the early 1770s, have more emotion and entail a larger scale than the earlier works. In particular, the development sections of the first movements are dramatic and employ sudden and unexpected changes of dynamics. The slow movements contain great warmth, and in the third movements Haydn frequently drew on Austrian folk songs and Baroque dance music. His changes of tonality contain great dramatic power.

11.44 Haydn, *Symphony No. 94 in G major*, first theme.

Among his late works the most famous is *Symphony No. 94 in G major* (1792), commonly known as the "Surprise Symphony" (Fig. **11.44**). The surprise is a very loud chord played by the full orchestra when it is least expected.

Mozart

Wolfgang Amadeus Mozart (1756–91), also an Austrian, was a child prodigy—he performed at the court of Empress Maria Theresa at the age of six. As was the case throughout the Classical period, aristocratic patronage was essential for musicians to earn a living, although the middle classes provided a progressively larger portion of commissions, pupil fees, and concert attendance. Mozart's short career (he died at the age of thirty-five) was dogged by financial insecurity.

His early symphonies are simple and relatively short, like those of Haydn, while his later works are longer and more complex. The last three are generally regarded as his

11.45 Mozart, *Symphony No. 40 in G minor*, first movement (excerpt).

greatest symphonic masterpieces, and *Symphony No. 40 in G minor* (Fig. **11.45**) is often referred to as the typical Classical symphony. This work and Nos. 39 and 41 have clear order and yet exhibit tremendous emotional urgency, which many scholars cite as the beginning of the Romantic style.

Mozart is also well known for his operas, and was especially skilled in *opera buffa*. *The Marriage of Figaro* is fast and humorous, with slapstick action in the manner of farce, but has great melodic beauty. In this quotation from the beginning of the opera (Fig. **11.46**) the main character, Figaro, is measuring the new bedroom his employer has allocated to him for his married life.

11.46 Mozart, *The Marriage of Figaro*, first theme of "Cinque ... dieci" duet.

In a totally different vein, the final movement of Mozart's *Sonata No. 11 for Piano in A* (music CD track 12) has always been a public favorite. Called the *Rondo alla Turca* or "Turkish Rondo," it has an exotic or "Turkish" character underlined by the main theme in A minor (Fig. **11.47**) that reappears throughout the rondo, softly:

11.47 W. A. Mozart. *Sonata No. 11 for Piano in A* (K. 331) "Turkish Rondo."

Beethoven

Ludwig van Beethoven (1770–1827) is often considered apart from the Classical period and treated as a singular transitional figure between Classicism and Romanticism. Beethoven wanted to expand the Classical symphonic form to accommodate greater emotional character. The typical Classical symphony moves through contrasting movements; Beethoven continued that but began to work toward using a single theme throughout, thereby unifying the work.

Beethoven's symphonies are significantly different from those of Haydn and Mozart. They are more dramatic and use changing dynamics more often for emotional effects. Silence, too, is employed as a device in pursuit of dramatic and structural ends. Beethoven's works are also longer. He lengthened both the development section of sonata form and the coda.

He also changed traditional numbers and relationships among movements. In the Symphony No. 5 no break occurs between the third and fourth movements. Beethoven's symphonies draw heavily on imagery, for example heroism in Symphony No. 3 and pastoral settings in Symphony No. 6. The famous *Symphony No. 5 in C minor*, for example, begins with a motif that Beethoven described as "fate knocking at the door." The first movement (allegro con brio) develops according to typical sonata form (see definition, p. 81; music CD track 13).

LITERATURE

Jonathan Swift represents the enlightened spirit in literature. An Anglo-Irish satirist and churchman, he wrote *Gulliver's Travels*, which mocks pomposity and woolly-headed idealism equally. His other famous work in prose, *A Modest Proposal*, took satire to the very edge of horror with its chillingly deadpan suggestion that the English should solve the "Irish Problem" by eating the babes of the poor.

A Modest Proposal
Jonathan Swift
1667–1745

For Preventing the Children of Poor People in Ireland from Being a Burden to Their Parents or Country, and for Making Them Beneficial to the Public

It is a melancholy object to those who walk through this great town or travel in the country, when they see the streets, the roads and cabin doors, crowded with beggars of the female sex, followed by three, four, or six children, all in rags and importuning every passenger for an alms. These mothers, instead of being able to work for their honest livelihood, are forced to employ all their time in strolling to beg sustenance for their helpless infants, who, as they grow up, either turn thieves for want of work, or leave their dear native country to fight for the Pretender in Spain, or sell themselves to the Barbadoes.

I think it is agreed by all parties that this prodigious number of children in the arms, or on the backs, or at the heels of their mothers, and frequently of their fathers, is in the present deplorable state of the kingdom a very great

additional grievance; and therefore whoever could find out a fair, cheap, and easy method of making these children sound, useful members of the commonwealth would deserve so well of the public as to have his statue set up for a preserver of the nation.

But my intention is very far from being confined to provide only for the children of professed beggars; it is of a much greater extent, and shall take in the whole number of infants at a certain age who are born of parents in effect as little able to support them as those who demand our charity in the streets.

As to my own part, having turned my thoughts for many years upon this important subject, and maturely weighed the several schemes of other projectors, I have always found them grossly mistaken in their computation. It is true, a child just dropped from its dam may be supported by her milk for a solar year, with little other nourishment; at most not above the value of two shillings which the mother may certainly get, or the value in scraps, by her lawful occupation of begging; and it is exactly at one year old that I propose to provide for them in such a manner as instead of being a charge upon their parents or the parish, or wanting food and raiment for the rest of their lives, they shall on the contrary contribute to the feeding, and partly to the clothing, of many thousands.

There is likewise another great advantage in my scheme, that it will prevent those voluntary abortions and that horrid practice of women murdering their bastard children, alas, too frequent among us, sacrificing the poor innocent babes, I doubt, more to avoid the expense than the shame, which would move tears and pity in the most savage and inhuman breast.

The number of souls in this kingdom being usually reckoned one million and a half, of these I calculate there may be about two hundred thousand couples whose wives are breeders; from which number I subtract thirty thousand couples who are able to maintain their own children, although I apprehend there cannot be so many under the present distresses of the kingdom; but this being granted, there will remain an hundred and seventy thousand breeders. I again subtract fifty thousand for those women who miscarry, or whose children die by accident or disease within the year. There only remain an hundred and twenty thousand children of poor parents annually born. The question therefore, is, how this number shall be reared and provided for, which, as I have already said, under the present situation of affairs, is utterly impossible by all the methods hitherto proposed. For we can neither employ them in handicraft or agriculture; we neither build houses (I mean in the country) nor cultivate land. They can very seldom pick up a livelihood by stealing till they arrive at six years old, except where they are of towardly parts; although I confess they learn the rudiments much earlier, during which time they can however be looked upon only as probationers, as I have been informed by a principal gentleman in the county of Cavan, who protested to me that he never knew above one or two instances under the age of six, even in a part of the kingdom so renowned for the quickest proficiency in that art.

I am assured by our merchants that a boy or a girl before twelve years old is no salable commodity; and even when they come to this age they will not yield above three pounds, or three pounds and half a crown at most on the Exchange; which cannot turn to account either to the parents or the kingdom, the charge of nutriment and rags having been at least four times that value.

I shall now therefore humbly propose my own thoughts, which I hope will not be liable to the least objection.

I have been assured by a very knowing American of my acquaintance in London, that a young healthy child well nursed is at a year old a most delicious, nourishing, and wholesome food, whether stewed, roasted, baked, or boiled; and I make no doubt that it will equally serve in a fricassee or a ragout.

I do therefore humbly offer it to public consideration that of the hundred and twenty thousand children, already computed, twenty thousand may be reserved for breed, whereof only one fourth part to be males, which is more than we allow to sheep, black cattle, or swine; and my reason is that those children are seldom the fruits of marriage, a circumstance not much regarded by our savages, therefore one male will be sufficient to serve four females. That the remaining hundred thousand may at a year old be offered in sale to the persons of quality and fortune through the kingdom, always advising the mother to let them suck plentifully in the last month, so as to render them plump and fat for a good table. A child will make two dishes at an entertainment for friends; and when the family dines alone, the fore or hind quarter will make a reasonable dish, and seasoned with a little pepper or salt will be very good boiled on the fourth day, especially in winter.

I have reckoned upon a medium that a child just born will weigh twelve pounds, and in a solar year if tolerably nursed increaseth to twenty-eight pounds.

I grant this food will be somewhat dear, and therefore very proper for landlords, who, as they have already devoured most of the parents, seem to have the best title to the children.

Infant's flesh will be in season throughout the year, but more plentiful in March, and a little before and after. For we are told by a grave author, an eminent French physician, that fish being a prolific diet, there are more children born in Roman Catholic countries about nine months after Lent than at any other season; therefore, reckoning a year after Lent, the markets will be more glutted than usual, because the number of popish infants is at least three to one in this kingdom; and therefore it will have one other collateral advantage, by lessening the number of Papists among us.

I have already computed the charge of nursing a beggar's child (in which list I reckon all cottagers, laborers, and four fifths of the farmers) to be about two shillings per annum, rags included; and I believe no gentleman would repine to give ten shillings for the carcass of a good fat child, which, as I have said, will make four dishes of excellent nutritive meat, when he hath only some particular friend or his own family to dine with him. Thus the squire will learn to be a good landlord, and grow popular among the tenants; the mother will have eight shillings net profit, and be fit for work till she produces another child.

Those who are more thrifty (as I must confess the times require) may flay the carcass; the skin of which artificially dressed will make admirable gloves for ladies, and summer boots for fine gentlemen.

As to our city of Dublin, shambles may be appointed for this purpose in the most convenient parts of it, and butchers we may be assured will not be wanting; although I rather recommend buying the children alive, and dressing them hot from the knife as we do roasting pigs.

A very worthy person, a true lover of his country, and whose virtues I highly esteem, was lately pleased in discoursing on this matter to offer a refinement upon my scheme. He said that many gentlemen of this kingdom, having of late destroyed their deer, he conceived that the want of venison might be well supplied by the bodies of young lads and maidens, not exceeding fourteen years of age nor under twelve, so great a number of both sexes in every county being now ready to starve for want of work and service; and these to be disposed of by their parents, if alive, or otherwise by their nearest relations. But with due deference to so excellent a friend and so deserving a patriot, I cannot be altogether in his sentiments, for as to the males, my American acquaintance assured me from frequent experience that their flesh was generally tough and lean, like that of our schoolboys, by continual exercise, and their taste disagreeable; and to fatten them would not answer the charge. Then as to the females, it would, I think with humble submission, be a loss to the public, because they soon would become breeders themselves; and besides, it is not improbable that some scrupulous people might be apt to censure such a practice (although indeed very unjustly) as a little bordering upon cruelty; which I confess, hath always been with me the strongest objection against any project, how well soever intended.

But in order to justify my friend, he confessed that this expedient was put into his head by the famous Psalmanazar, a native of the island Formosa, who came from thence to London above twenty years ago, and in conversation told my friend that in his country when any young person happened to be put to death, the executioner sold the carcass to persons of quality as a prime dainty; and that in his time the body of a plump girl of fifteen, who was crucified for an attempt to poison the emperor, was sold to his Imperial Majesty's prime minister of state, and other great mandarins of the court, in joints from the gibbet, at four hundred crowns. Neither indeed can I deny that if the same uses were made of several plump young girls in this town, who without one single groat to their fortunes cannot stir abroad without a chair, and appear at the playhouse and assemblies in foreign fineries which they never will pay for, the kingdom would not be the worse.

Some persons of a desponding spirit are in great concern about that vast number of poor people who are aged, diseased, or maimed, and I have been desired to employ my thoughts what course may be taken to ease the nation of so grievous an encumbrance. But I am not in the least pain upon that matter, because it is very well known that they are every day dying and rotting by cold and famine, and filth and vermin, as fast as can be reasonably expected. And as to the younger laborers, they are now in almost as hopeful a condition. They cannot get work and consequently pine away for want of nourishment to a degree that if at any time they are accidentally hired to common labor, they have not strength to perform it; and thus the country and themselves are happily delivered from the evils to come.

I have too long digressed, and therefore shall return to my subject. I think the advantages by the proposal which I have made are obvious and many, as well as of the highest importance.

For first, as I have already observed, it would greatly lessen the number of Papists, with whom we are yearly overrun, being the principal breeders of the nation as well as our most dangerous enemies; and who stay at home on purpose to deliver the kingdom to the Pretender, hoping to take their advantage by the absence of so many good Protestants, who have chosen rather to leave their country than stay at home and pay tithes against their conscience to an Episcopal curate.

Secondly, the poorer tenants will have something valuable of their own, which by law be made liable to distress, and help to pay their landlord's rent, their corn and cattle being already seized and money a thing unknown.

Thirdly, whereas the maintenance of an hundred thousand children, from two years old and upwards, cannot be computed at less than ten shillings a piece per annum, the nation's stock will be thereby increased fifty thousand pounds per annum, besides the profit of a new dish introduced to the tables of all gentlemen of fortune in the kingdom who have any refinement in taste. And the money will circulate among ourselves, the goods being entirely of our own growth and manufacture.

Fourthly, the constant breeders, besides the gain of eight shillings sterling per annum by the sale of their children,will be rid of the charge of maintaining them after the first year.

Fifthly, this food would likewise bring great custom to taverns, where the vintners will certainly be so prudent as to procure the best receipts for dressing it to perfection, and consequently have their houses frequented by all the fine gentlemen, who justly value themselves upon their knowledge in good eating; and a skillful cook, who understands how to oblige his guests, will contrive to make it as expensive as they please.

Sixthly, this would be a great inducement to marriage, which all wise nations have either encouraged by rewards or enforced by laws and penalties. It would increase the care and tenderness of mothers toward their children, when they were sure of a settlement for life to the poor babes, provided in some sort by the public, to their annual profit instead of expense. We should see an honest emulation among the married women, which of them could bring the fattest child to the market. Men would become as fond of their wives during the time of their pregnancy as they are now of their mares in foal, their cows in calf, or sows when they are ready to farrow; nor offer to beat or kick them (as is too frequent a practice) for fear of miscarriage.

Many other advantages might be enumerated. For instance, the addition of some thousand carcasses in our exportation of barreled beef, the propagation of swine's flesh, and improvement in the art of making good bacon, so much wanted among us by the great destruction of pigs, too frequent at our tables, which are no way comparable in taste or magnificence to a well-grown, fat, yearling child, which roasted whole will make a considerable figure at a lord mayor's feast or any other public entertainment. But this and many others I omit, being studious of brevity.

Supposing that one thousand families in this city would be constant customers for infants' flesh, besides others who might have it at merry meetings, particularly weddings and christenings, I compute that Dublin would take off annually about twenty thousand carcasses, and the rest of the kingdom (where probably they will be sold somewhat cheaper) the remaining eighty thousand.

I can think of no one objection that will possibly be raised against this proposal, unless it should be urged that the number of people will be thereby much lessened in the kingdom. This I freely own, and it was indeed one principal design in offering it to the world. I desire the reader will observe, that I calculate my remedy for this one individual kingdom of Ireland and for no other that ever was, is, or I think ever can be upon earth. Therefore let no man talk to me of other expedients: of taxing our absentees at five shillings a pound: of using neither clothes nor household furniture except what is of our own growth and manufacture: of utterly rejecting the materials and instruments that promote foreign luxury: of curing the expensiveness of pride, vanity, idleness, and gaming in our women: of introducing a vein of parsimony, prudence, and temperance: of learning to love our country, in the want of which we differ even from Laplanders and the inhabitants of Topinamboo: of quitting our animosities and factions, nor acting any longer like the Jews, who were murdering one another at the very moment their city was taken: of being a little cautious not to sell our country and conscience for nothing: of teaching landlords to have at least one degree of mercy toward their tenants: lastly, of putting a spirit of honesty, industry, and skill into our shopkeepers; who, if a resolution could now be taken to buy only our native goods, would immediately unite to cheat and exact upon us in the price, the measure, and the goodness, nor could ever yet be brought to make one fair proposal of just dealing, though often and earnestly invited to it.

Therefore I repeat, let no man talk to me of these and the like expedients, till he hath at least some glimpse of hope that there will ever be some hearty and sincere attempt to put them in practice.

But as to myself, having been wearied out for many years with offering vain, idle, visionary thoughts, and at length utterly despairing of success, I fortunately fell upon this proposal, which, as it is wholly new, so it hath something solid and real, and no expense and little trouble, full in our own power, and whereby we can incur no danger in disobliging England. For this kind of commodity will not bear exportation, the flesh being of too tender a consistence to admit a long continuance, in salt, although perhaps I could name a country which would be glad to eat up our whole nation without it.

After all, I am not so violently bent upon my own opinion as to reject any offer proposed by wise men, which shall be found equally innocent, cheap, easy, and effectual. But before something of that kind shall be advanced in contradiction to my scheme, and offering a better, I desire the author or authors will be pleased maturely to consider two points. First, as things now stand, how they will be able to find food and raiment for an hundred thousand useless mouths and backs. And secondly, there being a round million of creatures in human figure throughout this kingdom, whose sole subsistence put into a common stock would leave them in debt two millions of pounds sterling, adding those who are beggars by profession to the bulk of farmers, cottagers, and laborers, and their wives and children who are beggars in effect; I desire those politicians who dislike my overture, and may perhaps be so bold to attempt an answer, that they will first ask the parents of these mortals whether they would not at this day think it a great happiness to have been sold for food at a year old in the manner I prescribe, and thereby have avoided such a perpetual scene of misfortunes as they have since gone through by the oppression of landlords, the impossibility of paying rent without money or trade, the want of common sustenance, with neither house nor clothes to cover them from the inclemencies of the weather, and the most inevitable prospect of entailing the like or greater miseries upon their breed forever.

I profess, in the sincerity of my heart, that I have not the least personal interest in endeavoring to promote this necessary work, having no other motive than the public good of my country, by advancing our trade, providing for infants, relieving the poor, and giving some pleasure to the rich. I have no children by which I can propose to get a single penny; the youngest being nine years old, and my wife past childbearing.[6]

The eighteenth century's enlightened spirit brought the essay to the forefront as a means of criticizing society and religion. Its flexibility, brevity, and potential for ambiguity and allusions to contemporary situations made it an ideal tool for reformers throughout Europe and America. Among its adherents, Englishman Alexander Pope created in *An Essay on Man* (1733) a philosophical essay written in heroic couplets of iambic pentameter. The poem takes the form of four letters: (1) a survey of relations between humans and the universe, (2) a discussion of humans as individuals, (3) a discussion of the relationships between individuals and society, and (4) an exploration of questions involving the potential for happiness in individuals. In *An Essay on Man*, Pope describes the universe as a hierarchy of being that has humans, because of their ability to reason, at the top, above animals and plants. The brief excerpt that follows illustrates Pope's form and style in the piece.

An Essay on Man
Epistle I: Of the Nature and State of Man, With Respect to the Universe
Alexander Pope
1688–1744

ARGUMENT

Of Man in the abstract. I. That we can judge only with regard to our own system, being ignorant of the relations of systems and things. II. That Man is not to be deemed imperfect, but a being suited to his place and rank in the creation, agreeable to the general order of things, and conformable to ends and relations to him unknown. III. That it is partly upon his ignorance of future events, and partly upon the hope of a future state, that all his happiness in the present depends. IV. The pride of aiming at more knowledge, and pretending to more perfection, the cause of Man's error and misery. The impiety of putting himself in the place of God, and judging of the fitness or unfitness, perfection or imperfection, justice or injustice, of his dispensations. V. The absurdity of conceiving himself the final cause of creation, or expecting that perfection in the moral world which is not in the natural. VI. The unreasonableness of his complaints against Providence, while, on the one hand, he demands the perfections of the angels, and, on the other, the bodily qualifications of the brutes; though to possess any of the sensitive faculties in a higher degree would render him miserable. VII. That throughout the whole visible world a universal order and gradation in the sensual and mental faculties is observed, which causes a subordination of creature to creature, and of all creatures to man. The gradations of Sense, Instinct,

Thought, Reflection, Reason: that Reason alone countervails all the other faculties. <u>VIII.</u> How much further this order and subordination of living creatures may extend above and below us; were any part of which broken, not that part only, but the whole connected creation must be destroyed. <u>IX.</u> The extravagance, madness, and pride of such a desire. <u>X.</u> The consequence of all, the absolute submission due to Providence, both as to our present and future state.

Awake, my St. John! leave all meaner things
To low ambition and the pride of Kings.
Let us, since life can little more supply
Than just to look about us and to die,
Expatiate free o'er all this scene of man;
A mighty maze! but not without a plan;
A wild, where weeds and flowers promiscuous shoot,
Or garden, tempting with forbidden fruit.
Together let us beat this ample field,
Try what the open, what the covert yield;
The latent tracts, the giddy heights, explore
Of all who blindly creep or sightless soar;
Eye Nature's walks, shoot folly as it flies,
And catch the manners living as they rise;
Laugh where we must, be candid where we can,
But vindicate the ways of God to man.

I

Say first, of God above or Man below
What can we reason but from what we know?
Of man what see we but his station here,
From which to reason, or to which refer?
Thro' worlds unnumber'd tho' the God be known,
'Tis ours to trace him only in our own.
He who thro' vast immensity can pierce,
See worlds on worlds compose one universe,
Observe how system into system runs,
What other planets circle other suns,
What varied being peoples every star,
May tell why Heav'n has made us as we are:
But of this frame, the bearings and the ties,
The strong connexions, nice dependencies,
Gradations just, has thy pervading soul
Look'd thro'; or can a part contains the whole?
Is the great chain that draws all to agree,
And drawn supports, upheld by God or thee?[7]

Alexander Pope served as a model for an American poet, Phillis Wheatley. Perhaps of Fulani origin, in or near the current nation of Senegal, she came to America, captive, on the slaver "Phillis." At the age of seven, she was sold to John Wheatley, a Boston merchant. Recognizing her talent, the Wheatleys taught her to read and write not only in English but also in Latin. She read poetry, and at the age of fourteen, began to write. Her elegy on the death of George Whitefield (1770) brought her acclaim. With the 1773 publication of her *Poems on Various Subjects* in England, Phillis Wheatley's fame spread in Europe as well as America. She was freed in 1773 but remained with the Wheatley family as a servant and died in poverty. Her poetry follows Neoclassical style, has African influences, and reflects Christian concerns for morality and piety. In the short poem "On Virtue" the poet's language invokes imagery, figures, and allegory to make the moral quality of virtue a "bright jewel" and imbue it with personal characteristics. The unrhymed lines flow freely in iambic meter.

On Virtue
Phillis Wheatley
c. 1753–84

O Thou bright jewel in my aim I strive
To comprehend thee. Thine own words declare
Wisdom is higher than a fool can reach.
I cease to wonder, and no more attempt
Thine height t' explore, or fathom thy profound.
But, O my soul, sink not into despair,
Virtue is near thee, and with gentle hand
Would now embrace thee, hovers o'er thine head.
Fain would the heav'n-born soul with her converse,
Then seek, then court her for her promis'd bliss.
Auspicious queen, thine heav'nly pinions spread,
And lead celestial Chastity along;
Lo! now her sacred retinue descends,
Array'd in glory from the orbs above.
Attend me, Virtue, thro' my youthful years!
O leave me not to the false joys of time!
But guide my steps to endless life and bliss.
Greatness, or Goodness, say what I shall call thee,
To give me an higher appellation still,
Teach me a better strain, a nobler lay,
O thou, enthron'd with Cherubs in the realms of day.[8]

THINKING CRITICALLY

- Using the discussions of perspective and chiaroscuro in Chapter 1 (pp. 49 and 52) as a guide, compare how Leonardo's *Last Supper* (Fig. **11.8**) and Rubens's *Henry IV Receiving the Portrait of Maria de' Medici* (Fig. **11.33**) achieve depth of space.

- Using the text on style in the Introduction to Part II (p. 194) and the discussions on Renaissance and Baroque art in this chapter as guides, explain why Masaccio's *Tribute Money* (Fig. **11.1**) and Rembrandt's *Night Watch* (Fig. **11.34**) represent each style.

- Listen to the first movement of Vivaldi's "Spring" (http://www.classicalarchives.com/cgi-bin/n.cgi/prep/0/viv811.mid) and the first movement of Mozart's *Symphony No. 40 in G minor* (http://www.classicalarchives.com/cgi-bin/n.cgi/prep/3/sym40-1.mid) then compare the use of motif, melody, and texture in each work and explain how the pieces represent the Baroque and Classical styles, respectively.

- How are the Vivaldi and Mozart, just mentioned, analogous to the visual representations of the same styles—for example, to Bernini's *David* (Fig. **11.35**; Baroque) and David's *Oath of the Horatii* (Fig. **11.43**; Neoclassical)?

CYBER STUDY

RENAISSANCE:
—Visual Art: Europe
http://www.artcyclopedia.com/history/early-renaissance.html
http://www.artcyclopedia.com/history/high-renaissance.html
http://www.artcyclopedia.com/history/northern-renaissance.html
—Visual Art: Asia
http://www.kamat.com/kalranga/art/timeline.htm
http://www.asianart.org/exhibits/collect_jpn_2.htm
—Music
http://www.classicalarchives.com/early.html
—Theatre: Shakespeare; Marlowe
http://readroom.ipl.org/cgi/i/ipl/ipl.books-idx.pl?type=browseauthor&tq1=S
http://readroom.ipl.org/cgi/i/ipl/ipl.books-idx.pl?type=browseauthor&tq1=M

BAROQUE:
—Visual Art
http://www.artcyclopedia.com/history/baroque.html
—Music: Vivaldi, Handel, Bach
http://www.classicalarchives.com/index_1.html

EIGHTEENTH CENTURY:
—Rococo
http://www.artcyclopedia.com/history/rococo.html
—Neoclassicism
http://www.artcyclopedia.com/history/neoclassicism.html
—Musical Classicism: Mozart, Haydn
http://www.classicalarchives.com/index_1.html
—Literature: Swift, Pope
http://readroom.ipl.org/cgi/i/ipl/ipl.books-idx.pl?type=browseauthor&tq1=S
http://readroom.ipl.org/cgi/i/ipl/ipl.books-idx.pl?type=browseauthor&tq1=P

CHAPTER TWELVE

THE BEGINNINGS OF MODERNISM

c. 1800 to c. 1900

IMPORTANT TERMS

Guardian figure An artistic manifestation believed to protect the remains of the dead.

Animism The belief that a spirit exists in every living thing.

Romanticism A wide-ranging style and philosophy that emphasizes emotional appeal, personalization, and imagination.

Art song A solo musical composition for voice, usually with piano accompaniment.

Idée fixe A recurrent melodic motif representing a nonmusical idea.

Requiem A mass for the dead.

Gesamtkunstwerk A comprehensive work of art in which music, poetry, and scenery are all subservient to the central generating idea.

Realism A style of painting and sculpture based on the theory that the method of presentation should be true to life.

Impressionism A style in painting emphasizing the presence of color and the interrelated mechanisms of the camera and the eye. A musical style exemplified by Debussy, using reduced melodic development and gliding chords.

Post-Impressionism A very diverse and personal style of visual art typically concerned with capturing sensory experience and insisting on "art for art's sake" and a return to form and structure.

Art Nouveau A style of architecture characterized by the lively, serpentine curve and a fascination with plant and animal life and organic growth.

JAPANESE STYLE IN PRINTMAKING

In the nineteenth century, as Japan began to look westward, the style of the country's two-dimensional art began to evolve. Some of the changes can be seen in the works of two printmakers, Katsushika Hokusai (hoh-KOO-sigh; 1760–1849) and Ando Hiroshige (hee-roh-SHEE-ghay; 1797–1858).

12.1 Katsushika Hokusai, *The Great Wave off Kanazawa*, 1823–9. Polychrome woodblock print, 10 × 14¾ ins (25.5 × 37.5 cm). Victoria & Albert Museum, London.

HOKUSAI

Hokusai broadened subject matter to include all aspects of Japanese life. In particular, his prints document in detail the streetlife in and around Edo. His works, entitled *Manga*, fill fifteen volumes, which he began to publish in 1814. Full of vibrancy, virility, and humor, his works show humankind in all its contrasting nobility and gracelessness. In a woodcut from *Manga* he portrays acrobats in various attitudes (Fig. **12.3**). They seem oblivious of any observer, and their antics reveal an earthy forthrightness that seems totally at odds with the graceful power one would normally associate with them. They seem cartoonish caricatures, and yet there is vitality, energy, and suppleness within the unflattering representation.

In his landscapes, Hokusai forged new directions in Japanese art. *The Great Wave off Kanazawa*, for example (Fig. **12.1**), is a boldly colored rendering that is neither realistic nor idealized. While Mount Fuji reposes calmly in the background, the great wave breaks over the boats with raging fury, and the foam reaches out like grasping fingers to crash down on the fragile craft. There is a new sense of directness here, and yet Hokusai's response to natural forms and his decorative patterning lie firmly within the traditions of Japanese art.

HIROSHIGE

A similar freshness can be seen in the strongly colored landscape *Maple Leaves at the Tekona Shrine, Mamma* by Hiroshige (Fig. **12.2**). It shows deep space, using the

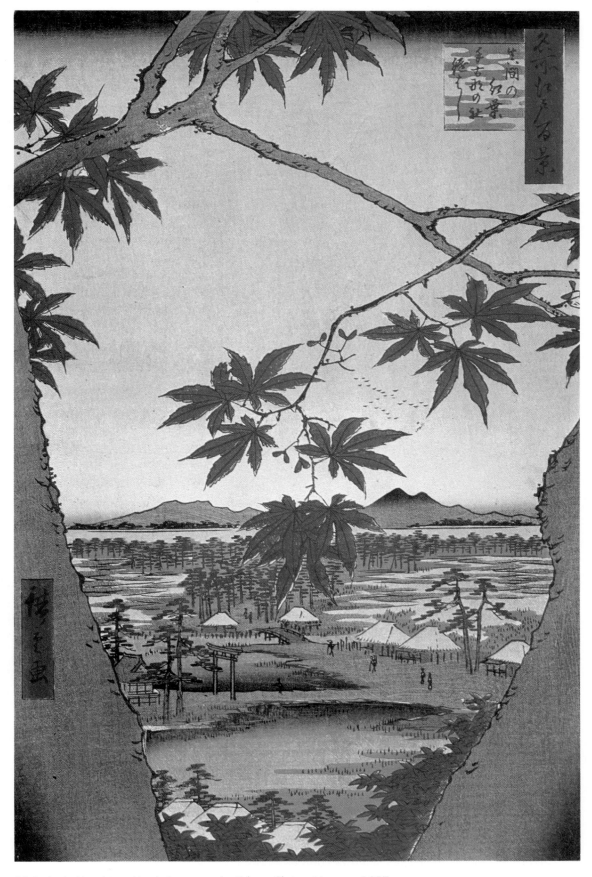

12.2 Ardo Hiroshige, *Maple Leaves at the Tekona Shrine, Mamma,* 1857.
Polychrome woodblock print, 13¾ × 9¾ ins (35 × 24 cm). British Museum, London.

12.3 Katsushika Hokusai, page from *Manga*, vol. 8, 1817. Woodcut, 9 × 5¾ ins (22.8 × 14.6 cm). British Museum, London.

AFRICA AND EARLY BLACK AMERICA

ART AND ANCESTOR WORSHIP

The nineteenth century, the focus of this chapter, brought significant changes to the entire world. Most certainly it changed Africa and African Americans. In tribal Africa at that time, animism and ancestor worship prevailed (the term "animism" is the belief that a spirit exists in every living thing). Ancestor worship takes a variety of forms, depending on the tribe, and its artistic manifestations also vary widely. One form is the *guardian figure*, used to protect the remains of the dead. In Gabon in Equatorial Africa, the Kota tribe of the nineteenth century produced polished metal figures which guarded large containers of skulls of ancestors—believed to be communal dwellings of ancestor spirits. The guardian figure in Figure **12.4** is in an abstract geometric style typical of the art of tribal societies. Despite its abstraction, the anatomical parts of the body are clearly defined. The entire design has been flattened into a single plane, and the work is perfectly symmetrical in balance. It has a calming effect: This guardian was clearly not intended to frighten the viewer. Compare it with the ancestor figure shown earlier in the book, Figure **2.6**.

foreground to "frame" the distance, and allowing the perspective to shift as described on page 50. The distance seems logical even though the colors and details are the same in foreground and background. Only the trees exhibit any degree of foreshortening. This pulls our vision back and forth in space as the red maple leaves—placed directly in our line of sight to the distance—constantly compete with middle ground and background for our attention. Thus, we are invited to focus on the series of huts staggered across a line, which divides the print into fourths. Downward deflecting leaves and a strong, dark border redirect us into the painting at the top, while the framing diagonals of the tree trunks carry us back into the lower fourth of the work. Hiroshige cleverly manipulates hue, value, and contrast to keep interest and control. The red leaves and complementary gray-green limbs and mountains strike a harmonious visual chord, and the ocher grass, thatched roofs, and lightened sky stand in contrast—both in tone and value—to create a counterpoint and to hold our vision stable in the center of the work.

12.4 Guardian figure of the Kota tribe, from Gabon, late 19th century. Wood, brass, ivory eyes, height 16⅝ ins (42.2 cm). Metropolitan Museum of Art, New York (Michael C. Rockefeller Memorial Collection, Bequest of Nelson A. Rockefeller).

12.5 Mask, from the Bamenda area, Cameroon, late 19th century. Wood, height 26½ ins (67.3 cm). Rietberg Museum, Zürich (Heydt Collection).

The animism of the Kota people is all-embracing—for example, trees have spirits that must be appeased before the tree can be cut down; the individual tree spirit merges with a general "tree spirit"; this in turn merges with a larger "life spirit." Spirits are believed to dwell in rivers, lakes, forests, the sun, the moon, wind, and rain. In dealing with the spirit world, tribal peoples act out relationships with the spirits in dances and other dramatic ceremonies. Sometimes they disguise themselves so as to assume the role of the spirit temporarily. In the Bamenda area of Cameroon, the traditional costume for these ceremonies features a prominent mask. The one shown in Figure 12.5 is typical. Like the guardian figure, it has a symmetrical composition and distinct detailing. Again the design is abstract while leaving anatomical details recognizable. The elevated eyebrows with their delicate arching lines give the mask a sophisticated and striking appearance. Its dignity and strength stem from its straightforwardness and the solidity of its detailing.

TRANSPORTATION TO AMERICA

The European colonization of Africa had a negative impact on African art. More important for art was the transportation of African culture to the Americas as a result of the slave trade that serviced the plantations of the American South. The blending of Euro- and African-centered cultures created a significant African American artistic heritage. It emerged publicly during and immediately after the American Civil War (1861–5), and has been felt most strongly in music.

AFRICAN AMERICAN MUSIC

African American music consists of three basic types: folk music, art music, and popular music. Each has its own idiom, function, and place in the sociology of African American culture. Folk music—for example, the spiritual—is anonymous in origin, orally transmitted, and shows the "expressive melodic and racial feeling, character, and expression of the people."[1] This was a profoundly social musical form that defined a coherent experience for a dislocated people, supported people in distress, occasionally contained coded language of rebellion and escape, and provided a subtle language for exploring emotional extremities. Art music has a technical tradition in the hands of a group of highly trained specialists involved in both creation and performance. Popular music—for example, blues, ragtime, jazz, and soul—combines the art and folk traditions. It concerns itself with the contemporary world, seeks novelty, and tends to be faddish. We will briefly examine some of the folk music of the African American tradition that is appropriate to the time-frame of this chapter.

As Northern soldiers, journalists, and missionaries arrived in the South toward the end of the Civil War, their reports created a new interest in and documentation of the culture of African Americans—especially their music. Numerous chronicles of this music can be found in newspaper and journal articles, letters, and other documents from the mid-1860s. In these lies the record of a musical heritage that expresses the joys and sorrows, thoughts and reactions of a people immersed in a struggle for freedom.

African Americans played numerous roles in the American Civil War: They were, for example, body servants for Southern officers, soldiers, cooks, hospital attendants, and railroad workers. Out of one unsuccessful attempt to organize freed men for military service came a plaintive song of regret:

Oh Lord, I want some valiant soldier,
I want some valiant soldier,
I want some valiant soldier,
To help me bear de cross.
For I weep, I weep,
For I weep, I weep,
I can't hold out;
If any mercy, Lord,
O pity poor me.[2]

On the eve of the expected Emancipation Proclamation, December 31, 1862, a prayer meeting and song service vigil held in the District of Columbia produced a spontaneous musical outpouring.

12.6 "The Old Ship of Zion," slave song.

By the end of the Civil War, nearly 200,000 African Americans had served as soldiers in 166 regiments. Nearly 20,000 had served as sailors—almost one quarter of the entire United States Navy. Casualties numbered around 70,000, with approximately 30,000 killed. African Americans fought well and sang well. They linked their military struggle with their belief in a kind and liberating God.

The songs of slavery and the American South fill volumes. Clearly, music formed the core of the African American's life and culture during the two centuries of bondage. There were slave songs, religious folk songs, camp meeting songs, and spirituals. Most had strong religious themes—for example, the slave song "The Old Ship of Zion" (Fig. 12.6).

The spiritual remains the most popular of the African American genres. A common misconception is that most of this music is in the minor key—it is not. It *is* a commentary on the awful state of the African American's daily life, yet it is full of patience for that life coupled with triumph in the life to come. Some songs focus on the present and some on the future, but the two were inexorably tied together, at least by implication. For example, in the spiritual "This World Almost Done" we hear the patient reminder,

> Brudder, keep your lamp trimmin' and a-burnin',
> Keep your lamp trimmin' and a-burnin',
> Keep your lamp trimmin' and a-burnin',
>   For dis world most done.
> So keep your lamp trimmin' [etc.]
>   For dis world most done.[3]

In "I Want to Go Home" the patience remains, but the final reward is proclaimed:

> Dere's no rain to wet you,
>   O, yes, I want to go home.
> Dere's no sun to burn you,
>   O, yes, I want to go home.

> O, push along, believers,
>   O, yes, I want to go home.
> Dere's no hard trials,
>   O, yes, I want to go home.
> Dere's no whips a crackin',
>   O, yes, I want to go home.
> My brudder on de wayside,
>   O, yes, I want to go home.
> O, push along, my brudder,
>   O, yes, I want to go home.
> Where dere's no stormy weather,
>   O, yes, I want to go home.
> Dere's no tribulation,
>   O, yes, I want to go home.[4]

The first 250 years of African American cultural history reflect a diversity of reactions: Sometimes the people howled in alarm; sometimes they fought back and learned the advantages of resistance. They certainly did not "accept" slavery and oppression. The music of the time reflected the mind of the people and their circumstances.

The influence of this outpouring of musical expression in the folk idiom has been pervasive, and it has become a significant part not only of African American culture, but of American culture as a whole. In 1914 Henry Edward Krehbiel asserted:

> Is it not the merest quibble to say that these songs are not American? They were created in America under American influences and by people who are Americans in the same sense that any other element of our population is American—every element except the aboriginal.[5]

NATIVE AMERICA

The aboriginal in this context means Native American, and in the nineteenth century Native American artists pursued many of the same goals as artists from any culture—they tried to evoke emotional responses in the viewer. But in the case of Native American artists, the viewer might be a supernatural being. Much of their art deals with religious matters, and its purpose is like that of prayer—to entreat a benign god or placate a hostile one. Tradition dictates the manner or form. In fact, in Native American culture a major criterion for "art" is how well the artist recognizes the force of tradition. Little room for artistic experimentation exists within the established tribal organization. However, there are exceptions, and artists such as Nampeyo, the Hopi potter, have been able to introduce new elements to the cultural tradition, perhaps solely by the force of their individual talent.

INFLUENCES

Naturally, many different factors have influenced Native American works of art. Function is one factor. Environment is another: The accessibility of materials has played an important role in determining the nature of Native American art. For example, availability of soapstone and lack of access to clay have meant that Inuit art is carved rather than ceramic. In addition, traditions have sometimes mixed as one people conquers another or as intertribal marriage occurs, thereby creating new traditions. Often, tribal groups such as the Hopi and Navajo share a common environment and lifestyle, and the function of their art is similar. Tradition and tribal integrity, however, keep their styles separate, and the works of both cultures remain distinguishable.

SYMBOLISM

The meaning of works of art from Native American cultures can prove baffling to someone raised in a Euro-centered culture. Native American artists do not draw merely to recreate a picture of something, for they understand that they could not draw a tree as perfectly as it could be made by the Creator. This spiritual consciousness finds its way into the works of art. "Therefore, it can be said that Indian art is not so much drawings, carvings or reproductions *of* an object, but more the representation of the spirit *within* it. In short, it embodies the essence of the subject as well as its appearance."[6] Native American art has a magical quality rather than a "meaning" in the sense that Western minds expect.

INUIT STYLE

In a wide band of the Arctic, stretching right across North America, hundreds of tribes comprise the Inuit (IH-noo-iht) culture. All of them are related to each other culturally and/or linguistically. Out of the bleak and inhospitable environment of the North—where the quest for survival would seemingly leave little room for artistry—comes a tremendously imaginative artistic tradition. The long Arctic winter nights have given individuals ample time to carve ivory obtained from walrus and killer whales and, more recently, stone. Because of the difficulty of obtaining materials, Inuit art tends to be small in scale. In the case of tusk ivory, it is of necessity larger at one end than at the other. Characteristic of Inuit art is humor: Caricatures found in the form of driftwood masks are common (Fig. 12.7). This mask was originally decorated with snow goose feathers. It is typical of the elaborate or grotesque dance masks that are widely crafted

12.7 Carved dance masks of the Inuit tribe, from Mamtrek, Alaska, late 19th century. Wood (originally decorated with snow goose feathers), 8½ × 4½ ins (21.6 × 11.4 cm). National Museum of the American Indian, Smithsonian Institution, Washington, D.C.

among the Inuit people. They depict a variety of subjects—sacred and secular, human and animal.

NORTHWEST COASTAL STYLE

The Pacific Northwest of North America produced stable Native American cultures. This is in great measure due to the abundance of resources and temperate climate, which figure prominently in the social and cultural fabric of the tribes. Fishing, hunting, and foraging produce ample means of sustenance, and therefore, the people of this region had no reason to cultivate crops or domesticate animals. Their cultures have tended to share certain features, probably because they traded and warred with one another. Artistic motifs are alike and they share a common religion, shamanism—an ancient form of magic, centered on wise, all-seeing men (shamans). (It is also shared with the hunting tribes of Siberia and various African cultures.) Although their pantheons and myths may differ, the Northwest tribes all acknowledge the power of shamans to contact the spirits of the forest and waters, to heal the sick, and to predict the future.

The rich forests of the area have provided Native American artists with a wealth of materials for sculpting.

12.8 Housepost, from Haida, Alaska, 19th century. Wood, height 11 ft 6½ ins (3.52 m). National Museum of the American Indian, Smithsonian Institution, Washington, D.C.

Huge spruce and cedar trees abounded for many centuries, and when steel knives were obtained from fur traders and used as tools, Northwest-coast artists excelled in producing magnificent totem poles, carved posts for wooden dwellings, masks, rattles, and other objects. Figure 12.8 shows a carved housepost that was used inside a wooden dwelling to support the roof and to give additional decoration to the interior. It depicts the sea bear and has a frog carved in each ear. It was presented as a token of respect to Chief Frog Ears of Sukkwan by the

12.9 Tlingit totem pole, Sitka, Alaska, late 19th century. Carved and painted wood.

people of a neighboring village. Proximity to the sea also provided abalone shells that were used as inlays to give luster to sculpted works.

Although many art objects from the area, such as masks, concern themselves with shamanistic religious rituals, a fair amount of art is secular. Like some African art, it is used to maintain the social fabric and bolster a ruler's power. In the Tlingit tribe, for example, communities are made up of a number of families, each of which has its own chief who inherits his rank from his mother. Carefully devised social customs oblige both men and women to marry outside their own clan. In this way a balance is established in which no one family achieves dominance. Nonetheless, chiefs compete fiercely with each other in displays of riches. Totem poles form a part of this ostentation, proclaiming prestige and family pride through genealogy—much like the coats of arms of the European aristocracy. Totem poles are carved from single tree trunks and often reach a height of 90 feet (27.4 m). Probably originating as funerary monuments, by the nineteenth century they had become fixtures adorning the exteriors of chiefs' houses.

Eagles, beavers, and whales appear on the totem poles (Fig. 12.9), in essence as crests that a chief inherited from his ancestors. The Tlingit do not worship these figures or have any supernatural relationship with them. They are governed by traditional artistic principles. One of these is that of bilateral symmetry—the designs on either side of the central axis are identical. Another specifies the transition from one motif to another: Each design must appear to grow from the one below. Thus, not only the overall vertical form of the totem pole, but also the design of its interior parts, leads the eye upward along its central axis. In our example, the patchwork of contrasting colors and upward striving line carry us with rhythmic precision from one motif to another until, finally, we reach the top. At the top, a darkly colored, triangular form and a strong horizontal capping band redirect the eye downward.

As historical documents that record the wealth, social position, and relative importance of the person who paid for them, totem poles are quite similar to sculptural records from other cultures. The ultimate function of such art was probably to act as a gift: "The life goal of many of these tribes involved the belief that the greatest value was to give away all of one's possessions."[7] The actual working out of such a philosophy created some interesting scenarios. The more one gave away, the greater was one's prestige. In turn, one's rival was more or less obliged to give back the same or more material wealth in order to prove greater disdain for possessions. As a result, totems and other goods were often burned, thrown into the sea, or otherwise destroyed. It even went so far

that slaves were occasionally killed and entire families sold into slavery.

LITERARY STYLE

Literacy among Native Americans began to take hold in the late eighteenth century as a result of missionary activity—particularly that of Methodists and Presbyterians—and a century later, increased interest in America's heritage gave rise to the publication of tribal histories written by Native Americans. Fiction writing among Native Americans appeared as early as 1823.

Between 1870 and 1920, Native American culture underwent tremendous change: Tribal autonomy decreased, and all tribes within the territory of the United States were confined to reservations. By the end of 1870, the federal government had become actively involved in Native American education, and a subsequent increase in literacy produced something of an intellectual elite. Numerous authors emerged, one of whom was "Bright Eyes" (Susette La Flesche). Her story "Nedawi" was first published in 1881 in a popular magazine for children. It arguably represents the first short story written by a Native American that is not a reworking of a legend. The author's gender testifies to the prominence of women in Native American (as well as American) literature. Describing a past way of life in nostalgic terms, "Nedawi" is representative of much of Native American fiction prior to 1920. The story emphasizes ethnocentric detail, has a strong moralistic tone, and appeals to young readers.

Nedawi
An Indian Story from Real Life
"Bright Eyes" (Susette La Flesche)

"Nedawi!" called her mother, "take your little brother while I go with your sister for some wood." Nedawi ran into the tent, bringing back her little red blanket, but the brown-faced, roly-poly baby, who had been having a comfortable nap in spite of being all the while tied straight to his board, woke with a merry crow just as the mother was about to attach him, board and all, to Nedawi's neck. So he was taken from the board instead, and, after he had kicked in happy freedom for a moment, Nedawi stood in front of her mother, who placed Habazhu on the little girl's back, and drew the blanket over him, leaving his arms free. She next put into his hand a little hollow gourd, filled with seeds, which served as a rattle; Nedawi held both ends of the blanket tightly in front of her, and was then ready to walk around with the little man.

Where should she go? Yonder was a group of young girls playing a game of *konci*, or dice. The dice were five plum-seeds, scorched black, and had little stars and quarter-moons instead of numbers. She went over and stood by the group, gently rocking herself from side to side, pretty much as white children do when reciting the multiplication table. The girls would toss up the wooden bowl, letting it drop with a gentle thud on the pillow beneath, the falling dice making a pleasant clatter which the baby liked to hear. The stakes were a little heap of beads, rings, and bracelets. The laughter and exclamations of the girls, as some successful toss brought down the dice three stars and two quarter-moons (the highest throw), made Nedawi wish that she, too, were a young girl, and could win and wear all those pretty things. How gay she would look! Just then, the little glittering heap caught baby's eye. He tried to wriggle out of the blanket to get to it, but Nedawi held tight. Then he set up a yell. Nedawi walked away very reluctantly, because she wanted to stay and see who would win. She went to her mother's tent, but found it deserted. Her father and brothers had gone to the chase. A herd of buffalo had been seen that morning, and all the men in the tribe had gone, and would not be back till night. Her mother, her sister, and the women of the household had gone to the river for wood and water. The tent looked enticingly cool, with the sides turned up to let the breeze sweep through, and the straw mats and soft robes seemed to invite her to lie down on them and dream the afternoon away, as she was too apt to do. She did not yield to the temptation, however, for she knew Mother would not like it, but walked over to her cousin Metai's tent. She found her cousin "keeping house" with a number of little girls, and stood to watch them while they put up little tents, just large enough to hold one or two girls.

"Nedawi, come and play," said Metai. "You can make the fire and cook. I'll ask Mother for something to cook."

"But what shall I do with Habazhu?" said Nedawi.

"I'll tell you. Put him in my tent, and make believe he's our little old grandfather."

Forthwith he was transferred from Nedawi's back to the little tent. But Habazhu had a decided objection to staying in the dark little place, where he could not see anything, and crept out of the door on his hands and knees. Nedawi collected a little heap of sticks, all ready for the fire, and went off to get a fire-brand to light it with. While she was gone, Habazhu crawled up to a bowl of water which stood by the intended fire-place, and began dabbling in it with his chubby little hands, splashing the water all over the sticks prepared for the fire. Then he thought he would like a drink. He tried to lift the bowl in both hands, but only succeeded in spilling the water over himself and the fire-place.

When Nedawi returned, she stood aghast; then, throwing down the brand, she took her little brother by the shoulders and, I am sorry to say, shook him violently, jerked him up, and dumped him down by the door of the little tent from which he had crawled. "You bad little boy!" she said. "It's too bad that I have to take care of you when I want to play."

You see, she was no more perfect than any little white girl who gets into a temper now and then. The baby's lip quivered, and he began to cry. Metai said to Nedawi: "I think it's real mean for you to shake him, when he doesn't know any better."

Metai picked up Baby and tried to comfort him. She kissed him over and over, and talked to him in baby language. Nedawi's conscience, if the little savage could be said to have any, was troubling her. She loved her baby brother dearly, even though she did get out of patience with him now and then.

"I'll put a clean little shirt on him and pack him again." said she, suddenly. Then she took off his little wet shirt, wrung it out, and spread it on the tall grass to dry in the sun. Then she went home, and, going to a pretty painted skin in which her mother kept his clothes, she selected the red shirt, which she thought was the prettiest. She was in such a hurry, however, that she forgot to close and tie up the skin again, and she carelessly left his clean shirts lying around as she had laid them out. When Baby was on her back again, she walked around with him, giving directions and overseeing the other girls at their play, determined to do that rather than nothing.

The other children were good-natured, and took her ordering as gracefully as they could. Metai made the fire in a new place, and then went to ask her mother to give her something to cook. Her mother gave her a piece of dried buffalo meat, as hard as a chip and as brittle as glass. Metai broke it up into small pieces, and put the pieces into a little tin pail of water, which she hung over the fire. "Now," she said, "when the meat is cooked and the soup is made, I will call you all to a feast, and Habazhu shall be the chief."

They all laughed. But alas for human calculations! During the last few minutes, a shy little girl, with soft, wistful black eyes, had been watching them from a little distance. She had on a faded, shabby blanket and a ragged dress.

"Metai," said Nedawi, "let's ask that girl to play with us; she looks so lonesome."

"Well," said Metai, doubtfully, "I don't care; but my mother said she didn't want me to play with ragged little girls."

"My father says we must be kind to poor little girls, and help them all we can; so *I'm* going to play with her if *you* don't," said Nedawi, loftily.

Although Metai was the hostess, Nedawi was the leading spirit, and had her own way, as usual. She walked up to the little creature and said, "Come and play with us, if you want to." The little girl's eyes brightened, and she laughed. Then she suddenly drew from under her blanket a pretty bark basket, filled with the most delicious red and yellow plums. "My brother picked them in the woods, and I give them to you," was all she said. Nedawi managed to free one hand, and took the offering with an exclamation of delight, which drew the other girls quickly around. Instead of saying "Oh! Oh!" as you would have said, they cried "Hin! Hin!" which expressed their feeling quite as well, perhaps.

"Let us have them for our feast," said Metai, taking them.

Little Indian children are taught to share everything with one another, so it did not seem strange to Nedawi to have her gift looked on as common property. But, while the attention of the little group had been concentrated on the matter in hand, a party of mischievous boys, passing by, caught sight of the little tents and the tin pail hanging over the fire. Simultaneously, they set up a war-whoop and, dashing into the deserted camp, they sent the tent-poles scattering right and left, and snatching up whatever they could lay hands on, including the tin pail and its contents, they retreated. The little girls, startled by the sudden raid on their property, looked up. Rage possessed their little souls. Giving shrieks of anger, they started in pursuit. What did Nedawi do? She forgot the plums, baby, and everything. The ends of the blanket slipped from her grasp, and she darted forward like an arrow after her companions.

Finding the chase hopeless, the little girls came to a standstill, and some of them began to cry. The boys had stopped, too; and seeing the tears flow, being good-hearted boys in spite of their mischief, they surrendered at discretion. They threw back the articles they had taken, not daring to come near. The did not consider it manly for big boys like themselves to strike or hurt little girls, even though they delighted in teasing them, and they knew from experience that they would be at the mercy of the offended party if they went near enough to be touched. The boy who had the dinner brought the little pail which had contained it as near as he dared, and setting it down ran away.

"You have spilt all our soup. There's hardly any of it left. You bad boys!" said one of the girls.

They crowded around with lamentations over their lost dinner. The boys began to feel remorseful.

"Let's go into the woods and get them some plums to make up for it."

"Say, girls, hand us your pail, and we'll fill it up with plums for you."

So the affair was settled.

But, meanwhile, what became of the baby left so unceremoniously in the tall grass? First he opened his black eyes wide at this style of treatment. He was not used to it. Before he had time, however, to make up his mind whether to laugh or cry, his mother came to the rescue. She had just come home and thrown the wood off her back, when she caught sight of Nedawi dropping him. She ran to pick him up, and finding him unhurt, kissed him over and over. Some of the neighbors had run up to see what was the matter. She said to them:

"I never did see such a thoughtless, heedless child as my Nedawi. She really has 'no ears.' I don't know what in the world will ever become of her. When something new interests her, she forgets everything else. It was just like her to act in this way."

Then they all laughed, and one of them said:

"Never mind—she will grow wiser as she grows older," after which consoling remark they went away to their own tents.

It was of no use to call Nedawi back. She was too far off.

Habazhu was given over to the care of the nurse, who had just returned from her visit. An hour or two after, Nedawi came home.

"Mother!" she exclaimed, as she saw her mother frying bread for supper, "I am so hungry. Can I have some of that bread?"

"Where is your little brother?" was the unexpected reply.

Nedawi started. Where *had* she left him? She tried to think.

"Why, Mother, the last I remember I was packing him, and—and oh, Mother! you *know* where he is. Please tell me."

"When you find him and bring him back to me, perhaps I shall forgive you," was the cold reply.

This was dreadful. Her mother had never treated her in that way before. She burst into tears, and started out to find Habazhu, crying all the way. She knew that her mother knew where baby was, or she would not have taken it so coolly; and she knew also that her mother expected her to bring him home. As she went stumbling along through the grass, she felt herself seized and held in somebody's strong arms, and a great, round, hearty voice said:

"What's the matter with my little niece? Have all her friends deserted her that she is wailing like this? Or has her little dog died? I thought Nedawi was a brave little woman."

It was her uncle Two Crows. She managed to tell him, through her sobs, the whole story. She knew, if she told him herself, he would not laugh at her about it, for he would sympathize in her troubles, though he was a great tease. When she ceased, he said to her: "Well, your mother wants you to be more careful next time, I suppose; and, by the way, I think I saw a little boy who looked very much like Habazhu, in my tent."

Sure enough, she found him there with his nurse. When she got home with them, she found her mother,—her own dear self,—and, after giving her a big hug, she sat quietly down by the fire, resolved to be very good in the future. She did not sit long, however, for soon a neighing of horses, and the running of girls and children through the camp to meet the hunters, proclaimed their return. All was bustle and gladness throughout the camp. There had been a successful chase, and the led horses were laden with buffalo meat. These horses were led by the young girls to the tents to be unpacked, while the boys took the hunting-horses to water and tether in the grass. Fathers, as they dismounted, took their little children in their arms, tired as they were. Nedawi was as happy as any in the camp, for her seventeen-year-old brother, White Hawk, had killed his first buffalo, and had declared that the skin should become Nedawi's robe, as soon as it was tanned and painted.

What a pleasant evening that was to Nedawi, when the whole family sat around a great fire, roasting the huge buffalo ribs, and she played with her little brother Habazhu, stopping now and then to listen to the adventures of the day, which her father and brothers were relating! The scene was truly a delightful one, the camp-fires lighting up the pleasant family groups here and there, as the flames rose and fell. The bit of prairie where the tribe had camped had a clear little stream running through it, with shadowy hills around, while over all hung the clear, star-lit sky. It seemed as if nature were trying to protect the poor waifs of humanity clustered in that spot. Nedawi felt the beauty of the scene, and was just thinking of nestling down by her father to enjoy it dreamily, when her brothers called for a dance. The little drum was brought forth, and Nedawi danced to its accompaniment and her brothers' singing. She danced gravely, as became a little maiden whose duty it was to entertain the family circle. While she was dancing, a little boy, about her own age, was seen hovering near. He would appear, and, when spoken to, would disappear in the tall, thick grass.

It was Mischief, a playmate of Nedawi's. Everybody called him "Mischief," because mischief appeared in every action of his. It shone from his eyes and played all over his face.

"You little plague," said White Hawk; "what do you want?"

For answer, the "little plague" turned a somersault just out of White Hawk's reach. When the singing was resumed, Mischief crept quietly up behind White Hawk, and, keeping just within the shadow, mimicked Nedawi's grave dancing, and he looked so funny that Nedawi suddenly laughed, which was precisely Mischief's object. But before he could get out of reach, as he intended, Thunder, Nedawi's other brother, who had been having an eye on him, clutched tight hold of him, and Mischief was landed in front of the fire-place, in full view of the whole family. "Now," said Thunder, "you are my prisoner. You stay there and dance with Nedawi." Mischief knew there was no escape, so he submitted with a good grace. He went through all sorts of antics, shaking his fists in the air, twirling suddenly around and putting his head close to the ground, keeping time with the accompaniment through it all.

Nedawi danced staidly on, now and then frowning at him; but she knew of old that he was irrepressible. When Nedawi sat down, he threw into her lap a little dark something and was off like a shot, yelling at the top of his voice, either in triumph at his recent achievements or as a practice for future war-whoops.

"Nedawi, what is it?" said her mother.

Nedawi took it to the fire, when the something proved to be a poor little bird.

"I thought he had something in his hand when he was shaking his fist in the air," said Nedawi's sister, Nazainza, laughing.

"Poor little thing!" said Nedawi; "it is almost dead."

She put its bill into the water, and tenderly tried to make it drink. The water seemed to revive it somewhat.

"I'll wrap it up in something warm," said Nedawi, "and maybe it will sing in the morning."

"Let me see it," said Nedawi's father.

Nedawi carried it to him.

"Don't you feel sorry for it, daughter?"

"Yes, Father," she answered.

"Then take it to the tall grass, yonder, and put it down where no one will step on it, and, as you put it down, say: 'God, I give you back your little bird. As I pity it, pity me.'"

"And will God take care of it?" said Nedawi, reverently, and opening her black eyes wide at the thought.

"Yes," said her father.

"Well, I will do as you say," said Nedawi, and she walked slowly out of the tent.

Then she took it over to the tall, thick grass, and making a nice, cozy little nest for it, left it there, saying just what her father had told her to say. When she came back, she said:

"Father, I said it."

"That was right, little daughter," and Nedawi was happy at her father's commendation.

Nedawi always slept with her grandmother and sister, exactly in the middle of the circle formed by the wigwam, with her feet to the fire-place. That place in the tent was always her grandmother's place, just as the right-hand side of the tent was her father's and mother's and the left-hand her brothers'. There never was any confusion. The tribe was divided into bands, and every band was composed of several families. Each band had its chief, and the whole tribe was ruled by the head-chief, who was Nedawi's father. He had his own particular band besides. Every tent had its own place in the band, and every band had its own particular place in the great circle forming the camp. Each chief was a representative, in council, of the men composing his band, while over all was the head-chief. The executive power was vested in the "soldiers' lodge," and when decisions were arrived at in council, it was the duty of its soldiers to execute all its orders, and punish all violations of the tribal laws. The office of "town-crier" was held by several old men, whose duty it was "to cry out" through the camp the announcements of councils, invitations to feasts, and to give notice of anything in which the whole tribe were called on to take part.

Well, before Nedawi went to sleep this evening, she hugged her grandmother, and said to her:

"Please tell me a story."

Her grandmother said:

"I cannot, because it is summer. In the winter I will tell you stories."

"Why not in summer?" said Nedawi.

"Because, when people tell stories and legends in summer, the snakes come around to listen. You don't want any snakes to come near us to-night, do you?"

"But," said Nedawi, "I have not seen any snakes for the longest time, and if you tell it right softly they won't hear you."

"Nedawi," said her mother, "don't bother your grandmother. She is tired and wants to sleep."

Thereupon Grandmother's heart felt sorry for her pet, and she said to Nedawi:

"Well, if you will keep still and go right to sleep when I am through, I will tell you how the turkeys came to have red eyelids.

"Once upon a time, there was an old woman living all alone with her grandson, Rabbit. He was noted for his cunning and for his tricks, which he played on everyone. One day, the old woman said to him, 'Grandson, I am hungry for some meat.' Then the boy took his bow and arrows, and in the evening he came home with a deer on his shoulders, which he threw at her feet, and said, 'Will that satisfy you?' She said, 'Yes, grandson.' They lived on that meat several days, and, when it was gone, she said to him again, 'Grandson, I am hungry for some meat.' This time he went without his bow and arrows, but he took a bag with him. When he got into the woods, he called all the turkeys together. They gathered around him, and he said to them: 'I am going to sing to you, while you shut your eyes and dance. If one of you opens his eyes while I am singing, his eyelids shall turn red.' Then they all stood in a row, shut their eyes, as he had told them, and began to dance, and this is the song he sang to them while they danced:

> Ha! wadamba thike
> Inshta zhida, inshta zhida,
> Imba theonda,
> Imba theonda.

[The literal translation is:

> Ho! he who peeps
> Red eyes, red eyes,
> Flap your wings,
> Flap your wings.]

"Now, while they were dancing away, with their eyes shut, the boy took them, one by one, and put them into his bag. But the last one in the row began to think it very strange that his companions made no noise, so he gave one peep, screamed in his fright, 'They are making 'way with us!' and flew away. The boy took his bag of turkeys home to his grandmother, but ever after that the turkeys had red eyelids."

Nedawi gave a sigh of satisfaction when the story was finished, and would have asked for more, but just then her brothers came in from a dance which they had been attending in some neighbor's tent. She knew her lullaby time had come. Her brothers always sang before they slept either love or dancing songs, beating time on their breasts, the regular beats making a sort of accompaniment for the singing. Nedawi loved best of all to hear her father's war-songs, for he had a musical voice, and few were the evenings when she had gone to sleep without hearing a lullaby from her father or brothers. Among the Indians, it is

the fathers who sing, instead of the mothers. Women sing only on state occasions, when the tribe have a great dance, or at something of the sort. Mothers "croon" their babies to sleep, instead of singing.

Gradually the singing ceased, and the brothers slept as well as Nedawi, and quiet reigned over the whole camp.[8]

THE INDUSTRIAL WEST: ROMANTICISM

In the late eighteenth century, Immanuel Kant proposed a philosophy that distinguished between a knowable world of sense perceptions and an unknowable world of essences. This reconciliation of philosophical extremes led to a nineteenth-century philosophy focused on the emotions. According to Kant, the real world, so far as humans could possibly rationalize it, is a mental reconstruction, an ideal world of the understanding. Thus, the nature of reality is of the nature of the mind—that is, ideal. This doctrine was called *Kantian idealism* and also *Romanticism* and its reaction against eighteenth-century rationalism permeated both philosophy and the arts. The emphases of Romanticism were individualism, imagination, free expression, of feeling, communion with nature, and the idea of the creative artist as visionary genius. Romanticism saw the artist as possessing ultimate insight into fundamental reality and revealing it, through impassioned self-expression, in a work of art that embodies, however imperfectly, a sublime ideal that transcends the ordinary world. Nature, wild and unspoiled, often became a metaphor for that idealism, and art was seen by some as the highest form of human endeavor.

PAINTING

Romantic painting reflected a striving for freedom from social and artistic rules, coupled with an intense introversion. Formal content was subordinated to expressive intent. As the French novelist Emile Zola (1840–1902) said of Romantic naturalism, "A work of art is part of the universe as seen through a temperament." Closely associated with the French critic and poet Charles Baudelaire (1821–67), Romanticism explored the capacity of color and line to affect the viewer independently of subject matter.

Many Romantic painters are worthy of note, but a detailed look at Ingres, Goya, and Bonheur will suffice for our overview (see also Géricault, p. 53). The art of Jean-Auguste-Dominique Ingres (AHNG-gruh; 1780–1867), and perhaps David as well, illustrates the confusing relationships and conflicts surrounding the Neoclassical and Romantic traditions in painting. Ingres's *Grande Odalisque*, or *Harem Girl* (Fig. **12.10**), has been called both Neoclassical and Romantic, and in many ways it represents both. Ingres professed to despise Romanticism, and yet his subject exudes Romantic individualism, exoticism, and escape. His sensuous textures appear emotional, not intellectual. At the same time, his line is Neoclassically simple, his palette is cool, and his spatial effects are geometric. The linear rhythms of his painting are precise and intellectual in appeal.

The Spanish painter and printmaker Francisco de Goya (GOY-ah; 1746–1828) used his paintings to attack the abuses perpetrated by governments—both the Spanish and the French. His highly imaginative and nightmarish works capture the emotional character of humanity and nature, and often their malevolence. *Execution of the Citizens of Madrid, May 3, 1808* (see Fig. **1.46**) tells a true story. On that date, the citizens of Madrid rebelled against the invading army of Napoleon. People were summarily executed. Using compositional devices to fragment the painting, Goya captures the climactic moment. It is impossible for the viewer to escape the focal point of the painting: the man in white who is about to die.

Goya leads us beyond the death of individuals here. These figures are not realistically depicted people. Napoleon's soldiers are not even human types. Their faces are hidden, and their rigid, repeated forms become a line of subhuman automatons. Goya is making a powerful social and emotional statement. The murky quality of the background strengthens the value contrasts in the painting, and this charges the emotional drama of the scene. Color areas have hard edges, and a stark line of light running diagonally from the oversized lantern to the lower border irrevocably separates executioners and victims. Goya has no sympathy for French soldiers as human beings here; his subjectivity fills the painting.

Rosa Bonheur (buh-NUHR; 1822–99) has been labeled both a Realist and a Romantic in style. Her subjects are mostly animals, and she draws out their raw energy. "Wading in pools of blood," as she puts it, she studied animal anatomy, even in slaughter houses. She was particularly interested in animal psychology. *Plowing in the Nivernais* (Fig. **12.11**) expresses the tremendous power of the oxen on which European agriculture depended before the Industrial Revolution. The beasts appear almost monumental, and each detail is precisely executed. This painting reveals Bonheur's reverence for the dignity of labor and humankind's harmony with nature.

12.10 Jean-Auguste-Dominique Ingres, *Grande Odalisque (Harem Girl)*, 1814. Oil on canvas, 35¼ × 63¾ ins (89.5 × 161.9 cm). Louvre, Paris.

Rosa Bonheur

One of the most significant and prominent women artists of the time, Rosa Bonheur (1822–99) focused her artistic attention almost solely on animals. Born in Bordeaux, France, she was the eldest of four children of an amateur painter. After early instruction from her father, she studied with Léon Cogniet (cuhn-YAY) at the École des Beaux-Arts (ay kohl day boh-ZAHR) in Paris, and soon began to specialize in animal subjects, studying them wherever she could. Her early paintings won awards in Paris, and in 1848 she won a first-class medal for *Plowing in the Nivernais* (Fig. **12.11**). By 1853 her work had reached full maturity, and she received high acclaim in Europe and the United States. Her paintings were much admired and she became widely known through engraved copies. She was also well known as a sculptor, and her animal subjects led to her success among her contemporary French sculptors.

Rosa Bonheur had an independent spirit, perhaps typical of the Romantic artist, and fought to gain acceptance on a level equal to that of male artists of the time. Her ability and popularity earned her the title of Chevalier of the Legion of Honor in 1865, and she was the first woman to receive the Grand Cross of the Legion. Befriended by Queen Victoria of Britain, who became her patron, Bonheur was also a favorite among the British aristocracy, although her last years were spent in France, and she died near Fontainebleau in 1899.

12.11 Rosa Bonheur, *Plowing in the Nivernais*, 1849. Oil on canvas, 5 ft 9 ins × 8 ft 8 ins (1.75 × 2.64 m). Musée Nationale du Château de Fontainebleau, France.

SCULPTURE

Romantic sculpture never developed into a uniform style. Those works not clearly of the Neoclassical and Rococo traditions show a generally eclectic spirit and a uniformly undistinguished character. There may be a reasonable explanation for such a phenomenon in Romantic idealism, whose strivings after nature and the far away and long ago cannot easily be translated into sculptural expression.

The term Romantic is often applied loosely to almost anything of the nineteenth century, and this is the case with the most remarkable sculptor of the era, Auguste Rodin (ruh-DAN; 1840–1917). Rodin's textures, more than anything else, reflect Impressionism (see p. 357)—his surfaces appear to shimmer as light plays on their irregular features. They are more than reflective surfaces—they give his works dynamic and dramatic qualities. *The Thinker* (Fig. **12.12**) shows the difficulty inherent in attempting to put into sculptural form what painters like Monet (muh-NAY) were trying to do with color and texture (see Fig. **12.27**). Although Rodin used

12.12
Auguste Rodin, *The Thinker*, first modeled c. 1880, executed c. 1910. Bronze, height 27½ ins (70 cm). Metropolitan Museum of Art, New York (Gift of Thomas F. Ryan).

a fair degree of lifelikeness, he nevertheless presented a reality beneath the surface.

LITERATURE

The beginning of the main phase of Romantic literature can be dated to around 1790. One characteristic was the tendency of writers, such as the Germans Johann Wolfgang von Goethe (1749–1832) and Friedrich Schiller (1759–1805), to form groups or partnerships. Britain produced major literary figures, especially poets: Wordsworth, Blake, Coleridge, Scott, Byron, Shelley, and Keats, of whom we will examine only Wordsworth.

William Wordsworth (1770–1850) charged the commonplace and everyday with transcendental and often indefinable significance. He created a new world of beauty through his closeness to nature and in the harmony he felt existed between humanity and nature. In 1795, he met the English poet Samuel Taylor Coleridge (1772–1834), and this friendship opened up his life and writing. Out of it came the *Lyrical Ballads*, which Wordsworth published anonymously along with four poems by Coleridge. Among these ballads, "Tintern Abbey" reveals Wordsworth's love of nature. That love is first seen as a sensuous animal passion, then as a moral influence, and finally as a mystical communion.

Lines Composed a Few Miles above Tintern Abbey, on Revisiting the Banks of the Wye during a Tour, July 13, 1798
William Wordsworth
1770–1850

Five years have past; five summers, with the length
Of five long winters! and again I hear
These waters, rolling from their mountain-springs
With a soft inland murmur.—Once again
Do I behold these steep and lofty cliffs,
That on a wild secluded scene impress
Thoughts of more deep seclusion; and connect
The landscape with the quiet of the sky.
The day is come when I again repose
Here, under this dark sycamore, and view
These plots of cottage-ground, these orchard-tufts,
Which at this season, with their unripe fruits,
Are clad in one green hue, and lose themselves
'Mid groves and copses. Once again I see
These hedge-rows, hardly hedge-rows, little lines
Of sportive wood run wild: these pastoral farms,
Green to the very door; and wreaths of smoke
Sent up, in silence, from among the trees!

With some uncertain notice, as might seem
Of vagrant dwellers in the houseless woods,
Or of some Hermit's cave, where by his fire
The Hermit sits alone.

These beauteous forms,
Through a long absence, have not been to me
As is a landscape to a blind man's eye:
But oft, in lonely rooms, and 'mid the din
Of towns and cities, I have owed to them
In hours of weariness, sensations sweet,
Felt in the blood, and felt along the heart;
And passing even into my purer mind,
With tranquil restoration:—feelings too
Of unremembered pleasure: such, perhaps,
As have no slight or trivial influence
On that best portion of a good man's life,
Into a sober pleasure; when thy mind
Shall be a mansion for all lovely forms,
Thy memory be as a dwelling-place
For all sweet sounds and harmonies; oh! then,
If solitude, or fear, or pain, or grief,
Should be thy portion, with what healing thoughts
Of tender joy wilt thou remember me,
And these my exhortations! Nor, perchance—
If I should be where I no more can hear
Thy voice, nor catch from thy wild eyes these gleams
Of past existence—wilt thou then forget
That on the banks of this delightful stream
We stood together; and that I, so long
A worshipper of Nature, hither came
Unwearied in that service: rather say
With warmer love—oh! with far deeper zeal
Of holier love. Nor wilt thou then forget,
That after many wanderings, many years
Of absence, these steep woods and lofty cliffs,
And this green pastoral landscape, were to me
More dear, both for themselves and for thy sake![9]

Jane Austen (1775–1817) lived and worked in the high years of the major English Romantics, but she shunned the Romantic cult of personality and remained largely indifferent to Romantic literature. She looked back to Neoclassicism and the comedy of manners as her sources, and her work portrays middle-class people living in provincial towns and going about the daily routine of family life—a life of good breeding, wit, and a reasonable hope that difficulties can be resolved in a satisfactory manner. She occasionally portrayed disappointments in love and threatened or actual seduction, but, somehow, these seem less important than the ongoing and routine conversations and rituals of daily life. Merely because she portrayed a quiet form of life does not mean, however,

that her characters lack depth or interest. She explored human experience deeply and with humor. She proved that one does not require spectacular events in order to provide engaging art.

Her early years produced a variety of works that parody the sentimental and romantic clichés of popular fiction. In her second period of writing, from 1810 on, she crowned her career with works such as *Emma* (1815), *Persuasion* (1818), and *Mansfield Park* (1813). *Emma* shows Jane Austen's ability to remain detached from her heroine, Emma Woodhouse, who represents self-deception, as she misreads evidence, misleads others, and discovers her own feelings only by accident. In her other works, Austen portrayed many gentle and self-effacing characters in the mode of her earlier masterpiece *Pride and Prejudice* (1813).

MUSIC

In an era of Romantic subjectivity, music provided the medium in which many found an unrivaled opportunity to express emotion. In trying to express human emotion, Romantic music made stylistic changes to Classical music, and although Romanticism amounted to rebellion in many of the arts, in music it involved a more gradual and natural extension of Classical principles.

As in painting, spontaneity replaced control, but the primary emphasis of music in this era was on beautiful, lyrical, and expressive *melody*. Phrases became longer, more irregular, and more complex than they had been in Classical music. Much Romantic rhythm was traditional, but experiments produced new meters and patterns. Emotional conflict was often suggested by juxtaposing different meters, and rhythmic irregularity became increasingly common as the century progressed.

Romantic composers emphasized colorful harmonies and instrumentation. Harmony was seen as a means of expression, and any previous "laws" regarding key relationships could be broken to achieve striking emotional effects. Harmonies became increasingly complex, and traditional distinctions between major and minor keys were blurred in chromatic harmonies, complicated chords, and modulations to distant keys. In fact, some composers used key changes so frequently that their compositions are virtually nothing but whirls of continuous modulation.

As composers sought to disrupt the listener's expectations, more and more dissonance occurred, until it became an important focus of the music. Dissonance was explored for its own sake, as a strong stimulant of emotional response rather than merely as a decorative way to get to the traditional tonic chord. By the end of the

MASTERWORK

Jane Austen, *Pride and Prejudice*

Pride and Prejudice (1813) contains little of the satire of works of the same period, but an ironic and sympathetic view of human nature and its propensity for comic incongruity. The narrative, which Austen originally titled "First Impressions," describes the clash between Elizabeth Bennet, the daughter of a country gentleman, and Fitzwilliam Darcy, a rich and aristocratic landowner. Austen reverses the convention of first impressions: "pride" of rank and fortune, and "prejudice" against Elizabeth's inferiority of family, hold Darcy aloof; while Elizabeth is equally fired both by the pride of self-respect and by prejudice against Darcy's snobbery. Ultimately they come together in love and self-understanding.

The central comedy of *Pride and Prejudice* lies in the fully developed character that reveals a sense of human realities and values. For example, in the character of Mr. Bennet, Austen makes a symbolic comment on intelligence that exists without will or drive. In her two opposing protagonists, Darcy and Elizabeth, who reflect the title of the book, Austen depicts character overlaid with class superciliousness and character abounding in independence and sharpness of mind that acts with prejudgment, wrong-headedness, and self-satisfaction. In all situations, Jane Austen remains detached, witty, and good-humored. Her disturbances are minor intrusions in an unshakable moral universe in which one can point out an entire range of human frailties and yet not despair.

In the story, as summarized in *The Bloomsbury Guide to English Literature* (Prentice Hall, 1990), Mr. and Mrs. Bennet belong to the minor gentry and live at Longbourn, near London. Mr. Bennet is witty and intelligent, and bored with his foolish wife. They have five daughters, whose marriage prospects are Mrs. Bennet's chief interest in life, since the estate is "entailed"—i.e. by the law of the period it will go on Mr. Bennet's death to his nearest male relation, a sycophantic clergyman called Mr. Collins. The main part of the story is concerned with the relationship between the witty and attractive Elizabeth Bennet and the haughty and fastidious Fitzwilliam Darcy, who at first considers her beneath his notice and later, on coming to the point of asking her to marry him, finds that she is resolutely prejudiced against him.

Elizabeth is subjected to an insolent offer of marriage by Mr. Collins and the arrogant condescension of his patroness, Lady Catherine de Bourgh, Darcy's aunt. In the end, chastened by finding in one another a fastidiousness and pride that equal their own and despite a family scandal, they are united.

Romantic period, the exhaustion of chromatic usage and dissonance had led to a search for a completely different type of tonal system.

Exploring musical color to elicit feeling was as important to the Romantic musician as it was to the painter. Interest in tonal color, or timbre, led to great diversity in vocal and instrumental performance, and the music of this period abounds with solo works and exhibits a tremendous increase in the size and diversity of the orchestra. We have many options in how we might go about exploring Romantic music, none of which we could pursue exhaustively. We will proceed by isolating some major genres and, within them, noting major composers as we pass. These choices remain arbitrary. More composers might be examined, but, again, this is a buffet: a sample provides a taste of the whole.

Lieder

In many ways, the "art song," or *Lied* (leed; see Chapter 3), characterized Romantic music. A composition for solo voice with piano accompaniment and poetic text allowed for a variety of lyrical and dramatic expressions and linked music directly with literature.

The burst of German lyric poetry in this period encouraged the growth of *Lieder*. Literary nuances affected music, and music added deeper emotional implications to the poem. This partnership had various results: some *Lieder* were complex, others were simple; some were structured, others were freely composed. The pieces themselves depended on a close relationship between the piano and the voice. In many ways, the piano was an inseparable part of the experience, and certainly it served as more than accompaniment, for the piano explored

Wer rei - tet so spät durch Nacht und Wind?

12.13 Franz Schubert, *The Erlking* (excerpt).

mood and established rhythmic and thematic material, and sometimes had solo passages of its own. The interdependency of the song and its accompaniment is basic to the art song.

The earliest, and perhaps the most important, composer of *Lieder* was Franz Schubert (1797–1828). Schubert's troubled life epitomized the Romantic view of the artist's desperate and isolated condition. Known only among a close circle of friends and musicians, Schubert composed almost one thousand works, from symphonies to sonatas and operas, to masses, choral compositions, and *Lieder*. None of his work was publicly performed, however, until the year of his death. He took his *Lieder* texts from a wide variety of poems, and in each case the melodic contours, harmonies, rhythms, and structures of the music were determined by the poem.

Schubert's song *Der Erlkönig* (*The Erlking*, 1815; music CD track 14; Fig. **12.13**) provides an excellent example both of Schubert's work and of Romantic music in general. The song consists of a musical setting of a poem about the supernatural by Goethe. Schubert uses a *through-composed setting*—that is, he writes new music for each stanza—in order to capture the poem's mounting excitement. The piano plays the role of an important partner in transmitting the mood of the piece, creating tension with rapid octaves and menacing bass motif. Imaginative variety in the music allows Schubert's soloist to sound like several characters in the dramatic development.

Who rides so late through the night and the wind?
It is the father with his child;
He folds the boy close in his arms,
He clasps him securely, he holds him warmly.

"My son, why do you hide your face so anxiously?"
"Father, don't you see the Erlking?
The Erlking with his crown and his train?"
"My son, it's a streak of mist."

"Dear child, come, go with me!
I'll play the prettiest games with you.
Many-colored flowers grow along the shore;
My mother has many golden garments."

"My father, my father, and don't you hear
The Erlking whispering promises to me?"

"Be quiet, stay quiet, my child;
The wind is rustling in the dead leaves."

"My handsome boy, will you come with me?
My daughters shall wait upon you;
My daughters lead off in the dance every night,
And cradle and dance and sing you to sleep."

"My father, my father, and don't you see there
The Erlking's daughters in the shadows?"
"My son, my son, I see it clearly;
The old willows look so gray."

"I love you, your beautiful figure delights me!
And if you are not willing, then I shall use force!"
"My father, my father, now he is taking hold of me!
The Erlking has hurt me!"

The father shudders, he rides swiftly on;
He holds in his arms the groaning child,
He reaches the courtyard weary and anxious:
In his arms the child was dead.

Translated by Philip L. Miller

Piano Works

The development of the art song depended in no small way on nineteenth-century improvements in piano design. The instrument for which Schubert wrote had a much warmer, richer tone than earlier pianos, and improvements in pedal technique made sustained tones possible and gave the instrument greater lyrical potential.

Such flexibility made the piano an excellent instrument for accompaniment, and, more importantly, made it an almost ideal solo instrument. As a result, new works were composed solely for the piano, ranging from short, intimate pieces, similar to *Lieder*, to larger works designed to exhibit great virtuosity in performance. Franz Schubert wrote such pieces, as did Franz Liszt (1811–86). Liszt was one of the most celebrated pianists of the nineteenth century and one of its most innovative composers. He enthralled audiences with his expressive, dramatic playing, and taught most of the major pianists of the next generation. He also influenced Richard Wagner (vahgh-nuhr) and Richard Strauss. His piano works include six *Paganini Études* (1851), concertos, and twenty *Hungarian Rhapsodies* based on Hungarian urban popular music rather than folk music. The technical demands of Liszt's compositions, and the rather florid way he performed them, gave rise to a theatricality, the primary purpose of which was to impress audiences with flashy presentation. This fitted well with the Romantic concept of the artist as hero.

The compositions of Frédéric Chopin (sho-pan; 1810–49) were somewhat more restrained. Chopin wrote

12.14 Frédéric Chopin, *Nocturne in E flat major*, Op. 9, No. 2, first theme.

almost exclusively for the piano. Each of his *Études* (AY-tood; studies) explored a single technical problem, usually set around a single motif. More than simple exercises, these works explored the possibilities of the instrument and became short tone poems in their own right. A second group of compositions included short intimate works such as preludes, nocturnes, and impromptus, and dances such as waltzes, polonaises, and mazurkas. (Chopin was Polish but lived in France, and Polish folk music had a particularly strong influence on him.) A final class of larger works included scherzos, ballades, and fantasies. Chopin's compositions are highly individual, many without precedent. His style is almost totally without standard form. His melodies are lyrical, and his moods vary greatly.

Chopin's nocturnes, or night pieces, are among his most celebrated works. His *Nocturne in E flat major* Op. 9, No. 2 (1833; music CD track 15) illustrates the structure and style of this sort of mood piece well. It has a number of sections, with a main theme alternating with a second until both give way to a third. The piece has a complex AA'BA''B'A'''CC' structure. The nocturne is in andante tempo, a moderate, walking speed, and begins with the most important theme (Fig. **12.14**).

The melody is very graceful and lyrical over its supporting chords. The contours of the melody alternately use pitches that are close together and widely spaced. The theme is stated, then immediately repeated with ornamentation. The second theme begins in the dominant key of B flat major and returns to E flat for a more elaborate repeat of the first theme. The second theme is restated, and followed by an even more elaborate restatement of the first theme, leading to a dramatic climax in the home key. A third theme is presented and then repeated more elaborately in the tonic key. The work ends with a short cadenza, which builds through a crescendo and finishes pianissimo, very softly.

Program Music

One of the new ways in which Romantic composers structured their longer works was to build them around a nonmusical story, a picture, or some other idea. Music of this sort is called "descriptive." When the idea is quite specific and closely followed throughout the piece, the music is called "programmatic" or "program music."

These techniques were not entirely new—we have already noted the descriptive elements in Beethoven's "Pastoral" Symphony—but the Romantics found them particularly attractive and employed them with great gusto. A nonmusical idea allowed composers to rid themselves of formal structure altogether. Of course, actual practice varied tremendously—some used programmatic material as their only structural device, while others subordinated a program idea to formal structure. Nevertheless, the Romantic period has become known as the "age of program music." Among the best-known composers of program music were Hector Berlioz (1803–69) and Richard Strauss (1864–1949).

Berlioz's *Symphonie Fantastique* (1830) employed a single motif, called an *idée fixe* (ee-DAY feex), to tie the five movements of the work together. The story on which the musical piece is based involves a hero who has poisoned himself because of unrequited love. However, the drug only sends him into semi-consciousness, in which he has visions. Throughout these visions the recurrent musical theme (the *idée fixe*) symbolizes his beloved. Movement 1 consists of "Reveries" and "Passions."

12.15 Hector Berlioz, from *Symphonie Fantastique*, fourth movement: A. "March to the Scaffold"; B. *idée fixe*.

Movement 2 represents "A Ball." "In the Country" is movement 3, in which he imagines a pastoral scene. In movement 4, "March to the Scaffold" (Fig. **12.15**; music CD track 16), he dreams he has killed his beloved and is about to be executed. The *idée fixe* returns at the end of the movement and is abruptly shattered by the fall of the axe. The final movement describes a "Dream of a Witches' Sabbath" in grotesque and orgiastic musical imagery.

Not all program music depends for its interest upon an understanding of its text. Many people believe, however, that the tone poems, or symphonic poems, of Richard Strauss require an understanding of the story. His *Don Juan*, *Till Eulenspiegel*, and *Don Quixote* draw such detailed material from specific legends that program explanations and comments are integral to the works and help to give them coherence. In *Till Eulenspiegels lustige Streiche* (*Till Eulenspiegel's Merry Pranks*), Strauss tells the legendary German story of Till Eulenspiegel and his practical jokes. Till is traced through three escapades, all musically identifiable. He is then confronted by his critics and finally executed. Throughout, the musical references are quite specific.

Symphonies

Beethoven's powerful symphonies strongly influenced nineteenth-century composers. Schubert, whom we just discussed as a composer of *Lieder*, wrote eight symphonies, one of which, the so-called "Unfinished" (B Minor) has a darkly Romantic style. Hector Berlioz's *Symphonie Fantastique* (see above) illustrated that a symphony could be written in an entirely different manner from Beethoven's. Felix Mendelssohn (1809–47) followed Classical tradition in most of his symphonies, but we should note that although Classical form was followed in many Romantic symphonies, the form was employed more as a means to a Romantically expressive end and not for its own sake.

An outstanding example of the Romantic symphony is Brahms's *Symphony No. 3 in F major* (1883). Composed in four movements, the work calls for pairs of flutes, oboes, clarinets, a bassoon, a contrabassoon, four horns, two trumpets, three trombones, two timpani, and strings—not an adventurous grouping of instruments for the period. Composed in sonata form, the first movement is allegro con brio (fast with spirit), and begins in F major (Fig. 12.16).

The exposition section closes with a return to the opening motif and meter, employing rising scales and arpeggios. Then, following Classical tradition, the exposition is repeated.

The development section uses both the principal themes, with changes in tonal colors, dynamics, and modulation. The recapitulation opens with a forceful

12.16 Johannes Brahms, *Symphony No. 3 in F major*, opening motif of first movement.

restatement of the opening motif, followed by a restatement and further development of materials from the exposition. Then comes a lengthy coda, again announced by the opening motif, and based on the first theme. A final, quiet, restatement of the opening motif and first phrase of the theme brings the first movement to an end.

Trends

The Romantic period also gave birth to new trends in music. The roots of such movements went deep into the past, but composers also wrote with the political circumstances of the century in mind. Folk tunes appear in these works as themes, as do local rhythms and harmonies. The exaltation of national identity was consistent with Romantic requirements, and it occurs in the music of nineteenth-century Russia, Bohemia, Spain, Britain, Scandinavia, Germany, and Austria.

Of all the composers of the Romantic period, the Russian Peter Ilyich Tchaikovsky (chy-KAWF-skee; 1840–93) has enjoyed the greatest popularity with his *1812 Overture* perhaps topping the list, followed closely by his *Nutcracker* ballet. In his First Symphony, he imitates the lyricism of Russian folk song, and the traits of the nineteenth-century Russian salon song can be found in his Fifth and Sixth Symphonies.

The *symphonic poem*, an offshoot of the symphony proper, was a term invented by Franz Liszt to describe a series of orchestral works he wrote which take their musical form and rhetoric from nonabstract ideas, some of them poetic and others visual. Other composers followed Liszt's lead, and the model proved especially popular in topics stemming from nationalistic sources, among them Smetana (*My Country*), Dvořák (*The Noonday Witch*), Borodin (*In the Steppes of Central Asia*), Sibelius (*Tapiola*), and Elgar (*Falstaff*).

Choral Music

Vocal music ranged from solo to massive ensemble works. The emotional requirements of Romanticism were well served by the diverse timbres and lyricism of the human voice. Almost every major composer of the era wrote some form of vocal music. Franz Schubert is remembered for his masses, the most notable of which is the *Mass in A flat major*. Felix Mendelssohn's *Elijah* stands beside Handel's *Messiah* and Haydn's *Creation* as a masterpiece of oratorio. Hector Berlioz marshaled full Romantic power for his *Requiem*, which called for 210 voices, a large orchestra, and four brass bands.

One of the most enduring popular choral works of the Romantic period is Brahms's *Ein Deutsches Requiem* (*A*

PROFILE

Johannes Brahms

Although he was born into an impoverished family, Johannes Brahms (1833-97) appears to have had a relatively happy childhood. His father was an itinerant musician, who eked out a meager living playing the horn and double bass in taverns and nightclubs. The family lived in the slums of Hamburg, Germany, but, despite their economic hardships, they retained close and loving family relationships. Early in life, Johannes showed evidence of considerable musical talent, and the eminent piano teacher Eduard Marxsen agreed to teach him without pay.

By the time he was twenty Brahms had gained acclaim as a pianist and accepted an invitation to participate in a concert tour with the Hungarian violinist Eduard Remenyi. The event was invaluable to the young Brahms, because it introduced him to Franz Liszt and Robert Schumann, and through Schumann's efforts Brahms was able to publish several of his compositions, which opened the door to the wider artistic world and launched his prolific career. Brahms gained experience as musical director at the little court of Detmold and as founder and director of a women's chorus in Hamburg, for which he wrote several choral works. His musical creativity showed a deep love of folk music and a sensitivity of expression. He mastered German *Lieder* and remained devoted to the Romantic style throughout his career, notwithstanding his fondness for clarity of structure and form based in the Classical style of the previous century.

Although Brahms wanted to stay in Hamburg, he was passed over for a position, and, feeling betrayed and neglected by his native town, he moved to Vienna. That city's rich musical ambience enriched his talent and experience, and he gained tremendous success, serving as director of the Vienna Singakademie and as conductor of the Society of Friends of Music. In 1875, he resigned his positions and spent the rest of his days in creative endeavors. For the next twenty-two years, he sacrificed his personal life in pursuit of his career, and the results gained him—in his own lifetime—recognition as one of the world's greatest artists.

His work spanned several idioms, from solo piano compositions and chamber music to full orchestral works. He was never interested in music for the stage nor in program music, but he reveled in symphonic compositions ruled by purely musical ideas, favoring absolute music.

German Requiem). Based on selected texts from the Bible, in contrast with the Latin liturgy of traditional requiems, Brahms's work is not so much a mass for the dead as a consolation for the living. It is principally a choral work—the solos are minimal: two for baritone and one for soprano—but both vocal and instrumental writing are very expressive. Soaring melodic lines and rich harmonies weave thick textures. After the chorus sings "All mortal flesh is as the grass," the orchestra suggests fields of grass moving in the wind. The lyrical movement, "How lovely is thy dwelling place," soars with emotion. Brahms's *Requiem* begins and ends with moving passages aimed directly at the living: "Blest are they that mourn." Hope and consolation underlie the entire work.

An important factor in Brahms's music is its lyricism and its vocal beauty. Brahms explored the voice as a human voice, and not as another instrument or some other mechanism unaffected by any restrictions, as other composers have done. His parts are written and his words chosen so that no voice is ever required to sing outside its natural range or technical capacity.

Opera

The spirit and style of Romanticism are summed up in that perfect synthesis of all the arts, opera. Three countries, France (especially Paris), Italy, and Germany, dominated the development of opera.

Paris occupied an important position in Romantic opera during the first half of the nineteenth century. The spectacular quality of opera and the size of its auditoriums had made it an effective vehicle for propaganda during the Revolution, and as an art form, opera enjoyed great popular appeal among the rising and influential middle classes.

A new type of opera, called "grand opera," emerged early in the nineteenth century, principally through the efforts of Louis Veron, a businessman, the playwright

Eugène Scribe, and Giacomo Meyerbeer, a composer. These three broke away from Classical themes and subject matter and staged spectacular productions with crowd scenes, ballets, choruses, and fantastic scenery, written around medieval and contemporary themes. Meyerbeer (1791–1864), a German, studied Italian opera in Venice and produced French opera in Paris. *Robert the Devil* and *The Huguenots* typify Meyerbeer's extravagant style; they achieved great popular success, although the composer Schumann called *The Huguenots* "a conglomeration of monstrosities." Berlioz's *The Trojans*, written in the late 1850s, was more Classically based and more musically controlled. At the same time, Jacques Offenbach (1819–80) brought to the stage a lighter style (*opéra comique*; see p. 93) in which spoken dialogue was mixed with the music. Offenbach used vaudeville humor to satirize other operas, popular events, and so forth. In between the styles of Meyerbeer and Offenbach there was a third form of Romantic opera, lyric opera. Ambroise Thomas (1811–96) and Charles Gounod (1818–93) turned to Romantic drama and fantasy for their plots. Thomas's *Mignon* contains highly lyrical passages, and Gounod's *Faust*, based on Goethe's play, stresses melodic beauty.

Early Romantic opera in Italy featured the *bel canto* style, which emphasizes beauty of sound, and the works of Gioacchino Rossini (1792–1868) epitomize this feature. Rossini's *The Barber of Seville* takes melodic singing to new heights with light, ornamented, and highly appealing work, particularly for his soprano voices.

Great artists often stand apart from or astride general stylistic trends while they explore their own themes. Such is the case with the Italian composer Giuseppe Verdi (1813–1901). With Verdi, opera is truly a human drama, expressed through simple, beautiful melody.

In what might be described as typical of Romanticism, Verdi dared to make an operatic hero out of a hunchbacked court jester—Rigoletto—whose only redeeming quality seems to be his great love for his daughter, Gilda. Rigoletto's master is the licentious duke of Mantua, who, while posing as a poor student, wins Gilda's love. When the duke seduces the innocent girl, Rigoletto plots his

death. Despite the seduction, Gilda loves the dissolute duke and ultimately gives her life to save his. Virtue does not triumph in this opera.

Act Three contains one of the most popular of all operatic arias, "La donna è mobile" ("Woman is fickle"; Fig. **12.17**; music CD track 17):

Woman is fickle
Like a feather in the wind,
She changes her words
And her thoughts.
Always a lovable
And lovely face,
Weeping or laughing,
Is lying.
Woman is fickle, etc.
The man's always wretched
Who believes in her,
Who recklessly entrusts
His heart to her!
And yet no one who never
Drinks love on that breast
Ever feels
Entirely happy!
Woman is fickle, etc.

Late in his career, Verdi wrote works such as *Aïda* (1871), grand operas of spectacular proportions built upon tightly woven dramatic structures. Finally, in a third phase, he produced operas based on Shakespearean plays. *Otello* (1887) contrasts tragedy and *opera buffa*—comic opera, not *opéra comique*—and explores subtle balances among voices and orchestra, together with strong melodic development.

Richard Wagner (1813–83) was one of the masters of Romantic opera. At the heart of Wagner's artistry lay a philosophy that has affected the stage from the mid-nineteenth century to the present day. His ideas were laid out principally in two books, *Art and Revolution* (1849) and *Opera and Drama* (1851). Wagner's philosophy centered on the *Gesamtkunstwerk* (geh-ZAMT-koonst-VAIRK), a comprehensive work of art in which music, poetry, and scenery are all subservient to the central generating idea. For Wagner, the total unity of all elements was supremely important. In line with German Romantic philosophy, which gives music supremacy over the other arts, music has the predominant role in Wagner's operas. Dramatic meaning unfolds through the *Leitmotif* (LYT-moh-TEEF), for which Wagner is famous, although he did not invent it. A *Leitmotif* is a musical theme that is tied to an idea, a person, or an object. Whenever that idea, person, or object appears on stage or comes to mind in the action, that theme is heard. Juxtaposing *Leitmotifs* gives

12.17 Giuseppe Verdi, "La donna è mobile," from *Rigoletto* (1851).

the audience an idea of relationships between their subjects. *Leitmotifs* also give the composer building blocks to use for development, recapitulation, and unification. The sweeping strains of an excerpt ("Liebestod") from the opera *Tristan und Isolde* (music CD track 18) can only suggest to us the power of Wagner's music.

Each of Wagner's magnificent operas deserves detailed attention. Anything we might say here by way of description or analysis would be insignificant compared to the dramatic power these works exhibit in full production. Even recordings cannot approach the tremendous effect of these works on stage in an opera house.

THEATRE

"The play-going world of the West End is at this moment occupied in rubbing its eyes, that it may recover completely from the dazzle of Thursday last, when, amid the acclamations of Queen Victoria's subjects, King Richard the Second was enthroned at the Princess's Theatre." Thus began the reviewer's comments in *The Spectator*, March 14, 1857. The dazzle of scenery, revivals, and a pot-pourri of uncertain accomplishments helped a stumbling theatre to keep up with the other arts that flourished through the early years of the nineteenth century.

Popularism and Historical Accuracy

Romanticism as a philosophy of art was its own worst enemy in the theatre. Artists sought new forms to express great truths, and they strove to free themselves from Neoclassical rules and restraints. They did, however, admire Shakespeare as an example of new ideals and as a symbol of freedom from structural confinement. Intuition reigned, and the artistic genius was set apart from everyday people and above normal constraints. As a result, Romantic writers had no use for any guide but their own imagination.

Unfortunately, the theatre operates within some rather specific limits. Many nineteenth-century playwrights penned scripts that were unstageable and/or unplayable, and great writers could not or would not abide by constraints of the stage, while the hacks, yielding to popular taste, could not resist overindulgence in phony emotionalism, melodrama, and stage gimmickry. As a result, the best Romantic theatre performances came from the pen of William Shakespeare, whose work was revived in a great rush of nineteenth-century antiquarianism.

Poor as it may have been in original drama, the Romantic period did succeed in loosening the arbitrary rules of Neoclassical convention. Thus, it paved the way for a new theatrical era in the later years of the century.

12.18 Charles Kean's production of Shakespeare's *Richard II*, London, 1857. Between Acts III and IV, the Entry of Bolingbroke into London. Contemporary watercolor by Thomas Grieve. Victoria & Albert Museum, London.

The audiences of the nineteenth century played a significant part in determining what took the stage. Royal patronage was gone, and box office receipts were needed to pay the bills. A rising middle class had swelled the eighteenth-century audience and changed its character. Then, in the nineteenth century, the lower classes began attending the theatre. The Industrial Revolution had created larger urban populations and expanded public education to a degree. As feelings of egalitarianism spread throughout Europe and America, theatre audiences grew, and theatre building flourished. To appeal to this diverse audience, theatre managers had to put on plays for the popular as well as the sophisticated taste if they wanted to make money, so to offer something for everyone, an evening's theatre program might contain several types of fare and last over five hours. The consequence was predictable. Fewer and fewer sophisticated patrons chose to attend, and the quality of the productions declined.

By 1850, theatres began to specialize, and sophisticated playgoers came back to certain theatres, although the multipart production remained typical until nearly the turn of the twentieth century. Audience demand was high, and theatre continued to expand.

After the Civil War a number of African American theatre companies emerged, featuring artists such as Anna and Emma Hyers, classically trained actors from California. In 1884, J. A. Arneaux founded the Astor Place Company of Colored Tragedians, who performed a repertory of Shakespearean plays. By the turn of the twentieth century, African Americans had made notable contributions to straight drama in the works of such playwrights as William Edgar Easton, who wrote historical plays.

Although theatre design was by now very diverse, some general similarities existed. Principally, the changes in nineteenth-century stages and staging were prompted by increased interest in historical accuracy and popular demand for depiction rather than convention. Before the eighteenth century, history had been considered irrelevant to art. Knowledge of antiquity that began with archeological excavations in Pompeii, however, aroused curiosity, and the Romantic dream of escape to the long ago and far away suggested that the stage picture of exotic places should be somehow believable. At first, such detail was used inconsistently, but, by 1823, some productions claimed that they were entirely historical in every respect. Attempts at historical accuracy had begun as early as 1801, and in France, Victor Hugo and Alexandre Dumas *père* insisted on historically accurate settings and costumes during the early years of the century. However, it was Charles Kean (1811–68) who brought the spectacle of antiquarianism in the London theatre to fruition in the 1850s (Fig. **12.18**).

The onset of accuracy as a standard for production led to three-dimensionality in settings and away from drop and wing scenery to the box set. The stage floor was leveled—since the Renaissance it had been raked—and new methods of shifting and rigging were devised to meet specific staging problems. Over a period of years, all elements of the production became integrated, much in the spirit of Wagner's totally unified artwork, the *Gesamtkunstwerk*. The distraction of numerous scene changes was eliminated by closing the curtain.

Melodrama

On the popular side, nineteenth-century theatre developed a Romantically exaggerated form called *melodrama*.

Melodrama (see Chapter 4) was popular throughout Europe and the United States. *Uncle Tom's Cabin*, based on the novel by Harriet Beecher Stowe (1852), took the stage by storm. The stage version was opposed by Stowe, but copyright laws did not exist to protect her. The play does retain her complex themes of slavery, religion, and love. The action involves a number of episodes, some of which are rather loosely connected. Characteristic of melodrama, *Uncle Tom's Cabin* places considerable emphasis on spectacle, the most popular of which at the time was Eliza's crossing of the ice with mules, horses, and bloodhounds in pursuit. The stage version of *Ben Hur*, meanwhile, went so far as to depict a chariot race, with live horses and moveable treadmills for the chariots to pass each other.

BALLET

In a totally unrehearsed move, a ballerina leaped from the tomb on which she posed and narrowly escaped a piece of falling scenery. This and other disasters plagued the opening night performance of Meyerbeer's *Robert the Devil* in 1831. The novelty of tenors falling into trapdoors, and falling stagelights and scenery, however, was eclipsed by the startling novelty of the choreography for this opera. Romantic ballet was at hand. To varying degrees, all the arts turned against the often cold formality of Classicism and Neoclassicism. The subjective (not the objective) viewpoint and feeling (rather than reason) sought release.

Two sources are helpful in understanding the Romantic ballet, the writings of Théophile Gautier (goh-TYAY) and Carlo Blasis (blah-SEE). Gautier (1811–72) was a poet and critic, and his aesthetic principles held first of all that beauty was truth, a central Romantic conception. Gautier believed that dance was visual stimulation to show "beautiful forms in graceful attitudes." Dancing for Gautier was like a living painting or sculpture—"physical

12.19 Illustrations from *The Art of Dancing*, 1820, by Carlo Blasis. The New York Public Library.

12.20 Marie Taglioni (1804–84). Engraving, 1834. The New York Public Library.

pleasure and feminine beauty." This exclusive focus on ballerinas placed sensual enjoyment and eroticism squarely at the center of his aesthetics. Gautier's influence was significant, and it accounted for the central role of the ballerina in Romantic ballet. Male dancers were relegated to the background, strength being the only grace permissible to them.

The second general premise for Romantic ballet came from *Code of Terpsichore* (tuhrp-SIH-kuh-ree) by Carlo Blasis (1803–78). Blasis was much more systematic and specific than Gautier—he was a former dancer—and his principles covered training, structure, and positioning. Everything in the ballet required a beginning, a middle, and an ending. The basic "attitude" in dance, which was modeled on Giovanni Bologna's statue of *Mercury* (Fig. 2.7), was to stand on one leg with the other brought up behind at a 90-degree angle with the knee bent. The dancer needed to display the human figure with taste and elegance. If the dancer trained each part of the body, the

result would be grace without affectation. From Blasis comes the turned-out position, which is still fundamental to ballet today (Fig. **12.19**; see also Fig. **6.2**). These broad principles provided the framework, and, to a great extent, a summary, of objectives for Romantic ballet: delicate ballerinas, lightly poised, costumed in soft tulle, and moving *en pointe*, with elegant grace.

The first truly Romantic ballet, *Robert the Devil* told the story of Duke Robert of Normandy, his love for a princess, and an encounter with the devil. The ballet contains ghosts, bacchanalian dancing, and a spectral figure who was danced by Marie Taglioni (tah-lee-OH-nee; Fig. **12.20**).

Taglioni went on to star in perhaps the most famous of all Romantic ballets, *La Sylphide* (sihl-FEED; 1832). Here the plot centered on the tragic impossibility of love between a mortal and a supernatural being. A spirit of the air, a sylph, falls in love with a young Scot on his wedding day. Torn between his real fiancée and his ideal, the sylph, he deserts his fiancée to run off with the spirit. A witch gives him a scarf, and, unaware that it is enchanted, he ties it around the spirit's waist. Immediately her wings fall off and she dies. She drifts away to sylphs' heaven. The young man, disconsolate and alone, sees his fiancée passing in the distance with a new lover on the way to her wedding. The Scottish setting was exotic, at least to Parisians. Gaslight provided a ghostly, moonlit mood in the darkened auditorium. Taglioni danced the role of La Sylphide like "a creature of mist drifting over the stage" (assisted by flying machinery). Her lightness, delicacy, and modest grace established the standard for Romantic style in dancing. The story, exotic design, and mood-evoking lighting completed the production style, a style that prevailed for the next forty years— "moonbeams and gossamer," as some have described it.

Choreographers of Romantic ballet sought magic and escape in fantasies and legends. Ballets about elves and nymphs enjoyed great popularity, as did ballets about madness, sleepwalking, and opium dreams. Unusual subject matter came to the fore. For example, harem wives revolt against their oppressors with the help of the "Spirit of Womankind" in Filippo Taglioni's *The Revolt in the Harem*, possibly the first ballet about the emancipation of women. Women appeared not only as performers and as subjects of the dance, however. They also began to come to prominence as choreographers.

The ballet *Giselle* (zhee-ZEHL; 1841) marks the height of Romantic achievement. With its many fine dancing roles, both for women and for men, it has been a favorite of ballet companies since its first production.

The ballet has two acts; Act I is in sunlight, and Act II in moonlight. During a vine festival in a Rhineland village,

Giselle, a frail peasant girl in love with a mysterious young man, discovers that the object of her affection is Albrecht, Count of Silesia. Albrecht is already engaged to a noblewoman. Giselle is shattered. She goes mad, turns from her deceitful lover, tries to commit suicide, swoons, and falls dead. In Act II, Giselle is summoned from her grave, deep in the forest, by Myrthe (MUHR-tuh), Queen of the Wilis, spirits of women who, having died unhappy in love, are condemned to lead men to destruction. (The word *wili* comes from a Slavic word for "vampire.") When a repentant Albrecht comes to bring flowers to Giselle's grave, Myrthe orders her to dance him to his death. Instead, Giselle protects Albrecht until the first rays of dawn break Myrthe's power.

In St. Petersburg, Russia, in 1862, an English ballet called *The Daughter of Pharaoh*, choreographed by Marius Petipa (peh-tee-PAH), sent Russian audiences into rapture. Petipa had come to Russia from France in 1842, and he remained a central figure in Russian ballet for almost sixty years. By the middle of the nineteenth century, ballet companies were flourishing in Moscow and St Petersburg. Dancers enjoyed positions of high esteem in Russia, as they did not in the rest of Europe.

In Russia, the influence of Petipa carried Russian ballet forward in a quasi-Romantic style. He shared the sentimental taste of his time, but his works often contained very strange elements and numerous anachronisms. Minor characters might wear costumes suggesting period or locale, but the stars wore conventional garb, often of Classical derivation. Prima ballerinas often appeared in stylish contemporary coiffures and jewels, even when playing the role of a slave. *Divertissements* (dee-vair-TEES-mawn)—light entertainments—were often inserted into a ballet. Petipa included many different kinds of dance in his ballets—Classical, character, and folk dance. His creative approach more than compensated for his anachronisms. As some have said in his defense, "No one criticized Shakespeare for having Antony and Cleopatra speak in blank verse."

From this Russian school came the ever-popular *Nutcracker* and *Swan Lake*. The scores for both were composed by Tchaikovsky. *Swan Lake* was first produced in 1877 by the Moscow Bolshoi and *Nutcracker* in 1892. *Swan Lake* popularized the *fouetté* (foo-eh-TAY), or whipping turn, introduced by the ballerina Pierina Legnani in Petipa's *Cinderella* and incorporated for her in *Swan Lake*. In one scene, Legnani danced thirty-two consecutive *fouettés*, and to this day that number is mandatory.

ARCHITECTURE

One of the characteristics of Romantic architecture is its borrowing of styles from other eras. A vast array of buildings revived Gothic motifs, adding a major element of fantasy to create the Picturesque style. Eastern influence and whimsy abound in the Royal Pavilion at Brighton,

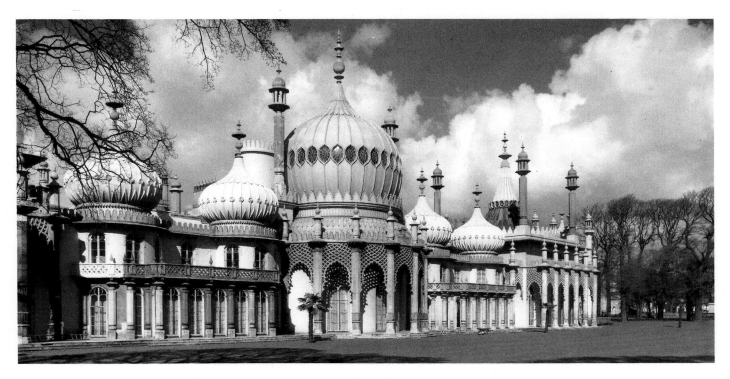

12.21 John Nash, Royal Pavilion, Brighton, England, remodeled 1815–23.

12.22 Sir Charles Barry and Augustus Welby Northmore Pugin, Houses of Parliament, London, 1839–52.

England (Fig. **12.21**), designed by John Nash (1752–1835). Picturesque also describes the most famous example of Romantic architecture, the Houses of Parliament in London (Fig. **12.22**). Significantly, its exterior walls function as a screen, and suggest nothing of structure, interior design, or usage—a modern tendency in architectural design. Conversely, the inside has absolutely no spatial relationship to the outside. Note, too, the strong contrast of forms and asymmetrical balance.

The nineteenth century was an age of industry, of experimentation and new materials. In architecture, iron, steel, and glass came to the fore. At first it took courage for an architect actually to display structural honesty by allowing support materials to be seen as part of the design. England's Crystal Palace (Fig. **12.23**) exemplifies the nineteenth-century fascination with new materials and concepts. Built for the Great Exhibition of 1851, this mammoth structure was completed in the space of just

12.23 Sir Joseph Paxton, Crystal Palace, London, 1851.

nine months. Space was defined by a three-dimensional grid of iron bars and girders, designed specifically for mass production and rapid assembly (in this case, disassembly as well—the entire structure was dismantled and rebuilt in 1852–4 at Sydenham). Like the Houses of Parliament, the Crystal Palace highlights the growing divergence of function (as reflected in the arrangement of interior spaces), surface decoration, and structure.

NEW STYLES IN EUROPE AND AMERICA

REALISM

A new painting style called *Realism* arose in the mid-nineteenth century. The term "reality" came to have special significance in the nineteenth century because the camera—a machine to record events, people, and locations—thrust itself into what had previously been considered the painter's realm.

Courbet

The central figure of Realism was Gustave Courbet (coor-BAY; 1819–77). He sought to make an objective and unprejudiced record of the customs, ideas, and appearances of contemporary French society. He depicted everyday life in terms of the play of light on surfaces, as seen in *The Stone Breakers* (Fig. 12.24). This painting was the first to display his philosophy to the full. Courbet painted two men as he has seen them, working beside a road. The painting is lifesize, and the treatment seems objective, and yet it makes a sharp comment on the tedium and laborious nature of the task. As a Social Realist, Courbet was more intent on political message than on meditative reaction.

Manet

Edouard Manet (mah-NAY; 1832–83) strove to paint "only what the eye can see." Yet his works go beyond a mere reflection of reality to encompass an artistic reality: Painting has an internal logic different from that of familiar reality. Manet thus liberated the canvas from competition with the camera. As indicated in the catalogue for

12.24 Gustave Courbet, *The Stone Breakers*, 1849. Oil on canvas, 5 ft 3 ins × 8 ft 6 ins (1.6 × 2.59 m). Formerly in the Gemäldegalerie, Dresden (destroyed 1945).

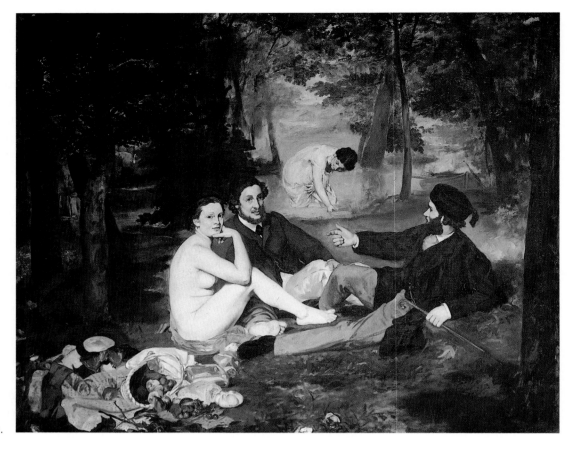

12.25 Edouard Manet, *Déjeuner sur l'herbe* (*The Picnic*), 1863. Oil on canvas, 7 ft × 8 ft 10 ins (2.13 × 2.69 m). Musée d'Orsay, Paris.

12.26 (*below*) Henry O. Tanner, *The Banjo Lesson*, c.1893. Oil on canvas, 48 × 35 ins (122 × 89 cm). Hampton University Museum, Hampton, Virginia.

an exhibition he produced when he was excluded from the International Exhibition in Paris in 1867, Manet believed that he presented in his art sincere—rather than faultless—perception.

His sincerity carried a form of protest—his impressions. To a certain extent Manet was both a conformist and a protester. He came from a comfortable bourgeois background and yet maintained a conviction about socialism. His work leans heavily on the masters of the past—for example, Raphael and Watteau—and at the same time explores completely new ground. He sought acceptance in salon circles while aiming to shock those same individuals. Striving to be a man of his own time, he rejected the superficiality he found in Romantic themes. He gave the reality of the world around him a different and more straightforward interpretation. As a result, he is often hailed as the first modern painter.

Déjeuner sur l'herbe (day zhuh-NAY syoor-lairb; Fig. 12.25) shocked the public when it first appeared in 1863. Manet sought specifically to "speak in a new voice." The setting is pastoral, as in Watteau (see Fig. 11.39), for example, but the people are real and identifiable: Manet's model, his brother, and the sculptor Leenhof. The apparent immorality of a naked frolic in a Paris park outraged the public and the critics. Had his figures been nymphs and satyrs, all would have been well; but Manet wanted both to be accepted by the official Salon, and to shock its organizers and visitors. The painting is modern while commenting upon similar themes of the past. But the intrusion of reality into the sacred confines of the mythical proved more than the public could handle.

Manet's search for harmonious colors, subjects from everyday life, and faithfulness to observed lighting and atmospheric effects led to the development of a style described in 1874 by a hostile critic as Impressionist.

Tanner

The first important African American painter, Henry O. Tanner (1859–1937), studied with the American Realist Thomas Eakins (1844–1916). *The Banjo Lesson* (Fig. 12.26) presents its images in a strictly realistic manner, without sentimentality. The painting achieves focus through contrast, with clarity in the central objects and less detail in surrounding areas. This technique reflects

contemporary experiments investigating the nature of perceptual experience. A natural phenomenon had been discovered: Only objects immediately in the center of our vision are in sharp focus, and the rest remain slightly out of focus. Tanner's skill can be seen in the way he has captured the atmosphere of concentration and the warm relationship of teacher and pupil.

IMPRESSIONISM

Painting

In France, the Impressionists created a new way of seeing reality, seeking to capture "the psychological perception of reality in color and motion." Manet is credited with the original concepts of the style. It emerged in competition with the newly invented technology of the camera, for the

12.27 Claude Monet, *Au Bord de l'eau, Bennecourt* (*On the Seine at Bennecourt*), 1868. Oil on canvas, 31⅞ × 39½ ins (81.5 × 100.7 cm). Art Institute of Chicago (Potter Palmer Collection).

12.28 Pierre-Auguste Renoir, *Moulin de la Galette*, 1876. Oil on canvas, 51½ × 69 ins (131 × 175 cm). Musée d'Orsay, Paris.

Impressionists tried to beat photography at its own game by portraying the essentials of perception which the camera cannot capture. The style lasted fifteen years in its purest form but deeply influenced all art that followed.

Working out of doors, the Impressionists concentrated on the effects of natural light on objects and atmosphere. They emphasized the presence of color within shadows and based their style on an understanding of the interrelated mechanisms of the camera and the eye: vision consists of the result of light and color making an "impression" on the retina. Their experiments resulted in a profoundly different vision of the world around them and a new way of rendering that vision. For them, the painted canvas was first of all a material surface covered with pigments and filled with small patches of color, which together create lively and vibrant images.

Despite the individualistic nature of the nineteenth century, Impressionism is as collective a style as any we have seen thus far. It reflects the common concerns of a relatively small group of artists who met frequently and held joint exhibitions. As a result, the style has marked characteristics which apply to all its exponents. The paintings are relatively small and use clear, bright colors. Composition appears casual and natural. Typical subjects include everyday scenes such as landscapes, rivers, streets, and cafés.

Au Bord de l'eau, Bennecourt (*On the Seine at Bennecourt*) (Fig. **12.27**) by Claude Monet (muh-NAY; 1840–1926) illustrates several of the concerns of the Impressionists. It portrays a pleasant, objective picture of the times, in contrast with the often subjective viewpoint of the Romantics. It suggests a fleeting moment—a new tone in an era when the pace of life has increased. Monet, along with Renoir and Berthe Morisot (bairt muh-ree-SOH), among others, was a central figure in the development of Impressionism.

12.29 Berthe Morisot, *In the Dining Room*, 1886. Oil on canvas, 24⅛ × 19¾ ins (61.3 × 50 cm). National Gallery of Art, Washington, D.C. (Chester Dale Collection).

Pierre Auguste Renoir (rehn-WAH; 1841–1919) specialized in portraying the human figure, seeking out what was beautiful in the body. His paintings sparkle with the joy of life. In *Moulin de la Galette* (Fig. **12.28**) he depicts the bright gaiety of a Sunday crowd in a popular Parisian dance hall. He celebrates the liveliness and charm of these everyday folk as they talk, crowd the tables, flirt, and dance. Sunlight and shade dapple the scene and create a floating sensation in light. There is a casualness here, a sense of life captured in a fleeting and spontaneous moment. A much wider scene seems to extend beyond the canvas—the composition is an open one, not formally composed like David's *Oath of the Horatii* (see Fig. **11.43**). Rather, we are invited to become part of the action. People are going about their everyday routine with no reaction to the painter's presence. As opposed to the Classicist, who focuses on the universal and the typical, the Impressionist seeks realism in "the incidental, the momentary and the passing."

The original group of Impressionists included a woman, Berthe Morisot (1841–95), on equal terms. Gently introspective, her works often focus on family members. Her view of contemporary life is edged with pathos and sentimentality. In *In the Dining Room* (Fig. **12.29**) she uses Impressionist techniques to give a penetrating glimpse of psychological reality. The servant girl has a personality, and she stares back at the viewer with complete self-assurance. The painting captures a moment of disorder: The cabinet door stands ajar with what appears to be a used tablecloth merely flung over it. The little dog playfully demands attention. Morisot's brushstroke is delicate, and her scenes are full of insight.

Music

In music, the anti-Romantic spirit produced a style analogous to that of the Impressionist painters. There was some direct influence from the Impressionist painters, but mostly Impressionism in music turned to the *Symbolist* poets for inspiration.

Ironically, Impressionist music's primary champion, Claude Debussy (deh-boo-SEE; 1862–1918), did not like to be called an Impressionist. In fact, this is not surprising, for the label had been coined by a severe critic of the painters and was intended to be derogatory. Debussy maintained that he was "an old romantic who has thrown the worries of success out of the window," and he sought no association with the painters. However, similar motifs can be seen. His use of tone color has been described as "wedges of color" applied in a similar way to painters' individual brushstrokes. He delighted in natural scenes and sought to capture the ◆ effects of shimmering light.

Debussy wished above all to return French music to fundamental sources in nature and move it away from the heaviness of the German tradition.

In contrast to his predecessors, Debussy abandoned chordal harmony's traditional progressions—perhaps his greatest break with tradition. Oriental influence is apparent in his use of the Asian five-tone scale and dissonance is common. Each chord is considered strictly on the merits of its expressive capabilities and apart from any context of tonal progression. As a result, gliding chords (repetition of a chord up and down the scale) became a hallmark of musical Impressionism.

Debussy reduced melodic development to short motifs—an analogy can again be drawn with the individual brushstrokes of the painters. Irregular rhythm and meter further distinguish his works. So, once more, form and content are subordinate to expressive intent. His music tends to suggest, rather than to state, and to leave the listener with ambiguity—with an impression. Key elements of his style are freedom, flexibility, and nontraditional timbres. His most famous composition is the *Prélude à l'après-midi d'un faune* (*Prelude to the Afternoon of a Faun*; see also p. 91), based on a sensual poem by the Symbolist Stéphane Mallarmé (mah-lahr-MAY; 1842–98). The piece uses a large orchestra, with emphasis on the harps and woodwinds, most notably in the haunting, chromatically sliding theme running throughout. Although freely ranging in an irregular 9/8 meter and virtually without tonal centers, the *Prélude* has a basically traditional ABA structure (music CD track 19).

POST-IMPRESSIONISM

In the last two decades of the nineteenth century Impressionism evolved gently into a collection of rather disparate styles called, simply, Post-Impressionism. In subject matter Post-Impressionist paintings are similar to Impressionist ones—landscapes, familiar portraits, groups, and café and nightclub scenes. The Post-Impressionists, however, gave their subject matter a profoundly personal significance.

The Post-Impressionists were deeply concerned about the formal language of art and its ability to capture sensory experience. They maintained the contemporary philosophy of art for art's sake and rarely attempted to sell their works. They did wish to share their subjective impressions of the real world, but moved beyond the Romantic and Impressionist world of pure sensation. They were more interested in the painting as a flat surface carefully composed of shapes, lines, and colors, an idea that became the foundation for most of the art movements that followed.

12.30 Georges Seurat, *Sunday Afternoon on the Island of La Grande Jatte*, 1884–6. Oil on canvas, 6 ft 9½ ins × 10 ft ⅜ ins (2.07 × 3.06 m). Art Institute of Chicago (Helen Birch Bartlett Memorial Collection).

The Post-Impressionists called for a return to form and structure in painting, characteristics they believed were lacking in the works of the Impressionists. Taking the evanescent light qualities of the Impressionists, they brought formal patterning to their canvases. They used clean color areas, and applied color in a systematic, almost scientific manner. The Post-Impressionists sought to return painting to traditional goals while retaining the clean palette of the Impressionists.

Seurat

Georges Seurat (suh-RAH; 1859–91) is often described as a Neo-Impressionist rather than a Post-Impressionist (he called his approach and technique *divisionism*). He took the Impressionist method of painting one step further. In his patient and systematic technique specks of paint are applied with the point of the brush, one small dot at a time. He used paint in accordance with his theories of optics and of color perception: *Sunday Afternoon on the Island of La Grande Jatte* (Fig. **12.30**) illustrates his concern for the accurate depiction of light and color. Its composition and depiction of shadow show attention to perspective, and yet Seurat willfully avoids three-dimensionality. As in much Post-Impressionist art, Japanese influence is apparent: Color areas are fairly uniform, figures are flattened, and outlining is continuous. Throughout the work we find conscious systematizing. The painting is broken into proportions of three-eighths and halves, which Seurat believed represented true harmony. He also selected his colors by formula. Physical reality for Seurat was just a pretext for the artist's search for a superior harmony, for an abstract perfection.

Cézanne

Paul Cézanne (say-ZAHN; 1839–1906) is considered by many as the father of modern art. *Mont Sainte-Victoire* (Fig. **12.31**) illustrates his concern for formal design with its nearly geometric configuration and balance.

12.31 Paul Cézanne, *Mont Sainte-Victoire seen from Les Lauves*, 1902–4. Oil on canvas, 27½ × 35¼ ins (70 × 90 cm). Philadelphia Museum of Art (George W. Elkins Collection).

12.32 (*below*) Paul Gauguin, *The Vision after the Sermon*, 1888. Oil on canvas, 28¾ × 36¼ ins (73 × 92 cm). National Gallery of Scotland, Edinburgh.

Foreground and background are tied together systematically so that both join in the foreground to create patterns. Simplified shapes and outlining occur throughout. Cézanne employed geometric shapes—the cone, the sphere, and the cylinder—as metaphors of the permanent reality that lay beneath surface appearance.

Cézanne tried to invest his paintings with a strong sense of three-dimensionality. His use of colored planes is much like Seurat's use of dots. He took great liberty with color and changed traditional ways of rendering objects, utilizing the cones and other geometric shapes just mentioned.

Gauguin

A highly imaginative approach to Post-Impressionist goals came from Paul Gauguin (goh-GAN; 1848–1903). He and his followers were known as Symbolists or Nabis (the Hebrew word for prophet). An artist without training and a nomad who believed that all European society and its works were sick, Gauguin devoted his life to art and wandering, spending many years in rural Brittany and the end of his life in Tahiti and the Marquesas Islands. His work shows an insistence on form and a resistance to realistic effects. *The Vision after the Sermon* (Fig. 12.32) has

Gauguin's typically flat, outlined figures, simple forms, and symbolism. In the background Jacob wrestles with the angel, as described in Genesis, the first book of the Bible. Meanwhile, in the foreground, a priest, nuns, and women in Breton costume pray. The intense reds of this work are typical of Gauguin's symbolic and unnatural use of color, used here to portray the powerful sensations of a Breton folk festival.

Van Gogh

We move now to look at the work of the Dutch Post-Impressionist Vincent van Gogh (1853–90). His emotionalism in the pursuit of form is unique. Van Gogh's turbulent life included numerous short-lived careers, impossible love affairs, a tempestuous friendship with Gauguin, and, finally, serious mental illness. Biography here is essential because van Gogh gives us one of the most personal and subjective artistic viewpoints in the history of Western art. Works such as *The Starry Night* (see Fig. 1.7) explode with frenetic energy manifested in the brushwork. Flattened forms and outlining reflect Japanese influence (see Fig. 10.50). *The Starry Night* exhibits tremendous power and controlled focus; dynamic, personal energy and mental turmoil. This work

12.33 Vincent van Gogh. *Harvest at La Crau (The Blue Cart).* 1888. Oil on canvas, 28½ × 36¼ ins (72.5 × 92 cm). Rijksmuseum, Vincent van Gogh, Amsterdam.

represents one of the earliest and most famous examples of Expressionism in painting. We will examine this in the next chapter.

Works such as *Harvest at La Crau* (*The Blue Cart*; Fig. **12.33**), which van Gogh produced in his Arles period, reflect an interest in *complementary colors* (colors on opposite sides of the color wheel—see Chapter 1). Unlike Seurat, for example, who applied such colors in small dots, van Gogh placed large color areas side by side. Doing so, he believed, expressed the quiet, harmonious life of the rural community. Notice that the brushwork in the foreground is active while the fields in the background are smooth. Subtle diagonals break up the predominantly horizontal line of the work.

ART NOUVEAU

In the 1890s and early 1900s a "new" art phenomenon occurred in Europe. Called "New Art" or Art Nouveau (ahrt noo-VOH), it grew out of the English Arts and Crafts Movement, emerging initially in response to a world's fair, the Paris Universal Exposition of 1889. Encompassing art, architecture, and design, Art Nouveau comprised a variety of examples, but typically it reflected the lively, serpentine curve known as the "whiplash." Overall, the style pursues a fascination with plant and animal life and organic growth. The influence of Japanese art is evident in Art Nouveau's undulating curves. In addition, the style incorporates organic and often symbolic motifs, treating them in a linear, relief-like manner.

Turning to the Paris Universal Exposition, the story of Art Nouveau emerges: The best known creation of the fair was and is the Eiffel Tower, designed by a civil engineer, Gustave Eiffel (1832–1923). The design for the tower was the winning entry in a contest for a monument to symbolize French industrial progress. At 984 feet (300 m), the tower stood as the tallest structure in the world at that time, its iron latticework resting on four huge legs reinforced by trussed arches similar to those Eiffel had used on his railroad bridges. The Eiffel Tower raised great

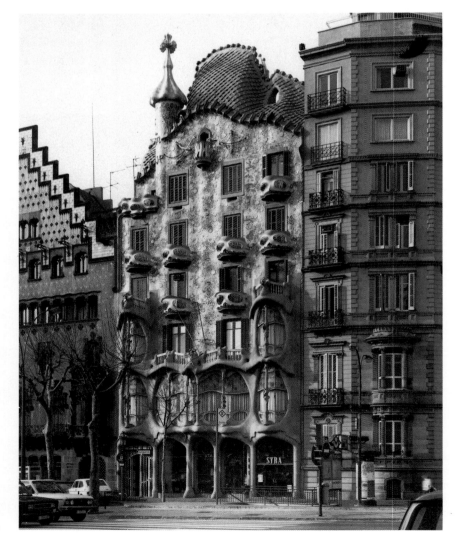

12.34 Antoni Gaudí, Casa Batlló, Barcelona, 1905–7.

A Personal Journey

ANTONI GAUDÍ, LA SAGRADA FAMILIA

The terrace of my hotel room in Barcelona, Spain, yielded a panoramic view of the city. A block away was Antoni Gaudí's Casa Batlló (Fig. **12.34**), and, in the distance, the twin, dark, mysterious, and honeycombed spires of Holy Family Cathedral (Fig. **12.35**) broke the skyline. Even from afar, it evoked curiosity.

In the park across the street from the cathedral I took in its scale. A few brownish leaves clung tenaciously to the branches of a tree, softening my view in the late December sunlight. A pond made the urban setting seem like countryside and gave the twisted features of the church façade a rustic, natural feeling, as if it were completely at home in its context. An old man sat on a bench reading his Sunday

paper and, nearby, a cadre of men, both old and young, engaged in the pantomimic ritual of the Spanish equivalent of bocce ball. Women with baby carriages and women with sewing sat on benches, absorbed in the moment. The cathedral watched silently over them like a patient mother. They, in turn, went about their activities seemingly oblivious to her presence. While I, the outsider, stood in awe and fascination, they regarded her presence benignly. I wondered how they felt about this controversial icon.

The Holy Family Cathedral (La Sagrada Familia [lah sah-GRAH-dah fah-MEEL-yah]) was built by hand. I say built, in the past tense, even though it remains unfinished after nearly 100 years of construction. Gaudí is dead, and the newer portions do not have the rough quality of the front. They are the products of modern thought and, perhaps out of deference to Gaudí, are markedly different from the sections he designed and built. They do, however, reflect the tone of his design. Gaudí made no plans for his work. He shaped it as he went, and his style—Art Nouveau—has not met with universal acceptance. To some it is ugly and too whimsical; to others it has an organic quality that makes it one with the environment. Personally, I like Gaudí's work. Its whimsy is a charm rather than a curse, and his work exemplifies how artworks can evoke complex responses. I find La Sagrada Familia captivating, creative, and reflective of skilled artisanship. The touch of the artist is obvious—something architecture does not always reveal. The Holy Family Cathedral appears difficult to be ambivalent about, its fanciful clutter appealing to me for many reasons I do not fully understand, any more than I understand why some people appeal to me and others do not. The basic question, though, is why? How much am I the cause of my reactions, and how much is Gaudí? Or is it something else, entirely?

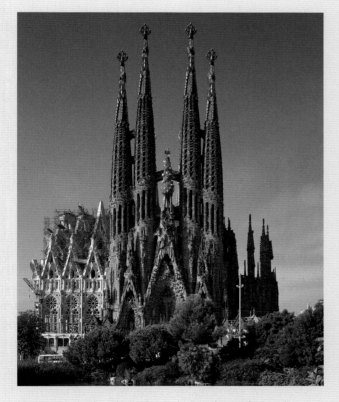

12.35 Antoni Gaudí, La Sagrada Familia (Holy Family Cathedral), Barcelona, begun 1883.

12.36 Louis Sullivan, Carson, Pirie, & Scott Department Store, Chicago, 1899–1904.

concern in many quarters as regards its influence on the future of art in conjunction with the industrial age. Art Nouveau constituted one response. It sought to reflect modernism but to do so without losing a pre-industrial sense of beauty. As a consequence, the use of organic forms and traditional materials such as wood and stone emerged.

The issues addressed by Art Nouveau ranged beyond French borders. In fact, it was a Belgian, Victor Horta (1867–1947), who launched the style. It spread throughout Europe, recognized by a variety of names in various countries: In Italy, *Stile floreale* ("floral style") and *Stile Liberty* (after the Liberty Department Store in London); in Germany, *Jugendstil* ("Youth Style"); in Spain, *Modernismo* (Modernism); in Vienna, *Secessionsstil* (after the secession from the Academy led by Klimt); in Belgium, *Paling Style* ("Eel Style"), and in France, a number of names including *moderne*. Eventually the name Art Nouveau settled on the movement after a shop in Paris (La Maison de l'Art Nouveau) that opened in 1895.

In France, where in Paris and Nancy the style proliferated, it was often called *style Guimard* after its leading practitioner, Hector Guimard (ghee-MAHR; 1867–1942),

whose many works include the famous entrance portals for the Paris Métro (subway). In Spain, the man perhaps best remembered as a champion of the style, Antoni Gaudí, transformed its characteristics into remarkable constructions. Two examples serve our purposes: Casa Batlló (baht-LOH; Fig. **12.34**) and La Sagrada Familia (Fig. **12.35**), both in Barcelona. Gaudí's approach took architecture in an astonishing direction: that of hand-crafted buildings made without plans other than what was in the head of the architect, and this effect clearly resonates from the two examples noted.

EXPERIMENTATION IN ARCHITECTURE

The new age of experimentation took nineteenth-century architects in a new direction—upward. Late in the period—not until a man named Elisha Graves Otis (1811–61) had invented a safe elevator—the skyscraper was designed in response to the need to create commercial space on limited property in burgeoning urban areas. At that period it was almost exclusively limited to America. Burnham & Root's Monadnock Building in Chicago (see Fig. **7.20**) is an early example and illustrates the trend toward thinking in a unified way about design, materials, and new concepts of architectural space. This prototypical "skyscraper" is all masonry—built completely of brick and requiring increasingly thick walls toward its base—which limited its possible height. Soon architects were able to erect buildings of unprecedented height (see the Sears Tower, Fig. **7.39**) without increasing the thickness of the lower walls. This was done by erecting structural frameworks (first of iron, later of steel) and by treating walls as independent partitions. Each story was supported on horizontal girders.

An influential figure in the development of the skyscraper and in the whole philosophy of modern architecture was Louis Sullivan (1856–1924). The first truly modern architect, he worked in the last decade of the nineteenth century in Chicago, then the most rapidly developing metropolis in the world. Sullivan designed buildings characterized by dignity, simplicity, and strength. Most importantly, he created a rubric for modern architecture by combining form and function: In his theory the former flows from the latter. As Sullivan said to an observer of the Carson, Pirie, & Scott building (Fig. **12.36**), "It is evident that we are looking at a department store. Its purpose is clearly set forth in its general aspect, and the form follows the function in a simple, straightforward way."[10]

THINKING CRITICALLY

- Enumerate the basic characteristics of Romanticism and then, touching upon the elements of each art form (discussed in Chapters 1–8), compare Goya's *Execution of the Citizens of Madrid, May 3, 1808* (Fig. **1.46**), Wordsworth's "Tintern Abbey" (p. 342), Chopin's *Nocturne in E flat major* (http://www.nifty.ne.jp/forum/fmidicla/mid/chonoc02.mid), and John Nash's Royal Pavilion (Fig. **12.21**) as representatives of the style.

- Explain how the styles of Realism, Impressionism, and Post-Impressionism are alike and/or different in the manner in which they utilize line, color, form, and personal emotion. Use examples from the text to illustrate your analysis.

- Compare Gaudí's Casa Batlló (Fig. **12.34**) and Sullivan's Carson, Pirie, & Scott Building (Fig. **12.36**) in terms of their basic stylistic approaches. In doing so, comment on line, scale, proportion, fenestration, structure, and expression of personal emotion. Give your own personal reaction to each building and explain why you feel as you do.

CYBER STUDY

JAPAN:
—Printmaking: Hokusai, Hiroshige
http://www.ibiblio.org/wm/paint/auth/hiroshige/

NATIVE AMERICA:
http://www.virtualmuseum.ca/English/Gallery/static/InuitSculpture_page1.html

WESTERN ROMANTICISM:
—Visual Art
http://www.artcyclopedia.com/history/romanticism.html
—Music: Strauss, Schubert, Chopin, Liszt, Wagner, Brahms, Berlioz, Tchaikovsky
http://www.classicalarchives.com/index_1.html
—Literature: Austen, Goethe, Wordsworth, Coleridge, Byron, Shelley, Keats, Blake
http://sunsite.berkeley.edu/alex/authors.html

NEW STYLES IN EUROPE AND AMERICA:
—Realism
http://www.artcyclopedia.com/history/realism.html
—Impressionism in Visual Art
http://www.artcyclopedia.com/history/impressionism.html
— Impressionism in Music: Debussy
http://www.classicalarchives.com/debussy.html
—Post-Impressionism
http://www.artcyclopedia.com/history/post-impressionism.html
—Art Nouveau
http://www.artcyclopedia.com/history/art-nouveau.html

CHAPTER THIRTEEN

PLURALISM: MODERNISM, POSTMODERNISM, AND BEYOND

1900 to the Present

IMPORTANT TERMS

Abstract Expressionism A painting style of the late 1940s and early 1950s, predominantly American, characterized by its rendering of expressive content by abstract or nonobjective means.

Cubism A style of art noted for the geometry of its forms, its fragmentation of the object, and its increasing abstraction.

Expressionism An art that stresses the psychological and emotional content of the work.

Fauvism An art movement characterized by its use of bold arbitrary color.

Futurism An art movement characterized by the desire to celebrate the movement and speed of modern industrial life.

Modernism Generally speaking, the various strategies and directions employed in twentieth-century arts to explore the particular formal properties of a given medium.

Pop Art A style arising in the 1960s characterized by its emphasis on the forms and imagery of mass culture.

Postmodernism A term used to describe the willfully plural, eclectic, and typically anti-modern forms of art of the late twentieth century.

Surrealism A style of art that emphasized dream imagery, chance operations, and rapid, thoughtless forms of notation that expressed the unconscious mind.

Serialism A system of musical composition emphasizing the tone row or twelve-tone technique.

Musique actuelle Cutting-edge music drawing on jazz and rock to create vibrant, lively, personalized expressions.

The one constant in the arts of the turbulent and phenomenal twentieth and into the twenty-first century is a seemingly inexhaustible quest for originality and freshness. Among the awesome contradictions of an age that witnessed the worst and the best that humanity is capable of, its vision of itself and where it was going is as troublesome as it was for our Paleolithic ancestors.

In contrast to the atmosphere of flurried change in the West, many cultures still make use of the traditional practices and techniques of their predecessors. The so-called "primitive" art of Africans and Native Americans in fact masks a web of complicated rituals, myths, and beliefs in which art plays a crucial role. Despite enormous differences between the function and style of tribal and Western art, the two-way flow of influence has been significant, particularly in the modern and postmodern era.

Increasingly, we recognize that even as our humanness unites us, there are manifold expressions of individuality in that togetherness. To paraphrase St. Paul the Apostle, the body that represents humanity is not all one part, whether ears or eyes or feet. It takes diverse members, each with a different purpose, to make a complete body. Thus, here at the beginning of the twenty-first century, the evidence, indeed, the celebration, of pluralism—of difference—remains an important theme, if perhaps a troubling one, because hidden within its apparent openness lies the potential for tribalization and separation.

NATIVE AMERICA
FICTION

As discussed in the last chapter, the period from 1870 to 1920 produced a profound change in Native American culture and circumstances. Confinement to reservations and an increase in formal education changed both the traditional way of life and, in particular, its oral transmission of culture. A frequent issue for both Native Americans and settlers was whether their cultures were incompatible. Cultural conflict was a common preoccupation and central theme for Native American writers, many of whom were of mixed ancestry and the products of the white educational system. Native Americans of mixed ethnicity were themselves popular subjects in the nineteenth and early twentieth centuries, and writers who focused in this way on the meeting point between the two cultures give us a profound insight.

Gertrude Bonnin, a South Dakota Yankton Sioux, who had a full-blooded mother and an Anglo-American father, wrote under the pen name of Zitkala-Sa (Red Bird). The mixed-culture protagonist of "The Soft-Hearted Sioux" (published in 1901) reflects the conflicts of a Native American caught between cultures. Unable to function in either world, he is given no alternative but to face a violent death.

The Soft-Hearted Sioux

Zitkala-Sa (Gertrude Bonnin)

1

Beside the open fire I sat within our tepee. With my red blanket wrapped tightly about my crossed legs, I was thinking of the coming season, my sixteenth winter. On either side of the wigwam were my parents. My father was whistling a tune between his teeth while polishing with his bare hand a red stone pipe he had recently carved. Almost in front of me, beyond the center fire, my old grandmother sat near the entranceway.

She turned her face toward her right and addressed most of her words to my mother. Now and then she spoke to me, but never did she allow her eyes to rest upon her daughter's husband, my father. It was only upon rare occasions that my grandmother said anything to him. Thus his ears were open and ready to catch the smallest wish she might express. Sometimes when my grandmother had been saying things which pleased him, my father used to comment upon them. At other times, when he could not approve of what was spoken, he used to work or smoke silently.

On this night my old grandmother began her talk about me. Filling the bowl of her red stone pipe with dry willow bark, she looked across at me.

"My grandchild, you are tall and no longer a little boy." Narrowing her old eyes, she asked, "My grandchild, when are you going to bring here a handsome young woman?" I stared into the fire rather than meet her gaze. Waiting for my answer, she stooped forward and through the long stem drew a flame into the red stone pipe.

I smiled while my eyes were still fixed upon the bright fire, but I said nothing in reply. Turning to my mother, she offered her the pipe. I glanced at my grandmother. The loose buckskin sleeve fell off at her elbow and showed a wrist covered with silver bracelets. Holding up the fingers of her left hand, she named off the desirable young women of our village.

"Which one, my grandchild, which one?" she questioned.

"Hoh!" I said, pulling at my blanket in confusion. "Not yet!" Here my mother passed the pipe over the fire to my father. Then she too began speaking of what I should do.

"My son, be always active. Do not dislike a long hunt. Learn to provide much buffalo meat and many buckskins before you bring home a wife." Presently my father gave the pipe to my grandmother, and he took his turn in the exhortations.

"Ho, my son, I have been counting in my heart the bravest warriors of our people. There is not one of them who won his title in his sixteenth winter. My son, it is a great thing for some brave of sixteen winters to do."

Not a word had I to give in answer. I knew well the fame of my warrior father. He had earned the right of speaking such words, though even he himself was a brave only at my age. Refusing to smoke my grandmother's pipe because my heart was too much stirred by their words, and sorely troubled with a fear lest I should disappoint them, I arose to go. Drawing my blanket over my shoulders, I said, as I stepped toward the entranceway: "I go to hobble my pony. It is now late in the night."

2

Nine winters' snows had buried deep that night when my old grandmother, together with my father and mother, designed my future with the glow of a camp fire upon it.

Yet I did not grow up the warrior, huntsman, and husband I was to have been. At the mission school I learned it was wrong to kill. Nine winters I hunted for the soft heart of Christ, and prayed for the huntsmen who chased the buffalo on the plains.

In the autumn of the tenth year I was sent back to my tribe to preach Christianity to them. With the white man's Bible in my hand, and the white man's tender heart in my breast, I returned to my own people.

Wearing a foreigner's dress, I walked, a stranger, into my father's village.

Asking my way, for I had not forgotten my native tongue, an old man led me toward the tepee where my father lay. From my old companion I learned that my father had been sick many moons. As we drew near the tepee, I heard the chanting of a medicine-man within it. At once I wished to enter in and drive from my home the sorcerer of the plains, but the old warrior checked me. "Ho, wait outside until the medicine-man leaves your father," he said. While talking he scanned me from head to feet. Then he retraced his steps toward the heart of the camping-ground.

My father's dwelling was on the outer limits of the round-faced village. With every heart-throb I grew more impatient to enter the wigwam.

While I turned the leaves of my Bible with nervous fingers, the medicine-man came forth from the dwelling and walked hurriedly away. His head and face were loosely covered with the loose robe which draped his entire figure.

He was tall and large. His long strides I have never forgot. They seemed to me then as the uncanny gait of eternal death. Quickly pocketing my Bible, I went into the tepee.

Upon a mat lay my father, with furrowed face and gray hair. His eyes and cheeks were sunken far into his head. His sallow skin lay thin upon his pinched nose and high cheek-bones. Stooping over him, I took his fevered hand. "How, Ate?" I greeted him. A light flashed from his listless eyes and his dried lips parted. "My son!" he murmured, in a feeble voice. Then again the wave of joy and recognition receded. He closed his eyes, and his hand dropped from my open palm to the ground.

Looking about, I saw an old woman sitting with bowed head. Shaking hands with her, I recognized my mother.

I sat down between my father and mother as I used to do, but I did not feel at home. The place where my grandmother used to sit was now unoccupied. With my mother I bowed my head. Alike our throats were choked and tears were streaming from our eyes; but far apart in spirit our ideas and faiths separated us. My grief was for the soul unsaved; and I thought my mother wept to see a brave man's body broken by sickness.

Useless was my attempt to change the faith in the medicine-man to that abstract power named God. Then one day I became righteously mad with anger that the medicine-man should thus ensnare my father's soul. And when he came to chant his sacred songs I pointed toward the door and bade him go! The man's eyes glared upon me for an instant. Slowly gathering his robe about him, he turned his back upon the sick man and stepped out of our wigwam. "Hā, hā, hā! my son, I cannot live without the medicine-man!" I heard my father cry when the sacred man was gone.

3

On a bright day, when the winged seeds of the prairie-grass were flying hither and thither, I walked solemnly toward the center of the camping-ground. My heart beat hard and irregularly at my side. Tighter I grasped the sacred book I carried under my arm. Now was the beginning of life's work.

Though I knew it would be hard, I did not once feel that failure was to be my reward. As I stepped unevenly on the rolling ground, I thought of the warriors soon to wash off their war-paints and follow me.

At length I reached the place where the people had assembled to hear me preach. In a large circle men and women sat upon the dry red grass. Within the ring I stood, with the white man's Bible in my hand. I tried to tell them of the soft heart of Christ.

In silence the vast circle of bareheaded warriors sat under an afternoon sun. At last, wiping the wet from my brow, I took my place in the ring. The hush of the assembly filled me with great hope.

I was turning my thoughts upward to the sky in gratitude, when a star called me to earth again.

A tall strong man arose. His loose robe hung in folds over his right shoulder. A pair of snapping black eyes fastened themselves like the poisonous fangs of a serpent upon me. He was the medicine-man. A tremor played about my heart and a chill cooled the fire in my veins.

Scornfully he pointed a long forefinger in my direction and asked, "What loyal son is he who, returning to his father's people, wears a foreigner's dress?" He paused a moment, and then continued: "The dress of that foreigner of whom a story says he bound a native of our land, and heaping dry sticks around him, kindled a fire at his feet!" Waving his hand toward me, he exclaimed, "Here is the traitor to his people!"

I was helpless. Before the eyes of the crowd the cunning magician turned my honest heart into a vile nest of treachery. Alas! the people frowned as they looked upon me.

"Listen!" he went on. "Which one of you who have eyed the young man can see through his bosom and warn the people of the nest of young snakes hatching there? Whose ear was so acute that he caught the hissing of snakes whenever the young man opened his mouth? This one has not only proven false to you, but even to the Great Spirit who made him. He is a fool! Why do you sit here giving ear to a foolish man who could not defend his people because he fears to kill, who could not bring venison to renew the life of his sick father? With his prayers, let him drive away the enemy! With his soft heart, let him keep off starvation! We shall go elsewhere to dwell upon an untainted ground."

With this he disbanded the people. When the sun lowered in the west and the winds were quiet, the village of cone-shaped tepees was gone. The medicine-man had won the hearts of the people.

Only my father's dwelling was left to mark the fighting-ground.

4

From a long night at my father's bedside I came out to look upon the morning. The yellow sun hung equally between the snow-covered land and the cloudless blue sky. The light of the new day was cold. The strong breath of winter crusted the snow and fitted crystal shells over the rivers and lakes. As I stood in front of the tepee, thinking of the vast prairies which separated us from our tribe, and wondering if the high sky likewise separated the soft-hearted Son of God from us, the icy blast from the north blew through my hair and skull. My neglected hair had grown long and fell upon my neck.

My father had not risen from his bed since the day the medicine-man led the people away. Though I read from the Bible and prayed beside him upon my knees, my father would not listen. Yet I believed my prayers were not unheeded in heaven.

"Hā, hā, hā! my son," my father groaned upon the first snow-fall. "My son, our food is gone. There is no one to bring me meat! My son, your soft heart has unfitted you for everything!" Then covering his face with the buffalo-robe, he said no more. Now while I stood out in that cold winter morning, I was starving. For two days I had not seen any food. But my own cold and hunger did not harass my soul as did the whining cry of the sick old man.

Stepping again into the tepee, I untied my snow shoes, which were fastened to the tent-poles.

My poor mother, watching by the sick one, and faithfully heaping wood upon the center fire, spoke to me:

"My son, do not fail again to bring your father meat, or he will starve to death."

"How, Ina," I answered, sorrowfully. From the tepee I started forth again to hunt food for my aged parents. All day I tracked the white level lands in vain. Nowhere, nowhere were there any other footprints but my own! In the evening of this third fast-day I came back without meat. Only a bundle of sticks for the fire I brought on my back. Dropping the wood outside, I lifted the door-flap and set one foot within the tepee.

There I grew dizzy and numb. My eyes swam in tears. Before me lay my old gray-haired father sobbing like a child. In his horny hands he clutched the buffalo-robe, and with his teeth he was gnawing off the edges. Chewing the dry stiff hair and buffalo-skin, my father's eyes sought my hands. Upon seeing them empty, he cried out:

"My son, your soft heart will let me starve before you bring me meat! Two hills eastward stand a herd of cattle. Yet you will see me die before you bring me food!"

Leaving my mother lying with covered head upon her mat, I rushed out into the night.

With a strange warmth in my heart and swiftness in my feet, I climbed over the first hill, and soon the second one. The moonlight upon the white country showed me a clear path to the white man's cattle. With my hand upon the knife in my belt, I leaned heavily against the fence while counting the herd.

Twenty in all I numbered. From among them I chose the best-fattened creature. Leaping over the fence, I plunged my knife into it.

My long knife was sharp, and my hands, no more fearful and slow, slashed off choice chunks of warm flesh. Bending under the meat I had taken for my starving father, I hurried across the prairie.

Toward home I fairly ran with the life-giving food I carried upon my back. Hardly had I climbed the second hill when I heard sounds coming after me. Faster and faster I ran with my load for my father, but the sounds were gaining upon me. I heard the clicking of snow-shoes and the squeaking of the leather straps at my heels; yet I did not turn to see what pursued me, for I was intent upon reaching my father. Suddenly like thunder an angry voice shouted curses and threats into my ear! A rough hand wrenched my shoulder and took the meat from me! I stopped struggling to run. A deafening whir filled my head. The moon and stars began to move. Now the white prairie was sky, and the stars lay under my feet. Now again they were turning. At last the starry blue rose up into place. The noise in my ears was still. A great quiet filled the air. In my hand I found my long knife dripping with blood. At my feet a man's figure lay prone in blood-red snow. The horrible scene about me seemed a trick of my senses, for I could not understand it was real. Looking long upon the blood-stained snow, the load of meat for my starving father reached my recognition at last. Quickly I tossed it over my shoulder and started again homeward.

Tired and haunted I reached the door of the wigwam. Carrying the food before me, I entered with it into the tepee.

"Father, here is food!" I cried, as I dropped the meat near my mother. No answer came. Turning about, I beheld my gray-haired father dead! I saw by the unsteady firelight an old gray-haired skeleton lying rigid and stiff.

Out into the open I started, but the snow at my feet became bloody.

5

On the day after my father's death, having led my mother to the camp of the medicine-man, I gave myself up to those who were searching for the murderer of the paleface.

They bound me hand and foot. Here in this cell I was placed four days ago!

The shrieking winter winds have followed me hither. Rattling the bars, they howl unceasingly: "Your soft heart! your soft heart will see me die before you bring me food!" Hark! something is clanking the chain on the door. It is being opened. From the dark night without a black figure crosses the threshold . . . . It is the guard. He tells me that tomorrow I must die. In his stern face I laugh aloud. I do not fear death.

Yet I wonder who shall come to welcome me in the realm of strange sight. Will the loving Jesus grant me pardon and give my soul a soothing sleep? or will my warrior father greet me and receive me as his son? Will my spirit fly upward to a happy heaven? or shall I sink into the bottomless pit, an outcast from a God of infinite love?

Soon, soon I shall know, for now I see the east is growing red. My heart is strong. My face is calm. My eyes are dry and eager for new scenes. My hands hang quietly at my side. Serene and brave, my soul awaits the men to perch me on the gallows for another flight. I go.[1]

POETRY

During the last thirty-five years of the twentieth century, Native Americans struggled to avoid succumbing to a sense of despair about their culture's demise—a seeping assimilation into the general American "melting pot." Writers, in particular, made the assault on such feelings a major focus of their works. In 1969, Scott Momaday's novel *House Made of Dawn* won a Pulitzer Prize and made a new generation of Native American writers aware of a powerful message: People caught between cultures can, despite a variety of problems, find ways to survive.

Paula Gunn Allen, perhaps representative of many Native American writers, believes that Momaday's book created a new future for her: It "brought my land back to me." She believes that she and many Native Americans suffer from "land sickness"—a deep sense of exile caused by the loss of her land and birthright. In passages from *House Made of Dawn* she found that she shared a familiarity with the places Momaday described: "I knew every inch of what he was saying." It gave her the strength and inspiration—the will—to continue. In her poem "Recuerdo" she creates images of movement, loss, and of searching. She looks for a sense of "being securely planted."

13.1 Lucy Lewis, ceramic bowl, from the Pueblo area, Acoma, New Mexico, 1969. National Museum of the American Indian, Smithsonian Institution, Washington, D.C.

Recuerdo
Paula Gunn Allen

I have climbed into silence trying for clear air
and seen the peaks rise above me like the gods.
That is where they live, the old people say.
I used to hear them speak when I was a child
and we went to the mountain on a picnic
or to get wood. Shivering in the cold air then
I listened and I heard.

Lately I write, trying to combine sound and memory,
searching for that significance once heard and nearly lost.
It was within the tall pines, speaking.
There was one voice under the wind—something in it
that brought me to terror and to tears. I wanted
to cling to my mother so she could comfort me,
explain the sound and my fear, but I simply sat,
frozen, trying to feel as warm as the campfire,
the family voices around me suggested I should.

Now I climb the mesas in my dreams.
The mountain gods are still, and still I seek.
I finger peyote buttons and count the stalks of sweetsage
given me by a friend—obsessed with a memory
that will not die.
I stir wild honey into my carefully prepared cedar tea
and wait for meaning to arise,
to greet and comfort me.

Maybe this time I will not away.
Maybe I will ask instead what that sounding means.
Maybe I will find that exact hollow
where terror and comfort meet.
Tomorrow I will go back and climb the endless mesas
of my home. I will seek thistles drying in the wind,
pocket bright bits of obsidian and fragments
old potters left behind.[2]

CERAMICS AND PAINTING

Pottery was the greatest of the prehistoric arts, and it continues almost completely as an aesthetic activity. Early pottery vessels, however, were designed for everyday use, and finishing techniques took second place to practical concerns—most important was to get the object into use. By the late twentieth century, time-honored traditions of Southwestern pottery rose in quality of finish and design to the status of high art. Thus, the culture has been sustained. Native American potters today, however, face the challenge of deciding on the degree to which younger artists should master—that is, replicate—traditional forms, as opposed to expressing individual creativity while still maintaining cultural traditions. Lucy Lewis's ceramic bowl (Fig. **13.1**) reflects this challenge. It follows the traditions of Acoma pottery but does not reflect traditional design.

Other Southwestern artistic forms include silversmithing—the popular silver and turquoise jewelry is still made—and sand painting. Sand paintings incorporate important religious meanings, and many rituals cannot be performed without them. The traditional materials of Native American art—indigenous and easily accessible—were supplemented in the twentieth century by standard Western media—for example, watercolor. In Figure **13.2** one of the foremost Navajo painters documents typical

13.2 Harrison Begay, *Women Picking Corn*, mid-20th century. Watercolor, 15 × 11½ ins (38.1 × 29.2 cm). National Museum of the American Indian, Smithsonian Institution, Washington, D.C.

Native American life. One characteristic aspect of Native American watercolor painting from the middle of the last century is this use of space: The painting stays on the surface plane and no background or spatial environment appears. The women and the corn are the only concerns. They are rendered in two dimensions with only the diminutive size of the woman on the left to hint at three-dimensional space or perspective. The horizon line, or viewer's eye level, is at the bottom of the painting.

MUSIC

As in the case of African tribal music, Native American music continues as an important part of cultural reality. For example, Inuit music has developed into an art form with complex rhythms using contrasting accents and meters. Its melodies are fairly conjunct, creating a gentle and undulating quality, but the style can be declamatory—similar to recitative in Western operas.

In Northwest-coast Native American music, only the owner of a song is permitted to perform it. However, it is possible to buy a song, to inherit it, or even to obtain it by murdering the owner. Additionally, songs are owned by secret societies within the tribes. In musical terms, Northwest Native American music is similar to some African music, using parallel harmonies sung by separate voices and *drone* notes (single notes sustained while the remaining parts sing on). Rhythms tend toward strongly percussive and intricate patterns.

Songs among the Southwestern Native Americans, especially the Pueblos, have a complex tonal system. They are based on six- or seven-note scales and stay at the low end of the register. This is in contrast to the music of the Plains Indians, who tend to use high pitches. Nearly every social occasion, holy day, and ceremony has its own special music.

AFRICA

African tribal art maintained its traditions into the early twentieth century. As we examine some final examples, let us review a few of its characteristics.

First of all, and perhaps unlike much of Western art, African art is made to be used—for example, it is frequently worn, as in the case of a mask or costume in a dance. The dance itself will have a ritual function: to ensure the continuity of the tribe. The rituals enact complex dramas of birth, succession of power, and initiation to adulthood.

Like art from all traditions—including much from Western culture—African art frequently serves a religious function, for religion permeates all facets of African life and death. Art is created to represent local deities and/or personal spirits, in the hope that they will grant favors to the worshiper in return for offerings and ceremonials. It can function as a device for divining the future and for worshiping ancestors—ancestor shrines often have figurative sculptures carved in honor of the dead. And it can symbolize concepts like family unity and character traits like aggression.

In addition, African art maintains a political function. Traditionally, tribal power was held both by a king and by a governing body of tribal elders who balanced the royal authority. In many regions, a queen mother (or another female relative of the king) also held a powerful position within the community. Frequently art objects were created to symbolize and sustain the ruling authority. Like Native American art—and Western art from such periods as the Baroque—African art often proclaims the wealth and power of the king. Often made from the richest of materials, works of art become proof positive of the king's majesty and his ability to commission works from the greatest artists.

Finally, although African artworks are primarily functional, this does not mean that beauty is not a consideration. Rarely does African art copy nature. Rather, we can think of it as conceptual—that is, artists emphasize the physical and symbolic characteristics of the essences, rather than the visible nature, of their subjects.

SCULPTURAL STYLE

Figures

Two carved figures of a dancing royal couple (Fig. 13.3) from the Bangwa Kingdom of Cameroon exemplify typically dynamic combinations of line, form, and texture. These cult images have a ritualistic purpose encompassing the appeasement of the spirit of the tree from which they were carved. The sculptor has captured the movement of two figures caught at a moment in a dance, complete with flexing legs and tightening muscles. The neck and chin of the female strain upward, showing tension filled with dynamic energy. Open mouths indicate that

the dance was accompanied by a song. Both sculptures—the female form, especially—seem to be built up out of ovoid sections although each was carved from one piece of wood. Smooth, sweeping curves create a dynamic rhythm, while the slender points of articulation between body parts heighten the intensity of motion.

Although these depictions suggest reality, they modify and stylize it. Like the figures of the ancient and Classical Greeks, these statues represent types rather than individuals. However, they are very human, with facial expressions that communicate individual human emotion and expression—although some proportions have been exaggerated, for example, the eyes in the male figure. The wooden surface has been polished to a degree of smoothness that suggests the play of light on real skin. Clothing and accoutrements represent the costume of the tribe. Both of these figures suggest youth and health. They seem powerful, alive, and in the prime of life. Despite their less-than-lifelike proportions, they communicate grace and flexibility—characteristics particularly admired by Africans in dancers.

The lengthy European presence in Africa has, in some cases, had a subtle influence on the construction of traditional tribal artifacts. The early twentieth-century figure in Figure 13.4, an animal from Loango in Congo Brazzaville, displays African symbolic significance but is made of European materials. This animal is called a *power figure*—it is a magical effigy. Its spines are iron nails and blades driven into a wooden core. The act of driving the nails and blades into the figure was thought to activate magic, used either to cure or kill. Because nails are of European manufacture, more than one expert has suggested that the concept of giving them supernatural power stemmed from the story of Christ's crucifixion, told by missionaries who first came to Africa after the

13.3 Dancing royal couple from Bangwa, Cameroon, early 20th century. Wood, height 34½ and 34¼ ins (87.6 and 87 cm). Harry A. Franklin family, on loan to the Los Angeles County Museum of Art.

13.4 Magic animal, from Loango, Congo Brazzaville, early 20th century. Wood, with iron nails and blades, length 35 ins (88 cm). Musée de l'Homme, Paris.

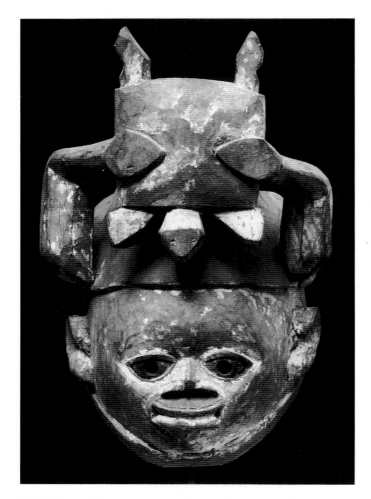

13.5 Yoruba Gelede mask headdress with carved turtle superstructure, from Benin, 20th century. Height 15 ins (38.1 cm).

great age of discovery in the sixteenth century. In fact, from the early sixteenth to the late seventeenth century, Christianity was the state religion in the area where these figures were found, but clearly traditional beliefs coexisted with it. Although these nails are European, iron had older ritual significance in Africa. The metal had been smelted from early times in northern Nigeria and was used widely in agriculture and warfare long before Christianity reached Africa. It is therefore likely that iron as a magical symbol predates Christian influence.

Whatever the case, this feisty animal bristles with life. Like a worried porcupine, it seems set in an aggressive posture, with quills poised at the optimum angle for attacking an enemy. The open mouth, extended tongue, and bulging eyes convey a sense of imminent action. Because the front legs slant backward, we feel that the animal is poised to spring forward.

Power figures like this one apparently had only a short lifespan. Unlike some others, these effigies were discarded once their original purpose had been achieved (or after

they had proven ineffective). Whatever their original intention, these works transcend anthropological speculation and have interest purely as works of sculpture. Their texture, line, and form surely communicate far more than their makers intended.

Headdress Masks

Headdress masks are widely used in African rituals, and the following example from western Africa gives some insight into their importance. The Yoruba headdress mask in Figure 13.5 was made for a tribal festival—Gelede—found only among the southwestern Yoruba peoples along the border between Nigeria and the Republic of Benin. Gelede is in the spring, from March through May, when the rains arrive. Coinciding with a time of vegetative renewal, the festival aims to renew the social condition of the tribe by honoring "the mothers."

Gelede masks such as this one represent elder Yoruba women in their dual role as "the mothers" and as witches: They have the power to create, but also to destroy. The term "the mothers" signifies the collective power of women and refers specifically to elderly women, female ancestors, and female deities. The power ascribed to them affects the fertility of the fields, the family, and the peace and prosperity of the community.

In this particular example, the head of one of "the mothers" is carved as a headdress with a turtle held above it by the jaws of two snakes which wrap around the headpiece. The headdress is daubed with white and red paint which gives the image a mottled texture, strengthening the three-dimensionality of the carving.

The Yoruba peoples' art represents the Guinea Coast Style Zone, and this large and diverse zone consists of several stylistic approaches of peoples who are principally farmers. Centralized political institutions and hierarchical organization characterize the region. The arts are used in secret societies; in representations of ancestors, protective images, and nature spirits; in funerary, initiation, and public entertainment performances; and in the service of traditional political institutions.

AFRICAN INFLUENCE ON WESTERN ART

The direct influence of African art can be seen in the early work of the Romanian sculptor Constantin Brancusi (brahn-KOOSH or bran-KOOZ-ee; 1876–1957). While his work borrows freely from African tribal motifs, the smooth, precise surfaces of much of his work seem to have an abstract, mechanistic quality. His search for essential form led to very economical presentations, often

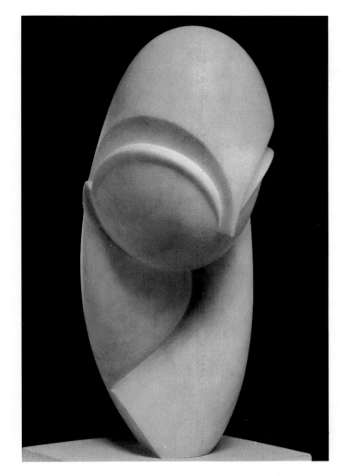

13.6 Constantin Brancusi, *Mlle. Pogany*, 1931. Marble on limestone base, height 19 ins (48 cm). Philadelphia Museum of Art (Gift of Mrs. Rudolphe Meyer de Schauensee).

death—and times and seasons—such as the new year and the new moon—have their own songs and dances.

The heritage of the tribe is communicated from generation to generation by means of song and dance. Thus, music plays a vital role in keeping alive the spirit and cohesiveness of society. Nearly every one of Africa's hundreds of tribes has its own individual musical characteristics. Because African music tends to be sung, the language of the tribe contributes its unique sounds and textures. This is especially true of the tone languages—those in which pitch helps to denote meaning. A particular word, when sung, must stay in a specific pitch range because to move into another pitch range would change its meaning.

Typically, the music of tribal Africa consists of short melodic phrases that are repeated, alternated, and varied in order to create longer melodies. Often a phrase is sung by a leader and then repeated in response by a chorus. Voices move in parallel chords—always consistent in their separation—and this gives African music its characteristic harmonic quality. Another interesting aspect of some African music is a drone held by one voice while a second voice sings a phrase; the drone then passes to the second voice while the first sings a phrase, and so on. Also typical is the use of complicated and contrasting rhythmic patterns. Quite often one voice or drum will maintain a duple meter while another works in triple meter against it. Harmonically, melodically, and rhythmically, African music is very complex not only across the range of tribes but also within specific tribal groups (music CD track 3).

ovoid and simple, yet animate. *Mlle. Pogany* (Fig. 13.6) has the enigmatic character of an African mask despite its superbly polished surface and the accomplished curves that lead the eye inward. The surface has a modern sleekness, and there is great psychological complexity here; and yet the tribal essence remains, reminding us of the work of Africans or Aboriginals.

AFRICAN TRIBAL MUSIC

Although African tribal music could have been introduced at any point, it has been placed here so that we can understand its continuing presence in African life. Music in Africa is truly universal: Its importance crosses all societal levels, from royalty to the common person. Every aspect of tribal existence has special music—for example, there is music for communicating news, for entertainment, for legal dealings, for hunting, and for working in the fields. Special life events—like marriage, birth, and

AFRICAN AMERICA

HARLEM RENAISSANCE

From 1919 to 1925 Harlem, a small enclave in New York City, became the international capital of African culture. "Harlem was in vogue" wrote the poet Langston Hughes (see p. 380). African American painters, sculptors, musicians, poets, and novelists joined in a remarkable artistic outpouring. The period became intensely controversial, its artistic merits attacked by some critics of the time as isolationist and conventional; the qualities of the Harlem Renaissance still provoke debate. Nonetheless, this period of intense creative activity by African Americans "gave the artists an identifiable artistic context for their work, propelled them to the forefront of the New Negro Movement, and inspired their art for the remainder of their careers."[3]

The artistic works of this period reached a national audience through exhibitions sponsored by the Harlem

Foundation. The movement explored several themes: African American heritage; the traditions of African folklore; and the daily life of African American people. In every case the Harlem Renaissance artists broke with previous African artistic traditions. They celebrated their history and culture and "defined a visual vocabulary for Black Americans."[4]

Intellectuals such as W. E. B. Du Bois, Alain Locke, and Charles Spurgeon spearheaded the movement. Among the notable artists were social documenter and photographer James van der Zee (1886–1983), painter Palmer Hayden (1890–1973), painter Aaron Douglas (1899–1979), painter William Henry Johnson (1901–70), painter Jacob Lawrence (b. 1917), sculptor Meta Vaux Warrick Fuller (1877–1968), and poet Langston Hughes (1902–67).

Painting

Palmer Hayden (Peyton Cole Hedgeman) trained at the Cooper Union in New York in 1919 and later at the Boothbay Art Colony. In 1927 he traveled to Europe and studied at the Ecole des Beaux Arts. His work was exhibited widely in New York and despite its symbols of ethnic heroism it drew heavy criticism from those who believed that his depictions mocked African American people and sustained negative stereotypes. Later in life he created the John Henry series, twelve oil paintings portraying the life and death of a folk hero. This was part of his focus on African American legends, which visually expressed the wealth of material from the African American oral culture of the rural South and from Africa itself. His main approach was to use folk themes to illustrate industrial America's dependence on the African American labor force.

Aaron Douglas, perhaps the foremost painter of the Harlem Renaissance, earned a bachelor of fine arts degree from the University of Nebraska and a master's degree from Columbia University. His training encouraged him to explore the rich vocabulary of African American myth and culture. His work is highly stylized, explores a palette of muted tones, and is well known through its appearance as illustrations and cover designs for many books by

13.7 Aaron Douglas, *Aalta*, 1936. Oil on canvas, 18 × 23 ins (45.7 × 58.4 cm). Carl Van Vechten Gallery of Fine Arts, Fisk University (Afro-American Collection of Art).

13.8 Jacob Lawrence, "One of the most violent race riots occurred in East St. Louis," Panel 52 from *The Migration Series*, 1940–1; text and title revised by the artist, 1993. Tempera on gesso on composition board, 12 × 18 ins (30.5 × 45.7 cm). The Museum of Modern Art, New York (Gift of Mrs. David M. Levy).

African American writers. His mural *Aspects of Negro Life*, at the New York Public Library's Cullen Branch, documents in four panels the emergence of an African American identity. The first panel portrays the cultural background in images of music, dance, and sculpture. The next two bring to life slavery and emancipation in the American South and flight to the cities of the North. The fourth panel returns to the theme of music. Among Douglas's wide variety of stylistic approaches, his realistic portrait of Aalta (Fig. **13.7**) provides a warm and relaxed composition. Its palette and expression show dignity, elegance, and stability.

William Henry Johnson trained at the National Academy of Design in New York, followed by a three-year fellowship in 1926 to study in Europe. Under the influence of the European Impressionists and Realists, his style grew in personal expressiveness. His many works focus on African American experience. Harlem, where he spent his childhood, is the central theme. Just prior to World War II his style changed again, moving from fully rounded to flat figures.

In Jacob Lawrence's works, such Modernist effects—for example, the flattening of space and the use of undifferentiated planes of color—are secondary to the need to convey an intelligible narrative to the viewer (Fig. **13.8**). Having trained at the Harlem Art Workshop and the American Artists' School in New York, he is a fine example of an artist acutely aware of his privileged position and, at the same time, his membership of a dispossessed and disadvantaged section of society.

Sculpture

Meta Vaux Warrick Fuller "was the first Black American artist to draw heavily on African themes and folklore for her subjects."[5] Years before the Harlem Renaissance, she began to express the pan-African ideals that later permeated the movement. After finishing graduate work at the Pennsylvania Museum and School for Industrial Arts, she studied in Paris at the Ecole des Beaux Arts and the Académie Colarossi. One of her mentors was the sculptor Auguste Rodin (see p. 342), and his influence can be seen in her impressionistic surface treatment of Romantic Realist subjects. Fuller built her own studio in Framingham, Massachusetts, and focused on themes dealing with antislavery and protests against injustice to African Americans. In one of the earliest works by an American focusing on the African heritage, her sculpture *Ethiopia Awakening* shows an Egyptian woman emerging from her embalming wrappings. "The work symbolically represents the emergence of Black cultural awareness from the 'wrappings' of ignorance and oppression, and the beginnings of the end of colonial rule in Africa."[6] Works such as *The Talking Skull* are based on African models and illustrate the confrontation of humans with death, a prevalent theme in her career.

Poetry

Langston Hughes is often referred to as the "poet laureate of Harlem." He portrays the life of the ordinary African American in the United States, catching with sharp immediacy and intensity the humor, pathos, irony, and humiliation of being black in America. His poetry particularly appeals to young people. He speaks of the basic qualities of life: love, hate, aspirations, and despair. Yet he writes with a faith in humanity in general. He interprets all life as it is experienced in the real world, as well as touching on the ideal. Hughes struggled within himself between what he wanted to express and what his audience expected him to write. Thus some of his work is militant, with broad sociopolitical implications.

Hughes received considerable attention as a poet as early as 1921 with his poem "The Negro Speaks of Rivers." In his novel *Not Without Laughter*, he creates a brilliant portrayal of an African American youth's passage into manhood. In the selections that follow, readers can sense something of the African American experience and perception of the universe.

Theme for English B

Langston Hughes

1902–67

The instructor said,

    Go home and write

    a page tonight.

    And let that page come out of you—

    Then, it will be true.

I wonder if it's that simple?

I am twenty-two, colored, born in Winston-Salem.

I went to school there, then Durham, then here

to this college on the hill above Harlem.

I am the only colored student in my class.

The steps from the hill lead down into Harlem

through a park, then I cross St. Nicholas.

Eighth Avenue. Seventh, and I come to the Y,

the Harlem Branch Y, where I take the elevator

up to my room, sit down, and write this page:

It's not easy to know what is true for you or me

at twenty-two, my age. But I guess I'm what

I feel and see and hear, Harlem, I hear you:

hear you, here me—we two—you, me, talk on this page.

(I hear New York, too) Me—who?

Well, I like to eat, sleep, drink, and be in love.

I like to work, read, learn, and understand life.

I like a pipe for a Christmas present,

or records—Bessie, bop, or Bach.

I guess being colored doesn't make me not like

the same things other folks like who are other races.

So will my page be colored that I write?

Being me, it will not be white.

But it will be

a part of you, instructor.

You are white—

yet a part of me, as I am a part of you,

that's American.

Sometimes perhaps you don't want to be a part of me.

Nor do I often want to be a part of you.

But we are, that's true!

As I learn from you

I guess you learn from me—

although you're older—and white—

and somewhat more free.

This is my page for English B.

Harlem

Langston Hughes

What happens to a dream deferred:

Does it dry up

like a raisin in the sun?

Or fester like a sore—

and then run?

Does it stink like rotten meat?

Or crust and sugar over—

like a syrupy sweet?

Maybe it just sags

like a heavy load.

Or does it explode?[7]

JAZZ

Probably the most significant African American contribution to music, *jazz* began near the turn of the last century. It is essentially made up of improvised variations on a theme. The earliest form—*blues*—went back to the music of the slaves. It consists of two rhythmic lines and a repeat of the first line (AAB). At the end of the nineteenth century, performers like Bessie Smith gave the blues an emotional quality, which the accompanying instruments tried to imitate.

At approximately the same time came *ragtime*, a form of piano jazz with a strict two-part form. Syncopation—the displacement of accent from the normally accented beat to the offbeat—played an important role in this style. Its most famous artist was Scott Joplin.

New Orleans, the cradle of jazz, also produced *traditional jazz*, featuring improvisation on a basic chord sequence. This was followed in the 1930s and 1940s by *Swing* and *Be-bop*. The term "Be-bop" was coined as a result of the characteristic long-short triplet rhythm that ended many phrases. Its prime developers were alto saxophonist Charlie "Bird" Parker (Fig. **13.9**) and trumpeter Dizzie Gillespie. Styles stemming from traditional jazz proliferated after World War II. There was a gradual move away from big bands to smaller groups and and a desire for much more improvisation. The *Cool Jazz* style developed in the early 1950s with artists like Miles Davis. Although the technical virtuosity of Be-bop continued, it also emphasized a certain lyric quality, particularly in the slow ballads. More importantly, actual tone quality was a major distinction, particularly in the wind instruments.

Were our space unlimited, we could look further into this African American form and include such gifted performers as Thelonius Monk, John Coltrane, and Cecil Taylor. John Coltrane, for example, has had a tremendous influence on African American society in the United States. Coltrane's personality and charisma are clear in his albums *A Love Supreme, Ascension Meditations*, and those that followed. These works acted as a significant spiritual reservoir for African Americans and have cast a hugely influential shadow over jazz ever since.

DANCE

The American dance scene has benefited from a number of exceptional choreographers of African American heritage who draw upon their culture. Among them is Alvin Ailey (1931–89), a versatile dancer whose company is known for its unusual repertoire and energetically free movements. Another form of dance that has its roots in Africa, but which draws upon the broad experiments of modern dance, is *jazz dance* (see Chapter 6). Like modern dance in general, its form and direction are still in flux. Nevertheless, stemming from sources as diverse and yet as allied as tribal Africa and the urban ghetto, it has seen significant activity and experimentation throughout the United States (see Figs. **6.8** and **6.9**). Pioneered by choreographers such as Asadata Dafora Horton in the 1930s and Katherine Dunham and Pearl Primus in the 1940s, jazz dance flourished at the end of the century under choreographers such as Talley Beatty and Derglas MacKayle.

LIBERATION IN THE THEATRE

Theatrical liberation of the African American began in the 1960s. One manifestation of the civil rights movement of the 1950s and 1960s was the angry, militant African Americans who espoused "Black consciousness." Many converted to the African Muslim version of Islam, and many longed for a completely separate "Black nation." Radical groups talked about destroying Western society. A number of African Americans turned toward Africa and

13.9 Saxophonist Charlie Parker in performance with Tommy Potter. Parker died prematurely in 1955, aged 35, but by that time he was already a legendary figure.

sought a new identity in the Third World. In the 1980s, there was a change in self-description from Black to African American.

Many of these ideas were expressed in the works of playwrights such as LeRoi Jones (who became Imamu Amiri Baraka). His plays dramatize the dangers of Blacks allowing Whites into their private lives and call for racial separation. Charles Gordonne's *No Place to Be Somebody* renews Baraka's cause, and espouses violence as legitimate action in the penetrating story of a fair-skinned Black searching for his own racial identity.

Many new African American theatre companies emerged in the 1960s. The Negro Ensemble Company, founded by Douglas Turner Ward, is one enduring example. It staged a moving production of *Home* by Samm-Art Williams. *Home* traces the ups and downs in the life of an African American Southerner named Cephus. Raised on a farm, he leaves for the big city. Convicted of draft evasion and sent to jail, he progresses to joblessness and welfare, disease and despair. Finally, he returns to the honest labor and creative values on the farm. The poetic language and the conventions of its production format give *Home* a unique and endearing quality. Cephus is played by a single actor, but all the other roles—old, young, male, female, Black, White—are played by two women who take on whatever role they wish by changing costumes. Sometimes they are characters in Cephus's journey and other times they act as a chorus, helping the audience to follow leaps in time and space. The chorus format helps the audience to see Cephus from the point of view of African American history and culture. Although Cephus is constantly on the move, the stage setting never changes, and although the actresses play several different roles, they never change. Through these devices, the playwright suggests that "home" is at hand all the time, waiting to be grasped. The force that stands in the way is unwillingness: to acknowledge one's inner yearnings, to accept help from others, and to extend oneself by choosing a path of peace instead of confrontation.

The son of a White father and a Black mother, August Wilson (b. 1945) writes with an ear tuned to the rhythms and patterns of the blues and the speech of African American neighborhoods. He founded the Playwrights Center in Minneapolis. His plays range from *Jitney* and *Ma Rainey's Black Bottom* in the 1980s to *Two Trains Running* and *Seven Guitars* in the 1990s. Wilson believes that the African American has the most dramatic story of all humankind to tell. His concern lies with the stripping away of important African traditions and religious rituals from Blacks by Whites. In plays such as *The Piano Lesson*, he portrays the complexity of African American attitudes toward themselves and their past. Both the blatant and the more subtle conflicts between Black and White cultures and approaches form the central core of Wilson's work and can be seen in plays such as *Fences*.

Fences treats the lives of African American tenement-dwellers in Pittsburgh in the 1950s. Troy Maxson, a garbage collector, takes great pride in his ability to hold his family together and to take care of them. As the play opens, Troy discusses his challenge to the union concerning Blacks' access to doing the same "easy" work as Whites. He is frustrated and believes that he has been deprived of the opportunities to get what he deserves—and this becomes a central motif. He describes his wrestling match with death in 1941 when he had pneumonia. He also tells of his days in the African American baseball leagues, barred from playing in the majors because of his race.

AMERICA AND EUROPE

EXPRESSIONISM

Visual Arts

Expressionism traditionally refers to a movement in Germany between 1905 and 1930, but used more broadly it applies to a focus on the joint reaction of artist and viewer to composition elements. Any element (line, form, color, and so on) can be emphasized to elicit a specific response. The artist consciously tries to stimulate a reaction specifically relating to his or her feelings about, or commitment to, the subject matter. Subject matter itself mattered little; what counted was the artist's attempt to evoke in the viewer a similar response to his or her own. In Max Beckmann's *Christ and the Woman Taken in Adultery* (Fig. 13.10), the artist's revulsion against physical cruelty and suffering is transmitted through distorted figures crushed into shallow space. Linear distortion, changes of scale and perspective, and a nearly Gothic spirituality communicate Beckmann's reactions to the horrors of World War I. In this approach, meaning relies on specific nonverbal communication.

The 1970s saw a continuation of Expressionism in the lyrical work of artists such as William T. Williams (b. 1942). *Batman* (Fig. 13.11) has a methodology that has been compared to jazz improvisation. In the carefully defined two-part structure, verticals subtly play across the dividing line to pull the work together. At the same time delicate traceries reinforce the basic structure and provide endless variations. The resulting texture is evocative, like

13.10 Max Beckmann, *Christ and the Woman Taken in Adultery*, 1917. Oil on canvas, 4 ft 10¾ ins × 4 ft 1⅞ ins (1.49 × 1.27 m). St. Louis Art Museum (Bequest of Curt Valentin).

cracking or peeling paint on a series of old boards. True to its Expressionist heritage, the work links the artist's memory with the experience of the viewer.

Theatre and Film

Expressionism found its way into the theatre in scenic design, as the painters' revolt against realism was adopted. But here we must tread carefully, because the theatre is both visual and oral. As regards concepts and plots, Expressionism was merely an extension of realism, and disillusionment often came to the fore. Yet it allowed playwrights a more adequate means to express their own reactions to specific items in the universe around them. The Swedish dramatist August Strindberg (1849–1912), for example, turns inward to the subconscious in Expressionistic plays such as the *Ghost Sonata*. In so doing, he creates a presentational rather than representational style.

Expressionism also found its way to America. Elmer Rice's play *Adding Machine* depicts Mr. Zero, a cog in the great industrial machinery of twentieth-century life, who stumbles through a pointless existence. Finding himself replaced by an adding machine he goes berserk, kills his employer, and is executed. Then, adrift in the hereafter, he is too narrow-minded to understand the happiness offered to him there. He becomes an adding machine operator in Heaven and finally returns to earth to begin his tortured existence all over again.

German Expressionism made its mark in film as well as in the visual and other performing arts, and in 1919 its best example, Robert Wiene's (VEEN-uh) *Cabinet of Dr. Caligari*, shook the world. Macabre sets, surrealistic lighting effects, and distorted properties all combine to portray a menacing postwar German world.

CUBISM

Between 1901 and 1912 a new approach to pictorial space emerged: *Cubism.* Cubist space violates all concepts of two- or three-dimensional perspective. In the past the space within a composition had been thought of as separate from the main object of the work. That is, if the subject were removed, the space would remain, unaffected. Pablo Picasso (1881–1973) and Georges Braque (brahk; 1882–1963) changed that relationship to one in which the artist tried to paint "not objects, but the space they engender." The area around an object became an extension of the object itself. If the object were removed, the space around it would collapse. Cubist space is typically quite shallow and gives the impression of reaching forward toward the viewer, thereby intruding into space outside of the frame. Essentially the style developed as the result of independent experiments by Braque and Picasso with ways of describing form. Perhaps newly evolving notions of the time–space continuum proposed by German physicist Albert Einstein (1879–1955) at this time helped to make their works more acceptable.

Picasso influenced the visual arts of the twentieth century more than any other individual. Born in Spain, he moved in 1900 to France, where he resided for most of his life. In Paris he was influenced by Toulouse-Lautrec and the late works of Cézanne (see p. 361), particularly in terms of their organization, analysis of forms, and assumption of different viewpoints. He focused on form kept within the frame. Mass was "built up within [the frame] like a box within a box"[8] (see Figs. **1.19** and **1.36**).

Very early on, Picasso began to identify deeply with society's misfits and cast-offs. He was able to express this strongly in his art. Depression characterized his works from 1901 until around 1904 or 1905. This is known as his Blue Period and was followed by his Rose Period (1904–6) "in which he was less concerned with the tragic aspects of poverty than with the nostalgic charm of itinerant circus performers and the school of make-believe."

13.11 William T. Williams, *Batman*, 1979. Acrylic on canvas, 6 ft 8 ins × 5 ft (2.03 × 1.52 m).
Collection of the artist.

Les Demoiselles d'Avignon (lay duh-mwah-ZEHL dah-veen-YAWN; Fig. **13.12**) has become the single most discussed image in modern art. Its simplified forms and restricted color were adopted by many Cubists, as they reduced their palettes in order to concentrate on spatial exploration. A result of personal conflicts on the part of the artist, combined with his ambition to be recognized as the leader of the avant garde, the painting deliberately breaks with the traditions of Western illusionistic art. The painter denies both Classical proportions and the organic integrity and continuity of the human body.

Les Demoiselles d'Avignon (Avignon in the title refers to a street in Barcelona's red-light district) is aggressive and harsh like the world of the prostitutes who inhabit it. Forms are simplified and angular, and colors are restricted to blues, pinks, and terracottas. Picasso breaks his subjects into angular wedges which convey a sense of three-dimensionality. We do not know whether the forms protrude out or recess in. In rejecting a single viewpoint, Picasso presents "reality" not as a mirror image of what we see in the world, but as images that have been reinter-

preted within the terms of new principles. Understanding thus depends on knowing rather than seeing in the literal sense. Cubism uniformly reduced its palette range, thereby emphasizing the exploration of space.

FAUVISM

The label "Fauves" (fohv; French for "wild beasts") was applied by a critic in response to a sculpture (exhibited in 1905) which seemed to him "a Donatello in a cage of wild beasts." Violent distortion and outrageous coloring mark the subjective expression of the Fauves. Their two-dimensional surfaces and flat color areas were new to European painting. The best-known artist of this short-lived movement was Henri Matisse (1869–1954). He tried to paint pictures that would "unravel the tensions of modern existence." In his old age he made a series of joyful designs for the Chapel of the Rosary in Venice, not as exercises in religious art but, rather, to express the almost religious feeling he had for life. *Blue Nude* (Fig. **13.13**), painted after the Fauves disbanded, illustrates the

13.12 Pablo Picasso, *Les Demoiselles d'Avignon*, Paris, June to July 1907. Oil on canvas, 8 ft × 7 ft 8 ins (2.44 × 2.34 m). The Museum of Modern Art, New York (Acquired through the Lillie P. Bliss Bequest).

wild coloring and distortion of Matisse and *Fauvism*. The painting takes its name from the energetically applied blues all over the figure as darkened accents. For Matisse color and line were indivisible. His bold strokes of color are both coloristic and linear stimulants, and also revelations of form. Matisse literally "drew with color." Underlying this work is Matisse's desire to express his feelings about the nude as an object of aesthetic interest, rather than to draw the woman as he saw her in life.

FUTURISM

New concerns for space turned, logically, to the potential of three-dimensional space. Technological developments and new materials also encouraged the search for novel forms characteristic of the age. Futurists in the visual arts searched for dynamic qualities; some sculptures even included moving parts. Others followed mechanistic lines, as people began to appreciate that many of the new machines of the era had sculptural form.

Unique Forms of Continuity in Space by Umberto Boccioni (boh-CHOH-nee; Fig. **13.14**) takes the mythological subject of Mercury, messenger of the gods (see Fig. **2.7**), and turns him into a futuristic machine. The overall form is recognizable and the connotations of the myth suggest subject matter. Nonetheless, this is primarily an exercise in composition of forms. The intense sense of energy and movement is created by the variety of surfaces and curves that flow into one another in a seemingly random yet highly controlled pattern. The overall impression is of a figure in motion, rather than of the figure itself.

ABSTRACTION

Abstract art contains minimal reference to natural objects—that is, objects in the phenomenal or natural world. In many ways abstract art contrasts with Impressionism and Expressionism in that the observer can read little or nothing in the painting of the artist's feelings about the universe. Abstract art seeks to explore the expressive qualities of formal design elements in their own right. These elements are assumed to stand apart from subject matter. The aesthetic theory underlying abstract art maintains that beauty can exist in form alone, and no other quality is needed.

Visual Arts

Piet Mondrian (1872–1944) believed that the fundamental principles of life consisted of straight lines and right angles. A vertical line signified active vitality and life; a horizontal line signified tranquillity, rest, and death. The crossing of the two in a right angle expressed the highest possible tension between these forces, positive and negative. *Composition in White, Black, and Red* (see Fig. **1.43**) explores Mondrian's philosophy in a manner characteristic of all his linear compositions. The painting's planes are close to the surface of the canvas, creating, in essence, no space, in contrast to the deep space of other styles. The palette is restricted to three hues. Even the edges of the canvas take on expressive possibilities as they provide additional points of interaction between lines. Mondrian believed that he could create "the equivalence of reality"

13.13 Henri Matisse, *Blue Nude* ("*Souvenir de Biskra*"), 1907. Oil on canvas, 36¼ × 55¼ ins (91 × 104 cm). Baltimore Museum of Art (Cone Collection, formed by Dr. Claribel Cone and Miss Etta Cone of Baltimore, Maryland).

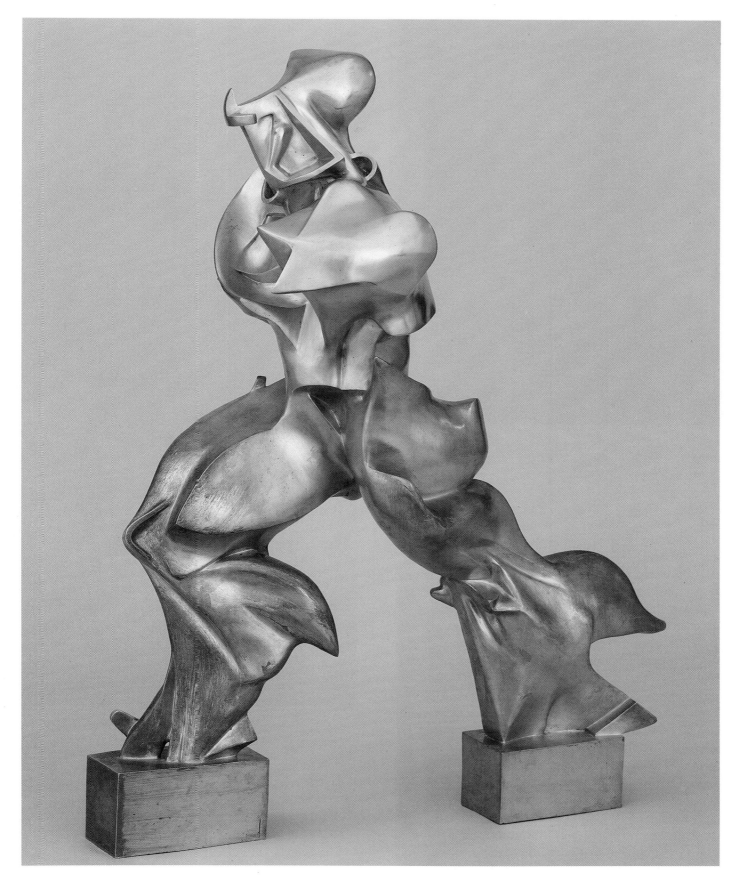

13.14 Umberto Boccioni, *Unique Forms of Continuity in Space*, 1913. Bronze (cast 1931), 43⅞ × 34⅞ × 15¾ ins (111.2 × 88.5 × 40 cm). The Museum of Modern Art, New York (Acquired through the Lillie P. Bliss Bequest).

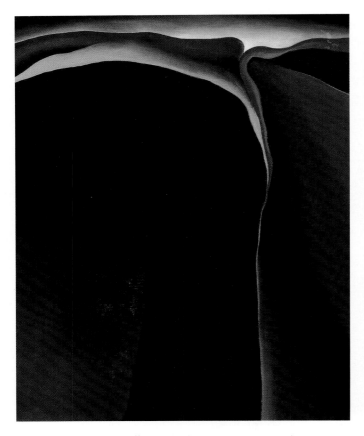

13.15 Georgia O'Keeffe, *Dark Abstraction*, 1924. Oil on canvas, 24⅞ × 20⅞ ins (63.3 × 53 cm). St. Louis Art Museum (Gift of Charles E. and Mary Merrill).

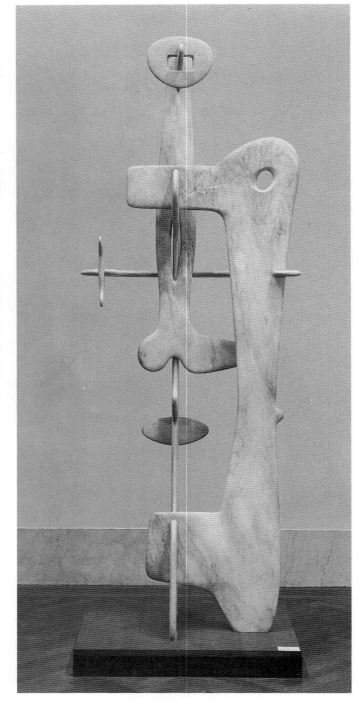

13.16 Isamu Noguchi, *Kouros* (in nine parts), 1944–5. Pink Georgia marble, slate base, height approx. 9 ft 9 ins (2.97 m). Metropolitan Museum of Art, New York (Fletcher Fund).

and make the "absolute appear in the relativity of time and space" by keeping visual elements in a state of constant tension.

The American Georgia O'Keeffe (1887–1986) was one of the most original artists of the twentieth century. Her imagery draws on a diverse repertoire of objects abstracted in a uniquely personal way. She takes, for example, an animal skull and transforms it into a form of absolute simplicity and beauty. In *Dark Abstraction* (Fig. 13.15) an organic form becomes an exquisite landscape which, despite its modest size, appears monumental. Her lines flow gracefully upward and outward with skillful blending of colors and rhythmic grace. Whatever the subject of the painting, it expresses a mystical reverence for nature. O'Keeffe creates a sense of reality that takes us beyond our surface perceptions.

Isamu Noguchi (noh-GHOO-chee; 1904–88), seemingly less concerned with expressive content than others, experimented with abstract sculptural design from the 1930s onward. His creations go beyond sculpture to provide highly dynamic designs which have inspired the choreography of Martha Graham, with whom he was associated for a number of years. Noguchi's *Kouros* figures

(Fig. 13.16) are an abstract response to archaic Greek sculpture, with exquisitely finished surfaces and exemplary technique.

The highly original mobiles of Alexander Calder (1898–1976; see Fig. 2.4) put abstract sculpture into motion. Deceptively simple, these colorful shapes turn at the whim of subtle breezes or are powered by motors.

Here is the discovery that sculpture can be created by movement in undefined space.

Objectivity returns in the work of Alberto Giacometti (jah-koh-MEH-tee; 1901–66). He explores the reality of the human figure and surface depiction and meaning, as can be seen in Figure **2.12**. Here form is reduced to its essence in a tortured fragmentation that appears to be a comment on the nature of humankind in the contemporary world.

Poetry

The Englishman Wystan Hugh Auden (1907–73) took abstraction into poetry. His main concerns in the 1930s were for humanity, society, and personal problems. His writings show a strong desire for pattern and order. In this early period he tends toward discussion, logic, and reasoning. In later works, Auden appears to have become disenchanted with Marx and Freud. These poems are marked by skepticism, irony, and a semireligious tone. In 1936 Auden traveled to Spain to support the left-wing cause in the Spanish Civil War. From 1948 until the mid-1950s, he experimented with symbolic landscape poetry, characterized by a syllabically counted line. Auden's writing was influenced by numerous factors, including Greek literature, Old English poetry, and the Icelandic sagas. He remains one of the major influences in twentieth-century British and American poetry.

In War Time
(For Caroline Newton)
W. H. Auden
1907–73

Abruptly mounting her ramshackle wheel,
Fortune has pedalled furiously away:
The sobbing mess is on our hands today.

Those accidental terrors, Famine, Flood,
Were never trained to diagnose or heal
Nightmares that are intentional and real.

Nor lust nor gravity can preach an aim
To minds disordered by a lucid dread
Of seeking peace by going off one's head.

Nor will the living waters whistle; though
Diviners cut their throats to prove their claim,
The desert remains arid all the same.

If augurs take up flying to fulfill
The doom they prophesy, it must be so;
The herons have no modern sign for No.

If nothing can upset but total war
The massive fancy of the heathen will
That solitude is something you can kill,

If we are right to choose our suffering
And be tormented by an Either-Or,
The right to fail is worth dying for,

If so, the sweets of victory are rum;
A pride of earthly cities premising
The Inner life as socially the thing,

Where, even to the lawyers, Law is what,
For better or for worse, our vows become
When no one whom we need is looking, Home

A sort of honour, not a building site,
Wherever we are, when if we chose, we might
Be somewhere else, yet trust that we have chosen right.[9]

SURREALISM

As the work of Sigmund Freud became popular, artists became fascinated by the subconscious mind. By 1924, a Surrealist manifesto stated some specific connections between the subconscious mind and painting. Surrealist works were thought to be created by "pure psychic automatism," whose goal was to merge reason and unreason, consciousness and the unconscious into an "absolute reality—a super-reality." Its advocates saw Surrealism as a way to discover the basic realities of psychic life by automatic associations. Supposedly, a dream could be transferred directly from the unconscious mind of the painter to canvas without control or conscious interruption.

Two directions of Surrealist art emerged. The metaphysical fantasies of Giorgio de Chirico (KEE-ree-koh; 1888–1978), for example, present fantastic, hallucinatory scenes in a hard-edged, realistic manner. In works such as *The Nostalgia of the Infinite* (see Fig. **1.45**), strange objects are irrationally juxtaposed: They come together as in a dream. These bizarre works reflect a world that human beings do not control. In them, "there is only what I see with my eyes open, and even better, closed."

Another Surrealist of this same direction was Mexican painter Frida Kahlo (KAH-loh; 1907–54). Her works (more than one third are self-portraits) are studies in great pain and suffering, both mental and physical. A bus crash at age eighteen resulted in the loss of her right leg. Works such as *The Broken Column* (Fig. **13.17**) portray a

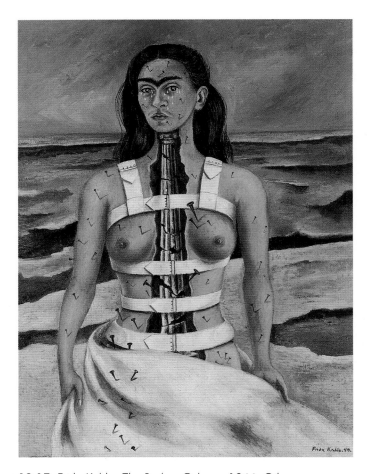

13.17 Frida Kahlo, *The Broken Column*, 1944. Oil on masonite, 15¾ × 12¼ ins (40 × 31 cm). Museo Dolores Olmedo, Mexico.

nightmarish quality typical of Surrealism—here a myriad of emotions, as the subject appears both as a sufferer and a savior. The broken column displayed in the open chasm of the torso juxtaposes a graphic architectural form, perhaps suggesting her own spine and brokenness, with her body itself, punctured by numerous nails and held together by a cloth harness. The self-portrait stands before a barren monochromatic landscape and darkened sky.

The second direction of Surrealism—the abstract—can be seen in works by Joan Miró (see Fig. **1.20**). These are based on spontaneity and chance, using abstract images.

REALISM

Painting

In the twentieth century, pictorial objectivity continued in the Realist tradition in the works of Grant Wood (1892–1942)—for example, *American Gothic* (see Fig. **0.4**), a celebration of America's heartland and its simple, hardworking people. There is a lyric spirituality behind the façade of this down-home illustration. The upward movement of the elongated forms is pulled together at the top into a pointed arch which encapsulates the Gothic window of the farmhouse and escapes the frame of the painting through the lightning rod, in the same sense that the Gothic spire released the spirituality of the earth into heaven at its tip. Rural American reverence for home and labor is fêted here with gentle humor. There is a capricious two-dimensionality. All objects, and the people, line up horizontally. There is no linear perspective in the middle ground, and so the buildings appear pressed against the backs of the farmer and his wife.

Film

World War II and its aftermath brought radical change to the form and content of the cinema. A film came out in 1940 that stunned even Hollywood. Darryl Zanuck and John Ford's version of John Steinbeck's *Grapes of Wrath* took the social criticism of Steinbeck's portrayal of the Depression and presented it visually, creating art through superb cinematography and compelling performances. Social commentary burst forth again in 1941 with two outstanding works, *How Green was my Valley*, which dealt with exploited coal miners in Wales, and *Citizen Kane*, about wealth and power, and thought by some to be the best film ever produced. The cinematic techniques of *Citizen Kane* forged a new trail. Orson Welles, director and star, and Greg Toland, cinematographer, brilliantly combined deep-focus photography, new lighting effects, rapid cutting, and moving camera sequences.

But as the war ended and Italy overthrew the yoke of Fascism, a new concept set the stage for the years ahead. In 1945 Roberto Rossellini's (rah-seh-LEE-nee) *Rome, Open City* graphically depicted the misery of Rome during the German occupation. It was shot on the streets of the capital using hidden cameras and mostly nonprofessional actors and actresses. Technically, the quality of the work was deficient, but the effectiveness of its objective viewpoint and documentary realism changed the course of cinema and inaugurated a style called *Neorealism*.

Theatre

Realism continued its strong tradition in the theatre throughout the postwar era, owing much of its strength to the works of the American playwrights Tennessee Williams (1912–83) and Arthur Miller (b. 1915). It has now expanded since its nineteenth-century conception in the works of Henrik Ibsen (*Ghosts*; *A Doll's House*) and George Bernard Shaw (*Pygmalion*; *Major Barbara*) to include more theatrical approaches, such as fragmented settings. Including many nonrealistic devices, such as

13.18 Jackson Pollock, *Autumn Rhythm*, 1950. Oil on canvas, 8 ft 9 ins × 17 ft 3 ins (2.67 × 5.26 m). Metropolitan Museum of Art, New York (George A. Hearn Fund).

symbolism, it has become broader and more eclectic, concluding that stage realism and life's realism are two separate issues.

Tennessee Williams skillfully blends the qualities of Realism with whatever scenic, structural, or symbolic devices are necessary to meet his goals. His plays, such as *The Glass Menagerie*, deal sensitively and poignantly with the problems and psychology of everyday people. Character development is thorough and occupies the principal focus as he explores the mental and emotional ills of our society. Arthur Miller, too, probes the social and psychological forces that destroy contemporary men and women in plays such as *Death of a Salesman*.

ABSTRACT EXPRESSIONISM

The first fifteen years following the end of World War II were dominated by a style called Abstract Expressionism. Beginning essentially in New York, it spread rapidly throughout the world. Like most modern styles, it is used with some variation among individual artists. Two characteristics can be identified. One is freedom from traditional use of brushwork, and the other is the exclusion of representational subject matter. Individual expression used to reflect inner life gave artists rein to create works of high emotional and dynamic intensity. The freedom of this style appears to relate to the optimistic postwar sense

of conquest over totalitarianism. By the early 1960s, when life was less certain and the implications of the nuclear age had sunk in, Abstract Expressionism as a force in art had reduced to a trickle.

The most heralded artist of this style was Jackson Pollock (1912–56). A rebellious spirit, he evolved a method of dripping and spilling paint onto huge canvases placed on the floor (Fig. **13.18**; see also Fig. **1.22**). Often called *action painting*, the controlled dripping gives a sense of tremendous energy, and a revolutionary concept of space, line, and form. Pollock rejected much of the European tradition in favor of cruder, rougher formal values identified with the American frontier. The term "action painting" (coined by an art critic) refers to active paint handling by the artist. Pollock indicated that he was more at ease with painting on the floor, believing that in that way he could literally be in the painting, and when in the painting, not aware of what he was doing. The result was pure harmony. Thus, Pollock found deep pleasure in the technique, which provided him with a sense of being fully absorbed in action and freed from any estrangement from the world.

The Abstract Expressionist tradition continues in the work of Helen Frankenthaler (frahn-kehn-TAH-luhr; b. 1928). Her staining technique, as seen in *Buddha* (Fig. **13.19**), consists of pouring color across an unprimed canvas, creating amorphous shapes which seem to float in space. The image has infinite potential meaning, apart from that suggested by the title. The very freedom of the form symbolizes our freedom to choose its associations. However, we are directed by the sensual quality of the work. Its fluidity and the nonlinear use of color give it softness and grace.

Abstract Expressionism proved ultimately to be an American movement. Nowhere else did anything even remotely comparable emerge during this time. However, by the early 1960s the style seems to have reached its zenith. An entirely new perception of reality—one of consumerism and affluence—began to sweep the world.

13.19 Helen Frankenthaler, *Buddha*, 1988. Acrylic on canvas, 6 ft 2 ins × 6 ft 9 ins (1.88 × 2.06 m). Private collection.

13.20 Roy Lichtenstein, *Whaam!*, 1963. Acrylic on canvas, 5 ft 8 ins × 13 ft 4 ins (1.73 × 4.05 m). Tate, London.

13.21 Claes Oldenburg, *Two Cheeseburgers, with Everything* (*Dual Hamburgers*), 1962. Burlap soaked in plaster, painted with enamel, 7 × 14¾ × 8⅝ ins (17.8 × 37.5 × 21.8 cm). The Museum of Modern Art, New York (Philip Johnson Fund).

Following Abstract Expressionism, and in some instances as a reaction against that type of painting, there came a veritable explosion of styles and movements: Pop Art, Op Art, Hard Edge, Primary Structures, Minimal Art, Post-Minimal Art, Environmental Art, Body Art, Earth Art, Video Art, Kinetic Art, Photo Realism, and Conceptualism. We have space to discuss only four of these.

POP ART

Pop Art evolved in the 1950s, and concerns itself above all with image in a representational sense. Subjects and treatments in this style come from mass culture and commercial design. These sources provide Pop artists with what they consider to be essential aspects of their visual environment. Pop Art is essentially an ironic reflection of the contemporary scene. The term "Pop" was coined by the English critic Lawrence Alloway.

Probably the compelling depictions of Roy Lichtenstein (1923–97) are the most familiar (Fig. **13.20**). These magnified cartoon-strip details use the Ben Day screen of dots by which colored ink is applied to cheap newsprint. Using a stencil about the size of a coin, the artist builds the image up into a stark and dynamic, if sometimes violent, portrayal.

Pop objects serve as source materials for Claes Oldenburg (b. 1929). *Dual Hamburgers* (Fig. **13.21**) presents an enigma to the viewer. What are we to make of it? Is it a celebration of the mundane? Or is there a greater comment on the age implicit in these objects? Certainly Oldenburg calls our attention to the design of ordinary objects by taking them out of their context and changing their scale.

HARD EDGE

Hard Edge or Hard Edged Abstraction came to its height during the 1950s. The work of Ellsworth Kelly (b. 1923) and Frank Stella (b. 1936) best illustrates this style: Flat color areas have hard edges which carefully separate them from each other. Essentially, Hard Edge is an exploration of design for its own sake. Stella often abandons the rectangular format in favor of irregular compositions to be sure that his paintings bear no relationship to windows. The shape of the canvas is part of the design itself, as

13.22 Frank Stella, *Tahkt-i-Sulayman I*, 1967. Polymer and fluorescent paint on canvas, 10 ft ¼ in × 20 ft 2¼ ins (3.04 × 6.15 m). Pasadena Art Museum, California (Gift of Mr. and Mrs. Robert A. Rowan).

13.23 Louise Nevelson, *Black Wall*, 1959. Wood, 112 × 85¼ × 25½ ins (264 × 216 × 65 cm). Tate, London.

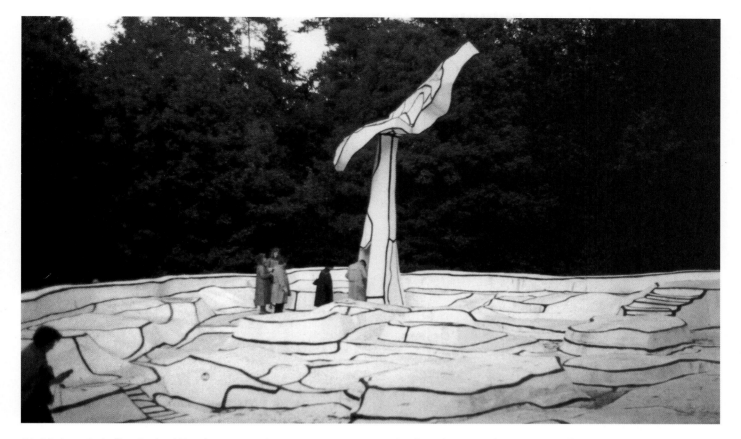

13.24 Jean Dubuffet, *Jardin d'Email*, 1973–4. Concrete, epoxy paint, and polyurethane, 66 ft 8 ins × 100 ft (20 × 30 m). State Museum Kröller-Müller, Otterlo, The Netherlands.

opposed to being a frame or a formal border within which the design is executed. Some of Stella's paintings have iridescent metal powder mixed into the paint, and the metallic shine further enhances the precision of the composition. *Tahkt-i-Sulayman I* (Fig. **13.22**) stretches 20 ft (6 m) across and intersperses wonderfully surging circles and half-circles of yellow and green, reds and blues. The intensity of the surface counters the grace of its form with jarring fluorescence. The simplicity of these forms deceptively counters the variety of their repetitions.

PRIMARY STRUCTURES

The Primary Structures movement pursues two main goals: extreme simplicity of shape and a kinship with architecture. It is the space–time relationship that distinguishes Primary Structures from other sculpture. The viewer is invited to share an experience in three-dimensional space by walking around and/or through the works. Form and content are abstracted to Minimalist qualities.

Louise Nevelson (1900–88), perhaps the twentieth century's first major woman sculptor, overcame the perception that sculpture was a man's profession because of

the heavy manual labor involved. In the 1950s she began using found pieces of wood to construct her own vision of reality—at first miniature cityscapes. Her work grew to larger proportions—for example, *Black Wall* (Fig. **13.23**), a relieflike wall unit painted a monochromatic flat black. These pieces suggest the world of dreams, but their meaning and logic remain a puzzle with intense appeal to the imagination.

ENVIRONMENTAL ART

Environmental Art creates an inclusive experience. In *Jardin d'Email* (zhahr-DAN deh-MEHL; Fig. **13.24**) by Jean Dubuffet (doo-boo-FAY; 1901–85), an area is made of concrete covered with white paint and black lines. It is capricious in form and surrounded by high walls. Inside the sculptural environment are a tree and two bushes made of polyurethane. We might conclude that Dubuffet has pushed the essence and boundaries of art to their limits. He has consistently opted for chaos, for *art brut*— the art of children, psychotics, and amateurs. The *Jardin d'Email* is one of a small series of projects in which he depicts the chaotic, disorienting, and inexplicable in three-dimensional form.

13.25 Judy Chicago, *The Dinner Party*, 1974–9. White tile floor inscribed in gold with 999 women's names; triangular table with painted porcelain, sculpted porcelain plates, and needlework, each side 48 ft (14.6 m). Courtesy the artist.

FEMINIST ART

During the 1970s the feminist artists of the Women's Art Movement attempted to break down old barriers. Substantially as a result of this movement, women began to achieve increased recognition in the art world in America and beyond. Marches, protests, the organization of women's cooperative galleries, active promotion of women artists, critical exploration by women art historians, and the development of a Feminist Art Program at the California Institute of the Arts, in 1971, brought about significant results. One of the founders of the CalArts program, Judy Chicago, provides a good example of the feminist perspective. At the end of the 1960s she began to use feminine sexual imagery to reveal the sexism of the male-dominated art world. *The Dinner Party* (Fig. **13.25**) records the names of 999 notable women, and pays homage to thirty-nine legendary women, including an Egyptian Queen and Georgia O'Keeffe (see p. 388). At each side of the triangular table are thirteen settings (the number of witches in a coven and the number of men at the Last Supper). The triangular shape is a symbol for woman. During the French Revolution it stood for equality. Each of the place settings at the table features a runner in a style appropriate to the woman it represents, in addition to a large ceramic plate. Included are traditional women's art forms such as stitchery, needlepoint, and china painting, which Chicago wished to raise to the status given to painting and sculpture. Suggestions of female genitalia throughout the painting are the artist's comment that that was all the women at the table had in common.

Susan Lacy, whose analysis of the roles played by artists we examined on page 15, collaborated with Leslie Labowitz in a performance piece (see Performance Art, p. 100) called *In Mourning and Rage* (1977) outside the Los Angeles City Hall to protest violence against women in American cities. This example of political art, which we discussed as a function of art on page 18, utilized the image of mourning in a stark and elaborate event designed to promote action. The artists secured media coverage and followed the event with a number of talk-show appearances, a rape hotline, and other related activities.

LATINO ART

Our focus throughout Part II of this book has been on "style." Nonetheless, there is merit, given the pluralism of the current age, in recognizing that we can also examine a spirit at work in art that presents its ethnic ethos prominently, even though it may fall into a stylistic category with works by artists of other cultural backgrounds. Such is the case with Latino art.

Painting

Diego Rivera (ree-BAY-rah; 1886–1957) revived the fresco mural as an art form in Mexico in the 1920s. Working with the support of a new revolutionary government, he produced large-scale public murals that picture contemporary subjects in a style that blends European and native traditions. The fresco painting *Slavery in the Sugar Plantation* (Fig. **13.26**) creates a dramatic comment on that chapter in Mexican history. The composition is

13.26 Diego Rivera, *Slavery in the Sugar Plantation, Tealtenago, Morelos* (detail), 1930–1. Fresco, 14 ft 3 ins × 9 ft 3 ins (4.35 × 2.82 m). Palace of Cortez, Cuernavaca, Mexico.

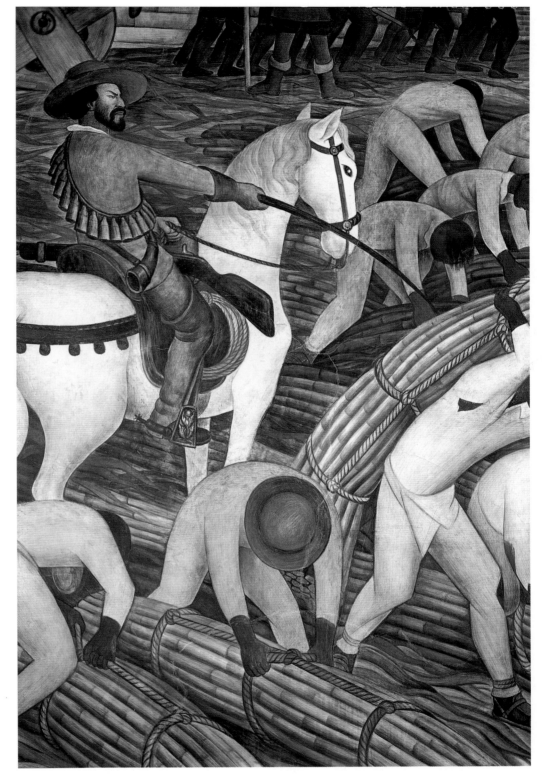

not unlike Goya's *Execution of the Citizens of Madrid, May 3, 1808* (see Fig. **1**.46). A strong diagonal sweeps across the work, separating the oppressed from the oppressor, and provides a dynamic movement stabilized by the Classically derived arcade framing the top of the composition. Rivera's wife, Frida Kahlo, whose work we dis-

cussed as an example of Surrealism (see p. 389), was one of the most celebrated painters of the early twentieth century. Her style reflects Mexican folk culture and her deep feeling for the power and beauty of folk art.

Rafael Ferrer (b. 1933), born in Puerto Rico, creates an exotic, mysterious world of the tropics in *El Sol Asombra*

13.27 Rafael Ferrer, *El Sol Asombra*, 1989. Oil on canvas, 5 × 6 ft (1.52 × 1.83 m). Courtesy Nancy Hoffman Gallery, New York.

(Fig. **13.27**). A lively palette dominates the painting, and the relationship of the central structure to those surrounding it gives the work a slightly unsettling sense of space. The painting has a surface flatness, given its simplified and flattened shapes and tonally even colors. Ferrer's use of light energizes the composition and creates an inviting series of patterns. The title of the painting means "the sun with shade or shadow," and we suspect a play on words because, although the title describes the work accurately, there is mystery in the lightness juxtaposed against the dark.

Jose Bedia (BAY-dee-ah; b. 1959), a Cuban painter and installation artist, draws the viewer into *Si se quiere, se puede* (*If you want to, you can*; Fig. **13.28**). The painting raises ideas about leaving Cuba, and the image of a man on a boat shaped like an anvil, coupled with the title and the restricted palette, raises questions to which the viewer wants to respond. The flat starkness and black and blue palette of Bedia's rendering create a confrontational and engaging image. We are left to ponder the larger issues.

Theatre and Poetry

Theatre of the Spanish-speaking communities of America reflects and serves a diverse population. It dates to the conquistadors and grew significantly during the civil rights struggles of the 1960s. In the summer of 1965, Luis Valdez joined Cesar Chavez to use improvisational theatre to underscore the plight of the migrant worker and give political impetus to the farm workers' strike in Delano, California. This led Valdez to form El Teatro Campesino (Farm Workers' Theatre). Using Valdez as a model, a number of other Chicano theatre groups appeared during the 1960s and 70s, including Jorge Huerta's (WAR-tah) Teatro de la Esperanza ("Theatre of Hope"). A number of Latino playwrights have emerged as well, including Estela Portillo Trambley.

The curious label *Nuyorican theatre* applies to Puerto Rican culture in New York, which typically deals with bilingual and working-class situations. This ethnic consciousness produces a diversity of street theatre, prison productions, and small non-profit Hispanic theatres such as Teatro Repertorio Español and the Puerto Rican Traveling Theatre. The term Nuyorican began to arouse negative responses when themes of crime, drugs, abnormal sexuality, and generally aberrant behavior became associated with the movement.

Nuyorican poetry came into being in the 1960s and 70s and currently enjoys a nationwide standing. Anthony Morales (b. 1981) represents the latest generation. He

13.28 Jose Bedia, *Si se quiere, se puede (If you want to, you can)*, 1993. Acrylic on canvas, 5 ft × 7 ft 6 ins (1.52 × 2.29 m). Collection of Robertson, Stephens, Inc., San Francisco. Courtesy George Adams Gallery, New York.

dedicated a poem read at the Nuyorican Poets Café, in New York City, to the founders of the stage where he stood—among them poet and playwright Miguel Piñero, subject of the film *Piñero* (2001), starring Benjamin Bratt:

> to those stoned crazy prophets of revolution,
> giving poetic solutions to political pollution,
> organizing rhythmic confusion of assimilation
> to this untied states nation of eggs, cheese and bacon
> upon wakin'.

Morales, a native of the Bronx, majored in English and Latino studies at Columbia University and speaks of the heroin-infested, crime-ridden, self-destructive world of Piñero. His literary tradition, like that of Piñero, comes from the Puerto Rican experience in the United States. "My poetry is about trying to make sense of the world, of being a young Puerto Rican male. ... We have incredible stories we got to tell." Piñero's play *Short Eyes* (1974)—a prison drama presented by Joseph Papp's Public Theater and at Lincoln Center—won the New York Drama Critics Circle Award for best American play. It was developed in a workshop at the Ossining Correctional Facility (Sing Sing), where Piñero was serving time for armed robbery. That year Piñero, known as Miky, helped found the Nuyorican Poets Café. Piñero died of cirrhosis of the liver in 1988, at age 41 (*New York Times*, January 2, 2002).

Cuban-American theatre emerged as early as the nineteenth century in the Cuban-American communities of New York City and Ybor City-Tampa. The Cuban Revolution of 1959, which brought Fidel Castro to power in Cuba, resulted in large-scale theatrical activity in Cuban-American communities throughout the United States, but principally in Miami and New York. This was primarily political theatre of exile, and themes often include acculturation, bilingualism, culture conflict, and the generation gap between immigrants and their US-raised children.

MODERNISM

Architecture

EXPERIMENTATION Structural expression and preoccupation with building materials dominated the early twentieth century, as it had the nineteenth. Of vital importance was reinforced concrete, or ferroconcrete. It had been in use since around 1850, but nearly fifty years elapsed before it emerged fully as an important architectural material. Auguste Perret (peh-reh; 1874–1954) single-mindedly set about developing formulas for building with ferroconcrete, and his efforts were influential in the works of those who followed. Some of the implications are evident in Perret's Garage Ponthieu in Paris (Fig. **13.29**). The reinforced concrete structure protrudes from the façade, and glass or ceramic panels fill the open spaces. The result is a certain elegance and a logical expression of strength and lightness.

Perret's contemporary, Frank Lloyd Wright (1867–1959; see Profile, p. 164), was one of the most innovative and influential of twentieth-century architects. While Perret encapsulated and continued earlier traditions, Wright initiated new ones. One of Wright's creations was the Prairie Style, developed around 1900 and drawing upon the flat landscape of the Midwest for its tone. Wright's Prairie houses reflected Japanese influence in their simple horizontal and vertical accents.

As assistant to Louis Sullivan (see p. 366), Wright was influenced in his pursuit of form and functional relationships. Wright attempted to devise practical arrangements for his interiors and to reflect the interior spaces in the exterior appearance of the building (see Fig. 7.38). He also tried to relate the exterior of the building to its context or natural environment. Wright designed some of the furniture for his houses; comfort, function, and design integration were his chief criteria. Textures and colors in the environment were duplicated in the materials, including large expanses of wood in both the house and its furniture. He made a point of producing multifunctional furniture—for example, tables also served as cabinets. All spaces and objects were precisely designed to present a complete environment. Wright was convinced that houses profoundly influence the people who live in them, and he saw the architect as a "molder of humanity." His works range from the simple to the complex, from the

13.29 Auguste Perret, Garage Ponthieu, Paris, 1905–6.

serene to the dramatic, and from interpenetration to enclosure of space. He always pursued experimentation: Exploration of the interrelationships of spaces and geometric forms marks his designs (see Fig. 7.22).

A new concept in design can also be seen in the works of Le Corbusier (see p. 169) in the 1920s and 1930s. He espoused a "domino" system of house construction, using a series of poured concrete slabs supported on slender columns. The resulting building was boxlike, with a flat roof which could be used as a terrace (see Fig. 7.31). Much machine-related art in the first half of the century sought depersonalization, but not Le Corbusier's design. Rather, it implied efficient construction from standard, mass-produced parts, logically planned for use in an efficient "house-machine."

INTERNATIONAL AND CORPORATE ARCHITECTURE It is hard to sample or overview the architecture of the late

MASTERWORK

Frank Lloyd Wright, Kaufmann House

Frank Lloyd Wright is one of the greatest American artists in any medium. His primary message is the relationship of architecture to its setting, a lesson that some modern architects seem to have forgotten. Wright's buildings seem to grow out of, and never violate, their environment.

One of his most inventive designs is the Kaufmann House, Fallingwater, at Bear Run, Pennsylvania (Fig. 13.30). Cantilevered over a waterfall, its dramatic imagery is exciting. The inspiration for this house was probably the French Renaissance château of Chenonceaux, built on a bridge across the River Cher. However, Fallingwater is no house built on a bridge. It seems to erupt out of its natural rock site, and its beige concrete terraces blend harmoniously with the colors of the surrounding stone. Wright has successfully married two seemingly dissimilar styles: The house is a part of its context, yet it has the rectilinear lines of the International Style, to which Wright was usually opposed. He has taken those spare, sterile boxes and made them harmonize with their natural surroundings.

Wright's great asset, and at the same time his greatest liability, was his myopic insistence on his own vision. He could work only with clients who could bend to his wishes. So, unlike many architects, whose designs are tempered by the vision of the client, what Wright built was Wright's, and Wright's only. Watch the Humanities CD: Architecture, Frank Lloyd Wright.

13.30 Frank Lloyd Wright, Fallingwater (Kaufmann House), Bear Run, Pennsylvania, 1936–7.

13.31 Ludwig Mies van der Rohe and Philip Johnson, Seagram Building, New York, 1958.

13.32 Pier Luigi Nervi, Small Sports Palace, Rome, 1957.

twentieth century. In a sense, the task is particularly difficult in this medium, because the human element of artistic creation has been blurred by architectural corporations, as opposed to individual architects. There is also a tendency for the contemporary observer to see a sameness in the glass and steel boxes of the International Style that dominate our cities and to miss the innovative design of, say, a housing project in an obscure locale.

World War II caused a ten-year break in architectural construction and, to a certain extent, separated what came after from what went before. However, the gap is bridged by the continuing careers of architects who achieved significant accomplishments before the war. Geographical focus shifted from Europe to the United States, Japan, and even South America. But the overall approach remained modern or international in flavor, which helps us to select a few examples to illustrate general tendencies.

As a type, the skyscraper saw a resurgence in the fifties, in a glass-and-steel box form. The rectangle, which has so uniformly—and, in many cases, thoughtlessly—become the mark of contemporary architecture leads us to one of its prewar advocates. The German architect Ludwig Mies van der Rohe (roh-uh; 1886–1969) insisted that form should not be an end in itself. Rather, the architect should discover and state the function of the building. His pursuit of those goals and his honesty in outwardly expressing the shapes of mass-produced materials— bricks, glass, and manufactured metals—was the basis for the rectangularization that is the common ground of twentieth-century architecture. His search for proportional perfection can be traced, perhaps, to the German Pavilion of the Barcelona Exposition in 1929 and was expressed in projects such as New York's Seagram Building (Fig. **13.31**).

Contemporary design has ultimately pursued the question formulated by the American architect Louis I. Kahn

(1901–74), "What form does the space want to become?" In the case of Frank Lloyd Wright's Guggenheim Museum (see Fig. **7.38**), space has become a relaxing spiral that reflects the leisurely progress one should make through an art museum.

The simple curves of the arch and dome characterize the work of two noteworthy architects. The unencumbered free space in their projects contrasts with the self-contained boxes of the International Style. Pier Luigi Nervi's Small Sports Palace (Fig. **13.32**) and Richard Buckminster Fuller's Climatron (see Fig. **7.21**) illustrate the trend toward *spansion architecture*, which stretches engineering to the limits of its materials.

Music

Modernism in music took no less radical a path from its nineteenth-century heritage than it did in painting and sculpture. Nevertheless, contemporary concert programs illustrate that response to works of art is always in the present tense. Our own responses to the meanings in works of art are those of today, whether the artwork was created this morning or 20,000 years ago. So we have the luxury of sharing experiences directly with Michelangelo, Shakespeare, Leonardo da Vinci, J.S. Bach, and the architects of Athens, as well as with artists of our own era who illuminate and comment upon the events and circumstances that surround us. Our contemporaries may, and do, choose to follow the traditions of the past and invent new ones.

Twentieth-century music took both paths. The radical one diverges from the past essentially in three ways. The first is rhythmic complexity. Prevailing tradition since the Middle Ages has emphasized grouping beats together in measures. The accents of duple and triple meters have helped to characterize and unify compositions. But Modernist composers have done away with these regular accents, choosing instead to employ complex, changing rhythms in which it is virtually impossible to determine meter, or even the actual beat.

The second change from the past concerns dissonant harmonies. Prior to the late nineteenth century, musical convention in the West centered upon consonance as the norm to which all harmonic progressions returned. Dissonance was used to disturb the norm. The late nineteenth century witnessed significant tampering with that concept. By the twentieth century composers were using more and more dissonance, focusing on it, and refraining from consonant resolution.

The third major change from the past was a rejection of traditional tonality and sense of key altogether. Traditional thinking held that one note, the *do* or tonic of a scale, was the most important. All music was composed with a specific key in mind. Modulations into distant or related keys occurred, but even then the tonic of the original key was the touchstone to which all progression related. In the twentieth century, many composers rejected that manner of systematizing musical sound and chose, instead, to reject any sense of tonal center. All twelve tones of the chromatic scale thus become equal, and the system is known as *twelve-tone composition*, which was later refined into *serialism*.

The more conservative path saw a transition from the nineteenth to the twentieth century in France that rode primarily on the works of one major composer, the Impressionist Claude Debussy (see p. 360). Debussy's style linked him closely with the French composer Maurice Ravel (1875–1937), who began as an Impressionist but became more and more Classical in orientation as years went by. However, even in his earlier works, Ravel did not adopt Debussy's complex sonorities. Ravel's *Bolero* exhibits strong primitive influences and the unceasing rhythm of Spanish dance music. More typical works of Ravel—for example, his *Piano Concerto in G*—use Mozart and traditional Classicism as their models. As a result of Ravel's tendencies and the similar concerns of other composers—a Classically oriented style was adopted by Camille Saint-Saëns (san-SAHN; 1835–1921), for example—music in the early twentieth century took a Neoclassical direction, maintaining the established conventions of Western music but rejecting both Impressionist and serialist developments.

The American composer William Schuman also took the more traditional path in the 1930s and 1940s. His symphonies have bright timbres and energetic rhythms and focus on eighteenth- and nineteenth-century American folklore. The eighteenth-century American composer William Billings figures prominently in the works of Schuman in the *William Billings Overture* and the *New England Triptych*, based on three pieces by Billings. *American Festival Overture* is perhaps Schuman's most famous composition.

Traditional tonality can also be found in the works of Russia's Sergei Prokofiev. Notwithstanding this, his *Steel Step* reflects the encroachment of mechanization during the 1920s. The machine as a symbol for tremendous energy and motion found its way into music; in the *Steel Step* Prokofiev intentionally dehumanizes the subject in order to reflect contemporary life.

HINDEMITH Experimentation and departure from traditional tonality mark the compositions of the German composer Paul Hindemith (hin-duh-muhth or hin-duh-miht; 1895–1963). Concerned with problems of musical organization, he formulated a systematic solution in the *Craft of Musical Composition*. His music is extremely chromatic—almost atonal. He used "tonal centers," but abandoned the concepts of major and minor keys. He hoped that his new system would become a universal music language, but it did not. He was, however, extremely influential in twentieth-century music composition, both as a composer and a teacher. His works are broad and varied, encompassing nearly every musical genre, including ten operas, art songs, cantatas, requiems, chamber music, sonatas, concertos, and symphonies.

BARTÓK The Hungarian composer Béla Bartók (bar-TAWK; 1881–1945) took another nontraditional approach to tonality. He was interested in folk music. His research into eastern European folk music is significant, because much of it does not use Western major/minor modality. Bartók invented his own types of harmonic structure, which could accommodate traditional folk melodies. He also used tonal centers, and his music is often harshly dissonant.

As nontraditional as some of his work is, however, Bartók also employed traditional devices and forms. His style was precise and tightly structured. He often developed whole movements from one or two very short motifs. His larger works are unified by repetition of thematic material throughout. Occasionally he even used the Classical sonata form. Textures in Bartók's works are largely contrapuntal, which gives them a melodic emphasis on the motifs that are being developed.

Rhythm is important in Bartók's music—it has great rhythmic energy, employing many different devices, such as repeated chords and irregular meters (always to generate impetus). His use of polyrhythms—that is, various juxtaposed rhythms—creates a nonmelodic counterpoint of unique quality. In part, this reflects the influence of folk song and dance. Bartók's compositions—many piano pieces (including three concertos), six string quartets, the *Concerto for Orchestra*, an opera entitled *Duke Bluebeard's Castle*, and others—all possess a wonderfully spontaneous freshness.

STRAVINSKY Nontraditionalism was followed in other quarters, and with *The Firebird* the Russian composer Igor Stravinsky (1882–1971) came to prominence in 1910. *The Rite of Spring* (music CD track 20) created an even greater impact a couple of years later. Both works were scores for ballets. *The Firebird* was a commission for the Russian impresario Sergei Diaghilev, and premièred successfully at the Paris Opéra, while *The Rite of Spring* caused a near riot and a great scandal as a result of its revolutionary orchestrations, dissonance, and driving primitive rhythms. The piece had a great impact on twentieth-century music.

In later works, Stravinsky adopted a Neoclassical style as he attempted to revive Baroque and Classical elements and forms, for example in the oratorio *Oedipus Rex* and the opera *The Rake's Progress*. Toward the end of his life Stravinsky also experimented with serialism.

SCHOENBERG The movement that drew the most attention in the first half of the twentieth century grew out of German Romanticism and took a radical turn into atonality, and the composer at its root was Arnold Schoenberg (SHUHRN-bairk or SHUHRN-buhrg; 1874–1951). Between 1905 and 1912 Schoenberg turned away from the gigantic Post-Romantic works he had been composing to a more contained style. He broke down the musical texture, alternating timbres swiftly and fragmenting rhythm and melody.

Although the word atonality (without tonality) is used to describe Schoenberg's works, he preferred the term pantonality—that is, inclusive of all tonalities. His compositions use any combination of tones without the necessity of having to resolve chordal progressions. He called that concept "the emancipation of dissonance."

By 1923 Schoenberg was composing in twelve-tone technique, in which a row or series of the twelve tones in an octave is used in order before any note can be repeated. The tone row can then be used upside down, backward, or upside down and backward. This serial arrangement can also be applied to rhythm and dynamics. The logical structure of the technique is mathematical and somewhat formalized, but it does maintain a complete absence of key sense, and a balance between emotion and mechanization. The important thing for a listener to understand about these works which stand outside conventional tonal organization is the fact that they contain their own internal logical order.

IVES AND COPLAND Ives and Copland were both Americans with experimental styles. Charles Ives (1874–1954) was so experimental and ahead of his time that many of his compositions were considered unplayable and did not receive public performances until after World War II. Content to remain anonymous, and financially able to do so, as he had a separate career working in insurance, Ives went unrecognized for many years. His melodies spring from folk and popular songs, hymns, and other, often familiar, material, which he treated in most unfamiliar ways. He experimented with quarter tones, polytonality, and polyrhythms. His rhythms are often irregular and without measure delineation except for an occasional bar line to indicate an accent beat. Some of the tone clusters in his piano music are unplayable without using a block of wood to depress all the necessary keys at once. Ives's experimentations, such as the *Unanswered Question*, employ ensembles placed in various locations to create stereophonic effects. For Ives, all music related to life's experiences and ideas, some of which were consonant and some dissonant, and his music reflected that philosophy accordingly.

Aaron Copland (1900–90) integrated national American idioms into his compositions. Jazz, dissonance, Mexican folk songs, and Shaker hymns all appear. The latter figure prominently in Copland's most significant work, *Appalachian Spring* (music CD track 21). First written as a ballet, it was later reworked as a suite for symphony orchestra. Some of Copland's music is reserved and harmonically complex, and some simple. He often used all the tones in the diatonic scale simultaneously, particularly in the opening chord of a work. Despite a diversity of influences, he achieved a distinctive personal style which is traditionally tonal. His manipulation of rhythms and chords was highly influential in twentieth-century American musical composition.

Dance

DUNCAN Romantic ballet had become conventional and static by the late nineteenth century. The remarkable Isadora Duncan (1878–1927) was to introduce a revolutionary new style. By 1905 she had gained notoriety for her barefoot and deeply emotional dancing. She was considered controversial among balletomanes and dance reformers alike.

Although an American, Isadora Duncan achieved her fame in Europe. Her dances interpreted moods suggested to her by music or nature. Her costume was loose and flowing, inspired by Greek tunics and draperies, and the fact that she did not wear dancing shoes was deeply significant—this unconventional approach stuck, and it continues to this day in the modern dance tradition she helped to form.

DENISHAWN Isadora Duncan's contemporary Ruth St. Denis and her husband, Ted Shawn, were to lay more substantial cornerstones for modern dance. St. Denis's dancing began as a strange combination of exotic, Oriental interpretations and Delsartian poses. (Delsarte is a nineteenth-century system originated by François Delsarte as a scientific examination of the manner in which emotions and ideas are transmitted. His overzealous disciples formed his findings into a series of graceful gestures and poses, which supposedly denoted specific things.) St. Denis's impact on dance was solidified by the formation with her husband of the Denishawn company and school to carry on her philosophies and choreography. Their headquarters were in Los Angeles. A totally eclectic approach to dance was followed—any and all traditions were included, from formal ballet to Oriental and American Indian dances.

GRAHAM First to leave Denishawn was Martha Graham (1894–1991), probably the most influential figure in modern dance. Although the term modern dance defies accurate definition and satisfies few, it remains the most appropriate label for the nonballetic tradition Martha Graham has come to symbolize. She maintains that artistic individualism is fundamental. "There are no general rules. Each work of art creates its own code." Even modern dance has come to include its own conventions, however, principally because it tries so hard to be different from formal ballet. Ballet movements are largely rounded and symmetrical. Therefore, modern dancers emphasize angularity and asymmetry. Ballet stresses leaps and bases its line on toework, while modern dance hugs the floor and dancers go barefoot. As a result, the early works of Graham and others tended to be rather fierce and earthy, as opposed to graceful. But beneath it all was the desire to express emotion first and foremost, disregarding the execution of conventional positions and movements on which ballet is based. Martha Graham has described her choreography as "a graph of the heart."

Her ballets, often concerned with the psychological exploration of mythological themes, include *Primitive Mysteries* and *Circe*. After the Depression, when social criticism formed a large part of artistic expression, Graham pursued topical themes concerning the shaping of America, including her renowned work to the music of Aaron Copland, *Appalachian Spring*. It dealt with the effects of Puritanism and depicted the overcoming of its fire and brimstone by love and common sense (see p. 143).

CUNNINGHAM Martha Graham's troupe produced a radical and controversial choreographer who broke with many of the traditions of modern dance (as flexible as those traditions have been). He incorporated chance elements into his choreography and has often been associated with the composer John Cage. Merce Cunningham (b. 1919) uses everyday activity as well as dance movements in his works. His concern is for the audience to see dance in a new light; his choreography is radically different from anyone else's. His works show elegance and coolness, as well as a severely abstract quality. Dances such as *Summerspace* and *Winterbranch* illustrate Cunningham's use of chance, or indeterminacy. He thoroughly prepares numerous options and orders for sets, which can then be varied and intermixed in different orders from performance to performance (sometimes the choices are made by flipping a coin). The same piece may thus appear different from one night to the next. Cunningham also treats space as an integral part of the performance and allows focus to be spread across various areas of the stage, unlike classical ballet which tends to concentrate its focus on center stage or downstage center alone. So Cunningham allows audience members to choose where to focus, as opposed to forcing that focus. Finally, he tends to allow each element of the dance to go its own way. As a result, the direct, beat-for-beat relationship that audiences have come to expect between music and footfalls in ballet and much modern dance simply does not exist.

LATER DEVELOPMENTS Since 1954, another graduate of Martha Graham's troupe (and also of Merce Cunningham's) has provided strong direction in modern dance. The work of Paul Taylor (b. 1930) has a vibrant, energetic, and abstract quality that often suggests primordial actions. Taylor, like Cunningham, often uses strange combinations of music and movement in highly ebullient and unrestrained dances such as *Book of Beasts*. Taylor's music often turns to Classical composers, such as Beethoven, and to specialized works like string quartets. The combination of such formal music with his wild movements creates challenge for the audience.

In a tradition which encourages individual exploration and independence, there have been many accomplished dancer/choreographers, among them Alvin Ailey (see p. 381) and Alwin Nikolais. Nikolais designs scenery, costumes, and lights and composes the music, as well as the choreography—his works tend to be mixed-media extravaganzas celebrating the electronic age. Often the display is so dazzling that the audience loses the dancers in the lighting effects and scenic environment. Twyla Tharp and Yvonne Ranier have both experimented with space and movement. James Waring has combined Bach and 1920s pop songs, florid pantomimes and abstractions, Romantic point work and modern dance.

ULTRARATIONALISM AND BEYOND

Avant-Garde Music

Music from the late 1950s until the early 1970s went to further extremes in "ultrarational" and "antirational" directions. At times the desire for novelty superseded most other considerations. The German composer Karlheinz Stockhausen (b. 1928), for example, became interested in the total manipulation of sound and the acoustic space in which the performance was to take place, as seen in works like *Gruppen*, for three orchestras. As he became more and more interested in timbre, he encompassed a greater variety of sound sources, both electronic and acoustic, in an interesting combination of control and noncontrol, as in *Microphonie I*.

The American Elliott Carter (b. 1908) has developed a highly organized approach toward rhythm, called metric modulation: The mathematical principles of meter, standard rhythmic notation, and other elements are developed in complex ways. The pitch content of Carter's music is highly chromatic, and his music requires virtuoso playing from both the individual and the ensemble. Like Stockhausen, he has written a work for three orchestras.

Experimentation with *microtones* has been of interest to Western music theorists throughout history and many non-Western cultures employ them routinely. Microtones can be defined as intervals smaller than a half step. Our system divides the octave into twelve equal parts. There seems to be no reason why the octave cannot be divided into 24, 53, 95, or any number of parts. The possibilities are limited only by the listener's ability to hear such intervals and the performer's ability to produce them. Alois Haba (1893–1973) experimented in the early part of the century with quarter tones (24 per octave) and sixth tones (36 per octave) and, as we have mentioned, so did Charles Ives. A number of instruments have been designed to produce microtones, and experimentation and composition have been carried out widely.

In an atmosphere of constant searching and experimentation, composers of the past few decades have often questioned the validity of traditional concepts of art in general and specifically the limitations of the traditional concert hall. The earlier work of John Cage and others led in a number of directions—including theatre pieces, multimedia or mixed media, so-called danger music, biomusic, soundscapes, happenings, and total environments

(which might include stimulation of all the senses in some way). Thus the definition of a composer as opposed to playwright, filmmaker, visual artist, and so on was often obscured.

Many mainstream composers continued writing from the late 1950s to the early 1970s. However, a noticeable element of controlled chance has found its way into the music of many of them. This period brought greater tolerance and acceptance on the part of composers for each other's varying viewpoints and musical styles, in a blending of avant-garde techniques with the mainstream.

Freedom from melodic, rhythmic, and formal restraints in jazz led to the free jazz art form of the 1960s. Saxophonist Ornette Colman (b. 1930) was one of the earliest proponents of such freedom. Others, such as John Coltrane (1926–67), developed a rhythmically and melodically free style based on modal materials, while Cecil Taylor (b. 1930) moved more toward chromaticism. In the mid to late 1960s a mature blend of this freedom was reached, with control and sophistication, in the *Bitches Brew* album by Miles Davis (1926–91). A number of musicians who originally worked with Miles Davis became leading artists in the 1970s, developing a style called jazz-rock, or fusion.

Polish composer Krzysztof Penderecki (pehn-duhr-EHT-skee; b. 1933) has striven to produce new sounds from traditional string instruments. He is widely known for both instrumental and choral works, including a major composition, the *Requiem Mass*, written in 1985. His *Polymorphia* uses twenty-four violins, eight violas, eight cellos, and eight double basses. Because of his experimentation with new techniques and sounds for strings, Penderecki has had to invent a whole new series of musical markings, listed at the beginning of each score. In actual performance, timings are measured by a stop watch and there is no clear meter. *Polymorphia* uses a free form with structure defined only by textures, harmonies, and string techniques. The piece is dissonant and atonal until the very end. It begins with a low, sustained chord in the bass. The mass of sound grows purposefully, with the entry of the upper strings, and then the middle register. Then comes a section of *glissandos*, which can be played at any speed between two given pitches—what amounts to improvisation. A climax occurs, after which the sound tapers off. Then a number of plucked-string effects are explored. Fingertips are used to tap the instruments, and the strings are hit with the palms of the hands (this has to be done gently so as not to damage the instruments). A second climax occurs. After another section in which sustained and sliding sounds are explored, a third climax is reached. The work ends with a somewhat surprising C major chord.

PROFILE

Richard Danielpour

Richard Danielpour (b. 1956) studied at the New England Conservatory and the Juilliard School and also trained as a pianist. Currently he is a member of the composition faculty at the Curtis Institute and the Manhattan School of Music. Speaking of his recent rise in the ranks of recognized composers, Danielpour reflected, "From the beginning, it was agonizing. It was like waiting for a Polaroid to develop, but the Polaroid took 10 years instead of 30 seconds." Indicative of his standing in the music world is his collaboration with Nobel Prize-winning writer Toni Morrison on a piece titled "Sweet Talk," premiered by Jessye Norman at Carnegie Hall.

In the early 1980s Danielpour moved away from the complexities of Modernism toward a more accessible style. As a result, his music's large and romantic gestures, brilliant orchestrations, and vibrant rhythms appeal to a wide cross-section of the public. In this regard, some critics have compared him to Leonard Bernstein, Aaron Copland, Igor Stravinsky, Dmitri Shostakovich, and other twentieth-century masters. "As I got older, I was aware of a number of different strands coming together in my music, rather than seeing myself on a mission with one particular ax to grind," he said. He calls himself an assimilator rather than an innovator. By utilizing familiar and unthreatening styles as a basis for his compositions, he has been able to win over even conservative audiences.

In the process of finding the means to express his message, Danielpour draws from many resources. "For me style is not the issue," he said. "It's how well a piece is written on a purely technical level. If other composers see themselves as superior just because their music may be more 'original,' that's O.K. That's not what I'm about." His "American-sounding rhythmic swagger," easy lyricism, and keen understanding of instrumental color create an appealing formula.

Although reluctant to discuss his music's spiritual component, he tends to label supposedly abstract instrumental works with intriguing, metaphysical titles. The movements of his Piano Quintet, for example, are "Annunciation," "Atonement," and "Apotheosis." Such titles, he admits, can be distracting. "Maybe it would be better not to have any at all," he said. When he does discuss spirituality in music, he doesn't hesitate to place himself in good company. "Some of my favorite composers," he said, "are also philosopher-composers who find themselves addressing questions about life and death in the very music they write: Mahler, Shostakovich, Bernstein."

He speaks of the creative process in spiritual and perhaps eccentric terms. "Where is the music received from?" he asked. "Where do your dreams come from? Composing is like being in a waking dream. To me the where is not important. It's intuition that has to lead the way and thinking that has to follow it. To speak of the mind first is worthless."

Perhaps typical of all professionals in today's music world, he has a sense of the business side of music. He knows about contracts and commissions and how to be in the right place at the right time. Nonetheless, Danielpour insists that he is no more active in self-promotion than his colleagues.[10]

Musique Actuelle

In the late 1990s, improvised music, viewed as the cutting edge of musical style, took the name *musique actuelle* (moo-ZEEK akt-yoo-EHL; meaning "current"). It freely draws on jazz and rock and elicits vibrancy, liveliness, and personal expression. It represents a number of subfactions from various localities such as New York, San Francisco, Vancouver, Chicago, and Montreal. Illustrative of this approach is Gianni Gebbia (b. 1961) and his trio, whose music reflects one of the heroes of musique actuelle, Evan Parker. Gebbia's music integrates three strains, American jazz, free improvising, and traditional Sicilian music. In musique actuelle there is often a strain of humor—for instance, the vocalist in Gebbia's trio might alternate between phrases reminiscent of opera and phrases utilizing nasal whines and fearsome guttural groans in two simultaneous pitches.

POSTMODERNISM

For more than twenty years, debates about Postmodernism dominated the cultural and intellectual scene in many fields. In aesthetic and cultural theory, arguments emerged over whether "Modernism" in the arts was or was not dead and what sort of "Postmodern" art was succeeding it. In philosophy, discussion centered upon whether or not the tradition of modern philosophy had ended and been replaced by a new "Postmodern" philosophy. Eventually, the Postmodern discussion produced new social and political theories, as well as theoretical attempts to define the multifaceted aspects of the Postmodern phenomenon itself.

Basically, discourses about Postmodernism raise issues that resist easy conclusions. Advocates for Postmodernism harshly criticize traditional culture, theory, and politics, and defenders of Modernism respond either by ignoring the challenges, attacking Postmodernism in return, or attempting to come to terms with new discourses and positions. Critics of Postmodernism contend that it is a passing fad, a specious invention of self-seeking intellectuals, or an attempt to devalue the liberating theories and values of Modernism.

In fact, there is no unified Postmodern theory, or even a coherent set of positions. Rather, we find great diversity among theories often lumped together as "Postmodern" and a great plurality—often contradictory—among Postmodern positions. We certainly do not have the space to trace the issue in depth, but we must, at least, acknowledge them "up front," as it were.

The questions, What is Modernism? and What is Postmodernism? are highly relevant to the twentieth century and its arts. "Modernity" is often conceptualized as the "modern age" and "postmodernity" as a term for describing the period that allegedly follows modernity. Modernity is a term for an historical period encompassing the epoch that follows the Middle Ages or feudalism. Modernism, then, might be defined as an attempt to overturn the feudal world and to produce a just and egalitarian social order that embodies reason and social progress. Modernity enters everyday life through the dissemination of modern art, the products of consumer society, new technologies, and new modes of transportation and communication that have constituted the modern world. "Modernism" could be used to describe the art movements of the modern age (Impressionism, art for art's sake, Expressionism, Surrealism, and other avant-garde movements), which have strong formalist bases.

Postmodern theorists, however, claim that in the contemporary high-tech media society, emergent processes of change and transformation are producing a new, "Postmodern" society that constitutes a novel state of history and novel socio-cultural formation which requires new concepts and theories. "Postmodernism" would describe those diverse aesthetic forms and practices that come after and break with Modernism and formalism. These forms include the architecture of Philip Johnson (see Fig. 13.31), the musical experiments of John Cage, the art of Andy Warhol, the novels of Thomas Pynchon, and films like *Blade Runner* or *Blue Velvet*. The debate centers on whether there is or is not a sharp conceptual distinction between Modernism and Postmodernism and the relative merits and limitations of these movements.

Therefore, Postmodernism begins with a loss of faith in the dreams of Modernism (the mindset that emerged during the Enlightenment, an optimistic faith in the idea that the methodology of science could lead to meaningful understanding of people). Postmodernism, however, does not suggest anything to replace Modernism. Rather, it invents a new and evolving language with words such as "metaphorical structuring," "deconstruction," and "metanarrative." As we work our way through this section, perhaps—just perhaps—this engaging and challenging dilemma will begin to coalesce for us.

Visual Arts

The period from the late 1960s through the 1980s witnessed a variety of reactions to the styles of the past—including the recent past of the twentieth century. Like the collective styles of the end of the nineteenth century, which were called Post-Impressionist, these "new" styles have been lumped together as Postmodernist although they seem to have no common thread. They are, generally speaking, highly individualistic, although some artists prefer to return art to the anonymity of pre-Renaissance times. One aspect of Postmodernist style appears to be a desire for recognizable content or meaning in works of art. Artists following this path are reacting to what they feel is a clutter and lack of content in previous styles. They seek to "make it new" and take great pains to be "different." The question of difference, however, has become complicated by the fact that many, such as the Postmodernist architects, take great delight in eclectically borrowing from the past. They mix old styles to create something "new."

One artist who represents this mélange of styles is the sculptor Joel Shapiro (b. 1941). He was born, raised, and educated in New York, and his art gradually evolved into the production of miniature clay, glass, copper, and lead pieces shaped objectively. One particular aspect of his works illustrates the art of the 1980s—the use of a variety of media, some of which are new and require new techniques. The mixing of media in previously untried ways provides new avenues of experimentation and mastery as well as providing works of art that look different from those of the past. Shapiro's works graduated from clusters of small geometric pieces—spread out on the floors of galleries where the actual space in which they were assembled became an important element—to large-scale stick figures exhibiting precarious balance, such as *Untitled* (Fig. **13.33**).[11] It is cast in metal but retains the texture and apparent construction methods of the wood from which it was originally made.

Architecture

Contemporary architecture has, like the other visual arts, turned in pluralistic directions. Past styles are also given new manifestations in Postmodern or Revisionist architecture. The Spanish architect Ricardo Bofill (boh-FEEL; b. 1939) and the Italian Aldo Rossi (1931–97) have both derived much of their architectural language from the past. As Bofill remarked, his architecture takes "without copying, different themes from the past, but in an eclectic manner, seizing certain moments in history and juxtaposing them, thereby pre-figuring a new epoch." We see this in his public housing development called, with typical grandiosity, the Palace of Abraxas (Fig. **13.34**). Here columnar verticality is suggested by glass and by cornice/capitals, which dynamically present characteristics of Classicism. Postmodern architecture focuses on meaning and symbolism: The past and ornamentation are acceptable; functionalism no longer controls. The Postmodernist seeks to create buildings "in the fuller context of society and the environment." Social identity, cultural continuity, and sense of place become foundations for art.

In a clear repudiation of the glass and steel box of the International Style and other popular forms in mainstream architecture, the design for the Pompidou (pahm-pee-doo) Center in Paris (Fig. **13.36**) turns the building inside out, externalizing its network of ducts, pipes, and elevators while hiding the internal structure, which has no fixed walls—temporary dividers can be arranged in any desired configuration. The bright primary colors of the exterior combine with serpentine, plexiglass-covered escalators to give a whimsical, lively appearance to a functional building. The Pompidou Center (also known by Parisians as the Beaubourg) has become a tourist attraction rivaling the Eiffel Tower and, although controversial, has wide popular acceptance.

Another contemporary departure from the Modern and International styles is Frank Gehry's Guggenheim Museum in Bilbao, Spain (Fig. **13.35**). The building's

13.33 Joel Shapiro, *Untitled*, 1980–1. Bronze, 4 ft ⅞ in × 5 ft 4 ins × 3 ft 9½ ins (1.34 × 1.62 × 1.15 m). Private collection.

13.34 Ricardo Bofill, Palace of Abraxas, Marne-la-Vallée, near Paris, 1978–93.

highly complex form would have been impossible to design without the use of computers. Comprising a member of interconnecting shapes, it uses limestone to contrast with bent forms covered in titanium. Glass curtain walls add light and transparency. It is like a work of sculpture set against the background of the city.

Dance

Rising in the Judson Dance Theatre of the 1960s, Postmodern dance, like the style in the other arts, seeks the interrelationships between art and life. The Judson Dance Theatre comprised an informal collective of experimentalists who rejected traditional choreography and technique in favor of open-ended scores and ordinary movement. Again, Postmodernism does not lend itself to descriptions of "typical" adherents, but one example surely is Deborah Hay (b. 1942), one of the style's pioneers. Ms Hay defines dance broadly as "the place where I practice attention. . . . It's a kind of alertness in my body that I have at no other time. So dance for me is about playing awake."[12]

13.35 Frank Gehry, Guggenheim Museum, Bilbao, 1991–7.

A Personal Journey

THE POMPIDOU CENTER

There's an old popular song that says "I love Paris in the springtime; I love Paris in the fall. I love Paris in the summer, when it sizzles; I love Paris in the winter, when it drizzles. I love Paris every moment—every moment of the year." That is a fair, if syrupy, summary of my feelings. There are, of course, parts of Paris that I like better than others, and some parts I have mixed feelings about. I love the little streets off the Boulevard St. Michel near the Seine filled with inexpensive Greek restaurants, but I don't particularly like the throngs of tourists they attract. I like the Saturday market in Rue Mouffetard, but don't care for the *bateaux mouches*, whose views from the Seine are not very illuminating. In a similar vein (although it may sound like heresy at this point in the text to make the following statement), I love

the arts, but I'm not thrilled by every piece of art I see. I do, however, feel the need to give any work of art its due, without preconception. Sometimes I connect; sometimes I don't.

I had read a good bit about Paris's Pompidou Center (Fig. **13.36**) prior to seeing it. The context, the Marais neighborhood around it, is predominantly seventeenth-century, and the Pompidou's Postmodern design was highly controversial, to say the least. The primary blues and reds of the pipes on its exterior and the industrial appearance of its façade stand in strong contrast to the subdued tones

13.36 Renzo Piano and Richard Rogers, Pompidou Center, Paris, 1971–8.

and character of its context. Having steeled myself with both sides of the argument, I was ready for my own journey to Les Halles, the old central Paris market, and the Pompidou Center that now sits nearby. When I arrived at the scene, my expectations received a rude shock. Nothing looked as anticipated. Actually, the Pompidou Center looked like its pictures, but the old market? It was a huge construction site, a vast wasteland. In comparison, anything that had a sense of completeness—specifically, the Pompidou Center—looked pretty good. Approached from the temporary chaos of a construction site, the Center did not seem quite the violator of context I had thought it might be.

In theory, at least, I found the concept of the museum's design intriguing: Put the infrastructure—heating, ventilation, and air conditioning (HVAC)—that usually takes up space inside, on the outside and leave the interior free and flexible. That seems like a reasonable idea. Paint all those pipes and structural members bright, primary colors to glorify them. I could understand that line of thinking as well. Fill the entire design with glass to add to its sense of space and light. There is logic in that rationale. Add such a design to a historic Parisian neighborhood. Was I stodgy and intolerant in my discomfort with that?

I've since returned to Les Halles and the Pompidou Center many times. Les Halles is now a large, underground shopping mall, and the surface, which was the old market, is now a park. The context seems more eclectic today than it did when the Center first appeared. The contrasts seem less harsh. The Pompidou Center still mildly ruffles the feathers of the architectural purist in me, but I remind myself to treat each case as individual, being careful to maintain standards but careful, also, not to jump too quickly to judgment.

Most of Hay's work is playful, and "Voil," a forty-minute solo piece, requires the dancer to gallop and prance, engage in awkward gesticulations, and do storytelling, vocalizations (tongue clicks and guttural rumblings), as well as other sorts of emotional outburst. The dance is "fierce, tentative, sorrowful, amazed, earnest, exasperated . . . [with] ugly faces and . . . silly kid's Stuff."[13]

Literature

Exemplary of Postmodernism in literature is Thomas Pynchon (b. 1937), an American novelist and short story writer, who combines black humor and fantasy to portray human alienation in the chaos of modern society. His masterpiece, *Gravity's Rainbow* (1973), is based on the idea of conspiracy and is filled with descriptions of paranoid fantasies, grotesque imagery, and esoteric mathematical language.

NEOABSTRACTION

By the mid-1980s young artists were seeking to make their mark by reacting against the Postmodernist trends. Many of them returned to abstraction and near-abstraction, including Hard Edge (see p. 393). These Neo-abstractionists, like the Postmodernists, make up a loose confederation of mostly individualistic approaches. An example is the work of Lynda Benglis (b. 1941), a painter who has turned to sculpture. Her work also represents

13.37 Lynda Benglis, *Passat*, 1990. Aluminum, 78 × 52 × 27 ins (198 × 132 × 68.5 cm). Paula Cooper Gallery, New York.

Process Art—that is, taking molten materials, letting them flow freely on the floor, and then adding color and/or shape to them. *Passat* (Fig. **13.37**) illustrates how she shapes knots, bows, and pleats into insectlike sculptures in shiny metal. Like the Postmodernists, Neoabstractionists borrow freely from others by modifying or changing the scale, media, or color of older works to give them a new framework and, hence, new meaning. Occasionally, the new meanings include sarcasm and satire and often comment on the decadence of contemporary American society.

"NEW" REALISM

The realistic style of the nineteenth century (see p. 355) returns from time to time, and in the new century we find its evidence in the work of a number of young painters. Some of these approaches employ conventional techniques and traditional approaches to figure depiction in order to illuminate personal and ethnic narratives, including political statements. In other cases, the "New" Realism searches for metaphorical connections between subject matter and ideas. What ties together this variety of individual approaches is the appearance of observable "reality" in the works. Illustrative of the "New" Realist tendency is Julie Roberts (b. 1963), a Welsh painter based in London. In works such as *The Little Girl Rosalia Lombardo, Embalmed* (Fig. **13.38**), she takes a close look at the realism and drama of human life and death. With detailed clarity and smooth brushstroke, she brings a powerful statement to the viewer, leaving much to the imagination while at the same time creating an effective tension between the paint surface and the disturbing suggestion of the images.

13.38 Julie Roberts, *The Little Girl Rosalia Lombardo, Embalmed*, 2000. Oil on canvas, 19¹¹⁄₁₆ × 19¹¹⁄₁₆ ins (50 × 50 cm). Courtesy Sean Kelly Gallery, New York.

THINKING CRITICALLY

- Using the elements and characteristics of poetry (see Chapter 8), analyze Paula Gunn Allen's poem, "Recuerdo" (see p. 373). What is your personal reaction to the poem and why do you feel that way?

- Using examples from the text to illustrate your point, compare a sculptural work from twentieth-century Africa with a painting from the Harlem Renaissance to develop an understanding of how the Black experience on two different continents may be alike or different, as seen through a work of art. What is your reaction to these works, and why?

- Using the elements of line and color as well as the characteristics of the styles discussed in the text, compare Picasso's *Demoiselles d'Avignon* (Fig. **13.12**) with Roy Lichtenstein's *Whaam!* (Fig. **13.20**). What is your reaction to these works, and what elements of the works cause it?

- Using the elements and principles of composition as well as the characteristics of the styles discussed in the text, compare Matisse's *Blue Nude* (Fig. **13.13**) with Georgia O'Keeffe's *Dark Abstraction* (Fig. **13.15**). What is your reaction to these works, and what elements of the works cause it?

CYBER STUDY

EXPRESSIONISM:
http://www.artcyclopedia.com/history/expressionism.html

CUBISM:
http://www.artcyclopedia.com/history/cubism.html

FAUVISM:
http://www.artcyclopedia.com/history/fauvism.html

FUTURISM:
http://www.artcyclopedia.com/history/futurism.html

ABSTRACTION:
http://www.artcyclopedia.com/history/neo-plasticism.html

SURREALISM:
http://www.artcyclopedia.com/history/surrealism.html

ABSTRACT EXPRESSIONISM:
http://www.artcyclopedia.com/history/abstract-expressionism.html

POP ART:
http://www.artcyclopedia.com/history/pop.html

NOTES

INTRODUCTION

1 Edwin J. Delattre, "The Humanities Can Irrigate Deserts," *The Chronicle of Higher Education*, October 11, 1977, p. 32.

CHAPTER FOUR

1 August Wilson, *Fences*, in Lee A. Jacobus, *The Bedford Introduction to Drama* (New York: St. Martin's Press, 1989), p. 1055.

2 Pierre Corneille, *Le Cid*, trans. and ed. John C. Lapp (New York: Appleton Century Crofts, 1955), pp. 36–7.

3 *American Theatre Magazine*, January 1991.

CHAPTER SIX

1 John Martin, *The Dance* (New York: Tudor Publishing Company, 1946), p. 26.

2 Agnes DeMille, *Martha, the Life and Work of Martha Graham* (New York: Random House, 1991), p. 261.

CHAPTER EIGHT

1 Alice Walker, "Roselilly," from *In Love & Trouble: Stories of Black Women* (Orlando: Harcourt Brace & Company, 1972), copyright © 1972 by Alice Walker, reprinted by permission of Harcourt, Inc.

2 Saki (H. H. Munro), *The Blood-Feud of Toad-Water: A West Country Epic*, from *Reginald in Russia and Other Sketches* (1910). Available online at http://www.ibiblio.org/gutenberg/etext99/rgrus10.txt

3 Goeffrey Chaucer, *The Canterbury Tales*, trans. J. Nicolson (New York: Crown Publishing Group, 1934), pp. 120–3.

4 William Shakespeare, Sonnet XIX (*Sonnets* published by Thomas Thorpe in 1609). Available online at http://www.ibiblio.org/gutenberg/etext97/wssnt10.txt

5 John Wesley, *God Brought Me Safe.*

6 Oliver Goldsmith, "The Benefits of Luxury, in Making a People more Wise and Happy."

7 William Shakespeare, "The Seven Ages of Man," from *As You Like It*, Act II, scene vii, 139–66.

8 Robert Frost, "Stopping by Woods on a Snowy Evening," from *The Poetry of Robert Frost*, ed. Edward Connery Lathem (New York: Holt, Rinehart & Winston, 1969). Copyright 1923, © 1969 by Holt, Rinehart, & Winston. Copyright 1951 by Robert Frost. Reprinted by permission of Henry Holt & Company.

9 K. L. Knickerbocker and W. Willard Reninger, *Interpreting Literature* (New York: Holt, Rinehart, & Winston, 1969), p. 218.

CHAPTER NINE

1 Common usage today has changed the references B.C. (Before Christ) and A.D. (*Anno Domini*, "the year of our Lord," i.e. after Christ) to B.C.E. (Before Common Era) and C.E. (Common Era).

2 Revised Standard Version Bible.

3 Homer, *The Iliad*, prose version by Andrew Lang, W. Leaf, and E. Myers (1883). Available online at http://www.ibiblio.org/gutenberg/etext02/iliab10.txt

CHAPTER TEN

1 In each Greek tragic contest a playwright was required to present four plays in succession—three tragedies and a satyr play.

2 Aeschylus, *Agamemnon*, trans. Peter D. Arnott, in *An Introduction to the Greek Theatre* (Bloomington: Indiana University Press, 1963), pp. 76–7.

3 The chorus was a distinctive feature of Greek drama, portraying the dual function (in the same play) of narrator and collective character responding to the actors.

4 Virgil, *Aeneid*, trans. Theodore C. Williams (New York: Houghton Mifflin, 1938), p. 1.

5 John Garraty and Peter Gay, *A History of the World*, 2 vols. (New York: Harper & Row, 1972), p. 209.

6 Revised Standard Version Bible (Oxford: Oxford University Press, 1977).

7 "Rings around the Pantheon," *Discover*, March 1985, p. 12.

8 Hugh Honour and John Fleming, *The Visual Arts: A History*, 4th edn. (Englewood Cliffs, NJ, and New York: Prentice Hall and Abrams, 1995), p. 94.

9 AOI: These three mysterious letters appear throughout the text. No one has ever adequately explained them, though every reader feels their effect.

10 *The Song of Roland*, trans. Frederick Goldin (New York: W. W. Norton, 1978).

11 Dante, *The Divine Comedy*, quoted in Cunningham and Reich, *Culture and Values*, vol. 1. (Harcourt Brace Jovanich College Publishers, 1994), p. 366.

CHAPTER ELEVEN

1 Baldassare Castiglione, *The Book of the Courtier*, trans. George Bull (London: Penguin Classics, 1967). Copyright © 1967 George Bull.

2 D. Redig de Campos, ed., *Art Treasures of the Vatican* (Englewood Cliffs, NJ: Prentice Hall, 1974), p. 7.

3 William Shakespeare, "To be, or not to be," from *Hamlet*, Act III, scene i.

4 Lilian Hornstein et al., *World Literature*, 2nd edn. (New York: Mentor, 1973), p. 155.

5 Germain Bazin, *The Baroque* (Greenwich, CT: New York Graphic Society, 1968), p. 30.

6 Jonathan Swift, "A Modest Proposal," in *The Norton Anthology of English Literature*, vol. 1, 3rd edn. (New York: W. W. Norton, 1974), p. 2094.

7 Alexander Pope, *An Essay on Man*, 1733–4. Available online at http://www.ibiblio.org/gutenberg/etext00/esymn10.txt

8 Phillis Wheatley, 'On Virtue', from *Poems on Various Subjects* (1773). Available online at http://www.ibiblio.org/gutenberg/etext96/whtly10.txt

CHAPTER TWELVE

1 Dominique-Rene de Lerma, *Reflections on Afro-American Music* (Kent, OH: Kent State University Press, 1973), p. 162.

2 William Allen, Charles Ware, and Lucy Garrison, *Slave Songs of the United States* (New York: A. Simpson, 1867), p. 50; in George R. Keck and Sherrill V. Martin, *Feel the Spirit* (New York: Greenwood Press, 1988), p. 3.

3 Bernard Katz, *The Social Implications of Early Negro Music in the United States* (New York: Arno Press and *The New York Times*, 1969), p. 26.

4 Katz, op. cit., p. 14.

5 Henry Edward Krehbiel, *Afro-American Folksongs* (New York: G. Schirmer, n.d. [c. 1914]), p. 26.

6 Frederick J. Dockstader, *Indian Art of the Americas* (New York: Museum of the American Indian Heye Foundation, 1973), p. 14.

7 Ibid.

8 Susette La Flesche, "Nedawi." Copyright © 1989 The Arizona Board of Regents. Reprinted from *The Singing Spirit*, ed. Bernd C. Peyer (Tucson: University of Arizona Press, 1991).

9 William Wordsworth, "Tintern Abbey," in *The Poetical Works of William Wordsworth* (New York: Houghton Mifflin, 1982), pp. 91–3.

10 Helen Gardner, *Art Through the Ages* (New York: Harcourt Brace Jovanovich, 1980), p. 760.

CHAPTER THIRTEEN

1 Zitkala-Sa (Gertrude Bonnin), "The Soft-Hearted Sioux." Copyright © 1989 The Arizona Board of Regents. Reprinted from *The Singing Spirit*, ed. Bernd C. Peyer (Tucson: University of Arizona Press, 1991).

2 Paula Gunn Allen, "Recuerdo," from *Shadow Country* (Los Angeles: University of California, American Indian Studies Center, 1982). Copyright © 1982 Regents of the University of California. Reprinted from Joseph Bruchac, *Survival This Way* (Tuscon, AZ: University of Arizona Press, 1987), p. 3.

3 "Harlem Renaissance, Art of Black America." Exhibition book for the traveling exhibition under the auspices of the American Federation of Arts, 1989.

4 Ibid.

5 Ibid.

6 Ibid.

7 Langston Hughes, "Theme for English B" and "Harlem," from *The Collected Poems of Langston Hughes* (New York: Alfred A. Knopf, 1994). Copyright © 1994 by the Estate of Langston Hughes.

8 H. W. Janson, *A Basic History of Art*, 5th edn. (Englewood Cliffs, NJ, and New York: Prentice Hall and Harry N. Abrams, 1995), p. 682.

9 W. H. Auden, "In War Time." From *The English Auden: Poems, Essays and Dramatic Writings*, ed. Edward Mendelson (London: Faber & Faber, 1968).

10 *New York Times*, January 18, 1998, Section 2, p. 41.

11 Otto G. Ocvirk et al., *Art Fundamentals*, 7th edn. (Madison, WI, and Dubuque, IA: Brown & Benchmark, 1994), p. 309.

12 *New York Times*, May 30, 1997.

13 Ibid.

GLOSSARY

Cross-references are indicated by *italic* type.

a cappella. Choral music without instrumental accompaniment.

ABA. In music, a three-part structure that consists of an opening section, a second section, and a return to the first section. See also *ternary form*.

abacus. The uppermost member of the *capital* of an architectural *column*; the slab on which the *architrave* rests.

absolute music. Music that is free from any reference to nonmusical ideas, such as a text or program. See also *program music* and *tone poem*.

absolutism. The system or doctrine of government by which the ruler has unlimited powers; despotism.

abstract. *Nonrepresentational*; the essence of a thing rather than its actual appearance.

Abstract Expressionism. In art, a style of *nonrepresentational* painting that combines *abstract forms* with *Expressionist* emotional values.

abstraction. A thing apart; that is, removed from real life.

Absurdism. In drama and prose fiction, the view that the human condition is profoundly and unalterably absurd and indecipherable, giving rise to feelings of purposelessness and bewilderment. The movement arose after World War II in opposition to the beliefs and values of traditional culture and literature.

academic Neoclassicism. A style of the late eighteenth and early nineteenth centuries, particularly in France, and exemplified by the work of such painters as Jacques Louis David, who was not only influenced by *Classical art* but took Classical themes for his subject matter. See also *Neoclassicism*.

accelerando. In music, a gradual increase in *tempo*.

accent. (1) In music, a stress that occurs at regular intervals of time. (2) In the visual arts, any device used to highlight or draw attention to a particular area.

accentual-syllabic. A form of poetry in which the *rhythm* depends on there being a fixed number of syllables in each line.

acrylic. An artist's *medium* made by dispersing pigment in a synthetic medium.

action painting. A form of *Abstract Expressionism*, in which paint is applied with rapid, vigorous strokes or even splashed or thrown on the canvas.

adagio. A musical term meaning slow and graceful.

additive. (1) In sculpture, those works that are built. (2) In color, the term refers to the mixing of *hues* of light.

aerial perspective. The indication of distance in painting through the use of light and atmosphere. See also *linear perspective* and *perspective*.

aesthetic. Having to do with the pleasurable and beautiful as opposed to the useful.

aesthetics. A branch of philosophy dealing with the nature of beauty and art, and their relation to experience.

affective. Relating to feelings or emotions, as opposed to facts.

aleatory. Chance or accidental. Such music cannot be predicted beforehand, but depends for its form on statistical or computerized processes during the performance.

allegory. Expression by means of symbols to make a more effective generalization or moral commentary about human experience than could be achieved by direct or literal means.

allegretto. A musical term denoting a lively *tempo*, but one slower than *allegro*.

allegro. A musical term meaning brisk.

alliteration. A sound structure in which an initial sound is repeated for effect.

altarpiece. A painted or sculptured panel placed above and behind an altar to inspire religious devotion.

alto. In music, the lowest female voice.

ambulatory. A covered passage for walking, found around the *apse* or choir of a church.

amphora. A two-handled vessel for storing provisions, with an opening large enough to admit a ladle and usually fitted with a cover.

anapestic. One of the four standard feet in poetry. Two light syllables are followed by a stressed syllable. See also *foot* and *meter* (1).

andante. A musical term meaning a medium leisurely, walking *tempo*.

andantino. A musical term meaning a *tempo* a little faster than *andante*.

appoggiatura. In music, an ornamental note or series of notes above and below a tone of a *chord*.

apse. A large niche or niche-like space projecting from and expanding the interior space of an architectural form such as a *basilica*.

aquatint. An *intaglio* printmaking process in which the plate is treated with a resin substance to create textured tonal areas.

arabesque. A classical ballet pose in which the body is supported on one leg, and the other leg is extended behind with the knee straight.

arcade. A series of *arches* placed side by side.

arch. In architecture, a structural system in which space is spanned by a curved member supported by two legs.

architrave. In *post-and-lintel* architecture, the *lintel* or lowest part of the *entablature*, resting directly on the *capitals* of the *columns*.

arena theatre. A theatre in which the audience surrounds the stage.

aria. An elaborate solo song found primarily in operas, *oratorios*, and *cantatas*.

art brut. The name given by the French painter Jean Dubuffet to art created by anyone from outside the art world, such as children, prisoners, and the mentally ill.

art song. A vocal musical composition in which the text is the principal focus.

articulation. The connection of the parts of an artwork.

aryballus. An Incan bottle-shaped pot with a pointed bottom, which fell over when empty. The word is also used for the round, narrow-necked container used in Greece, apparently to hold perfumed oil.

assemblé. In ballet, a leap with one foot brushing the floor at the moment of the leap and both feet coming together in fifth position at the finish.

assonance. A sound structure employing a similarity among vowels but not consonants.

atmospheric perspective. The three-dimensional space in a painting, especially when achieved through the use of *aerial perspective*.

atonality. The avoidance or tendency to avoid tonal centers in musical compositions.

avant-garde. French for "advanced guard." A term used to designate innovators, whose experiments challenge established values.

balance. In composition, the equilibrium of opposing or interacting forces.

ballad. A song or poem that tells a story in short *stanzas*; a narrative version of a folk song.

balletomane. A term used by ballet enthusiasts to refer to themselves. A combination of ballet and mania.

balloon construction. Construction of wood using a skeletal framework. See also *skeleton frame* and *steel-cage construction*.

Baroque. A seventeenth- and eighteenth-century style of art, architecture, and music that is highly ornamental.

barre. A wooden railing used by dancers to maintain balance while practicing.

barrel vault (tunnel vault). A series of *arches* placed back to back to enclose space.

bas relief. *See low relief.*

basilica. In Roman times, a term referring to building function, usually a law court; later used by Christians to refer to church buildings and a specific form.

battement jeté. A ballet movement using a small brush kick with the toe sliding on the floor until the foot is fully extended about two inches off the floor.

bay. A vertical division of the exterior or interior of a building, marked by piers, windows, *buttresses*, and so forth.

bearing-wall. A form of construction in which the wall supports itself, the roof, and floors. See also *monolithic construction*.

beats. In music, the equal parts into which a *measure* is divided.

Be-bop. A style of *jazz*, popular between about 1945 and 1955, characterized by complex *rhythms* and instrumental virtuosity. Shortened to "bop."

bel canto. Italian for "beautiful singing." A style of singing in which beauty of tone and perfect technique are preeminent.

binary form. The *form* of a piece of music with two sections.

biography. A written account of a person's life.

biomorphic. Representing life *forms* as opposed to geometric forms.

blues. Music of Black American folk origin, melancholy and often in 12-bar sequences.

bridge. In music, a passage of subordinate importance, played between two major *themes*.

bridging shot. In film, a shot inserted at editing to cover a break in continuity.

buttress. A support, usually an exterior projection of masonry or wood, for a wall, *arch*, or vault.

cadence. In music, the specific harmonic arrangement that indicates the closing of a phrase.

canon. In music, a type of *polyphony* in which a *melody* is repeated by each voice or instrument as it enters after a brief interval.

cantata. A short composition for *orchestra* and chorus, sometimes also with soloists.

cantilever. An architectural structural system in which an overhanging beam is supported at only one end.

capital. The transition between the top of a *column* and the *lintel*.

cast. See *sculpture*.

catharsis. The cleansing or purification of the emotions through the experience of art, the result of which is spiritual release and renewal.

cella. The principal enclosed room of a temple; the entire body of a temple as opposed to its external parts.

chaîné. A series of spinning turns in ballet utilizing a half turn of the body on each step.

changement de pied. In ballet, a small jump in which the positions of the feet are reversed.

character Oxfords. Shoes worn by dancers which look like ordinary street shoes but are actually specially constructed for dance.

chiaroscuro. Light and shade. In painting, the use of highlight and shadow to give the appearance of three-dimensionality. In theatre, the use of light to enhance *plasticity* of human and scenic form.

chord. Three or more musical tones played at once.

choreography. The composition of a dance work; the arrangement of patterns of movement in dance.

chroma. The degree of *saturation* or purity of a color or *hue*.

chromatic scale. A musical *scale* consisting of half steps or semitones.

cinéma verité. Candid camera; a television-like technique of recording life and people as they are. The hand-held camera, natural sound, and minimal editing are characteristic.

cinematic motif. In film, a visual image that is repeated either in identical form or in variation.

cire-perdue (lost-wax). A method of casting metal in a mold, the cavity of which is formed of wax, which is then melted and poured away.

Classic. Specifically referring to Greek art of the fifth century B.C.E.

Classical. Adhering to traditional standards. May refer to Greek and Roman art in which simplicity, clarity of structure, and appeal to the intellect are fundamental.

clerestory. The upper stage or portion of the *nave* walls of a church or *basilica*, located above an adjoining roof and admitting light through a row of windows.

coda. A passage added to the end of a musical composition to produce a satisfactory close.

cognitive. Facts and objectivity as opposed to emotions and subjectivity. See also *affective*.

collage. An artwork constructed by pasting together various materials, such as newsprint, to create *textures* or by combining two- and three-dimensional media.

colonnade. A row of *columns* usually spanned or connected by *lintels*.

color wheel. A circle or wheel in which the primary colors—yellow, red, and blue—are separated by secondary and tertiary colors, so that, for example, red and blue are separated by red-violet, violet, and blue-violet. The wheel shows the complementary color of each primary color—for example, green is opposite to red, yellow is opposite to violet, and blue is opposite to orange.

column. A cylindrical post or support, which often has three distinct parts—base, shaft, and *capital*.

complementary colors. Colors that lie opposite each other on a *color wheel*.

composition. The arrangement of line, *form*, *mass*, color, and so forth in a work of art.

compression. In architecture, stress that results from two forces moving toward each other.

compressive strength. The ability of a material to withstand crushing. See also *tensile strength*.

concerto. A composition for *orchestra* and, usually, one soloist.

concerto grosso. A composition for *orchestra* and a group of soloists.

conjunct melody. In music, *melody* consisting of notes close together in the *scale*. The opposite of *disjunct melody*.

consonance. The feeling of a comfortable relationship between elements of a composition. Consonance may be physical and/or cultural in its ramifications.

contrapposto (counterpoise). In *sculpture*, the arrangement of body parts so that the weight-bearing leg is apart from the free leg, thereby shifting the hip/shoulder axis.

conventions. The customs or accepted underlying principles of an art.

Cool jazz. A form of *jazz* playing characterized by a restrained, relaxed style.

Corinthian. A specific Greek architectural *order* with a *column* employing an elaborate leaf motif in the *capital*.

cornice. A crowning, projecting architectural feature.

corrales. Spanish for "playhouses."

Council of Trent. The council of the Roman Catholic Church, held at Trent in northern Italy, between 1545 and 1563. It condemned the Protestant Reformation and began the Counter- or Catholic Reformation.

counterpoint. In music, two or more independent *melodies* played in opposition to each other at the same time. See also *homophony*, *monophony*, and *polyphony*.

countersubject. In music, a subsidiary *theme* played at the same time as the subject (main theme) of a *fugue*.

crescendo. An increase in loudness.

crosscutting. In film, alternation between two independent actions that are related thematically or by plot to give the impression of simultaneous occurrence.

cruciform. Arranged or shaped like a cross.

Cubism. A movement and style of art of the early twentieth century in which objects are represented as assemblages of geometric shapes.

curvilinear. Formed or characterized by curved lines.

cutting. The trimming and joining that occurs during the process of editing film.

cutting within the frame. Changing the viewpoint of the camera within a shot by moving from a long or medium shot to a close-up, without cutting the film.

dactylic. One of the four standard feet in poetry. A stressed syllable is followed by two light syllables. See also *foot* and *meter* (1).

decrescendo. A decrease in loudness.

deësis. An artwork representing Christ in majesty seated between the Virgin Mary and John the Baptist.

demi-hauteur. A ballet pose with the leg positioned at a 45-degree angle to the ground.

demi-plié. In ballet, a half-bend of the knees in any of the five positions.

dénouement. The section of a play's structure in which events are brought to a conclusion.

depth of focus. In film, when both near and distance objects are clearly seen.

design. A comprehensive scheme, plan, or conception.

detachment. Intellectual as opposed to emotional involvement. The opposite of *empathy*.

development. In *sonata form*, the second section in which the *themes* of the *exposition* (1) are freely developed. See also *recapitulation*.

diatonic minor. The standard musical minor *scale* achieved by lowering, by one half step, the third and sixth notes of the diatonic or standard major scale.

differential focus. See *rack focus*.

diptych. (1) A painting or other artwork in two panels, hinged so that it can be closed like a book. (2) A painting consisting of two individual panels or canvases. See also *triptych*.

direct address. In film and theatre, when a character addresses the audience directly.

disjunct melody. In music, *melody* characterized by skips or jumps in the *scale*. The opposite of *conjunct melody*.

dissolve. In film, to make an object or person appear or disappear from view.

dissonance. The occurrence of inharmonious elements in music or the other arts. The opposite of *consonance*.

divertissement. A dance, or a portion thereof, intended as a diversion from the idea content of the work.

divisionism. The juxtaposition of tiny dots of unmixed paints, giving an overall effect of color when mixed optically by the viewer's brain. Also known as *pointillism*.

documentary. In photography or film, the recording of actual events and relationships using real-life subjects as opposed to professional actors.

dolly shot. In film, a shot taken by moving the camera, which is mounted on a "dolly," toward or away from an object or person.

dome. An architectural form based on the principles of the *arch* in which space is defined by a hemisphere used as a ceiling.

dominant. In music, the fifth note of the *scale* in relation to the *key* note. For example, in the scale of C (major or minor) the dominant note is G. See also *tonic*.

Doric. A Greek architectural *order* with *columns*

having no base and only a simple slab as a *capital*.

drone. In music, a pipe or pipes sounding a note or notes of fixed *pitch*, continuing as a permanent bass, especially on various forms of bagpipe.

drypoint. An *intaglio* process in which the metal plate is scratched with a sharp needle-like tool.

dynamics. The various levels of loudness and softness of sounds; the increase and decrease of *intensities*.

eclecticism. In design, a combination of examples of several differing *styles* in a single composition.

editing. The composition of a film from various shots and sound tracks.

elevation. In dance, the height to which a dancer leaps.

embossing. The creation of raised designs in the surface of, for example, paper, leather, or metal.

empathy. Emotional and/or physical involvement in events to which one is a witness but not a participant.

empirical. Based on experiment, observation, and practical experience, without regard to theory.

en pointe. See *on point.*

engaged column. A *column*, often decorative, which is part of, and projects from, a wall surface.

engraving. An *intaglio* process in which sharp, definitive lines are cut into a metal plate.

entablature. The upper portion of a *Classical* architectural *order* above the *column capital.*

entrechat. In ballet, a jump beginning from fifth position in which the dancer reverses the legs front and back one or more times before landing in fifth position. Similar to the *changement de pied.*

ephemeral. Transitory; not lasting.

epic. A long narrative poem in heightened *style* about the deeds and adventures of a hero.

episode. In music, a subordinate section occurring between entries of the subject in a *fugue.*

epistolary narrative. A work of *fiction* in which the narrative is conveyed wholly by the exchange of letters. Examples include *Clarissa* by Samuel Richardson and *Les Liaisons dangereuses* by Laclos.

esprit d'escalier. French, meaning "spirit of the stairs." Remarks, thought of after the fact, which could have been *bons mots* had they been thought of at the right moment; witty remarks.

essay. A short literary composition on a single subject, usually presenting the personal views of the author. Essays can be formal or informal.

establishing shot. In film, a long shot at the beginning of a scene to establish the time, place, and so forth. See also *master shot.*

etching. An *intaglio* process; lines are cut in the metal plate by an acid bath.

étude. French for "study." In music, an instrumental piece, usually solo, to train or demonstrate the performer's technique.

existentialism. The name given to a group of philosophies that hold that humans are completely free and wholly responsible for their actions, which is the reason for the sense of dread and anguish they feel.

exposition. (1) The first section of *sonata form*, in which the first subject (in the *tonic key*) and second subject (in the *dominant* key), also sometimes further subjects, are played and often repeated. See also *development* and *recapitulation.* (2) The first statement of the subject of a *fugue* by all players in turn.

Expressionism. A movement in art, literature, and drama of the early twentieth century, in which artists attempted to express emotional experience rather than impressions of the external world. It was characterized by the distortion of reality and the use of symbols and stylization.

façade. The front of a building or the sides if they are emphasized architecturally.

farce. A theatrical *genre* characterized by broad, slapstick humor and implausible plots.

Fauvism. A *style* of painting, developed in the early twentieth century, characterized by the vivid use of color.

fenestration. Exterior openings, such as windows and archways, in an architectural *façade.*

ferroconcrete (reinforced concrete). Concrete reinforced with rods or mesh of steel.

fiction. A literary work created from the author's imagination rather than from fact.

fluting. Vertical ridges in a *column.*

flying buttress. A semidetached *buttress.*

focal point (focal area). A major or minor area of visual attraction in pictures, *sculpture*, dance, plays, films, landscape design, or buildings.

foot. In poetry, a group of syllables forming a metrical unit. See also *anapestic, dactylic, iambic, meter* (1), and *trochaic.*

foreground. The area of a picture, usually at the bottom, that appears to be closest to the viewer.

form. The shape, structure, configuration, or essence of something.

form cutting. In film, the framing in a successive shot of an object that has a shape similar to an image in the preceding shot.

forte. A musical term meaning loud.

found object. An object taken from life that is presented as an artwork.

frame. In film, a single or complete image.

frame-tale. A literary device with a preliminary narrative in which one or more of the characters tells a tale. *The Arabian Nights Entertainments* was an early example.

fresco. A method of painting in which pigment is mixed with wet plaster and applied as part of the wall surface.

frieze. (1) The central portion of the *entablature* between the *architrave* and *cornice.* (2) Any horizontal decorative or sculptural band.

fugue. Derived from a Latin word meaning flight. A conventional musical composition, vocal or instrumental, in which a *theme* is developed by *counterpoint*, each voice or part entering successively and in imitation of each other. See also *exposition* (2).

full-round. See *sculpture.*

galliard. A lively court dance in $\frac{3}{2}$ time of the sixteenth and early seventeenth centuries; usually associated with a *pavane.*

genre. (1) A category of artistic composition characterized by a particular *style, form,* or

content. (2) A style of painting representing an aspect of everyday life, such as a domestic interior or a rural scene.

geodesic dome. A dome-shaped framework constructed from short, straight, lightweight bars that form a grid of polygons.

geometric. Based on man-made patterns, such as triangles, rectangles, circles, ellipses, and so on. The opposite of *biomorphic.*

Gesamtkunstwerk. A complete, totally integrated artwork; associated with the music dramas of Richard Wagner in nineteenth-century Germany.

gestalt. A whole; the total of all elements in an entity.

glyptic. Sculptural works emphasizing the qualities of the materials from which they are created.

gopura. The monumental gateway to a Hindu temple.

Gothic. A style of architecture based on a pointed-*arch* structure and characterized by simplicity, verticality, elegance, and lightness.

gouache. A *watercolor medium* in which gum is added to ground opaque colors mixed with water.

grand jeté. In ballet, a leap from one foot to the other, usually with a running start.

grand plié. In ballet, a full bend of the knees with the heels raised and the knees opened wide towards the toes. May be done in any of the five positions.

grande seconde. A ballet pose with the leg in second position in the air.

grave. In music, a *tempo* marking meaning slow.

Greek cross. A cross in which all arms are the same length.

Gregorian chant. See *plainchant.*

groin vault. The ceiling formation created by the intersection of two tunnel or *barrel vaults.*

ground. (1) A surface to which paint is applied. (2) The coating material in which lines are scratched to produce designs in such processes as *etching.*

guardian figure. A figure made by ancestor-worshiping societies to watch over (guard) the remains of dead tribe members.

hagiography. The written life of a saint or other religious figure.

harmony. The relationship of like elements, such as musical notes, colors, and repetitive patterns. See also *consonance* and *dissonance.*

Hellenistic. Relating to the time from Alexander the Great to the first century B.C.E.

heroic. Larger than life size.

hierarchy. Any system of people or things that has higher and lower ranks.

hieratic. (1) Of or used by priests. (2) Of or concerning Egyptian, Byzantine, or Greek traditional styles of art.

homophony. A musical *texture* characterized by chordal development supporting one *melody.* See also *counterpoint, monophony,* and *polyphony.*

horizon line. A real or implied line across the picture plane, which, like the horizon in nature, tends to fix the viewer's vantage point.

hue. The spectrum notation of color; a specific, pure color with a measurable wavelength.

There are primary hues, secondary hues, and tertiary hues.

hypostyle. A hall with a roof supported by rows of *columns*.

iambic. One of the four standard feet in poetry. A light syllable is followed by a stressed syllable. See also *foot* and *meter* (1).

icon. Greek for "image." Used to identify paintings that represent the image of a holy person.

iconography. (1) A set of *symbols* conventionally associated with a subject, such as the iconography of Christianity. (2) The meaning assigned to a set of images or symbols according to a particular convention.

idée fixe. A recurring melodic *motif.*

identification. See *empathy.*

igneous rock. A very hard rock, such as granite, produced by volcanic or magmatic action and usually too hard to carve. See also *sedimentary rock* and *metamorphic rock.*

impasto. The painting technique of applying pigment so as to create a three-dimensional surface.

improvisation. Music and other art forms, produced on the spur of the moment or spontaneously.

inciting incident. In the theatre, an event or decision that creates a complication leading to the resolution of the drama.

intaglio. The printmaking process in which ink is transferred from the grooves of a metal plate to paper by extreme pressure.

intensity. (1) The degree of purity of a *hue.* (2) In music, theatre, and dance, that quality of *dynamics* denoting the amount of force used to create a sound or movement.

interval. The difference in *pitch* between two tones.

intrinsic. Belonging to a thing by its nature.

Ionic. A Greek architectural *order* with a *column* that employs a scroll-like *capital* with a circular base.

iris. In film and photography, the adjustable circular control of the aperture of a lens.

isolation shot. In film, the isolation of the subject of interest in the center of the frame.

jamb. The upright piece forming the side of a doorway or window frame.

jazz. Music of African American origins, characterized by *syncopation, improvisation,* and a regular rhythm.

jazz dance. A form of dancing arising partly from African dance customs, and with a strong, improvisational nature, that developed into American social and entertainment dances, such as the Charleston, the jive, and the jitterbug.

jeté. In ballet, a small jump from one foot to the other, beginning and ending with one foot raised.

jump cut. In film, the instantaneous cut from one scene to another or from one shot to another; often used for shock effect.

key. A system of tones in music based on, and named after, a given tone—i.e., the *tonic.*

keystone. The central stone at the summit of an *arch, rib,* or vault, locking the whole together.

kouros. An archaic Greek statue of a standing, nude youth.

krater. A bowl for mixing wine and water, the usual Greek beverage.

kylix. A vase turned on a potter's wheel; used as a drinking cup.

Labanotation. A system of writing down dance movements.

lap dissolve. In film, the simultaneous fade in and fade out of two scenes so that they briefly overlap.

largo. In music, a *tempo* notation meaning large, broad, very slow, and stately movement.

Latin cross. A cross in which the vertical arm is longer than the horizontal arm, through whose midpoint it passes.

legato. In music, a term indicating that passages are to be played with smoothness and without break between the tones.

leitmotif. A "leading *motif*" used in music to identify an individual, idea, object, and so on. Associated with Richard Wagner.

lekythos. An oil flask with a long, narrow neck adapted for pouring oil slowly; used in funeral rites.

lento. A musical term indicating a slow *tempo.*

libretto. The words or text of an opera or musical.

linear perspective. The creation of the illusion of distance in a two-dimensional artwork through the convention of line and foreshortening. That is, the illusion that parallel lines come together in the distance. See also *aerial perspective* and *perspective.*

linear sculpture. Sculptural works emphasizing two-dimensional materials.

lintel. The horizontal member of a *post-and-lintel* structure in architecture.

lithography. A printmaking technique, based on the principle that oil and water do not mix, in which ink is applied to a piece of paper from a specially prepared stone.

lost-wax. See *cire-perdue.*

low relief (bas relief). Relief *sculpture* in which figures and forms project only slightly from the background.

madrigal. A secular part song, originating in Italy.

magnitude. The scope or universality of the *theme* in a play or film.

mambo. A South American dance, similar to the rumba.

manipulation. A sculptural technique in which materials such as clay are shaped by the skilled use of hands.

masonry. In architecture, stone or brickwork.

mass. (1) Actual or implied physical bulk, weight, and density. (2) The most solemn rite of the Roman Catholic liturgy, often set to music for liturgical use.

master shot. In film, a single shot of an entire piece of action. See also *establishing shot.*

measure. A division of music, marked by vertical lines (bar lines). See also *meter* (2).

medium. The process employed by the artist. Also, the binding agent that holds pigments together.

melisma. A group of notes sung to a single syllable.

melodrama. A theatrical *genre,* characterized by stereotyped characters, implausible plots, and emphasis on spectacle.

melody. In music, a succession of single tones.

metamorphic rock. A rock such as marble that is formed by natural forces such as heat, pressure, or chemical reaction. See also *igneous rock* and *sedimentary rock.*

metaphor. A figure of speech by which new implications are given to words.

meter. (1) Any form of poetic *rhythm,* determined by the number and length of feet in a line. See also *foot.* (2) In music, the regular succession of rhythmical impulses or *beats.*

metronome. In music, an electrical or mechanical instrument for sounding the number of *beats* per minute and thereby fixing the *tempo* of a composition.

microtone. In music, all *intervals* lying between the semitones of the 12-note tuning system.

mime. In dance or theatre, gestures and expressions that imitate human or animal activity, character, and so on without using words.

Minnesänger. A German lyric poet or singer of the twelfth to fourteenth centuries. See also *troubadour* and *trouvère.*

mise-en-scène. The complete visual environment in the theatre, dance, and film, including setting, lighting, costumes, properties, and physical structure of the theatre.

mobile. A constructed structure whose components have been connected by joints to move by force of wind and motor.

mode. A particular *form, style,* or manner.

modeling. The shaping of three-dimensional *forms.* Also the suggestion of three-dimensionality in two-dimensional forms.

modern dance. A form of concert dancing relying on emotional use of the body, as opposed to formalized or conventional movement, and stressing human emotion and the human condition.

modulation. A change of *key* or *tonality* in music.

monolithic construction. A variation of *bearing-wall* construction in which the wall material is not jointed or pieced together.

monophony. In music, a musical *texture* (2) employing a single *melody* line without harmonic support. See also *counterpoint, homophony,* and *polyphony.*

montage. The process of making a single composition by combining parts of others. A rapid sequence of film shots bringing together associated ideas or images.

monumental. Works actually or appearing larger than life size.

Moog synthesizer. See *synthesizer.*

motet. A short, unaccompanied, *polyphonic* work for choir.

motif (motive). In music, a short recurrent melodic or rhythmic pattern. In the other arts, a recurrent element.

musique concrète. A twentieth-century musical approach in which conventional sounds are altered electronically on tape to produce new sounds.

narthex. A porch or vestibule at the main entrance of a church.

nave. The great central space in a church. See also *transept.*

Neoclassicism. Various artistic *styles* in art, literature, music, and so forth, that borrow the devices or objectives of *Classical* art.

Neoplatonism. Any of the schools of philosophy based on modified Platonism, but especially that developed by the followers of Plotinus in the third century C.E.

Neorealism. A movement, especially in Italian literature and film after World War II and in the tradition of *verismo*, in which superficially naturalistic works are informed by a degree of populism and sentimentality.

nirvana. In Buddhist philosophy, the state of perfect blessedness attained by the extinction of individual existence and the absorption of the soul into the supreme being.

nonobjective. Without reference to reality; may be differentiated from "abstract."

nonrepresentational. Without reference to reality; including *abstract* and *nonobjective.*

novel. A fictional prose narrative of considerable length, with a plot that unfolds through the actions, speech, and thoughts of the characters.

objective camera. A camera position based on a third-person viewpoint.

objet d'art. A French term meaning "object of art."

octave. In music, the distance between a specific *pitch* vibration and its double; for example, concert A equals 440 vibrations per second, one octave above that pitch equals 880 v.b.s., one octave below equals 220 v.b.s.

on point (en pointe). In ballet, a specific technique utilizing special shoes in which the dancer dances on the points of the toes.

opera buffa. A comic opera, dating from the eighteenth century, and depicting characters drawn from everyday life; the opposite of *opera seria.*

opéra comique. An opera with spoken dialogue. It is not necessarily humorous, as, for example, Bizet's *Carmen* and Beethoven's *Fidelio.*

opera seria. An opera, on a tragic or heroic theme, dating from the eighteenth century.

operetta. Light opera, with spoken dialogue and often a humorous or light-hearted theme.

opus. A single work of art.

oratorio. A semi-dramatic work, often on a religious *theme,* for *orchestra* (2), choir, and soloists.

orchestra. (1) The circular area in an ancient Greek theatre used by the chorus. (2) A large instrumental musical ensemble.

order. In architecture, one of the systems used by the Greeks and Romans to decorate and define their buildings. See also *Corinthian, Doric,* and *Ionic.*

overtones (overtone series). The additional sounds automatically stimulated by a vibrating body. See also *sympathetic vibration.*

palette. In the visual arts, the composite use of color, including range and *tonality.*

pan. In film, to follow a moving object with the camera.

pantheon. A Greek word meaning all the gods of a people.

pao-chia system. In China, a system of mutual familial responsibility.

parallel development. The use in film of *crosscutting* between scenes of contemporaneous action, often for ironic effect.

pas. In ballet, a combination of steps forming one dance.

pas de deux. A dance for two dancers.

pathos. The "suffering" aspect of drama usually associated with the evocation of pity.

patina. The film, usually greenish, that forms on the surface of copper and bronze as a result of oxidation; also known as verdigris and aerugo. The word is also used for the gloss produced by age on wood and other surfaces.

pavane. A stately court dance in $\frac{3}{4}$ time; it usually follows a *galliard.*

pedal point. In music, a sustained note, usually in the bass, above or around which *harmonies* change.

pediment. The typically triangular roof piece characteristic of *Classical* architecture.

pendentive. A triangular part of the vaulting which allows the stress of the round base of a *dome* to be transferred to a rectangular wall base.

persistence of vision. The continuance of a visual image on the retina for a brief time after the removal of the object.

perspective. The representation of distance and three-dimensionality on a two-dimensional surface. See also *aerial perspective* and *linear perspective.*

Philosophes. The collective name given to a group of eighteenth-century writers and thinkers, who believed in the power of reason and disliked repressive traditions.

photojournalism. Photography of actual events that may have sociological significance.

piano. A musical term meaning soft or quiet.

picaresque novel. A style of literature dealing with the episodic adventures of a rogue.

pirouette. In ballet, a full turn on the toe or ball of one foot.

pitch. In music, the quality of a sound—its highness or lowness—which is governed by the number of vibrations per second emanating from the source of the sound.

plainchant (Gregorian chant). The liturgical chant to Latin texts, sung in unison and used since the Middle Ages; also known as plainsong,

plan. An architectural drawing of a building as seen from above that reveals in two dimensions the arrangement and distribution of interior spaces and walls, as well as door and window openings.

planographic process. A method of printing from a flat surface, such as *lithography.*

plasticity. The capability of being molded or altered. In film, the ability to be cut and shaped. In painting, dance, and theatre, the accentuation of dimensionality of form through *chiaroscuro.*

platemark. The ridged or embossed effect created by the pressure used in transferring ink to paper from a metal plate in the *intaglio* process.

poetry. A literary work designed to convey a vivid and imaginative sense experience through the use of condensed language selected for its sound and suggestive power and meaning, and employing specific technical devices, such as *meter* (1), *rhyme,* and *metaphor.* There are three major types of poetry—narrative, dramatic, and lyric.

pointillism. In art, a kind of French Impressionism in which color is applied in tiny dots or small, isolated strokes. Forms are visible only from a distance. Also known as *divisionism.*

polyphony. In music, the combination of two or more independent melodic lines. See also *counterpoint, homophony,* and *monophony.*

polyrhythm. In music, the use of contrasting *rhythms* at the same time.

porcelain. A variety of hard, non-porous, translucent ceramic ware, made from kaolin, feldspar, and quartz or flint.

port de bras. The technique of moving the arms correctly in dance.

portico. An open or partly enclosed roofed space, usually serving as an entrance and often the centerpiece of a *façade.*

post-and-lintel. An architectural structure in which horizontal pieces (lintels) are held up by vertical *columns* (posts).

post-Columbian. The word used to denote the history, architecture, culture, and so forth of the Americas after Columbus landed there. See also *pre-Columbian.*

post-tensioned concrete (prestressed concrete). Concrete using metal rods and cables under stress or tension to cause structural forces to flow in predetermined directions.

power figure. A figure regarded by tribal societies as a repository of magic, which could be activated by the insertion of nails.

precast concrete. Concrete cast in place using wooden forms around a steel framework.

pre-Columbian. The word used to denote the history, architecture, culture, and so forth of the Americas before Columbus landed there. See also *post-Columbian.*

presto. A musical term denoting a rapid *tempo.*

prestressed concrete. See *post-tensioned* concrete.

program music. Instrumental music that interprets, narratively and descriptively, a story or picture. See also *absolute music* and *tone poem.*

proportion. The relation, or ratio, of one part to another and of each part to the whole with regard to size, height, width, length, or depth.

proscenium. A Greek word meaning "before the *skene.*" The plaster arch or "picture frame" stage of traditional theatres.

protagonist. The leading person or character in a work of literature, theatre, or film.

prototype. The model on which something is based.

putto (plural putti). A representation of a naked child, especially a cupid or cherub, particularly in Renaissance art.

pyramidal structure. In film and dance, the rising of action to a peak, which then tapers to a conclusion.

quadrille. (1) An American square dance. (2) A European ballroom dance of the eighteenth and nineteenth centuries.

rack focus (differential focus). In film, when an object is clearly shown while the remainder of the scene is out of focus.

ragtime. A kind of American music, mostly composed and popular from about 1890 to 1914, and characterized by fast, even time and strong *syncopation.*

Realism. A style of painting, sculpture, and theatre based on the theory that the method of presentation should be true to life.

recapitulation. In *sonata form*, the third section in which the *exposition* (1) is repeated, often with variations. See also *development*.

recitative. Sung dialogue in opera, *cantata*, and *oratorio*.

rectilinear. In the visual arts, the formed use of straight lines and angles.

register. A range or row, especially when one of a series.

reinforced concrete. See *ferroconcrete*.

relative major. In music, the sharing of a common *key* signature by a major and a minor key. For example, G major is the relative major of E minor (both have one sharp). Similarly, E minor is the relative minor of G major.

relevé. In ballet, the raising of the body to full height or half-height during the execution of a step or movement.

relief. See *sculpture*.

relief printing. The process in printmaking by which the ink is transferred to the paper from raised areas on a printing block.

representational. Objects that are recognizable from real life. See also *abstract* and *nonrepresentational*.

requiem. A *mass* for the dead.

rest. In music, silence. The notation used in scores to indicate the absence of sound from a performer or group of performers.

rhyme. A sound structure coupling words that sound alike.

rhythm. The relationship, either of time or space, between recurring elements of a composition.

rib. In a vault system, a slender architectural support projecting from the surface.

rib vault. A structure in which *arches* are connected by diagonal as well as horizontal members.

ritardando. A musical term indicating a decrease in *tempo*.

ritornello. In a Classical *concerto*, the return of the full *orchestra* after a solo passage.

Rococo. A style of architecture and design, developed in France from the *Baroque* and characterized by elaborate and profuse ornamentation, often in the form of shells, scrolls, and the like.

Roman cross. A cross with a long vertical arm and a shorter horizontal one; also known as a *Latin cross*.

rondo. A form of musical composition employing a return to an initial *theme* after the presentation of each new theme.

ronds de jambe à terre. In ballet, a rapid semicircular movement of the foot in which the toe remains on the floor and the heel brushes the floor in first position as it completes the semicircle.

round. In music, a vocal piece in which the same *melody* is sung at the same *pitch* but at different times by a group of singers. See also *canon*.

rubato. A style of musical performance in which the performer treats the *rhythm* of a piece with a degree of freedom.

satire. (1) The use of ridicule, irony, or sarcasm to hold up to ridicule and contempt vices, follies, abuses, and so forth. (2) A work of literature that uses satire (1).

saturation. In color, the purity of a *hue* in terms of whiteness; the whiter the hue, the less saturated it is.

scale. (1) In music, a graduated series of ascending or descending tones. (2) In architecture, the *mass* of the building in relation to a given measurement, such as the human body.

sculpture. A three-dimensional art object. Among the types are: cast, which is created from molten material in a mold; relief, which is attached to a larger background; full-round, which is freestanding; and built or assembled, which is created by the addition of, often, prefabricated elements.

sedimentary rock. A rock such as limestone or sandstone that is formed by erosion and deposition. See also *igneous rock* and *metamorphic rock*.

sequence. In music, the repetition of a phrase at a higher or lower *pitch* than the original.

serial music. A twentieth-century musical style utilizing the tone row and serialization of *rhythms*, *timbres*, and *dynamics*.

serigraphy. A printmaking process in which ink is forced through a piece of stretched fabric, part of which has been blocked out; for example, silk-screening and stenciling.

sfumato. In oil painting, the creation of soft, delicately blended effects by the gradation of one tone into another.

shape. A two-dimensional area or plane with distinguishable boundaries.

short story. A short *fictional* work of prose, focusing on unity of characterization, *theme*, and effect.

silhouette. A form as defined by its outline.

silk-screening. See *serigraphy*.

skeleton frame. Construction in which a skeletal framework supports the building. See also *balloon construction* and *steel-cage construction*.

skene. The stage building of the ancient Greek theatre. See also *proscenium*.

sonata. In music, an instrumental piece, usually in three or four movements and usually for one or two players.

sonata form. A type of musical structure usually used in the first movement of a *sonata*. The three parts are the *exposition*, *development*, and *recapitulation*.

song cycle. A group of *art songs* combined around a similar text or *theme*.

sonority. In music, the characteristic of *texture* resulting from chordal spacing.

spansion architecture. A style of architecture that takes to the extreme the horizontal distance between the supports of a bridge, *arch*, and so forth.

spine (superobjective). In the theatre, the motivating aspect of a character's persona that an actor seeks to reveal by physical means.

staccato. In music, the technique of playing so that individual notes are detached and separated from each other.

stanza. The group of lines of verse forming one of the divisions of a poem or song, usually consisting of four lines and having a regular arrangement of *rhyme* and *meter*.

static. Devoid of movement or other dynamic qualities.

steel-cage construction. Construction using a metal framework. See also *balloon construction* and *skeleton frame*.

stereotype. A conventional, formulaic, and usually oversimplified conception, opinion, or belief.

stippling. Applying small dots of color with the point of a brush.

stream of consciousness. A narrative form in fiction that attempts to capture the whole range and flow of a character's mental processes.

strophic form. Vocal music in which all *stanzas* of the text are sung to the same music.

stucco. A plaster used as a finishing and protective covering on walls. A mixture including lime and powdered marble was used extensively in Europe for relief decorations (see *sculpture*) from the sixteenth century.

Sturm und Drang. German for "storm and stress." The Romantic movement in late eighteenth-century German literature, developed in opposition to French *Neoclassicism* and characterized by the cult of genius and a return to "nature."

style. Those characteristics of a work of art that identify it with an artist, a group of artists, an era, or a nation.

stylization. Reliance on conventions, distortions, or theatricality; the exaggeration of characteristics that are fundamentally verisimilar.

stylobate. The foundation immediately below a row of *columns*.

substitution. A sculptural technique utilizing materials transformed from a plastic, molten, or fluid into a solid state.

subtractive. (1) In *sculpture*, referring to works that are carved. (2) In color, referring to the mixing of pigments as opposed to the mixing of colored light.

suite. In music, a group of compositions, originally in dance style, to be played in succession.

superobjective. See *spine*.

Surrealism. A movement in art developed in the 1920s in which artists and writers gave free rein to the imagination, expressing the subconscious through the irrational juxtapositions of objects and *themes*.

suspension construction. In architecture, the use of steel cables to suspend bridges, walkways, and the like.

Swing. A kind of *jazz* music, popular between about 1935 and 1945, characterized by strong, driving *rhythms*, and improvised *counterpoint*, and played by big bands.

symbol. A form, image, or subject, standing for something else.

symbolism. The suggestion through imagery of something that is invisible or intangible. In art and literature, the word refers especially to the French and Belgian writers and artists of the late nineteenth century who rejected realism and sought to express ideas, emotions, and attitudes by the use of symbolic words, objects, and so on.

symmetry. The balancing of elements in designs by placing physically equal objects on either side of a center line.

sympathetic vibration. The physical phenomenon of one vibrating body being set in motion by a second vibrating body. See also *overtones*.

symphony. A large musical ensemble; a symphony *orchestra* (2). Also, a musical composition for orchestra, usually consisting of three or four movements.

syncopation. In a musical composition the displacement of *accent* from the normally accented beat to the offbeat.

synthesis. The combination of independent factors or entities into a compound that becomes a new, more complex whole.

synthesizer (Moog synthesizer). An electronic instrument that produces and combines musical sounds.

systematic rationalism. In the seventeenth century, a system developed to explain the universe in both secular and religious terms.

tempera. An opaque *watercolor medium*, referring to ground pigments and their color binders, such as gum, glue, or egg.

tempo. The rate of speed at which a musical composition is performed. In theatre, film, or dance, the rate of speed of the overall performance.

tensile strength. The internal strength of a material that enables it to support itself without bending under tension. See also *compressive strength*.

ternary form. In music, the form of a movement in three sections. See also *ABA*.

terra-cotta. An earth-brown clay used in ceramics and *sculpture*.

tessitura. The general musical range of the voice in a particular composition.

texture. (1) In visual art, the two- or three-dimensional quality of the surface of a work. (2) In music, the melodic and harmonic characteristics of the composition.

theatricality. Exaggeration and artificiality. The opposite of lifelikeness.

theme. The general subject of an artwork whether melodic or philosophical.

thrust theatre. A theatre in which the stage projects into the auditorium so that the audience is seated on three sides of the stage.

timbre. The characteristic of a sound that results from the particular source of the sound. The difference between the sound of a violin and the sound of the human voice is a difference in timbre; also called tone color.

tint. A color or *hue* that has been modified by the addition of a small amount of another color.

toccata. A composition, usually for organ or piano, intended to display technique.

tonality. (1) In music, the specific *key* in which a composition is written. (2) In the visual arts, the characteristics of *value*.

tondo. A painting in a circular format.

tone poem. An orchestral work, on a symphonic scale, written to interpret musically something non-musical, such as a work of literature; also called symphonic poem. See also *absolute music* and *program music*.

tonic. In music, the root tone or note (do) of a *key*; also sometimes called the keynote. See also *dominant*.

tracking. In film, when the camera is moving in the same direction and at the same speed as a person or object.

traditional jazz. In the style of the early twentieth century, as distinct from modern jazz, which developed from *Be-bop*.

tragedy. A serious drama or other literary work in which conflict between a protagonist and a superior force (often fate) concludes in disaster for the protagonist.

tragicomedy. A drama combining the qualities of *tragedy* and comedy.

transept. The crossing arm of a *cruciform* church, in contrast to the *nave*, to which it is at right angles.

transverse arch. In Romanesque and *Gothic* architecture, an *arch* separating one bay of a vault from another.

travertine. A hard limestone, found in Italy, used as a building material and for outdoor *sculpture*.

triad. A *chord* consisting of three tones.

triforium. An arcaded wall passage, above the *arcade* but below the *clerestory* and facing the *nave* of a Romanesque or *Gothic* church.

triptych. An artwork in the form of a set of three panels with related subject matter, often designed as an *altarpiece*. See also *diptych*.

trochaic. One of the four standard feet in poetry. A stressed syllable is followed by a light syllable. See also *foot* and *meter*.

trompe l'oeil. French for "trick of the eye" or "fool the eye." A two-dimensional artwork, executed in such a way as to make the viewer believe that three-dimensional subject matter is being perceived.

trope. (1) In music, a type of interpolation into the traditional liturgical *plainchant*. (2) In theatre, a dramatic elaboration of the *mass*.

troubadour. A lyric poet or poet-musician who performed songs of courtly love and chivalry at the courts of southern France, Provence, Catalonia, and northern Italy in the eleventh to thirteenth centuries. See also *Minnesänger* and *trouvère*.

trouvère. A narrative poet, especially in northern France, between the eleventh and fourteenth centuries. See also *Minnesänger* and *troubadour*.

tunnel vault. See *barrel vault*.

tutu. A many-layered, short, stiff skirt worn by a ballerina.

twelve-tone technique. A twentieth-century *atonal* form of musical composition associated with Arnold Schoenberg.

two-shot. In film, a close-up of two people.

tympanum. The open space above the door beam and within the arch of a medieval doorway.

value (value scale). In the visual arts, the range of *tonalities* from white to black.

vanishing point. In *linear perspective*, the point on the horizon toward which parallel lines appear to converge and at which they seem to vanish.

variation. The repetition of a *theme* with minor or major changes.

verisimilitude. The appearance of reality in any element of the arts.

verismo. Italian for "realism." A word applied to late nineteenth-century Italian operas with contemporary, often violent, plots and everyday settings.

vivace. A musical term denoting a vivacious or lively *tempo*.

virtuoso. Referring to the display of impressive technique or skill by an artist.

waltz. A dance in $\frac{3}{4}$ time.

watercolor. (1) A pigment or coloring agent mixed with water for use as a paint. (2) An artwork produced with this medium.

wipe. In film, a line passes across the screen, eliminating one scene as it reveals the next.

wood engraving. A relief printing made from a design cut in the butt of the grain.

woodcut. A relief printing executed from a design cut in the plane of the grain.

ziggurat. In Mesopotamia, a stepped, rectangular tower, topped by a temple.

BIBLIOGRAPHY

Abcarian, Richard, and Marvin Klotz (eds.). *Literature, the Human Experience*. New York: St. Martin's Press, 1998.

Acton, Mary. *Learning to Look at Paintings*. London: Routledge, 1997.

Ambrosio, Nora. *Learning About Dance* (2nd edn.). Dubuque, IA: Kendall Hunt, 1999.

Anderson, Jack. *Dance*. New York: Newsweek Books, 1974.

Andreae, Bernard. *The Art of Rome*, New York: Abrams, 1977.

Arnheim, Rudolph. *Art and Visual Perception: A Psychology of the Creative Eye*. Berkeley: University of California Press, 1997.

Arnheim, Rudolph. *Film as Art*. Berkeley: University of California Press, 1992.

Arnott, Peter D. *An Introduction to the Greek Theatre*. Bloomington: Indiana University Press, 1963.

Artz, Frederick. *From the Renaissance to Romanticism*. Chicago: University of Chicago Press, 1962.

Bacon, Edmund N. *Design of Cities*. New York: Viking Press, 1976.

Bazin, Germain. *The Baroque*. Greenwich, CT: New York Graphic Society, 1968.

Benbow-Pfalzgraf, Taryn. *International Dictionary of Modern Dance*. New York: St James Press, 1998.

Bobker Lee R. *Elements of Film*. New York: Harcourt Brace Jovanovich, 1979.

Booth, Michael. *Victorian Spectacular Theatre 1850–1910*. Boston: Routledge & Kegan Paul, 1981.

Bordwell, David, and Kristin Thompson. *Film Art: An Introduction*. Reading, MA: Addison-Wesley, 1996.

Braider, Christopher. *Refiguring the Real: Picture and Modernity in Word and Image: 1400–1700*. Princeton, NJ: Princeton University Press, 1993.

Brindle, Reginald Smith. *The New Music: The Avant-Garde Since 1945*. London: Oxford University Press, 1975.

Brockett, Oscar G. *History of the Theatre*. Boston: Allyn & Bacon, 1968.

Brockett, Oscar G.. *The Essential Theatre* (5th edn.). New York: Holt, Rinehart, & Winston, 1992.

Cameron, Kenneth M., and Patti Gillespie. *The Enjoyment of the Theatre* (4th edn.). Boston, MA: Allyn & Bacon, 1996.

Campos, D. Redig de (ed.). *Art Treasures of the Vatican*. Englewood Cliffs, NJ: Prentice Hall, 1974.

Canaday, John. *What Is Art?* New York: Alfred A. Knopf, 1990.

Cass, Joan. *Dancing Through History*. Englewood Cliffs, NJ: Prentice Hall, 1993.

Chadwick, Whitney. *Women, Art, and Society*. New York: Norton, 1991.

Ching, Frank D. K., and Francis D. Ching. *Architecture: Form, Space, & Order* (2nd edn.). New York: John Wiley & Sons, 1996.

Cook, David A. *A History of Narrative Film*. New York: Norton, 1996.

Le Corbusier. *Towards a New Architecture*. New York: Dover, 1986.

Corner, James S. *Taking Measures Across the American Landscape*. New Haven, CT: Yale University Press, 1996.

Davis, Phil. *Photography*. Dubuque, IA: William C. Brown, 1996.

Dean, Alexander, and Lawrence Carra. *Fundamentals of Play Directing*. New York: Holt, Rinehart, & Winston, 1990.

De la Croix, Horst, Richard G. Tansey, and Diane Kirkpatric. *Gardner's Art Through the Ages* (9th edn.). San Diego, CA: Harcourt, 1991.

De Lerma, Dominique-Rene. *Reflections of Afro-American Music*. Kent, OH: Kent State University Press, 1973.

Diehl, Charles. *Byzantium*. New Brunswick, NJ: Rutgers University Press, 1957.

Dockstader, Frederick J. *Indian Art of the Americas*. New York: Museum of the American Indian; Heye Foundation, 1973.

Ernst, David. *The Evolution of Electronic Music*. New York: Schirmer, 1977.

Finn, David. *How to Look at Sculpture*. New York: Harry N. Abrams, 1989.

Frampton, Kenneth. *Modern Architecture: A Critical History* (3rd edn.). London: Thames and Hudson, 1992.

Gardner, Helen. *Art Through the Ages* (9th edn.). New York: Harcourt Brace Jovanovich, 1991.

Garraty, John, and Peter Gay. *A History of the World* (2 vols.). New York: Harper & Row, 1972.

Giannetti, Louis. *Understanding Movies* (2nd edn.). Englewood Cliffs, NJ: Prentice Hall, 1996.

Giedion, Sigfried. *Space, Time and Architecture: the Growth of a New Tradition* (5th edn.). Cambridge, MA: Harvard University Press, 1967.

Gilbert, Cecil. *International Folk Dance at a Glance*. Minneapolis, MN: Burgess Publishing, 1969.

Gilbert, Creighton. *History of Renaissance Art Throughout Europe: Painting, Sculpture, Architecture*. New York: Abrams, 1973.

Glasstone, Victor. *Victorian and Edwardian Theatres*. Cambridge, MA: Harvard University Press, 1975.

Golding, John. *Visions of the Modern*. Berkeley, CA: University of California Press, 1994.

Grabar, André. *The Art of the Byzantine Empire*. New York: Crown Publishers, 1966.

Graziosi, Paolo. *Paleolithic Art*. New York: McGraw-Hill, 1960.

Griffiths, Paul. *A Concise History of Avant-Garde Music*. New York: Oxford University Press, 1978.

Grimm, Harold. *The Reformation Era*. New York: Macmillan, 1954.

Groenewegen-Frankfort and Bernard Ashmole. *Art of the Ancient World*. Englewood Cliffs, NJ: and New York: Prentice Hall and Abrams, n.d.

Grout, Donald Jay. *A History of Western Music* (rev. edn.). New York: W. W. Norton, 1973.

Hamilton, George Heard. *Nineteenth and Twentieth Century Art: Painting, Sculpture, Architecture*. New York: Abrams, 1970.

Hartnoll, Phyllis, and Peter Found (eds.). *The Concise Oxford Companion to the Theatre* (2nd edn.). New York: Oxford University Press, 1992.

Hartt, Frederick. *Art* (4th edn.). Englewood Cliffs, NJ, and New York: Prentice Hall and Abrams, 1993.

Hartt, Frederick. *Italian Renaissance Art* (3rd edn.). Englewood Cliffs, NJ, and New York: Prentice Hall and Abrams, 1987.

Hawkes, Jacquetta, and Sir Leonard Wooley. *History of Mankind: Prehistory and the Beginnings of Civilization*. New York: Harper & Row, 1963.

Held, Julius, and D. Posner. *17th and 18th Century Art*. New York: Abrams, n.d.

Helm, Ernest. *Music at the Court of Frederick the Great*. Norman, OK: University of Oklahoma Press, 1960.

Henig, Martin (ed.). *A Handbook of Roman Art*. Ithaca, NY: Cornell University Press, 1983.

Heyer, Paul. *Architects on Architecture: New Directions in America*. New York: Walker and Company, 1978.

Highwater, Jamake. *Dance: Rituals of Experience* (3rd edn.). New York: Oxford University Press, 1996.

Hitchcock, Henry-Russell. *Architecture; Nineteenth and Twentieth Centuries*. Baltimore: Penguin, 1971.

Honour, Hugh, and John Fleming. *The Visual Arts: A History* (4th edn.). Englewood Cliffs, NJ, and New York: Prentice Hall and Abrams, 1995.

Hornstein, Lilian, G. D. Percy, and Sterling A. Brown. *World Literature* (2nd edn.). New York: Mentor, 1973.

Hubert, J., J. Porcher and W. F. Volbach. *The Carolingian Renaissance*. New York: George Braziller, 1970.

Hyman, Isabelle, and Marvin Trachtenberg. *Architecture: From Prehistory to Post-Modernism/The Western Tradition*. New York: Harry N. Abrams, 1986.

Janson, H. W. *History of Art* (5th edn.). Englewood Cliffs, NJ, and New York: Prentice Hall and Abrams, 1995.

Jones, LeRoi. *Black Music*. New York: William Morrow, 1967.

Kamien, Roger. *Music: An Appreciation* (5th edn.). New York: McGraw-Hill, 1995.

Katz, Bernard. *The Social Implications of Early Negro Music in the United States*. New York: Arno Press and *The New York Times*, 1969.

Keck, George R., and Sherrill Martin. *Feel the Spirit*. Westport, CT: Greenwood Press, 1988.

Keutner, Hubert. *Sculpture: Renaissance to Rococo*. Greenwich, CT: New York Graphic Society, 1969.

Kjellberg, Ernst, and Gosta Saflund. *Greek and Roman Art*. New York: Thomas Y. Crowell, 1968.

Kramer, Jonathan D. *Listen to the Music: A Self-Guided Tour Through the Orchestral Repertoire*. New York: Schirmer Books, 1992.

Krehbiel, Henry Edward. *Afro-American Folksongs*. New York: G. Schirmer, n.d. (c. 1914).

Lee, Sherman. *A History of Far Eastern Art* (4th edn.). Englewood Cliffs, NJ, and New York: Prentice Hall and Abrams, 1982.

Lippard, Lucy R. *Pop Art*. New York: Oxford University Press, 1966.

Lloyd, Seton. *The Archaeology of Mesopotamia*. London: Thames & Hudson, 1978.

Mango, Cyril. *Byzantium*. New York: Charles Scribner's Sons, 1980.

Marshack, Alexander. *The Roots of Civilization*. New York: McGraw-Hill, 1972.

Martin, John. *The Modern Dance*. Brooklyn: Dance Horizons, 1965.

McDonagy, Don. *The Rise and Fall of Modern Dance*. New York: E. P. Dutton, 1971.

McLeish, Kenneth. *The Theatre of Aristophanes*. New York: Taplinger Publishing, 1980.

Muthesius, Stefan. *The High Victorian Movement in*

Architecture 1850–1870. London: Routledge & Kegan Paul, 1972.

Nesbitt, Kate (ed.). *Theorizing a New Agenda for Architecture: An Anthology of Architectural Theory 1965–1995*. New Haven, CT: Princeton Architectural Press, 1996.

Newton, Norman T. *Design on the Land: the Development of Landscape Architecture*. Cambridge, MA: Harvard University Press, 1971.

Nyman, Michael. *Experimental Music: Cage and Beyond*. New York: Schirmer Books, 1974.

Ocvirk, Otto G. et al. *Art Fundamentals* (7th edn.). Madison, WI, and Dubuque, IA: Brown & Benchmark, 1994.

Ostransky, Leroy. *Understanding Jazz*. Englewood Cliffs, NJ: Prentice Hall, 1977.

Pfeiffer, John E. *The Creative Explosion*. New York: Harper & Row, 1982.

Pignatti, Terisio. *The Age of Rococo*. London: Paul Hamlyn, 1969.

Politoske, Daniel T. *Music* (5th edn.). Englewood Cliffs, NJ: Prentice Hall, 1992.

Powell, T. G. E. *Prehistoric Art*. New York: Frederick Praeger Publishers, 1966.

Preble, Duane. *We Create, Art Creates Us*. New York: Harper & Row, 1976.

Rasmussen, Steen Eiler. *Experiencing Architecture*. Cambridge, MA: MIT Press, 1984.

Read, Benedict. *Victorian Sculpture*. New Haven, CT: Yale University Press, 1982.

Rice, David Talbot. *The Art of Byzantium*. New York: Abrams, n.d.

Richter, Gisela. *Greek Art*. Greenwich, CT: Phaidon, 1960.

Robertson, Martin. *A Shorter History of Greek Art*. Cambridge, MA: Cambridge University Press, 1981.

Roters, Eberhard. *Painters of the Bauhaus*. New York: Praeger Publishers, 1965.

Ryman, Rhonda. *Dictionary of Classical Ballet Terminology*. Princeton, NJ: Princeton Book Company, 1998.

Sachs, Curt. *World History of the Dance*. New York: W. W. Norton, 1937.

Savill, Agnes. *Alexander the Great and His Times*. New York: Barnes and Noble, 1993.

Schonberger, Arno, and Halldor Soehner. *The Rococo Age*. New York: McGraw-Hill, 1960.

Sherrard, Philip. *Byzantium*. New York: Time, 1966.

Sitwell, Sacheverell. *Great Houses of Europe*. London: Spring Books, 1970.

Sorell, Walter. *Dance in its Time*. Garden City, NY: Doubleday Anchor Press, 1981.

Sporre, Dennis J. *The Art of Theatre*. Englewood Cliffs, NJ: Prentice Hall, 1993.

Sporre, Dennis J. *The Creative Impulse* (5th edn.). Upper Saddle River, NJ: Prentice Hall, 2000.

Sporre, Dennis J., and Robert C. Burroughs. *Scene Design in the Theatre*. Englewood Cliffs, NJ: Prentice Hall, 1990.

Stanley, John. *An Introduction to Classical Music Through the Great Composers & Their Masterworks*. New York: Reader's Digest, 1997.

Stearns, Marshall, and Jean Marshall. *Jazz Dance*. New York: Macmillan, 1968.

Steinberg, Cobbett. *The Dancing Anthology*. New York: Times Mirror, 1980.

Steinberg, Michael. *The Symphony: A Listener's Guide*. New York: Oxford University Press, 1995.

Summerson, John Newenham. *Classical Language of Architecture*. Cambridge, MA: MIT Press, 1984.

Thompson, Kristin, and David Bordwell. *Film History: An Introduction*. New York: McGraw-Hill, 1994

Tirro, Frank. *Jazz: A History*. New York: W. W. Norton, 1977.

Trythall, Gilbert. *Principles and Practice of Electronic Music*. New York: Grosset & Dunlap, 1973.

Vacche, Angela Dalle. *Cinema and Painting: How Art Is Used in Film*. Austin, TX: University of Texas Press, 1996.

Van Der Kemp, Gerald. *Versailles*. New York: Vendome Press, 1977.

Wheeler, Robert Eric Mortimer. *Roman Art and Architecture*. New York: Praeger Publishers, 1964.

Yenawine, Philip. *How to Look at Modern Art*. New York: Harry N. Abrams, 1991.

Zarnecki, George. *Art of the Medieval World*. Englewood Cliffs, NJ: Prentice Hall, 1975.

Zorn, Jay D. *Listen to Music*. Englewood Cliffs, NJ: Prentice Hall, 1994.

INDEX

Prelims and Introduction
Page 8 The Art Archive/©Estate of Diego Rivera
0.1 AKG London
0.2 A/B ©Christo 1997. Photo: Wolfgang Volz
0.6 Alinari
0.7 ©The British Museum, London
0.9 VAG (UK) Ltd.

Chapter 1
1.1 Photograph ©The Board of Trustees, The National Gallery of Art, Washington. 1991.150.1.a. Photo: Dean Beasom
1.2 Photograph ©The Board of Trustees, The National Gallery of Art, Washington. 1986.82.1. Photo: Dean Beasom
1.3 Photograph ©The Board of Trustees, The National Gallery of Art, Washington. 1979.41.1. Photo: Dean Beasom
1.4 Courtesy Bernice Steinbaum Gallery, Miami, FL. Photo: Adam Reich
1.5 Photograph ©The Board of Trustees, The National Gallery of Art, Washington. 1942.9.670. Photo: Dean Beasom
1.7 Digital Image ©2002 The Museum of Modern Art, New York/Photo Scala, Florence
1.14 ©Thomas Hart Benton Trust/VAGA New York/DACS London 2000
1.19 Digital Image ©2002 The Museum of Modern Art, New York/Photo Scala, Florence. ©Succession Picasso/DACS 2003
1.20 ©Succession Miro, DACS 2003
1.22 Digital Image ©2002 The Museum of Modern Art, New York/Photo Scala, Florence. ©ARS, New York and DACS, London 2003
1.34 Digital Image ©2002 The Museum of Modern Art, New York/Photo Scala, Florence. ©Salvador Dali, Gala-Salvador Dali Foundation, DACS, London 2003
1.35 RMN
1.36 ©Succession Picasso/DACS 2003
1.43 Digital Image ©2002 The Museum of Modern Art, New York/Photo Scala, Florence. ©Mondrian/Holzman Trust, c/o Beeldrecht, Amsterdam, Holland
1.45 Digital Image ©2002 The Museum of Modern Art, New York/Photo Scala, Florence. ©DACS 2003

Chapter 2
2.4 ©ARS, NY and DACS, London 2003
2.5 Giraudon, Paris
2.6 ©The British Museum, London
2.10 ©Christo 1997. Photo: Wolfgang Volz
2.8 and 2.11 Hirmer Fotoarchiv, Munich
2.12 Digital Image ©2002 The Museum of Modern Art, New York/Photo Scala, Florence. ©ADAGP, Paris and DACS, London 2003
2.13 Digital Image ©2002 The Museum of Modern Art, New York/Photo Scala, Florence. ©DACS 2003
2.27 Rheinisches Bildarchiv, Cologne. Courtesy of Heaton Sessions, Stone Ridge, New York

Chapter 3
3.11, 13 Trudy Lee Cohen, Philadelphia

Chapter 4
4.6, 9, 11, 12 University of Arizona Theatre
4.7, 8 Old Globe Theatre, San Diego
4.10 State University, New York
4.13 University of Illinois
4.14 University of Iowa Theatre
4.15 Black Star, New York. Photo: Steve Schapiro

Chapter 5
5.1 ©ADAGP, Paris and DACS, London 2003
5.2, 4 B.F.I., London
5.3 ©Universal Pictures, a Division of Universal Studios Inc. All Rights Reserved

Chapter 6
6.1 Dee Conway Ballet and Dance Picture Library
6.6 Dee Conway Ballet and Dance Picture Library

6.7 Linda Rich, Addlestone, U.K.
6.8, 9 Roger Greenawalt, Langhorne, PA
6.10 Dee Conway Ballet and Dance Picture Library
6.11 Hulton Deutsch

Chapter 7
7.1, 23 Britain on View (B.T.A.), London
7.2 A.C. & R. John Donat, London
7.5 Hirmer Fotoarchiv, Munich
7.14, 33 A.F. Kersting, London
7.20 Library of Congress
7.21 Wayne Andrews/ESTO, Mamaroneck
7.22 Ezra Stoller/ESTO, Mamaroneck. ©ARS, NY and DACS, London 2003
7.26 Wayne Andrews, Chicago. ©ARS, NY and DACS, London 2003
7.27 Ralph Liebermann, North Adams, MA
7.28, 31 ©FLC/ADAGP Paris/DACS London 2003
7.29 Norman McGrath, New York
7.32 Giraudon, Paris
7.34, 36 Scala, Florence
7.37 Washington Area Convention and Visitors Association
7.38 Solomon R. Guggenheim Museum/Robert E. Mates ©ARS, NY and DACS, London 2003

Chapter 8
8.1 Range Pictures, London/Bettmann Archive, New York/U.P.I.

Part II
II.2, 4 ©Succession Picasso/DACS 2003
II.3 Digital Image ©2002 The Museum of Modern Art, New York/Photo Scala, Florence
II.5, 7 Novosti, London

Chapter 9
9.2, 4 Colorphoto Hans Hinz, Allschwil, Switzerland
9.9 Courtesy University of Pennsylvania Museum, Philadelphia
9.15, 17 A.F. Kersting, London
9.22 Hirmer Fotoarchiv, Munich
9.27 RMN-Hervé Lewandowski

Chapter 10
10.2, 3, 9, 11, 18, 19, 21, 22, 26 Alinari, Florence
10.6, 31 Hirmer Fotoarchiv, Munich
10.7, 14, 24 A.F. Kersting, London
10.16, 28 Scala, Florence
10.20 Fototeca Unione, Rome
10.29 Sonia Halliday Photographs, Weston Turville, U.K.
10.33 RMN
10.44 Ancient Art and Architecture Collection, London
10.51 Todaiji, Nara
10.52 Jean Dieuzaide, Toulouse
10.53 Clive Hicks, London
10.54 Bulloz, Paris
10.56 Britain on View (B.T.A.), London
10.58, 60 Giraudon, Paris
10.59 Photo: J. Feuille, CNMHS, Paris

Chapter 11
11.4, 6, 8, 35 Alinari, Florence
11.3, 9, 32 Scala, Florence
11.5, 39, 40, 43 RMN
11.10 Hirmer Fotoarchiv, Munich
11.18 Courtesy The Bodleian Library, University of Oxford. MS.Arch.Selden.A.1,fol.2r
11.19 The Art Archive/National Anthropological Museum Mexico/Dagli Orti
11.21 The Bridgeman Art Library. Photo: Miranda Talbot
11.22 The Bridgeman Art Library. American Museum of Natural History, New York
11.23 Photograph by Schecter Lee ©1986 The Metropolitan Museum of Art
11.24 ©The British Museum, London
11.36 Robert Harding Picture Library, London
11.42 Weidenfeld & Nicolson Archives, London

Chapter 12
12.2, 3 ©The British Museum, London
12.10, 25, 28 RMN
12.21, 22 A.F. Kersting, London
12.24 Bridgeman Art Library, London
12.27, 30 Photograph ©1990. Art Institute of Chicago. All rights reserved
12.35 ©InigoBujedo Aguirre, London.

Chapter 13
13.5 Eric Robertson, Robertson African Arts, New York
13.6, 24 ©ADAGP, Paris and DACS, London 2003
13.8 Digital Image ©2002 The Museum of Modern Art, New York/Photo Scala, Florence. Courtesy of the artist and Francine Seders Gallery, Seattle, WA
13.9 David Redfern Photography, London
13.10 ©DACS 2003
13.12 Digital Image ©2002 The Museum of Modern Art, New York/Photo Scala, Florence. ©Succession Picasso/DACS 2003
13.13 ©Succession H. Matisse/DACS 2003
13.14, 21 Digital Image ©2002 The Museum of Modern Art, New York/Photo Scala, Florence
13.15, 18, 22, 30 ©ARS, NY and DACS, London 2003
13.17 The Art Archive/Dolores Olmedo Mexico/Nicolas Sapieha
13.18 Photograph ©1998 The Metropolitan Museum of Art, New York
13.19 André Emmerich, New York
13.20 ©The Estate of Roy Lichtenstein/DACS 2003
13.22 ©ARS, NY and DACS, London 2003
13.24 ©ADAGP, Paris and DACS, London 2003
13.25 Photo: Donald Woodman
13.26 The Art Archive/©Estate of Diego Rivera
13.27 Courtesy Nancy Hoffman Gallery, New York
13.28 Courtesy George Adams Gallery, New York. Photo: Don Queralto.
13.29 F.R. Yerbury Collection, London
13.31 Ezra Stoller ©ESTO, Mamaroneck
13.36 Cement and Concrete Association, Slough, U.K.
13.35 Courtesy Guggenheim Bilbao Museoa. Photo: Erika Barahona Ede
13.37 ©DACS, London and VAGA, NY 2003
13.38 Courtesy Sean Kelly Gallery, New York